Using a World Wide Web Browser (Netscape for Windows 95)

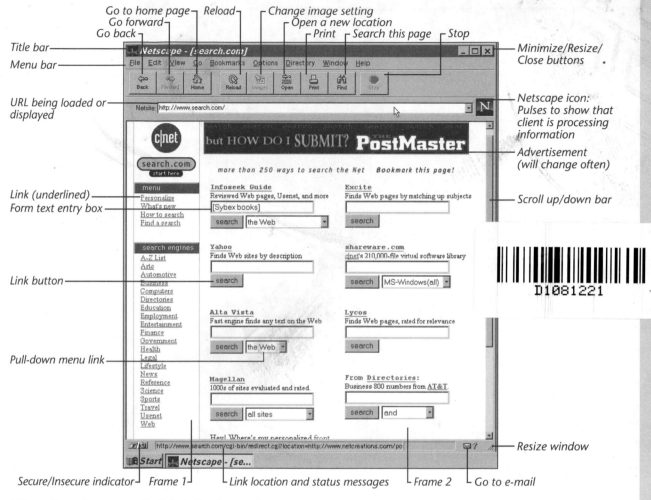

Go to home page
Go forward
Go back
Reload
Change image setting
Open a new location
Print
Search this page
Stop

Title bar
Menu bar

Minimize/Resize/Close buttons

URL being loaded or displayed

Netscape icon: Pulses to show that client is processing information

Advertisement (will change often)

Link (underlined)
Form text entry box

Scroll up/down bar

Link button

Pull-down menu link

D1081221

Secure/Insecure indicator
Frame 1
Link location and status messages
Frame 2
Go to e-mail
Resize window

Tips for Successful Web Searches

1. Read the help or syntax information to get hints on how to best formulate your query. For example, can you say "Dogs AND Breeding" to get information about breeding dogs?

2. Use lowercase letters to help the search engine do better matching of your text with text on the pages it's searching.

3. Use specific language rather than general. For example, if you are interested in tools to help research your family history, search on "genealogy" rather than "family tree." The second string will likely get you information on Family Values, Arbor Day, and other unrelated topics. There might be genealogy information in the search results, as well, but you'd have to wade through the rest to find it.

4. If the search engine presents findings with ratings for relevancy, find out what those ratings mean: do they rate for keywords, number of times the search term appears in the document, or some other rating system? This will help you sort through the results more efficiently.

5. Be patient! Most search engines are searching through millions of references to find your information. This can take a few minutes. Start your search, and then sit back and enjoy a moment of free time in your busy day while the search engine does your work for you!

Mastering
the Internet

Mastering™ the Internet

Second Edition

Glee Harrah Cady

Pat McGregor

SYBEX®

San Francisco • Paris • Düsseldorf • Soest

Associate Publisher: Carrie Lavine
Acquisitions Manager: Kristine Plachy
Developmental Editor: Dan Brodnitz
Editor: James A. Compton
Technical Editors: Juli Geiser, Mark Butler
Graphic Illustrators: Cuong Le, John Corrigan
Desktop Publisher: Franz Baumhackl
Desktop Publisher Liaison: Molly Sharp
Production Coordinator: Kimberley Askew-Qasem
Indexer: Matthew Spence
Cover Designer: Design Site
Cover Photographer: Dennis O'Clair/Tony Stone Images

Screen reproductions produced with Collage Plus.

Collage Plus is a trademark of Inner Media Inc.

SYBEX is a registered trademark of SYBEX Inc.

Mastering is a trademark of SYBEX Inc.

TRADEMARKS: SYBEX has attempted throughout this book to distinguish proprietary trademarks from descriptive terms by following the capitalization style used by the manufacturer.

Netscape Communications, the Netscape Communications logo, Netscape, and Netscape Navigator are trademarks of Netscape Communications Corporation.

Every effort has been made to supply complete and accurate information. However, SYBEX assumes no responsibility for its use, nor for any infringement of the intellectual property rights of third parties which would result from such use.

"Hobbes' Internet Timeline" copyright © 1993-96 by Robert H. Zakon. Reproduced by permission.

"Internet Standards for Business Users" copyright © 1994-96 by Daniel P. Dern. Reproduced by permission.

Brevard County (Florida) School District "Acceptable Use Policy" reproduced by permission.

"Bill of Rights and Responsibilities for the Electronic Community of Learners" reproduced by permission of EDUCOM.

"Policy: Proper Use of Information Resources, Information Technology, and Networks at the University of Michigan" reproduced by permission of the University of Michigan.

"Four11 Acceptable Use Policy" copyright © 1994–96 Four11 Corp. Reproduced by permission.

"General Hints for the New Online User" reproduced by permission of Hilarie Gardner.

"K–12 Internetworking Guidelines" reproduced by permission of the Internet Engineering Task Force.

"Electronic Access to Potentially Offensive Material and Pornography" reproduced by permission of Virginia E. Rezmierski.

"Internet Content Regulation in the Telecommunications Act of 1996" reproduced by permission of Piper & Marbury, L.L.P.

A portion of Appendix H appeared in a somewhat different form in *Web Browsing with Netcom NetCruiser*, copyright © 1996 Pat McGregor and Glee Harrah Cady, published by Prima Publishing (916-632-4432).

Library of Congress Card Number: 96-67622

ISBN: 0-7821-1893-3

Manufactured in the United States of America

10 9 8 7 6 5 4 3 2 1

From Glee:

To my parents, Glenn and Dee Harrah, for believing in me.
In memory of the best writer and teacher I have known,
Frank Cullison Cady
1944–1993

From Pat:

To Roy and Susy Odum, for letting me stay up all night writing,
and to my first and most-loved online community,
the Gazebo/Waldenites.

Acknowledgments

Dan Brodnitz, our developmental editor at Sybex, has a great sense of humor. He needed it.

Jennie Brown, no longer a novice Internet user, helped her mother figure out what was interesting to kids and teens and what wasn't. In addition, she and her cousin *Robert Hodkinson* of Bradford University helped revise and rework the chapter on MUDs.

Brian and Kevin Cady lived through yet another one of Mom's "seemed like a good idea at the time" projects without too much complaining.

Judi Clark provided unflagging encouragement, good illustrations, taxi service, and companionship as well as server space and HTML advice.

Jim Compton, our editor at Sybex, helped us make things clearer for you to understand, and asked critical questions at the right points.

Daniel Dern and *David Peal* provided inspiration, insight, and impetus. Without them this book would likely never have happened.

Joe Gelinas, User Advocate for the Information Technology Division at the University of Michigan, was invaluable as a research assistant, critical reader, and provider of key bits of information, particularly on troubleshooting Net connections and tricks of the trade. He researched and wrote the chapter on communications software.

Doug Busch, Keith Core, Tony Cox, Sally Hambridge, Brian Hayden, George Moakley, Robert Noth, and *Jeff Sedayao* of Intel Corporation provided invaluable insight into corporate Intranets and new technologies.

Brendan Kehoe helped think things through, answered e-mail at odd hours with questions like "What's the URL for the thing with the charts?", and gave us navigation advice for the big scary world of publishing.

Jeff Marraccini researched and revised the chapter on Internet Relay Chat and Talk. A long-time professional lurker of the Internet (and a talented electronic musician), Jeff is the System Administrator of the popular OAK Repository and software archive, `oak.oakland.edu`, managed by Oakland University's Academic Computing Services.

Glenn McGregor, VP of Engineering at Lloyd Internetworking, spent hours making sure that all the applications we needed to make the screen shots for this book were installed and working on the various machines, UNIX and otherwise, that we used. He also read many chapters and drew many diagrams on napkins to help keep us on track.

Duncan McGregor gave love and hugs while Mom and Glee slaved over hot computers.

Jennifer Tifft, of Sybase, Inc., and *Richard Smiley* of the Sacramento Public Schools, newcomers to the Net, kept us focused on the needs of real people instead of network nerds. *Mike Andrews* of the Oklahoma Department of Transportation shared insights from the government side of networking, and a lot of good jokes.

Joe and Peggy Thomas, of the Thomas Group, despite having to share a copy of the book, read the first edition as complete neophytes to networking, and gave us good feedback on what worked and what needed more explanation.

Much of the modem, SLIP, and PPP troubleshooting sections of this book come from the collective wisdom of the network consultants and systems administrators at MichNet, the University of Michigan, NetManage, CICNet, Cygnus Support, Lloyd Internetworking, and Netcom. We are particularly grateful to *Bob Williams, Pritish Shah, Laura Bollettino, Mark Davis-Craig, Christine Wendt, Howard Chu, Sarah Stapleton-Gray, Brian Smith, Kathy Madison,* and *Rhana Jacot* for the collection and distillation of this wisdom, and for permission to use some of their consulting tip sheets in pulling all this information together.

Other valuable tidbits, insights, and work which we could build on come from members of various Internet Engineering Task Force Working Groups, especially the User Services Area of the Internet Engineering Task Force (IETF).

Discussions with *Kael Loftus* and *Steve Covington* as well as *Eric Olson* of Netcom's staff helped to greatly clarify our thinking. And *Judie Sassali-Hayes,* Glee's great boss, supplied the environment in which continued learning is possible.

Glee's association with the Interactive Services Association and Project OPEN gave us additional insight into the public policy arena that is affected and being affected by the Internet. Particularly helpful were *Bill Burrington* and *Lucy Winkler* of AOL, *Eric Lee* of AT&T, *Steve Heaton* of CompuServe, *Jack Krumholtz* of Microsoft, and *Brian Ek* of Prodigy as well as *Bob Smith* and *Sara Fitzgerald* of the ISA. The policy arena is one populated by brilliant attorneys. Some of them (besides those in the preceding list, of course) who need to be singled out for their contributions are *Melissa A. Burke* of Pillsbury, Madison, & Sutro; *Bruce Ennis*, *John Morris*, and *Anne Kappler* of Jenner & Block; and the especially helpful team of *Ron Plesser* and *Jim Halpert* from Piper & Marbury. You can read some of Plesser and Halpert's work in the Appendix on the Telecommunications Act of 1996. Finally, being brilliant isn't always enough :-). You need to communicate that brilliance. Fleishman Hillard helps others communicate to our own best advantage. We thank their San Francisco (particularly *Curt Kundred*) and Washington offices for that help.

Special mention still goes to *Peter Kaminski*, formerly a software developer at Netcom and now running Nanospace, who provided thoughtful and considered answers to grand philosophical questions as well as an FTP client that worked so we could move the materials back and forth.

Ed Vielmetti of First Virtual, and *Brian* and *Connie Lloyd* of Lloyd Internetworking provided invaluable information and insight into how businesses get started using the Internet and how to solve their problems. Lloyd Internetworking also provided insight into K–12 networking solutions, as well as the Internet connections and host accounts that let us exchange chapters in the book.

Final thanks go to the freelancers and Sybex staffers who made up the editorial and production team for this edition of the book: *Mark Butler* evaluated the technical content, and *Juli Geiser* tested all the instructions and URLs; both made many valuable suggestions. Desktop publishing wizard *Franz Baumhackl* responded with flexibility, promptness, and good sense to the book's evolving needs; *Kim Askew-Qasem* proofed more than a thousand pages with enthusiasm and attention to detail; and *Dan Schiff*, *Scott McDonald*, *Molly Sharp*, and *Catalin Dulfu* also moved mountains to speed this book on its way.

Contents at a Glance

Table of Contents

Preface to the Second Edition

Why are we doing this again? Well, the Internet is different today from what it was a mere year-and-a-half ago. We then thought that we could declare victory and take a few deep breaths. Well, we were wrong. The Internet changes so quickly that between the time we write this preface and the time the book reaches you, many new ideas, sites, and tools will be available to all of us. Fortunately, we're pretty flexible. We hope that the tools, tips, and hints that we give will help you find the things that will excite you to find your own appropriate use of the Internet.

Glee Harrah Cady, Palo Alto, California

Pat McGregor, Cameron Park, California

May 1996

Introduction

communicate (verb transitive) **1. a.** To convey information about; make known; impart: *communicated the new data to our office* **b.** To reveal clearly; manifest: *"Music ... can name the unnamable and communicate the unknowable"* (Leonard Bernstein) **2.** To spread (a disease, for example) to others; transmit: *a carrier who communicated typhus.* (verb intransitive) **1.** To have an interchange, as of ideas **2.** To express oneself in such a way that one is readily and clearly understood: *"That ability to communicate was strange in a man given to long, awkward silences"*(Anthony Lewis) **3.** To receive Communion **4.** To be connected: *apartments that communicate.*

The Internet as Communication Medium

These definitions come from *The American Heritage Dictionary of the English Language*, 3rd edition. Except for the third definition of the intransitive verb form (and there are those who would no doubt feel it applies, too), all of the definitions can be applied to using and enjoying the use of the global Internet, whether as information consumers or as information providers.

Most of us are both consumers and providers at different times. Sometimes we take both roles simultaneously. This book will help you function effectively in both capacities.

Included in this book are two types of notes that will serve you as tools in exploring the Internet: MasterWords and Warnings. MasterWords give definitions, anecdotes, or pointers to more information. Warnings, obviously, point out potential pitfalls.

 WARNING Like the ocean, the Internet is vast and ever-changing. No one is truly its master; no one has plumbed its depths *in toto;* no one knows everything about it, because it changes on a daily basis. But, like master navigators, you can learn to chart the familiar seas and figure out how to safely travel the unfamiliar ones, bringing back treasure and new information with every trip.

Why Is Everyone Talking about the Internet?

We Internet users care passionately about it. We talk about our e-mail, some new trick we've discovered, some neat new technology we've found out about—and those folks who haven't discovered it, who feel uncomfortable using it, or who haven't ever found a good use for it look at each other with raised eyebrows. We continue to be excited and amazed at the wonderful things that others are doing and that we might do. We want to excite you about the possibilities, too. That's what this book is *really* about.

Who Is This Book For?

If you have never used the Internet before, this book will help you get started. Both of us were beginners once, and we've gotten feedback from other Net neophytes on ways to improve our text to make sure newcomers won't get lost. All we expect is that you know how to turn your computer on, how to load software onto it, and run at least one application in your operating system or environment, whether that's DOS, Windows, the Mac, or UNIX. We don't, for example, show Windows or Mac users how to work with the Clipboard. If you've not yet used a computer, or are just beginning, we encourage you to develop the basic skills before you begin using this book to explore the Net.

But if you do have the basic computer skills, you're ready to begin. When you finish reading the book, you'll be netsurfing like a pro: you'll be able to converse fluently with e-mail and the instantaneous communication services such as IRC and Talk, read and reply to network news, explore the world of vast resources using Gopher and the World Wide Web, and more.

If you've been using the Net for a while and know how to use your modem to connect to a network, then you're probably familiar with basic Internet services such as e-mail, the Web, Gopher, and FTP. You are probably not afraid to explore and try things out. This book can help you learn to use the Net more efficiently and more enjoyably. For more experienced users, we've included special hints and tips for shortcuts and troubleshooting. We hope you'll use this book as a well-thumbed reference to services, providers, and troubleshooting tips.

If you're thinking about putting your company, organization, or school online, we offer special sections about becoming an Internet presence, from how to assess your needs to strategies for developing good employee use policies. We will arm you to understand the new world you're entering into, and help you assess how best to proceed.

If you're interested in publishing information on the Net using the World Wide Web and/or Gopher, we provide step-by-step instructions and valuable insights for building those resources.

If you're a systems administrator, network protocol programmer, or professional network consultant, you probably know most of the facts in this book. We think you might enjoy some of our insights and learn a tip or two.

What's in This Book?

We've written this book to serve the broadest possible range of Internet users. Thus, we don't expect that all of you will want to read every chapter or appendix from beginning to end. Here's a quick guide to help you find the parts of the book that best meet your needs, current and future.

Part I: Becoming an Effective Internet User

This first section of the book builds your knowledge from the ground up: What is a network? How did the Internet get started? What can I do with it? Here we help you build skills to navigate the Net and understand its strengths and limitations.

▶   In **Chapter 1,** we introduce basic networking and data communication concepts. You'll learn about various kinds of networks, how they interconnect, and what the underlying principles of the Internet are.

▶   Developing a conceptual framework for something as immense as the Internet helps you understand it. The best way to understand the Internet is not by its technology but by its potential for communication. In **Chapter 2,** we describe the various Internet services and applications in the light of how they help you communicate.

▶   How do you find things on the Internet? How are the names or addresses of computers chosen, and what do they mean? Is there a difference in how computers find each other, and how people locate resources on the Net? **Chapter 3** answers all these questions and more.

▶ Getting on the Internet is not as simple as ordering phone or cable service—or at least not yet. In **Chapter 4**, we discuss the ways you can get connected, from a simple phone line and modem for home use to a high-speed dedicated link for your business or organization. Included in this section are tips on assessing your needs for network connectivity and some tips on comparing network providers and the services they offer.

▶ **Chapter 5** gives you information on some of the more popular software packages available for desktop computers, what the packages will and won't do for you, and how to get the software in the first place.

▶ The previous chapters are about making the connection: getting a connection from the Internet into your home or office. Once that basic connection is made, **Chapter 6** will tell you about your options for software and services: what can you use at home, how you can turn your desktop computer into an Internet host, what you can do with a traditional host-dial account.

▶ Where do I park? What's the speed limit? Where do I find the rulebook? Do I need a license? Just as in learning to drive, you need to know the rules of the road. On the Information Superhighway, the rules aren't always written down online, so we put them in **Chapter 7**.

Part II: The Internet Toolkit

In the second group of chapters we examine each of the major Internet services: e-mail, FTP, Telnet, the World Wide Web, Gopher, search engines and related tools, Usenet newsgroups, FAQs, Internet Relay Chat and Talk, and MUDs.

▶ **Chapter 8** covers electronic mail, or e-mail—one of the most popular services on the Internet. Friends, coworkers, even heads of state use e-mail to communicate. How can you get started? What's the best way to make sure your message gets through? How can you manage e-mail so that it won't overwhelm your work flow? Here we discuss both the basics and the advanced skills for using e-mail, including ways to diagnose bounced messages and get them back on track.

▶ Once you've mastered e-mail, you need to know how to get to other resources and bring your treasures home with you. FTP, or File Transfer

Protocol, lets you bring files across the Net to your own desktop. In **Chapter 9,** we teach you how to move one or many files and do it in the fastest, most efficient way. Telnet is the Internet's tool for interacting directly with other hosts on the network. This chapter shows you how to establish your connection correctly and make sure you can work efficiently once you're there.

▶ The hottest services on the Internet are the World Wide Web and Gopher, simply because they are so easy to use. These two major services use the principle of discovery by serendipity, but you shouldn't have to discover them by chance. **Chapter 10** introduces the Web and hypermedia. Just point and click your way around the globe with your graphical browser.

▶ **Chapter 11** demonstrates how easy it is to use Gopher to find information. Choose what you want from the vast global information menu.

▶ Not even Columbus really knew he was in the right spot when he set off to discover India and stumbled into the New World instead. How can an Internet navigator feel confident of finding cool things to do (and being able to get back to them whenever she wants)? **Chapter 12** tells you the best way to find and keep track of people as well as resources.

▶ Usenet News is one of the biggest sources of conversation, information, and entertainment on the Internet, yet without some guidance you can get lost in this world, either by information overload or by falling prey to a rude individual. In **Chapter 13,** we discuss how to read and reply to news, how to filter the flood of information to get what you want, and what courtesies are expected by your fellow news readers.

▶ What about in-line skating? How do I display Chinese text within my Web browser? Is there a place to get the Barney patch for DOOM? Where can I get information on special education for disabled children? How many episodes of "Married with Children" are there, and who starred in each? Hundreds of questions are asked and answered each day on the Internet. The system of Frequently Asked Questions records these answers so you can get them (and not feel foolish for asking something that has been asked a hundred times before). **Chapter 14** tells you what FAQs are, where to get them, and how to contribute to them.

▶ Some conversations on the Internet are immediate and personal. IRC (Internet Relay Chat) and Talk are two ways to communicate right now, without the delay of e-mail, with folks around the world. **Chapter 15** talks about how to do it, what the rules are, and what the bonuses of instantaneous communication are.

▶ Once solely the province of hackers and role-playing gamers, Multiple User Domains (and their various cousins) are moving into the corporate world as a place to hold meetings between scattered employees, stimulate creativity, and generate team spirit. **Chapter 16** explains how MUDs work, how to get into them and move around in them, and what the attraction is.

Part III: Becoming an Information Provider

Once you've mastered the Internet basics, you will want to become a provider of information as well as a consumer. In Part III, we'll show how to use the basic tools to build an Internet presence for your organization, be it a commercial corporate entity, school, or nonprofit organization. We also discuss management and planning issues that you should consider; that is, what connection options exist, how to develop your own appropriate usage policies, and how to incorporate appropriate system security right from the start.

▶ How do you put your business or organization on the Net? What can you do with a network connection, and how do you make sure you come up with appropriate policies for employee use of your connection? **Chapter 17** is for business people, administrators, and anyone who wants to get their organization connected without encountering potholes on the Information Highway.

▶ The Internet has been called one of the greatest boons to education since the library, but how do you make use of that resource? Why should you get your school connected? In **Chapter 18** we talk about funding your connection, share case histories of schools who are successfully using the Net, and share strategies for effective use of the Internet in the lives of our schoolchildren.

▶ Even a vast resource like the Internet has limits. Acceptable use policies help guide us all to courteous, legal, ethical use of the resources, and help define what is and isn't appropriate on the Net. In **Chapter 19** we discuss what constitutes a good policy, how to integrate your network policies with other organizational policies, and how to get compliance without being a network cop.

▶ Once you're connected and everything is working smoothly, you'll want to use the Network to distribute information: one of the reasons you got on the network in the first place. In **Chapter 20** you'll learn how to build a "gopher hole," "spin" a Web site, or set up a mailing list. Step-by-step instructions, as well as philosophical and legal considerations, make the job easier.

▶ If you are one of the many people interested in using the Internet for commerce, you'll want to know what's possible. In **Chapter 21** we discuss what kinds of businesses are working well today, what kinds of payment processes are available, and so on. The electronic market could be yours to use for buying or selling.

Part IV: Internet Resources

Whether you're exploring the Net for business, education, or pleasure, you'll want to know where to find the most interesting, useful, or just plain fun resources that are now available. The chapters in Part IV present some of our favorites.

▶ **Chapter 22** is an annotated list of cool resources we want to share with you. Here we have the best of the best. We list libraries, indexes, newsgroups, Web pages, and on and on. Every user of the Net can benefit by using these basic resources.

▶ More and more specialized resources are appearing on the Net. **Chapter 23** includes the information resources provided by governments and businesses, including state and federal agencies, storehouses of important documents, and commercial resources.

▶ **Chapter 24** shows where teachers and students can turn to find curriculum modules, teaching guidelines, support groups and pen-pals, projects to join or observe, or research resources.

▶ Playing on the Net can be fun and educational. What time is it in Tanzania? Will they close the schools because of snow tomorrow? Where can I find other folks who like the same music I do? How many Cokes are left in the Stanford Coke machine? Who won the National Hockey league finals in 1987? Where's the best collection of computer games on the Net? **Chapter 25** offers cool resources for kids (of all ages).

Part V: An Internet User's Glossary

The Internet has generated a whole new language. In the Glossary we have collected hundreds of network terms (including those aggravating acronyms) and defined them for you in human-understandable language.

Appendices

As Appendices, we've collected several documents, written or compiled by authorities on various aspects of the Internet, that shed light on topics raised earlier in the book.

▶ What were the scientific and social developments that contributed to the Internet? When did the first connections get made? **Appendix A** presents Hobbes' Timeline, a classic and still-evolving online project that will help you understand how a wide array of influences shaped the Net as we know it, and continue to shape the Net our children will use.

▶ **Appendix B** presents the standard netiquette document. You'll want it to be part of your network education. In addition, we include guidelines for "Safe and Smart" computing, particularly directed at preserving your privacy in a computer-filled world.

▶ When you plan your network, you'll be swamped with new terms, new concepts, and new technologies. **Appendix C**'s guide to Internet protocols and technology, specifically designed with the business user in mind, will help you better understand what the technical issues are surrounding your new network installation.

▶ **Appendix D** presents an exceptional paper, titled "Internetworking Guidelines for K-12" that describes everything you need to know to get your school online, from technology to policies. We couldn't do it any better, so we included the paper here.

▶ In **Appendix E**, one of the nation's top university computing policymakers discusses the administrative and personal dilemmas faced by college and university administrators when dealing with tough issues such as pornography, harassment, and inappropriate materials on the Internet.

▶ The special intricacies of using the Windows 95 operating system as an environment for Internet access are explained in **Appendix F**.

▶ **Appendix G** is a summary and analysis of the Communications Decency Act of 1995, prepared by the law firm of Piper and Marbury.

▶ **Appendix H** shows how to use the software included on the accompanying CD-ROM.

Becoming an Effective Internet User

CHAPTER 1

What Is the Internet?

FEATURING

Chapter 1
What Is the Internet?

WHAT is the Internet? There is no single, generally agreed-upon answer to this question, because the Internet is different for each of us:

▶ *It is a set of computers talking over fiber optics, phone lines, satellite links, and other media.*

▶ *It is a place where you can talk to your friends and family around the world.*

▶ *It is a place to get cool game demos.*

▶ *It is an ocean of resources waiting to be mined.*

▶ *It is a place to do research for your thesis or a business presentation.*

▶ *It is a place where "crackers" and other shady characters lurk, waiting to wreak havoc.*

▶ *It is unlimited commercial opportunity.*

▶ *It is a world-wide support group for any problem or need.*

▶ *It is a gold mine of professionals in all fields sharing information about their work.*

▶ *It is hundreds of libraries and archives that will open to your fingertips.*

▶ *It is the ultimate time-waster.*

▶ *It is the technology of the future that will help make our lives, and those of our children, brighter.*

All of these answers are right; none of them is complete. Today the Internet is much more than it was in the 1980s, and in five more years it will have grown so far that the cool toys we use today will be the ancient grandparents of the tools in use then. But there are some ways to talk about the Internet on which we can all agree.

GROWTH OF THE INTERNET

In 1989, fewer than 12 million packets (or pieces) of information passed through the Internet. In December 1992, 25 *billion* packets were transferred, and by November 1994, more than 100 billion packets of information were flowing across the fiber and computer links of the NSFNET (then the principal backbone of the Internet within the United States). Here's a quick look at the growth in several of the Internet's most widely used services on that network from December 1992 to April 1995 when the NSFNET was shut down. (You'll learn about these services in various chapters throughout this book.)

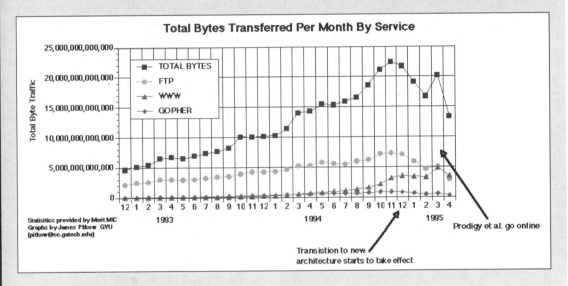

To be technically correct, we can say that the Internet is "the network formed by the cooperative interconnection of computing networks." In fact, the word "Internet" was coined from the words "interconnection" and "network." What this jargon means is that hundreds of connecting networks, usually made up of differing kinds of computers and different technologies, are put together so smoothly that the individual parts appear to be one network. These connected networks usually use the *TCP/IP (transmission control protocol/internet protocol)* communications suite.

Protocols are the rules that the networks all use to understand each other. The various protocols are sets of technical specifications that let computers exchange information, no matter what kind of computers they are, or what kind of technology hooks them together. Vendors of software and hardware want their products to be useful on the Internet, and so they make sure those products understand the Internet protocols and operate within them. The term *interoperability* has been coined to describe this ability of disparate types of hardware and software to work together under a common set of rules. Interoperability is a hot market commodity today, and so you'll see the term in advertising and product reviews for all kinds of computer products.

MASTER WORDS   TCP/IP and the various protocols that are used on the Internet are important underlying concepts for the Net. But unless you need to configure TCP/IP software on a computer, all you need to know is that they exist: the specific techniques need not be important to you.

People often say "It's on the Internet" to describe where some information is located. In that sense, the word *Internet* refers to the services that can be reached using the interconnected networks. Some of those services include:

▶ library catalogs

▶ Usenet "news groups" and electronic mailing lists—forums in which you can discuss any of thousands of topics with people who share your interests

▶ archives of free or shareware software

▶ customer service information for commercial companies

▶ free information on nonprofit and political organizations

▶ text of books, papers, and historical documents

and much, much more.

The Internet is also the community of people who work together to use the networks. The Internet is a cooperative effort of many people and organizations, all working to enhance the Net by their participation. It's important to realize that people don't just use the information on the network—by contributing to electronic mailing lists, by building information services and archives of various kinds, all the users of the Internet are information providers. You will be, too.

Who Owns It?

No one owns the Internet.

It was not funded by any single person, service, corporation, university, or government. *Every person* who makes a connection, every group whose Local Area Network (LAN) becomes connected, owns a slice of the Internet.

Because we have grown used to the model of centralized, cooperating utilities, such as the phone companies and the electric companies, we can comfortably compare the Internet to a utility. For example, there is phone service in almost every part of the United States. With a phone company, each person who wants telephone service contacts a local area service provider. The service provider provides a "hook-up" from the residence or business to the service network. The person wanting service actually provides the telephone instrument and the connections within the residence or business.

As long as you want to place calls to other telephones only within your local area, you don't need anything else. However, if you want to place a call to someone in another area, you need to purchase services from a long distance service provider. The local area provider supplies the connection from the local network into the long distance network. This arrangement allows you to connect to telephones almost anywhere in the world. Moving among networks of computers works much the same way (which is not surprising since the telephone networks—that is, the physical cables—are being used to connect the computers).

No Single Entity Owns the Internet

But lots of people care about it. Later in this chapter you'll learn about the organizations that set standards for the Internet.

Each computer connected is owned by someone or some enterprise. The owner of the connected equipment therefore "owns" a piece of the Internet. The telephone companies "own" the pieces that carry the packets (blocks of information). The service providers "own" the packet routing equipment. So, while no one person or entity owns the Internet, all who use it or supply materials for it play a part in its existence.

What Is a Network, Anyway?

The formal definition of a network is: "a data communications system that interconnects computer systems at various sites. A network may be composed of any combination of LANs (Local Area Networks), MANs (Metropolitan Area Networks), or WANs (Wide Area Networks)." But what does that mean to the user?

At its simplest, a network consists of two computers or devices with a length of wire between them, letting them communicate. At its most complex, as in the Internet, a network is a globe-spanning, heterogeneous mix of technologies and operating systems. Figure 1.1 illustrates several kinds of networks.

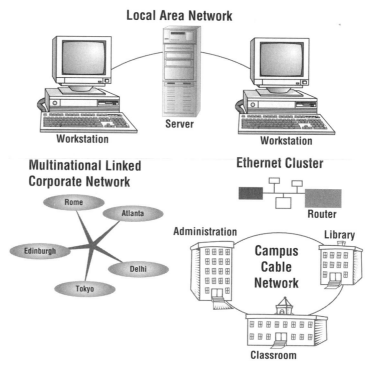

Figure 1.1   What is a network?

"A Network of Networks"

The Internet mostly connects networks of computers. Think of a corporate-wide network: each department has a LAN that allows it to share files and maybe a printer or two. Several departments, working together, interconnect their networks so that information may be shared more easily among the departments. These "regional" networks are interconnections based on geography (same city, same state, same group of states) or function (accounts-receivable grouped with accounts-payable into an accounting network, for example).

Then the regional networks are connected together onto a corporate network, sometimes called a *backbone*. So, there is a user connected to a local Net; a local Net connected into a regional Net; and regional nets connected to a backbone.

This is actually the way the modern Internet grew: the collection of organizations of various kinds shown in Figure 1.2, with backbones connected to each other at physical network meeting points called *gateways*, illustrates the global Internet. We say "global" because networks from most countries with some sort of telephone service infrastructure are connected to it. Practically, this means people can use their computers on their local networks to send messages or exchange files with people using computers in another company or in another state, in another region, in another country: anywhere, in fact, that is connected.

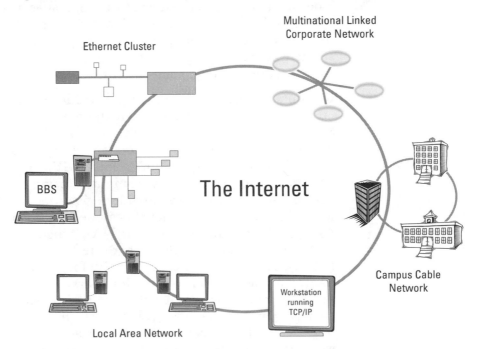

Figure 1.2   *A network of networks.*

MASTER WORDS   For several years, commercial use of the Internet was contro-versial. Discussion raged about whether businesses could use the Net to do business: to solicit customers, to support those customers, to adver-tise, to communicate with their remote offices. For a long time, the major backbone of the Internet was supported with tax dollars, by way of grants from the United States National Science Foundation. In the past few years, commercial Internet providers have sprung up, opening the potential and resources of the Internet to businesses of all sorts and their customers. Probably you are one of those customers: if you're not con-nected to a university or other educational organization, you probably got your Internet connection through a commercial provider.

How Is the Internet Administered?

To many people's surprise, there really is no central administration to the Internet.

The Internet has been described as cooperative anarchy: each individual network has its own rules and its own organization chart. But communication between networks can't happen without cooperation, and so there are committees and working groups hard at work all the time to make sure the Beast hangs together.

Of course, there are formal bodies within the Internet that perform coordinating functions. They include the InterNIC Registration Services (rs.internic.net) for Internet Administration in North America, The rs-Internic is a cooperative agreement with the United States National Science Foundation (NSF) to register the domains, names, and addresses of new computers being added to the network. Internet service providers provide registration service and assistance for each new connected network under the auspices of the Internet Assigned Numbers Authority (IANA), which is in turn chartered by The Internet Society (ISOC) and the Federal Networking Council (FNC). The InterNIC charges a fee for the registration of domain names to help cover their administrative costs. Internet service providers may pass that fee along to their customers or include it as part of their own services. This fee was instituted by the agency that provides InterNIC registration services and may change when the registration services cooperative agreement (with NSF) is renegotiated or otherwise redone in 1998.

Network operations are coordinated in North America by the North American Network Operators Group (NANOG). Security matters are addressed by Computer Emergency Response Teams (CERT) which are in turn coordinated by the Forum of Incident Response and Security Teams (FIRST).

Much of the cooperative efforts happen under the auspices of The Internet Society. You can join the Society yourself and be a part, too. You'll find more information about them at `http://www.isoc.org` on the World Wide Web.

Each individually connected network maintains its own user policies and procedures—who can be connected, what kind of traffic the network will carry, and so on. Each manages its own network—engineering the network, choosing to provide particular services or not. And each network cooperatively carries the traffic from its connected networks to gateways and from gateways to its connected networks.

The technical rules (protocols) are agreed upon after a process of proposal, trial, and discussion in the networking community. No one person can "lay down the law" to the rest of the community, because there is no law and there is no one person.

MASTER WORDS When you read this formal description, you might imagine calm committee meetings full of men and women in business attire, discussing and passing rules for the Internet. Not a chance: the 800–1200 folks who help plan and administer the Internet would be horrified to think they'd turned into a bunch of "suits." At the Internet Engineering Task Force (IETF) meetings, held three times a year, T-shirts and flannels, chinos and jeans are the uniform of the day, and beards and balding domes compete with acne and skater cuts. The meetings are frequently loud and argumentative, and standing around in the hallways debating the fate of the Internet is a time-honored tradition. It's true that most attendees at the IETF are traditional male programmer types, but women (and suits) are coming up fast in the halls of Internet power. Catering an IETF meeting requires good relations with the local Coca-Cola distributor and a direct line to the local cookie factory. IETF participants can go through about three times as many catered goodies as an equivalent number of, say, accountants.

How Does the Internet Work?

At the simplest level, there is one user sitting in front of one computer on a network. Let's say that this person is in Durham, England. Let's also say that this person wants to get information to another person in Seattle, Washington. Now, if these people are in the same company, using some corporate-wide e-mail system, the first person just enters in the name of the second person as it is known to the corporate e-mail system—usually, a user name. This serves as an address for the electronic message, and the Send command has the e-mail system deliver the message to the second person.

If our English networker is called Hilary, his address on the company system might be simply `hilary`. His coworker in Seattle, Sue, would likely just be `sue`.

Again, let's compare this to a telephone system. Within the same local company and exchange, some telephone systems allow you to dial a digit or two to reach someone else also connected to the same local system. If the two people are not on the same exchange, then (within the United States, anyway) you will need to dial the full seven digits and perhaps a three-digit area code.

If the two people are *not* on the same e-mail system, whether or not it is corporate-wide, the message needs to have some extension that serves the same function as the full seven digits plus the area code in the phone number. This address extension is found following the @ sign in an Internet e-mail address. For example, `totn@npr.org` is the complete Internet address for the staff of the National Public Radio show *Talk of the Nation*. This type of address is spoken of as the *fully qualified* address—this means that it has all the parts to let it be delivered from anywhere on the network.

Let's look at Hilary and Sue again. Hilary's full address might be: `hilary@durham.org`. Sue's full address is: `sue@seattle.org`. (These are fictitious addresses used for example only.)

Once a message has an address on it, the interconnected Internet systems take over. The e-mail handling system on the sender's computer packages the message and prepares it for "shipping." The message is broken up into small pieces called "packets." The packets are all addressed to the final destination. The path from Durham, England, to Seattle, Washington, may have many different networks in it. In fact, the packets that contain the message may not all travel the same path.

 MASTER WORDS Packets are one of the basic units of measurement on the Internet. Packets have different sizes, depending on what application "packed" them. You can think of them as envelopes or suitcases full of information.

Along the possible paths are special-purpose computers called *routers*. These computers do nothing but look at network addresses and figure out from the address what is the current best route to the destination address. Once the packets reach their destination, they are reassembled into the original message.

Routers make their decisions based on information that is constantly reaching them from all over the Net. They hear from other routers about links that are down, about others that may be congested and slow, or about routers that are no longer accepting packets for certain destinations. Each packet's destination and proposed route is evaluated individually, in the blink of an eye, and sent off along the best route for that particular packet at that particular moment. Figure 1.3 shows how Hilary's message to Sue might look as it is being routed.

The same sort of decision-making is made for all packets that traverse the Internet. Each time a packet reaches a router, its address is examined and the packet is forwarded either to another router nearer its ultimate destination or to that destination if the router is the final router on the path. The destination computer is the one that unpacks the packets, throws away the "envelopes," and hands off the e-mail message (or the Gopher menu instruction, or the file transfer request, to the appropriate program on the destination machine).

 MASTER WORDS The concept of packets flying off from your workstation and being reassembled correctly at the other end, no matter what route the individual pieces take to get there, is the basic idea underlying Internet technology.

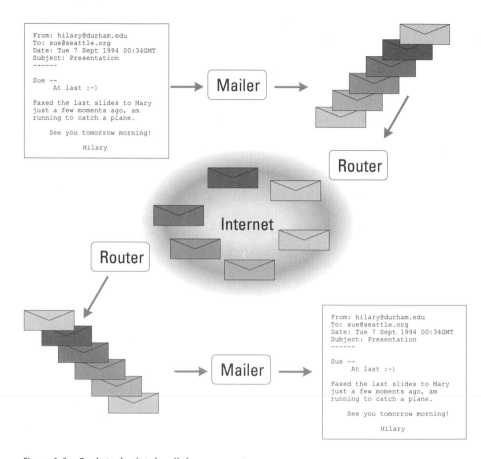

Figure 1.3   Packets don't take all the same route.

Being Connected as a Node vs. Connecting to a Host

Being *connected* to the Internet means that your computer system or network is actually a *node* on the Internet. It has an individually assigned Internet address, and client programs running on the computer system can take full advantage of the computer's capabilities. Your workstation is a peer of every other computer on the Net, be it another personal computer dialed in with a modem, or a large UNIX installation with a hundred users currently signed onto it. Your workstation, depending on the software, can do many of the most useful functions of the Internet: *e-mail, Gopher, WWW, FTP.* You can communicate, and all on your own. Figure 1.4 shows several kinds of nodes on a network.

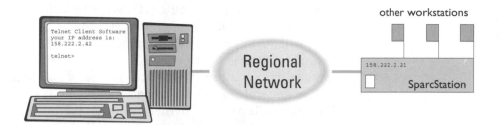

Figure 1.4   A node can be any device on the network.

MASTER WORDS   A *node* is any "addressable device" attached to a computer network. This means It has a separate, distinct Internet address and can be
reached by other computers and devices on the Net. Printers, file servers,
workstations, and packet-routing devices are all nodes. Your computer,
when you link it to the Net with TCP/IP software, also becomes a node.
You can reach other devices, and they can reach you.

In contrast, if you connect to and log into a *host*, and then use *its* functions to reach out onto the Internet, you are using *your* computer as a
terminal to reach another computer. Usually host connections are
designed to use very simple text-based interactions—not the more
sophisticated Graphic User Interfaces (GUIs) we'll see in later chapters
of the book—because those interactions are possible on the slowest and
oldest equipment that potential users are likely to have. This is how you
will interact with computers to which you *Telnet*. (Information Services
such as CompuServe and America Online, however, may offer custom
software that lets you work with a Graphic User Interface even though
your connection is through a host.)

MASTER WORDS   *Telnet* is a major Internet application. Telnet is the tool that
delivers you to the front door of other networks, other services, and other
resources. You use Telnet to connect from your workstation or node to
another node. You can think of Telnet, in the Internet Information
Highway metaphor, as the car that gets you places. Internet application
suites frequently include a Telnet client.

If you are using your computer as a terminal to someone else's computer, you are restricted to the interactions possible between that other

computer and your computer. Those interactions are governed by the host computer. Even if your workstation is capable of other interactions, you won't be able to use them from the host computer. A good example of this is Compuserve's CIM graphical user interface. CIM works to help you use the services provided by Compuserve. It doesn't work as general-purpose Internet application software. Conversely, the Netscape Web browser, which is a general-purpose World Wide Web browser, can display the Compuserver Web pages, but you cannot use it to connect to the proprietary Compuserve Forums. *Client* software on your own computer usually takes advantage of the strengths of your computer in combination with the information provided by the *server*. We cover how these two kinds of connections work, and their advantages and disadvantages, in Chapter 4.

Are You Being Served?—Clients and Servers

The concept of *client/server* computing has particular importance on the Internet because so many popular programs are built using this design. A *server* is a program that "serves" (or delivers) something, usually information, to a client program. A server usually runs on a computer that is connected to a network. The size of that network is not important to the client/server concept—it could be a small local area network or the global Internet. The server is designed to interact with a client program or client programs so that people using the system can determine whether the information they want is there, and if so, have it sent. You, the end user, don't have to take care of most of the underlying operations necessary to get the information: the server and client programs do that for you.

 MASTER WORDS   Popular client/server software includes Pegasus and Eudora e-mail software; TurboGopher and WinGopher; Netscape, Emissary, and QMosaic World Wide Web software, Fetch (a Macintosh file transfer program), and Novell NetWare file server software.

A client program is designed for a particular computing platform (for example, Windows, Macintosh, UNIX) to take advantage of the strengths of the platform. The client software is designed to make you comfortable: it uses interface elements just like the ones you use to do word processing or a spreadsheet, or even to play a game. Good

Part
I

Becoming an Effective
Internet User

Internet application client software is available for most computers being manufactured and sold today.

Using your familiar computer environment, the client may help you locate servers of interest, send a query, process the query results, and display them using the tools familiar to you. For example, if you use the Macintosh program Fetch, the screens and push buttons look like other programs you use on the Macintosh. Similarly, if you use a Windows program like WFTP (shown in Figure 1.5), you'll see a version of the familiar Windows interface.

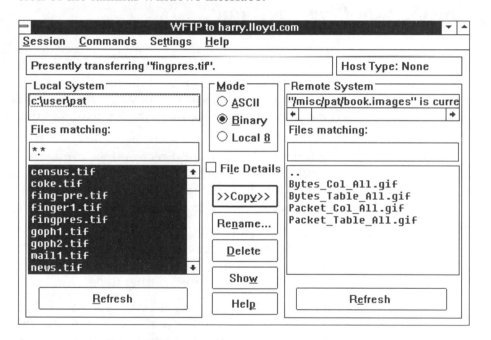

Figure 1.5   *A Windows-based FTP client.*

MASTER WORDS   Your *environment* is the *user interface* you see: the menu bars at the top of the screen, whether you click on icons or type in the names of programs you want to use, whether there are buttons or pull-down screens to give you choices, and so on. Internet application programmers try to write client software that looks just like those interfaces. The ultimate goal is that eventually, you won't need to know whether what you are doing happens on your computer or on one a hundred miles away: the client/server software will look just like everything else, and the transaction will take place just as quickly as everything else you run.

The advantage of this type of design is that a server with multiple client programs only has to store the information in one format: the various client programs can present it to different users in different places who are using different computers. The client program creates the data presentation. This ensures that the information looks familiar to the person making the request. It also spreads the cost of presenting the information: computing resources used in developing the presentation are consumed by the person who made the request.

Anyone Can Play—and Pay

An important part of the cooperative nature of the Internet is the provision of information that is "free" via the network. "Free" information means that you may use the information (within the bounds of copyright law, of course) without paying a fee. However, the Internet itself *is not free*. Someone, somewhere is paying for the part of the network each of us uses.

Sometimes the fees are direct and we are aware of them, like those charged by the Internet access providers like Netcom or PSI. Direct provider fees range from all-inclusive monthly fees to itemized connect time, basic service, e-mail, or per-attachment costs.

Sometimes the fees are direct, but you are not aware that you are paying for Internet access with them. For example, if you are a college student and you are charged a "computing services" fee, some part of that money pays for your Internet usage.

Sometimes the fees are paid by the enterprise that you work for, when your company is connected. Sometimes the fee is paid indirectly, when you use a service sponsored by a government. The government may have received money from you in the form of taxes which are in turn being used to provide the service.

With all of these different models of payment and provision, it's no wonder we say that "Anyone can play—and pay."

A Brief and Biased Historical Review

Here's a short history for those of you who would like a brief review of how the Internet got where it is now. Other books address this topic in greater detail, and we refer you to them if you would like more information. Robert Hobbes Zakon has collected a timeline, which we've included as Appendix A for further reference.

ARPAnet

While the interest in science and technology was fueled by the competition that began with the Sputnik satellite, from the networking point of view, it all started with the ARPAnet and a few resourceful computer scientists who wanted to share files among people working on the same or similar projects. ARPA is the acronym for Advanced Research Projects Agency of the United States Department of Defense. In order to share information and research results, and to collaborate more easily on papers, scientific colleagues and the people who worked to support their efforts connected together computers at initially a very few research universities and research laboratories.

From the few connected institutions, word spread about the value and ease of collaborative work and, over time, more and more people connected their research institutions to each other. They also began to connect the manufacturers of equipment, computers, and software used to support the scientific and research mission. For over twenty years, this network served the research community well, and it grew each year as more people moved out from the larger, earlier-connected institutions to smaller institutions.

The trend toward connection followed the general trend of more-affordable technology, as technology itself became more available to the general populace. As part of the continuing expansion and enhancement of the ARPAnet, the TCP/IP protocols came to replace the older, less powerful protocols. The idea behind TCP/IP was to connect unlike things together in a way that made using the equipment more transparent, so that users didn't have to understand the inner workings of each particular computer and its native operating system. The official change to TCP/IP happened in 1983. In the same year, the ARPAnet split into the MILNET (for military network), which served the defense community, and the ARPAnet, which served the research and education community.

Today you can send e-mail to folks on MILNET, and access information in other limited ways from their hosts, but it is still essentially an independent network. For security reasons, the MILNET administrators have built an e-mail-only gateway, and backup security structures to protect the US defense information from attack by folks with malicious or destructive intent. If any of the automatic triggers sends a message that MILNET is under attack, the "firewall" slams down, severing all contact with the rest of the network. Modern companies have taken this concept to their own security installations. Many corporate networks now have firewalls and "bastion" hosts to protect their systems and data. (A "bastion" is a curtain wall or other defensive structure on a castle.)

Supercomputing Centers

In the mid-1980s, the National Science Foundation looked to form a shared resource of supercomputing centers that could be used by researchers at multiple institutions. At that time, a supercomputer was a very rare and expensive thing: not every institution, even among the research universities, could afford to buy these very costly things, nor could they necessarily afford to maintain the environment and the support staff necessary to run a supercomputer center. However, many institutions and their research scientists needed access to such computing power. The National Science Foundation (NSF), an agency of the United States Federal government, conceived of and funded a small number of supercomputer centers, strategically located geographically throughout the United States, which could be used by many researchers.

The supercomputer centers ranged from the San Diego Supercomputer Center (SDSC) in San Diego, California to the Cornell Theory Center at Cornell University in Ithaca, New York. Each center was to furnish computing power and staff resources to a group of institutions that were organized either along geographic lines or by common research interests.

The original plan called for scientists to prepare their computing problems on the computers at their home institutions and then travel to the regional supercomputer centers. However, it became apparent that traveling to the supercomputer centers was less desirable for researchers than remaining at their institution with their own research staffs and familiar tools (not to mention being able to fulfill their numerous other responsibilities). So NSF thought to provide a high-speed connection among the supercomputer centers and then from home institutions to the centers. In 1987, high-speed was considered a 56 Kbps (56,000 bits per second) connection. But it soon became obvious that even that speed was inadequate for the demand.

RELATIVE LINE SPEEDS

Connection speeds have changed in the past 10 years at, well, blinding speed. In 1987, whole colleges and universities shared a 56 Kbps line, and many felt too much of the capability of the line (its *bandwidth*), was going to waste. Today many Internet users believe that 56 Kbps is just the right speed for connecting a personal workstation to the Net in order to view color graphics. (If pressed, we might graciously share the connection with another workstation or two.)

As an example of the difference that line speeds can make, consider the Oxford English Dictionary (OED), whose most recent edition is estimated to have 41.5 million words in it. Here's how long it would take to transfer the OED at various common Internet line speeds:

RATE	TRANSFER TIME
9600 bps	9.6 hours
14,400 bps	6.4 hours
28,800 bps	3.2 hours
56,000 bps	1.6 hours
128,000 bps	25.9 minutes
T1 (1.544 million bps)	3.6 minutes
T3 (45 million bps)	0.92 seconds

NSFNET

The NSFNET was the first step along that path of increased demand. As more and more researchers exchanged data and collaborated on papers using data from the supercomputer centers, more people wanted to get involved. Scientists told scientists in other disciplines. Scientists told their colleagues in medicine. Scientists told their colleagues in the arts and the humanities.

Soon many, many people were devising very useful things to be done with a network. Demand began to grow rapidly. The NSFNET backbone needed to be replaced with something faster. In 1990–91, the initial backbone was replaced with the very fast T1 NSFNET.

 MASTER WORDS   **T1 and T3 are terms used to describe network bandwidth. You can find out more about network bandwidth in Chapter 4.**

This created a new problem, in that not every scientist was located at an institution that could connect to the NSFNET backbone that connected the supercomputer centers. But the NSF proposed and funded intermediaries that would help with this problem.

Figure 1.6 shows graphically the amount of data that flowed across the NSFNET backbone and to each of the supercomputer centers. It was created using actual data for each router on the Net and then superimposing the resulting figure over a map of the United States.

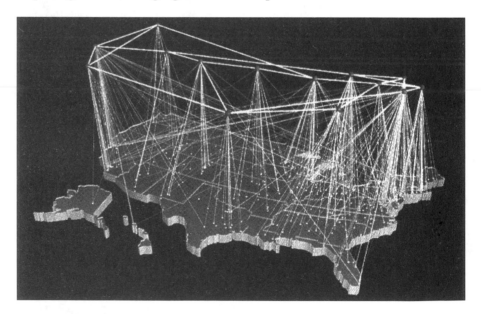

*Figure 1.6   **NSFNET traffic superimposed over the US map.***

The T3 NSFNET backbone was retired in April 1995. Its network interconnection functions were replaced by Network Access Points (NAPs). There are several of these (San Francisco, New York/Philadelphia,

Washington DC, and Chicago). The Washington NAP is also MAE-EAST (Metropolitan Area Exchange) and FIX-East (Federal Internet Exchange). The San Francisco NAP also connects MAE-West, FIX-West, and a CIX (Commercial Internet eXchange) interconnection. There are more interconnection points in the US, most notably one in Los Angeles that connects ESnet (Energy Sciences Net), CERFnet and Los Nettos.

Midlevel Regional Networks

The NSF conceived of the *Midlevel Regional Networks*, which were networks that served regions by connecting the institutions both with each other and with the NSFNET backbone. Now, instead of a researcher at Colorado State University in Fort Collins dialing into a modem at the University of Illinois in Urbana-Champaign, the researcher would connect from Fort Collins to his regional network (Westnet), and Westnet would connect to the NSFNET backbone, and the packets would be carried on the network to Urbana-Champaign.

Some of the original Midlevel Regional Networks were

CERFnet	(Southern California)
NorthWestNet	(Pacific Northwest)
NYSERNet	(New York State)
NEARNET	(New England)
SURANet	(Southern Seaboard)
MichNet	(Michigan)
BARRNet	(Northern California)
SesquiNet	(Texas)

Most likely, the original connections would have been from a communications processor added to a college campus academic computing system. Most campuses did not consider global networking when they designed their campus computing resources: most networks were based around a mainframe academic computing system. The sudden growth in popularity of networked communications caught most universities unprepared.

The basic academic computing system at most colleges and universities would have supported some sort of electronic mail system and some method of moving files to departmental computing systems, if such systems existed. Sometimes, it was the scientific community's departmental systems that carried the networking burden for the research community because the larger academic system might not have been able to connect to the network. Physics and Electrical Engineering/Computer Science departments frequently led the way to Internet connectivity on their campuses.

Local/Campus/Enterprise Nets

The increasing demand for connections, the availability of more powerful desktop computers, and the advances in networking technology all contributed to the continued growth of local and campus networks and to the growing number of companies with their own networks. These became "third-level" networks connected into the Internet. Now the network really was *interconnected.* The campus researcher AND the corporate administrative support person AND the home-office entrepreneur were connected into first-level networks based on departments in companies or universities, or based on geographical proximity, or based on organizational function within larger organizations.

Originally, the goal was for a person sitting at home to have her home computer connected directly to a larger computer, emulating a terminal. This became common in many workplaces. Because of the growth of networking technology, our worker can now connect directly to her machine in her office or to a computer across the globe. Her local network is connected to her campus or enterprise network, which is connected to a midlevel network or commercial service provider. This intermediate network can deliver packets to other networks connected through it or can transfer packets to the tertiary-level backbones.

Commercial Service Providers

The most recent development in the Internet's history, and the one that may have brought *you* into the picture, is the rise of commercial service providers.

With the impetus provided by influential people within the United States Federal Government networking community and within the human network of interested people, the value of networked information became more obvious to the general populace. People who were not affiliated with institutions of higher education wanted to send messages and exchange files. People who worked for connected enterprises wanted to be able to exchange messages with other enterprises who were not connected.

But the NSF and other operators of government-sponsored network backbones continued to be concerned about the appropriateness of carrying commercial or non-mission-oriented traffic on their networks. Specifically, the people at NSF were concerned that tax dollars not be spent to favor one commercial enterprise over another. A less restrictive alternative was needed.

Several companies not affiliated with the US government were started to provide access to these newly interested customers. Some of the commercial providers grew out of organizations that provided networking expertise to the research and education community. Some of the companies grew out of organizations whose networking expertise came from other types of networks. Some of the companies grew out of smaller providers of host computing systems. Several of these companies worked together to form the Commercial Internet eXchange (CIX), an organization that allowed the exchange of commerical traffic among its member networks. With the availability of network interconnections that were not based on the NSFNET, the concern about inadvertent and unintentional subsidies was lessened and the way was cleared for commercial traffic not related to research and education.

IAB/IETF—Standards and Agreements

All of the Internet works because of the standards and agreements forged by the Internet Engineering Task Force (IETF). The IETF creates the "prototypes" of the "design by prototype" engineering model. In the Internet environment, new ideas in networking technology go through these steps:

▶ Conceive and design a useful thing.

▶ Share it with a few colleagues to refine the design.

▶ Design and implement a trial to prove the concept.

▶ Improve the design based on feedback from the trial.

▶ Disperse the implementation details widely so that other people can test it.

▶ After everyone agrees that it works, document the refined design as a standard.

The IETF is a part of the Internet Architecture Board (IAB) upon which sit some of the guiding lights of internetworking (those jeans-and-T-shirt-clad men and women we talked about before). The IETF is charged with designing, implementing, and deploying the Internet itself. Another part of the IAB is the IRTF, the Internet Research Task Force, which is charged with looking into the future of Internetworking.

The IETF meets in person three times each year, but much of the important activity happens in the working groups, which "meet" in mailing lists and Usenet news groups to discuss (well, argue about, really) the whole scope of Internet architecture and support:

▶ the fine points of routing protocols

▶ the definitions of words to put into a glossary for users

▶ security issues

▶ technical details for end-to-end connectivity

and the many other issues that keep the Internet functioning behind the scenes. People representing the network services providers; the computing and networking equipment manufacturers; the fiber optic cable manufacturers; and the user services people who try to answer user's questions and provide training all meet to solve the current and future problems. It is an extremely cooperative effort.

What the Internet Isn't—Other Nets and Services

You will find references to many other kinds of services as you cruise the Net: you'll see e-mail addresses from other places and read conversations where people talk about other services. These services may not be part of the Internet, even though they may be linked to it, because they do not run the same protocols as the Net. Often they simply have a gateway between their service and the greater Internet. We are beginning to see more integration of these services into the Internet as their customers begin to demand more complete access to Internet resources.

CompuServe, AOL, Prodigy, MSN, and Genie

These commercial, for-fee services are the consumer information-service providers. Specializing in discussion forums, airline reservation systems, encyclopedias, and the like, these services deployed private networks throughout the US and Canada to provide services to individual consumers.

With the rise in popularity of the Internet, more cross-connections have sprung up. It is now possible to send electronic mail from and to these services from the Internet. Subscribers to these services may pay surcharges for their electronic mail and may pay surcharges to receive mail from or send mail to the Internet.

CompuServe has long been the home of discussion forums for some vendors of computing and telecommunications equipment. It is an excellent service for business people and is particularly strong in its collection of databases.

> **WARNING** There may be additional charges for receiving and sending Internet-originated e-mail if you are a user of one of the commercial information serves. There may also be strict message length limits. It may not be possible to successfully subscribe to electronic mailing lists that originate on the Internet (you'll learn about these mailing lists in Chapter 13) without spending a large amount of money. It is not always possible to send file attachments (like formatted documents and spread-sheets) through the gateways between the Internet and the commercial information services. Since the products that are available from the information services change in response to user demand, you will want to confirm with your service exactly what you are able to do.

America Online (AOL) has recently been specializing in newspapers and discussions focused on current news. It is a middle ground between the business orientation of CompuServe and the home orientation of Prodigy. Prodigy, which in 1995 reworked its user interface to be based on World Wide Web delivery, has professional hosts for some of their forums and provides contributions from professionals in many fields to add to the value of the discussions. Each service is designed to serve a specific information market and the offerings of the services will change with time as the wishes of the marketplace dictate. All these services now provide access to and from the Internet (via e-mail, WWW, and newsgroups).

WARNING   All online service providers are interested in making sure their users receive the services they want. This means that the service offerings change frequently. For example, America Online now delivers an Internet service, GNN—Global Network Navigator. This changes their provision of services dramatically. We recommend that you investigate thoroughly each type of service to see which one fits your anticipated needs best—and then remember to watch the announcements made by your service provider and the services others provide. In such a swiftly changing environment, the service that best meets your *current* needs should be your choice.

MSN (or The Microsoft Network) was originally envisioned to be a separate online information service like AOL or Compuserve. Its introduction (and integration) with the Windows 95 operating system made it a natural service to investigate for the operating system's new users. Now it, too, is becoming less a separate service and more a view through which its customers can access the Net. Its appeal is its provision of specific content. We anticipate that this content will become available (for a fee) to users of other providers' systems—that MSN will be an "information-full" destination on the Net, like the New York Times or ESPN's Sportsnet.

GEnie had a relatively early separate user interface that worked with some of the more graphically oriented small computers like the Atari.

In general, though, the basic difference between these commercial services and the Internet is that the services provide coherent environments. Someone selects and presents the information. The Internet is not a coherent environment, and until additional ways of indexing are invented and deployed, discovering the information available takes a little work.

Luckily for users, the tools for accessing information over the Internet are improving constantly. If you learn to use the tools we present in the book, your search for information will be much easier and even a lot of fun.

FidoNet and BBSs

Bulletin Board Systems (BBSs) have long been used to connect small, local conferencing and e-mail systems to one another using "store-and-forward" technology. As the name implies, store-and-forward systems allow you to send a message at any time, without worrying about whether the recipient will be ready to retrieve it at exactly that moment—they can pick it up at their convenience. You don't establish a direct connection. By contrast, in client/server networking you need to make such a connection, in "real time." This type of network can work on either a small scale or a very large scale. Frequently these systems are run by volunteer systems operators (sysops). More and more, these BBSs have either gateways to the Internet or actual network connections to it. FidoNet is a network of bulletin board systems. Each FidoNet node calls the next node on the network to send the files queued for transmission. This is file-oriented (rather than packet-oriented) transmission. The term used to describe this type of transmission is "store and forward." Each file is moved to the next computer in the path, where it is stored and then forwarded to the next computer until all the computers have the information.

WARNING Small BBS operators have been cited and arrested for storing pornography and other materials on their systems. In an explosively controversial case, a BBS in Milpitas, California, was offering erotic material for users to download to their home systems. A prosecutor in Tennessee, who was able to download this material into a computer in Tennessee, tried and convicted the BBS operators under Tennessee pornography laws. Small system operators are easy targets for enforcement officials because they frequently don't have the resources to hire expensive lawyers, and they also believe that because they are small they won't be noticed. If you use a BBS that has erotic or other material that may skirt the edge of legality, beware: If this system is ever captured by law enforcement, information about you, who you correspond with, and whatever material you have been storing on the BBS will also be captured. No matter whether the information you are storing is acceptable under your own community standards, if people can access it through the Net, it can be judged by the standards of the community in which *they* live. Whatever you put out there may be illegal somewhere.

Usenet/Net News

Usenet is a community of bulletin board systems that is a separate system, although it is closely allied with the Internet and the Internet community. In fact, much of the information on Usenet travels on the

Internet using a protocol called NNTP (network news transport protocol). Usenet grew out of the loosely interconnected network of UNIX sites, where the software to run "Net News" was developed.

You'll find more in Chapter 13 about Net News and newsgroups. The important thing to know is that by copying files from one bulletin board to another, many, many thousands of people can contribute their thoughts to the thousands of Usenet news forums. No one specific method is used to transmit each and every contribution. The contributions are accepted at the millions of Usenet sites around the world and passed on and back to the other sites. It is a cooperative effort of each and every site that is connected to and by the Usenet.

BITNET and CSNET

BITNET and CSNET were parallel and complementary efforts to the ARPAnet. BITNET (or Because It's Time Network) connected a number of the larger computers used for academic and administrative computing among universities throughout the world. Originally, BITNET operated between IBM mainframes, although software modifications to allow BITNET technology to work on other mainframe operating systems were written.

BITNET originally transferred information in a format which mimicked computer punch cards: the punch-card images were reassembled at the remote end and turned back into files. BITNET's logical organization remains today, long after much of the traffic on the network is actually made into packets and transported on the Internet.

CSNET stood for the Computer + Science Network. It remained an important part of the networking community until the end of the 1980s, when the network itself was dismantled and the organization was merged with the administration of BITNET to form CREN (Corporation for Research and Educational Networking). The folks at CSNET were pioneers in the development of user services in networking: they were particularly good at helping their users understand how to use the network well.

MCIMail, AT&TMail, and SprintMail

MCIMail and AT&TMail are e-mail and conferencing services provided by some of the same companies that provide long-distance telephone services. MCIMail was a relatively early entry into the electronic mail provider market, and its addresses are interestingly constructed to resemble telephone numbers.

These services usually offer a method of exchanging e-mail with the Internet. They aren't really networks themselves, but information services that grew out of efforts of the telephone carrier companies to provide added value and attract a different type of client.

 MASTER WORDS   SprintMail has a gateway to the Internet, operated by Merit Network, Inc., who also operate MichNet, the Michigan midlevel network. But CompuServe users cannot take advantage of this gateway: SprintNet, because of its competition with CompuServe, rejects any CompuServe mail that passes through the gateway.

Dialog, Dow Jones News/Retrieval, Lexis-Nexis and West

Dialog Information Services (a division of Knight Ridder Information) and Dow Jones News/Retrieval are two of the information providers whose databases are available via Internet doorways. In these cases, the Internet does indeed serve as an Information Highway, but it only delivers you to the front door of these services, which have long provided dial-up access to their databases. You can find out about their services on the World Wide Web but you'll need to connect to their services via a service like Telnet.

Dialog and Dow Jones are fee-based services. You must have arranged for an account in advance; you are charged either for time spent on the service, for materials retrieved, or a combination. It is possible to spend quite a bit of money searching these services for information if you do not know how to frame the search properly.

Dialog users pay fees based on a combination of connect time and records retrieved. Dialog provides a large number of databases and their indexes, for searching by experienced professional researchers. In general, Dialog's services are best employed by trained searchers who can design "search arguments" to best find the information you seek.

While some of the material indexed by Dialog is also present in the Dow Jones News/Retrieval system, Dow Jones specializes in information for businesses: articles from the business press and stock information are the specialties of this group. Like Dialog, this service was originally available through a private network and a combination of other connection options. Dow Jones expanded into using the Internet when they became aware how many of their academic customers were already connected to the Internet.

Lexis and Nexus contain Legal, News, and Business information archives, operated by Reed Elsevier. There is a gateway from the Internet; like Dialog and Dow Jones, these are specialized, fee-based services.

West Publishing and their WESTLAW service have been experimenting with providing legal news via the World Wide Web. They also provide a searchable interface to their *West's Legal Directory*. This interface is available to anyone who can connect to their Web pages.

The Game of Life

Watching the Internet grow has been a little like a popular time-eater on many mainframes in the 70s and 80s: The Game of Life. In Life you develop figures on a grid, set the game running, and see whether your figures will grow into a stable configuration, grow and expand, or eventually eat each other and die.

The Internet's phenomenal growth in just the past few years has been much like that game: from a few groups doing really exciting projects in isolation; to a point where advertisements in most general-interest newsmagazines like *Time* carry World Wide Web site addresses and newspapers regularly run columns about new and interesting things to do on the Net. The Net is continuing to grow explosively, new services are springing up all around us, and there appear to be plenty of rich resources to keep it growing. As more and more people discover that the Internet can be theirs to use—to communicate better, to get better information for their work and play—the Net can only continue to grow.

For beginners, netsurfing (a common metaphor for exploring the Net) has never been easier. With the advent of the World Wide Web, Gopher searching tools, and graphical interfaces that let you use familiar tools to do your work, communicating, finding and distributing information, and sharing really cool resources on the Net is much simpler than it was even five years ago. School kids and grandparents are surfing the Net and coming up with treasures to make life more interesting and easier.

For those who have been watching the development of the Net through the popular media, or even swimming in the shallows, there are exciting things on the horizon: the development of audio and visual conferencing; more countries getting better connections; more schools, small businesses, and nonprofit organizations getting linked in so they can talk to each other, and provisions in many broad, sweeping bills in the US Congress to include a data infrastructure along with the social or economic advantages of the legislation.

There have been some scary moments for all of us: the Morris worm, when the newspapers and radio waves were full of reports about how the worm was going to bring down the entire network (and did, in fact, bring down large chunks of it); and the security scares of sniffers, when lots of folks discovered that even having a password wasn't good enough, because someone might steal it. But we have also learned how to protect ourselves and our data better. We learned we didn't live in a small town anymore: we'd better lock our doors and our cars and take the keys with us.

We're out of the infancy of the Internet, and into the toddlerhood. It's an exciting time of growth and learning, and occasionally we may fall and bump our nose. But the opportunities, and the adventure, are there for everyone.

CHAPTER 2

Picking a Model of the Internet

FEATURING

The Internet as a medium for personal communications

Type I Internet Communications (one-to-one)

Type II Internet Communications (many-to-many, nonauthoritative)

Type III Internet Communications (many-to-many, possibly authoritative)

Type IV Internet Communications (one-to-many, authoritative)

Chapter 2

Picking a Model of the Internet

LIKE anything else, the Internet is easier to learn about if you can develop a model that helps you think about it. When we study the theory of any subject, we first learn to develop maps that enable us to return to the same departure point and then perhaps start off in another direction, mapping new areas as we travel. Each time we review our knowledge, we add enhancements to our notes, and while we don't necessarily end up with something as valuable as the *Journals of Lewis and Clark*, we do add to our own body of knowledge and to our own understanding. Sometimes we are able to borrow from one discipline to help our understanding of another, and all of us borrow from the ideas of other individuals we know.

For the authors of this book, the value of the Internet lies in the way people communicate with each other. When we were planning this book, we talked about why we wanted to share our knowledge of the Internet with you. For both of us, the important element is not the resources you can use, the things you can get, or the limitless commercial opportunities available on the Internet. It's the ability to communicate quickly— to get information to one or many people efficiently and effectively.

Communication is the key.

Communication happens between people, not between machines. Machines, fiber optics, modems, and software are not the heart of this resource. It's people, and the ways they communicate, that intrigue us.

Getting Personal over the Net

To understand why the authors are so excited about the Internet, you need to understand a little about how we use it.

When we first met, Pat was a consultant for MichNet (the regional Internet for Michigan) and Glee came to the NSFNET Information Services group at Merit. It became apparent to us that we were alike in some fundamental ways. The most important of them was that we are *people* people, and that good communication between people was one of the cornerstones of all our relationships.

We are both readers, as well as parents, writers, and journalists. Our training and inclination lead us to use every tool at our disposal to communicate. And so we came to use the networks.

Glee's first use of networks was as part of a problem-solving effort in the larger community of her work life. She used networking tools—file sharing, e-mail, talk functions—as simply one option to improve communication and solve problems.

Glee is one of the people who helped start the process of getting library card catalogs online; first, just for the use of folks within the library walls, and then for the world to access. She's helped develop not only the technology to share information about acquisitions and circulation, but the policies to keep that information flowing within the comfort zones of the folks who have to baby-sit it.

As her career expanded, and as networking technology evolved, communications via the network became one of the easiest and cheapest ways to keep in touch. It's a lot easier in the middle of a hectic working day to dash off a note to a collaborator at another university via e-mail than to type it up, put it in an envelope, find a stamp, and remember to stick it in the mailbox. And Glee's work has always put her in contact with folks all over the world: when Pat met her she was corresponding regularly and fluently over the bewildering array of e-mail networks with folks Pat had only heard of by name or seen mentioned in footnotes or resource lists.

Glee introduced Pat to the world of interest-based mailing lists: lists about mystery writers, journalism, and parent resources. Pat used to think Glee knew everything; now Pat realizes that she simply knows who to ask, over the expanding net of people online.

Electronic Lifelines

This wide network of correspondents and friends became a lifeline when Glee's husband Frank was diagnosed with cancer. Glee turned to her friends and contacts, and found medical information, support groups, people to help with financial planning and legal matters. And she found a way to be surrounded by loving friends who were accessible without regard to time zones, work schedules, or physical location.

(No, electronic communities can't take the place of people being there to help with cooking and visits. Virtual hugs can't replace strong arms and shoulders. But they can go a long way, especially when the networks let you link up with so many people and keep you in touch with people you haven't seen in years.)

Frank was able to keep working for a long time after his illness became acute, because he could use a computer that connected him to the exceptional University of Michigan campus network right from his bedside in the UM Hospital. And we could talk to him daily, keep him involved with the details of life around him, and be reassured about him the same way.

After Frank's death, Glee's network of people on the Net was one of her best support groups. And when she decided to go back to California from Michigan, they helped with everything from moving arrangements to school registration, arranging lunches, and welcoming parties. After she left, she and Pat still talked. It seemed to Pat that their friendship was kept strong, like those of the ladies in the Victorian epistolary societies, by the letters they exchanged via e-mail.

Teething on Data Communication

For Pat, computer networks started as a way to stay home and do college homework on icy Massachusetts winter evenings. She used a 300 bps modem to dial into the Massachusetts State College System infant network and type programs (and term papers!) into the DEC 20 mainframe. Her fellow students left messages in files, where they traded notes on eighteenth-century literature and programming algorithms.

When Pat went to work for the Michigan State University College of Agriculture, she discovered online information systems and e-mail. She could talk to all of the state's 80 counties at once, with one message, or talk to individual staff members about their computing problems. Pat was excited with the power of easily accessible information. Her group set up an exchange listing for farmers who wanted to either sell or buy hay in Michigan's severe drought, creating online newsletters, system notices, and a database of all the Cooperative Extension Service bulletins.

From there it was a tiny step to staff conferencing, electronic postmastering, anonymous FTP, and all the other tools we had at hand at MichNet. Pat is not sure which was more fulfilling: teaching folks at other universities about the ease and utility of communicating via the network, or doing it. She watched as more and more colleges and universities came online via Merit, and then we saw the NSFNET Information team not only teaching about the ocean of resources available on the Net but building some of those resources.

Now Pat, too, is living in California. (She got the job that brought her there answering an online job announcement in the MSEN Gopher server. She faxed a copy of her resumé, sent an e-mail letter of introduction, and had a phone interview less than four hours later.) She and her husband are co-owners of a small Internet service provider in Northern California. She has used e-mail to talk to her teenager in Michigan, she touches bases with her husband and several family members using the UNIX program `talk`, she corresponds at least daily with several friends around the world, and Glee and Pat have planned this book together over e-mail.

Not Consumers, but Communicators

As we explore the Internet in the next few years, and as some of the wild expansion starts to slow down and the bewildering flurry of TLAs (three-letter acronyms) and competing technologies shake out, people will begin to see that the point is not being consumers of resources, but communicators.

Teachers in schools linked to the Internet find that kids who previously had no interest in verbal communication are learning to read and write. Why? Because they are communicating with their peers over e-mail and conferencing systems, and they have to be able to communicate effectively using written language to get the respect of the people who matter to them. We've struggled to encourage literacy in our children: perhaps computers, and the ability to communicate, will be the best incentive.

PC magazine's Jim Seymour has written about the death of David Alsberg. Alsberg was a friend he had come to know only over the Net, but his tragic shooting death affected hundreds, perhaps thousands who knew his integrity, his involvement with humanity, and his passionate beliefs only from his online participation. Seymour talks about the community of friends and colleagues on the Net, and how the virtual involvement of these people with one another had created real feeling links between them.

In another example, a woman named Judy's first baby was due in January, 1996. Her mom and dad are both dead, and her only brother lives in Canada. Her husband was on duty in Eastern Europe, and she hadn't seen him in several months. Her friends on the newsgroups have not only talked over her pregnancy day by day, but one of the folks in Europe found a way to get e-mail from her husband, Steve, forwarded over the Internet to Judy. They were able to talk almost daily, instead of the infrequent letters she got from him via military mail.

Sandy, a labor assistant who lives within about 50 miles of Judy, volunteered to be her coach for the birth in case Steve couldn't get back. They met in person for the first time in the parking lot at the childbirth education classes, but they had been exchanging e-mail for weeks, and felt like they'd known each other for years. (As we went to press, we learned that the delivery went well, with no complications. It took about 36 hours to reach Judy's husband, but he called back via Red Cross as soon as he got the news.)

Finally, we saw the power of network-mediated communications when Pat's friend and co-worker at Cygnus Support, Brendan Kehoe, had a terrible car accident the morning of December 31, 1993. He was hospitalized, in a coma, and initial reports said that the injury was in the part of the brain that controls language functions. It was thought this talented programmer and writer (author of *Zen and the Art of the Internet*) might not be able to speak again. E-mail bulletins began to go out. Electronic mailing lists were formed.

Jeffrey Osier, another co-worker, went from California to Pennsylvania to help Brendan and his family, and almost immediately someone volunteered a network connection to help him stay in touch. Cygnus put up public information files and mail reflectors so people could get automatic updates, like the one shown in Figure 2.1, pulled from Jeffrey's messages back to Cygnus. Brendan not only recovered but, as you can see from the picture from his World Wide Web page in Figure 2.2, is back to work and doing well.

Pat handled mail from hundreds of people sending good wishes to Brendan, and much of it was from people who, like him, had suffered closed-head trauma. Some of them had found that the Internet was a godsend: they could communicate effectively even when they had lost the power to speak. We discovered, once again, what we had always known: The most important use of the network is to communicate. To make the connection between people, and let them share information, feelings, and concern for one another.

Everything else is just technology.

```
┌──────────────────────────────────────────────────────────────┐
│ ─  WTNVT: Session harry to host harry.lloyd.com          ▼ ▲  │
├──────────────────────────────────────────────────────────────┤
│ Session  Edit  Commands  Settings  Help                    ▲  │
│ harry-pat[~]>finger brendan@cygnus.com                        │
│ [cygnus.com]                                                  │
│ Login name: brendan              In real life: Brendan Kehoe  │
│ Directory: /cygint/s1/users/brendan    Shell: /usr/unsupported/bin/bash │
│ Last login Fri Aug 19 07:42 on ttyq4 from zen.org            │
│ New mail received Sat Aug 20 00:33:21 1994;                  │
│   unread since Fri Aug 19 16:58:17 1994                      │
│ Project: Make 1994 finish itself much better than it got started. │
│ Plan:                                                         │
│                                                               │
│   ''Think where man's glory most begins and ends,            │
│     And say my glory was I had such friends.''               │
│   -- ''The Municipal Gallery Revisited'' by W. B. Yeats      │
│ harry-pat[~]>                                                 │
│                                                               │
└──────────────────────────────────────────────────────────────┘
```

Figure 2.1   **An update on Brendan via Finger.**

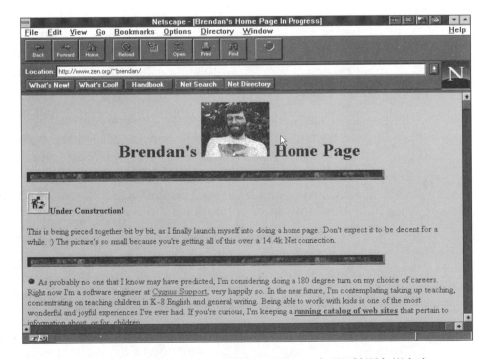

Figure 2.2   **Brendan is completely recovered, as this picture on the World Wide Web shows.**

Communication Is the Key

The Internet can be described using several kinds of theories. Computer scientists have a variety of technical models of the Internet; these largely describe the mechanisms which facilitate communication, but they don't aid in understanding how and why communication happens on the Internet. For us, the theories about communication prove most useful in understanding the tools and interactions in cyberspace.

Communication theories talk about how information is disseminated, who is providing it, and how trustworthy that information is. This is precisely what we need to know about information we get via the Internet.

Elementary communication theory describes the methods of communication as falling into a very few categories: one provider to one recipient, one provider to many recipients, and many providers to many recipients. Rob Raisch of the Internet Company (raisch@internet.com) developed an applied taxonomy for Internet tools that defined the types of online communication outlined below.

Communication Method	Tools	Type
One-to-one	E-mail, talk	Individual communication
One-to-many	Gopher, WAIS, WWW, mailing lists	Distributed communication
Many-to-many	Usenet news, IRC	Collaborative communication

As part of Raisch's taxonomy, he placed the various Internet tools in the appropriate categories.

Daniel P. Dern (ddern@world.std.com) developed a slightly different matrix when he described the tools in terms of communication activities instead of communication types, as shown here:

Communication Method	Tools	Activities
One-to-one	e-mail, anonymous FTP	Narrowcasting: explicit delivery/Respond to requests
One-to-many	Gopher WWW, anonymous FTP, Usenet news	Broadcasting/Publishing

Both of these groupings are helpful in seeing possibilities, but two-dimensional matrices (even with three columns!) are not really adequate to describe communication via the Internet, particularly the important additional concepts of temporality, public versus private communication, and the authoritativeness (trustworthiness) of the information received. We've made our own attempt here:

Type	Communication	Non-Simultaneous	Interactive/ Simultaneous
Type I	Private; individual to individual recipient; may be authoritative	e-mail including prepared e-mail auto-responses; individual files placed for FTP; files displayed by Finger, WWW sites with prearranged passwords or accounts	talk, "tell" in MUDs
Type II	Public; many contributors to many recipients; non-authoritative	Unmoderated mailing lists; unmoderated Usenet newsgroups	IRC; MUDs and MUSEs, Pow-Wow
Type III	Public; many contributors to many recipients; may be authoritative	Moderated mailing lists; moderated Usenet newsgroups	CU-SeeMe, Maven, Mbone, VAT
Type IV	Public; published contributions to many recipients; authoritative	Web pages; Gopher servers; corporate/ organizational files placed for FTP and Finger; searchable databases	Broadcast messages on systems and networks

---

MASTER WORDS   In the next chapter and beyond we will be showing you samples of the different types of tools we describe. To identify the location in cyberspace we are displaying, we'll use a notation called a *Uniform Resource Locator (URL)*. A URL tells you the tool and Internet address where the information can be found. For example, the URL `http://www.eff.org` tells you to use a World-Wide Web browsing tool (that's what the *http:* means) to find the information at the address `www.eff.org`. You'll learn more about URLs later on.

Looking Over the Tools

As with any kind of framework, there are cases where the frame cannot be bent to fit. In the case of Internet tools, there is one glaring omission from the tools so nicely placed in the box above: Telnet. Figure 2.3 shows a sample Telnet session.

 MASTER WORDS   Remember that we talked about Telnet in the last chapter. If the Internet is the Information Highway, Telnet is the automobile or vehicle we use to get us to the various resources on the Net.

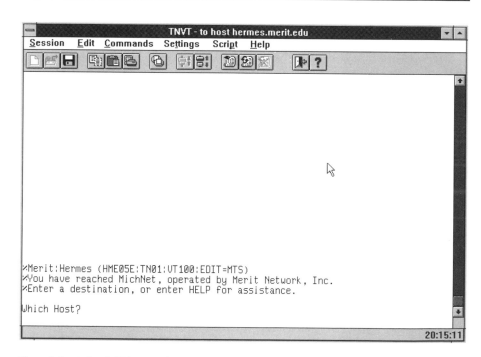

Figure 2.3   A simple Telnet session to the Merit/MichNet Gateway.

Telnet is an anomalous case because rather than searching, retrieving, indexing, or displaying data or information, it simply allows you to transport your point of view. Telnet logs you in to another computer system as if your computer system were a terminal.

The tools for the category we've labeled "Interactive/Simultaneous, Public" are also hard to pin down, because they are still evolving. The developing use of the MBONE (Multicast Backbone) system for audio broadcasts over the Net begins to fit this box when it is used to broadcast conference proceedings and meetings. A start at conferencing systems for relatively inexpensive desktop systems is the program CU-SeeMe developed at Cornell University. Used effectively by the Global Schoolhouse Project (`http://k12.cnidr.org/gsh/gshwelcome.html`) CU-SeeMe has been used to link classrooms in shared activities quite successfully using Macintosh and Windows machines in the schoolroom, connected via the Internet.

Early use of the video software demonstrated that audio was necessary, too. George H. Brett of CNIDR (The Clearinghouse for Networked Information Discovery and Retrieval) tells how the kids began writing signs and holding them up to the cameras so they could "talk" to their connected colleagues. Charley Kline of the University of Illinois contributed Maven, an audio tool for the Macintosh, that has been incorporated into later versions of CU-SeeMe for that computer. VAT and nv, audio and video conferencing tools, provide similar function on UNIX workstation computers.

That said, the matrix is useful in discussing how and why people want to use the Internet, because it describes the number of respondents, the validity of the information in communication, whether the communication is public, and whether it is interactive—all the things you need to know about communicating on a network.

"Can We Talk?": Type I Internet Communications

E-mail, e-mail auto-responses, FTP, files displayed by Finger, private accounts on World Wide Web pages, and Talk are all Type I Internet communications.

E-Mail

The most common of the communication methods used by people on the Internet is the private letter, written by one individual to another (on any subject and in any language), and sent between any two connected Internet sites or through an Internet e-mail gateway to or from a service which provides an Internet gateway. Figure 2.4 shows a typical e-mail message. E-mail is the subject of Chapter 8.

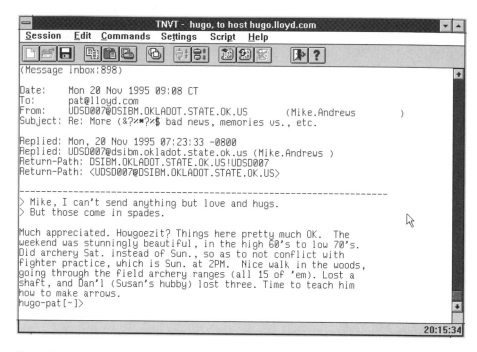

Figure 2.4   ***A typical e-mail message.***

As a recipient, you need to evaluate the information in the message by the same criteria you would use to judge the value of a similar communication received in a letter, phone call, or fax. It may be valid, or it may be rumor. Since (generally) e-mail is unmonitored, only you can judge. Remember, the only difference between e-mail and these other methods of communication is that it is occasionally easier to send e-mail than it is to make a telephone call, and sometimes it is less expensive.

Trustworthy or Not?

How should you evaluate the validity of the contents of an e-mail message? Ask yourself the following kinds of questions:

▶   Who was the sender?

▶   Was this person someone you know?

▶   Was it someone you can believe wholeheartedly?

▶   Was it someone who is an expert in the field being discussed?

▶ Is this letter in response to something you sent? If yes, is the response appropriate for the type of query?

If none of these things are true, and the sender is not known to you, is the message in response to something you "said" somewhere on the Net? If yes, is the message an appropriate response?

You can sort your e-mail using much the same criteria that you use with your postal mail. Some gets answered immediately, some gets put by until more information or time is available to answer it, some is saved for reference, and some gets deleted immediately.

Contact with Strangers

There are several reasons you may receive more e-mail than paper mail from people you do not know. E-mail is private and easy to send; you may not receive the e-mail immediately and be able to respond; and the sender need not actually be in the room with you or talk with you in person.

For example, Bill Gates, founder of Microsoft, once had his e-mail address published in an article that appeared in the national press. His mailbox was inundated. We're betting that he had that e-mail address changed almost immediately.

During the first debates about gays in the military, CompuServe reported that the CompuServe e-mail address of President Bill Clinton, which was set up during his 1992 presidential campaign but was not set up to handle mass quantities of e-mail, was receiving over 400 e-mail messages per hour. The mailbox soon ran out of disk space, and more had to be hastily allotted. Because the White House wasn't set up to handle e-mail yet, each of these messages had to be printed out to be sorted and dealt with.

Other e-mail users may send you mail because they associate your e-mail address with a product or idea that they believe you know about. You may be a published expert in some field. If your e-mail address becomes known, you may receive inquiries asking your opinions about ideas in your field, or from people seeking advice. In the Internet community, such inquiries are common and people generally reply. If you do not wish to reply, you need not. Or you may just reply that you prefer not to answer unsolicited mail.

Safety at a Distance

We have systems set up to handle problems with annoying or obscene paper letters or phone calls, but some people don't know what to do if they get e-mail that they find inappropriate. E-mail may contain messages that are rude or suggestive because the sender knows that it is relatively safe to act without consideration for the recipient. You may be nothing more than just a few characters on the screen to the sender.

 MASTER WORDS   If you receive offensive e-mail, respond promptly with a request that you not receive further e-mail from this person. If the sender continues to send e-mail you do not wish to receive, contact the postmaster at the site from which the mail is sent. Just as with paper mail or phone calls, there are policies in place at almost every e-mail provider to prevent people from sending you e-mail you do not want. The electronic postmaster, whose tasks are actually much like his or her paper mail colleagues, is there to assist you.

Is It Really Confidential?

Finally, e-mail, while private between individuals, should not necessarily be considered privileged. If you really need to say something that must remain absolutely confidential, you probably shouldn't say it in e-mail. Some systems administrators monitor e-mail via automated programs to look for key words, which indicate that illicit or commercially damaging e-mail is being sent. If you don't know whether your e-mail is being monitored, find out. Some e-mail systems automatically file copies of all e-mail you send. Sometimes e-mail *bounces* (is undeliverable for any number of reasons) and your e-mail will end up in the mailbox of a postmaster along the route. Sometimes your recipient will print your message and the printed copy will lay near the printer for others to read. Your recipient may forward it on to someone else, without thinking about your privacy or your concerns. All sorts of things that you didn't intend to happen, can happen. Remember: Never send anything via e-mail you wouldn't want to see posted on the cafeteria bulletin board!

E-Mail Auto-Responses

The e-mail equivalent of the direct response postal card is the prepared e-mail auto-response. The message is a composed one, especially prepared as an automatic answer to any e-mail that gets sent to that address.

There are two common uses for this type of message. The first is to notify the sender that the receiver may not answer the e-mail for some time—like when you are away from your e-mail system. If you (and your correspondents) are lucky, the automated program that sends these messages will only send a response once per week to each individual e-mail address that it receives messages from.

The other use is to distribute messages about products or services of a particular organization. When you send messages to an address like info@clue.org, you will most likely receive an individual piece of e-mail delivered to your mailbox that will explain the types of clues that you can obtain from this organization, perhaps where to get them and how much you would be charged if you wanted to purchase one. The message will usually contain something that will tell you where to get more information.

Sometimes people get creative with automatic e-mail responses. At Cygnus Support in Mountain View, California, folks who sent e-mail to xmastree@cygnus.com got the response shown in Figure 2.5.

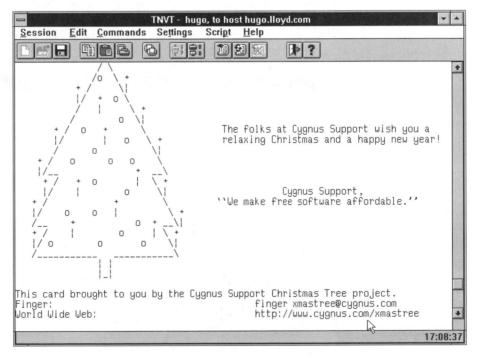

Figure 2.5   *The Cygnus Christmas Tree sends e-mail back automatically.*

FTP

FTP is an Internet tool that copies a file from one Internet site to another. FTP stands for both file transfer protocol and file transfer program, the specific program that implements the transfer. With the Internet address or domain name of a site, you can use FTP to connect to a specific location on that site (specific directory path and file name) and copy a file containing information to or from your computer for your own use. This activity is individual and private, although many FTP sites log (or register) file copy transactions either for market research or as security precautions. In the case of individuals sharing information, the file was prepared and stored specifically for you by the person distributing the information.

FTP is one of the ways the authors shared our work in writing this book—a splendid example of individual communication. One of us would prepare a file for transmission and then send e-mail to the other which contained the name of the file and its location. We used a special kind of security to make sure that no one could access this information without our permission, by using a special form of FTP program that requires a password before allowing access to the FTP directory. Figure 2.6 shows how we copied files from one workstation to the computer we used as a host.

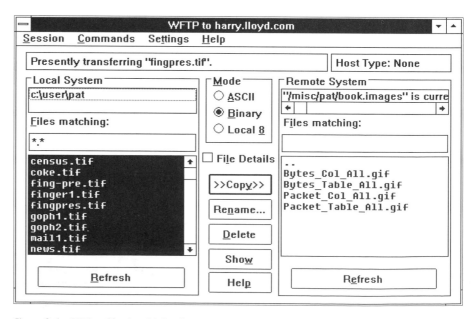

Figure 2.6   FTPing files for this book.

FTP does not require that both individuals be logged into connected networks during the file transmission. This makes FTP an asynchronous or nonsimultaneous activity. When Pat prepared files for Glee to receive, she would sometimes place them in the wee hours of the morning, and Glee would grab them off the FTP machine in mid-morning or late afternoon. Their computers didn't have to both be logged in at the same time.

 MASTER WORDS   While FTP does not need the sender and recipient to be logged into their respective computers at the same time, it does require that both sites be connected at the same time. If either host goes down (stops working or crashes), the FTP transaction will halt. One of the best times to use FTP is overnight. Start the transfer just before you go to bed, and let it work overnight while you sleep.

Please note: FTP can also be used for mass distribution. We will discuss how it functions in that capacity in Chapters 9 and 16.

Files Displayed by Finger

The Finger command displays the contents of a file associated with a particular user ID at a particular Internet site. Not all sites support access to information files via the Finger command. Some sites don't support Finger because they wish to preserve the privacy of their user community. Some sites don't support access via the Finger command for security reasons. And some sites don't support it because the operating system they use makes it difficult to support this type of access. For sites that do support such access, sending

```
finger skywalker@tatooine.org
```

will usually return information about whether that user ID is being used at that moment, and whether the user has mail waiting to be read. Lastly, it will display the contents of a .plan file. This file can contain any information that the file owner wishes. Some people use this file to convey information about sports scores or climatic conditions or earthquake activity. Both Internet sites need to be on the network to support the transaction, but the user being fingered need not be connected to the network to have information conveyed to the requester. Figure 2.7 shows a typical .plan file.

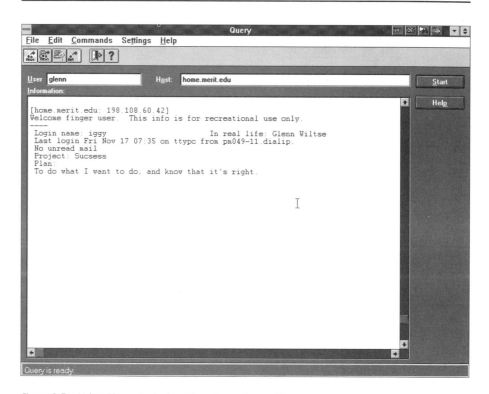

Figure 2.7   Using Finger to find out how to send e-mail to someone.

Web Pages with Private Access

It is possible to create World Wide Web pages where only one individual (or the holder of a special password or account) has access to the
information on a specific page. We see public examples of this with
services such as Wells Fargo Bank, United Parcel Service, Federal
Express, and so on.

As you can see in Fig. 2.8, you must type in your account number, secret code or other code known only to you (arranged ahead of time with the information provider). In this example, we use a UPS tracking number as the private information from the UPS Web server (http://www.ups.com).

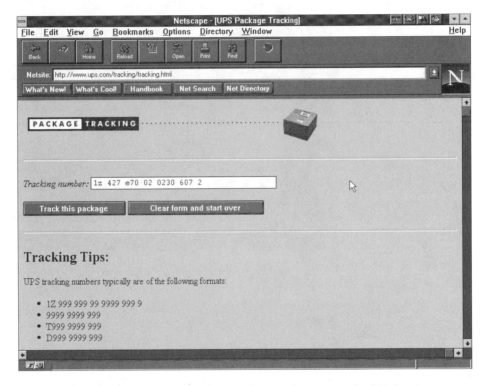

Figure 2.8   You must type in a UPS tracking number to gain access to the UPS database.

Once we type in the number, we can get information on our package's delivery (shown in Figure 2.9).

Obviously, we had to use a fairly public service for this example. Several companies use this sort of password-guarding on their internal networks to safeguard confidential information.

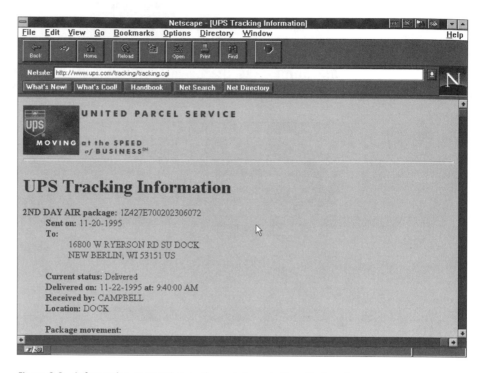

Figure 2.9   Information concerning package delivery is then displayed.

Talk

E-mail, FTP, and Finger are asynchronous. That is, the two communicating parties need not be connected to the Internet at the same time in order to exchange information. E-mail delivery systems, for example, store your messages until you connect and ask to see them. The synchronous or interactive equivalent to e-mail is Talk, discussed in Chapter 15.

Talk is also private communication between two individuals. The individuals can be connected through any two Internet sites and the content of the messages is not monitored. Talk is simultaneous: it does require that both parties be connected at the same time. Figure 2.10 shows a typical Talk session. Conversations, or Talk sessions, may be initiated by any party with a request. The recipient of the request may accept the invitation and begin a conversation. If you don't want to talk, you simply don't respond to the invitation. In the "Sex in Cyberspace" stories, there seem to be hints of lots of unwanted approaches to talk across the Internet. Since there is no way to monitor content, it is unclear how many uses of Talk are private in a way that should stay private. Talk can be very useful, however, for the sort of quick check needed between housemates as to who is going home to feed the cats or who is dropping by the store to pick up the milk. In other words, Talk is appropriate for ephemeral conversations—those just for fun—or for quick communications among co-workers and colleagues. Talk is for the sort of communication that doesn't need to be recorded for posterity.

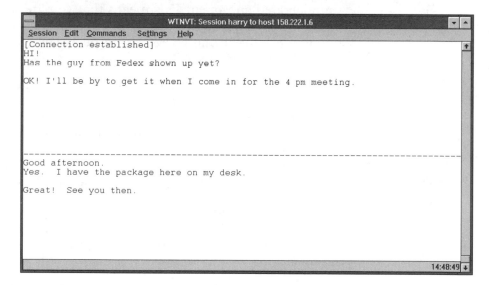

Figure 2.10 **Beginning a Talk session.**

"Citizens' Band (CB) Internet": Type II Internet Communications

Perhaps the most talked-about aspect of Internet communications is the very public communications that take place on unmoderated mailing lists or within unmoderated newsgroups. These communications come from many contributors and are distributed to many recipients. While the information contained in them may be very useful, in general the information is not authoritative. That means that, while the person giving the information may have the best of intentions, the information may not be true. Much of the discussion will be subjective: one person's opinion versus another's. Again you will need to learn to filter the information and find out what is useful and trustworthy.

Unmoderated Mailing Lists

A mailing list is a list of e-mail addresses. A message sent to a mailing list is re-sent to each e-mail address on the list. Many of the mailing lists (groups of people who wish to receive the same information) are unmoderated and open. This means that you are welcome to join (or subscribe to) a list and to post your contributions to the list. You may also unsubscribe at will. Therefore, the people who read the list will vary widely from time to time.

There will probably be a charter or statement of purpose and some general statements about what topics are acceptable to the mailing list and what topics are not. In general, while you may make contributions that are off topic, if you persist, others on the list will attempt to enforce the "rules" via peer pressure—e-mail to you personally and to the list suggesting that you keep to the topic. It is best to find a list that is discussing the topic in which you are interested.

Mailing lists are simply an extension of e-mail—easily copying a single mail message to many potentially interested persons, using e-mail as the transmission medium. As such, this type of communication is non-simultaneous.

 MASTER WORDS   "Spamming" of a mailing list or newsgroup has unfortunately become an unpleasant part of life for Internet navigators. A mailing list or newsgroup has been "spammed" when someone sends one or many copies of off-topic mail to the list. Spammers are generally taken care of by the list maintainer or other folks with authority, but it can be annoying.

Unmoderated Usenet Newsgroups

A newsgroup is similar to a BBS or bulletin board system but one that has been copied to hundreds of computers throughout the world. People read a newsgroup on some local site and post their contributions to that local site. The contributions are then copied to the other sites which carry that particular newsgroup. Like unmoderated mailing lists, unmoderated newsgroups may be read and contributed to by any-one who can receive the newsgroup. You may subscribe to the news-group and post your own contributions. Also, as with mailing lists, it is possible to contribute to a newsgroup without actually following the newsgroup (reading the group consistently to understand the tenor of the discussion), but this is considered rude and you may well receive e-mail stating that opinion with varying degrees of vigor. Figure 2.11 shows a typical news item.

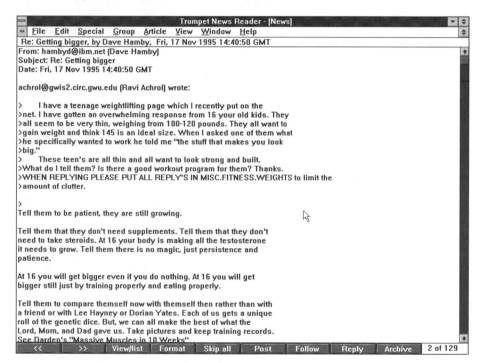

Figure 2.11   A typical news item on an unmoderated group.

Each newsgroup has a charter that states the topic for discussion and the type of contributions that the newsgroup entertains. Again, a single off-topic posting usually will be tolerated as long as it does not con-tinue. If the posting is clearly off-topic, particularly if it is construed as a commercial posting, complaints will be sent to the postmaster at your site. Depending on the policies of your site, you will probably be warned that you are not observing the charter of the group and you will be asked to stop. Some sites will take away your privileges if you persist in inappropriate postings.

Newsgroups are transmitted automatically. The messages are copied to each computer that runs news servers and that accepts and transmits postings for particular groups. Net News is cooperative and no site is required to accept the news feed for each and every newsgroup. Because each message is copied individually as part of a batch of messages, the communication is not simultaneous. Postings may take several days to reach all the sites that carry a particular group.

Usenet is the subject of Chapter 13.

IRC

IRC stands for Internet Relay Chat and it can best be compared to CB (Citizen's Band) radio. From an IRC server, you elect to join a channel. In IRC, each participant's contributions are displayed on the screens of all the others taking part in a conversation. Physically, this can be quite disconcerting until you are experienced enough not to be bothered by entering data into an environment where you can't really see what you have written until you press the Enter key.

In IRC, you can join an existing conversation or try to start one of your own. The topics being discussed will be as varied as the people participating. When you join, your name (or nickname) will be announced to others on that channel. Therefore, while you can be anonymous (by using a nickname that will hide your real identity) you cannot read without being seen (called "lurking") as you can in mailing lists and newsgroups. Others will know that another person is there watching and listening.

IRC is definitely individual and simultaneous. There can be few or many participants at any given time.

IRC is discussed in Chapter 15.

MASTER WORDS   One of the most fascinating uses of IRC came during the Gulf War when participants in Tel Aviv, inside their plastic-sealed living rooms and bedrooms, kept the rest of the world informed about the progress of the Iraqi attack on their city. IRC participants could "hear" first-hand accounts of sirens, bomb impacts, and the spectacular Patriot-SCUD explosions over the city. They also learned how teens and older people felt, living in danger of poison gas, huddled in their homes for what little protection they offered. The humanity of the people in the war became personal for a generation removed from the realities of Vietnam or the radio broadcasts from the London Blitz.

MUDs and MUSEs

MUDs (Multi-User Dungeons) and MUSEs (Multi-User Simulation Environments) are contributions from the gaming community. When you participate in these shared worlds, you communicate with others who are simultaneously taking part.

The difference between MUDs or MUSEs and IRC is not in the number and type of participants, nor in the general technology used. It's that MUDs and MUSEs postulate rules and environments that are shared. The environments may be imaginary or not. You may participate as yourself or as a character you construct (by your own rules or by the rules of the world you wish to share). In these shared worlds, the characters you construct walk around and converse with other characters created by other participants. Most of the shared worlds are intended for recreational use, but some are educational. Some corporations and think tanks are beginning to use this technology to have multi-level discussions not bounded by physical location or time zones. And some of the shared environments have been running for years (although not with exactly the same participants, of course).

MUDs are the subject of Chapter 16.

"Tower of Babel": Type III Internet Communications

Some mailing lists and newsgroups are moderated. Moderation is not intended to make the postings more or less authoritative, but to make sure the postings stick to the topic. The moderator may be the person who started the mailing list or newsgroup, or it may be someone selected later. The duties of the moderator vary according to the available software and the nature of the group. Since only mailing lists and newsgroups are moderated, this type of communication, like all unmoderated mailing lists and newsgroups, is nonsimultaneous.

Moderated Mailing Lists

All messages sent to a moderated mailing list go directly to a moderator. The moderator then determines whether the message should be sent on to the list. The moderator will forward the message or return it with a message explaining that it was inappropriate. Moderated mailing lists, like their cousins the moderated newsgroups (see below), are one answer to repeated spamming.

Participants in a moderated mailing list will never receive a request to subscribe accidentally posted to the entire list. This is the easiest of decisions that a moderator makes, and the easiest for mailing list participants to understand. In a large mailing list, one with several hundred participants, missent subscription requests cause needless messages to be sent, wasting everyone's time with useless transmissions.

Of course, moderators sometimes face more difficult decisions—for example, whether to forward a posting that contains a request for information about something not quite on topic. Many moderators will let a discussion that is off topic continue for several days and then intervene by sending a message to the list reminding the participants of the purpose of the list. This way, a list intended to discuss murder mysteries does not end up being dominated by discussions of the names of the participants' cats and dogs for longer than a day or two.

UNDERSTANDING BANDWIDTH

Bandwidth is a technical term that describes the capacity of the physical network to carry traffic. It comes from radio technology, where it described how wide a radio channel or *band* was—how much information could be transmitted on it.

Today networkers use bandwidth to describe not only the amount of data that can be transmitted over a network link (remember the OED table in Chapter 1?), but the amount of information available in a message. You may well see messages that talk about "emotional bandwidth" in e-mail messages or other on-line information sources. This describes how difficult it is to tell the speaker's emotions from the letters on the screen.

Experienced networkers are very jealous of their bandwidth, and some can get pretty rude if they think you're wasting time, resources, or money.

Moderated Usenet Newsgroups

Similar decisions are made by the moderators of newsgroups. Moderators are found particularly in the *.announce newsgroups. Because these groups are intended for announcements, an effort is made to make certain that the postings are appropriate for the newsgroup. Participants reading the group ba.announce (Bay Area Announce) want to be certain that posted announcements are for events in the next week or so and in the geographical location of the San Francisco

Bay Area. The moderators reject postings that are not timely or not taking place in the Bay Area. This activity makes the postings authoritative; that is, trustworthy.

MBONE

MBONE (Multicast BackbONE) is an emerging technology. MBONE is one type of audio and video transmission over the Net. The group of engineers, scientists, and user services folks who are working on the structure of the Internet itself are experimenting with broadcasts of their conferences over MBONE. Speeches, news conferences, and other informational events have also been broadcast. Listeners all over the world could hear the conference proceedings right at their workstations.

When listening to an MBONE conference, you can hear many people discussing their views in real time, and hundreds of other listeners are hearing it, too. (It does indeed sometimes resemble the cacophony of the Tower of Babel.)

Because MBONE requires special routing hardware and software right now, it's not interactive, nor is it available to everyone. But within the next few years MBONE promises to become truly interactive, allowing video conferencing among multiple participants from their workstations anywhere on the Internet.

CU-SeeMe, Maven, and VAT

CU-SeeMe, a video client/server program, and its companion audio program, Maven (for the Macintosh), come closer to the dream of a "picture telephone" over the Internet. CU-SeeMe was originally developed for the Macintosh and later also made available for Windows. CU-SeeMe can be used point to point (one machine connected to just one machine) or by using one of the reflector servers, you can get one-to-many or many-to-many conferences. With the CU-SeeMe client program, you can connect to a server and communicate! CU-SeeMe client programs can be senders or receivers or both. Receiving is simpler, of course, requiring only the client software and an Internet connection. Sending requires more equipment: a video board, a camera, and software to capture and transmit the video information.

Maven audio capabilities are built in to the later versions of the CU-SeeMe client programs for the Macintosh (Version 0.7 and later). More information and the programs themselves can be found at `ftp://ftp.gated.cornell.edu/pub/video`. Maven can be found at `ftp://k12.cnidr.org/pub/Mac`. Other programs of interest to people using Macintosh computers in the classroom will also be found there.

 MASTER WORDS   Integrated audio and video can require a connection at 56 Kbps or higher, or the video transmissions may be jerky and the audio signals may not be transmitted without the loss of significant amounts of information. This means that you can run the programs at slower speeds, but the audio will not be intelligible. An alternative is to use CU-SeeMe to transmit the video and use a direct telephone connection between two points or an audio conference call between multiple points. With speaker telephones, this method can sometimes be quite effective. Newer technologies such as VDOLive and ReadAudio (video and audio transmission programs) are now working at lower modem speeds. Each week, new ideas and new technologies become available that will make real time pictures and voice over the Internet more readily available.

CU-SeeMe reflectors are run on UNIX systems that are enabled for Multicast transmission. This requires the cooperation of your network administrator and your network provider. Not all network providers offer multicast service.

Another available audio conferencing tool is VAT, available for some UNIX workstations (Some Sun SparcStations, some Silicon Graphics workstations, some DECstations, and others). VAT supports both point-to-point and broadcast of audio using either multicast or unicast IP.

VAT is available from `ftp://cs.ucl.ac.uk/mice/videoconference/vat`. There is a Web page with a little information about VAT available at `http://www-mice-nsc.cs.ucl.ac.uk/mice-nsc/tools/instal-vat.html`.

nv is a similar concept in video conference tools for UNIX workstations. It is available for Sun workstations with videopix and parallax framegrabbers, Silicon Graphics workstations with Indigo framegrabbers, and DECstations with Jvideo framegrabbers. More information is available from Ron Frederick (`frederic@parc.xerox.com`). The nv program is available itself from `ftp://cs.ucl.ac.uk/mice/videoconference/nv`.

It is possible for people running VAT to participate in audio conferences with people running Maven. The CU-SeeMe to VAT connections are being investigated.

"The Internet Daily Planet":
Type IV Internet Communications

The final type of communication that can be found on the Internet consists of the public, published contributions of individuals and companies that can be received by many recipients, and that may be thought of as authoritative. In effect, this is rather like a book, a directory, a magazine, or a radio or television broadcast.

Some authority has exercised editorial control over the content of this type of communication. The content represents an official statement, information about a product or a service, editorial or procedural matters, art work, catalogs, calendars for schools, colleges or universities. In short, these are published works intended for general or specific consumption, using the tools of the Internet for the communication medium.

Broadcast Messages

There is only one type of communication in this category that is truly simultaneous: the broadcast message that is used by a system or network operator to communicate about the state of the network or system itself with everyone currently using it. Broadcast messages are sent from an operator to every person using a system at that time.

Broadcast messages are usually warnings about unusual activities such as system instabilities or outages. They are transmitted this way to reach the maximum number of affected people as quickly as possible.

World Wide Web Pages

The World Wide Web, discussed in Chapter 10, is a distributed, hypertext collection of clients and servers that link a page to other pages throughout the global Internet. A page is simply a title, a collection of information, and pointers (hyperlinks) to other information. You view it using a client program, which connects you to a server. Depending on the client you have, you can see color representations of lighthouses and other art work, hear audio clips from recorded music, see movie clips, or fill out survey forms. For example, Figure 2.12 shows a picture from the Le WebMuseum Collection, which contains many of the pictures housed in the Louvre museum. Page designers publish their pages, leaving you to decide whether or not to view them at some subsequent time.

World Wide Web pages have become the glossy catalogs and magazines of the Internet community. Some pages are published by colleges and universities and serve as interactive catalogs representing their institutions. Other pages are catalogs of jewelry or shoes. And some pages are published materials that describe the person who designed and built the page. Pages representing institutions and enterprises are authoritative; that is, they are authorized by the company or enterprise and can be trusted.

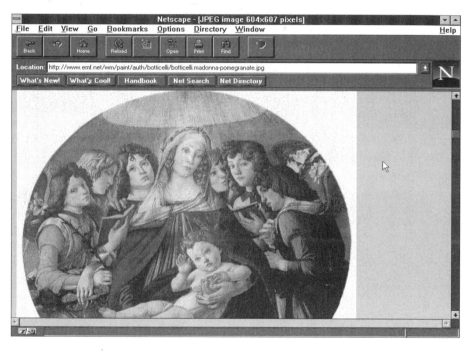

*Figure 2.12   **One of the images available through the Le WebMuseum page.***

MASTER WORDS   Both Pat and Glee have Web pages you can look at. Look at Glee's pages by using a WWW client to find `http://www.manymedia.com/glee`. Pat can be reached by going to `http://www.lloyd.com/~patmcg`. Try it out!

Gopher Servers

Gopher, discussed in Chapter 11, is another method of publishing material on the Internet that spread quickly thanks to its ease of use.

Gopher is a menu-driven client/server program that allows you to connect to files and display them on your own system, or to transmit image files encoded for other clients, such as gif or tif image files. Gopher lets you link to and display menus and files from other Gopher servers throughout "gopherspace," making it unnecessary to gather all the information needed and place it on a single server. Figure 2.13 shows the U.S. government's Gopher server at the National Archives.

Since access to Gopher clients is provided by almost any site that has Internet access, it is easy to find. Using Gopher usually means entering the word gopher and pressing the Enter (↵) key, and then pressing Enter again for each menu choice. It is one of the easiest Internet tools to use.

Most Gopher clients support a bookmark function, making it easy to return to a useful server without traversing a complicated menu tree. Gopher's ease of use and near ubiquity make it a popular platform for delivering information that can be structured into directories of files with menu pointers. Gopher can also link other servers and services, making serendipitous discovery very likely and interconnected travels easy.

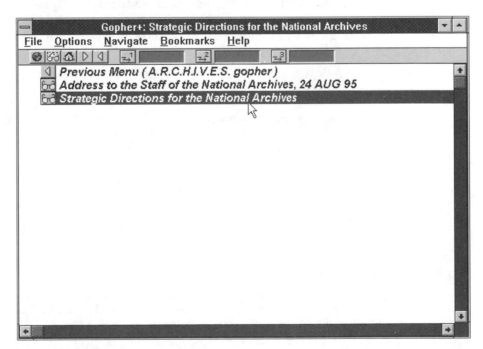

Figure 2.13 **The National Archives Gopher server.**

MASTER WORDS   If you have an account on an Internet host, type gopher at the main prompt. If you have a specific Gopher client that runs on your home or office workstation, such as WinGopher or TurboGopher, click the icon to launch the application. If you don't specify a particular server, these clients will take you to the Mother Gopher in Minnesota. From the first menu, you will see the possibilities for traveling via Gopher all over the Internet. Try it out!

Files Placed for FTP

Remember the automatic response e-mail communication? An organization's automatic response message frequently includes instructions for how to obtain more information about the organization and its services. Those instructions may well tell you how to receive another type of nonsimultaneous, published communication: information files placed for anonymous FTP. These files, like those in Web pages and in gopher-space, are prepared specifically for the convenience of others. The requester explicitly asks for it, so there is no question that it was wanted. No one asks for information they don't want to receive. Figure 2.14 gives an example of how to start an anonymous FTP session.

USING ANONYMOUS FTP

Anonymous FTP lets you get information off a host without having to have an account on that host. To use an anonymous FTP service, the transaction generally goes like this:

```
ftp ftp.anyhost.com
Connected to ftp.anyhost.com.
Enter login: anonymous
Anonymous identity accepted, enter full e-mail address as
password: yourname@yourhost.edu
ftp>
```

and you're in!

Anonymous FTP users do not have full run of the system, and are usually granted only limited access to files on that system. The use of the e-mail address helps with security and marketing research.

The biggest problem with anonymous FTP can be learning to spell *anonymous*! Therefore, many FTP servers will also accept a login ID of *FTP*.

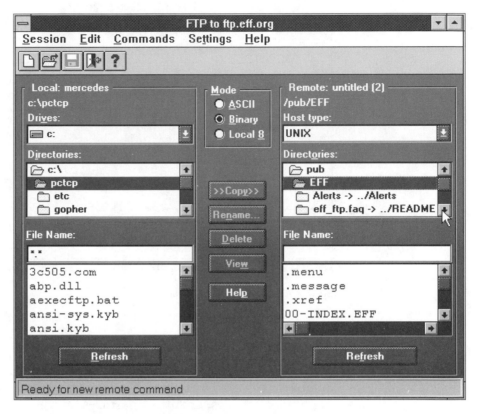

Figure 2.14 **Starting an anonymous FTP session to the Electronic Freedom Foundation (eff.org).**

Information Displayed by Finger

Above we listed how information can be displayed as the result of a Finger command. If you so choose, you can set up specific user IDs that will enable you to publish information about services and status, for example. The only difference between public and private publishing with Finger is whether the published information represents an entity rather than a person. Figure 2.15 shows a fun use of Finger—checking the status of the Coke machine at Carnegie Mellon University.

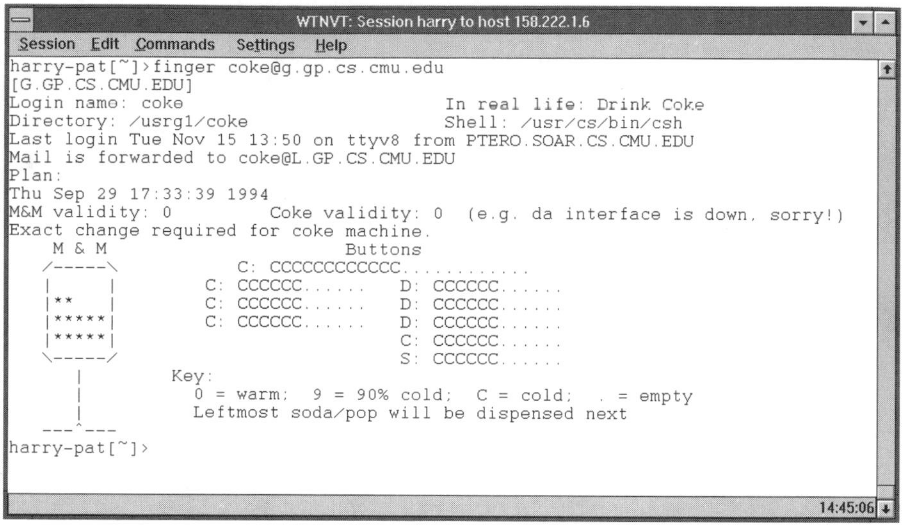

```
┌─────────────────────────────────────────────────────────────────────────┐
│ ═                     WTNVT: Session harry to host 158.222.1.6      ▼ ▲  │
├─────────────────────────────────────────────────────────────────────────┤
│ Session  Edit  Commands   Settings   Help                                 │
├─────────────────────────────────────────────────────────────────────────┤
│harry-pat[~]>finger coke@g.gp.cs.cmu.edu                              ↑   │
│[G.GP.CS.CMU.EDU]                                                          │
│Login name: coke                        In real life: Drink Coke          │
│Directory: /usrg1/coke                  Shell: /usr/cs/bin/csh             │
│Last login Tue Nov 15 13:50 on ttyv8 from PTERO.SOAR.CS.CMU.EDU            │
│Mail is forwarded to coke@L.GP.CS.CMU.EDU                                  │
│Plan:                                                                      │
│Thu Sep 29 17:33:39 1994                                                   │
│M&M validity: 0          Coke validity: 0  (e.g. da interface is down, sorry!)│
│Exact change required for coke machine.                                    │
│     M & M                    Buttons                                      │
│   /------\          C: CCCCCCCCCCCC............                           │
│   |      |        C: CCCCCC......  D: CCCCC......                          │
│   |**    |        C: CCCCCC......  D: CCCCC......                          │
│   |***** |        C: CCCCCC......  D: CCCCC......                          │
│   |***** |                         C: CCCCC......                         │
│   \------/                         S: CCCCC......                         │
│      |          Key:                                                      │
│      |            0 = warm;  9 = 90% cold;  C = cold;  . = empty          │
│      |          Leftmost soda/pop will be dispensed next                  │
│   ___^___                                                                 │
│harry-pat[~]>                                                              │
│                                                                           │
│                                                             14:45:06  ↓   │
└─────────────────────────────────────────────────────────────────────────┘
```

Figure 2.15   **Fingering the Coke machine at CMU.**

Searchable Databases

A more specific kind of published information can be provided with databases and search engines. Many databases on the Internet, including library catalogs, archives of articles, and books on-line, have their own specific interface. Database interfaces, or search programs, are called search engines.

Using one of the other Internet tools (such as Gopher or WWW) or using a specific client tailored for that database, you can publish information that users specifically request. Database publishing allows the user to access indexes to materials, making sure that the user gets what he or she wants more quickly, with fewer false starts.

Expanding the Matrix

Many resources exist only to tell you how to take advantage of what the Internet has to offer. Most of them take the viewpoint that you are primarily a consumer of information; that you are mostly interested in what you can get from the Net.

And you can get a lot—one of the great boons of an Internet connection is the ability to access information and data quickly, in usable chunks, and without having to physically go anywhere to get it. While working on a chapter for this book one morning, we were able to simultaneously receive copies of documents we wanted to reference, technical information we needed to abstract and describe, and letters of permission to reprint many things included in this book. Research and data gathering over the Internet is changing the scope of many projects, including the education of our children. We think this is a very good thing.

But for us, and we hope for you, too, getting things is only part of the Internet's value. Being able to communicate effectively, to share your views and hear the views of others, to receive information from others and to distribute information you want others to have, brings the richness of the Internet's potential to life.

CHAPTER 3

Locations in Cyberspace: Domains and Addresses

FEATURING

Chapter 3

Locations in Cyberspace: Domains and Addresses

As you begin working on the Internet, you're likely to run into the term *cyberspace*. *Cyber* comes from the 50s term *cybernetics*, which was used to describe electronic control systems and has come to refer more broadly to computers in general. *Space* hearkens back to the 60s terms *inner space, head space,* and so on—in other words, metaphorical space rather than physical space. But whether the term was coined by computer hackers or science fiction writers (both claim credit), *cyberspace* describes where you are when you are traversing the virtual geography of the Internet.

Just as in our physical lives we need some way to tell other people where things are, in the Internet's cyberspace we have to have a way to tell people how to find us or how to locate the interesting resources we have found. There are two kinds of addresses in the Internet: *Domain Names* and *IP Addresses*.

Once you figure out how to find the computer, host, or service in cyberspace, you can move on to e-mail addresses and other services that depend on knowing the address.

MASTER WORDS   With the advent of Gopher, WWW, and other servers that give you menu-driven access to services, you will find yourself using domain addresses less as you explore the network. More and more often you will need to know *only* a URL (Uniform Resource Locator) if you have to know *anything at all*. Most URLs have a domain name embedded in them, and you'll need to know that name. Many Internet clients (the software that helps you do things) have *bookmark* functions, which remember the URL for you. However, if your eventual goal is to become an *Internet Information Provider*, you should understand the Domain and IP address systems that underlie the user clients.

The Domain Name System (DNS)

People (unlike computers) like using names that mean something to them, that they can remember easily, and that have something to do with the language they speak. So when the people in the IETF who designed the addressing system were planning the way Internet users would interact with each other, they used a system using what look like words. These words roughly map to a parallel system of addresses called *Internet Protocol (IP) Addresses,* which we describe below. Every computer on the Internet has both a domain name and an IP address, and when you use a domain name, the computers translate that name to the corresponding IP address.

The names of the *domains* describe organizational or geographic realities. They indicate what country the network connection is in, what kind of organization owns it, and sometimes further details.

Since the folks who designed this system were computer programmers, who tend to think hierarchically, the Domain Name System organizes names into hierarchies, as shown in Figure 3.1, similar to the directory structures in a computer file system.

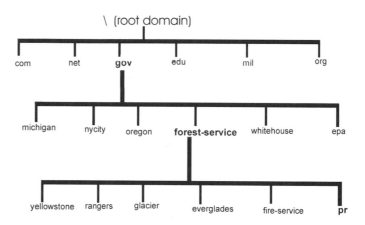

Figure 3.1 Domain name hierarchies.

Non-Geographic Domains

There are six common top-level domain types that are non-geographical:

.com for commercial organizations, such as `netcom.com`, `apple.com`, `sun.com`, etc.

.net for network organizations, such as `internic.net`

.gov for parts of governments within the United States, such as `nasa.gov`, `oklahoma.gov`, etc.

.edu for organizations of higher education, such as `sjsu.edu`, `ucsc.edu`, `mit.edu`, etc.

.mil for nonclassified military networks, such as `army.mil`, etc. (The classified networks are not connected to the wider Internet.)

.org for organizations that do not otherwise fit the commercial or educational designations, such as `eff.org`, `farnet.org`, etc.

Each domain has a number of hosts, as shown in the analysis published by the Internet Info company (`http://www.webcom.com/~walsh`), illustrated in Figure 3.2.

Don't be fooled! Because domain names are political rather than simply geographical, machines that are owned by the same organization but are located far apart can be named similarly. For example, `tweedledum.cygnus.com` is a machine owned by Cygnus Support, as is `canth.cygnus.com`. But `tweedledum` lives in Boston, with a physical

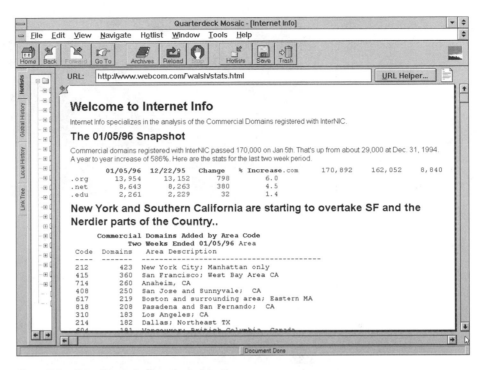

Figure 3.2   Growth rate in domain registrations.

wire connection to the national service provider BBN Planet, and `canth` is in Mountain View, California, and is physically connected to a network cooperative called *The Little Garden*. Never assume location from the domain name of the computer!

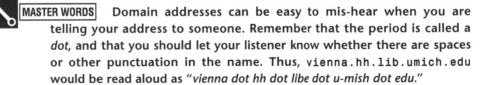

MASTER WORDS   Domain addresses can be easy to mis-hear when you are telling your address to someone. Remember that the period is called a *dot*, and that you should let your listener know whether there are spaces or other punctuation in the name. Thus, `vienna.hh.lib.umich.edu` would be read aloud as *"vienna dot hh dot libe dot u-mish dot edu."*

Geographic Domains

The geographically based top-level domains use two-letter country designations. For example, `.us` is used for the United States, `.ca` for Canada (not California), `.uk` or `.gb` for the United Kingdom or Great Britain, and `.il` for Israel.

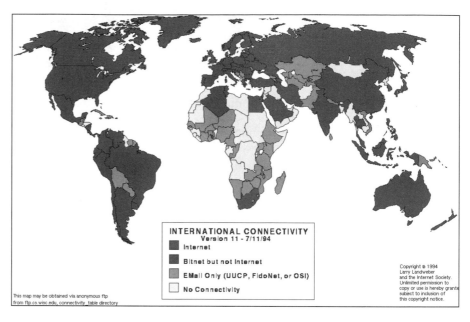

Figure 3.3 **Country connectivity by available services.**

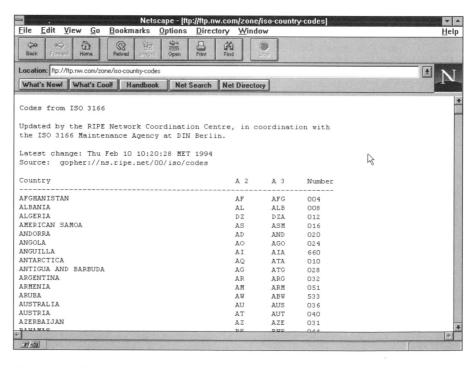

Figure 3.4 **A Web page listing the various country codes.**

An amazing number of countries are connected to the Net, as evidenced by Larry Landweber's map of country connectivity, in Figure 3.3.

Figure 3.4 shows the Web page listing the ISO Country Codes. You can see the complete list at `ftp://ftp.nw.com/zone/iso-country-codes`

Solving the Name Puzzle

In a complete (*fully qualified*) domain name, the part furthest to the right is the top level domain, representing either a type of organization or a country. As you read in from the right, the name gets more specific until you reach the name of the individual host computer. For instance:

`rubens.anu.edu.au`

is the name of a computer. It is in Australia (the geographically based domain is au), in the educational area (edu), at the Australian National University (anu), and the host computer is named `rubens`.

The best-planned names describe where in the organizational structure of the company or organization the owner of the machine can be found. For example:

`doc.cis.myuniversity.edu`

would show that this host or server is in the documentation department of the Computer Information Services Division at My University, which is an educational organization.

Some organizations let the person who uses the computer most name the machine something distinctive. So, you might see a server or host name that says something about the person's interests, such as:

`terminator.itd.umich.edu`

and

`predator.itd.umich.edu`

(These guys are Arnold fans!) or

`taliesin.sybase.com`

(this person studies Welsh poetry?) or

`bach.julliard.edu`

for the music lovers among us.

While it is possible to have very long domain names for machines (such as `birth12.maternity.womens.chicago.org`, and no, this doesn't really exist), such names would not be easy to remember and type. Most systems can be planned with simpler and easier names for the computers and local networks in the organization.

 MASTER WORDS   When the Domain Naming scheme was first being hashed out, the Internet was based mostly in the United States. So the original domain naming tree did not have a geographic domain for the United States. Today it does, but many US domain names do not have the `.us` on the end; that part is implied. Hosts and services in other countries have the country code appended.

IP Addresses

Connected nodes on the Internet have names and addresses that obey certain conventions. We've already talked about the Domain Name System, designed to be easy for humans to read and remember. In a wider sense, every node on the Net, every end point (which might be a computer or a dial-in modem), has a unique identifying address. These unique identifiers are called *Internet Protocol (IP) Addresses*.

The computer or server is known as a *host*, and the IP address, which identifies its physical network connection, is known as the *host address*. The IP address can be difficult to remember, is easy to enter incorrectly, and will not necessarily remain the same if someone needs to reorganize his or her network. The difficulty with these addresses is what led to the creation of DNS names, which map IP addresses to a set of more easily remembered words.

The IP address is a set of numbers that expresses the exact physical connection between a computer and the network on the Internet. In some senses you can think of them in the same way you think about telephone numbers: a phone number uniquely describes your connection to the telephone network.

What Do All Those Numbers Mean?

IP addresses contain four sets of numbers separated by periods or dots. These combined parts are unique on the network and allow it to know specifically which computer is to receive which electronic packet as well as from which specific computer the electronic packet came.

IP addresses look like this:

```
35.1.1.42
```

or

```
154.154.34.245
```

Unlike domain names, these addresses are now primarily read and managed by computers. IP addresses are organized from left to right, with the left-hand octet describing the largest network organization, and the rightmost octet describing the actual network connection.

To make this easier, let's go back to the telephone number analogy:

```
+1 415 555 1212
```

When we look at this number, we decipher where it is and what it means starting at the left. The **+1** tells me I am accessing the United States long-distance service. The **415** says I am looking for a number in California, specifically in the Bay area. **555** is a number owned by the local phone service, and **1212** is specifically the directory information service.

IP addresses work somewhat similarly but are more complex than phone numbers because there are literally millions of network connections possible and because IP addresses are intended for use by computers rather than people. Given an IP address that looks like this:

```
154.135.186.235
```

we can untangle it similarly. First, though, some explanations. Each of the parts of this address—the numbers between the periods—is called an *octet*. Octet is a word that comes out of computer science, and each octet has a value of 8 bits within the computer. When the four octets of the address are added together, the total address has a value of 32 bits. Using the various combinations of these octets, several million unique identifiers can be assigned. (You don't need to know much more about the computer math if you are not going to be doing network programming. But you'll hear the term from people who do know the jargon, and it's nice to know what they're talking about.)

Classes of Networks

Just as with our phone number, we can look at the leftmost octet and determine something about the network. Network addresses are divided into classes, which are assigned depending on the size of the physical network. The class of address (A, B, or C) determines the number of network connections that can be linked to the physical network. The value of the first octet tells us what class the network is in, and how large the physical network that underlies the numbers is. The first octet is sometimes called the *network address* or *net number*. Figure 3.5 gives a snapshot of the number of hosts and domains in the three network classes.

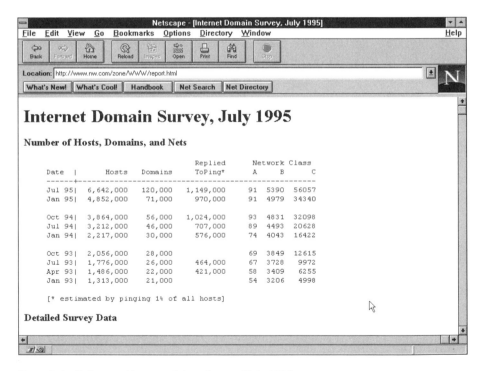

Figure 3.5   Estimate of hosts and domains as of July 1995.

Class A: Over 16 Million Served

Class A network addresses are assigned to major service providers—the big regional or national nets. NEARNET, Sprint, ANSnet, Merit, and AT&T are examples of organizations with Class A network numbers.

Class A numbers have a first octet with a value of 1–126. There can only be 126 Class A nets, but each can have up to 16,777,214 hosts. Following are some sample Class A addresses.

IP Address	Who Is It?
54.0.0.0	Merck Pharmaceuticals
36.0.0.0	SU-Net
12.0.0.0	AT&T

Class B: Larger Nets

Class B addresses go to organizations with larger nets, such as universities or large businesses. They have a first octet value between 128 and 191. The first two octets in a Class B address describe the network itself, and the second two identify the host. There are 16,382 possible network identifiers, and each has a potential of 65,534 connections. Some Class B addresses are shown below:

IP Address	Who Is It?
128.29.154.1	Mitre Corporation
128.54.16.1	University of California at San Diego
147.174.1.5	Southeastern Louisiana University
132.162.32.243	Oberlin
129.34.129.4	IBM Watson Research
140.147.2.12	Library of Congress
148.129.129.10	Census Bureau

Running Out of Room: the Class B and C Crisis

Class C addresses have first octet values of 192–223. The first three octets are used for the network numbers and the last octet is the host number. Since smaller networks are likely to be the most numerous, this class is where most networks will be assigned. There are over 2 million potential network numbers in Class C, but each can support only 254 hosts. Originally, Class C addresses were intended for small company networks, K-12 schools, and single machines that weren't connected to other, larger nets.

In the past few years, however, the original *address space* (the blocks of addresses originally allotted) has gotten cramped. Although the original designers had assumed that there would never be more than 126 Class A nets, and 16,382 Class B nets, we're quickly running out of address room. Some larger companies are getting multiple Class C addresses, and a new method of doing routing and other services for those addresses has been devised. This new routing protocol is called CIDR (Classless Internet Domain Routing).

The list below shows a few of the many Class C addresses.

IP Address	Who Is It?
192.216.246.0	Stanford Federal Credit Union
198.200.160.0	Berkeley Unified School District
192.195.245.3	University Microfilms
198.137.240.10	Whitehouse.gov
199.0.132.66	National Public Radio

Other Classes

Class D addresses, with a first octet value of 224–239, are reserved for *multicasting,* which is a way of grouping addresses so that you can send messages to them all at once. It's something like a mailing list for host addresses.

Class E addresses, 240–247, are reserved for future use.

Interim Solutions: Classless Internet Domain Routing, or CIDR

As we mentioned before, the phenomenal growth of the network is causing a crisis in the number of network addresses available. This is only the first problem. The second is the potential overload of major routers in the Internet backbones. The number of routes that were registered with the NSFNET prior to its termination exceeded 50,000, but today's off-the-shelf routers cannot effectively deal with more than approximately 30,000 routes. Internet planners and researchers are looking into many ways to solve the problem, and in fact have proposed a "Next Generation" of Internet addressing. In the meantime, however, there is only one technique in wide use that is capable of preventing overload of the major backbone routers. That technique is known as aggregation, or CIDR.

CIDR is essentially the "clumping" under a single network address of all the addresses that are served by that network number. This allows the major networks (such as Sprint, MCI, ANSNet, etc.) to carry a single route that leads to many different networks, just as a single Class C network leads you to all of the hosts on that Class C network.

The Internet's Next Generation of Addressing (IPng)

Growth is the basic issue that led to the need for a next generation of IP addressing. When IP addressing was first considered, the growth of the Internet and the limitations of the addressing scheme were not as obvious as they are today, with 20/20 hindsight.

The IETF (the Internet planners) consider that the current addressing scheme serves what could be called the computer market. The following paragraphs are excerpted from the proposal for the next generation of IP addressing (available on the World Wide Web at `http://playground.sun.com/pub/ipng/html/ipng-main.html`):

> The computer market has been the driver of the growth of the Internet. It comprises the current Internet and countless other smaller internets which are not connected to the Internet. Its focus is to connect computers together in the large business, government, and university education markets. This market has been growing at an exponential rate. One measure of this is that the number of networks in current Internet (40,073 as of 10/4/94) is doubling approximately every 12 months. The computers which are used at the endpoints of internet communications range from PC's to Supercomputers. Most are attached to Local Area Networks (LANs) and the vast majority are not mobile.

> The next phase of growth will probably not be driven by the computer market. While the computer market will continue to grow at significant rates due to expansion into other areas such as schools (elementary through high school) and small businesses, it is doubtful it will continue to grow at an exponential rate. What is likely to happen is that other kinds of markets will develop. These markets will fall into several areas. They all have the characteristic that they are extremely large. They also bring with them a new set of requirements which were not as evident [earlier in the development cycle]. The new markets are also likely to happen in parallel with one another. It may turn out that we will look back on the last ten years of Internet growth as the time

when the Internet was small and only doubling every year. The challenge for an IPng is to provide a solution which solves todays problems and is attractive in these emerging markets.

Nomadic personal computing devices seem certain to become ubiquitous as their prices drop and their capabilities increase. A key capability is that they will be networked. Unlike the majority of today's networked computers, they will support a variety of types of network attachments. When disconnected they will use RF wireless networks, when used in networked facilities they will use infrared attachment, and when docked they will use physical wires. This makes them an ideal candidate for internetworking technology as they will need a common protocol which can work over a variety of physical networks.

These types of devices will become consumer devices and will replace the current generation of cellular phones, pagers, and personal digital assistants. In addition to the obvious requirement of an internet protocol which can support large scale routing and addressing, they will require an internet protocol which imposes a low overhead and supports auto configuration and mobility as a basic element. The nature of nomadic computing requires an internet protocol to have built in authentication and confidentiality. It also goes without saying that these devices will need to communicate with the current generation of computers.

Another market is networked entertainment. The first signs of this emerging market are the proposals being discussed for 500 channels of television, video on demand, etc. This is clearly a consumer market. The possibility is that every television set will become an Internet host. As the world of digital high definition television approaches, the differences between a computer and a television will diminish. As in the previous market, this market will require an Internet protocol which supports large scale routing and addressing, and auto configuration. This market also requires a protocol suite which imposes the minimum overhead to get the job done. Cost will be the major factor in the selection of an appropriate technology.

Another market which could use the next generation IP is device control. This consists of the control of everyday devices such as lighting equipment, heating and cooling equipment, motors, and other types of equipment which are currently controlled via analog switches and in aggregate consume considerable amounts of electrical power. The size of this market is enormous and requires solutions which are simple, robust, easy to use, and very low cost. The potential pay-back is that networked control of devices will result in cost savings which are extremely large.

IPng Advantages

IPng is a new version of the Internet Protocol, which will someday replace the current addressing strategy.

IPng was designed to take an evolutionary step from the current system, which is called *IPv4*. In this step, however, IPng will remain compatible with the current system. The designers did not throw out functions and tools that worked well, although functions that were no longer needed or do not work well were removed.

The biggest advantages in IPng are:

▶ Expanded Routing and Addressing Capabilities

▶ IPng increases the IP address size from 32 bits to 128 bits. Without getting into the math, this will allow for millions more addresses.

▶ IPng includes capabilities that will provide support for authentication, data integrity, and confidentiality. As these are prime needs for the Internet now, and certainly in the future, this is an excellent change.

You as a user may not see major changes in the way the Internet functions when the new IP addressing schemes are put into place, but your Internet service provider will be able to provide you with better—faster and more dependable—service.

Unsnarling the Tangles

So, let's go back to our sample address:

    154.135.186.235

We now know that this is a Class B address (remember, the first octet is 154, between 128 and 191). Looking at the very last octet, 235, we know that this is the physical point on the network where this host or service is connected. Just as with the phone number, the address 154.135.186.235 pinpoints a specific, unique address.

There are two problems with human beings using these numeric IP addresses to reach hosts and services. First, they're hard to remember and easy to type incorrectly. Second, if a specific computer gets moved to some other physical connection point (say, if the machine gets moved to a new office down the hall, or even across the country!), its network IP address will change. This is why the DNS addresses are mapped onto the IP addresses. The only thing you need to know is how to reach a translator machine for this mapping. Sometimes you put a numeric address into the software on your workstation so it can reach a DNS translator directly; sometimes the modem pool or other network hardware is connected to a computer that knows how to do this translation.

WARNING   If you get a message from your system administrator notifying you of an impending IP address change for a DNS server, don't ignore it! If you don't know what it means or what you need to do about it, ask. Otherwise, you could suddenly find yourself cut off from the network.

What Do I Need to Know?

As a general user, you'll usually never have to know anything about IP addresses. You'll only need to know about IP numbers if you do any of the following:

▶ Set up your office or home workstation to use IP communications software.

▶ Call back into your home workstation or a computer service you use regularly from an unfamiliar server (see the tip below).

▶ Help plan for your local area network.

▶ Set up your own information services.

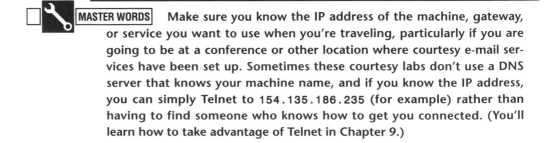

MASTER WORDS   Make sure you know the IP address of the machine, gateway, or service you want to use when you're traveling, particularly if you are going to be at a conference or other location where courtesy e-mail services have been set up. Sometimes these courtesy labs don't use a DNS server that knows your machine name, and if you know the IP address, you can simply Telnet to 154.135.186.235 (for example) rather than having to find someone who knows how to get you connected. (You'll learn how to take advantage of Telnet in Chapter 9.)

CHAPTER 4

Options for Connecting

FEATURING

Chapter 4
Options for Connecting

THIS chapter shows how to choose the type of Internet connection that best meets your needs. You should read it if any of the following statements describe your situation:

You don't have access to the Internet at this time.

You have access through your work or organization and want to obtain access at home to further your personal interests.

You already have a personal account and want to learn more about how to connect your business, school, or organization.

You may actually have access without knowing it. It may be that your organization has an Internet connection, but the connection hasn't been made available to your department; or a connection is available but the word hasn't spread yet; or someone's been working on it and the installation isn't yet complete and therefore hasn't been announced. So if you are part of a larger enterprise, you might go and check with the systems people and see what they can make available to you. After investigation, if the answer is still "my organization is not connected," then you'll want to read this chapter.

Whatever your motivation, there are a few criteria that will make your search for the appropriate type of connection easier.

What Do You Want to Do?

If a simple e-mail connection is your primary need, your options are wider than if (for example) you plan to offer audio files on an Internet server. Throughout this chapter you'll learn about what you can do with each of the basic connection types.

Where Are You Geographically Located?

In general, Internet service providers serve some geographic areas and not others. Some service providers offer services throughout the United States. Some provide services to a specific local region, like the Bay Area in California or the Boston, MA, metropolitan area. You will need to contact still other providers if you are outside the United States.

Determining Which Provider Is for You

Choosing a provider of network services involves the same process as with any other type of service provider.

First determine what services you want to purchase—just what type of access do you need and what type of equipment do you have? Are you trying to connect only one computer, or a LAN? Is there information your organization wants to make available to the public?

Then, determine who among the providers can deliver those services in a manner you consider effective.

When you have the potential providers located, you need to consider the level of service you wish to purchase and the costs for those services. For Internet services costs, mostly you pay for the connection itself, not for what you do with that connection (although like everything else on the Internet, that too may change).

With the information you have gathered, you can determine which provider is best for you.

At the end of this chapter, you'll find a list of network providers who sell connections to large regions or across the entire United States. Some provide international access.

BUT ISN'T IT FREE?

There is no such thing as a free connection to the Internet. Someone, somewhere is paying the bills for the equipment, the software, the routing, the network engineers, the telephone lines, and so on.

You will hear that universities in the United States have "free" connections. This is just not true. All the universities run their own networks. They have significant investments in equipment and management to connect smaller networks (for example, departmental networks) into something like a campus-wide network backbone (or larger bandwidth network) that can carry more traffic. Some universities have been working for years to connect their major academic departments to their networks. Many universities are working to build network connections into the residence halls for their students. Some fund extensive computing laboratories where students without personal computers can go to use the equipment and the Internet. The physical network is expensive to install and maintain. The software to route packets must be written (by employees) or purchased from a vendor. The computers that are used to route the packets must be purchased. The employees who install the connections or watch the network to make sure it continues to function must be paid their salary and benefits. Someone must have paid for the computers that are used for access and the software licenses for that access. And we haven't even routed a packet off the campus yet!

Most universities belong to a regional research and education network. The fees for these vary, but they are typically thousands of dollars per year. Each regional network needs to maintain its physical and logical network and therefore needs to pay for equipment, physical infrastructure, and people costs, too. These networks are membership organizations and, while some of the costs for the regional networks were originally met by the National Science Foundation (as were some of the universities' expenses, for that matter), the members are paying at least part of the expense. Some of the regional networks are, in turn, paying gateway fees to the owners of the larger national network backbones. These networks also have personnel and equipment expenses that must be met.

So how can anyone say all this is free? Well, if you are an individual user on one of these campuses, you are possibly not being billed directly for your access. It might be included in your student computing fees, for example, or your student registration fees, or, if you are an employee, as part of the general expense of running the department for which you work. Many universities like to think of access to networks and computing as an academic overhead expense similar to the costs incurred in maintaining an academic library. These costs are shared across the organizations, but the individual user may not see them.

What Equipment Do You Have (or Plan to Obtain)?

If you want to connect your department's Local Area Network (LAN) to the Internet, you will need different software and hardware than if you want to have dial-up access through your personal computer and modem at home. Throughout this chapter you'll learn about hardware and software requirements for different connection types.

How Much Are You Willing to Budget for Your Internet Access?

Rate structures vary widely from "free" and fixed-cost, terminal-emulating accounts to high-speed connections to very large servers. If you haven't much experience with the Internet, you might want to start out with a lower-cost account and learn how to use the Internet effectively for your organization before you invest in a lot of equipment.

Dial-Up Connections

If you have a computer, some communications software, a telephone line, and a modem, you can connect to the Internet. The types of connections listed here are in order of least complicated (in the level of equipment and software necessary) and least expensive to most complicated and most expensive. The major ways that you can link to the Net using dial-up are:

Host/terminal connection (shell accounts)

Individual computer TCP/IP link

Dial-up or on-demand TCP/IP link through your LAN

Each of these has variations, of course, and we discuss them individually below.

MODEMS

In order for your computer to communicate over telephone lines with another computer, the information you wish to send or receive must be converted into electrical impulses that can be sent over the connection. The device that makes that happen is a *modem* (**mo**dulator/**dem**odulator). You'll learn more about working with modems in Chapter 6, but here's a quick look at what they do and what to look for when buying one.

The higher the number of bits per second the modem will transmit, the faster you will receive the information. But because the modem is translating your signals into a carrier language, it is necessary to have a translator that "speaks the same language" on the other end. Therefore, you need to select a modem that speaks to your service provider, or select a service provider that can speak to your modem.

Some modems provide the extra service of data compression. If your modem compresses in a way not understood by your service provider, you will not be able to take advantage of the compression. There are standards for these compression algorithms, and many manufacturers build modems to these standards. There are also proprietary protocols that will make effective transmissions even faster. The disadvantage of these proprietary protocols is that both ends of the transmission must have the same type of modem. If you use standard transmission protocols, you will be able to transmit data to and from most service providers.

A good rule of thumb is to purchase the fastest modem that you can reasonably afford (and that is not speaking a proprietary language). Modem technology is changing rapidly and there are now (in early 1996) 28.8 Kbps modems using compression protocols readily available for about $150. Just a year or so ago, those same modems cost around $400. This means that many people can afford to buy 28.8 Kbps modems that will run at 38.6 Kpbs, which makes using graphical interfaces quite a bit more enjoyable.

Currently, 14.4 modems running at 19.2 Kbps are considered "acceptable but slow." The speed of change in technology is such that twelve months ago these modems were considered "fast."

Today's "fast" is defined by a telephone service called ISDN or "Integrated Services Digital Network." This service (which requires special switches and equipment on your part, the part of your telephone provider, and the part of your Internet Service provider) can be run as fast as 128 Kbps. You can see for yourself that this is much faster than 14.4 or 9.6. ISDN services have been around for ten years or so but they've not been deployed widely. Local telephone carriers are now better prepared to help you acquire these services, which make full-motion video over the Internet much more practical. You'll want to talk first to your local telephone carrier to see if this service can be provided in your area. If it can, the next thing to do is to talk with Internet service providers to see if they can provide the appropriate service. Do make certain that you understand the rate structure from both the telephone provider and your Internet service provider. The rates can vary widely and can be sensitive to both distance and traffic. This means you may face quite expensive bills, so you'll want to understand what you are buying.

Host/Terminal Connection (Shell Accounts)

In a host/terminal connection, your computer acts as if it were a terminal directly connected to some Internet host. You use a terminal emulation program that can make your computer act like a VT100 terminal. (A VT100 terminal is the lowest common denominator of emulation; it's the simplest to implement, and a terminal that can display visual information.) The program signals your modem to dial and handles the transfer of characters from your computer to the host computer and back. Your connection is at one remove; that is, the host computer is the one that is "on the Internet." This means that when you transfer files using FTP (discussed in Chapter 9), for example, the files are transferred to the host. You will then need to download the file to your computer using your communications program.

What Types of Users Is This Best For?

Host-terminal connections are best for

People on limited budgets.

People who don't need constant connectivity.

People who don't want to manage systems and network connections themselves.

People who may need to connect from many different locations and who don't have access to a network system that supports dynamic TCP/IP addressing. (*Dynamic addressing* supplies you with a different TCP/IP address depending on where you are connected from. Some software and security systems are not configured to support these differing addresses.)

People who may want to connect via the Telnet program to a host from some other host on the network in order to obtain a specific service.

If you have access to the Internet from your work location and you want to have a personal Internet account, a host-dial connection works well, too. This is because you can use Telnet to connect to your personal account from your work site. Host-dial connections are appropriate for entry-level users because they allow inexpensive access while you learn what your future needs will be.

What You Can Do with It

This depends directly on the features offered on the host computer. If the host offers a Gopher client, you will be able to use it. If the host offers a World Wide Web client, you will be able to use it. You will read and send your electronic mail to and from the host computer. Some host accounts will support your use of programming-language compilers. Some host accounts will allow you to store files on their disk drives or make available information via anonymous FTP. Typical service providers offer e-mail, access to newsgroups, Gopher, WWW, Telnet, FTP, Finger, Netfind, and Internet Relay Chat. Some providers offer a menu interface to these applications to make them easier for the new user to operate.

What You Cannot Do with It

Most host/terminal connection accounts do not offer graphical interfaces; you interact with the host by typing commands rather than by clicking on icons. You will, however, be able to download graphics to your computer, where you can use your own graphical viewing programs to see the images. A host/terminal connection does not allow you to "serve" information that is on your computer. You will need to move the information from your computer to an Internet-attached host. With a terminal connection, you will not be able to take advantage of any multitasking features of your computer: a terminal connection is a one-thing-at-a-time operation, so you cannot (for example) download a file and also be connected to a library catalog for searching at the same time.

What Will It Cost?

Host-terminal accounts are usually the least expensive type of Internet connections. Restricted host accounts (e-mail only, for example) may be quite inexpensive. You might be able to find them for less than $10 per month. Some services offer unlimited connect-time (the amount of time you are connected to their network and host) for a flat fee of less than $20 per month. Others offer a lower account fee and charge for connect time.

The lowest fees will be available from services called "freenets." These are volunteer and cooperative services created to provide access to others who might not have it available. A typical freenet account will cost around $20 to $30 per year. This type of account is generally restricted to a relatively short period of time within a time cycle, e.g., one hour of connect time per day or week. This allows the freenet to provide wider access with a small staff and not too much equipment.

What Do I Need to Know to Use It?

You'll need to understand how to connect your computer to your modem and how to run your terminal software. You'll need a basic understanding of the features offered on the host computer. The most difficult part for many newcomers is learning how to give the host computer the correct command to accomplish what you want to do. In this book you'll find that information for all of the most important Internet services. And in many cases, the user interfaces for the host computers have been (or are being) improved so that it is less necessary to know all the ins and outs of the UNIX operating system, which is used on many Internet hosts. As with many things we do, practice does indeed make us more effective, if not perfect.

Types of Host-Dial Connections

Local Dial   The local number host-dial connection is the least expensive type available. (Unfortunately, this kind of connection is not available in all areas.) With an access point that is a local telephone call from your geographical location, a telephone connection that does not incur measured time costs, and a flat rate Internet service, you may stay connected to your provider's system for long periods without incurring extra charges.

Long Distance Dial, Connection Services, or Public Data Networks   If you are not located where you can reach a service provider with a local call, you will need to consider whether a long distance call, a connection service, or a public data network is best for your connection. These are not really Internet service provider accounts but other ways of establishing your connection. Some nationwide service providers offer 1-800 or 1-900 service and essentially pass their costs through to you. This can be more expensive than simple long distance. A connection service is one that offers local or 800/900 access and then, once you are connected, lets you use Telnet to connect from the terminal server to your Internet service. This type of connection may be flat-rate, too. Investigate the speed at which you are allowed to connect. If the speed is very low, it might be less expensive to connect via long distance using a faster transmission speed, because you will be connected for less time.

Another connection method is that of a public data network like CompuServe's Packet Network or SprintNet. These services offer connections to local access points that may be more convenient for you. Be sure to investigate how fast these connections are because they might not offer the type of service that will serve your needs.

 MASTER WORDS   When investigating providers, be sure to request a complete list of local access points. Because of the structure of regulated telephone tariffs, it may be less expensive for you to dial an out-of-state point than to connect to the geographically nearest point. For example, if you happen to be located in Lake Tahoe, California, on the California/Nevada border, the nearest local access point for many service providers is Sacramento, California. The day rate (8 AM to 5 PM) for connections from Lake Tahoe to Sacramento is 40 cents per minute. However, if you call Las Vegas, Nevada, or Phoenix, Arizona, or Denver, Colorado, or even Raleigh, North Carolina, the day rate from one long distance carrier is around 27 cents per minute. This is a significant savings.

Telnet from Another Internet Site   Sometimes you may want a personal account on a commercial provider, but you do not have a modem at home. Or, say, your commercial provider does not have a local phone access number but you can reach it from other Internet sites using Telnet (further explained in Chapter 9). Or, suppose your local campus or regional network offers local dial-up from which you can make an Internet connection to another host. These are all ways to use the Internet itself to facilitate reaching your host service provider.

Telnetting from another Internet site is the same as a local call from the expense point of view. You need to be connected to some system that offers Telnet. It may be from a connection provider or from another Internet site (some people maintain accounts with more than one Internet service provider because of features that are offered on one and not on the other). Again, these connections may be a local call for you. Or you might not call at all. For example, you could Telnet in from your work site. In this case, you are most likely using the connections provided for your work, such as a LAN or an enterprise TCP/IP network, to your own advantage.

Restricted Access Accounts   If you are seeking only e-mail access, or perhaps a combination of e-mail with a few Usenet newsgroups (discussed in Chapter 13), a restricted-access account may be the best choice. These are offered by some freenets (community access host systems), for example, whose equipment budgets aren't large so they offer fewer newsgroups. There are also public-access UNIX sites or bulletin boards, whose general purpose is for some special interest: a local government bulletin board, or one devoted to providing information about health care. These sites may offer inexpensive e-mail access.

Yet another variation of this type of account is the gateway from an information provider. America Online offers its own services (chat rooms, files, and so on) as well as access to newsgroups and e-mail to Internet users. Prodigy offers an Internet e-mail gateway, as does CompuServe. All the information service providers offer access to the World Wide Web. Some of these services may be charged at a premium rate over the regular service. The premium may well be less than the cost of a connection to an Internet service provider, however, if you need or want the information service anyway.

Individual Computer TCP/IP Link

An individual computer TCP/IP link allows your computer to function as an Internet host. It's your host running whatever software you elect to run, providing only the service you've chosen to provide. These links are called either SLIP (for serial line Internet protocol) or PPP (for point-to-point protocol) links. Both types of links will handle dial-up. Both can take advantage of software techniques that condense or "compress" the data being transmitted so that transferring information to your computer is less complicated.

Although you might feel nervous at first about setting up and running your own Internet host, it's not rocket science. And most TCP/IP-based software for desktop computers is designed to work just like the other software you use on that machine. For example, Windows-based applications have the same kind of pull-down menus, dialog boxes, and error messages as your other applications. The same holds true for Macintosh or X-terminal applications.

What Types of Users Is This Best For?

People who want the benefits of working in a computing environment they are already familiar with while being connected to the Internet are candidates for this type of connection. People who want to use a graphical WWW browser, direct file transfer, or PC-based mail services that depend upon direct Internet connectivity need to use this type of service.

What You Can Do with It

With an individual link, using dial IP access, you have the benefits of direct e-mail (with multiple mailboxes if your e-mail software supports that), some sort of newsgroup access, and, again depending on the software you are running, the full suite of Internet tools—Telnet for connecting to other machines, FTP for transferring files directly to your machine, Finger for looking up information on people and organizations, and usually, an Internet browser or two for Gopher and WWW (text and image-viewing services). With this link you can run one of the graphical World Wide Web browsers like NCSA's Mosaic, Netscape Communications' Netscape, or Cornell Law School's Cello.

With your computer directly connected, you can transfer files directly to your personal computer, rather than to an intermediate host owned by an access provider. In contrast, if you have a host-based account, you must transfer the file from the source to your host, and then download it to your personal machine.

What You Cannot Do with It

There are only a few limitations on what you can do with an IP-based link.

The disk space available is limited to that on your local computer, unless you also have an account with a public access site. If you have a slower link (28.8 Kbps or less) you probably won't want to have people accessing your host via FTP, Telnet, Gopher, or WWW, even if your software and link will support that access, because their access will slow down your own use of the link. And for you *real* programmer types, you won't have access to UNIX compilers this way, unless you are already running UNIX on your local computer. You'll need to have an account with some public access site.

What Will It Cost?

Dial-up IP connections for individuals can run less than $20 per month (although most providers charge somewhat more than this). Some service providers charge a flat fee. Others charge a fee that includes a certain number of connect hours in the monthly fee and charge extra if you use more than that number of hours. Still others charge a monthly fee and charge a per-hour usage fee.

The best way to compare costs is to make a chart of the various options, and then talk to other folks using the services about how they use the service. Depending on what you want to do, differing charging structures may make more sense for you. For example, if you want to be online for long periods of time (if you want to participate in online forums, interactive communications, or spend a lot of time looking at resources at other sites), a flat-rate service is best for you. If, on the other hand, you want to upload and download files, including e-mail, and then get off the connection to process those files, a per-hour fee or minimum-use fee structure would suit you best.

What Do I Need to Know to Use It?

As of this writing, it is still not simple to install an individual SLIP or PPP connection. You will need to understand the basics of TCP/IP—what a default gateway is, what an IP address is, and so on. Fortunately, books like this are available to help you. Furthermore, vendors like Spry are offering "Internet in a box" products, designed to make the installation and connection process easier for nontechnical folk.

A TIP FOR TRAVELERS

If you travel frequently and want to have your portable computer directly connected to the Internet, you will need to investigate services and software that provide dynamically assigned IP addresses. If you have an IP address that is assigned permanently to your connection, you will need to call that specific access point to connect. For example, if you are usually connected through Washington, DC, and you travel to Las Vegas for a meeting, you will need to dial Washington if you have a static IP address. A service that provides dynamic IP addressing, however, may provide you access in Las Vegas. Another way around this is to have a combination account. Some service providers will provide a host-dial account that can access their network at various points as part of their SLIP or PPP connection accounts. Then you use the SLIP or PPP connection when you are at your home site and your host-dial connection when you are traveling.

Dial-Up or On-Demand TCP/IP Link through Your LAN

A dial-up link from your LAN is the intermediate step between individual dial-up and a dedicated high-speed link. It is therefore somewhat like dial-up and somewhat like having a direct link.

The main difference between this type of connection and one to your individual computer is that the TCP/IP software runs on the LAN server, and your connection is to the server. (A LAN for purposes of this discussion includes PC and Mac-based networks, such as Banyan, Novell, or AppleTalk, or a UNIX-based server with Ethernet links.) A TCP/IP connection through a LAN, either on a dial-up connection or a direct connection, is the most common type of IP connection, much more common than a personal dial-up IP connection. (We talk about dedicated links in the next section.)

With a dial-up or on-demand connection to your LAN, software in your server dials up your service provider when you tell the server you want to make a network connection. It may also dial into the network on a regular schedule to exchange e-mail.

What Types of Users Is This Best For?

A dial-up or on-demand connection is best for users who would like to exchange e-mail with the Internet from the e-mail system running on the LAN, but who do not have a lot of Internet traffic. Or for the user who only occasionally wants to use an Internet service. For example, a small law office might want only occasional access to a server that contains court decisions or governmental data. Other than that, the users would like to exchange e-mail with other lawyers and perhaps belong to a mailing list dealing with legal issues. These uses are similar to individual uses, and dial-up connections would be a reasonable choice. Dial connections are intermittent. They must be initiated by someone or by some program. They can meet busy signals from the provider's system. But they can be much less expensive than a dedicated link.

What You Can Do with It

A dial-up link to your server will allow you (if your network has an e-mail gateway) to exchange e-mail with Internet users, using your regular LAN-based mail software.

Beyond that, the client software you choose and the LAN server TCP/IP software you choose will dictate which Internet functions you can use. There are LAN clients for many of the Internet tools like Telnet, Gopher, FTP, and so on. A particular advantage of an FTP client on a LAN server is that files transferred there are available to all users of the LAN, just like any other shared file. Because the file space available on a shared server is usually larger than on the individual computers hooked into the LAN, you may be able to transfer larger files than you would be able to transfer to your individual machine.

Your LAN server may allow more than one person on the LAN to connect to the Internet at the same time. This is, of course, one of the many benefits of shared resources.

What You Cannot Do with It

The limitations of this type of connection are the same as for individual TCP/IP connections. The speed of the connection may limit your activity. There may not be clients for all the Internet functions for your particular type of LAN. (Check your applications menu or icons, or ask your systems administrator which network applications are available to you.) In addition, unless you have a very fast line and very fast server software, you will experience delays and congestion if several people try to use the Internet services at the same time.

What Will It Cost?

Costs for this type of connection vary widely. For the individual end user, a connection through a workplace LAN may not be charged to you directly. Students and faculty at schools and universities may have to pay some sort of technology fee in order to use computer resources, even if they are not connected to the Internet. If you are the business owner or the person who pays the bills for that workplace LAN, you will need to evaluate your costs carefully. Some providers base their fees on the number of connections within your LAN. Some providers base their fees on a flat rate. Some providers see no difference between this type of connection and one that is on an individual computer. Careful investigation of the providers available to you will be necessary to determine the actual costs for what you have in mind. (At the end of this chapter we include a list of regional and national providers, whom you can contact for cost and service information. You may have other, local providers available in your area.)

What Do I Need to Know to Use It?

For this type of connection, you will need a knowledgeable network administrator who can configure the TCP/IP software for your particular LAN and train people how to use the connection.

Dedicated Link Connections

A *dedicated link* is a permanent connection over a telephone line between a modem and a modem or a router and a router. A *router* is a specialized computer that reads the addresses of each TCP/IP packet and sends the packet to its destination. At lower transmission speeds (up to 28.8 Kbps), modems are used. At higher speeds (56 Kbps and above), routers are used. With a dedicated link, your personal computer or LAN is connected to the Internet at all times.

 MASTER WORDS   How many people and workstations are connected to the Net? Let's look at the numbers. Some estimates say there are 9 million individual users; others say there are 24 million. The January 1996 host count by Network Wizards was 9.4 million Internet hosts. One of the largest direct Internet service providers has more than 350,000 users. America Online has more than 5 million users. One thing that everyone agrees on is that the growth continues to be large.

What Types of Users Is This Best For?

A full, dedicated, high-speed network connection is best for organizations that want to provide information to the Internet and desire a 24-hour, 7-day connection. In general, this type of connection is best for a larger organization that is serving many internal as well as external customers. Smaller organizations may do better by obtaining individual accounts with a service provider and using the services of an information publishing organization.

What You Can Do

With a permanent connection, you have all the basic Internet applications available to you. Once you have installed the software on your end of the link, the basic Internet tools and resources are always at your fingertips. However, with this type of connection it is relatively easy to become an information provider yourself. (Becoming an information provider is discussed in Part II.) You could set up your computer or your network server to be accessible to anyone connected to the Internet 24 hours a day, 7 days a week. This makes it easier for your customers to obtain information or support, or for information about your organization or school to be made available. (Remember that to make information available, or to access information over the Net, still requires that you install and run Internet tools on your end of the connection. Some of these are more complex to run well than others—particularly those tools that allow others to get to your information, such as servers for file transfer, Gopher, and World Wide Web access.)

What You Cannot Do with It

This connection is what is described as a "full" connection. There are no features available to the Internet that you cannot use. You may choose not to use some of them for security, privacy, or policy reasons, but there is nothing you *cannot* do.

What Will It Cost?

Full connection costs have four components:

1. the network connection charge

2. the local loop (or *tail circuit*) charge (the charge for the physical line to your site)

3. the necessary one-time hardware and software and setup charges

4. recurring maintenance costs

    Network connection fees vary based on the speed of the connection. A 14.4 Kbps connection can cost less than $150 per month. (Note, however, that many providers are moving away from direct connections at this speed, because of the popularity and availability of dial-up modems that handle these speeds.) A T1 (or 1.5 Mbps) connection can run more than $1000 per month. A T3 (45 Mbps) connection can cost even more than that.

    The local loop charges also vary with the speed of the connection and with distance from your Internet access provider's network access point. (These are sometimes called *points of presence* or *POPs*.) Local line charges are usually based on cost per mile or cost per foot from the point of presence. In general, however, because local rate and line charges are "tariffed" (or set by Public Utilities Commissions), there will not be much difference among providers.

    Some of you will have several choices of provider in your geographical area, some only one. It largely depends on the competition for data services in your area, the remoteness of your location, and other local and regional regulations. Be sure to compare the services of several providers if there is more than one provider for your area.

One-time hardware and software costs vary widely depending on what's available from your provider, what you already have, what discounts you can get from vendors, and so on. Your best bet is to get several estimates and compare carefully. If you do not feel comfortable deciding what's the best deal for you, consider hiring a network consulting firm. Ask your provider candidates who they work with, or ask other businesses who they used or were happy with. In calculating recurring costs, you should not neglect to consider personnel training, salaries, and benefit costs for the people it will take to maintain your server and network connection. People with the requisite technical knowledge are in high demand and can command high salaries. If you choose to train someone already on your staff to troubleshoot and maintain your connection, you must consider the lead time for the person to learn the necessary skills, the training costs, and the costs incurred in reassigning some of that person's tasks to another staff member. It is important for you to consider all your recurring costs when contemplating a network connection.

HOW MANY STAFFERS WILL IT TAKE TO MAINTAIN YOUR RESOURCE?

In general, your support staff varies based on what you are doing and how many people you are supporting.

For an office of 1–10 workstations, expect one part-time systems administrator and one person who knows what to do in a pinch (someone who knows where the manuals are and knows the appropriate system passwords).

For 10–20 workstations, plan on two part-time systems administrators or one full-time and one part-time admininistator (and if you are providing online resources for customers, one full-time person to handle those resources).

For 20–50 workstations, you need two full-time administrators (and a vacation or emergency backup), and at least one part-time internal customer support person. If you also support external clients or have online resources, you need at least one full-time person to handle that support (preferably, one person to handle maintenance of the resource and another to answer customer questions).

Once you get beyond 50 workstations, you will need a network administration department, and the manager you hire for that job will be best able to determine how many staff are necessary to keep you up and running smoothly.

What Do I Need to Know to Use It?

Using your own network connection well requires several kinds of skills. You need people who know how to design and present information using the Internet tool kits (such as Gopher, WWW, and FTP archive software). You need people who know how to build and maintain networks themselves and are able to work with the network engineers of your service provider to find and repair problems. And, finally, you need to have people who understand how to use the Internet tools to find information that will be needed by your organization.

Information Publishers (Dial-up)

Electronic information publishing is one of the ways to make your organization's information available without requiring the initial outlay of resources (time as well as money) that comes with obtaining a full Internet connection. Essentially, having your information published is "out-sourcing" the development, presentation, and maintenance of the information server to a company that takes your materials and works with you to design an appropriate presentation of your material on the Internet.

Besides designing the presentation, an information publisher can also publish your information on the Internet. For example, Internet Distribution Services of Palo Alto, CA, Ecommerce of Columbus, OH, or The Internet Company of Cambridge, MA, will design and build a series of pages for the World Wide Web for you (the Web is discussed in Chapter 10). You can then contract with these companies to publish the pages on their server or present them on your own server. If they publish the pages, there is no need for your company to manage its own network connection. This option is particularly attractive to organizations that are not ready to maintain their own connections, or don't want to do so. With an information publisher, you can use lower-bandwidth, lower-cost connections for your personnel and yet still reap the benefits of maintaining a presence on the Internet.

What Types of Users Is This Best For?

Organizations that want an Internet presence and aren't ready (or don't want) to manage their own connections can benefit from this service. So, too, can small or geographically distant organizations for whom the cost of a full connection would be prohibitive.

What You Can Do with It

Information publishers generally support access through Gopher and/or WWW. Some will also provide access to FTP libraries, so that you can store material for your clients/customers to download. Finally, an information publisher may file domain registration forms for you and manage the publishing system as if it were in your network domain. This means that to the user, the computer system managed at the publisher's location would carry a domain address that identified it as part of your organization's domain. For example, if SmallCo, Inc., wanted to have a Web server but didn't want to maintain their own machine, they could contract with NetPublishers, Inc., to handle the Web server and information. The Web server would be running on NetPublisher's machine, `clients.netpub.com`. However, SmallCo could advertise to their customers that they had a Web server running at `www.smallco.com`.

What You Cannot Do with It

Usually information publishers will have secure systems, so you will not be able to give accounts on that machine for your customers to log in to, for example. You may be able to leave materials on the system (perhaps by anonymous FTP, for example) for the publisher to convert into Web or other server information.

What Will It Cost?

Costs can vary widely. They will include both development costs and recurring management costs. You can compare the recurring management costs to those you would incur if you wished to manage your own server and network connections.

What Do I Need to Know to Use It?

You need only be able to select a publisher that meets your needs.

A List of Information Publishers

On the accompanying CD you'll find a partial list of companies providing various information-publishing services. We make no recommendations of any of these services by providing this list. In choosing which services to include, we have selected those who have high-speed links, offer a wide variety of services, or who are addressing a specialty market.

Comments and service descriptions are provided by the companies themselves, or taken from their marketing literature. We make no guarantees of accuracy. Prices are subject to change. Many of the companies offer services beyond the Web information-publishing services listed here; contact them for further information.

A complete list of providers is maintained by Mary E. S. Morris of Finesse Liveware (`marym@finesse.com`). You can obtain a copy of her list using:

Anonymous FTP: `ftp://ftp.einet.net`. Then choose /pub/INET-MARKETING/www-svc-providers.

E-mail: `wwwproviders@finesse.com`—no message needed.

NetNews: Routine posts to: `alt.internet.services` and `comp.infosystems.www.providers`.

How Big a Connection Do I Need?

To answer that question, you first need to understand what "big" means in terms of data transfer capabilities.

Measurements

Data transfer speeds are usually expressed in bits per second. Sometimes you may see faster speeds expressed in bytes (or thousands of bytes) per second. A byte is roughly the equivalent of a single character. (There are 8 bits in a byte. A single bit is represented by either a 1 or a 0. These digits are our visual representation of the on/off impulses that are carried on the network.)

Note that we said *network*, not *wire*. Many times a network is not a wire. The medium may be copper wire in some places. It may also be a fiber optic link, a microwave link, or a radio transmission; in short, any method that can be used to carry the impulses. The network providers and the telephone companies continually strive to improve the transmission media and the rules by which the data are carried. As an example, in the late 1980s, when the NSFNET was implemented, the ultra-high speed connection that was estimated to be appropriate (considering availability, current technology, and costs) was a 56 Kbps connection. At that time, the connection was considered "state-of-the-art."

Almost before the connections were completed, the demand exceeded the ability of the network to carry the traffic. So the T1 NSFNET was proposed. T1 transfers data at the rate of 1.544 Mbps (1.5+ million bits per second). This was *so* fast and could carry so much more data that some people believed the expense in implementation and recurring costs would not be practical—the network, they believed, would be underutilized. Instead, what happened is that new applications were developed and more and more new users were connected; and the T1 network, too, became saturated.

The T3 NSFNET was begun. The T3 rate is 45 Mbps. The network designers had, however, learned well. Before the T3 NSFNET backbone was fully operational, designers and researchers had begun work on additional technologies to meet the needs of as-yet-unanticipated applications.

In talking about how much traffic can go over a network connection, you will hear the term *bandwidth*. As originally used in radio and television, it defines the range of a frequency, or band, that signals can be carried on. Carried over into data networking, bandwidth describes the amount of information that can be carried on a specific connection. Extremely fast connections have a lot of bandwidth: a great deal of information can be carried on those links. Applications that require high bandwidth include audio, video, and graphic-intensive applications such as World Wide Web.

BITS AND BYTES: A QUICK SUMMARY

Files are measured in bytes:

KB = kilobytes = thousand bytes

MB = megabytes = million bytes

GB = gigabytes = trillion bytes

Transfer speeds are measured as bits:

byte = 8 bits

*Estimating Bandwidth:
How Wide a Band Do I Need?*

The answer to this question depends entirely on what information you want to move. There are enormous differences in file size for different kinds of information:

Type of Information	Typical File Size
e-mail message	2.2 KB
longer document (20 pages)	44 KB
Graphic image	330 KB
1 minute of audio	475 KB
1 minute of video	2400 KB

Network connections are sometimes called pipelines. This helps us visualize how we transfer data. You can think of the data as a liquid you are pouring into a pipe. Data to be transferred is contained; that is, it is of fixed size: the user or even the user's application may not report what the exact size of the data is, but the transfer protocols themselves use the size information to make sure that the transfer is complete and correct. Because the amount of data is known and the size of the pipeline can be known, it is possible to estimate how long it will take to move your data through a pipe of a specific size.

 MASTER WORDS   Some service providers offer what they call "bitpipe" service. This means that they simply provide a wire over which bits can be pushed. You provide all the maintenance and programming expertise.

Now think about the *kind* of information you want to move. Let's say we have an e-mail message of approximately 2.2 KB. Remember, we need to multiply by 8 to count the number of bits: 2.2 KB × 8 bits/byte = 17,600 bits. If we divide that by 2400 bps (considered an *extremely slow* modem in 1996) we arrive at 17600/2400 or a little less than 7.5 seconds. At 2400 bps, it doesn't really matter if we round off this way, because the speed is relatively slow and it's hard to optimize sufficiently well so that the "extra" seconds used are really noticeable.

However, if we take that same message and send it at 9600 bps (a typical faster modem rate), it will take only 1.83 seconds. Table 4.1 summarizes the difference in transfer rates.

RATE	TRANSFER TIME	IMPROVEMENT
2400 bps	7.3 seconds	(base)
9600 bps	1.83 seconds	3.98 times faster
14400 bps	1.22 seconds	5.98 times faster
28800 bps	0.61 seconds	11.97 times faster
56 Kbps	0.314 seconds	23.24 times faster
1.5 Mbps	0.0113 seconds	646.01 times faster
45 Mbps	0.00039 seconds	1871.79 times faster

Table 4.1   Relative Speeds of an E-Mail Message of 2.2 KB

MASTER WORDS   The strength of a TCP/IP connection is that each packet can be routed through any open point in the connected networks. This allows transmission, even if some point in the connected network becomes unavailable during the transmission itself. The weakness of packet routing is that since no particular packet is guaranteed to traverse any particular network route, no one can guarantee that your packets will have the same bandwidth available to them from the beginning to the end of their route. So if you want to move data from point A to point B, you need to consider the bandwidth of the networks between those two points. If you are considering purchasing a T1 connection, but the network to which you wish to deliver information has a 56 Kbps connection, the network can only deliver information to the destination effectively at 56 Kbps. The data will queue on the network and will take longer to deliver than if there were a T1 connection all the way through.

Diagnosing Congestion and Bandwidth Problems

Once you begin to gain expertise in file transfers and other network information transfers, you will begin to care even more about the bandwidth between you and your target. Particularly if you want to get information from a host that's behind a slow link, or if you find your-self on a very congested connection, you'll want to know how to con-nect to and use more efficient connections. You may not care during the early days of your Internet exploration (although we know you will be frustrated if you get stuck on a really slow resource). If you care about estimating bandwidth and about understanding bottlenecks and congestion, these next paragraphs are for you.

In packet routing, you may not know all the points in the network between the starting and ending points. But you can ask in general about the bandwidth of your network provider, about the bandwidth of their connection into the larger Internet, or their connection into parallel networks.

The easiest method for figuring bandwidth is for you and the other party to be served by the same provider and know the bandwidth of all the net-work connections between your two points. Then you just need to look at three factors: your connection to the network provider, the provider's network bandwidth, and the connection to the target destination. The smallest number will be the effective throughput rate. If you are not con-nected through the same service provider, the exercise remains the same, but finding out all the possible bottlenecks becomes more difficult.

Here's a simple exercise in determining bandwidth: SmallCo is con-nected to the Net at 56 Kbps. This means that their link is capable of handling 56,000 bits per second of information. If the whole pathway was running at this speed, it would take 2.3 minutes to transfer 1 mega-byte of data, about the same as a full 3.5" high-density diskette.

Their network provider has a backbone speed of T1 (1.5 million bits per second). If the whole pathway was running at T1, it would take .08 minutes to transfer the data.

SmallCo wants to transfer this file to MyCustomer, who has an account on HappyBBS, which has a 14,400 bps link to the same net-work provider.

The data leaves SmallCo's machine at 56,000 bits per second. When it gets to the network backbone, it speeds up to T1 speeds. But when it gets to the link at HappyBBS, it has to slow down to 14,400 bps.

The most important thing to remember here is that the data can't be transferred faster than the slowest link. Thus, it takes 9 minutes to transfer the data from SmallCo to MyCustomer's account space on HappyBBS.

Choosing a Provider of Dial-up Internet Services

Finding Who the Providers Are The easiest way to do this is to ask someone you know who is already connected about their provider. Find out if you need to be a member of some organization or if anyone can join. Ask them if they like the service provided. Would they recommend that service or some other one instead? If you ask them nicely, maybe you can get this person to obtain information for you on the Internet itself.

One of the best places to find information is via the Gopher servers and WWW pages offered by the providers themselves.

Many of the providers also have automated e-mail replies in response to an e-mail message to the address `info@provider.com`, e.g. `info@netcom.com` or `info@lloyd.com`. If e-mail is sent to that address, an e-mail reply will be sent describing the offered services.

Another place to look on the Web is `http://www.thelist.com`. There are other lists, of course. You can find many of them by going to a search or directory service like Yahoo (`http://www.yahoo.com` on the Web) and looking under Internet Service Providers, Indices or Lists.

Don't forget that many providers will be listing themselves in your telephone book and running advertisements in your local newspapers. Finding the right Internet service provider is much like looking for any other kind of service provider. Look in all the places you'd look to find an accountant, for example.

Criteria to Consider

Here are some questions you might consider in choosing a dial-up service provider:

> **What type of account is it?** IP dial or host-based/shell?
>
> **What is the setup fee for the account?**
>
> **What is the fixed monthly charge?**
>
> **How many connect hours are included?**
>
> **What is the charge for the extra connect hours?**
>
> **What is the telephone charge** to connect to the provider's network?
>
> **What other costs are there?**

What is the availability of my connection? (That is, are there time restrictions? Are there dial-up numbers in a wide variety of locations? Do they have enough dial-up ports that I will not have many busy signals?)

What kind of assistance is available when things go wrong?

Choosing a Provider of Dedicated Internet Services

Finding Who the Providers Are   The process for finding a provider of a dedicated Internet connection is the same as for finding one for a dial-up account; you just look in slightly different places.

Remember to consider the costs of the dedicated service carefully: a glance at our provider's list and their various charges will help you understand more fully how expensive a dedicated line can be.

Again, asking your acquaintances and people in similar organizations who have Internet connections for the name of their providers is a good idea.

For dedicated connections, an additional source for access providers is the D-list. You'll find it on the Internet by sending e-mail to dlist@ora.com. This list was developed by Susan Estrada for her book, *Connecting to the Internet* (O'Reilly, 1993), which is devoted entirely to the topics discussed in this chapter.

Criteria to Consider

Here are some questions you should ask in choosing a service provider for a dedicated connection:

What is the speed of the connection proposed?

What is the installation charge?

What is the monthly recurring connection fee?

What is the monthly local loop charge?

What is the separate cost of the required equipment?

What other costs are there?

What is the availability of the type of connection you want?

What kind of assistance is available when things go wrong?

Is training offered?

How secure is the connection? Does it provide what you need?

Can you get a service guarantee? If so, what is it?

What are the long-term prospects for the viability of the provider? Will they be in business next year?

With the answers to these questions and an up-to-date list of network service providers, you should be well-equipped to pick a provider that is appropriate for you. The following list will help you get started.

Selected North American Internet Service Providers

Here is a sampling of Internet service providers, with phone numbers and e-mail addresses so you can contact them directly for current prices and service availability. All of these providers offer multistate, national, or international service. Area codes are included where available. The list is adapted from "Dern's Selected Internet Service Providers," copyright © 1996 Daniel Dern. (Daniel Dern is available at ddern@world.std.com.)

AlterNet

Area: US and International

Voice: 1-800-488-6384

URL: http://www.alter.net

E-mail: info@alter.net or sales@alter.net

ANS (Advanced Network & Services)

Area: US

Voice: 1-800-456-8267

URL: http://www.ans.net

E-mail: info@ans.net

FAX: 703-758-7717

BBN Planet

Area: US

Voice: 1-800-472-4565

URL: http:/www.bbnplanet.com

E-mail: net-info@bbnplanet.com

FAX: 617-873-3599

CERFnet

Area: Western US and International

Voice: 800-876-2373, 619-455-3900

E-mail: sales@cerf.net or infoserv@cerf.net

FAX: 619-455-3990

CICnet

Area: Midwest US (MN, WI, IA, IN, IL, MI, OH; area codes 312, 313, 708, 800)

Voice: 800-947-4754 or 313-998-6703

URL: http://www.cic.net

E-mail: info@cic.net or annp@cic.net

FAX: 313-998-6105

Digital Express Group

Area(s): Greater DC/Baltimore, Southern California, NYC, NJ (area codes 201, 202, 212, 215, 301, 302, 410, 412, 516, 609, 610, 703, 718, 804, 908, 914, 917)

Voice: 1-800-969-9090

URL: http://www.digex.net

E-mail: info@digex.com

FAX: 301-345-6017

NETCOM

Area: US and International

Voice: 1-800-353-6600 or 408-983-5950

URL: http://www.netcom.com

E-mail: info@netcom.com or personal@netcom.com

Fax: 408-241-9145

PSI Inc.

Area: US and International

Voice: 800-82PSI82 or 703-620-6651

URL: http:www.psi.com

E-mail: info@psi.com

FAX: 1-800-FAXPSI1

Uunorth

Area: 416, 604, 905, 807 area codes (Canada)

Voice: 416-225-8649

E-mail: info@uunorth.north.net

CHAPTER

5

Communication Software

FEATURING

Chapter 5

Communication Software

COMMUNICATION software (sometimes called terminal emulation software) enables your computer to communicate with another computer. Communication software is commonly used in combination with a modem. The software offers you a way to give commands to the modem, to dial the other computer's modem, and then to issue commands and receive responses from the remote computer. (We discuss modems in Chapter 6.)

There are many packages available today. They fall into two categories: terminal (used for accessing most host/shell account systems) and TCP/IP-based (which let your computer become a host on the Internet). The "dumb terminal" packages, like ProComm Plus for DOS/Windows and VersaTerm for the Macintosh, use your computer as a terminal—a keyboard and a display—attached to the remote machine. TCP/IP-based communication packages establish your computer as a workstation on a network.

Note: The term "dumb terminal" does not impugn the CPU power or computing wizardry of your very expensive workstation. It simply means that the packages emulate the early computer terminals, which had no intelligence of their own: they were essentially a video display and a keyboard, and all the computing was handled by the computer at the remote end. If you are connecting to a host or shell account, this is all the smarts you need.

What Kind of Software Should I Select?

The kind of software you choose will depend upon how you want to use your computer and the services available from your service provider. Many providers expect you to have dumb terminal communication software, or will provide their own proprietary communication software, and so give you a host or shell account. (CompuServe, America Online, and Delphi are examples of this kind of provider. Netcom and some other providers offer both host accounts and network accounts.) As TCP/IP-based communication software has become more common, more network service providers will deliver services based upon TCP/IP networking. For example, America Online also offers a version of their service that runs over TCP/IP. It's called GNN for Global Network Navigator.

TCP/IP-based communication software uses either SLIP (Serial Line Internet Protocol) or PPP (Point-to-Point Protocol). Special-purpose software, like PC Remote, uses a proprietary protocol that only works with its own server. Netcom's NetCruiser software is a hybrid; it uses standard protocols but connects specifically to the Netcom servers and will only talk to Netcom.

SLIP is the older protocol, but PPP is meeting with greater success. SLIP works only with IP, the Internet Protocol. PPP works with IP, AppleTalk, IPX (Novell's NetWare connectivity protocol), as well as others. The one you choose will depend upon which one your provider offers. If they offer both, you can choose the program whose interface you prefer. There is little difference between the protocols from a user's perspective. They both accomplish the same thing. It's like selecting an automobile for transportation. You choose the one whose features best fit your own needs.

There are many communication software packages available, both from commercial sources and from the public domain archives, and more are becoming available all the time. Support is likely to be better for the commercial packages, but the public-domain software has a significant initial cost savings. You should base your choices on what you want to do, what works well with your local provider's network, and what kind of support you can get for the software. If you are good at troubleshooting, and enjoy watching e-mail or news for tidbits of information, one of the public-domain packages may suit your needs very well. If you want point-and-click with phone support and little tinkering, go for a commercial solution.

Looking for Features

Different communication packages will have different features. Three of the most important are dialing functions, terminal emulation, and file transfer. You will also want to look into other network functions, and how easily the package is installed and configured.

TCP/IP Protocol Package (Underlying Network Software)

Some packages offer only clients such as Telnet, FTP, and WWW, and require you to use another communication package to establish the dial-in connection. PC and clone client packages often use WinSock (for Windows Sockets), a standard networking interface for Microsoft Windows. Windows 95 includes WinSock software and several clients as part of the basic operating system.

Macintosh computers use Apple's MacTCP, with another package using either SLIP or PPP to establish a link over the modem. Newer versions of the Macintosh operating system use Open Transport instead of MacTCP.

Dialing Functions

A basic terminal package integrates the dialing functions with the terminal interface. You will type in the commands to make the connection from the same screen that you read information from your provider on. A TCP/IP-based communication package, however, separates the modem-dialing functions from the rest of the programs. The dialer establishes a link that the other pieces of the package can then use to request services from, and provide services to, the network.

Terminal Emulation

A terminal package should offer at least a VT 100 emulation. It may emulate other terminals, such as the DEC VT220, as well. Like the terminal package, the Telnet client should emulate a VT 100, at least. Other terminal emulations may also be available. If the package includes an emulator of the IBM 3270 terminal, it will usually be as a separate application.

File Transfer

Since you will probably want to download files at least occasionally, the software you get should support file transfer protocols as well. If you are getting basic terminal software, some common file transfer programs to look for are Kermit, X-modem, Y-modem, and Z-modem.

A TCP/IP-based communication package should include at least an FTP client.

Gopher and WWW Clients

You will not be happy long without Gopher and WWW clients, as well. Look for a package that offers the complete suite of clients (or be sure and install the complete range if you are retrieving separate clients from the Net). Fortunately, most of the packages now available include a Web browser. Some, like Netscape, Attachmate's Emissary, or Microsoft's Internet Explorer, are Web browsers that include the full suite of functions within them.

Other Network Functions

Other network clients, like Finger, Talk, Whois, and Internet Relay Chat, may also be provided. A complete package will also include servers for applications like Finger and FTP, and possibly others, that will let other people request information from your machine.

Installation and Configuration

When looking for software, whether public-domain or commercial, remember to take into account the ease of installation and maintenance. If you are not a tinkerer, you should get a package that has an installation and configuration script or menu, rather than one that requires you to hand-edit a configuration file. Installation for some packages is done from a window with point-and-click features (called a *Graphic User Interface,* or *GUI).*

What's Available

To get the best product for your needs, your best bet is to contact your provider and find out what their users have had good experiences with. Ask your friends. Read the reviews in the trade journals and magazines.

Operating systems vendors are beginning to provide TCP/IP packages, either in the basic operating system (Microsoft's Windows 95) or as an add-on (IBM's OS/2 Connection Pack). These packages provide the basic (PPP) connectivity and, usually, a Telnet and FTP client, but you will have to get additional clients from other sources.

Some of the packages currently available are listed below. Note that many of the packages are based on some other vendor's connection software.

For example, the Internet Membership Kit is based on Netmanage's Chameleon software. Other common bases are Netcom's NetCruiser and Spry's Air series.

Underlying Network Software

Many TCP/IP software packages need underlying network software, sometimes called *drivers* or *dialers* to work with a full Internet connection. Two of the best for dial-up use are Trumpet Winsock and MacPPP.

Trumpet Winsock

As we said above, many PC and clone client packages use WinSock, a standard networking interface for Microsoft Windows. If your TCP/IP software supports WinSock, that means it can also run any WinSock-compatible program you acquire. Trumpet Winsock is a very reliable and strongly tested (as well as being shareware) TCP/IP driver. The most recent version is 2.1 or above and includes PPP support; Trumpet Winsock has had SLIP support for several years. The package is available by anonymous FTP from FTP.trumpet.com.au (yes, this really is in Australia). Trumpet's implementation of WinSock is in the directory /winsock.

Other versions of WinSock are available, some with commercial packages.

MacPPP

MacPPP is a PPP implementation for the Macintosh. MacTCP is a driver that underlies many Macintosh communications packages (and if you don't have it you must get it separately), but MacTCP needs MacPPP to work over a modem. MacPPP is essentially just a dialer and PPP implementation. MacPPP is available by anonymous FTP from merit.edu, in the directory /pub/ppp/mac. Merit Networking, Inc., has licensed MacPPP to others. These alternate versions have been distributed by their authors.

Terminal Packages

These packages offer terminal emulation and file transfer, and are mostly useful with host-dial or shell accounts.

VersaTerm for Macintosh

ProComm

WinQVT

Windows Terminal

VersaTerm

A full-featured terminal communication package for the Macintosh, VersaTerm offers several file-transfer protocols, including Kermit, X-modem, Y-modem, Z-modem, and MacBinary. The most recent versions include SLIP support. VersaTerm also works with the Comm Toolbox in Macintosh System 7.

ProComm

A full-featured terminal communications package for DOS/ Windows, ProComm offers several file-transfer protocols, including Kermit, X-modem, Y-modem, and Z-modem. The latest version includes Winsock-compliant Telnet and FTP clients. Unfortunately, ProComm does not include a TCP/IP stack. You will have to install one yourself (see the section above on Underlying Network Software).

WinQVT

A DEC VT220/102/52 terminal emulator and communications program that runs under Microsoft Windows. It offers Kermit, X-modem, Y-modem, Z-modem, and CompuServe B-Plus file transfer protocols.

Windows Terminal

A DEC VT100 terminal emulator that runs under Microsoft Windows, Terminal is a simple communications program. It offers X-modem and Kermit file transfers along with reasonable dialer features.

TCP/IP-Based Packages

The software packages in this section are generally full or large suites of Internet clients, rather than single-function clients.

Emissary (Attachmate Internet Products Group)

Explore (FTP Software, Inc.)

Internet Chameleon (NetManage Inc.)

Internet_in_a_box (Spry, Inc.)

LAN Workplace for DOS (Novell)

NetCruiser (Netcom)

Quarterdeck Internet Suite (Quarterdeck)

SuperTCP (Frontier Technologies)

NCSA Suite (public domain)

Emissary (Attachmate Internet Products Group)

Emissary is an integrated suite of TCP/IP applications that is designed to be used by the individual user on a single machine or on a larger Local Area Network (LAN). It uses the single-screen approach that is familiar to users of other Windows-based applications and provides strong local and remote file management. It includes e-mail, Usenet, Telnet, and Web browsing features as well as a Web page editor. Available commercially, via telephone order, and via the Web at `http://www.twg.com`. Trial version downloadable.

Explore (FTP Software, Inc.)

Explore is a full suite of TCP/IP applications, offering news, e-mail, Telnet, and FTP along with the Mosaic World Wide Web browser. Explore includes PPP and Winsock. Available from computer retailers.

Internet Chameleon (NetManage Inc.)

A full suite of TCP/IP applications. The Chameleon Sampler has Telnet, FTP, a WWW browser, and other clients. Several packages are available from Chameleon, all of which include PPP and WinSock. The Sampler is sometimes available for free, but the other products are full commercial versions.

Internet_in_a_box (Spry, Inc.)

A full suite of TCP/IP applications, including PPP and WinSock support. "Internet in a Box for Kids" includes SurfWatch, a program that blocks sites deemed by the publishers to contain sexual or other indecent material. "Mosaic in a box" offers just Mosaic and Spry's dial-up software, based on PPP and Winsock. All three are available at computer retailers.

LAN WorkPlace for DOS (Novell)

A suite of TCP/IP and NetWare applications for Microsoft Windows. It includes PPP and WinSock support. The latest version adds

Netscape as the World Wide Web browser. Available at authorized Novell resellers.

Minuet

Minnesota Internet Users Essential Tool is an integrated package of TCP/IP tools, including a news reader and Telnet, electronic mail (using the POP protocol), Gopher, FTP, and Finger clients, for DOS. SLIP, but not PPP, is available separately. It is available by anonymous FTP on boombox.micro.umn.edu, in the directory pub/pc/minuet.

NetCruiser (Netcom)

A SLIP-based proprietary package, NetCruiser includes most of the major Internet applications in the form of a Windows-based Graphical User Interface. Newer versions of NetCruiser (Versions 1.6 and later) let you use other clients as well as the Netcom clients for Internet access, once the connection to Netcom is established. NetCruiser is available for free, but will only work with Netcom, with whom you must purchase an account. Once you have a version of NetCruiser, you can download the newer ones from Netcom. Also available via download from the Web at http://www.netcom.com.

Quarterdeck Internet Suite (Quarterdeck)

A complete suite of TCP/IP applications, including PPP and Winsock. Quarterdeck Mosaic bundles Mosaic with Quarterdeck's dial-up PPP software. Available at computer retailers.

SuperTCP (Frontier Technologies)

A full suite of TCP/IP applications for Microsoft Windows. It includes PPP and WinSock support. Available at computer retailers.

NCSA (public domain)

A collection of network clients, including Telnet, FTP, WHOIS, and others, written at the National Center for Supercomputing Applications (NCSA), University of Illinois, Champaign-Urbana. There are versions for both the Macintosh and DOS. They all require a TCP/IP connection, over either Ethernet or PPP; and they do not include the communications software, so you will need to get one of the underlying network software packages we describe above. The NCSA suite is available at most large FTP archives.

TCP/IP-Based Separate Clients

The software packages in this section are programs that require you to have a separate TCP/IP dialer/driver package.

Trumpet Newsreader (Trumpet)

winQVT/Net

Fetch for Macintosh (FTP only)

Mosaic

Netscape

Trumpet Newsreader (Trumpet)

An excellent news reader for Microsoft Windows (illustrated in Chapter 13, which discusses Usenet News). The package is available by anonymous FTP from FTP.trumpet.com.au, in the directory /wintrump.

WinQVT/Net

An Ethernet-TCP/IP version of WinQVT. It does not include its own transport, requiring a third-party packet driver or WinSock implementation.

Fetch for Macintosh

Fetch is an excellent FTP client for the Macintosh. It requires a TCP/IP connection, such as is available with MacPPP and MacTCP. It is available by anonymous FTP from FTP.dartmouth.edu, in the directory /pub/mac. (One of Fetch's endearing features is the dog icon, which runs faster or slower depending on how quickly the transfer is proceeding.)

Mosaic

A World Wide Web client originally written by the National Center for Supercomputing Applications (NCSA), at the University of Illinois, Champaign-Urbana. There are versions of NCSA Mosaic for UNIX, Windows, and Macintosh. NCSA Mosaic is available by anonymous FTP from FTP.ncsa.uiuc.edu. Like NCSA Telnet, NCSA Mosaic requires a TCP/IP connection and does not include the communication software. Various commercially distributed versions of Mosaic (licensed by NCSA) are also available; these are often enhanced versions of the original NCSA Mosaic. You'll find versions of it commercially available identified by some variation of the Mosaic name. Some versions will require separate TCP/IP and communication software.

Netscape

A World Wide Web browser. Like Mosaic, it has versions for UNIX, Windows, and Macintosh. The original developers of Mosaic left the University of Illinois and continued development on their own. Netscape's most recent versions (2.0 and higher) include e-mail, threaded news software, and Telnet support. One of Netscape's largest drawing cards is its set of security features, which allow for encrypted transfer of information (such as credit card numbers) to and from secure Netscape WWW servers. Netscape offers several versions of its browser in the different types listed here for a number of different computer platforms (Windows 3.x, Macintosh, Windows 95, and UNIX).

An educational or evaluation browser, which is free but which expires on a regular basis so that new software must be downloaded. This version is not a secure client.

Netscape Navigator Personal Edition, which includes the underlying network software and dialer support as well as the secure browser.

Other Packages and Trends

In addition to these packages, some computer and modem manufacturers have begun bundling TCP/IP communications software with their products. For example, Hewlett Packard's Pavilion and Acer America's Aspire computers each come with several access programs like Netcom's NetCruiser and America Online access already installed. However, be aware that some of these packages are set to connect to the information services like CompuServe or America Online; they do not necessarily include PPP or SLIP communications. CompuServe and America Online now include connections from their proprietary software through to the Internet at large (but not necessarily via TCP/IP). Prodigy is now Web-based. America Online has its Information Service and its Internet-only access service, GNN. CompuServe has its CompuService Information Manager (CIM) and its more recently announced SPRYNET, an Internet-only access service.

CHAPTER

6

Once You're Connected: Working with Direct and Dial-Up Links

FEATURING

Basic concepts and vocabulary for
data communications

Using and troubleshooting a direct link

Using and troubleshooting a dialup link

Working with SLIP and PPP

Chapter 6

Once You're Connected: Working with Direct and Dial-Up Links

I N the previous chapters we discussed the criteria you need to consider in choosing how you want to be connected to the Internet and what types of software you may want to obtain. You learned that there are basically two ways to make a network connection: the *direct* (or *dedicated*) *link* and the *dial-up link*. As the names imply, a *direct link* has a continuous connection from your workstation to the computer or network, and a *dial-up link* is one you initiate by dialing into a modem over a phone line.

In general, you are more likely to have a direct connection to a router or LAN (Local Area Network), and a dial-up connection to a modem pool that lets you access either a LAN, a BBS, or a general-access launching point from a network service provider. Because of cost, most direct connections are at offices, dormitories, or workstation clusters, and most home systems use some variety of dial-up.

The good news about direct and dial-up connections is that, in most cases, you can use similar communications software no matter how you are connected. You will need to configure the software to know whether to wake up a modem or a direct connection, but the basic settings remain the same.

In this chapter we talk about the basic characteristics of direct and dial-up connections, and offer some simple troubleshooting tips.

What You Need to Know First (Datacom 101)

The following section is a review of basic data communications terms and theory. If you're already familiar with these concepts, feel free to go on to the section that describes your type of connection, either "Plugged In: Using a Direct Link," or "Reach Out and Touch the Net: Using a Dial-up Connection."

 MASTER WORDS   Many of these concepts apply whether you have a direct connection or a dial-up link, or host-dial or TCP/IP-based software. Because of differences in technology between host-dial and TCP/IP-based software, some of these concepts apply more to one technology than the other.

Host-Dial versus TCP/IP Connections

When we discuss *direct* versus *dial-up* connections, we're talking about a difference in the physical wire connection to the Internet. Another fundamental distinction between types of connection has to do with the protocols used to govern the connection. *Host-dial* communications have been in use for over 35 years, successfully connecting users to their computers and to their network providers. Host-dial connections allow you to become a terminal on your provider's network, usually connected to a host or terminal server. You can have a session where you use Internet tools such as Telnet or FTP, but the actual work of using those tools is handled by the server or host you are signed on to.

There are several names for host-dial type connections. You may see them called:

dumb terminal

shell account

terminal or TTY

host connection

asynchronous, or asynch

The other variety of connection is *TCP/IP-based,* in which software running in your workstation allows you to act as an Internet host, using the standard set of TCP/IP tools such as Gopher, Telnet, FTP, World Wide Web, and so on.

You can have either of these two varieties of connections with either sort of physical connection. Table 6.1 shows how the four possible combinations are generally used.

	Direct Link	**Dial-up Connection**
Host-Dial	Traditional mainframe link, as well as some LANs; passing away	CompuServe, AOL, etc., as well as many older dial-up providers
TCP/IP-Based	Most common LAN and WAN links	Home users, those dialing onto LANs at work, most commercial consumer providers

Table 6.1.   Host-Dial vs. TCP/IP Software

Host-Dial Connections

Host-dial users generally have no "smarts" in their terminals beyond the simple visual session management, and some don't have even that much control. Their high powered workstation acts just like an old-fashioned printing terminal. For this reason, this kind of access is also called "dumb terminal" access.

Most host-dial dial-up users have a limited range of Internet services available *end-to-end;* that is, they must Telnet or connect to a host that handles the Internet services for them. Most have some method of file transfer (such as Kermit or screen capture), but usually they cannot FTP a file from a distant service directly to their machine. They must, instead, FTP it to their host, and then download it from the host to their local workstations.

The most common host-dial connection these days is into a bulletin board system or other host on which you can do work such as read mail or use a client such as Gopher or World Wide Web (WWW). Many network providers, however, are now using some sort of network access server, which allows users to dial into the network, but which has no particular services itself. Many network access servers that accept host-dial connections (not all of them do) will let you use Telnet, WWW, or Gopher to reach other services, but you don't have access to file space, FTP, or e-mail services from the server itself. Figure 6.1 illustrates both types of host-dial sessions.

Host-Dial Connection

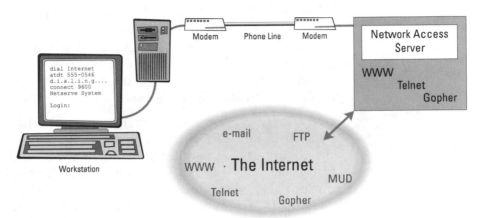

User logs into a network access server, on which network clients such as Telnet, WWW, and Gopher run.

Usually there is no file space for FTP or download; the user generally Telnets to a BBS or host for e-mail and FTP services.

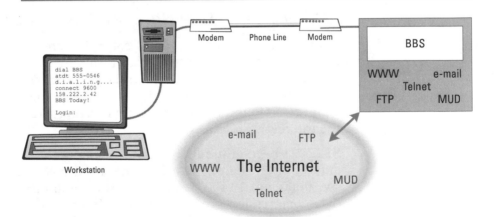

User logs into a bulletin board or other host. Internet clients such as Telnet, FTP, e-mail, and network news run on the host.

Users usually have file space; downloading of files or pop mail services is available.

Figure 6.1.   Host-dial sessions.

TCP/IP-Based Connections

The user with TCP/IP software on her computer is leveraging all the computing power of her own machine, turning it into a true Internet host in the process. With the right client software, you can use Telnet, FTP, WWW, and so on, without an intervening host. Most folks particularly like the ability to use their computer to get their electronic mail, using e-mail client software.

In a TCP/IP connection, you make a connection to the network (either by a direct link or dial-up). The network access server (the name for the computer that handles your physical connection to the network; sometimes the same kind of computer that host-dial users connect to, but not always) "authenticates" you (establishes your identity) and "authorizes" you (checks to see which services you are allowed to use). Then, that computer drops into the background, and your own computer takes over the client side of the services you want to access. The network access server is still working silently in the background, handling routing requests, some DNS requests, and sometimes the flow control for your session, but in general your workstation is in charge of it all. Figure 6.2 illustrates a typical TCP/IP session.

SLIP and PPP: True Network Interactions

SLIP (Serial Line Internet Protocols) and PPP (Point-to-Point Protocols) are software tools that turn your connection from "dumb terminal access" to full-fledged Internet node. This software negotiates the rules for your connection with the Internet access point you're connected to, and it takes care of packaging your data so that it meets the Internet standards.

SLIP has been around for many years, but it was painful and unpleasant to work with over very slow lines (under 9600 bps). Once inexpensive 9600 and 14400 baud modems came on the market, along with data compression protocols (which eliminate the "wasted" space in a packet and make smaller packets which can be transmitted more rapidly), SLIP metamorphosed from something that more or less worked to a powerful method of real-time data interaction.

PPP software may be easier for the user to configure, since PPP can automatically determine the network address assigned to it. The user does not need to type that information into a configuration file. Another advantage of PPP is that it allows for better compression of

TCP/IP-based Connection
(two-stage process)

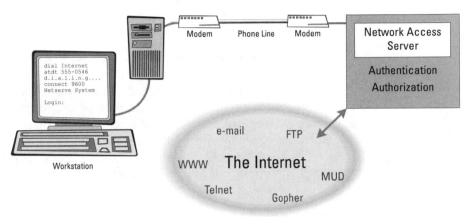

```
dial Internet
atdt 555-0546
d.i.a.l.i.n.g....
connect 9600
Netserve System

Login:
```

Modem   Phone Line   Modem

Network Access
Server

Authentication

Authorization

e-mail   FTP

WWW   **The Internet**

                        MUD

Telnet   Gopher

Workstation

> User dials into a network access server; goes through
> an authentication and authorization process.

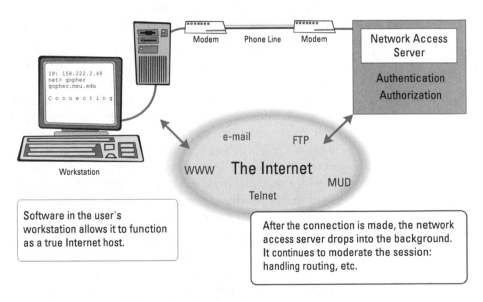

```
IP: 158.222.2.48
net> gopher
gopher.msu.edu

C o n n e c t i n g
```

Modem   Phone Line   Modem

Network Access
Server

Authentication

Authorization

e-mail   FTP

WWW   **The Internet**

                        MUD

Telnet

Workstation

> Software in the user's
> workstation allows it to function
> as a true Internet host.

> After the connection is made, the network
> access server drops into the background.
> It continues to moderate the session:
> handling routing, etc.

Figure 6.2. **Using a TCP/IP-based software package.**

the data in your session, which makes for faster throughput of your data. One final advantage of PPP is that it allows for authentication and authorization of the user as the connection is being established, rather than after the user connects to a network access box. PPP is, therefore, a more secure protocol.

Even though PPP is newer, both protocols serve the same function for the user. They transport information directly to your computer from some other Internet-connected computer. Choosing between the two protocols is like choosing what type of car to drive. You may find that your choices are restricted to one protocol or the other by the type of software you chose, the offerings of your provider, or some other factor. You will still be able to use the Internet effectively, just as most cars (even ones you might not like) will transport you from one place to another.

Modems

Hundreds of thousands of Internet users make their connection to the Net via a dial-up modem and communications software running on their personal workstation. The purpose of a modem (*mod*ulator-*dem*odulator) is to translate the digital signals that computers use to store and transmit information into the analog signals that telephone lines (or radio data systems) use to transmit information.

Digital systems represent information in the form of discrete voltage levels (typically 0.5v is "on" and 0v is "off") that correspond to the binary (base 2) digits 1 and 0. Combined into binary numbers, these bits form the building blocks of all information stored and processed by your computer. Communications systems are designed to transmit information in the form of *analog* voltages, which vary continuously over a range of values. (If you think of a light switch, with its two states—on and off—as illustrating the concept of a digital device, then a radio volume dial, with its continuous range of settings, would be analog.) A modem, then, makes the translation so that the computers on both ends of the connection can understand each other.

A network that allows dial-in access provides one modem at its end, while a user who dials in provides the other. These modems have to be compatible to be able to communicate. When you get your account with your provider, they should tell you what modems your modem is compatible with. When you purchase your modem, look for one compatible with a wide range of modems. We'll look at other important criteria later in the chapter.

Parity

In data communications, the word *parity* refers to a simple means of checking for errors in data transmitted. Parity only provides for the detection of errors; not for their correction. (It is also possible to add mechanisms to allow for retransmission of data, but the parity mechanism itself does not specify that. Error correction is merely the combination of error detection plus retransmission when an error is detected.) Many modern communications protocols, such as PPP and SLIP, do not use parity for error checking, because the information is checked for transmission errors in other ways.

With TCP/IP-based communications software to access the Internet, you should set up your communications software to use No parity. In this kind of parity, the parity bit is used by the communications software for other purposes. (See the discussion of an 8-bit data path below.)

If you are using standard "host-dial" communications to reach the Net, you will use either No parity or Even parity.

Data Bits per Character

Information sent from one computer to another is divided into pieces, known as characters (or bytes). Characters are made up of bits, and the number of bits per character depends on whether one bit per character is reserved for parity.

Most communications software used today will use No (None) parity: 8 bits per character (may be listed 8-N-1).

8-Bit Data Path

If you use TCP/IP-based software, you'll need to be able to set up your software to run in what is called "8-bit" mode, or an "8-bit data path." To understand this, you need to know something about how data is encoded for transmission over networks.

Most networks use ASCII (American Standard Code for Information Interchange) characters in their communications. ASCII is a means of encoding the roman alphabet, Arabic numbers, and various punctuation and control information using seven data bits. Traditional ASCII defined character encodings for 7-bit values, and assumes that one bit of each character is reserved for a different purpose (such as parity).

The new ASCII standard defines a way to encode the alphabet, numerals, and punctuation and control information using the eighth bit as part of the character.

Old host-dial or "dumb terminal" connections used ten bits for each character: a start bit (which signaled the beginning of the character), seven bits for the character information itself, a stop bit (which signaled the end of the character), and a parity bit (which helped in error detection).

Since modern protocols handle some of the control functions outside of the basic character set (they use a different error correction method, for example), they use the extra eighth bit to send more information, such as control or formatting characters.

To create an 8-bit data path, you need to be using no parity (because you want to free up the parity bit for use in information).

Duplex

When you access a remote computer, the characters you type are displayed on your screen so that you can see what you are typing. This is called *echoing*. There are two ways to handle echoing: older terminals could display everything as soon as you typed it (Half Duplex mode), or the computer at the remote end can send each character back to your screen as soon as it is received (Full Duplex mode).

Full Duplex is used in almost every network you'll encounter. You may be able to set this parameter in your software: if so, it will usually be called something like Full-Duplex, FDX, or Remote Echo in your terminal emulator program. It will usually be set to Full Duplex as the default, and you should leave it that way. If not, set it to Full Duplex and forget it.

Carriage Returns and Line Feeds

Whenever you send a carriage return, you expect the cursor to move to the next line. The software in most networks provides a line feed (harking back to the days of printing terminals) with each carriage return sent or received. When you set up your terminal emulator program, be certain to turn auto-linefeed off, or to set the end-of-line character to just carriage return, or else all the information that prints on your screen will be double-spaced.

Usually this will be a problem only when you are using dial-up, particularly into bulletin board systems. It is possible to encounter this in a LAN setup, but it is much rarer (and usually is a result of someone fiddling with the software without knowing what they are doing).

Flow Control

Flow control is something like running a hose into a bucket. When you are filling the bucket, you want to slow down the hose early enough that the remaining water in the hose goes into the bucket rather than onto your feet. After you've emptied the bucket into your kid's pool, you turn the hose back on, and wait a few seconds for the water flow to come back up to full strength.

In a computer network, flow control tells the computer at one end to stop sending data until the computer at the other end has finished processing it.

When flow control is turned on, the workstation or modem on the receiving end can send a message to the other computer to tell it to stop sending information until the message comes to start again. These messages are called flow control signals. You can do the same thing manually with most host-dial software by pressing Control-S to stop the flow of information and Control-Q to start it again.

Two Kinds of Flow Control

In today's communications, you can get two main kinds of flow control. One kind is handled by your communications software. In this kind (sometimes called *software flow control* or *in-band flow control*), the software inserts control sequences into the data traffic itself to tell the computer at the other end to start and stop sending data. You can't get an 8-bit clear data path if you use this kind of flow control, so you can't use TCP/IP-based software with it.

The other kind of flow control is called *hardware flow control* or *out-of-band flow control*. Hardware flow control uses two of the wires in your modem cable itself to tell the modem to start or stop sending information. Since it's not in the data stream, it's called "out of band" flow control. And since it's handled by the hardware itself, it's called "hardware" flow control.

When you look for a modem to use with your TCP/IP-based software, be sure to get one that supports hardware flow control.

Plugged In: Using a Direct Link

In the past, a direct link meant a cable that ran from your dumb terminal (a terminal that couldn't do anything but be an interface to the computer) to the mainframe computer. This link didn't depend on the phone lines being up and, as long as the mainframe was up, was always connected.

Today the concept is the same: a line plugs into the back of your computer and connects you directly to your computing resources, as shown in Figure 6.3. However, what happens on the other end of the line has changed somewhat.

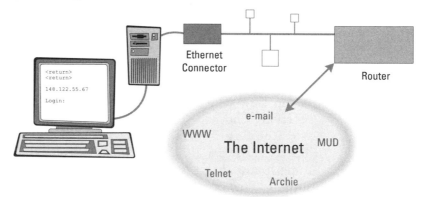

*Figure 6.3.   **A direct link.***

Today you are more than likely working on a personal computer or workstation that can do more all by itself on your desktop than the mainframe could twenty years ago. To link up with the network, you run special software on the workstation that handles the interface to the network. If you have a direct link, that cable plugged into the back of your workstation puts you in contact with some network instantly. You could have one of the following kinds of connections:

Ethernet hooked into a router (the type of connection shown in Figure 6.3).

AppleTalk hooked into a router.

Novell, Banyan, or other LAN connection, which in turn talks to an Internet gateway.

SLIP connection with a leased phone line that hooks you into a router connection or local network.

Direct connections tend to require moderately expensive equipment, such as Ethernet installations, routers, repeaters, and so on. The phone or fiber line usually runs at higher speeds: 56,000 bits per second (also called 56K, or 56 Kilobits per second) to over a million bits per second (T1, or 1.54 million bits per second). These high-speed phone lines are very expensive, and so direct connections that use them are usually shared among several users, or they are reserved for users sending very large amounts of data (graphics, sound, and so on) over the network for long periods of time.

Direct connections are also used for file servers, Gopher servers, World Wide Web servers, FTP archives, and other services that have lots of traffic all the time.

A variation on the direct link is demand dial-up (which we discussed in Chapter 4). When you are using an application on your workstation that does not require connection to the Internet, the link to the Internet is down; when you use an application that requires a link to the Internet, software in your system or your LAN server brings up the dial-up link and makes a connection to a node somewhere else on the Net. These links usually use a moderate-speed dial-up—9600 bps to 56K—and are not usually used for systems with a great deal of traffic.

Again, Chapter 4 discussed how to assess your needs for a connection and decide what sort of a direct connection suits you, and your organization or business, best.

Troubleshooting a Direct Link

Let's start with the easy problems. Beware! Troubleshooting directly connected links can involve getting under your desk or behind a cabinet to look for wires and jacks. Wear comfortable clothes and take along an adventurous attitude. If you work your way through each of the tips here, and you still have the problem, contact your systems administrator or someone who is good at debugging these things.

 WARNING Checking and connecting or disconnecting network wires (and other troubleshooting techniques) have the potential to bring down your whole local network. Some network administrators prefer that no one but them or their staff touch network hardware. If you are in an environment where you have network administrators, check with them before you touch any hardware.

This is by no means an exhaustive list of remedies for problems on direct links; we could write whole books just on those topics. But it should help you get started, and give you good information to give to your repair center or help service if you still can't locate the trouble.

The Connection Won't Wake Up

Particularly in corporate or group settings, you may have gotten a notice about scheduled maintenance time, changes about the network, or other happenings which may affect the network. Be sure to read and remember those notices! But assuming your system hasn't been "taken down" for scheduled maintenance, here are some possibilities:

0. **Go back to square one:** Is the computer connected to the jack, plug, Ethernet box, or whatever, and are all the cables screwed or clamped securely? Is the power turned on in the computer and all your peripheral equipment?

1. **Wrong speed?** Make sure that your communications program is set for the same speed as the connection you're attached to.

2. **The network is dead.** Ask next door or in the next cubicle if they have a live network connection. If you can see your router, server or the console for your LAN, look to see if it has any lights flashing or warning messages printed on it. If you are not the systems administrator, you may decide not to touch this equipment if it doesn't appear to be working. Once you've called for help, there's nothing much else you can do to troubleshoot this problem.

3. **Wrong settings** in your communications software. Go back to the basic instructions, and check to see that your communications software is set up correctly. Pay close attention to speed, protocols, and parity.

4. Your **network address** is wrong or has changed. Check the instructions you were given to make sure that your communications software has the correct network address for your machine. This should be in a menu called something like "Connections," "Configuration," "IP settings," or "Setup." Depending on your software, it may be in a file with the string "config" in the name. Look at that file carefully to make sure the address is correct.

> **WARNING**   Never edit a configuration file unless you have made a copy, called a backup, first. Copy the "config" file into a file called "config.old" or "config.bak" on PC-based systems, or some helpful similar name on other systems. This will let you restore your old configuration in case you make a mistake editing the file. If you have any doubt about undertaking this project, get someone knowledgeable to help you.

5. Someone **upstream** of you has disconnected the cable leading to you. Walk around to your co-workers and look for someone near you who has a live connection. Look for the wire that goes to your machine. If you find a place where it has been disconnected, you can *try* reconnecting it. Warning! Most systems administrators prefer to be called if you find a loose connection.

6. Your network connection is improperly **terminated.** Some network connections, particularly AppleTalk and some Ethernet connections, go through a small box with two jack holes that look like phone jacks. These boxes connect near the wire leading to your computer. Both holes should be filled; *how* they are filled depends on your location in your network and the particular configuration of your network. The easiest to troubleshoot on your end is the Local Talk network. (Other network wiring and configurations are more difficult for end users to troubleshoot, so we do not include tips on them here.)

   If you are the last person in line on the circuit, there will be a dummy plug, called a terminator, in one of the holes to indicate to the routing equipment that this is the end of the line. These plugs look like plastic phone jacks with little washers connected to them. If you don't have one, look to see if it's been pulled out (check on the floor around your work area). Contact your systems administrator or repair office.

   If there is someone downstream from you on the network, you should have two wires coming out of the network connection box. One leads to your computer, and the other goes on to the next person's connection. Look for a pulled-out wire near the connection box or mixed in with the other cables. If you don't find it, contact your systems administrator or repair office.

The Connection Wakes Up but Won't Go Anywhere

Sometimes your communications software comes up and tries to make a connection, but never succeeds. Your connection is live (or awake) on your end, but there's nobody home on the other end.

You get an error message that you can't find the network. There are several possible reasons for this:

1. Your **network server** is dead. Ask next door or in the next cubicle if they have a live network connection. If you can see your server or the console for your LAN, go look to see if it has any lights turned on or warning messages printed. If you are not the systems administrator, you may decide not to touch this equipment if it doesn't look as if it is working.

2. Your network **gateway** or **router** has changed addresses. Check back through your e-mail and other memos to find that message you threw out from the systems administrator about DNS changes over the weekend. Check your software or network instructions to find out what the backup or default gateway address is, and reset your software to find it. (The gateway addresses are the network addresses of the routers or other computers that handle DNS, routing, and other connection mechanics. If your software isn't talking to the right box, your session won't do anything.)

3. Your **software has the wrong address** for the gateway or router. Check your setup file or configuration file for the default gateway address. (Remember to back up the configuration file before you change it!)

4. Your local connection is OK, but **you are cut off from the world.** Perhaps you can get to your local gateway or your local router, but there is a problem in the greater network past that point. There's nothing you can do about this, but sometimes telling your systems administrators is a blessing, because they haven't noticed yet. (Be gentle when you let them know: you may be the first person to tell them, but you could also be the hundred-and-first.)

You can issue commands, and the session looks like it's working, but it never makes a connection. Here again there are several possibilities to consider:

1. Your software is **improperly configured.** Check to make sure that your communications software has the correct network address for your machine. This should be in a menu called something like "Connections,"

"IP settings," or "Setup." Depending on your software, it may be in a file with the string "config" in the name. Look at that file carefully to make sure the address is correct. Check the gateway and router default addresses, too.

2. The service you are trying to reach is **down or unreachable.** Ask a neighbor or someone else on the Net if they can reach the service from their workstation. (If they can, you need to contact your support line or systems administrator for assistance.)

3. The **DNS server** or other **routing** equipment/software is down or broken. Contact your support line or systems administrator for assistance.

Garbage on the Screen

The causes and solutions here depend on what the garbage looks like.

Do you see x's, f's, nonprinting characters, or graphics characters? You may be accessing a system that needs a different **parity** than the one you have set. This is most likely with host-dial, non-TCP/IP systems. Check the instructions for dialing in: check your modem or software settings. Most common settings are *8-N-1* (eight data bits, no parity, one stop bit) or *7-E-1* (seven data bits, even parity, one stop bit). Figure 6.4 shows an example of a connection with the wrong parity.

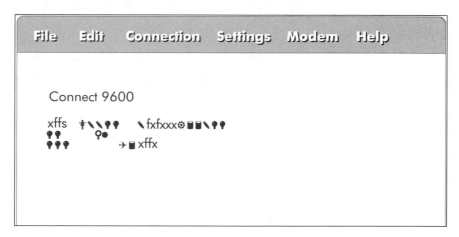

Figure 6.4.　Incorrect parity on a connection.

Do the words look like a foreign language? In other words, the pattern looks like it should be words, but the characters are not in English. Check your parity and bit settings. Although most networks require you to connect, the Internet using 8 data bits and no parity, some require that you use 7 data bits and even parity. Figure 6.5 shows sample data with incorrect parity and data bit settings.

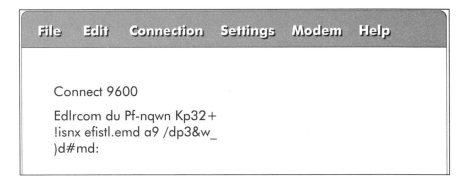

File   Edit   Connection   Settings   Modem   Help

Connect 9600

Edlrcom du Pf-nqwn Kp32+
!isnx efistl.emd a9 /dp3&w_
)d#md:

*Figure 6.5.   **Incorrect parity and data bit settings.***

Is the garbage sporadic or in rhythmic patterns, occurring unexpectedly and at random locations on your screen?   Although it's very unusual on a direct connection, this can happen. The most likely source is **noise** either on your physical connection wire or in the electrical system of your house or office. If you don't have a surge and noise protection power strip or control center for your computer equipment, buy one.

Figure 6.6 shows sporadic garbage in a connection.

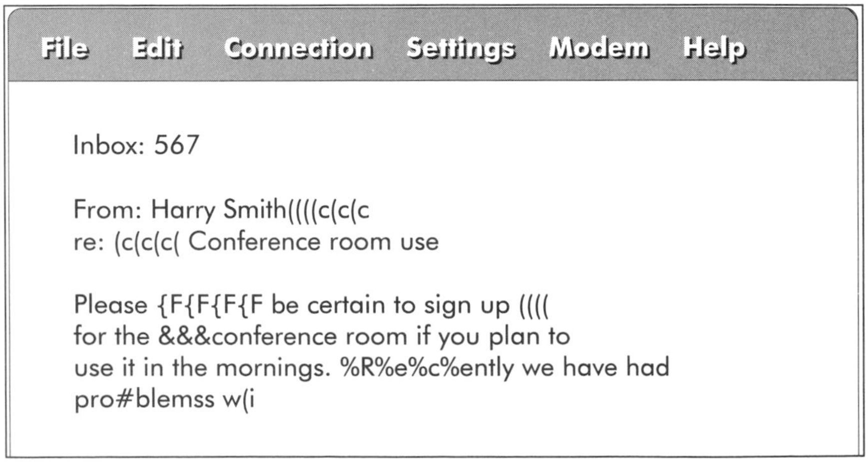

File   Edit   Connection   Settings   Modem   Help

Inbox: 567

From: Harry Smith((((c(c(c
re: (c(c(c(Conference room use

Please {F{F{F{F be certain to sign up ((((
for the &&&conference room if you plan to
use it in the mornings. %R%e%c%ently we have had
pro#blemss w(i

*Figure 6.6.   **Noise in an otherwise normal connection.***

Causes of data-corrupting noise include:

Worn shielding on your cabling, and another cable (or heavy power line) running close to it.

A big electric motor operating nearby (usually something like a refrigerator, a generator, or a vacuum).

An incandescent or fluorescent light or a radio on the same circuit as your computer.

Bad weather (such as high winds, rain, snow, thunderstorms, tornadoes), particularly if your network runs between buildings.

There's usually not much you can do about line noise, but here are a few suggestions:

Buy a noise and power surge protector for your computer equipment.

Wait until the weather clears (or move to a different climate).

Move the electric motor, the light or radio, or the computer to a different electrical circuit.

Check the wires and cables around your computer carefully for breaks, cracked or torn insulation, or other problems. (They may have gotten pinched, crushed, or had heavy objects set on them.)

Ask the physical plant or help desk folks for assistance.

Reach Out and Touch the Net: Using a Dial-up Link

Our goal here is to help you better understand the instructions you've gotten from your dial-up provider. We can't give detailed instructions on how to access every possible provider, but we *can* give you the benefit of our experience in dialing into a lot of providers to help you understand what's happening when you dial up. In this section we talk about pitfalls to avoid, tricks to get better performance, and how to troubleshoot your connection.

Choosing a Modem

A modem is an essential link between your computer and your dial-up service provider, so it's vital that you select one that meets your needs. Here are some of the most important considerations.

MASTER WORDS   One very nice feature to look for as you decide on a modem is whether it can be configured to support either host-dial or TCP/IP-based communications.

Communication Speeds

Most modern dial-in modems operate at 9600, 14,400 or 28,800 bits per second (sometimes incorrectly called the *baud rate*). The higher the number, the more bits it can push across your data pipe per second.

Technology for modems is changing so quickly that the speeds get higher and higher every year, and the older and cheaper modems (which are much less expensive) are consequently out of date almost before you get them out of the box.

The usual rule of thumb for figuring out how long it will take your file to go across a communication line is based on your communication speed. Generally, you can divide that rate by eight to find out how many characters per second are going across the line. Thus, for a 14,400 bps line, you are actually sending 1800 characters across the line every second. This is because there are roughly eight bits per character. (We'll talk later about data compression, but even with compression, this ratio holds most of the time.)

In reality, because of slow connections, line noise causing your computer to retransmit your data, and other *overhead* on the line, you'll almost never get your line to run as fast as it is rated for. But you can come close.

Modem Standards

When looking at modems, you need to be concerned with the following attributes: speed, error correction, data compression, and Hayes-compatibility.

Speed   In general, you want to buy the fastest modem you can afford when you buy a new modem. We recommend you purchase a 14,400 or 28,800 bps modem.

Error Correction   We recommend that you look for a modem that supports the V.42 protocol for error correction. This protocol has largely supplanted MicroCom's MNP4 protocol, which also supports error correction.

One reason for the rising popularity of the V protocols is that they are more easily configured for use with TCP/IP-based software. Another is that more and more modem manufacturers are incorporating them into their modems, avoiding the use of MicroCom's proprietary software.

Data Compression   We recommend that you look for a modem which supports the V.42*bis* protocol for data compression. This protocol has largely supplanted MicroCom's MNP5 and MNP10 protocols, which also supports data compression. Modems equipped with MNP protocols cannot handle data that you have already compressed (for example, with the ZIP program) as well as the V.42*bis*. The V.42*bis* modems recognize that the material is already compressed and do not attempt to compress it further.

Hayes-Compatibility   The Hayes modem company created a set of commands for use in talking to the modem (the "Hayes command set" or "AT command set") that has become accepted as a *de facto* standard. This standardization of one command set (and other commands in the same format) allows users to familiarize themselves with new modems quickly. Practically every modem you encounter today will be Hayes-compatible.

Sum it up

Here's a quick summary of the modem standards.

Modem Speed	Basic Protocol	Error Correction	Data Compression
14,400	v.32	v.42	v.42bis
28,800	v.34	v.42	v.42bis

Starting the Link: Using the Modem

Most modems sold now are autodialing modems—you can type commands from the keyboard to make your modem dial the telephone and establish a connection to the computer at the other end of the line. Figure 6.7 shows such a connection.

Many software packages even support dialing scripts to let you press one function key or click on one icon and make a connection to your dial-up provider.

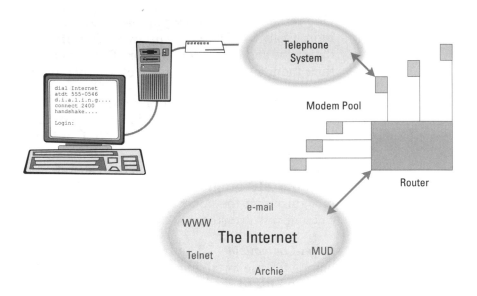

Figure 6.7. **Making the dial-up connection with a modem.**

 WARNING Never put your password in a dialing script. That would allow anyone who sat down at your computer (or who stole it from your car, home, hotel room, or office) to access the network using your identity. Make sure you have to type your password in every time you start your script unless you are completely confident of the physical security of your computer.

The best modems indicate what is happening at every step of a dial-in session. You can track the progress of the call in any of several ways: lights that indicate the modem's status, a speaker that allows you to listen to the progress of your call, or, in graphical user interface (GUI) programs, a phone ringing or a status bar. Your modem sends signals to your software which may appear as on-screen messages or status bars.

While your modem is dialing, for instance, you may hear the dial tone and then ringing, and see something like "Dialing" with the periods coming one at a time as a graphic reminder of the progress.

When the modem on the other end answers, you may hear the two modems start to hiss or "sing" to one another to make the connection.

Once your modem makes the connection to another computer, you may see something like "Connect 9600" (or whatever speed you are using).

The best source of information about your modem is the manual that came with it, and the help line or service number provided by the manufacturer. Many trouble calls can be eliminated if you just read the manual!

 MASTER WORDS   Friends, roommates, and family members can be the death of a dial-up session. If you can arrange it, don't connect your modem to a phone line that someone else may try to use while you're on-line! If someone picks up another phone on the same line you're using, your session will be at best mangled (junk characters will appear on your screen) and at worst abruptly disconnected. Call-waiting is another enemy of the dial-in session. The tones used to indicate that another call is coming in can completely disconnect your modem session. Either have the service removed from your phone line (or don't get it installed on your modem line), or be sure to disable it before you start a session. Instructions for disabling call-waiting are in the front of most United States phone books or are available from your local phone provider. (In most areas, you press *70 to disable call-waiting.)

Using a Calling Card with a Modem

Once you figure out how to dial your modem from home, you can put the steps in a dialing script and more or less forget them. But you may want to use a calling card at some point to charge your call. How do you do that?

Why Use a Charge Card?

You will probably make most of your modem calls from the comfort of your own home, using your own telephone to call a local number. But you may hear of a service that is only available by a long distance telephone call, or you may live in a city that doesn't have a local dial-in system.

And there are times when you will need to make a long distance call and be either unwilling or unable to charge the call to the phone number you are calling from. For instance, you've had a long commute from the office and now have to dial in to the office network to get a bit more work done. While there are other options (like paying for the call yourself), you might prefer to put the call directly on the company's calling card.

Or you might be out of town on a business trip and need to pick up the latest information for a proposal due the next morning. You could charge the call to your hotel room, but then you won't be able to control which long-distance company the hotel uses. So you will want to use your telephone charge card.

MASTER WORDS   Hotel rooms are common places to make modem calls. Some hotels and motels still have old-fashioned switchboards that do not allow you to make phone calls with your modem. Luckily, most of these hotels have installed special phone areas which have direct lines outside for you to use. If in doubt, check with the switchboard operator. Asking for a "modem friendly" room when you check-in is a good idea, too.

Setting Up the Card Transaction

Charging a voice long-distance call to a card is relatively easily. You dial your long-distance company's local access number (or its 800 number, if it doesn't have a local access number), wait for the beeps, dial the number you want to call, wait for a few more beeps, and then punch in your card number. It all goes very quickly and easily.

But you're a person. You know that you may have to wait a longer or shorter time this call than you did last call. Computers aren't that smart. For them, a dialing script has to be set up to work the same no matter what the phone company decides to do. A modem can't hear the beeps that would tell it to send the next string of digits. And there's no button we can push to tell the modem that's it time to send the next stream of digits into the telephone system. So we have to find another way to keep from entering a number before the telephone company's switch is ready to receive it. (Remember, a digit sent too early is lost, so we have to start over. And hope we get it right this time.)

So making a charge call over a modem is a process of trial and error.

Telling the Modem to Wait

Fortunately, the command set for today's modems includes the ability to tell the modem to pause. Simply adding a comma to the dial string will cause the modem to wait a bit before entering the next digit.

Putting commas between the three separate number strings will allow the telephone switches sufficient time to process the preceding number before receiving the next one.

But while this solution is simple, it's not the whole story. The length of the pause will vary from one modem to the next. Some modems may pause for as long as four minutes for a comma, while others may pause for less than half a second. So you will have to look in your modem's manual to find out how long your modem pauses. (The manual may even tell you how to set the length of the pause.)

MASTER WORDS   Again, it's important that you read the manuals. Getting familiar with your modem documentation is one of the most useful things you can do, especially if you travel a great deal.

Even with this piece of information, the quest is not yet over. There is still the question of how long the telephone system will take to respond to each number and thus be ready for your modem to send the next set. *The only way to discover this information for your telephone company is to experiment.*

To start, you might try making the call by hand, noting how long it takes for the beeps to come back. There is no need to be extremely precise at this stage; it is better to err a little on the too-late side than on the too-soon side. Once you have an idea of how long it takes the telephone system to be ready for the next string, you can calculate the number of commas you need to add between the pieces.

MASTER WORDS   If you think you will be traveling and using your modem from many phones, be sure to buy a modem that lets you listen to the dialing process. Those little beeps, whistles, and hisses are great helpers when trying to debug a dialing script!

Adding More Numbers

Your dial string now looks something like this:

```
ATDT18005551234,,02025559876,,,234567890987654321
```

The first two letters, AT, are the "attention" command, which alerts the modem to expect a command. The next two letters, DT, tell the modem to "Dial" a "Tone" call. (If your telephone is a rotary instrument, you will probably need to change the T to a P, for "Pulse-dialing.") Then comes the long-distance company's access number, a pause, the number you want to call (usually preceded by a zero to signify that it will require special processing, in this case charging to a calling card), another pause (slightly longer), and finally your calling card's authorization code. (For this example, I've chosen a random string of numbers. I hope I didn't get your number!)

> **WARNING**   Read the instructions that came with your calling card. Some cards require your personal access code first; some in the order that we have above. As they say in the Usenet newsgroups, YMMV (your mileage may vary).

Other Help

You will probably have to try several times to get the right number of commas for each pause. Once you have it right, though, you will not want to have to recreate it from scratch. Your communication software should include the capability to store numbers you dial frequently. (If it doesn't, you might consider finding a new one; there are many available, both commercially and as shareware, for every computer.) After storing a number, you will be able to make your credit-card calls quickly and easily.

Your modem may offer some other commands that would make these kinds of calls easier. For instance, it may offer a W command, to wait for a second dial tone. It may offer an @ command, to wait for a period of silence (like the comma, the length of the period varies and you may be able to set it). The @ command may require a ring before waiting, so it might not be as useful as we could hope.

Pitfalls

If you have been working with your modem while reading this, you may have found that this complex string of digits won't be accepted by your modem yet. That's because two eleven-digit telephone numbers, a fourteen-digit authorization code, several commas, and "ATDT," not to mention the final Return (also called Enter) keystroke at the end of the line, total a bit more than the 40 characters most modems can accept on a command line. (Some modems may not count the

"AT" and Return as part of the command line subject to the 40 character limit.) Spaces are usually ignored, but hyphens and parentheses are counted. Fortunately, a semicolon as the last command on the line (that is, the last character before the Return) tells the modem to return to command mode after dialing, so a second command line, with the rest of the command, can be entered. Thus, to use the command line given above, you would enter something like

```
ATDT18005551234,,02025559876,,;<RETURN>
ATDT23456789098765<RETURN>
```

Of course, you may need to use some of the other configuration commands for your modem, like disabling error detection or data compression, so the command line may have to be broken up into more pieces. Because there are so many good modems manufactured, we can't describe each one exactly. There are more than 500 commonly available modems! You'll need to check what we've said here against the information that came with your modem. If your modem information differs from what we present here, please use the information from your modem manufacturer. It's much more likely to work.

Dial-up Troubleshooting

No matter what kind of modem you have, or whether you're running TCP/IP software or traditional host-dial communications programs, these tips should help you solve most basic modem woes.

Garbage on the Screen

As with direct connections, the causes and solutions here depend on what the garbage looks like.

Do you see x's, f's, nonprinting characters, or graphics characters? There are several possibilities here:

1. You may be dialing into an **autospeed modem**. Some modems can accept calls from modems of different transmission speeds but must be told which speed to use. Synchronize your modem with the autospeed modem by:

   ▶ setting your communications program for automatic answer-back (see your software manual for instructions), or

   ▶ pressing Enter twice a few seconds after your call is answered.

2. You may be accessing a system that needs a different **parity** than the one you have set. This is most likely with host-dial, non-TCP/IP systems. Check the instructions for dialing in: check your modem or software settings. Most common settings are *8-N-1* (eight data bits, no parity, one stop bit) or *7-E-1* (seven data bits, even parity, one stop bit).

    Do the words look like a foreign language?   See the diagnosis and solution in the direct connection troubleshooting section.

    Is the garbage sporadic or in rhythmic patterns, occurring suddenly and at random locations on your screen?   Again, this is most likely **noise** on either your phone line or in the electrical system of your house. Data-corrupting causes of noise specific to dial-up connections include:

    A noisy or static-filled telephone line (if it sounds static-filled when you talk on it, or if people mention a noise problem when they talk to you, the computers will be trying to make sense of the static along with your data).

    A microwave oven operating near the computer or phone jack where your modem plugs in.

    A noisy or outmoded phone switch at your telephone company.

    Bad weather (such as high winds, rain, snow, thunderstorms, tornadoes).

    Someone picking up your telephone receiver.

    There's usually not much you can do about line noise, but here are a few suggestions:

    Buy a noise and power surge protector for your computer equipment, including the modem.

    Hang up and try again for a better connection.

    Wait until the weather clears (or move to a different climate).

    Remind others in your house or workplace not to use your phone while your modem connection is open.

    Turn off call-waiting, if you have it.

    Ask your telephone company to check your line (only if none of the other suggestions reduces the line noise). Remember that it may cost you money, depending on what service you are paying for.

Becoming an Effective
Internet User

Your modem dials but doesn't make a connection.

There are several possible causes:

1. **Wrong modem speed?** Make sure that your communications program is set for the same speed as the modem you're calling into.

2. Some network providers use varying **protocols** on their networks. Not all are the same. You may have one (most commonly MNP) enabled when the modem on the other end is looking for another protocol. Be sure your setup is appropriate.

3. Your connection may be too **noisy**. See the section on line noise, above.

4. **Your dial script or modem initialization string is incorrect.** Your software may be waiting for a string which will never appear, or your host or network access server may be waiting for a response which your software doesn't send.

5. The problem may be with your **service provider's modems.** There's not much you can do about this. If you can't *ever* establish a connection, or if it's always noisy and you've tried everything else, call the help desk or consulting number for your provider.

 MASTER WORDS To see if the modems at the other end are at fault, and if you have two phone lines, call the modem number with your regular voice line. If the modems "ring open," that is, ring and never pick up, you'll know it's definitely their problem. If you get a busy signal, or an answer, leave the voice line off the hook, tying up the modem, and try dialing with your modem line. You may be able to bypass a bad modem this way.

The modem doesn't dial at all.

Try the following diagnostic path:

0. **Go back to square one:** Are the modem and the computer connected, and all the cables screwed or clamped securely? Is the modem connected to the wall jack? Is the power turned on in the modem?

1. Get to the **modem command level** (the place where you can type commands directly to the modem) and type the modem-ready command, **AT** (see your communications software documentation for specific instructions on how to issue modem commands). Do the

characters you typed appear on your screen? Does the modem respond **OK** or **0** (zero)? If not, your workstation and modem aren't speaking to one another. Make sure that your modem is turned on and connected to your telephone line. Use the correct dialing command for your type of telephone—typically **ATDT** for a touch-tone phone, **ATDP** for a pulse-dial phone.

2. If you're working on a DOS (including Windows) computer, make sure that your modem is plugged into your computer's **serial port** and that your communications software is looking for the modem on the correct port. Do this by checking the menu for your modem or communications software settings. Most modems should be on COM1 but sometimes your computer will be configured with the modem on COM2.

3. Type your modem's dialing command all in UPPERCASE. (For example, **ATDT 555-0123** instead of **atdt 555-0123**.) Some modems require this.

4. Reset the modem to **factory defaults**. That is, reset it to the way the modem manufacturer set it up when it was sold. Sometimes there is a physical switch on external modems to do this: sometimes you have to issue a command from the keyboard. In many modems, the command to type is **AT&F** or **AT&F1**. Look at the owner's manual to find out how to reset the modem, then start your communications software up and try again. (Some newer modems have factory default settings for both host-dial communications and TCP/IP-based software. Check to be certain you're set up for the right type of communications.)

5. **Swap components** with a friend. Find someone with a modem that you know works. Have her bring it over, including her power and serial cables. *One at a time,* swap the components in this order: power cable; modem; serial cable. This is a good way to see if you have a defective component.

6. Make sure that you've connected your modem to your computer using the right kind of **cable**. This is a very unlikely problem if you are working at home by yourself, but it might happen if you work in a place where lots of cables are floating around and people are regularly using various cables to connect computers and components.

7. **Call a friend** who is good at data communications and offer them dinner if they'll help troubleshoot your modem problem.

Working with SLIP and PPP

Both SLIP and PPP are available from many commercial vendors and from several public-domain sources. Some common workstation packages are from commercial sources—Chameleon, VersaTerm, and FTP software's various packages. Some are from public domain archives—NCSA Telnet, and MacSamson. Check the list of public-domain archive sites on the accompanying CD-ROM for a starting place to look for these software packages.

We have some troubleshooting tips for some of the packages, but you should talk to the people at your network provider about which one seems to work best for them. If you are connected via a corporate LAN or other connection in your workplace, your local network administrator or other expert will probably know what's best for you (and may already have installed everything you need in your workstation).

Before Setting Up an IP Connection

Setting up your SLIP or PPP link can be tricky the first time or two. There are some basic pieces of information you need to get started, and it's better to gather them before you even sit down to try to start up the software. They are:

The IP address you have been assigned.

The default IP address (numbers, not words) of your IP gateway.

The IP address and domain name (both numbers and words) of your domain name server.

If you intend to use an e-mail client or read Usenet news via newsreader software, you also need to know:

The domain name (words, not numbers) of your e-mail server.

The domain name (words, not numbers) of your Net News (NNTP) server.

Some applications also ask that you have a Net *mask,* or default broadcast address, in your configuration file. Experienced consultants suggest that the mask should be **255.255.255.0,** although users who plan to use Trumpet (a news reader) should set the mask address to **0.0.0.0.**

There are distinct differences between setting up a PPP link and setting up a SLIP link. One advantage of PPP is that you need less information to set it up: because PPP has advanced negotiation processes built into the protocol itself, it can find out what IP address you have been assigned, and what the gateway address is, without your having to preconfigure it. To configure most SLIP software, you need to build this information into the configuration script or file. (Some SLIP software has a configuration script that tries to recognize the IP address when it is written on the screen, but not all do.)

MASTER WORDS   If you are dialing in, you may or may not have an assigned IP address. Some systems assign you an IP address depending on what physical modem you connect to in the modem pool (a method called *dynamic addressing*); some assign you a telephone number that corresponds to the IP address you will be given; some assign you an IP address, which you configure into your software and which will be the same no matter what modem you call into. Be sure you understand how your system works before you start to place the call.

Starting Up the Dial-up IP Link

Dialing into an IP link is similar to dialing into a traditional host-dial link, except that you will see the IP protocol handshaking going on—you may well see a series of IP addresses being exchanged on your screen. (Handshaking is essentially how the network confirms the settings on your workstation and sets up everything that needs to be in place to let your workstation act as a network host. Information is exchanged and agreed upon, hence the reference to handshakes.)

It's good to take care of a few bits of business before you start to dial the phone.

Make sure your flow control setting in your startup menu is set to **Hardware**, not software.

Be sure you've properly entered the configuration information into your configuration file or script. Be especially certain that you have not put your own IP address into the default gateway field, should you be required to give either one.

Starting Up Your Direct IP Link

In many ways a direct IP link is easier to set up than a dial-up IP link because the step of correctly configuring your modem is eliminated. But you still need to have some of the same business taken care of before you start:

Make sure your flow control setting in your startup menu is set to **Hardware,** not software.

Be sure you've properly entered the **configuration information** into your configuration file or script. Be especially certain that you have not put your own IP address into the default gateway field, should you be required to give either one.

Make sure your **line speed** and your **software settings** match.

Be sure that the **software driver** for your Ethernet or AppleTalk (or whatever kind of physical wire you're tied into) is running and configured. You may well need to have had a special card installed in your workstation to handle these types of media. If you don't think this has been done, go back to square zero: call your systems administrator or local expert.

Troubleshooting a SLIP or PPP Link

It's impossible to give a comprehensive list of troubleshooting tips here. Each network expert has her own, and some depend as much on the idiosyncrasies of a particular network or connection as any tried and true method. Some even seem to depend on what your mother may have called "holding your mouth right"—bewilderingly, some tricks may work for one person and not for another. But these will give you some hints to try in debugging your connection.

As in the modem list, this set of tips may not work for all problems, and you may need to call in a support person. But if you document what you tried and what the results were, the support person may be better able to solve the problem. For more comprehensive troubleshooting, contact your local network provider or join a newsgroup or e-mail discussion for your particular software.

> **MASTER WORDS**   A fast search of available newsgroups turns up the following list where you can get help for communications software: `comp.sys` `.amiga.datacom`, `comp.protocols.ppp`, `comp.dcom.modems`, `comp` `.emulators.announce`, `comp.os.ms-windows.apps.com`, `comp.os` `.ms-windows.networking.tcp-ip`, and `comp.sys.mac.comm`. You should also read `news.answers` to find the Frequently Answered Question lists for your particular software.

My modem dials, but I never get a connection.   Try the following diagnostic steps:

1. Are you using the right **parity, with hardware flow control enabled?** Rhana Jacot of CICNet says, "SLIP requires a totally transparent, 8-bit data path, and normal flow control will not work! Use RTS/CTS (Request To Send/Clear to Send) hardware flow control. If you are using a Macintosh and MacTCP, be sure your modem cable is a hardware-handshaking cable, where the limited number of serial control pins out of the Macintosh are used for handshaking, instead of detecting and controlling the flow rate of the modem."

2. Is your dialing **script** correct? Pritish Shah, a consultant for CICNet, says, "Most errors occur in the script where the script is expecting a particular string but gets some other input from the server—then it just keeps waiting and waiting. This is usually solved by carefully matching what the server is sending and what the script is expecting (to the very last capitalization and space). To figure that out, log in via terminal software, do a manual login and then note every line sent (basically doing by hand what the script is supposed to do)." Another good way to capture this information is to send the screen to your printer, or capture the window in a file, either by a screen capture routine or by using cut and paste. If all else fails, use paper and pencil!

3. Are you **configured for SLIP?** Some new software (such as Chameleon, VersaTerm, and FTP software) can run in either SLIP or PPP, and some in Host-dial mode. Double-check that you're configured for the correct protocol.

4. Do you have the right **device drivers** loaded? Most SLIP (and PPP) packages use at least one device driver, and you need to make sure that your configuration files call these drivers (and, more importantly, that they are installed on your workstation). This problem will need

either a very patient phone consultant or a good friend to come and help you figure it out.

5. If you're using a DOS computer, are you using **SuperTCP** or **Chameleon** to link to an IP network, and another communications software package to link to other networks? Although they perform very well in most instances, both of these packages will take over the COM ports and not release them for use by other applications. This is a design feature of the software, and you cannot switch back and forth between other communications applications without rebooting your machine.

I get a connection and everything handshakes, but nothing ever happens. Consider the following possibilities:

1. Is *your* IP address in the **gateway address** box? Bob Williams of NetManage, the folks who make the Chameleon software, offers this tip: "If the user makes a mistake, like putting their own IP address in under default gateway, they will get very fast pings, and nothing else." If you have made this mistake, your software is trying to talk to itself instead of the network, and is getting (predictably) nowhere.

2. Do you have the correct **DNS IP address** in your configuration file? TCP/IP software talks to a server called a DNS server to get the translation between IP addresses and domain names done. This lets you use domain names in your connection commands rather than IP addresses. If your DNS server, and your backup DNS server, are not listed correctly, your connection will spin its wheels waiting for routing assistance from the network.

3. Is your **DNS server** up? The only way to tell this is to set up an alternate DNS server in your configuration file. Be sure to back up your configuration file before making any changes. (Macintosh software users frequently have a list of alternate DNS servers in their software already; DOS and Windows users should try this solution only when extremely confident of their skills.) If you swap DNS servers, and your connection works, either you had the wrong address typed in or the original server is not responding. (If you're curious, you can *ping* the DNS server you were trying to reach once you make a solid connection, if your software supports Ping. Type **ping** and you should see at least the response "<host name> is alive.") If you don't have an alternative DNS server, your only hope at this point is to call your help center.

4. Did you try to force your software to use a particular gateway? Did you write in an incorrect IP address for your workstation? PPP negotiates its IP address and the address of the gateway that it uses, so if you have preconfigured these incorrectly your session may hang.

I get a connection and handshaking, but all that ever happens is a message telling me that something has "timed out."   Try the following diagnostic steps:

1. Check your **DNS address**. It's likely that the machine you are trying to reach is listed incorrectly. If there are no typos, there's a chance that the primary machine is not up, and you'll need to try using a secondary machine.

2. Check your configuration file to see **how many times** your connection tries to get connected before giving up. If the network is really congested, you may need to increase the number of *retries*. In some applications, you may need to explicitly set a parameter to do this.

3. Check your dialing script. It may be waiting for a line it can never receive, and timing out while it waits.

I get a connection, but it prints in bursts or with a very slow echo rate.   Try the following:

1. Make sure you have selected the **proper modem type.** For example, selecting a Hayes modem when you actually have Telebit equipment can produce these symptoms. Another possible reason may be selecting too high a baud rate. Up to speeds of 19,200 bps, no special settings usually need to be changed. To use compression and/or modems that run above that rate, you'll need to see your documentation or call your support line.

2. Check for **line noise** (see the section on troubleshooting modems above).

3. The network itself may be very **congested**. Switch to an alternate resource (another service with the same information), or, if that is not possible, log off, go for lunch, and try again later.

4. Is your **DNS server** up? The only way to tell this is to set up an alternate DNS server in your configuration file. See the suggestions for testing a DNS server earlier in this section.

CHAPTER 7

Observing the Rules of the Road

FEATURING

Chapter 7

Observing the Rules of the Road

ALTHOUGH a lot of people are tired of the "Information Highway" metaphor for the Internet (in part, because the Internet is so much more than just a highway system: it's the villages and libraries and newspapers and parking lots as well), we can compare traffic rules and regulations to the kinds of rules and agreements that govern the Internet.

Just as with the Interstate Highway system, there were fewer rules at the beginning, when the resource was used less; and there are more now, when all of us are competing for the same resources. While some network hackers, wizards, and cowboys lament the need for more rules, in general a little common courtesy and respect will get you most places you need to go.

Rules for Traveling the Internet

When you drive an automobile from one town to another, you need to be aware that the rules of the road may be slightly different in each of the areas through which you travel. There may be differences in where you are allowed to park, in whether turning right after stopping at a red light is permitted, or in speed limits, for example.

When you travel the Internet, the same sorts of things can differ, depending on the network and the host systems you are using. Some hosts and services permit only a certain number of connections at one time and will refuse any more until some of the resources being used are freed. Some networks allow commercial messages; some do not allow them.

Most network providers and hosts or bulletin board services (BBS) have Terms and Conditions by which you agree to abide. Some of them are called AUPs (Appropriate Use Policies). Some are called contracts or user policies. The rules for your network are spelled out there. You may have signed such a policy as part of getting your account, or as part of your employment agreement. It is a good idea to be familiar with these rules.

For example, the systems administrators at Lawrence Livermore National Laboratory, a big research center, discovered that one of their employees was using Livermore file space as a place where people could exchange erotic images via the Net. This was certainly against their policies, and the employee knew it. Needless to say, the employee was promptly fired.

In general, usage policies for connected networks and services are posted on each service or host. Read the "message of the day" or "banner" messages at the entrance to each service. These messages will tell you of policy changes or locations of important information. If you don't think you're well-informed about the policies you are working under, ask your systems administrator about them.

In all cases, it is against the law to use networks for illegal purposes. For example, child pornography and the distribution of it is illegal in the United States. Simply storing child pornography (either in text or graphic form) on your computer is not legal; if your systems administrator finds it, he or she must destroy it and contact the authorities. Using your computer network to arrange for the sale of drugs is not acceptable, for the same reasons.

Why Do I Care?

When traveling the interstate highways in America, particularly in the high summer tourist season, you'll sometimes encounter a nasty backup that stretches for miles. As you inch your way along, you'll discover that several lanes are being condensed down, and that people are trying to merge into one lane.

Some folks merged over as soon as they saw the signs telling them to do so. Out by the warning signs, the overall speed stays up. The early mergers cheerfully wave to folks to merge in before them. And if someone lets you in, you're more inclined to let someone merge in ahead of you, as well.

As you get closer to the point where everyone *must* be funneled into one lane, the congestion and confusion get worse.

Closer in, some have waited a while, but still merge in before it becomes urgent. And some race right up to the last car-length before their lane ends, then honk wildly for others to let them in. If the driver who's currently at the head of the line is feeling generous and pleasant, a choppy merge takes place. If not, a game of chicken happens, where the guy who wanted to save a few minutes sticks his nose into the traffic, and the guy who's mad because of Guy Number 1's rudeness threatens to take his bumper off.

As a consequence, the whole line of traffic clogs up. Had everyone just merged over when the signs directing them to first appeared, it's likely that much of the traffic jam could have been avoided. And, with it, lots of steamed tempers and irritated drivers, who then go on to fight with folks at every place they stop for the rest of the day.

On the network, just as in this example, both rudeness and courtesy are contagious. Rudeness, or using outright illicit or banned behavior, can clog up the network for all of us. Just as in everyday life, there are two sorts of "rules" for the Internet: those which govern our physical access and those which govern appropriate behavior.

Sharing Your Toys

Being rude about resources and physical access can lead to increased restrictions and, in some cases, to the resource being shut down. If modem access is scarce and you "lunch" a line (grab one early in the day and never break the connection, even when you're not using it), the normal pattern of use is disrupted, and even more people have problems getting a line. They complain: some of them grab lines and hold onto them, and soon the resource is tied up almost continuously. Everyone sends nastygrams to the system operators.

In some cases the systems operator can see who has been abusing the system and deal with that person. But in many cases, all they can do is collect statistics and figure out what to do.

Management looks at the stats to see if there really is a shortage, sees all these lines tied up all day (rather than the normal pattern of connects and disconnects), and either institutes a policy to limit continuous connect time, charges more (in order to buy more modems), or decides to limit access to folks with *legitimate* use as defined by the usage policies. Everybody loses.

Although it may be hard to believe, there really is an ocean of resources on the Internet. Most of us only "surf" or "cruise" around on the top, hardly touching the vast amount of things available. There seems to be plenty to go around, especially with the growing interest in providing services. If one service gets clogged up or overused, either they'll expand to let all the users who are trying to access it get in, or a competitor will spring up, offering a similar service. Since your biggest goal with the Internet is communication—getting or distributing information—these market forces are to your best advantage in the long run. Getting greedy isn't.

The other kinds of uses that are governed on the Internet have to do with appropriate use. They include things such as: respect of copyright, commercial use on a noncommercial system, employee privilege on business systems, and so on.

New Laws and Their Challenges

In early 1996, US President Bill Clinton signed into law the Telecommunications Act of 1996. This law has many facets. It is *extremely* complex, and there are very few people who can (or will want to) understand all its ramifications. The law reforms telecommunications regulatory environments that have been around since the mid-1930s.

Telecommunications is a term that covers a vast array of businesses. It includes the telephone-based communications: personal and business, single line and huge corporate telephone systems. Telephony covers many things we've come to take for granted in our environment in the United States: communications via modem, facsimile transmissions, the calls made by persons, 800 and 900 number services; automatic fax-back services, mobile (cellular and otherwise) telephone services, etc. Telecommunications also includes television and radio broadcasting, satellite transmissions of news feeds, and regulations that pertain to the cable broadcasting business. Essentially, telecommunications can mean any kind of electronic signal that is conveying a message from one point to another using electronic means. The Federal Communications Commission (FCC) has jurisdiction over telecommunications within the United States. You can find out more about the commission by visiting its pages on the World Wide Web. These pages are located at

```
http://www.fcc.gov
```

The Telecommunications Reform Act initiates changes to the rules under which the FCC has been governing the telephone and broadcasting environment for a long time. For example, there are rules about something called "media concentration." The law, protecting the interest of the people, demanded that no one organization can own more than so many newspaper and radio and television stations in one "media market." A single publisher could not then own all or nearly all the published voices in a single city. Thus when a newspaper bought a television station, it might have to sell a radio station. Or if a television and radio station bought a newspaper or another radio station, it would have to choose which of the "voices" it would own. The media concentration rules now allow television networks, previously limited to owning stations that reach a total of 25 percent of the nation's televisions, to reach 35 percent. The FCC's prohibition on TV networks owning a cable TV company (or vice versa) are also lifted. So is the existing statutory prohibition on same market TV station/cable system cross-ownership. However, the FCC's rule prohibiting same market TV station/cable system cross-ownership is not altered. You can see that there will be lots of work in trying to make sure that new owners of stations and cable systems will be obeying the new law and regulations.

Another large change is in the rules defining which types of telephone companies can provide which types of services. Before the new law was enacted, in the United States we had two types of telephone companies. There are the long distance carriers (Inter eXchange Carriers or IXCs) like AT&T, MCI, and Sprint. There are the local carriers (Local eXchange Carriers or LXCs—sometimes called RBOCs, short for Regional Bell Operating Companies). The two types of companies were formed by the forced breakup of AT&T. The breakup of AT&T came from a judicial decision that AT&T held too much of the communications business in the United States and that monopoly was not in the best interest of the people. Thus, competition was allowed in the long-distance market, enabling the formation of MCI and Sprint from small ideas to very large businesses. The local carriers maintained their monopolies but were required to carrier the local traffic to the long distance carriers networks. Long-distance carriers were not allowed to compete with Local carriers. Local carriers did not face competition in their geographically defined business areas. Which services the carriers could offer and where were all part of the regulated environment. The judge in the case was Judge Harold Green and his decisions are termed the Modified Final Judgment or MFJ.

The new law will change all these assumptions and rules. Competition will be allowed in the local markets. The telephone companies will be allowed to offer new services, perhaps with less regulatory oversight. The law will now permit power companies to enter the telephone and information service market, too. At this time, the FCC is extremely busy setting the stage, developing the new rules under which services can and will be offered. The sidebar (prepared by Piper and Marbury) shows the schedule under which the FCC will be releasing the new regulations. Except for the fact that the rules are changing very fast, no one can say what will happen next. It's a very exciting time.

In general, the effect on the ordinary user of telecommunications services is most likely to be more choices of services at more choices of cost.

TELECOMMUNICATIONS ACT OF 1996: STATUTORY DEADLINES FOR MAJOR REQUIRED FCC ACTIONS

1996:

By March 8, 1996*: (one month)

Institute and refer to a Federal-State Joint Board a proceeding to recommend changes to universal service regulations.

FCC chairman shall appoint chairman of the board of directors of the Telecommunications Development Fund.

By May 8, 1996: (three months)

Prescribe an alternate dispute resolution process that could be used to establish industry standards for telecommunications or customer premises equipment.

By June 8, 1996: (four months)

Issue regulations to allow cable operators to aggregate their equipment costs into broad categories.

By August 8, 1996:

Complete all actions necessary to establish regulations implementing the interconnection and related requirements of section 251 for LECs and incumbent LECs.

Adopt rules on geographic uniformity of subscriber interexchange rates.

Issue regulations to enforce prohibition on LEC use of calls received by providers of alarm monitoring services for marketing purposes.

Promulgate regulations to prohibit restrictions that impair a viewer's ability to receive video programming services through devices designed for over-the-air reception of television broadcast signals, multipoint distribution service, or direct broadcast satellite services.

Prescribe regulations on open video systems.

Complete inquiry on levels of closed captioning on video programming, and submit report to Congress.

Commence inquiry to examine use of video descriptions on video programming.

Revise regulations to prevent unfair billing practices for information or services provided over toll-free telephone calls.

Complete action in ET Docket 93-62 to prescribe and make effective rules regarding the environmental effects of radio frequency emissions.

Executive branch will prescribe procedures for access to federal property for CMRS operators.

By September 8, 1996: (seven months)

Complete proceeding on availability of advanced telecommunications capability to all Americans.

By November 8, 1996: (nine months)

The Federal-State Joint Board must make its recommendations to the FCC on changes to universal service regulations.

Take all actions necessary (including any reconsideration) to prescribe regulations to promote competition among pay phone service providers.

1997:

By February 8, 1997: (one year)

Prescribe regulations to require incumbent LECs to share infrastructure with qualifying carriers for provision of universal service.

Promulgate rules on procedure to be used by a public utility holding company to petition FCC to become an "exempt telecommunications company."

Television rating code for v-chip technology to take effect if FCC, in consultation with other parties, determines that distributors of video programming have not, by one year of enactment, established voluntary rules for rating video programming and agreed voluntarily to broadcast signals that contain ratings.

By May 8, 1997: (15 months)

Complete a single proceeding on universal service to implement the recommendations of the Joint Board.

Complete a proceeding to identify and eliminate market entry barriers for entrepreneurs and other small businesses in the provision and ownership of telecommunications services and information services, or in the provision of parts or services to providers of telecommunications services and information services.

By August 8, 1997: (18 months)

Develop guidelines in conjunction with Architectural and Transportation Barriers Compliance Board for accessibility of telecommunications and customer premises equipment to persons with disabilities.

Prescribe regulations on closed captioning and video programming.

1998:

By February 8, 1998: (two years)

Prescribe regulations to govern the charges for pole attachments used by telecommunications carriers to provide telecommunications services when the parties fail to resolve a dispute over such charges.

By August 8, 1998: (30 months)

Initiate a notice of inquiry on the availability of advanced telecommunications capability to all Americans. Conduct regular proceedings on this issue thereafter.

2000:

By February 8, 2000: (four years)

By rule or order, may extend sunset of separate affiliate safeguards on BOC interLATA information services.

2001:

By February 8, 2001: (five years)

Report to Congress on the implementation of the broadcasters' ancillary or supplementary services fee (under program to be established by FCC—no time frame set).

Regulations governing charges for pole attachments become effective.

2006:

By February 8, 2006: (10 years)

Conduct evaluation of the advanced television services program.

Variable:

Complete any proceeding to implement Joint Board universal service recommendations subsequent to the initial proceeding within 1 year of receiving them.

Report to Congress every three years starting 5/8/2000 on any regulations prescribed to eliminate small business market entry barriers and identify for Congress the statutory barriers to be eliminated.

Act on any application of a company to become an "exempt telecommunications company" within 60 days of receipt.

Review and act on complaints concerning failures by BOCs to meet conditions for interLATA approval within 90 days.

May extend sunset of safeguards on BOC manufacturing services or interLATA telecommunications services three years from interLATA authorization by FCC.

Following initial report to Congress on the broadcasters' ancillary or supplementary services fee, annually advise Congress on the amounts collected pursuant to such program.

Any carrier, or class of carriers, may petition the FCC to forbear from regulating the carrier(s) or any service offered by the carrier(s). Any such petition will be deemed granted if the FCC does not act on it within one year.

Prepared by Piper & Marbury L.L.P., 1200 19th Street, N.W., Washington, D.C.

Ron Plesser and Jim Halpert

---

* All dates based on 2/8/96 enactment.

Note: The FCC has yet to release its official schedule of rulemaking proceedings that it will undertake to implement the provisions of the Act. Many proceedings will involve a Notice of Proposed Rulemaking, as well as active participation from industry and the public.

Why Might This Law Affect You?

One important part of the new Telecommunications law is Title V of the act, which includes something called the Communications Decency Act of 1995 or CDA.

The general tone of the act was to deregulate—provide fewer rules to encourage competition so that competition would benefit the consumer. This title is not like that—it enacts additional regulations. The major provisions, which all resulted from amendments tacked on to the bill in committee or on the House or Senate floor, address content of telephone communications, online communications, cable transmissions, and TV broadcasts. Specifically, Title V addresses:

1. obscene, indecent or harassing use of telecommunications devices (other than computers);

2. use of interactive computer services to send or to display indecent material to minors;

3. use of interactive computer services to traffic in obscenity;

4. protections from civil liability for interactive computer services that screen, or enable users to screen, objectionable content;

5. sexually explicit cable programming; and

6. "V-chip" technology and rating systems to screen objectionable video programming.

The first provision here changes the word "telephones" in the older law to "telecommunications devices." This allows people who harass others using fax machines or other kinds of devices (pagers?) to be prosecuted. Specific provision for harsher penalties is made if the harassment is directed at a minor (someone under 18 years of age).

Blocking technologies have been used in cable systems for some time. The provisions in this act make the penalties harsher for transmission of certain kinds of sexually oriented broadcasts, further provide for blocking of such programs at no charge on the request of the consumer/subscriber, and allow cable operators to refuse to transmit this kind of material. If you wish to block this material, you may find it easier because of this law. You will still need to be informed about what channels you wish to have blocked.

"V-chips" are for television broadcast program blocking. You will buy a V-chip-enabled television if you buy one in the next year or so. The

"V" stands for violence and the thrust of the provisions are to require that content providers include a rating about the sexual and violent program composition along with the content. Then a "standard blocking" technology could "read" the rating and then block the program if a consumer chooses to do so. If you wish to keep violent or sexually oriented broadcast material out of your home, you will be able to program your television so that it will not show programs with specific ratings. You will still need to choose to program your television and you will need to be informed about the rating system.

Another section contains a narrow set of changes to existing federal obscenity law to clarify that it prohibits the knowing use of "an interactive computer service" to import, transport, or receive obscene material and certain abortion-related information in interstate or foreign commerce. Planned Parenthood swiftly challenged the reproductive information portion of the law. That is the first of the three big court actions to either define or overturn these portions of the law.

Indecency under the Act

Indecency in this law is defined as material that "in context, depicts or describes, in terms patently offensive as measured by contemporary community standards, sexual or excretory activities or organs." Indecency is criminal under this law. It is specifically against the law to make "knowing use of an interactive computer service to display indecent material in a manner available to minors, or knowing use of such a service to send indecent material to a specific minor." The law also prohibits facilities providers from knowingly and intentionally permitting use of their facilities for either of the above purposes. Violations are punishable by up to two years in prison and/or a fine under the federal criminal code.

People who specialize in First Amendment rights believe that this definition is too vague. What, in a global environment, constitutes community? It's clear that what might be acceptable in some cosmopolitan, metropolitan areas would not be acceptable in more conservative, farming communities, for example. That which is acceptable to some Americans might not be acceptable to some from Singapore or Denmark. What might be acceptable in the Netherlands might not be acceptable in the United States.

How do you know whether someone is a minor? (Let's not forget that on the Internet, you can pretend to be another and it is very difficult to spot these pretenses.) It has generally been accepted that minors do not have credit cards or debit accounts in their own names. Thus, if you require someone to give you a credit card number or the number of a debit account, and you can verify that the account exists and is held by that person, you are somewhat protected. However, not everyone has access to credit card validations. Nor is everyone who would like to have a Web page or post to a newsgroup able to predict who will see that page.

And from a service provider's point of view, it's difficult to know what your customer is doing on that Web page. Service providers have some protection under this law, but many are nervous about what their liability will be under this new law. The Stratton Oakmont v. Prodigy Services case (`http://www.mbc.com/prodigy.html`) is one where Prodigy was held liable for certain things posted on their service by a customer even though they didn't know what was happening. The court ruled that because Prodigy had sought to keep the "seven dirty words" from postings on the service, they had become a publisher rather than a distributor of information and were therefore responsible for the posting. This decision prompted legislators to try to make it easier for service providers to operate without necessarily being held responsible for what the customers do without the provider's knowledge.

COMMUNITY STANDARDS AND THE GLOBAL INTERNET

In late 1995, CompuServe's offices in Munich, Germany were visited by special state-based police who are responsible to the Prosecutor's office. These police desired to know more about specifically listed newsgroups that CompuServe carried to its general consumer customers. These newsgroups were generally those that carry erotic material in image form. Because CompuServe's servers were in the United States, and not in Germany alone, and because German law would hold CompuServe's German employees responsible for corporate actions, CompuServe chose to remove access to the questioned newsgroups. Because CompuServe was unable to block access to the groups for Germany alone, all CompuServe customers were unable to access these newsgroups.

There was an uproar. The German officials clarified and reclarified their positions. CompuServe clarified and reclarified its positions. The newsgroups remained blocked for all CompuServe customers until CompuServe was able to provide access to a blocking program. When CompuServe deployed the blocking program, each customer was able to select their own wanted materials, and CompuServe again provided access to all the newsgroups.

Because of the seriousness of the challenge to constitutionally protected speech, two more cases were filed according to the provisions for expedited review provided by the Telecommunications Act.

The second case was brought by a coalition of groups and people including the Electronic Frontier Foundation

```
http://www.eff.org
```

The American Civil Liberties Union

```
http://www.aclu.org
```

Human Rights Watch

```
gopher://gopher.humanrights.org:5000/11/int/hrw
```

and the Electronic Privacy Information Center

```
http://www.epic.org
```

Attorney General Janet Reno and the Justice Department have agreed not to initiate investigations or prosecutions under the law while the three judge panel in the Eastern District of Pennsylvania considers the constitutionality of the law. In this case the plaintiffs assert that

"1. ... the Act is unconstitutional on its face and as applied because it criminalizes expression that is protected by the First Amendment; it is also impermissibly overbroad and vague; and it is not the least restrictive means of accomplishing any compelling governmental purpose.

"2. In addition, plaintiffs assert that the Act violates the constitutional right to privacy encompassed in the First, Fourth, Fifth, and Ninth Amendments because it criminalizes private "e-mail" computer correspondence to or among individuals under the age of 18 if the correspondence is deemed "patently offensive" or "indecent."

"3. Plaintiffs further assert that the Act in effect prohibits the right to anonymous speech, guaranteed by the First Amendment, for vast portions of the computer networks.

"4. Finally, plaintiffs American Civil Liberties Union, Planned Parenthood Federation of America, Inc., and others also assert that 18 U.S.C. §1462(c), both before and after amendment, is unconstitutional on its face because it violates the First Amendment by criminalizing the distribution or reception of any information via "any express company or other common carrier, or interactive computer service" of "information ... where, how, or of whom, or by what means any ... drug, medicine, article, or thing designed, adapted, or intended for producing abortion ... may be obtained or made.""

COMPARE AND CONTRAST

(Written for the Internet Society Publication, *On the Internet,* Copyright 1996, Glee Harrah Cady)

The rabid discussions of the recent attempts to regulate the Internet's content in order to protect ourselves and our children from harmful and/or offensive material have caused many of us to question our own beliefs. People who generally consider themselves "liberal" or "moderate" have found themselves arguing for less government regulation—generally considered a more "conservative" stance in the United States. In contrast, people who generally consider themselves "conservative" have found themselves arguing for stringent government regulation, a position generally taken by "big government liberals." Feelings have been running high as each side fears that a "win" by the other will tilt the development of the Internet in directions that none of us can predict.

I think it interesting to compare and contrast two of the legislators who have had considerable influence over the legislation about which we all spend hours discussing, fretting, worrying, and trying to understand the implications—The Telecommunications Act of 1996 and the Communications Decency Act of 1995 which was contained within it. The two men (one Senator and one Representative; one Democrat and one Republican) have fascinating similarities and differences.

The first, Senator James Exon, is a Democrat from an agricultural, wide-open plains state, Nebraska. He is an experienced legislator whose opinion is sought because he is an independent legislator, not always inclined to vote the party line. He recently announced that his current term (his third) would be his last as a senator. He'll retire when his term is complete in 1997. He'll be 75 then. Sen. Exon has served in the senate since 1979. He also served two terms as Nebraska's governor.

He is the parent of three and the grandparent of eight and comes from a business background.

He serves on the Armed Services; Budget; and Commerce, Science, and Technology Committees. He's the ranking Democrat on the Budget Committee and is fiscally conservative—one of the Democrats who early favored passage of a balanced budget amendment. Senator Exon made the passage of a balanced budget amendment a priority for the 104th Congress.

Senator Exon also codeveloped a proposal (with Sen. Domenici, R.-N.M.) for a line-item veto, later dropped for other methods of passing legislation and having the President sign it into law. In the 103rd Congress, Senator Exon, with Senator Grassley (R.-Iowa), proposed an amendment to the budget to cut an additional $26.1 billion in spending—the proposed cuts surprised observers because of Senator Exon's long support of Defense spending. Eventually, a compromise plan that included $13 billion in cuts passed.

On the Armed Services Committee, Senator Exon reviews the military in which he served. He rose from his enlistment as a private to finish his service as a master sergeant. He served in the Pacific in World War II. He generally is regarded as "pro-Pentagon" and has supported the US position on the Persian Gulf War. He has been widely quoted about his opposition to gays serving in the military. He has argued for money for the B-2 bomber and yet successfully sponsored a measure to restrict US testing of nuclear weapons. He's worked on legislation for AMTRAK, for truck safety, for care in transportation of hazardous materials, for railroad safety, and for promoting Ethanol as a fuel. He sponsored a bill that designated the Niobrara River a National Scenic River.

His notoriety or celebrity in Internet circles comes from "The Exon Amendment," a measure intended to ensure that the same standards of decency are applied to telecommunications networks as are applied to the telephone. His most famous quotation deals with not wishing the "information superhighway" to become "a red-light district" in reference to areas where the sale of sex is denoted by red lights. You can read the text of the Amendment (S.314) itself via the Library of Congress Thomas Legislative Search System at

```
http://thomas.loc.gov
```

and the speech Senator Exon made when he introduced it at

```
http://www.infi.net/pilot/extra/exonspeech.html
```

Senator Exon clearly and passionately believes that it is government's responsibility to protect children from the inappropriate material that exists on the Net.

Rick White, on the other hand, is a Freshman Representative—one of the large class of Republican legislators who journeyed to Washington at the beginning of 1995. He's from the 1st Congressional District in the state of Washington, a relatively affluent district with an educated electorate. His district includes Redmond and the surrounding suburbs of Seattle, where there are many high-technology companies. He, too, voted for passage of the balanced budget amendment.

He's an Internet user himself—he characterizes himself as an "avid user." You can send him e-mail at repwhite@hr.house.gov. As a caring father of four relatively young children, he uses the Net to stay in touch with his family who remain in their Washington state home. He's stated clearly that he intends to limit himself to five terms. Rep. White is an attorney specializing in business law who before his election was a partner in the Seattle firm of Perkins Coie. He was born in Indiana in 1953, studied Government and French at Dartmouth College, and graduated from Georgetown's Law School. He also studied Philosophy at the Pantheon-Sorbonne in France.

Representative White serves solely on the House Commerce Committee. He is assigned to the Telecommunications and Finance subcommittee and the Commerce, Trade and Hazardous Materials subcommittee. The Commerce Committee is his only committee assignment because the Committee is classified as an "exclusive" committee by the House.

In contrast to James Exon's position that children should be protected by governmental regulation, Rick White believes that the better way is to educate parents and empower them to use that education and newly developing technologies on behalf of the children. Rep. White believes that parents and children together should explore and learn from the Net and that parents should instill their own political, cultural, and moral values rather than having to explain the values of someone else. This position is consistent with his habit of taking at least one of his children with him while he was campaigning in an attempt to spend more time together.

You can read Rep. White's Open Letter to the Internet Community. He wrote it on behalf of the "Internet Freedom and Family Empowerment Act." The text of his letter can be found at

```
http://www.eff.org/alerts/white_hr1555_120495_net.letter
```

Here he explains the Cox/Wyden/White amendment in contrast to the Hyde amendment. Rick White believes the "harmful to minors" phrase (which describes material that is sexually explicit and generally without artistic, political, or social value) is a more effective weapon to use against people who would make such material available to children. Thus, the amendment was attractive to law officers who believed they could effectively prosecute with this law. The amendment was also popular with people who worried that their own values were not shared with those who might be setting the legal standards.

Two legislators, both parents, trying to do the best for their constituents and for the Internet users everywhere. Isn't it interesting how their approaches could be so different?

The last case was filed several days later. A coalition representing a broad spectrum of Internet users, libraries, publishers, content providers and access providers filed a lawsuit on Monday February 26, 1996 in a Federal Court in Philadelphia, PA, seeking to overturn the act. The challenge argues that the Internet is a unique communications technology which deserves First Amendment protections at least as broad as those enjoyed by the print medium.

The group, known as the Citizens Internet Empowerment Coalition is coordinated by the Center for Democracy and Technology

```
http://www.cdt.org
```

America Online

```
http://www.aol.com
```

and the American Library Association

`http://www.ala.org`

and others. Its 35 members include libraries, book publishers, newspaper publishers, editors, advertisers, commercial online service providers, ISPs, nonprofit groups, and civil liberties advocates.

The CIEC complaint describes the history of the Internet and outlines how the network operates, intending to educate the court on how the Internet functions and why the broad content regulations imposed by the CDA threaten the very existence of the Internet as a viable medium for free expression, education, and commerce. Among other things, the CIEC challenge argues that:

▶ The Internet is a unique communications medium that deserves First Amendment protections at least as broad as those afforded to print media.

▶ Individual users and parents, not the federal government, should determine for themselves and their children what material comes into their homes based on their own tastes and values.

▶ The CDA will be ineffective at protecting children from "indecent" or "patently" offensive material online.

The CIEC challenge is separate from the case brought by the ACLU, etc. The CIEC case will reinforce the ACLU's efforts while focusing on the unique nature of the Internet and alternatives to government content regulations. ACLU and CIEC attorneys are closely coordinating their efforts, and the case has been consolidated.

Note: Glee Cady is an active member of CIEC. She filed a declaration describing communications on the Internet that is based in part on material that appears in Chapter 2 of this book. That declaration is part of the request for a preliminary injunction.

What Will Happen Next?

It's hard to say. Everyone expects the cases to move quickly. The cases may even be decided by the time you read these words. If so, you can write your own ending. Watch on the Net itself—that's your best source of information.

Copyright

In mid-1994 Dave Barry, the humor columnist, and his publisher proposed discontinuing the distribution of his columns over the Net. Why? Because one of his publisher's employees got a copy of one of Barry's columns, passed along fourth- or fifth-hand in e-mail—forwarded from the Clarinet news subscription service which had been publishing them electronically. His publishers (and Barry, presumably) felt that his potential to earn money was being diluted because of promiscuous theft of his copyrighted material off the Internet. Some of us may actually have to start reading the paper again to find Barry's columns. :-)

It's hard to remember that copyright law and intellectual property law still obtain even though materials may not be represented in some physical form like paper. It's too easy to just forward the file in e-mail to your buddy, or a set of buddies, or squirrel it away in an FTP archive or display it on your personal Web page or even dump it down to a newsletter or other publication.

But we must learn to respect copyrighted material in electronic format as much as we do that on paper or in broadcast media. Some day many of us may be making our livings solely from electronic publication, and the ground rules for that are being set now.

Remember that the materials obtained under license from news services, for example, may not be altered or used without permission. A shareware computer program obtained by downloading from a program archive may ask for a registration fee as part of its license agreement. You are ethically obligated to pay the fee if you use the program. If there's a copyright statement at the beginning of the document, software program, or other material, read it and respect it.

Copyleft

You may well run into something called *copyleft* on your travels about the Internet. Copyleft is a concept that has come out of the GNU (Gnu's Not UNIX) project, which is working on creating free software versions of most UNIX programs and utilities. The folks who work with the GNU project believe that the *source* code for every program ought to be available to everyone to use and modify. (This is a very simplistic description of the GNU project. For a more complete description, send e-mail to gnu@prep.ai.mit.edu.) Documentation and other works associated with the GNU project are *copylefted*, which means that the owner, while still retaining the copyright, has granted everyone the right to copy and use it, as long as acknowledgment is made, and *everyone else is free to use that material again in their own works.*

If you encounter copylefted materials and wish to use them for some purpose, be sure to read the provisions carefully to ensure that you use the materials appropriately.

 MASTER WORDS Several authors have put their books up on the Internet under copylefting terms. To find them, FTP to `ftp.eff.org`, log on as anonymous, and look in the directory. Among the writers whose work you'll find there are Bruce Sterling, Shari Steele, and William Gibson.

Commercial Use

What about commercial use of the Internet?

Commercial use is, roughly defined, traffic that supports business or trade rather than academic research or instruction. Want ads, service ads, software support, e-mail hotlines, and distribution of reports and financial data for large corporations can all be described as commercial use.

Positions on commercial use have changed dramatically in the last three years. Several years ago, anything traveling the old NSFNET backbone (which was most of the traffic on the still-infant Internet) had to either be academic or in support of academic research. Some networks, primarily those funded largely with academic research funds, still have restrictions on commercial traffic. But almost all of us can find an alternative provider these days, if we want to pass commercial traffic.

The interconnected networks of the Commercial Internet eXchange (CIX) were created to explicitly pass commercial transactions. But since the demise of the NSFNET backbone, most Internet service providers are connected to a commercial provider these days, rather than through an academic system.

Commercial use of certain other networks that have significant support from the United States Federal or other governments may be restricted to activities in support of research and education. Unfortunately, the definitions of support, commercial use, research, and education are not really clear, and the definitions that do exist are changing. Usually you can assume that running your own personal commercial service on the computer system of your employer or college or academic system will be against their policies. You will want to seek out one of the many other systems on which such uses are more than acceptable, they're encouraged.

The best thing to do is to be aware that there may be restrictions and try to abide by the Acceptable Use Policy (AUP) of each network. Consult with your systems administrator, employer, or university computing service if you are in doubt about the way you propose to use your service.

For-Fee Services

Some services use the Internet to deliver you to their front door and then begin charging for their use, others do not charge. Services that charge for their usage are well-marked. You will need to make account arrangements with these services before you can use them. There will be signs at the front door of these services to tell you how to open an account.

A Few Words about Netiquette

The American Heritage Dictionary defines etiquette as "the practices and forms prescribed by social convention or by authority." It lists etiquette, propriety, decorum, and protocol as being roughly equivalent words that refer to codes governing correct behavior.

Netiquette is the term that Internet users have developed to describe the personal protocol that helps us participate in the networked society. Such protocols are not, unlike the remainder of the TCP/IP protocol suite, formally written down, but they are essential to the well-being of the society as a whole. Netiquette provides the guidelines that allow us, for example, to agree to disagree. Mostly, being a good networked citizen is being a responsible person: not wasting resources; being aware of and observing restrictions that are placed on some Internet resources; observing the posted rules; remembering that on the Net, you are in public.

Remember the angry drivers in the scenario up above? On the Interstates, usually, these drivers are content to dole out a few well-chosen words and gestures, and then the flow of traffic whisks them away.

Unfortunately, if you're going to start being rude to someone on the Internet, they can archive your words and argue with you for a long time. In Internet terms, this is called a *flame war,* and no one really benefits from it. (Some of them can be incredibly creative and take the art of subtle insult to amazing levels. Such things are better seen from the peanut gallery, though.)

One of the pluses of the growing networked community is that some of the old-timers, and some of the newcomers who had to discover all the unwritten rules themselves, have started writing down some of the rules, customs, and conventions that govern interaction on the Internet. There are even newsgroups for newcomers these days:

news.answers	An amazing collection of Frequently Asked Questions show up here—a must read for everyone.
news.announce.newusers	This is where the Netiquette postings show up.
news.newusers.questions	This is where the Frequently Asked Questions lists, or FAQs, for many newsgroups are posted.

 MASTER WORDS   One of the newer RFCs (the standards and documentation of the Internet, written by members of the Internet Engineering Task Force—IETF) is on netiquette. It reminds us that we as users are ultimately responsible for our own actions on the Net. We've included it as part of Appendix B at the end of the book. This document, or something like it, can serve both as personal reference and as the cornerstone of a corporate or organizational policy on appropriate and courteous use of the Net.

Joy in Diversity

One of the most exciting things about the Internet is how easy it is to communicate and really get to know folks who are not very much like you. Glee has a regular e-mail exchange with a fellow in Europe whom she met through her work at Netcom; he's thoroughly European and about 5 years older than her oldest son. Through one of the mailing lists she reads, Pat has met a woman who works as a janitor and is running for public office; this woman has six children and worked her way off welfare. Nearly everybody hangs out on the Net.

The most exciting thing about all this communicating is that it's impossible to tell from the bits on the screen the gender, race, age, financial status, sexual orientation, political affiliation, or class of the person who's writing. Until they choose to reveal those details, all you know about someone is what they are saying. And so we get a chance to really get to know people without the barriers that our reflexive preconceptions and prejudices can impose.

We can learn to like or dislike someone based on their expressed beliefs, the language they use, their sense of humor, their concern for others. We can make friends with folks in much different situations than ourselves, and perhaps learn about the lives that other folks live away from the Net.

There is something of the soapbox about some network communications: if some person who is being a pest or annoyance—but who is *not* breaking any rules or laws—wants to keep sending out obnoxious messages, he or she can do it. Extreme views on both ends of the spectrum are very common: both extreme friendliness and civility, and extreme rudeness. We learn to revel in the one and ignore (sometimes aided by technological tools) the other.

Honesty and Hidden Faces

There are problems with the ability to hide something of ourselves, of course. A 1994 Doonesbury cartoon series showed two of the characters—good friends in the non-virtual universe—corresponding over a bulletin board *without knowing that they knew each other.* One of the characters pretended to be a gay man, and before he knew it, the two were involved in a hot romance over the Net, resulting in emotional pain for both of them. It pointed out that, because we can choose to hide those parts of ourselves we don't want to reveal, there is a potential for deception.

There have been notorious cases where pedophiles were trying to seduce schoolchildren over the Net; where men masqueraded as women and vice versa; where thieves engaged unsuspecting victims in conversations, found out vacation plans or other information, and robbed the victim. These are the high-profile cases: they make sensational news stories, so we see much more of them than we do the other side. We don't hear as much about the fundraisers that happen spontaneously when the news gets out that someone has lost their home in a fire, the deep and abiding friendships that spring out of mutual interests on the Net, or the marriages and successful romances.

It's important to remember that the Internet is a mirror of life: there are good people and jerks; kindness and rudeness; political action and apathy; and excitement and boredom. In general, the good and positive outweigh the bad—just like in our everyday, noncomputer lives. We just don't hear about it as much.

 MASTER WORDS When you start reading news, or subscribe to a mailing list, you *can* post things anonymously. There is an anonymous server at anon .penet.fi (in Finland) that will strip off all machine generated identifying marks on your postings (although if you leave your real name at the bottom it doesn't do much good). For more information, send e-mail to help@anon.penet.fi.

Pardon Me, You're Reading over My Shoulder

Privacy concerns are one of the biggest controversies in the computer industry today, and now that more and more of us are living parts of our lives over the Net, privacy concerns are reaching out and touching us all:

Do you dial into your bank to check your balance and make payments?

Do you send confidential company reports over the network, including spreadsheets or graphics?

Do you send e-mail to your mother, close friend, or lover?

Do you buy products or request quotes via e-mail from on-line vendors?

Do you read a newsgroup pertaining to your religious beliefs, sexual orientation, hobbies, or political leanings?

Do you keep personnel records on-line in your company LAN?

Do you participate in a MUD, MOO, or MUSE? A chat line? A CB group? IRC?

If you can answer "yes" to even one of these questions, you need to think about how much of your privacy you want to protect from others on the Internet.

This is not meant to scare you. We all want to close the blinds from time to time, to keep other people from looking in our windows. It's easier to forget on the Net than in our living rooms that other people can see what we're doing.

Hilarie Gardner (calliope@well.com) has published a good set of guidelines for new users of the Internet, included in Appendix B. Even some of us old-time users can benefit from thinking about these concerns.

More and more people are becoming concerned that the world is now so interlinked, with so many of our day-to-day transactions handled by computers, that no one will be able to have private interests or be able to even spend money without that expenditure being tracked. There are several key areas of privacy concerns: two of the most important are personal information and safety, and the sale of private information. We'll cover the sale of private information when we talk about setting policy in later chapters.

 MASTER WORDS   **If you are interested in finding out more about computer-related privacy and civil-liberties risks, you can read the RISKS mailing list. RISKS is available on Usenet as comp.risks.**

Who Knows What about Me?

If you have an account on a networked machine, chances are people can find out quite a bit about you just by checking out your account remotely with a network utility called *Finger* (we talk about it in Chapter 9). Depending on what you yourself have implemented, and what your systems administrator has done, quite a bit can be found with just this one simple tool.

Let's take Pat as an example.

Pat's been published in several computing journals with a reference saying she works at the University of Michigan. Let's suppose that someone tried to Finger her at U-M. What might they have seen in return?

```
home>>finger pat.mcgregor@umich.edu
[umich.edu]
X.500 Finger Service
```

```
One exact match found for "pat.mcgregor":
"Patricia O Mcgregor, Information Technology Division,
Faculty and Staff"
        Also known as:
                Patricia O Mcgregor 1
                Patricia O Mcgregor
                Patricia Mcgregor
                Pat Mcgregor
        e-mail address:
                pat@lloyd.com
        Fax number:
                +1 313 747 3185
        Business phone:
                +1 313 747 0416
        Business address:
                Merit / UMnet
                2901 Hubbard - Pod G
                Ann Arbor, MI 48109-2016
        Title:
                Computer Systems Consultant II, UM-Net
        Uniqname:
                patmcg
        Description:
                Consultant for Merit Technical Support group,
                working with MichNet and UMnet. Editor of the
                MichNet News. Bradley Childbirth Educator,
                amateur medievalist.
    home>>
```

This entry is pretty much out of date: Pat hasn't worked for U-M since late 1993. (U-M was keeping the listing as a courtesy and as a forwarding service.) But you can see from this that anyone who wanted to find her could have found out not only her e-mail address, but her phone number and the building where she worked. They could also learn something of her personal interests.

Pat knew that this information was accessible and chose not to edit it. She decided to take the relatively small risk that someone might decide to stalk her or call her with harassing phone messages in order to make it easy for people who needed or wanted to locate her for business or personal reasons. She chose not to make her home information accessible, however, to protect the privacy of herself and her family.

MASTER WORDS   The University of Michigan is aware that this information is available about many people connected with the University, and runs a large publicity campaign regularly to educate those associated with the school that this information is available. Because of the potential for harassment of several kinds, private information about students is not available via Finger unless the student explicitly includes it.

We discover from our initial Finger session that Pat's e-mail address is pat@lloyd.com. Let's try Fingering that and see where we get.

```
home>>finger pat@lloyd.com
[lloyd.com]
Login name: pat    In real life: Pat McGregor
Directory: /home/furry/pat
Shell:/usr/local/bin/tcsh
On since Jul  8 15:49:39 on ttyp2 from pickle.lloyd.com
No unread mail
No Plan.
```

This is a more typical UNIX-style Finger response. We can tell that Pat has a log-in ID on the machine furry and that she was, at the time the screen dump was taken, on-line. We can tell she logged into lloyd .com remotely over the Internet from a machine called pickle. Of importance for you, if you have sent her mail, is the fact that it looks like she has read everything that has been received by her mailer. You can tell that her real login ID is pat (and if you were a hacker interested in breaking into her account, this would give you a starting place to poke holes).

Not much other information is available about Pat from this Finger session. (If you're excited about the UNIX operating system, you can tell she's using a tcsh shell interface to UNIX, and what her home directory is called.) The systems administrators at lloyd.com have, for security reasons, chosen not to implement the features that would let you see what Pat has in her personal information file (called a *.Plan* file; the name comes from old UNIX days when folks would store their current working information in their planning file).

Not every system administrator has disabled this feature. Many times, you'll find something like this when you Finger someone:

```
home>>finger pat@inkwell.com
[inkwell.com]
Login name: pat    In real life: Patricia McGregor
Directory: /home/users/pat  Shell: /usr/
unsupported/bin/tcsh
Last login Wed May  4 18:43 on console
New mail received Fri Jul  8 15:50:08 1994;
              unread since Thu Jul  7 09:34:25 1994
Plan:
============================================================


Pat McGregor                        Inkwell Publications


              Speaker-to-Programmers
              pat@inkwell.com


     1937 Pelican Drive, Mountain View, CA 94444
              (415) 123-4567(voice)
              (415) 777-3456 (fax)


 "That's how freedom will end: not with a bang, but with
 a rustle of file folders. If you love any of your
 rights, defend all of them!"


 --Joe Chew, on the Net
```

Again, we can learn quite a bit about how to find Pat: something she has chosen deliberately to allow. We can see her work phone, her work fax, where her office is located, and that she hasn't read her mail in the last day.

The point of this extended discussion is to remind you that *unless you take steps to prevent it,* quite a bit of information about you is casually available on the Net. If you want to find out just how much, ask your systems administrator.

MASTER WORDS   We can hear you now: "Just how do I *find* my systems administrator?" Many systems have a mailbox called "postmaster" or "admin" where a real human being reads the mail. If all else fails, send to "root."

Some women in particular are concerned about harassing strangers finding out their work addresses, phone numbers, and so on. Hilarie Gardner's advice in her column helps you make decisions about what you want to allow to be private and what to make public.

ONLINE INFORMATION ABOUT SECURITY

Electronic Freedom Foundation: If you are interested in finding out more about privacy and freedom on the network, send e-mail to `info@eff.org`. This is the general mailbox for the Electronic Freedom Foundation, an organization which has as one of its concerns the protection of personal privacy in the age of the Internet. They also have a World Wide Web page available at `www.eff.org`.

The Internet PRIVACY Forum: The Web page of the Internet PRIVACY Forum describes the forum as a "moderated digest for the discussion and analysis of issues relating to the general topic of privacy (both personal and collective) in the 'information age' of the 1990's and beyond. Topics include a wide range of telecommunications, information/database collection and sharing, and related issues, as pertains to the privacy concerns of individuals, groups, businesses, government, and society at large." The discussion is distributed via e-mail. You can find out more about it by reading the Web page available at `http://www.vortex.com/privacy.html`.

The Privacy Rights Clearinghouse of the Center for Public Interest Law: This organization maintains a Web presence courtesy of ManyMedia. There you will find brief information, more links, and contact information for the Clearinghouse.

The Electronic Privacy Information Center: This is a public interest research center in Washington, DC Their Web page, including the current "hot" privacy issues, can be found at `http://www.epic.org`. E-mail to `info@epic.org` for general information.

cAsE Sensitivity and Password Privacy

Just as we discover the joy of diversity in people on the Internet, we also discover the challenges of working in a *heterogeneous networking environment*. Each computer and network in the global Internet operates in its own environment. You will see many different kinds of operating systems and commands. These days, most systems have good on-line help available; in most cases, you'll see the information on how to access it in the first screen you come to. Understanding something about these operating system features can help you maintain security.

 MASTER WORDS In many library catalog systems, the help and logoff information appears in the very first screen you access, and never again! Be sure and take note of it: copy it down if you think you'll forget.

Case sensitivity means that it matters whether a letter is typed in upper- or lowercase. Some operating systems don't care, others are particularly picky. One way to make sure that your e-mail gets through to someone on another system is to type everything in lowercase: i.e., barney@tv.org rather than Barney@TV.org. The rules that programmers must apply in accepting e-mail (if they want to be able to send and receive Internet mail) say that no matter what the internal system says, incoming mail must be accepted if it's in all lowercase.

UNIX

In many cases, the systems and services you reach from the Internet are running the UNIX operating system. UNIX began in a time of very slow computer terminals for use by people who were impatient typists. Consequently, good command interface design consisted of maximum information conveyed in very few keystrokes. This led to the single-letter, case-sensitive command structure that makes it difficult to learn UNIX quickly. UNIX systems also are case sensitive in the Login ID or User name. The Login ID must be lowercase in most UNIX environments. File names can also be mixed upper- and lowercase letters. To retrieve a file, if you are entering the file name rather than clicking on the name in a list of files, you must enter its name exactly.

The good aspect of this is that it's easier to make your password secure in an environment where the operating system is case-sensitive. A password of more than seven characters, typed with a mixture of upper- and lowercase letters, is harder for someone to accidentally (or even with some deliberation) type in, even if you do use a dictionary word for your password (a big no-no, because most folks who try to crack password files do so with huge dictionaries and programs that try them all out).

The most useful help systems on UNIX systems are called *man pages,* short for manual pages. The complete documentation for many system utilities can be accessed through the man pages. To ask for help, type

```
man man
```

This peculiar-looking command gives you instructions on using the man facility itself.

 MASTER WORDS   For help with UNIX commands, use a Web browser (see Chapter 11) to access http://www.nova.edu/Inter-Links/UNIXhelp/TOP_.html. This Web server provides information about UNIX and how to use it.

Other Systems

Non-UNIX systems have their peculiar features, too. IBM MVS and VM systems, for example, cannot have file names longer than eight characters per name segment, leading to some interesting names where vowels are deleted so that the file name can convey something about the content of the file. These systems, however, treat upper- and lowercase commands equally, giving the same result no matter how the command is entered.

This means that you cannot safeguard your files or your passwords by using mixed case on one of these systems. You must depend on something more robust, such as making sure your file permissions are set correctly or that the files are hidden.

Take Off and Explore

Although using the Internet can be confusing and overwhelming when you're first getting started, if you keep the simple rules of courtesy in mind, you can feel your way along pretty easily. Just remember these few guidelines:

Read the road signs as you come to them.

Be polite and respectful of other's property and privacy.

Keep a road map (a notepad) by your side to copy down the host address of fun or useful things, so you can find them again.

Learn how to use bookmarks and hot lists in clients such as Gopher and WWW.

Read the help files.

Read the Terms and Conditions.

Remember that you probably can't break the computer— don't be afraid to explore and try something new.

The Internet Toolkit

CHAPTER

8

Electronic Mail: Exchanging Messages with Other People

FEATURING

How electronic mail works
_____

Troubleshooting e-mail
_____

Using mail software
_____

Using your word processor for e-mail
_____

Managing e-mail and your work flow
_____

Finding e-mail addresses
_____

mail reflectors, mailing lists, and list servers
_____

Chapter 8

Electronic Mail: Exchanging Messages with Other People

ELECTRONIC mail (abbreviated "e-mail") is the service most people use first in networking, whether they are on a local LAN or on a service connected to the global Internet. It is *the* most commonly used service on the Internet, perhaps because of how convenient it is. It's easier to send e-mail than paper mail: no stamps, no searching for an envelope—just type and send! e-mail allows us to send a message to another computer without requiring that the receiving person be "at home" (logged into the destination computer) at the time the destination system actually receives the e-mail. Thus, e-mail is more like "talking" to an answering machine or a voice mail system than it is like a telephone conversation. And it can seem like playing telephone tag, because you send a message to your friend, who reads it after you go home, and then you read the answer later before you go to bed (or even after you go back to work the next day).

Most important, as you can see in Figure 8.1, e-mail is familiar and easy because it looks like a memo, a note to a friend, or a formal report, only on screen instead of on paper.

It is called e-*mail* because it is similar to the paper mail that the postal service delivers:

You put it into an electronic envelope and address it.

You hand the message off to someone else (the network) to be delivered.

You may not know when the e-mail is read.

If you address your message incorrectly, you get it back in your mailbox.

If the recipient leaves a forwarding address, the e-mail system will keep trying to route it to her until it runs out of forwarding locations.

Your message will be returned if the network is unable to deliver your e-mail. (This is called *bounced* mail because it "bounces" back to you.)

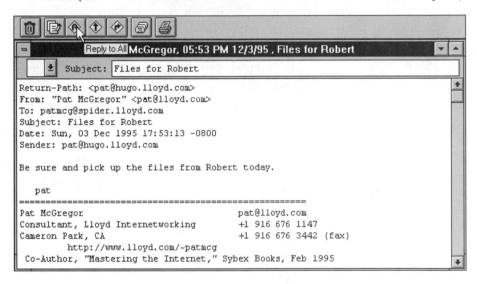

```
Reply to All McGregor, 05:53 PM 12/3/95 , Files for Robert

Subject: Files for Robert

Return-Path: <pat@hugo.lloyd.com>
From: "Pat McGregor" <pat@lloyd.com>
To: patmcg@spider.lloyd.com
Subject: Files for Robert
Date: Sun, 03 Dec 1995 17:53:13 -0800
Sender: pat@hugo.lloyd.com

Be sure and pick up the files from Robert today.

    pat
=====================================================
Pat McGregor                          pat@lloyd.com
Consultant, Lloyd Internetworking     +1 916 676 1147
Cameron Park, CA                      +1 916 676 3442 (fax)
        http://www.lloyd.com/~patmcg
Co-Author, "Mastering the Internet," Sybex Books, Feb 1995
```

Figure 8.1. **E-mail looks much like any other note or message.**

There are some other similarities to the paper stuff the post office puts in your mailbox:

Anyone who knows your address can send e-mail to you.

Friends you haven't seen in a long time can keep in touch with you.

You can get so much e-mail that you have trouble reading it all.

If you subscribe to them, electronic "magazines" or mailing lists can give you a much wider point of view about the world around you.

Commercial companies can send you advertising or "junk" mail (this is less true on academic systems, but such mail can slip through).

If you go on vacation, your mailbox can fill up.

Your mail can be delivered to, and read by, someone for whom it wasn't intended for.

There's no guarantee that every piece of e-mail you get will be pleasant and friendly. (But, as of yet, there are not very many electronic bills!)

Because e-mail does travel over computers and computer networks instead of in trucks and airplanes, it's important to remember some differences between e-mail and paper mail:

Because e-mail is so easy to handle (remember, no stamps or envelopes to hunt for), it is very easy for other people to pass around or forward on. Your e-mail may reach people you did not intend to see it.

Because computers and computer networks have "glitches," your e-mail may end up in the hands of a computer postmaster or someone who handles bounced e-mail.

Because e-mail is so easy to reply to, you may send off fast and snappy responses that may not say all you wanted, or you may say something you will regret later.

 MASTER WORDS   Remember the first rule of electronic mail: If you wouldn't want to see it posted on the lunchroom bulletin board, don't send it in an e-mail message.

What about Privacy?

Although e-mail has the *potential* to be terribly public, in reality, most e-mail gets read only by the sender and the intended recipient. For example, when Pat was one of the electronic postmasters at the University of Michigan, they estimated that something like 30,000 e-mail messages were transmitted per day across campus—on a slow day. Fewer than 75 per day of those messages ended up in the postmaster's mailbox for handling. That's 0.25%—so there's very little chance your e-mail will go astray.

Even if your message bounces back to you, chances are no one but you will see it. Unless something goes terribly wrong, most bounced messages are handled by the computers involved without human intervention.

Lots of people communicate with their friends and loved ones via e-mail every day. In general, it's probably not a good idea to get graphic about your reunion with your significant other over e-mail, just in case it does bounce. But there are lots of ways to talk personally without being worried about your messages being publicly displayed.

Even if your message does get sent to a postmaster for handling, it's not likely that he or she will read it and take it home to share with friends. Most postmasters are too busy to go looking for people's private e-mail to read, and most of them have respect for your privacy. It's part of their professional ethical system.

 WARNING Read the information you get from your e-mail service provider carefully (or ask to see the e-mail confidentiality information before you sign up). Some businesses have a policy of no private e-mail on their machines; they do not, therefore, hesitate to scan your mail. Some e-mail providers have automated programs that scan for key words (such as obscenities, root or daemon commands, hot topics such as "pornography," "cracker/hacker," and so on) in e-mail, and they will read or discard your e-mail if it contains one or more of those words. Make sure you know what you're signing up for.

Interconnected but Not All Alike

There are many different electronic mail systems that use the Internet as a delivery service. Some electronic mail enters or leaves the Internet from the commercial information providers like CompuServe and MCIMail. Most e-mail enters or leaves the network from an e-mail system on a connected network node.

These e-mail systems are supported by a local computing system administration and are chosen based on criteria important to the local service area or business. Any e-mail system that allows Internet addressing can let mail traverse the Internet if the networks at either end are set up correctly and their e-mail systems can put the e-mail in Internet-compatible format.

How Does E-Mail Work?

Let's review how e-mail works. As an example, we'll use the piece of e-mail between Hilary and Sue that we talked about in Chapter 1.

Hilary is in Durham, England, and he wants to get information to Sue in Seattle, Washington. Now, if these people are in the same company, using some corporate-wide e-mail system, Hilary just enters Sue's login on the company e-mail system as her address. Hillary's address on the company system might just be `hilary`. His coworker in Seattle, Sue, would likely just be `sue`. When Hilary types or clicks the Send command, the corporate e-mail system delivers it to the correct mailbox without sending it outside the system. This is the easiest kind of e-mail addressing.

MASTER WORDS   Not all e-mail user IDs or addresses are first names or initials. On some systems it will be your account number, your employee number, or some other randomly assigned user ID. Smaller systems tend to use names or initials; larger ones have to find a way to provide each user with a unique identifier.

In fact, people on CompuServe, GEnie, Netcom, America Online, and many other large providers can use this simple form of addressing, because even though they do not all work together, or live in the same town or country, their mailboxes are all handled by one single e-mail system.

MASTER WORDS   Hilary and Sue's messages might well have to go over the Internet in order to reach each other, since they are so far apart. If they were in the same building, their messages might not leave the building's computer system to be delivered. But because they are part of the same corporate e-mail system, Sue and Hilary usually don't have to know anything but each other's login name to exchange mail. The corporate e-mail system handles the routing and more complicated addressing, if any.

However, it is likely that Sue and Hilary are *not* on the same e-mail system. They need to know more in order to get e-mail to one another. They have to add something onto the login name to indicate what machine the e-mail is to go to. This address extension, found following the @ (at) sign in an Internet e-mail address, is called the *fully qualified* address—this means that it has all the parts it needs in order to be delivered from anywhere on the network.

MASTER WORDS   If you send messages to people, but they can't *reply* to those messages, your e-mail system might not be putting your fully qualified address on the FROM line; it might say `joe` instead of `joe@aol.com`. Ask your correspondents to dump your message, including the headers and all the incomprehensible bits, into a new message back to you, with your full address in the TO line. When it comes back, you can see what is going out to your friends.

Let's go back to Hilary and Sue. Hilary's full address might be: `hilary@durham.ac.uk`. Sue's full address is: `sue@seattle.org`. (These are fictitious addresses used for example only. The `ac.uk` is a British addressing convention that means "Academic, United Kingdom." It corresponds to the `.edu` and `.us` extensions in the United States.)

Once a message has an address on it, the interconnected Internet systems take over. The e-mail handling system on the sender's computer packages the message and prepares it for "shipping." The message is broken up into small pieces and put into envelopes called "packets." The packets are all addressed to the final destination. No matter what path or paths the packets with the bits of Hilary's message in it take, they are all reassembled in the correct order by the e-mail machine at Sue's end. Figure 8.2 illustrates the process.

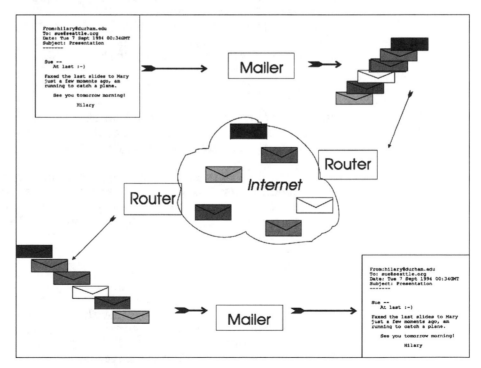

Figure 8.2. *An e-mail message, broken into packets, takes many routes to its destination.*

Understanding the Mail

Let's look at an e-mail message and dissect the bits. This is e-mail from Jeff Marraccini, who helped us on the book.

```
(Message inbox:398)
Date:  Sun, 14 Aug 1996 22:58:35 -0400 (EDT)
To:   pat@lloyd.com (Pat McGregor)
From: Jeff Marraccini <jeff@Vela.ACS.Oakland.Edu>
Subject: Re: IRC!

Return-Path: Vela.ACS.Oakland.Edu!jeff
Return-Path: <jeff@Vela.ACS.Oakland.Edu>
In-Reply-To: <mOqZgtJ-0005awC@lloyd.com> from "Pat McGregor"
at Aug 14, 96 07:50:29 am
Organization: Oakland University, Rochester, MI U.S.A.
X-Mailer: ELM [version 2.4 PL21]
Mime-Version: 1.0
Content-Type: text/plain; charset=US-ASCII
Content-Transfer-Encoding: 7bit
Content-Length: 588

--------------------------------

Pat McGregor (pat@lloyd.com) writes:
>I haven't had a chance to get it out of the FTP archive but
>I'll do that today and let you know.

I may be hard to reach starting on Tuesday and ending on
next Sunday, as I'm going on a small vacation before the
crunch hits. If you need to reach me, I'll hopefully be
able to check e-mail every other day, or leave a message
on my cellular phone.

Thanks,

Jeff
—
Jeff Marraccini         jeff@vela.acs.oakland.edu <- Work
Senior Computing Resource Admin  jeff@nucleus.mi.org<-Home
Oakland University                   +1 810 370-4542
Rochester, MI 48309 "The Computer is your Friend." —Paranoia
```

 MASTER WORDS   What if you use a GUI mail tool such as Eudora or cc:Mail? How can you find the headers in those tools? Frequently there will be a separate attachment (called external headers) or a menu item to let you see the headers.

Addressing

The first section is just like a memo or paper mail letter: it tells us who the message is from, who it goes to, what it's about, and when it was sent.

```
Date:  Sun, 14 Aug 1996 22:58:35 -0400 (EDT)
To:    pat@lloyd.com (Pat McGregor)
From:  Jeff Marraccini <jeff@Vela.ACS.Oakland.Edu>
Subject: Re: IRC!
```

Jeff's mailer is more user-friendly than some; it inserts real names with the e-mail addresses. This isn't so necessary with the kind of addresses that Jeff and Pat have: you can see at least something of their names from the user name.

Part II

The Internet Toolkit

 MASTER WORDS   User names (the part before the @ sign) can be pretty obscure. For example, take `MSO4147@med.ge.com`—we can't tell who this is from without a translation. Or consider the standard CompuServe address: `7041.89321@compuserve.com`. Both GE and CompuServe (and many other systems) use account numbers or employee numbers or some other gibberish string as user names. For this reason, you'll want to use your mailer's "alias" or "address book" functions to help you remember how to reach your friends. We'll talk about that soon.

You may also see these cryptic items in the address block of a message: CC and BCC. CC means "carbon copy," and it's pretty much the same as in a paper letter or memo. You are including the person listed in that line as a courtesy or for their information. Be careful about CC-ing the world on an e-mail message. Some people regard this as rude or excessive. Worse, they may not want to see all the responses that are generated by a mass mailing (or, if they are on CompuServe, they will be charged for this mail which they did not solicit and may not want).

BCC means "blind carbon copy." It's like making an extra photocopy of a memo or letter and dropping it in someone's in-box without letting the official recipients know you did it. Some people always BCC themselves in order to have a copy of everything they send out. BCC recipients usually get a notice that this is a blind carbon. Most mailers strip out the BCC line even for the recipients, so they can't tell who else may have gotten a blind carbon. The official recipients, of course, don't know that anyone else has gotten a copy.

Think carefully before BCC-ing someone on a message. It's possible to encourage gossip or to spread information indiscriminately with BCC, and hurt someone else. Additionally, if you spread information that is incorrect, and don't send the BCC recipient any follow-up messages correcting the information, you could be responsible for whatever bad results follow. Keep in mind the saying, "What goes around, comes around."

We can tell from the Subject line that this is a reply or a forwarded message: many mailers add "Re:" to indicate that this message *refers* to another.

Deciphering Headers

The next part of the message is where e-mail is different from paper mail. With e-mail, you can tell exactly how the message got to you from your correspondent. With paper mail, you only know that the carrier delivered it. You don't know what happened in the middle (and usually, with paper mail, you don't much care).

With e-mail, you know a lot. For example, you can see, perhaps, that an intermediate mailer held onto your message for several days before passing it along, which might explain why a message was delayed. You can see who handles the mail exchanges for your correspondent (which is sometimes more esoterically interesting than useful).

 MASTER WORDS   Do you really care about headers? 99% of the time, probably not. The headers you care most about are From:, To: and CC:, the time the message was sent, and the Subject. You may even care about the Content-Length, because that tells you if the sender has written the Great American Epistle. But if the mail gets screwy, or if things don't go as expected, knowing something about the headers can be very useful.

You can read even more in bounced messages, which we'll look at next.

```
Return-Path: Vela.ACS.Oakland.Edu!jeff
Return-Path: <jeff@Vela.ACS.Oakland.Edu>
In-Reply-To: <mOqZgtJ-0005awC@lloyd.com> from "Pat McGregor"
at Aug 14, 96 07:50:29 am
Organization: Oakland University, Rochester, MI U.S.A.
X-Mailer: ELM [version 2.4 PL21]
Mime-Version: 1.0
```

```
Content-Type: text/plain; charset=US-ASCII
Content-Transfer-Encoding: 7bit
Content-Length: 588
```

These lines, called "*headers*," tell us, in order:

How to get reply mail or bounced messages back to Jeff (the "Return-path"):

```
Return-Path: Vela.ACS.Oakland.Edu!jeff
```

The machine name or number of the message that Jeff replied to, and what time Pat sent the message:

```
In-Reply-To: <mOqZgtJ-OOO5awC@lloyd.com> from "Pat
McGregor" at Aug 14, 94 07:50:29 am
```

What organization or company Jeff works for and where it's located:

```
Organization: Oakland University, Rochester, MI U.S.A.
```

What kind of mailing software he's using:

```
X-Mailer: ELM [version 2.4 PL21]
```

What version of MIME his mailer is using, (MIME lets some of us include word-processing files, audio and other interesting material in e-mail):

```
Mime-Version: 1.0
```

And, in context of the MIME version, what kind of encoding the message is in (in this case it's plain text):

```
Content-Type: text/plain; charset=US-ASCII Content-
Transfer-Encoding: 7bit
```

Finally, how many characters are in the message:

```
Content-Length: 588
```

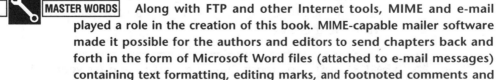

MASTER WORDS Along with FTP and other Internet tools, MIME and e-mail played a role in the creation of this book. MIME-capable mailer software made it possible for the authors and editors to send chapters back and forth in the form of Microsoft Word files (attached to e-mail messages) containing text formatting, editing marks, and footnoted comments and questions—information that can't be included in a simple ASCII file.

Scoping the Body

Next comes the body of the message. First, a line of hyphens (-) tells the computer that all the headers are done. Then, Jeff's message.

```
------------------------------------
Pat McGregor (pat@lloyd.com) writes:
>I haven't had a chance to get it out of the FTP archive but
>I'll do that today and let you know.

I may be hard to reach starting on Tuesday and ending on
next Sunday, as I'm going on a small vacation before the
crunch hits. If you need to reach me, I'll hopefully be
able to check e-mail every other day, or leave a message
on my cellular phone.

Thanks,

Jeff
```

 MASTER WORDS   Two important rules for composing text in your messages: (1) Keep your line length down below 75 characters. Some mailers truncate longer lines. (2) DON'T SHOUT AT YOUR FRIENDS in e-mail! (That is, don't use ALL CAPS.)

Here we see one of the ways that people in the Internet keep track of what they are talking about.

In this message, Jeff repeats part of Pat's message so that she can remember the *context* of these messages. The greater-than signs (>) show the text that came from Pat's message. This method of including context can be accomplished on almost any mailing system. The documentation (or a consultant or systems administrator) can help you figure out the automated way to do it. If all else fails, you can do it by hand using your editor.

 MASTER WORDS   Too much quoted material can drive your recipient nuts. Try not to quote an entire message in your message and just say, "Thanks!" or "I agree." at the end.

Signing Off

Many systems let you append a signature block to your message automatically. Jeff's looks like this:

```
—
Jeff Marraccini           jeff@vela.acs.oakland.edu  <- Work
Senior Computing Resource Admin  jeff@nucleus.mi.org<- Home
Oakland University               +1 810 370-4542
Rochester, MI 48309 "The Computer is your Friend." —Paranoia
```

This is an ideal Internet signature block: four lines or less, with Jeff's real name and his e-mail address(es), how to reach him should e-mail fail, and a saying that expresses something of his personal philosophy. This block of text, also called a *sig*, can be used in both e-mail and Usenet.

We use signature blocks because of the hazards of computerized e-mail. Even though your mailer may start off with your correct address in the headers, that address may get corrupted or changed as it passes through several other mail machines on the way to the final destination. As a precaution, always include your real name and e-mail address at the bottom of your mail. This way, your correspondents know the right way to reach you.

Signatures are as individual as the people who send the messages. Some include "ASCII Art," pictures of airplanes or the state the person is from or some other symbolic representation of the person. Some include a funny saying or meaningful quote. It's best not to let your sig get out of hand: 4–6 lines is probably enough.

 MASTER WORDS *"So, how do I get a signature block included in my message?"* Unfortunately, we can't tell you here in this book, since we can't know which of hundreds of mail programs you may be using. The exact technique for creating a signature block depends on the mailer software you're using, so check your documentation. If you can't find the information you need, either on-line or in paper form, you can at least demonstrate to your system administrator that you've attempted to do so.

Bounce-O-Grams: Troubleshooting E-Mail

Sometimes a message bounces (or is returned) right back to you. Sad, but true. Most commonly the cause is either a wrong user name or a wrong host name. Most mail bounces come from typos and misspellings.

Unknown User

Let's look at a bounce message where we typed the wrong user name.

```
Date:  Mon, 15 Aug 96 07:55 PDT
To:    pat
From:  <MAILER-DAEMON@lloyd.com>
Subject: mail failed, returning to sender

Return-Path: MAILER-DAEMON
Return-Path: <MAILER-DAEMON>
Reference: <mOqa3Ri-0005awC@lloyd.com>


------------------------------------------
¦------ Failed addresses follow: ------¦
pam@cluebus.com .. transport smtp: 550 <pam@cluebus.com>...
User unknown
¦------ Message text follows: ------¦
Received: by lloyd.com (Smail3.1.28.1 #3)
id mOqa3Ri-0005awC; Mon, 15 Aug 96 07:55 PDT
Message-Id: <mOqa3Ri-0005awC@lloyd.com>
Sender: pat (Pat McGregor)
From: "Pat McGregor" <pat@lloyd.com>
To: pam@cluebus.com
Subject: Test message
Date: Mon, 15 Aug 1996 07:55:30 -0700
Sender: pat

This is a test.
```

The first part of this message looks a lot like the good message from Jeff earlier. That's because this is a well-designed message from a computer personality: the mailer dæmon (pronounced "DEE-mon").

MASTER WORDS The term "dæmon" is an example of programmer humor. Dæmons are the servants in the afterlife. For a programmer, the worst punishment imaginable would be to handle repetitive support tasks day after day after day. So they write little helper programs to do these horrible things for them. Dæmons return bounced mail, make sure that programs that are supposed to run at certain times "wake up" and run, and so on.

Mailer dæmons are getting more sophisticated these days. Many tell you what the problem is, as this one does:

```
------------------------------------------
|------ Failed addresses follow: ------|
pam@cluebus.com ...transport smtp: 550 <pam@cluebus
.com>... User unknown
|-------- Message text follows: --------|
```

This error message tells you several things. First, there is the address we typed in: pam@cluebus.com. There is no pam user ID on the cluebus machine. This is probably where the error is: we either mistyped the name or didn't use the correct user ID.

Second, we know how the message got sent to the destination machine. Our machine used a network protocol called SMTP, or Simple Mail Transfer Protocol. The SMTP server on our machine talked to the SMTP server on cluebus to ask if there was a user named pam. And cluebus replied:

```
    550 <pam@cluebus.com>... User unknown
```

Whenever you see a line in a bounced message that starts with 550, you know it's an error message, telling you what went wrong with the delivery.

So, our mailer returned the message to us. You'll notice that this message is from the daemon on our own system. That's because it queried cluebus before it sent the message over. When it heard back from cluebus that the user name pam was wrong, it didn't even send the message out, just returned it to our mailbox.

This mailer did something user-friendly—it gave us our whole message back. That doesn't always happen: sometimes the postmaster who programmed the mailer daemon didn't think the message, no matter what it was, should be retransmitted (in case there was a bigger problem and a second or third postmaster would have to see the message). This is to protect your privacy.

MASTER WORDS   With e-mail, if you can't afford to lose the message—if you need to know what you sent, or you are paranoid about losing it if it bounces or your system goes down—write the message in a file first. Save the file carefully, either with your word processor or in a plain text file on your computer system. Then load the message into your mailer and send it. You still have a copy in case of calamity. In the last section of this chapter you'll see how to use your word processor to create and save e-mail messages.

Unknown Host

The second most common problem is sending a message to a host that doesn't exist. Unfortunately, most mailer dæmons can't tell what you mean when you type something incorrectly, so they just return the message:

```
Date:  Mon, 15 Aug 1996 11:00:40 -0400
To:    <bruce@wayne.com>
From:  MAILER-DAEMON@uunet.uu.net (Mail Delivery Subsystem)
Subject: Returned mail: Host unknown (Name server: gothom
.gov: host not found ***)

Return-Path: uunet.uu.net!MAILER-DAEMON
Return-Path: <MAILER-DAEMON@uunet.uu.net>


------------------------------------------------------
The original message was received at Mon, 15 Aug 1996
11:00:38 -0400
from boss.wayne.com [225.225.225.0]

   --- The following addresses had delivery problems ---
<gordon@gothom.gov> (unrecoverable error)

   --- Transcript of session follows ---
501 <gordon@gothom.gov>... 550 Host unknown (Name server:
gothom.gov: host not found)

   --- Original message follows ---
Return-Path: <bruce@wayne.com>
Received: from wayne.com by relay2.UU.NET with SMTP
id QQxdbo05621; Mon, 15 Aug 1996 11:00:38 -0400
Received: by wayne.com (Smail3.1.28.1 #3)
```

```
id mOqa3Wf-0005awC; Mon, 15 Aug 96 08:00 PDT
Message-Id: <mOqa3Wf-0005awC@wayne.com>
Sender: bruce@wayne.com (Bruce Wayne)
From: "Bruce Wayne" <bruce@wayne.com>
To: gordon@gothom.gov, kent@dailyplanet.com
Subject: Test message
Date: Mon, 15 Aug 1996 08:00:36 -0700
Sender: bruce@wayne.com

Hi, Commissioner

Here's another test.

                    bruce
```

In this rejection, the mailer dæmon couldn't find the host `gothom.gov`, so it passed it along to a system whose DNS server knows more addresses: `uunet.uu.net`. The uunet machine had never heard of "gothom," either, so it returned the message directly to the sender, with this error message:

```
--- The following addresses had delivery problems ---
<gordon@gothom.gov> (unrecoverable error)


   --- Transcript of session follows ---
501 <gordon@gothom.gov>... 550 Host unknown (Name server:
gothom.gov: host not found)
```

The "unrecoverable error" simply means that the mailer couldn't pass the message along to a machine that could fix the problem or further deliver the message, and so it bounced.

However, we also know that the message probably *did* get through to `kent@dailyplanet.com`, since that address was not listed in the list of problematic hosts.

Now, since the mailer daemon doesn't know what Bruce was trying to do, it can't tell him that he sent to "*gothom*" instead of "*gotham.*" Bruce will have to puzzle that out for himself. Sometimes these typing errors are the easiest ones to miss.

"It's Not My Fault!"

The third most common cause of a bounce is a problem at the other end. For example, some systems have limits on the amount of disk space a user can have. If your friend has not cleaned out his mailbox recently, and has exceeded his allotment of space, your message to him may bounce.

Or, the system may be down. Most systems administrators make arrangements with another host to "spool" or hold their mail for three to seven days in case the first machine goes down. After that, the mail is returned.

 MASTER WORDS   Some systems have very eccentric hours. One United States governmental machine is turned off every evening at 7 P.M. and is not turned back on until 6 the next morning, and it's shut down over weekends. Mailing list administrators with many subscribers on that machine have learned not to send messages that will arrive during this machine's down time, so that they will not be flooded with bounced messages. If you repeatedly send messages to a friend on Friday and they bounce, but messages sent on Mondays go through, suspect a weekend shutdown.

Another common problem at the other end is a DNS (Domain Name System addressing) problem. Perhaps the destination machine has changed its IP address and the DNS servers haven't been updated. Perhaps the destination machine is OK but the DNS server for it is down. There isn't much you can do about these except try again.

Fixing the Problem

As you're probably guessing, there isn't much you can do about bounced mail, although the more you learn about why it happens, and how to read bounced mail messages, the better you get at correcting what you can correct.

Here are some hints to help you with e-mail.

Before you send the message off, look carefully at the To: line or the CC: line. Make sure you've spelled things right.

Use the address book or aliases feature for your mailer. This way you don't have to remember those long complicated e-mail addresses every time—you can just type joe or sally.

Don't be discouraged. Try again. Sometimes bounces come from temporary outages or glitches. (That's why it's good to save your message if it's critical.)

Send a copy to yourself of any important messages.

Mail Software

There are half a hundred different kinds of e-mail software available these days. They are generally of two kinds: e-mail services that are available on a host you access either by Telnet or a direct link; and e-mail software that runs on your personal workstation.

There are blends of these two kinds of services: some people use e-mail software that lets them store and handle their e-mail in their workstations (or their laptops), but they need to connect to a host where their e-mail is delivered. The host waits for them to call for it to be downloaded to their personal computer.

We're going to talk about just two kinds of e-mail software: Pine, which is a user-friendly mail interface found on lots of BBSes and hosts, and Eudora, a personal workstation software. There are many other kinds of interfaces and software. But these two illustrate the two main differences in mail handling.

With Pine, you explicitly run the Pine interface and deal with your mail. If you have multiple windows, you can leave a Pine window running, but otherwise you go into Pine, handle your mail, and go back out to your other tasks.

Eudora runs like any other application on your machine. You launch it and work within it. You can leave it running in the background to deliver your mail and look for new mail, or shut it down to save on phone expenses.

Basic E-Mail Functions

There are only a few basic functions in e-mail, and almost all mailers handle them. They are:

Read

Compose (new messages)

Reply (to messages you've received)

Forward (messages you've received)

Refile (save the message away)

Delete

Other handy functions allow you to work more efficiently:

Include or attach (other files in your work)

Address book or aliases (remember human names for common addresses)

Sort your mail by any given category: sender, date, subject, and so on.

We'll talk about the most basic of these commands with our two chosen mailers.

 MASTER WORDS   Using any kind of mail on a UNIX system requires that you know how to use some sort of system editor. As part of getting up to speed on any new system, find out where you can get a personal tutorial on the editor, or take an introductory or other class on using the editor. You'll be glad you did.

Using Pine to Handle Your Mail

Pine is a very nice mailer. It's easy to learn, it has familiar controls (menus, graphic presentations), and it simplifies many of the tasks of handling e-mail. It runs on many UNIX machines, as well as many BBSes and other hosts. Pine has a graphic user interface, which lets you see your menus and all your choices of options at once.

Pine lets you use the functions we listed above, but you don't have to remember what the commands are, as Pine is menu-driven. Figure 8.3 illustrates the Pine main screen.

Receiving Your Mail with Pine

When you call Pine (by typing pine at the command prompt in your main session), your mail is automatically incorporated into your in-box, as illustrated in Figure 8.4. Then, you can call up a menu of available mail to choose which ones you want to read. When you highlight and choose a message, it appears in a new window.

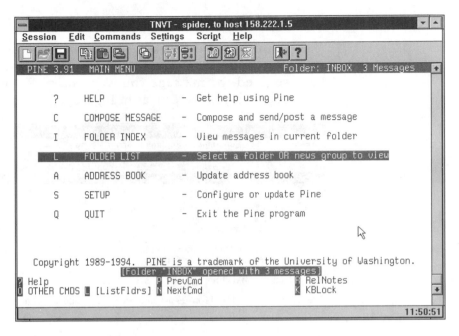

Figure 8.3. **The Pine main screen.**

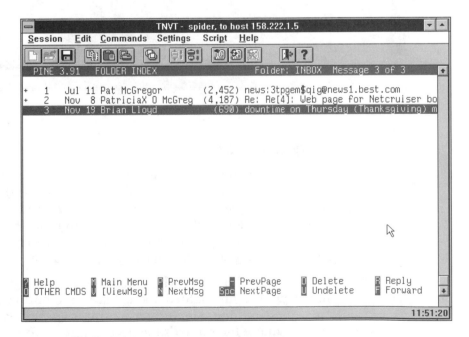

Figure 8.4. **The Pine inbox.**

Reading Messages in the Inbox

You can highlight the messages you want to read by using the arrow keys. New, unread messages will have a "N" next to them. When you have selected the message you want, press Return and the message will appear on your screen, as in Figure 8.5.

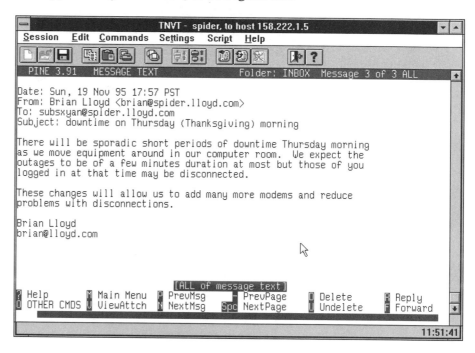

Figure 8.5. ***Reading a new message.***

Replying to a Message

If you want to reply to this message, you can press R (or use the arrow keys to highlight the command you want to use). Pine will ask you some useful questions, such as *Reply to all recipients?* Read the list of recipients carefully. You may not want to send this reply to a mailing list of folk who do not know you. Or, you may want to make sure everyone who got the first message gets your response. Be careful.

You may also be asked whether to *Include message text?* This question shows up in a highlighted status bar at the bottom, just as the recipients question does. Including the message text is very useful if you want to quote the sender's message and reply to bits of it with context.

If you're just saying "thanks" or some other brief reply, you can probably say "no" to this question.

Once you've answered these two questions, Pine gives you a pre-filled in reply template to write your answer in, as you can see in Figure 8.6. The recipient's address and the sender's signature are already filled in, and the cursor is waiting at the correct position to start typing. Type in your response.

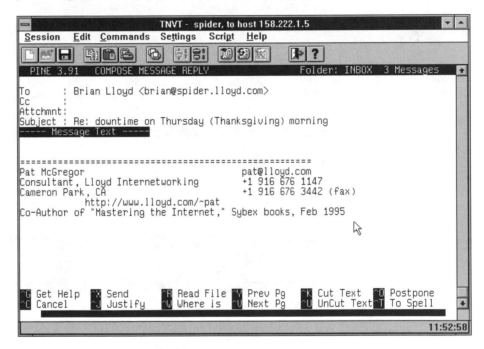

```
┌──────────────────────────────────────────────────────────────────────┐
│ —          TNVT - spider, to host 158.222.1.5                    ▼  ▲  │
│ Session  Edit  Commands  Settings  Script  Help                        │
│ ┌──┐ ┌──┐┌──┐  ┌──┐┌──┐┌──┐  ┌──┐ ┌──┐┌──┐   ┌──┐┌──┐┌──┐    ┌──┐ ┌──┐  │
│ └──┘ └──┘└──┘  └──┘└──┘└──┘  └──┘ └──┘└──┘   └──┘└──┘└──┘    └──┘ └──┘  │
│  PINE 3.91   COMPOSE MESSAGE REPLY              Folder: INBOX  3 Messages│
│ To      : Brian Lloyd <brian@spider.lloyd.com>                         │
│ Cc      :                                                              │
│ Attchmnt:                                                              │
│ Subject : Re: downtime on Thursday (Thanksgiving) morning              │
│ ----- Message Text -----                                               │
│                                                                        │
│                                                                        │
│ =====================================================                  │
│ Pat McGregor              pat@lloyd.com                                │
│ Consultant, Lloyd Internetworking    +1 916 676 1147                   │
│ Cameron Park, CA                     +1 916 676 3442 (fax)             │
│          http://www.lloyd.com/~pat                                     │
│ Co-Author of "Mastering the Internet," Sybex books, Feb 1995           │
│                                                         ▷               │
│                                                                        │
│ ^G Get Help   ^X Send      ^R Read File ^Y Prev Pg  ^K Cut Text  ^O Postpone│
│ ^C Cancel     ^J Justify   ^W Where is  ^V Next Pg  ^U UnCut Text^T To Spell│
│                                                               11:52:58 │
└──────────────────────────────────────────────────────────────────────┘
```

Figure 8.6. **Pine creates a reply form for you.**

If you want, you can use the spell-checker to look over your note. If not, simply press Ctrl+X to send the message. Pine will confirm that you really want to send the message, as shown in Figure 8.7.

Composing New Messages

If you want to send a new message, choose the "C" option from the main menu. Pine will give you a clean message template to write in, as shown in Figure 8.8. You can move from field to field using the arrow keys.

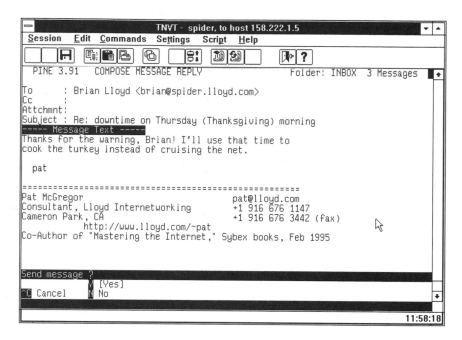

Figure 8.7.   Pine confirms that you are ready to send the message.

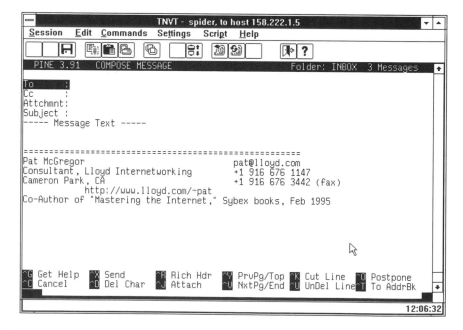

Figure 8.8.   The Pine blank message form.

You can add secondary recipients in the "CC" line, or specify a file to attach to the message. Type in the body of your message just the way you did in a reply. When you are ready to send the message, you choose either the spell checker or Ctrl-X to send, just as in the reply example.

Using the Pine Address Book

Pine gives you an address book function, where you can store people's e-mail addresses linked to a name you can remember easily. That way, you don't have to remember their whole e-mail address to send mail to them. You can also save alternate addresses for folks who get mail at both home and work.

The address book listing looks like Figure 8.9.

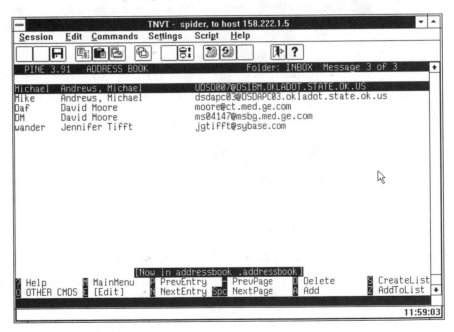

Figure 8.9. Pine's address book lets you store addresses and remember them easily.

Adding Names to the Address Book

You can insert new addresses in your address book easily. Press **A** and Pine will prompt you for the recipient's full name, nickname, and e-mail address. The new address will show up in your address book.

You can use the address book from the Reply or Compose windows if you don't remember someone's address. Simply type the nickname in the To: line, or press the menu for Address Book to choose recipients by highlighting their names.

Using Eudora Mail from Your Workstation

No matter whether you read mail from home or from work, you may use your PC as a full Internet node, and send and receive your e-mail from your desktop. In contrast, if you use a program like Pine you will have to link to another machine to receive, compose, and send your messages. On Eudora you can do all that from your desktop.

 MASTER WORDS   In most cases, you will be receiving your Eudora mail from a POP (Post Office Protocol) server on your Internet provider's network. If that machine is unreachable, you can compose mail on your desktop or write replies to mail you already have, but you will not be able to send that mail or get new letters until the server comes back up. The good news is that keeping their servers up is a high priority for most providers, however.

Configuring Eudora

Unlike Pine, you will need to tell Eudora to go and get messages for you from your local server (unless you've configured your own machine to be your mail server). To get Eudora running properly, you need to set it up to have the correct addresses and server information.

To configure Eudora, you need to know:

▶ Your POP server address (usually in the form name@server.domain, like harry@pop.network.net)

▶ The real name you want to put on your messages (for example, Harry Harrison)

▶ The address of your SMTP (simple mail transfer protocol) server.

Your Internet provider should be able to give you this information.

In Figure 8.10, we start the process of configuring Eudora. When you first install Eudora on your system, this is the menu that will first pop up, but you can go back and change the setup information any time you want to or need to.

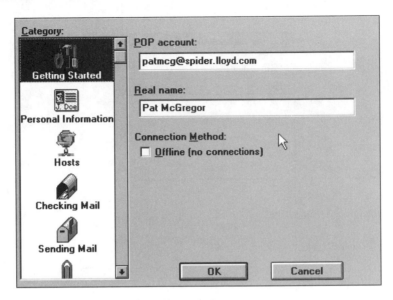

Figure 8.10. **Starting the configuration of the Eudora client on your system.**

As you progress down the settings menus, you can set up how often your system will check for mail, how the system alerts you that you have new mail, and whether mail is sent immediately off the system or waits until a specific time. You'll have to think of your own needs to figure out the best way to configure your system. Do you want to keep the link up for a long time? Or work in bursts of connections? Trial and error may be the best way to find the optimum configuration for your usage patterns.

Reading New Mail with Eudora

When you start up Eudora, it will make a connection to your POP server and bring down new mail for you. Or, you can make it check for new mail manually, as shown in Figure 8.11.

When Eudora finds new mail for you and has brought it down, it will send you a notification, as in Figure 8.12.

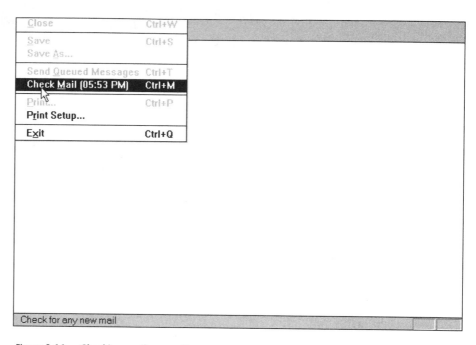

*Figure 8.11.   **Checking mail manually.***

*Figure 8.12.   **Mail Call!***

Eudora, like Pine, gives you a list of mail in your mailbox, as shown in Figure 8.13. The list of mail you haven't handled yet is called your "inbox." You can click on the message you want to read.

The message you've chosen comes up in a new window. You can delete, reply, forward, or file the message. Figure 8.14 shows a typical message window in Eudora. As you can see, we plan to reply to this message.

Replying to Mail with Eudora

When the reply comes up, you can highlight and delete the sections you don't want to send back. This works much as it does in your word processing software. Type in your reply and then send the message.

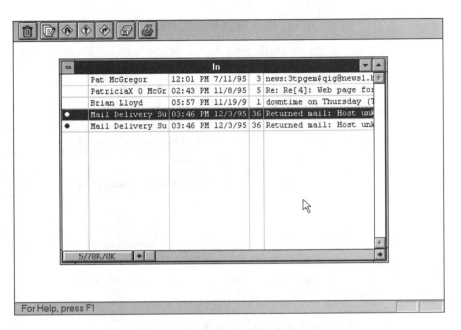

Figure 8.13. *The inbox list lets you choose which messages to read.*

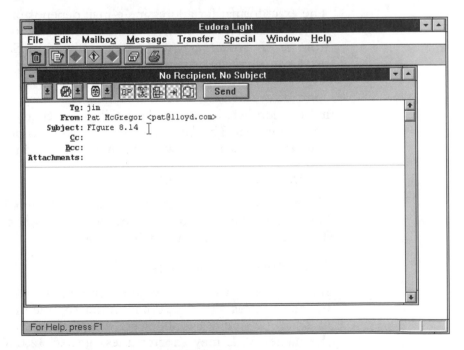

Figure 8.14. *A new message window in Eudora.*

Using the Address Book

Like Pine and most other mail-handling software, Eudora has an address book function (essentially, a small database) that lets you save e-mail addresses and find them easily by nicknames. Figure 8.15 shows how to create new entries in the address book.

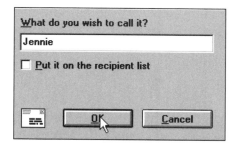

Figure 8.15. **Adding new entries in the address book.**

Addressing E-Mail Messages

The exact format for addressing e-mail depends on the network or mail service your correspondent is using. The information that follows came from *The Inter-Network Mail Guide* modified by Scott Yanoff (`yanoff@ csd4.csd.uwm.edu`), original by John J. Chew. It represents the aggregate knowledge of the readers of the newsgroup `comp.mail.misc` and many contributors elsewhere. While we have made every effort to make sure the information here is correct, these things can change with lightning speed on the Internet. The *Inter-Network Mail Guide* is posted monthly on the newsgroup *news.answers,* with the changes highlighted.

To Another Internet User

If the person to whom you wish to send e-mail is known as `p.leia` at `base.endor.org`, you put the address `p.leia@base.endor.org` in the To: line of your electronic mail message.

To an America Online User

If the person to whom you wish to send e-mail is known as `H Solo`, you put the address `hsolo@aol.com` in the To: line of your electronic mail message. Be sure to use all lowercase letters and remove all spaces from the name. AOL may shorten messages to 32,000 characters (8000 characters for PCs). AOL changes all nonalphabetic and numeric characters to spaces except for the newline character. AOL users are limited in the number of pieces of Internet mail in their mailbox at one time, and so if your correspondent on AOL does not keep up with reading and deleting mail, new incoming Internet mail may bounce. In an emergency, you can request assistance by sending electronic mail to postmaster@aol.com.

To an AT&T Mail User

If the person to whom you wish to send e-mail is known as solo, you put the address solo@attmail.com in the To: line of your electronic mail message.

To an MCI Mail User

If the person to whom you wish to send e-mail is known as Han Solo (123-4567), you can send to 1234567@mcimail.com or HSolo@mcimail.com (if HSolo is unique) or Han_Solo@mcimail.com (if Han Solo is unique), or to Han_Solo/1234567@mcimail.com (if Han Solo is NOT unique). Be sure to use the underscore (shifted hyphen) character between the first and last names.

To a CompuServe Mail User

If the person to whom you wish to send e-mail has the CompuServe account number 71234,567, enter the address as 71234.567@compuserve.com in the To: field. You can enter *compuserve* as any combination of upper- and lowercase letters. To reach the postmaster, contact *postmaster@compuserve.com*.

To a GEnie User

If the person to whom you wish to send e-mail is known as solo, enter the address as solo@genie.geis.com in the To: field. To reach the GEnie postmaster in an emergency, send to postmaster@genie.geis.com.

To a Prodigy User

If the person to whom you wish to send e-mail is known as 1234AB5, enter the address as 1234AB5@prodigy.com in the To: line. In an emergency, you can reach the Prodigy system postmaster by sending e-mail to postmaster@prodigy.com.

To a Sprint-Mail User

If the person to whom you wish to send e-mail is known as Han Solo at Millennium, enter the address as `/G=Han/S=Solo/O=millennium/ADMD=TELE-MAIL/C=US/@Sprint.COM` in the To: field. You can obtain help by telephoning 1-800-827-4685.

For Information on Sending Mail to Other Networks

If the network you need to reach isn't listed here, try looking it up in the complete *Inter-Network Mail Guide* on-line. The guide is available via anonymous FTP at `csd4.csd.uwm.edu` in the pub directory. The file is named `internetwork-mail-guide`. Or, as we said earlier, you can look for it in the newsgroup *news.answers*.

Using Your Word Processor for E-Mail

There are two main reasons why you may want to use your word processor to write the messages you send via e-mail. The first is familiarity. If you are like most people, one of the first applications you installed on your machine was a word processor. You have probably become very familiar with its strengths and weaknesses. The second reason is that it's cheaper to write your messages off-line. Most dial-in services charge for *all* of the time you spend connected. Drafting and revising messages can consume a lot of time, so you will probably prefer to spend that time while *not* connected. Moreover, your mailer's built-in word processing options are likely to be fairly limited; without those shortcut keystrokes, your message may take even longer to write.

Avoiding Common Problems

There are a few features of your word processor that you should avoid using in text destined for e-mail, because they probably won't be translated successfully. You have probably discovered many ways to enhance text with your word processor. You might underline important ideas or italicize titles. Perhaps you even use boldface occasionally. Unfortunately, you can't know what kind of machine your correspondent will be using to read your e-mail missive, so most of these features will not be available in your e-mail. Your correspondent may not have the correct software to display the beautiful effects you have included. Some of the effects may even backfire. For instance, "smart" quotation marks get mistranslated and show up as capital letters, R, S, and U, when the file is saved as plain text.

Another feature that often causes trouble is the Tab key. While tabs are very useful for aligning text, the tab character is sometimes interpreted as an instruction to ring the terminal's bell. If you have ever received a message that made your machine beep madly, tab characters were probably the cause.

Fortunately, there are alternatives to using these features. You can use spaces to align your tables. Leading and trailing underscore characters ("_") will indicate _underlined_ words. You might use asterisks to mark *boldface* or *italicized* phrases.

Also, you may want to set the left and right margins to allow no more than 70 characters on a line, including spaces. This way, you can be sure your message will appear on your correspondent's screen with the same line breaks as on your screen.

Saving the Text

Once you've written your message, the next step is to save it in a format that can be sent as e-mail, to avoid mistranslation problems. Your word processor's proprietary format includes information about the typeface, the size of the letters, and so forth. None of this information will be needed for your e-mail, and your mailer program will probably not be able to understand your word processor's codes. So you will have to save your text without them.

Your word processor should offer a "Save As" or "Save File As Type" option for specifying different file formats. Once you've located this option and its list of available formats, select "text with line breaks." Many word processors treat a paragraph as simply one long line of characters. Since most modern computers can display only 80 characters on a line (and some older ones can display even fewer), these long "lines" may be truncated (cut off at the 81st character) or "wrapped" at odd places. Your correspondents will find these lines hard to read.

By choosing "text with line breaks," you are telling your word processor to treat each line displayed on your screen as a separate paragraph. If your document is displayed nicely on your screen, it should be displayed in much the same way on your correspondent's screen.

Transferring the Text

The next step is to get your missive into an e-mail message. What you do at this point depends on your type of Internet connection and the software environment you're working in.

Macintosh and Windows users connected directly to the Internet (probably on a LAN) can use the clipboard to copy the word processor text and paste it into a message in the mailer program, or use whatever technique the mailer program provides for attaching a file. (These techniques vary from program to program; see your documentation.) DOS users with a dedicated link can also use the mailer's "attachment" commands. Once you've done that, your message is ready to send.

With a dial-up connection to a service provider, however, you need to transfer the file from your machine to the service provider's host computer.

If you have downloaded files via your service provider, you will only need to reverse that process to upload your files. If you are not familiar with downloading files, you will first have to find out which file transfer systems are available from your service. Some common options are Kermit, X-modem, Y-modem, and Z-modem. If you are using PPP or SLIP, and so have a TCP/IP connection, you will use FTP, the Internet's File Transfer Protocol, to move your files between machines. Let's take the easy one first; we'll start with FTP.

FTP

One of the pieces of your PPP (or SLIP) package should have been an FTP client. Although FTP clients have many names, a common one is "FTP" or some variant. For instance, the MS-DOS Telnet package available from the National Center for Supercomputing Applications (NCSA) at the University of Illinois—Urbana/Champaign calls its FTP client "ftpbin." Novell has named the FTP client included with their LAN WorkPlace for DOS package "Rapid Filer." The Macintosh FTP client from Dartmouth College is called "Fetch." Both Fetch and Rapid Filer automate many of the processes of transferring a file by FTP, so to give you the whole story we will use NCSA's FTPBIN to describe FTP, which doesn't offer automation.

After your PPP (or SLIP) connection is established, change directories ("cd") to the one containing the NCSA software. Then, enter the command

```
ftp host.domain
```

replacing *host.domain* with the name of the machine you log on to. FTP will start up; when the connection is established, you will see a Name: prompt. Enter your user name on that machine. You will then be prompted for your password. After your password is accepted, you should be in your usual file space on that machine. Enter the FTP command `type ascii` to set the type of file transfer to plain text. The remote machine will report that the file type has been set to either "ASCII" or "text," depending upon how the system administrator has set it up. Enter the command

```
put filename1 filename2
```

replacing *filename1* with the name of the file you saved in your word processor (using the full pathname, for example, C:\DOCS\MESSAGE .TXT) and *filename2* with the name you want it to have on the remote machine. When the file transfer is completed, type **bye** or **quit** to close the connection. Your file has now been copied to the machine you use for e-mail. You can now log on to the remote machine in the usual way (with Telnet, for instance) and use the file in an e-mail message.

Kermit, X, Y, and Z-Modem

Kermit, X-modem, Y-modem and Z-modem are all similar to each other. First you establish a connection to your e-mail service. Next you start the file transfer program on the remote machine (that is, your e-mail service's machine), specifying the kind of transfer (text, or ASCII, rather than binary) and the name of the file to receive. Then you start the file transfer program on your local machine, specifying the kind of transfer (text again), and finally you specify which file you want to transfer. When the transfer is completed, you can shut down the file transfer programs; your file has now been copied to the machine you use for e-mail. Let's look at VersaTerm, a communications program for the Macintosh, and Kermit for a specific example.

After dialing in to your service with VersaTerm and logging on in your usual fashion, enter the command to start Kermit, probably something like

```
Kermit
```

to begin the file transfer process. Next, enter `set file type text`. The remote machine should respond `Text filetype set`. Now that the type of file to be transferred has been specified, enter the command *receive filename2*, replacing *filename2* with the name you want the file to have on the remote machine. The remote machine is now ready to accept your file.

Go into VersaTerm's File menu and make sure that the option Text Kermit is available. If it isn't (and some of the other choices are Mac XModem, Text XModem, Binary XModem and MacBinary XModem), select whatever is showing and then, from the resulting dialog box, choose Text Kermit and click OK.

Now go back into the File menu and select Send File. VersaTerm's next dialog box will let you browse the disk to find the file you want to transfer. After selecting the file, and clicking the Add button to put it in the Send Files window, click the Send button to begin the transfer. When the transfer is complete, all of the dialog boxes close, and you will again be at your service's prompt. You can now enter quit to close the Kermit program. Your file has been copied to the remote host.

Keeping Yourself Sane (or, Mail Handling in the Information Age)

If you've ever been to one of those productivity seminars, you'll remember that they told you to keep a wastebasket right next to where you stand and look at your mail when you get home or come into the office. "Don't handle the same piece of mail twice." This rule holds for handing e-mail, too. In fact, many of the techniques that help keep you from going crazy dealing with the paper that comes across your desk will help you manage your e-mail.

These guidelines won't work for some of us who are so addicted to e-mail that we read everything, and go answer the mail call every time it goes off. But even we addicts can benefit from some discipline in our mail handling.

Don't Turn On Mail Call—Limit Your Reading of Mail.

In the average office, we have at *most* two paper mail deliveries a day: internal office mail and external mail. There may be a courier delivery at odd times, as well. But the point here is that we handle our paper-mail by doing it in batches.

If you get lots of e-mail during the day, and you find it's breaking up your day and affecting your productivity, you may need to be more disciplined with it—control it instead of letting it control you. Turn off the automatic notification feature that pops up and whistles at you seductively every time a new message comes in. Only read mail at certain times of day. Some folks like to read mail when they first come in, after lunch, and again about an hour before they go home.

Skim the Subject Lines and Trash Judiciously

Look at the subject lines. *If there are things that are obviously of no interest to you, toss them unread.* This rule assumes that you don't have a psychological need to read everything just to be sure you haven't missed something. ;-) Many people do not open all the junk mail that comes to their houses; similarly, you do not have to read all the e-mail that comes to you.

For example, if you own a Macintosh and are on a mailing list about children's software, you can delete anything that comes in about PC software. Or, if you are on a street rod list but don't want to travel outside your own region, you can toss announcements about meets in other areas.

Use Subjects That Make Sense This system depends, of course, on people using intelligent subject lines. Some major corporations where e-mail is the main communication medium have adopted e-mail guidelines asking employees to use subjects that say something useful. Several of these companies call this "decision-enabling subjects," so that you can tell from the subject line whether you are interested in the message.

You can help this process along; if you get a message with a non-helpful subject but to which you want to respond, don't be afraid to change the subject. If the subject originally said

```
Orientation Session
```

but the message is really about whether new people are getting acclimatized to the company, you should feel free to change the subject to something like:

```
Helping New Hires Fit In (Was: Orientation Session)
```

This will help everyone, not just you, make better use of their time reading e-mail.

Read Messages in Reverse: Newest to Oldest

If you read your messages in this order, you can delete or file items you have already dealt with. This also keeps you on top of the most current developments.

Handle E-Mail as Few Times as Possible

Take Action Now When reading mail, there will be some items that come to you for information only; you don't have to respond. Do whatever you're going to do with them immediately, be it forwarding it to another person or group, filing them in an electronic folder, trashing it, or printing it.

Use Folders to Help You Prioritize Let's say you don't have time to read and respond to all your mail at the moment. Let's also say that this is a common fact of your life. How do you handle it?

First of all, tell yourself that it's OK not to answer every message right away. The one from your boss marked "urgent" or the one from your mother probably needs attention soon, but most messages don't have to be answered right away. (And, when you do, using prioritization will help you have enough time to do it!) One of the beauties of e-mail is that it's asynchronous: the sender and the receiver do not have to be online at the same time to communicate. You can put off answering e-mail.

Some people use electronic folders to help them. They use a sorting method that helps them figure out what to do with their messages. You can set up several folders (how many depends on you) to help you prioritize your mail. Some typical folders are:

hot (do something with this message *today!)*

soon (do something with this message in the next couple of days)

research (you need more information before you can answer this)

cooloff (this message made you so mad you don't want to answer it right away)

pass-along (someone else needs to handle this message)

As with any system, you have to use this one for it to be effective. As part of your normal work load, you have to process these messages or else the whole thing is useless.

 MASTER WORDS Beware of folders that are temporary! If you're using cc:Mail, MS Mail, or another LAN-based mailer system, check to see if you're using *folders* on a system mail post office or *archives* on your hard disk. Mail in folders on the system mail post office is usually deleted to conserve file space; sometimes this is every 15 or 30 days. Mail in your inbox will likely disappear on that schedule, as well. The only guaranteed permanent storage is on your hard drive. (Be sure and include your mail archives in your backup schedule.) Temporary folders are fine for things that will be processed soon and can be thrown away, but don't get an unpleasant surprise by using them for permanent storage.

Use filters   Some mailers will sort your mail for you automatically when you open your mailbox, based on rules you've set up. For example, if you want all the mailing list mail about that children's software to go into a separate folder so you can read it later, you might set up a filter that takes any mail which came to the mailing list name and puts it in a folder before you even see it. Or, mail from your boss might go into a folder with BOSS! as the name.

Unsubscribe

If you find yourself getting lots of mail from a mailing list and always throw it away unread, either with a filter or by hand, consider whether you need to be on that list. If it were a paper item, like a newspaper or a magazine, you would probably cancel your subscription if you hadn't read any of the magazines in a year. Do the same thing with e-mail mailing lists.

If it's a work list and you think it's politically appropriate, ask the sender if you need to be on the distribution list. If it's a public mailing list, send in an unsubscribe request. (See the section later in this chapter on mailing lists for help in unsubscribing.) If it's something you didn't subscribe to (like a friend who always sends along dumb jokes or political commentary or other things you aren't interested in), send a note to the sender and politely ask them to stop.

If you're going to be away from your mailbox for more than a day or two, you may want to unsubscribe from heavy-volume lists. Most lists are archived somewhere, anyway, so you can go back and check out what you missed.

Take Out the Trash

If, after following all the rules, you still have more than one screen of messages in your mailbox, you need to spend more time on your e-mail, or find a way to get less. For some of us, more than 50 messages in our inbox is a disaster. Just as you would if your desk got piled with things you needed to do, you need to take care of your e-mail regularly. Once you've done all the regular processing, you have to do the rest.

Pat starts from the bottom of the inbox (the oldest messages) and re-reads each message to see what has to be done. If a message has sat around for several days and she still can't figure out whether she's supposed to answer it, file it, trash it, or take it to dinner, she usually sends a note to the sender asking if she needs to respond, and if so, how.

And, just as you would do with your paper files, go through your electronic folders on a regular basis and clean out what doesn't need to be there. Some folks visit every folder once a month, or when folders get over 200 messages or 1000. Set a schedule that makes sense to you, and adjust as necessary.

Interesting E-Mail Addresses

Now that you know a little bit about e-mail, here are some fun places to send mail.

E-Mail to the White House

For those of you who would like to communicate with the current United States executive officer, the Clinton administration has encouraged you to e-mail the president or the vice president with your thoughts on the issues that affect us all. Do not expect to get anything but a form reply, but you can address your comments to

    president@whitehouse.gov

or

    vice.president@whitehouse.gov

You can receive a summary of White House press releases. To find out more, send e-mail to publications@whitehouse.gov with the body of the message containing send info.

Almanac E-Mail Information Service

The United States Department of Agriculture operates an e-mail information service called Almanac. To find out more about it, send e-mail to almanac@esusda.gov with the message send guide. The message send catalog will ask the server to send you a catalog of available information. The USDA also operates a Gopher server at esusda.gov. Figure 8.16 shows typical information available from the Almanac service.

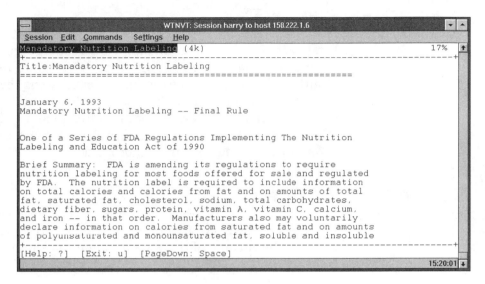

Figure 8.16. Almanac service information from the USDA.

Books for Young People

Scholastic Press, a publisher of books for young people, maintains a mailing list for reviews of new and interesting books. (e-mail mailing lists are discussed later in this chapter.) It is called the BookBrag mailing list. The address for the mailing list server is:

```
bookbrag-request@scholastic.com
```

Send an e-mail message to this address with the body of the message as follows:

```
subscribe bookbrag yourfirstname yourlastname
```

Talking Back to National Public Radio

If you have wanted to talk back to NPR, here are a few addresses of specific programs:

Program	Address
Talk of the Nation	totn@npr.org
All Things Considered	atc@npr.org
Science Friday (Ira Glass)	scifri@aol.com
Fresh Air	freshair@hslc.org
Weekend All Things Considered	watc@npr.org
Weekend Edition/Sunday	wesun@npr.org

Shakespeare Online

Interested in an online Shakespeare reading group? Join Michael Conner's Shakespeare reading group. The group reads one play per month. The first half of the month is spent reading the play individually; the second half of the month the play is discussed by e-mail. Volunteers take turns leading the discussion. Feel free to join, volunteer as a leader or just lurk and learn. Everyone is welcome. Send e-mail to YORTMTC@ henson.cc.wwu.edu if you are interested.

Finding E-Mail Addresses

In Chapter 12 we talk about finding people and things online. Here we will talk about some of the ways to find e-mail addresses using specific Internet tools.

Using Address Directories in Gopher

Many Gopher menus include selections that point to various types of electronic address directories. Choose WorldWide Directory Services. Look at the choices, and read the descriptions and the help information provided to see if one might fit your needs. Choose among the entries for the directory most likely to fit your needs.

Searching for Usenet Addresses

If you think your correspondent has ever posted to Usenet News, you might be able to find their exact address if you know a little about their name and address. Send e-mail to mail-server@rtfm.mit.edu with the message

```
send usenet-address/name
```

where *name* is one or more words separated by spaces. For example, if you were interested in finding out whether award-winning Star Trek writer Peter David has ever posted to a Usenet newsgroup, you would send this message:

```
send pdavid@/peter david
```

you would discover that David has, indeed, posted many times to newsgroups. This server works better when you give it more material to work with, so you should list all the words you think might appear in the address. Neither the order of the words nor their case is important to the server. You can send multiple requests in one e-mail message.

Each request should appear on a separate line. The server may return more than one match, but it will never return more than 40 matches.

For more information, send a message containing

```
send usenet-addresses/help
```

Part
II

LURKING

Lurking describes the activity of reading mailing list posts and newsgroup articles without participating in the group. In spite of the name, lurking is a recommended activity, at least for the first few weeks that you read in a particular area. Taking the time to see the kind of discussion that occurs in a particular networked community will give you an idea of the type of posting to which the community likes to respond. For more on appropriate posting, see the discussion of netiquette in Chapter 7. For more on newsgroups, see Chapter 13.

The Internet Toolkit

The IBM Mail Exchange Directory

Advantis and the IBM Information Network provide e-mail access to the IBM Mail Exchange directory server. The IBM Mail Exchange allows its subscribers to exchange mail with a wide range of office systems. The directory contains address book details of those subscribers to the service who have granted public access to that information. It contains entries for users (typically commercial users) in more than 60 countries.

You can search on any of the following items:

Name (last name, first name or initial)

User ID (IEA)

Organization name

Telephone number

Country

You specify one or more keywords and parameters in the body of an e-mail message to

```
whois@ibmmail.com
```

The server answers several basic styles of query:

```
WHOIS Sm*
```

will retrieve results for names beginning with the characters Sm.

```
WHOIS ! userid
```

will retrieve results for the user ID *userid*. Note that user ID searches need to begin with the ! character.

```
WHOIS Smith
Phone 813*
```

will retrieve results with the name Smith and a telephone number beginning with 813. The wildcard character (*) can be used at the beginning or the end of a telephone number, but not in both places.

```
WHOIS Smith
ORGANIZATION ABC
```

will retrieve results with the name Smith from the ABC organization.

```
WHOIS Smith
COUNTRY US
```

will retrieve results with the name Smith and the country code US. Send HELP in the body of your message for more instructions.

Mail Reflectors, Mailing Lists, and List Servers

Mailing lists are a specialized type of e-mail, a hybrid of e-mail (which is individual) and Usenet News (which is seen by many). Lists are delivered specifically via e-mail to the individual mailboxes of the individuals who subscribe to the list. You can choose to participate in many mailing-list communities on the Internet. When you find a list you like, you "join" it by sending mail to the list administrator. A mail reflector is the name of the mailbox to which you send e-mail when you want to send it to all of the people who read the list. The reflector receives the e-mail and "reflects" it to the members of the mailing list. Maintaining mailing lists is one of the many tasks of a systems administrator. When the list administrator is aided by a computer program that helps with list management, that program is called a *list server*. LISTSERV is a representative example.

About LISTSERV

LISTSERV is the name of a specific program developed by Eric Thomas. Like other list servers, it allows a user to send electronic mail to addresses like these:

```
listserv@kentvm.kent.edu
listserv@cunyvm.cuny.edu
listserv@is.internic.net
```

Sometimes the lists are *moderated*. This means that the messages sent by the subscribers to the rest of the list are read by a person before they are forwarded on to the remainder of the list. The moderator may choose not to send a message on to the list. Large lists are frequently moderated so that mailing errors do not get sent on to all the people reading the list, or so that messages that are "off the topic" of the list are not sent to the list.

Using a "-request" Petition

Another style of list subscription is the "-request" petition. This is an address constructed from the name of the mailing list, the -request modifier and the @fully.qualified.domain Internet address. This message may be read by a person or by a program; the address does not tell you which. Your e-mail message would be something like

```
To: starwars-request@academy.endor.org
```

in the address portion of your message. In the body of the message you put

```
subscribe starwars yourfirstname yourlastname
```

This would subscribe you to the mailing list.

Do not assume that because a mailing list is served from a particular host computer, the list will always remain there (or that the organization that owns the computer necessarily supports or agrees with the discussion on the mailing list). Sometimes people start lists from a particular computer and the goals of the list do not match the goals of the host organization. In that case the list will move or change its nature. Sometimes list traffic becomes too heavy for the original list server to handle adequately, so either the list is moved or the traffic becomes restricted in some way.

How to "Talk" to List Servers

If the address for subscribing to a mailing list begins with the words LISTSERV, LISTPROC, or MAJORDOMO, you should assume that you are communicating with a program that manages the list, not a person. This means you should not include extraneous information, like punctuation or signature files. These can confuse the programs. These programs usually ignore anything you put in the subject line of your e-mail message.

Always be careful to send your electronic mail requests to the list server, not to the list itself; that is, to `listserv@nodename`, *not* `list@ nodename`.

When you *unsubscribe* from the list, you must unsubscribe from the same e-mail address that you subscribed from. If you are no longer able to do that, you will need help from the list owner. You can find out about the owners of the list by sending the command `review <listname>` to the LISTSERV program.

COMMON LISTSERV COMMANDS

`SUB(scribe) <listname> <yourfirstname> <yourlastname>`

`UNSUB(scribe) <listname>`

`Signoff <listname>`

`set nomail <listname>`

When this command is accepted, the listserver will not send you mail. To receive mail again, send the **set mail <listname>** command.

`set conceal <listname>`

Similar to an unlisted telephone number, this command hides your name on the subscription list. Sending the command **set no conceal** will reset the default.

Sending the command **Info Refcard** will cause the ListServ program to send you a list of commands.

How to Search for Mailing Lists

There is a searchable list of BITNET mailing lists maintained at Nova University. Use the Web to go to `http://alpha.acast.nova.edu/cgi-bin/lists`. This link opens a search. Enter your search word into the dialog box and press Enter. This search returns literal matches. For example, entering the word **bird** will return citations for the mailing lists about bird-watching (BirdChat, and so on), and mailing lists that feature discussion of cars (T-Birds and Firebirds), and a mailing list that deals with the Blackbird fighter plane.

How to Get the BITNET "List of Mailing Lists"

The BITNET network maintains a list of all the BITNET mailing lists that are known to its network nodes. You can request that the BITNIC (BITNET Network Information Center) computer send you that list. To do so, send e-mail to `listserv@bitnic.educom.edu` with the message:

Command	Action
`get bitnet userhelp`	to receive a longer explanation of BITNET
`help`	to receive a short list of commands
`info refcard`	to receive a command reference card
`info ?`	to receive a list of ListServ information guides
`list global`	to receive the complete list of BITNET mailing lists

In addition, many BITNET lists are cross-posted to Usenet (discussed in Chapter 13). You can look in the list of newsgroups available from your provider for groups with the name pattern *bit.** or *bitnet.**.

Publicly Accessible Mailing Lists

The FAQ "Publicly Accessible Mailing Lists" is posted in multiple parts to the newsgroup `news.announce.newusers`. This FAQ has a list of all the Internet mailing lists (it is a companion list to the BITNET list of lists, above). See Chapter 13 if you need help reading these newsgroups. There is also a World Wide Web page that reflects these lists. You can use the Web to jump there by entering `http://www.ii.uib.no/cgi-bin/paml` in the center dialog box from the display of any Web page. For more information about using the Web, see Chapter 10.

New Patent Titles Mailing List

Greg Aharonian offers a free service to anyone who can receive e-mail from the Internet. The service is a weekly mailing of all patents issued by the Patent Office during the last week (or more specifically, all of the patents listed in the most recent issue of the USPTO Patent Gazette).

Please include some information on what you do and how you might use this patent information. Send your requests to: `patents-request@world.std.com`.

Other Special Interest Mailing Lists

You can subscribe to these lists using the "-request" technique described above.

For people who enjoy leisure reading: `SFLOVERS@uga.edu` and `DOROTHYL@kentvm.kent.edu` are discussions of science fiction and mystery fiction respectively.

For people who enjoy discussing computer gaming:

    `GAMES-L@brownvm.brown.edu`

For people who enjoy discussing the game of golf:

    `GOLF-L@ubvm.buffalo.edu`

For people who are interested in genealogy:

    `ROOTS-L@ndsuvm1.nodak.edu`

CHAPTER

9

FTP and Telnet

FEATURING

Chapter 9
FTP and Telnet

FTP and Telnet are two of the most common tools you'll use on the Internet. FTP (File Transfer Protocol) lets you move files around; these may be either files that are specifically intended for you or files that are placed for general consumption. Telnet connects you to other computers.

About FTP: the File Transfer Program

FTP is the abbreviation used for the *file transfer protocol* and the file transfer programs that use the protocol. File transfer simply means sending a copy of a file (not a message) from one computer to another. Examples of files include spreadsheets, digitized photographs, sounds, compiled programs, or document files from a word processing program.

If you want to send a copy of a file from your computer to another computer, you use the FTP program in *upload* or *put* mode. More frequently people use the *download* or *get* mode; for example, to retrieve public-domain computer programs.

There are two methods for using FTP. In one method, you sign on to the *remote host* with your own account or ID and transfer files. In the other, you sign on as a guest or as an anonymous user and transfer files. This method is called "anonymous FTP." With anonymous FTP, your privileges on the host system will be severely limited for security reasons. That's because hosts that provide anonymous FTP do so specifically to make certain files available to anyone who wants them. To use it, you connect using the login ID anonymous, guest, or ftp and use your e-mail address as a password. The use of your e-mail address helps the FTP provider track who is interested in which materials, and it provides a trace in case of a security problem.

You can find a FAQ on Anonymous FTP via anonymous FTP itself at

    rtfm.mit.edu

and it is regularly posted to

    news.newusers.questions

and several *.answers newsgroups. (See Chapter 14 for more information about FAQs.)

Anonymous FTP is a convenient tool for making information and other files available to the public. Hundreds of sites currently use it to provide resources; you can find the most current listing of selected sites via the Web. The easiest way to do that is to go to the Yahoo site:

    http://www.yahoo.com

Click on Internet, and then click on FTP. From Yahoo's FTP menu you can find several entry points that will present a list of FTP sites in different formats.

How to Use FTP

Except for the initial act of signing on, regular FTP and anonymous FTP are almost identical in the way you use them. With regular FTP, you sign on to the host site with your account or user name and password. With anonymous FTP, you type the word **anonymous** as your user name and your e-mail address for the password. Some graphical interface programs will automatically connect to FTP sites using anonymous FTP. When you connect to an FTP site using a Web browsing program (read more about that in Chapter 10), you will be connected using anonymous FTP.

There are two basic kinds of FTP clients: GUI (Graphical User Interface) and line-mode clients. With a GUI client you use your mouse or arrow keys to manipulate the transaction. In line mode you type the commands at a system or FTP prompt.

Connecting to the Host

You use FTP with an FTP client—a program that manages the transmissions for you. If you are using a graphical client program, it will have pull-down menus or point-and-click buttons. You start this client by pulling down a menu or clicking on an icon. Look for the Open or Connect dialog box. Type the name of the host in that box; then press Enter or click OK to send the connect command across the network.

If you are using a UNIX shell system, you'll be using a line-mode client. You start it from the regular system prompt on your host account. To access an FTP site, you type:

ftp *hostname.domain*

Many FTP sites have the prefix *ftp* in front of their regular host name, so that you can access the FTP server directly. For example, to access Merit, Inc.'s anonymous FTP server and get the statistics and educational material stored there, you would type:

ftp nic.merit.edu

Once you are connected, you will see a screenful of introductory information, as in Figure 9.1. You may then be asked for your user name and password. Type (your responses are in **bold** type):

Login: **anonymous**

password **<supply your e-mail address here>**

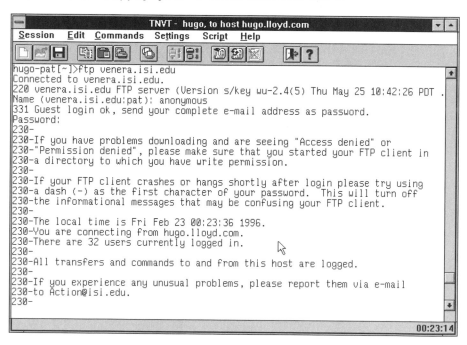

Figure 9.1. *Starting a line-mode anonymous FTP session to venera.isi.edu.*

Most line-mode FTP clients will give you a list of available commands if you type **help** or **?** at the FTP> prompt. Graphical interface clients usually have a Help system.

MASTER WORDS   Many line-mode FTP programs have a utility built in that will let you track the progress of your file transfer in line mode. It's called *hash*, because it prints out # signs (*hash marks*) to show you how much of your file has transferred. It's a good idea to enter the hash command as the first thing you do when you start a line-mode FTP session. Simply type **hash** at the FTP> prompt. Some systems will respond with the number of transferred bites each hash mark represents; some simply return you to the FTP> prompt. Graphical clients frequently report the number of bytes transferred and the total number of bytes in a status display. Sometimes this is done simply by percentage, too.

Finding What You Need

Once you have connected to a host you will want to get a listing of the materials available, like that shown in Figure 9.2. This will give you an idea of what's available on the system. If you see a file called "index" or "Read.Me" (or some variant), it is usually a general information document.

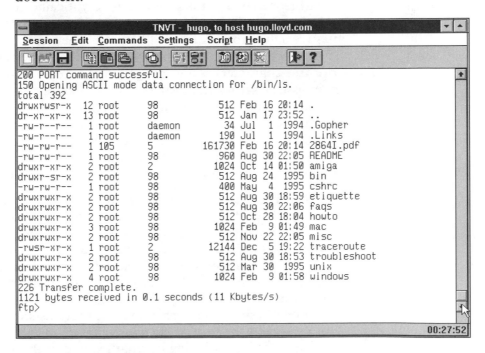

Figure 9.2.   A typical directory listing.

If you are using a graphical interface, look for instructions about finding and manipulating directory listings.

In line mode you can get a listing by typing the UNIX directory command:

```
ls
```

Most line-mode FTP clients will give you a list of available commands if you type **help** or **?** at the FTP> prompt. Graphical interface clients usually have a Help system.

What a UNIX File/Directory Listing Tells You

Here is a sample directory listing from a file archive hosted on a remote computer using the UNIX operating system. Many of the archive sites are hosted on UNIX machines, so this may help you understand what the directory listing says:

```
drwxr-xr-x  2 glee    512   Jan 8 22:95   foom
-r-r-xr-  1 brian  165418   May 3 95    game.zip
```

The first series of letters describes (cryptically) the file type and permissions set for the directory or file. If the first character is a **d**, the item is a directory. A file will have a hyphen in this position. The next characters describe the security permissions. They are in three groups of three characters. The first group of three characters describes the permissions set for the owner. The **r** indicates permission to read. The **w** indicates permission to write. The **x** indicates permission to execute from. The second group of three characters describes the permission set for a group of login IDs of which the owner is a part. The third group of three characters describes the permission set for the world—that is, everyone who has access to this host computer.

Let's apply this to our sample directory. The first entry, foom, is a directory (that's what the d means). The second, third, and fourth letters are rwx. This means the directory can be written (that is, changed) by the owner, who can read every file in the directory and can also execute (run) programs stored in it. Next we have r-x. This means that the owner's group can read files and execute the programs, but not write or change anything. Finally, we have -x. This means that the rest of the users on the system can execute any programs stored in the directory, but can't read the files or change anything. In fact, general users can't even get a directory listing of what's stored in this directory: they have to know a program is there to use it. (This isn't as strange as it sounds: UNIX lets you link files together and so users might think they were executing a file stored elsewhere when it really lives in this directory.)

The second entry, game.zip, has more limited permission. It is a file, not a directory (there is a hyphen in the first position). The owner can read it, but cannot change or execute it. The group can read and execute it. The rest of the world can read it but not change or execute it.

For anonymous FTP to work, the **r** must be present in the eighth character position. That is, the world must have permission to read the file. If you are the file owner, or your login ID is part of the defined group with the file owner's login ID, you may transfer the file if the **r** is present in the second or fifth character.

To be able to write a file to a directory, there must be a **w** in the appropriate character position.

The name of the file owner is the next piece of information. If the file owner is named something like root or wheel, you are looking at the description of a file managed by the system administrator for that system. The size of the file in bytes is listed. The date that the file was last stored appears next. If the file was modified in this calendar year, the time that the file was stored may be listed. Otherwise, the year that the file was modified is displayed.

Finally, the name of the file finishes up the description line.

Most FTP archive owners want you to be happy using their resource, and so they use the conventions listed earlier in naming their files. However, a few rogues do exist, and so it's important to check the INDEX or README files when you access a new archive.

WARNING   Some clients will display the names of *all* files in the directory. Others will not show the *hidden* files. Usually *hidden* files will be preceded by a period (dot); e.g., ".mailbox". If your FTP client allows you to manage your files (that is, erase or rename them), be very careful not to delete these hidden files unless you are quite certain their removal will not remove a function that you want. Erasing the file ".mailbox" will definitely remove your incoming e-mail.

Moving Around with FTP

After you see the top-level directory of materials available (and you read the index or the README), you may need to move into a lower-level directory to retrieve your file. Each lower level directory will contain an index or README file to describe its contents. The line-mode command to change directories is:

```
cd directory-name
```

With a line-mode client you can find out where you are by using the UNIX "print working directory" command. Type **pwd** to find out what directory you are in.

With a graphical client, the directories are probably displayed in a layout similar to your folders or your File Manager or Windows Explorer. You can scroll, point, and click your way through the directory listings. The next higher level directory (frequently called the parent directory) can be represented by two periods (dots) followed by a slash:

```
../
```

Getting Files to You

Many files stored for FTP are in ASCII, or plain text, format. But some are programs, visual images, or sounds. It's important that you know what kind of file you are getting, because you have to tell the FTP client what *mode* to transfer the file in. There are two modes for transferring files in FTP. ASCII mode is used for plain text and PostScript files. Binary mode (also, confusingly, called I mode on some servers) is for everything else. Here's a list of the common types of files and the modes in which you should retrieve them.

.Z files are UNIX files that are compressed and require you to execute the UNIX uncompress utility before you can use them. Retrieve these files in binary mode.

.gz files are UNIX files that are compressed by the UNIX GNU gzip utility program and will need to be processed before you can use them. Retrieve these files in binary mode.

.tar files are UNIX files that are in the UNIX tape archive format and need to be processed with the UNIX tar utility before you can use them. They should be retrieved in binary mode.

.tar.Z files are compressed UNIX tar files that require application of the uncompress utility followed by the tar utility. Retrieve these files in binary mode.

.hqx files are compressed Macintosh files. These files should be retrieved in binary mode and then processed by a Macintosh decompression program.

.sit files are Macintosh files processed by the Stuffit program. Retrieve them in binary mode.

.zip files are DOS files compressed by a zip utility. These files need to be decompressed (unzipped) before you can use them. Retrieve these files in binary mode.

.com files are executable files for DOS computers. They should be retrieved in binary mode.

.exe files are executable files for DOS or VAX/VMS computers. They should be retrieved in binary mode.

.ps files are PostScript files that must be viewed with a PostScript viewer or printed on a PostScript printer. These files should be retrieved in text/ASCII mode.

.c files are C programming language source code. These files should be retrieved in text/ASCII mode.

.h files are C programming language header files. These files should be retrieved in text/ASCII mode.

.gif files are files in Graphics Interchange Format. These files should be retrieved in binary mode.

.mpeg files are video files. They need to be played with a video player. These files should be retrieved in binary mode.

.jpg files are graphics files in a compressed format. These files should be retrieved in binary mode.

.txt files or files that have no special suffix are plain text files that can be displayed or printed without requiring processing by any utility. These files should be retrieved in text/ASCII mode.

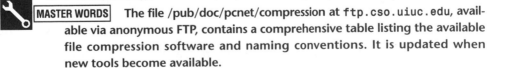

MASTER WORDS   The file /pub/doc/pcnet/compression at `ftp.cso.uiuc.edu`, available via anonymous FTP, contains a comprehensive table listing the available file compression software and naming conventions. It is updated when new tools become available.

Using a graphical client, you'll most likely select BINARY or ASCII by clicking the appropriate button. To turn ASCII mode on in a line-mode FTP session, type **ASCII**. To turn BINARY on, type **BIN.** Most FTP sessions start up by default in ASCII mode.

Most commonly, you will be bringing files down to your local workstation or the host on which you have an account. You will use the get or mget commands.

get   To bring a single file down to your local host or workstation, type the command:

    get *filename*

This will initiate the file transfer from the server to your local system. Don't forget to include the extension (if any) after the filename.

MASTER WORDS   If you want to look at a short file, such as a README or an index file, there are a couple of "short cuts" you can take. With a graphical client, look for a "view" command. With line mode on a UNIX host, you can use UNIX syntax and your pager to look at it right from your FTP session. Type get filename | more to "pipe" (that's the UNIX name for the vertical rule [|]) the file into the UNIX page reader, *more.*

mget   Sometimes you want to transfer a number of files at the same time. For example, if you are transferring JPEG images, they frequently are broken up into linked but separate files, because of their size. Or you may want to get several PostScript files at once.

mget is a UNIX program used in line mode to do *m*ultiple *get*s. You use it almost like you use get, except that mget takes advantage of the UNIX (and DOS) pattern matching facility. You can use the asterisk (*) in place of the variable parts of the filename.

For example, if you want a bunch of JPEG files about tigers, you might want to look for all the files that match the pattern tigr*.jpeg. The * will usually stand in for a number or a series of letters.

Once you have examined the directory and decided which files you want, type:

    mget *filepattern*

Figure 9.3 shows an mget session, requesting files with the pattern
audio.* and using hash to measure the transfer's progress.

 WARNING   It is extremely important to know whether you want to use
ASCII or binary mode when you are transferring files with mget, or you will
waste time and bandwidth and end up with files filled with gibberish.
Always transfer all the files that need the same mode in the same mget
operation; if you need both ASCII and binary transfers, you'll need to run
mget twice. Some FTP clients are smart enough these days to read the
extension and guess the file type, but not all are. Be sure and set the mode
before you begin the mget.

```
┌─────────────────── WTNVT: Session harry to host harry ──────────── ▼ ▲
 Session   Edit  Commands   Settings   Help                               ↑
ftp> hash
Hash mark printing on (8192 bytes/hash mark).
ftp> mget *audio*.*
mget ietf-audiocast-article.ps? y
200 PORT command successful.
150 Opening ASCII mode data connection for ietf-audiocast-article.ps (177682 by.
##########################
226 Transfer complete.
local: ietf-audiocast-article.ps remote: ietf-audiocast-article.ps
184247 bytes received in 57 seconds (3.2 Kbytes/s)
mget ietf-audiocast.txt? y
200 PORT command successful.
150 Opening ASCII mode data connection for ietf-audiocast.txt (21761 bytes).
###
226 Transfer complete.
local: ietf-audiocast.txt remote: ietf-audiocast.txt
22123 bytes received in 19 seconds (1.2 Kbytes/s)
ftp>
ftp>
ftp>
ftp>
ftp>
ftp>
ftp> █
                                                              12:41:25 ↓
```

*Figure 9.3. **The mget command in operation.***

Moving Files from You to Somewhere Else

Sometimes you will want to place a copy of a file on another host,
either to share it with someone or to put it into a public archive or to
move your html source files to a Web server. Then you use the put or
mput commands.

WARNING   You will not be able to copy a file into a directory or onto a host if you do not have *write permission* for that host or directory. Some FTP sites do not allow any anonymous FTP users to write (copy) files into their archives. You will need to have an account on that system to *put* files on such hosts.

put   The put command works just like get, only in reverse. Check what your file mode should be (ASCII or BINARY), set the appropriate type, and then send it away. Here's a line-mode example:

```
hash
set ascii
put index.html
```

The little hash marks will march across the screen, and your file will slip away across the Internet to its new home.

 MASTER WORDS   Remember, unlike the DOS command MOVE or the UNIX mv command, FTP's put and mput do not *move* the file from one place to another: they merely *copy* it.

Using your graphical FTP client to move files *to* a server will work similarly to moving files *from* a server, just in reverse. Look for the transfer mode (ASCII or BINARY) settings, make sure that you are connected to the correct host and in the appropriate directory, and then click on Send or Put or some similar command button.

mput   Just as mget retrieves multiple files with one command, mput sends multiple files. Again, you check what your file mode should be (ASCII or binary), set the appropriate type, and then send them away. Figure 9.4 illustrates a typical mput session.

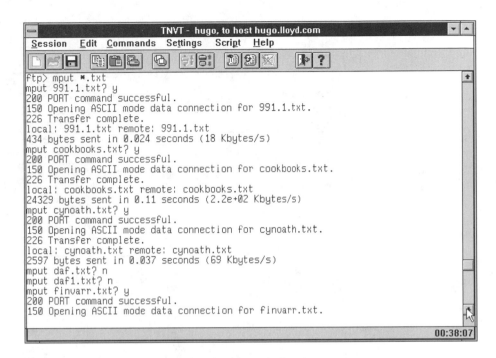

Part
II

The Internet Toolkit

Figure 9.4. Using mput from a vt100 (dumb) terminal session.

GUI FTP Clients

Many of the most modern TCP/IP-based Internet clients that you run from your desktop have graphical interfaces. That is, they will run in either the standard Macintosh or Windows-like formats. These clients are extremely easy to use because they have menus that help you remember how to do things.

Signing On

Most of these clients have a menu of hosts you have used regularly, or they let you type the name of the FTP service you wish to use into a response box. You can also type in your user name and password at the same time. The client generally handles passing along these bits of information for you.

One such client program is FTP Software's WFTP. Figure 9.5 shows the start of a WFTP session.

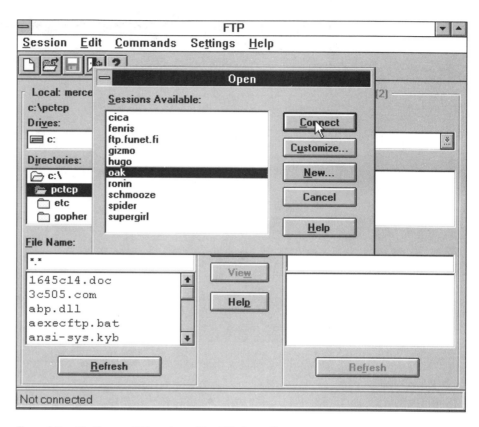

*Figure 9.5. **Starting an FTP session with a Windows client.***

Getting Files

When you sign on, you will see a list of files available. Some clients show you both the available files on your local workstation or host as well as those on the remote host; some show you only the remote host unless you explicitly ask for a local listing. In general, you select the file mode in which you want to transfer the files, highlight the names of the file or files you want to transfer, and then click on the direction you want to send the files (in this case, to you). Figure 9.6 shows a typical WFTP transfer session.

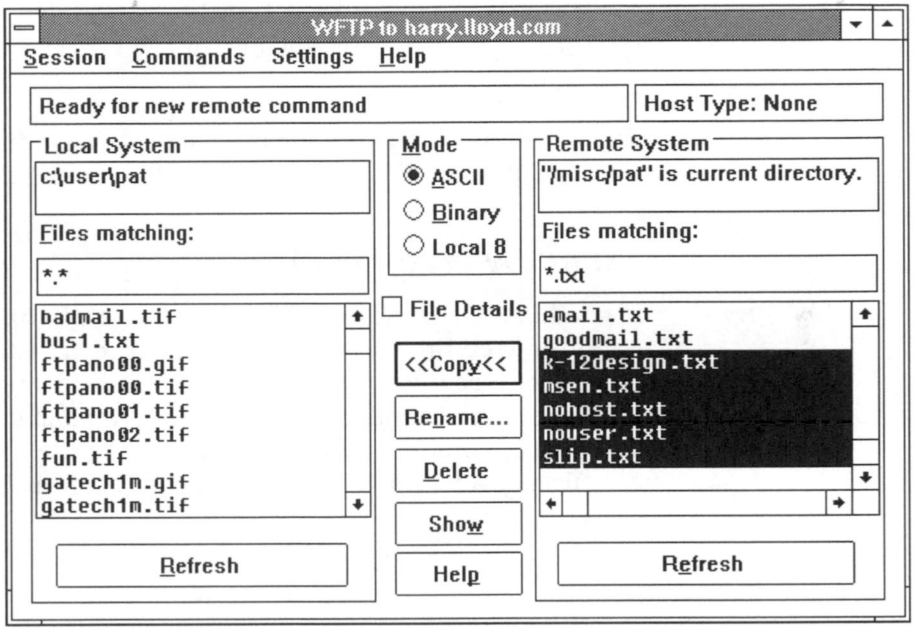

Figure 9.6. Transferring files using FTP Software's Windows client.

Placing Files

Putting a file on a remote host is very simple with these GUI clients: you click on the arrows for the direction in which you want to copy the files (from you to the remote host) or on a button labeled something like Put.

Again, you can transfer either a single file or multiple files with most clients. But remember that the file *modes* must be identical for all types if you are transferring several files.

NCFTP

NCFTP is an improved line-mode program for anonymous FTP that doesn't require you to be able to spell *anonymous*. It also automatically enters the e-mail address (derived from the user ID and host name) as the password. It's intended to be an easy and efficient "front end" to the traditional FTP programs.

Check with your systems administrator to see if NCFTP has been installed on your host or site; or just enter

```
ncftp oak.oakland.edu
```

at the system prompt. If you are connected to the Oakland University FTP archive, you'll know that NCFTP is running on your system.

Using the Web for FTP

If you have a Web client (either line mode's Lynx or one of the many graphical Web browsers), you can use it to transfer files *to* your computer. Web browsers are usually capable of dealing with several different types of protocols including FTP as well as http and Gopher. You can read more about this in Chapter 10. To use most Web browsers to download a file using FTP, enter the URL of the host preceded by the keyword ftp:

```
ftp://ftphost.domain
```

wherever you can enter a new URL for navigation. (Note that some browsers, such as Oracle's PowerBrowser, will put the ftp:// in for you automatically. Try it out.) In line-mode clients, that will be at the browser prompt. In a graphical client, it will be in the appropriate dialog box. To connect to the Washington University in St. Louis Software Archive via FTP, enter

```
ftp://wuarchive.wustl.edu
```

in the appropriate place for your client, and press Enter. You'll be connected via FTP to the archive. Use your browser's movement commands, buttons, or arrows to see what is available. When you find a file you want to transfer, select it via your browser (highlight it, for example) and press Enter or click OK. The file will be transferred to your computer. Your new file will be stored in the location you've specified in your browser's preference settings.

Interesting FTP Sites

Some places to go with FTP include:

Extensive archives of computer source code: for Windows at

```
ftp.cica.indiana.edu
```

(Indiana University); for Macintosh computers at the SUMEX-AIM system in the Stanford University in California domain; for

DOS and Amiga machines (among others) at

  `wuarchive.wustl.edu`

(Washington University in St. Louis, Missouri) or

  `oak.oakland.edu`

(Oakland University in Rochester, Michigan). Note that many archives now operate Web sites that are a bit easier to navigate. You may want to check the Web first.

Information Source Lists: The Internet and Computer-Mediated Communication (AKA The December list), compiled by John December (`decemj@rpi.edu`) at host

  `ftp.rpi.edu`

(Rennselaer Polytechnic Institute, Troy, New York) in the /pub/communications/ directory; also available via the Web at

  `http://www.rpi.edu/Internet/Guides/decemj/text.html`.

This file is a list of pointers to information describing the Internet, computer networks, and issues related to computer-mediated communication (CMC). Special Internet Connections (AKA The Yanoff list) is another list that contains many resources of potential interest. Scott Yanoff compiles and updates it and the list is posted frequently across the Net. It can be reached via anonymous FTP from the host

  `csd4.csd.uwm.edu`

(University of Wisconsin, Madison, Wisconsin) or via the World Wide Web. One place you can find it is at the Stanford Linear Accelerator Center:

  `http://slacvx.slac.stanford.edu:80/misc/`
  `internet-services.html`.

The "original" can be found at

  `http://www.uwm.edu/Mirror/inet.services.html`.

Connected countries: If you'd like to know what countries are connected to the global Internet and how, you can get a file of information collected by Larry LandWeber. It's in the directory /connectivity_ table/ on the host

  `ftp.cs.wisc.edu`

(University of Wisconsin).

Part II

The Internet Toolkit

State Government: For information from the Legislature of the State of California, FTP to

`leginfo.public.ca.gov`

or Gopher the University of California at Santa Cruz's Infoslug system

`scilibx.ucsu.edu`

From their main menu, choose "The Community," then "Guide to government," and then "US, State and Local." This menu will present a number of choices for government information.

The charters for many of the Usenet newsgroups can be found at

`ftp.uu.net`

in the \usenet\ directory.

Telnet

People who are in one location frequently want to use a computer in another location. Perhaps they are on a business trip and want to read their e-mail. Perhaps they want to access data on the computer in another branch or in the main office. Perhaps they want to look at a library catalog to see if a certain book has been published. Perhaps they want to use one of the services of the information providers such as Dialog or Mead Data Central. Telnet is the Internet tool that lets you travel from your own workstation out into cyberspace to "land" on another computer.

You can also use Telnet to get to services, such as Gophers, line-mode Web servers, and libraries, even if you do not have clients for those servers on your own host system. (See Chapter 10 for information about the Web and Chapter 11 for information about Gopher.)

When you are connected to a remote host via Telnet, you interact with that computer and operating system and issue commands as if you were directly connected (via wires) to that computer. Your session acts as if it were a terminal session connected to the remote host.

Using Telnet

Telnet is one of the simplest tools on the Internet. To open a line-mode session with a remote host from a system prompt, type:

`telnet hostname`

You should see the welcome or login banner for the host.

If you have already started the Telnet program, you may see a prompt for the Telnet program itself: `telnet>`. If you are at such a prompt, type:

    open *hostname*

and, again, you should see the login prompt. Figure 9.7 shows the beginning of a line-mode Telnet session.

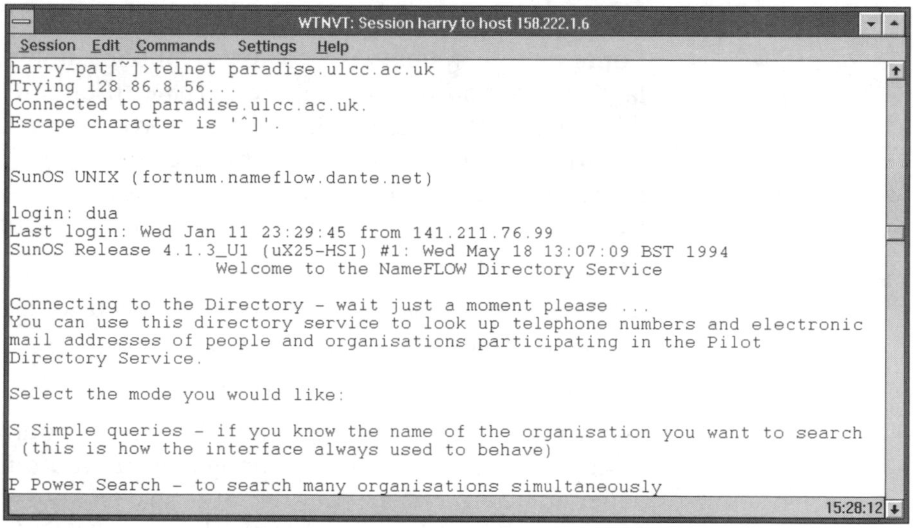

```
                    WTNVT: Session harry to host 158.222.1.6
 Session  Edit  Commands   Settings   Help
harry-pat[~]>telnet paradise.ulcc.ac.uk
Trying 128.86.8.56...
Connected to paradise.ulcc.ac.uk.
Escape character is '^]'.


SunOS UNIX (fortnum.nameflow.dante.net)

login: dua
Last login: Wed Jan 11 23:29:45 from 141.211.76.99
SunOS Release 4.1.3_U1 (uX25-HSI) #1: Wed May 18 13:07:09 BST 1994
                  Welcome to the NameFLOW Directory Service

Connecting to the Directory - wait just a moment please ...
You can use this directory service to look up telephone numbers and electronic
mail addresses of people and organisations participating in the Pilot
Directory Service.

Select the mode you would like:

S Simple queries - if you know the name of the organisation you want to search
 (this is how the interface always used to behave)

P Power Search - to search many organisations simultaneously
                                                                    15:28:12
```

Figure 9.7. Beginning a simple Telnet session to the Paradise directory service.

If you are using a graphical Telnet client, you may be able to save short names for commonly used hosts or services, as in Figure 9.8.

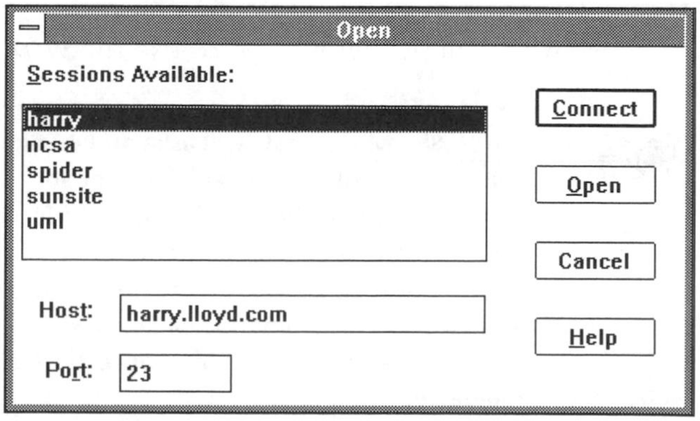

```
                            Open
 Sessions Available:
                                              Connect
 harry
 ncsa
 spider                                        Open
 sunsite
 uml
                                              Cancel

   Host:  harry.lloyd.com                       Help

   Port:  23
```

Figure 9.8. Opening a connection with a graphical Telnet client.

Telnet sessions may be established directly by typing the command explicitly, or through an intermediary such as Gopher or WWW. There are directories that you will find on the Internet that list remote services. These directories will list the appropriate command to use, including the appropriate domain and/or Internet address. If a remote service is publicly accessible, you may not need a user account on the remote system.

tn3270

Some remote systems (some library public catalog systems, in particular) require you to use a different Telnet program to connect properly. This program, called tn3270, causes your computer to appear to be ("emulate") an IBM 3270 computer terminal (instead of using the more common VT100 emulation). If you need to connect to one of these systems, you may need to Telnet to a public site that offers a tn3270 program.

Two clues will tell you that you might need to use tn3270. The first is a message that says

```
Connection closed by foreign host.
```

consistently. This message indicates there is trouble between your two systems. Naturally, there are many reasons you might receive this message, including that the remote host is not currently available. However, if you suspect that the host is an IBM system, think about trying tn3270.

The second clue is a ...connected ... message returned from the remote host, containing the letters VM or MVS in the welcome message. This indicates that you are connected to an IBM system. If the interaction between your computer and the remote host doesn't go well, you probably need to use tn3270.

 MASTER WORDS Many hosts will ask you what kind of terminal emulation you are using when you first make a connection. Usually these hosts tell you what kind of emulator they think you are using and ask you to confirm (or enter a different emulation). It is particularly important to respond correctly to these prompts, because otherwise your screen will not look correct, and your keyboard commands will probably not behave in an expected way. If you don't know how to respond, type a question mark (?) and see the online help.

Once you are connected to this type of system, you will be presented with menus and forms that expect you to "fill in the blanks." When you have completed your form, send it to the remote host by pressing Enter. tn3270 maps your keyboard to the keyboard of the 3270 terminal. Many systems that use these terminals use the Program Function (PF) keys and the Clear key to communicate special commands to the program. It is particularly important to tell the tn3270 program that you have a VT100 terminal when you start the program. Then, once you are connected, you will need to figure out how the keys on the 3270 keyboard are represented. Usually Tab will move you through the input areas. Try the arrow keys. If they don't work, you can use Tab. Usually the tn3270 Enter is the Enter key on your keyboard and also the one on your numeric keypad.

For the function keys, try the F1, F2, ... keys across the top of your keyboard. If they work, the screen display will change or you will get a message like "PF4 undefined." If they don't work, try Escape+1 for PF1, and so on.

To clear the screen, try Ctrl-Home, Ctrl-l, or Ctrl-z.

Any Port in a Storm

A *port* is rather like a transmission channel on a radio. It is the place at which the application on the remote or host computer "listens" for connection requests to a particular application. Gopher usually uses port 70. Telnet usually uses port 23. FTP usually uses two ports, one of which is port 21. Services can use other port numbers to direct connections to specific applications. If you are given a specific port number, place the number after the host name in a command-line interface, or in the "port" box in a GUI or dialog box interface.

 MASTER WORDS Curious about geographic location as well as location in cyberspace? Can't remember your mother's zip code? Need to find out the longitude and latitude of your office building? Telnet to

martini.eecs.umich.edu 3000

where you will be connected to the machine called martini in the Electrical Engineering Computer Science domain at the University of Michigan, using port 3000. This is the Geographic Name Server. Once connected, you can enter a place name or a zip code. In return, you will receive a short display of information available about that place. No special login sequence is needed. There is online help.

Hytelnet

An important tool for working with Telnet is Hytelnet. Canadian Peter Scott, developer, singer/songwriter, and librarian extraordinaire, has designed and implemented this DOS program, which presents menus of library catalogs and other resources that allow public access through Telnet. Other good people have come along and produced client programs for other platforms—Windows, UNIX, VMS, and Macintosh. The particular advantage of Hytelnet for you as a user is that the specific information about a library or service is remembered by the program, and you need not keep track of it yourself. If Hytelnet is not already on your system, you can use it via

```
http://moondog.usask.ca/hytelnet/
```

or

```
gopher://liberty.uc.wlu.edu/11/internet/hytelnet
```

For more information about the program itself, use your Web browser to go to the Hytelnet information page at

```
http://www.lights.com/hytelnet/
```

You may want to download a version to run on your own DOS machine. You can get that from

```
ftp://ftp.usask.ca/pub/hytelnet/pc/latest/hyteln69.zip
```

or

```
http://www.lights.com/hytelnet/hyteln69.zip
```

Pointers to the Windows, Macintosh, UNIX, and VMS versions will be found at the Hytelnet information page.

Using the Web for Telnet

Some Web browsers have Telnet clients built in; others rely on you setting your preference files so that the browser can find your separate Telnet client. In either case, your Web browser may be capable of connecting to another Internet host using Telnet. To try this, open your Web browser and enter

```
telnet://books.com
```

in the dialog box or command line where your Web browser receives navigation information (the place where you put the address where you want the browser to go). Your browser will open a Telnet session (perhaps in another window, perhaps not; this will depend on the browser itself) to Book Stacks Unlimited, a bookstore. You can follow the directions to look at their offerings and perhaps find a book you'd like to read.

Interesting Telnet Sites

These sites offer products, services, and/or discussions. When you Telnet to these sites, use the login name specified for the service. Be prepared to register your name, address, and perhaps e-mail address on entry to these services.

Argonne National Laboratory in Illinois offers an educational service called Newton. To reach it, Telnet to

```
newton.dep.anl.gov
```

If you need agricultural information, try Cornell's Extension Network. To reach CENET, Telnet to

```
empire.cce.cornell.edu
```

There is a backgammon server at

```
fraggel65.mdstd.chalmers.se
```

on port 4321.

You can play bridge (live!) by Telnetting to

```
vanderbilt.okbridge.com
```

port 1729. You will receive a welcome message and be asked to select an account name. You need an e-mail account somewhere to play.

MichNet and its members maintain several interesting Gophers as well as other interesting services. Telnet to

```
hermes.merit.edu
```

and then, at the "Which Host?" prompt, type HELP. Some of the most interesting services include UM-Weather, which has forecasts and current information as well as educational programs and curriculum ideas for teachers; the MSU Gopher, which has a library of voice recordings; the libraries of many of Michigan's colleges and universities; and many others.

Telnet to

```
books.com
```

to find a bulletin board system (BBS) that is the bookstore Books Stacks Unlimited.

Telnet to

```
pac.carl.org
```

to find book reviews and a journal article fax service.

Telnet to

```
classroom-earth.ciesin.org 2010
```

to find the Global change education bulletin board.

Pilots! Telnet to

```
duats.fsdgte.com
```

to get a complete weather briefing; with your pilot's certificate number, you can even file your flight plan.

CHAPTER 10

Threading Your Way through the World Wide Web

FEATURING

Chapter 10

Threading Your Way through the World Wide Web

THE tools we have talked about so far have a significant limitation—in order to use them you must already have an address for a host computer or the name of the file or person you're interested in. This chapter is about serendipity and starting points: the World Wide Web. The Web has done the most to excite the interest of ordinary, non-technical people in the possibilities of the Internet. The World Wide Web offers views of cyberspace that don't require you to have an exact address, to know exactly what you are looking for, or to type a command with exactly the right characters in order to find something. You start from some point (and it doesn't really matter too much which point), and you can wander around in cyberspace just by taking "jumps" or links to connections that interest you from the display at which you are looking.

Once you're connected to the Web, you don't need to know the address of the page that you wish to reach as long as you can find a page to which it is linked. When you are viewing a Web page, you see visually distinct "links" to other Web pages. The links may be underlined, for example, or displayed in a second color. Or, you may click on an icon or picture and be connected from there.

1994 and 1995 were the years of fastest growth on the Internet. The widespread interest in the Internet has come about because of the ease of use of Web browsers, the fantastic variety of pages and topics available using the Web, and the rise in low-cost access available to more and more people.

The World Wide Web

The World Wide Web (also called WWW, or W3, or simply the Web) is a tool that helps you to find and retrieve information, using links to other WWW pages. Web links are stored within the page itself and when you wish to "jump" to the page that is linked, you select the "hotspot" or "anchor." This technique is sometimes called *hypermedia* or *hypertext*. If you've used a Windows- or Macintosh-based help system in which you click on an underlined phrase to jump to that topic, you're already familiar with hypermedia. Figure 10.1 shows the "home page" (starting point) for the Web, from the World Wide Web Consortium, the organization that maintains the standards that enable us to use (and develop with) this terrific Internet tool.

The outrageous growth of the Web has come thanks to the ability to build information resources that let you point to a wide variety of links, unconstrained by the formality of a menu. Sometimes it is very difficult to organize your information into a series of menus. Sometimes your information is best represented by lists within paragraphs of description, or by an image, or by a list of items that have associated paragraphs of description. And sometimes it's nice to just click on a map of the world to select the information servers located in Italy.

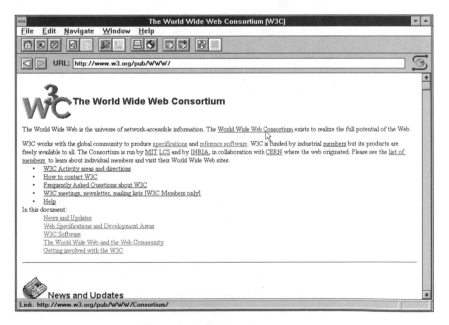

Figure 10.1. **The Web Community "home page."**

WWW, because of its ability to incorporate FTP, Gopher, and other tools, has become the most widely used Internet navigation tool. Add to this the snazzy graphic interface and point-and-click capability, and we see the beginnings of a truly democratic Internet interface. You can even become a Web page publisher yourself. We cover how to get started in Chapter 20 later in this book.

WWW clients on the Internet can display pages from any of the nearly 1 million Web servers. Each time you choose a link, WWW connects to the appropriate server, retrieves the next page wanted, and returns control to the local client. Once the document has been retrieved, the link is broken. This means that the server does not have to keep the link open while you read the document. WWW is thus an efficient method of finding and using information widely dispersed throughout the world. Figure 10.2 shows the beginning of the geographically organized list of Web servers.

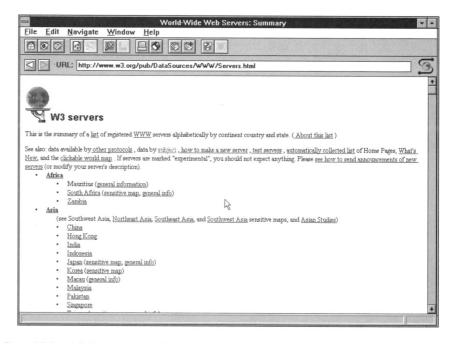

Figure 10.2.   **A listing of known Web pages in the world.**

Web pages are truly multimedia: they may contain text, graphic images, moving pictures, sound files, and other types of electronic information. Figures 10.3 through 10.7 show the variety of graphic images available on the Web.

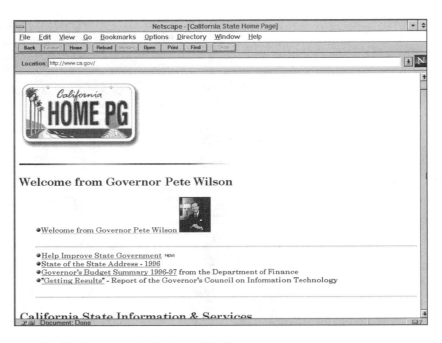

Figure 10.3. *The Home Page for the State of California.*

Figure 10.4. *The Future Fantasy Bookstore in Palo Alto, California.*

Figure 10.5.   *Kevin & Kell, the first cyberspace-only comic strip.*

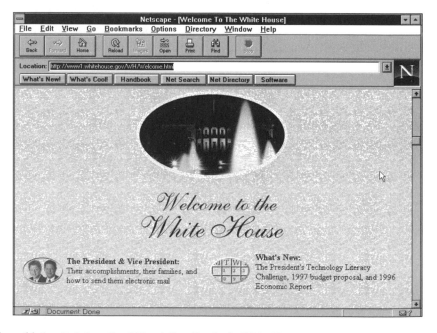

Figure 10.6.   *An Interactive Citizen's Handbook: the White House.*

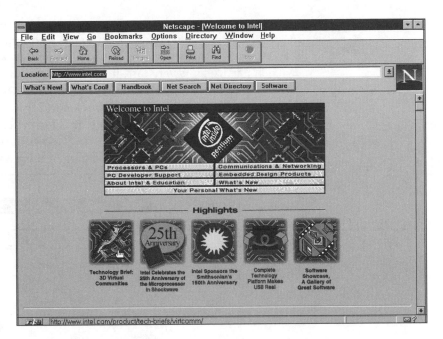

Figure 10.7. **The Intel home page.**

Not all Web clients can handle all the various media available. Even if your client can process the information, your particular configuration may not be able to display it. For example, Figure 10.8 is a display of the White House home page, only shown through the line-mode browser Lynx rather than the graphic display tool Netscape used in Figure 10.6. You can see text only, rather than the pictures (although you can download the pictures and display them if you have a local GIF viewer).

Fortunately, the designers of the clients know about this limitation and make allowances for differing configurations. If a page contains something that the client cannot process, it will not attempt to display it. Some well-known Web clients include Cornell Law's Cello, University of Kansas' Lynx (used for the text-based illustrations in this chapter), Netscape Communications Corporation's Netscape (illustrated throughout this book), IBM's OS/2 Explorer, and the National Center for Supercomputer Applications (NCSA) Mosaic. You'll see how to find these programs shortly.

MASTER WORDS   Why would anyone want to use a nongraphical browser, in this day of fancy graphics and exciting point-and-click interfaces? Because Lynx, in particular, is very fast. It accesses pages and displays them more quickly than most graphical browsers. It has all the other features that people like in browsers (such as bookmarks, printing, mailing a document, and so on), and it runs on the lowest-common-denominator machines. Some people use Lynx for fast access to text information. It's a second tool in the toolbox, next to a graphical browser.

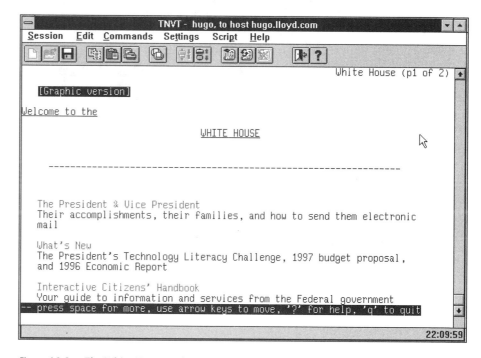

Figure 10.8.   The White House Web page through a Lynx Web browser.

Many Web pages now include forms you can fill out or database front ends to let you search for specific patterns or words. Most let you send e-mail or comments on the Web page itself. Many let you mail the page text or a graphic from the page to yourself or a friend. Not all browsers can handle the forms in these pages: most of the graphical front ends are "forms-capable," but many of the simple line-mode interfaces (like the "www" tool) are not.

COOL WEB PAGES WITH ADVANCED FEATURES

There are a lot of really nifty pages out there with animated graphics, blinking colors and signs, frames, and shifting images. We can show you static pictures of them, but it's just a teaser. Unfortunately, you have to use a browser that will see these things, and in most cases you will need to use Netscape version 1.1 or above. The wizards at Netscape have developed many new Web features, and a lot of Web page designers are incorporating them. The other Web browser companies are catching up, but not as quickly as you might like.

Some fun places to go and see cool graphics and effects are:

What	URL
The Batman Forever home page	http://www.batmanforever.com
The Levi-Strauss home page	http://www.levi.com
The Silicon Graphics home page	http://www.sgi.com
The Netscape home page	http://home.netscape.com

The Levi-Strauss home page uses programming to shift its images:

The World Wide Web was originally developed at CERN, the high-energy physics research center in Switzerland. The Web interface is designed so that you can choose to follow a Web "filament" around the Web as far as you like by selecting a spot on the "page" displayed on your screen. The locus of the WWW system is the "home page." This is the place from which the server to which you are connected starts.

Most browsers, such as Netcom's NetCruiser, Netscape Navigator, or Mosaic, start you at their home page. You can reset this in the options for your particular client, either for your own home page or some other place. The ultimate home page for WWW is the home page at W3.Org:

```
http://www.w3.org
```

It's the first illustration in this chapter, if you'd like to go back and review.

Giving Web page citations, called URLs (Universal Resource Locators), lets you indicate the filament of the Web you wish to follow; alternatively, you may jump directly to particular points on the Web.

If you have never used the Web, the easiest way to find out more about it is to take a tour. You could try the A to Z Tour page that Lycos put together to illustrate the depth and breadth of information available via the Web. Start whatever client you have available by opening the page:

```
http://a2z.lycos.com
```

From this page, you can jump to any of a varying set of links organized by topics like "Art and Humanities." Then you can choose among lower-level topics like "Museums." Finally you can browse through an alphabetical listing of museums or you can jump directly to the beginning letter of the museum you have in mind. And remember that you can also use your Web browser to connect to Gopher and FTP sites, as well as ones on the Web. You can go to and use Gopher and FTP servers with your Web client by simply indicating the type of server in the URL. To go to a Gopher, for example, enter

```
gopher://gopher.netcom.com/
```

or

```
gopher://gopher.isoc.org/
```

wherever your client allows you to specify a particular URL. Similarly, to go to an FTP server, enter (for example)

```
ftp://ftp.uu.net/
```

in the dialog box.

More introductory information about the Web can be found at the W3.Org Web site, where the information originally gathered at the CERN laboratory in Switzerland now resides. You might want to see how many ways there are to reach that page by using the information you have so far to navigate.

Finding Web Clients

As with Gopher, you may already have access to a WWW browser client. If you have a host account on someone else's system, try typing **lynx** or **www** at the main system prompt.

Below is a list of WWW client software available for most common systems. You will need to bring them to your computer via anonymous FTP, and install them (following the instructions in the Readme and doc files). Unless otherwise listed, the following browser clients are available via anonymous FTP from the archive at `info.w3.org`.

Windows and Win95 Web Browsers

Netscape Netscape exploded onto the scene early in 1995. It was designed by some of the folks who did the early work on the Mosaic browser, but they wanted improve on that design and to create a successful business built around their ideas. They were successful. Netscape is a full-featured, forms-capable browser, and many users like the way it handles inline graphics and other media better than the other three Windows browsers. In fact, many of the innovations are now migrating to other browsers. You can get a free copy of Netscape for evaluation or educational use, or buy a copy of the Netscape Personal Navigator. Figure 10.9 shows the Netscape home page.

You can get Netscape in several ways: First, you can FTP it from the main Netscape archive at

```
ftp.netscape.com
```

or get it from one of the many mirror sites. (If the main Netscape FTP site is seriously congested, you will see a list of alternative mirror sites that Netscape has licensed.) You will probably want to get your evaluation copy from a mirror site, as the main Netscape FTP site is always remarkably busy.

You can also buy Netscape's Personal Navigator or Netscape Gold (the newest edition) from your local computer store.

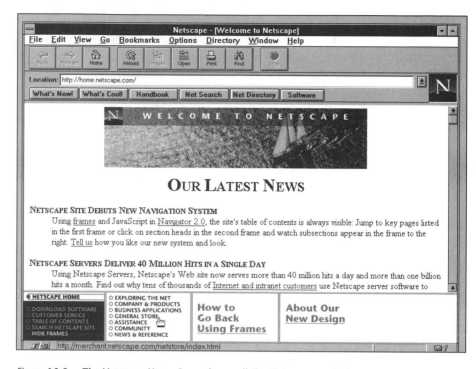

*Figure 10.9.   **The Netscape Home Page shows all the Netscape products.***

The advantage to the commercial versions is one of the features which makes Netscape a very exciting product. Along with the browser, the Netscape team has developed a WWW server which will protect the information you are sending over the wire by encrypting it. This means that businesses, for example, can take your charge card number over the Net, with reduced fear that it will be stolen.

In addition, the newest commercial versions of Netscape include an editor that helps you create your own WWW pages.

To install Netscape if you are running Windows 3.1 or Windows for Workgroups (WFW), you must use the 16-bit Navigator even if you have Win32 installed. If you are running Windows 95 or Windows NT, use the 32-bit Navigator. To run the 32-bit Navigator, you must have a 32-bit TCP/IP stack. Both Windows 95 and Windows NT provide 32-bit TCP/IP stacks that you can set up. If you need help setting up the TCP/IP stack in Windows 95, see

```
http://www.windows95.com
```

MASTER WORDS   Just how dangerous is it to transmit your charge card number over World Wide Web? There are widely differing opinions about this. Netscape and several of the other companies selling secure browsers have had their encrypted cracked, but they have immediately fixed problems that were found. You should know that the "cracking" was done by very talented computer programmers who made an inspired guess and had access to large computing power. In order for this to happen to your encrypted message, it would need to be intercepted AND the message encryption would have to be cracked. Some folks feel that you should never send charge or financial information over the network, as there is a chance that someone will intercept it. Others feel that there is no more danger in transmitting your charge number over a secure browser than there is in handing it to a clerk in a store (who may make an extra charge slip while you aren't looking) or calling a catalog company and ordering over the phone. You'll need to make your own choices. However, some basic common-sense rules do apply: do not send passwords, charge card numbers, or other critical information over unsecured browsers, and never put them in unencrypted e-mail.

If you are running Netscape on Windows 3.1 or WFW, you'll also need Winsock software from another source, either software supplied by your network vendor or a publicly available package such as Peter Tattam's Trumpet Winsock. Netscape has been used successfully with Winsocks from all leading software vendors. Winsock is available via anonymous FTP from

```
ftp.cica.indiana.edu
```

Sybex's *Surfing the Internet with Netscape* (Daniel A. Tauber and Brenda Kienan, 1995) provides complete information for getting and using the Netscape Web browser and includes TCP/IP software on disk in the form of Chameleon Sampler. The book's second edition, *Surfing the Internet with Netscape Navigator 2* (1996), covers the latest version of Netscape; its companion disk provides a different selection of Web resources.

Cello   This program allows you full access to the information resources of the Internet. It can run World Wide Web, Gopher, FTP, CSO/ph/qi, and Usenet News retrievals, and it runs other protocols (WAIS, Hytelnet, Telnet, and TN3270) through external clients and public gateways. It can be used to view hypermedia documents, including inline images, text, and digital sounds and movies. Cello runs under Microsoft Windows on any IBM PC with a 386SX chip or better. You will get better performance with at least 4 megabytes of RAM and a 16 MHz or faster chip. You'll also need Winsock software from another source, either software supplied by your network vendor or a publicly available package such as Peter Tattam's Trumpet Winsock. Cello has been used successfully with Winsocks from all leading software vendors. Winsock and Cello are available via anonymous FTP from

```
ftp.cica.indiana.edu
```

Mosaic for Windows   NCSA Mosaic is a full-featured, forms-capable WWW browser. It supports World Wide Web, Gopher, and FTP directly, and other protocols either by emulation or through public gateways. Mosaic for Windows runs under Microsoft Windows on any IBM PC with a 386SX chip or better. You will have better performance with at least 4 megabytes of RAM. You'll also need Winsock software from another source, either software supplied by your network vendor or a publicly available package such as Peter Tattam's Trumpet Winsock. Mosaic for Windows is available via anonymous FTP from

```
ftp.ncsa.uiuc.edu
```

in the /PC/Mosaic/ directory. Other forms of Mosaic are available commercially; see Chapter 5.

WinWeb   A full-featured, graphical WWW browser employing a standard Windows interface. To install it you will need Windows 3.1 and 4 megabytes of RAM. You should also have 5 megabytes of space free on your hard drive to install the software. EINet WinWeb is available by anonymous FTP from

```
ftp.einet.net
```

Terminal-Based Browsers

You will probably already find these installed on your host-based account; if not, consult your local systems administrator to get them installed.

www Line Mode Browser   The CERN Line Mode Browser is a character-based World Wide Web Browser. It is developed for use on hosts that support VT100 terminal emulation. Binary files are available for most UNIX varieties and many other platforms; the filename will look like www*.tar.Z, where * identifies the particular platform.

Lynx Full Screen Browser   This is a hypertext browser for VT100s using full screen, arrow keys, highlighting, and so on. It is much preferred over the www line mode browser. Sources and precompiled binaries are available for rs6000, sun3, sun4, NeXT, VMS (multinet). The software is available by anonymous FTP from

```
ftp2.cc.ukans.edu
```

Macintosh Web Browsers

Netscape for Macintosh Netscape is available for Macintosh as well as DOS/Windows and UNIX platforms. You can get a free copy of Netscape for evaluation or educational use, or buy a copy of the Netscape Personal Navigator.

You can get Netscape in several ways: First, you can FTP it from the main Netscape archive at

```
ftp.netscape.com
```

or get it from one of the many mirror sites. (If the main Netscape FTP site is seriously congested, you will see a list of alternative mirror sites that Netscape has licensed.) You will probably want to get your evaluation copy from a mirror site, as the main Netscape FTP site is always remarkably busy.

You can also buy Netscape's Personal Navigator or Netscape Gold (the newest edition) from your local computer store.

Mosaic for Macintosh Like its cousins, NCSA Mosaic for Macintosh is a full-featured, forms-capable browser. It is available via anonymous FTP from

```
ftp.ncsa.uiuc.edu
```

Samba A basic browser, available from W3.Org. It does not support many of the advanced WWW features. To install Samba on your system, you must install MacTCP (at least version 1.1.1, to avoid a bug in earlier versions). The binary can be picked up from

```
ftp.w3.org
```

on the /ftp/pub/www/bin/mac/ directory by anonymous FTP.

MacWeb This is EINet's full-featured World Wide Web client. EINet MacWeb is available by anonymous FTP from the host named

```
ftp.einet.net
```

in the file named /einet/mac /macWeb.latest.sea.hqx. In order to run MacWeb, your Macintosh must be configured with System 7 and MacTCP 2.0.2 (MacTCP 2.0.4 is recommended). Use StuffIt Expander (or an equivalent program) to de-binhex and expand the archive.

How to Navigate within the Web

When you start most Web clients, you begin with the display of a home page. This page could be one that points to descriptions of the organization that sponsored the development of the client. Or it could be one you constructed from links that are meaningful and useful to you.

If your organization has a home page, displaying it when each client is called up onto the display screen is a good way to remind people where they "are" in the Web. Many companies have a home page for their internal internet (sometimes called an "Intranet"), and their home page comes up when anyone on the internal net starts up a browser.

 MASTER WORDS   If your organization doesn't have a home page, you might want to recommend constructing one. Every organization on the Internet should have a home page. Presenting a home page allows you to tell other Internet users who you are, where you are, and what your organization does. You can list the products or services that you provide, and you can present links to information about your organization. This book's companion CD includes a list of "information publishers"—companies that will construct and maintain a Web page for your organization. The fees they charge vary widely. Chapter 20, "Building the Resource," shows how to construct your own Web page and offers examples of well-designed Web pages.

From the home page you can move to any link by moving your cursor to the hotspot or anchor. To take the jump, click your mouse or Press Enter.

Most Web clients also provide a method of moving directly to a specific page. This is called "Opening a URL" (pronounced by some as *yew-are-el* and by others as *earl*). To do this, you open the client, and then enter the URL in the space provided. If you are using NetCruiser, enter the URL in the center dialog box at the top of the screen page. If you are using Lynx, type **g** for "go," followed by the URL. Figure 10.10 shows opening a location in Netscape, and Figure 10.11 shows how to open the same location or URL in Lynx.

MASTER WORDS   URLs are frequently case-sensitive. Remember that the part after the host name is the complete file name for the file you want to retrieve. If you fail to connect to a specific Web page on a direct jump, chances are you've mistyped the URL.

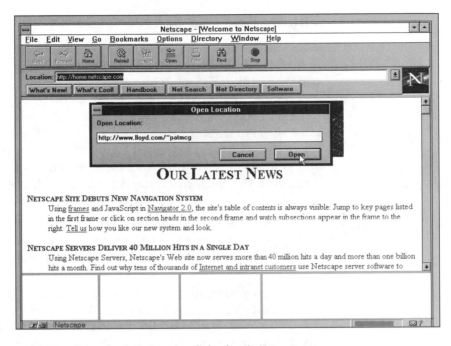

Figure 10.10.   Using the Open Location dialog box in Netscape.

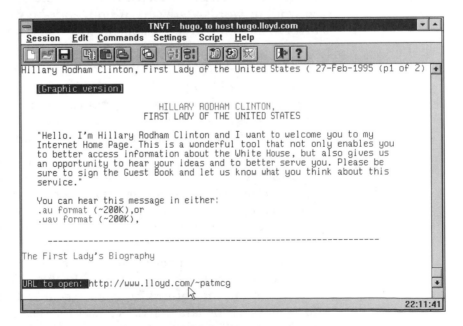

Figure 10.11.   Opening the same URL in Lynx.

Things You Can Expect to Do

Web clients offer some other features besides connecting you to documents and other files. At the simplest, each variety of Web server will let you print a file. You can choose to print it to a printer, to a file, or you can send it to yourself by e-mail. All of these are in the Print menu on most clients. You can also choose to save these items as PostScript files, HTML (Hypertext Markup Language, the Web source format), or just plain typescript. Some clients move the desired files to a host system, and you will need to download them to your local machine. Others save directly to the local machine. Again, you will need to consult the help files in your client software to see how it can best serve you.

 MASTER WORDS   Some clients save the pages in HTML format so that you can use the page locally as a jump point, either as you saved it or as you modified it.

Sometimes your don't really want to store the page itself, you just want to be able to get to it again directly. In large documents, it is nice to be able to go quickly to a specific known point, or to see whether a specific word or string is present in the file. To serve this function, many Web clients have a search capability. You select the Search option and enter the word or words you want to find, and the Web client moves your cursor to the point in the document where that word appears.

Getting Back to a Place You've Found

You can also add to your bookmark list. In many Web browsers this called the *hot list, bookmarks,* or *favorites.* Under the Navigation menu in most browsers, or in the toolbar across the top, look for an item that lets you add the current displayed page to the hot list.

 MASTER WORDS   Want to create a Web page with your favorite spots in it? Use your bookmark list! Most browsers store their bookmarks in HTML format. You can copy the file, transfer it to your Web server, and create a Web page. See Chapter 20 for more information on creating HTML documents.

For navigation within a page and within a server, Web clients use commands like Forward or Down as well as Back or Up. This means you can move around in the "history" of your recent Web travels. Back returns you to the page you last visited. Forward will take you to the next page in your history of Web travels, if you have returned back along the path; it's meaningless unless you have a history path to travel. You can continue to choose Back until you reach the point at which you entered the Web for the current session. This page is called "home" for the session.

The final important thing to learn how to do with your Web client is to stop the display of a very long page. Sometimes you will start the display of a page that contains so much information that you decide you don't want to wait for it to be delivered to your client. You should be able to choose some sort of Halt, Stop, or Abort command that will stop the current activity and redisplay the currently loaded page. Look for a "stop sign" or something like that at the top of the page.

Global Links

Table 10.1 shows some fun links and interesting entries from around the Globe.

Description	URL
Clickable Map of the World	`http://www.vtourist.com/webmap`
An Entry Point for Asia	`http://coombs.anu.edu.au/WWWVL-AsianStudies.html`
Australia's Matilda in Cyberspace	`http://snazzy.anu.edu.au/Matilda/start.html`
Pictures from Brazil	`http://guarani.cos.ufrj.br:8090/Rio/Todas.html`
Information about Italy	`http://www.pi.cnr.it/NIR-IT`
Information about Japan	`http://fuji.stanford.edu/XGUIDE`
Information about the Netherlands	`http://www.tno.nl`
Information about Norway	`http://www.service.uit.no/homepage-no`
Information about Peru	`http://www.rcp.net.pe/rcp.html`
Information about Portugal	`http://s700.uminho.pt/Portugal/general_info.html`
Russian and Eastern European Studies	`http://www.pitt.edu/~cjp/rees.html`
United Nations UNICEF	`gopher://gopher.unicef.org/`
Le WebMuseum	`http://mistral.enst.fr/~pioch/louvre`

Table 10.1. **Global Links for Worldwide Information**

You Can Do It All from a Web Browser

Eighteen months ago, Web browsers were fun tools, but you still needed to have lots of other Internet tools: today, if you pick the right browsers, you hardly need anything else. The WWW browser or client software can incorporate many of the other Internet protocols. The URL tells you what protocol is being used, as shown in Table 10.2.

URL	What You're Doing
`http://www.lloyd.com`	Access a WWW page.
`ftp://ftp.oak.oakland.edu`	Open an FTP session to an FTP archive.
`gopher://gopher.msu.edu`	Access the Gopher server at Michigan State University.
`telnet://hermes.merit.edu`	Telnet to the Hermes Merit Gateway.
`news://<newserver.host>`	Read news from a news system to which you have access. News systems are generally restricted to the subscribers to a particular service and not accessible to the general public.
`mailto://glee@netcom.com`	Send an e-mail message from your browser.

Table 10.2. **URL Formats for Accessing Other Internet Tools**

Sometimes you'll need a helper application, such as a Telnet application, to Telnet from within your browser. Look at your OPTIONS or CUSTOMIZE menu to find out how to let your browser know what Telnet client to use. Then, you don't need to call it separately to go Telnetting off. The browser calls the Telnet client for you.

FTP

With your browser, you can FTP material from most online archives. Even the biggest FTP archives, such as the Oak archive at Oakland University, have a WWW interface, as shown in Figure 10.12. Click on the material you want to download, and it comes to your desktop. The URL is

```
oak.oakland.edu
```

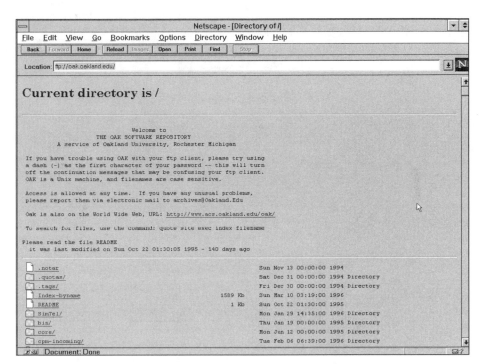

Figure 10.12. Downloading software from the Oak repository using Mosaic.

Gopher

Want to access a gopher server? Use your browser. Figure 10.13 shows what accessing the UNICEF gopher:

```
gopher://gopher.unicef.org/
```

looks like using Mosaic.

Telnet

Telnet from your browser is especially interesting if you want to be able to explore MUDs (Multiple User Dungeons) from your browser. (See Chapter 16 for information about MUDs and MUDding.) In Figure 10.14 we are Telnetting to the SchMOOze Educational MUD:

```
telnet://arthur.rutgers.edu:8888
```

using Netscape.

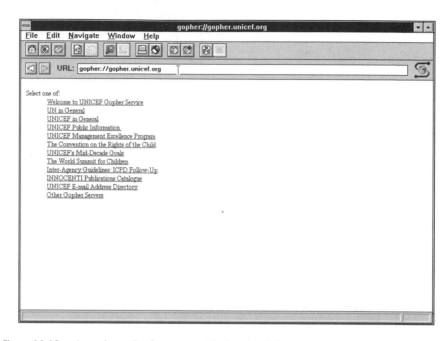

Figure 10.13.   *Accessing a Gopher server with the Mosaic browser.*

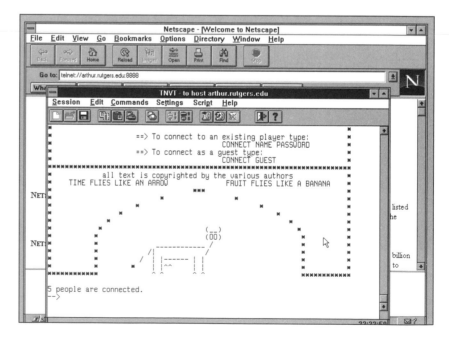

Figure 10.14.   *Telnetting to SchMOOze from Netscape.*

Reading Network News

Reading news from your browser is easy. Some people still prefer to use a newsreader because of the advanced capabilities, such as threading, that are available with newsreaders, but for most of us reading news off a browser is satisfactory. (Netscape Navigator versions 1.2 and above have a satisfactory threading method for reading news.) One advantage to reading news from the browser is that if someone includes a reference to a Web page URL in the news page, you can click on that URL and go visit the page right away. Figure 10.15 shows what reading news looks like from Netscape.

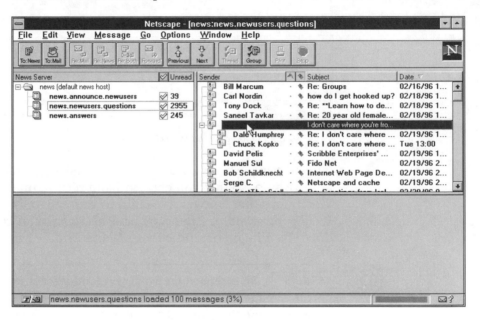

*Figure 10.15.   **Reading the news.newusers.questions newsgroup from Netscape.***

Sending E-Mail

Sending mail from your browser is one of the more exciting capabilities. Suppose you want to tell a friend about a really cool page—you don't need to write down the URL and send a separate message later, or even cut-and-paste the URL from the page over to your mail software. Using the MAIL option, or a "mailto:" URL, you can send either the URL or a copy of the text to your friend. In Figure 10.16 you can see sending e-mail from Netscape.

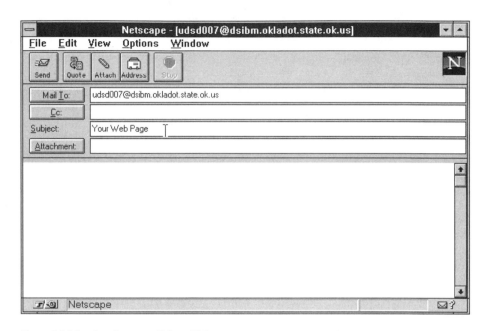

Figure 10.16. **Sending e-mail from Netscape.**

The Netscape browser 2.0 (commercial version) has mail software built right in, so that you can send and receive mail from your browser. Watch for other software to build in this capability in 1996 and 1997. Earlier versions of Netscape had a connection to e-mail, too. Pull down the File menu and choose "Send Mail" or press Ctrl-M.

 WARNING Be careful about what you send around the Internet in e-mail. Not all pages on the WWW are available for casual distribution. Look carefully for the copyright symbol (©). If you see one, read the text attached. If in doubt, just send the URL to folks and let them look for themselves.

Listening to the Radio and Other Sound

You can also listen to sound from your browser, if your PC or workstation has sound capability. And there are hundreds of sites taking advantage of this capability. For example, the White House Web page

```
http://www.whitehouse.gov
```

has recorded messages from the President, Vice President, and First Lady.

There are two ways to hear sound: download and play a sound file, or listen to something called "Real Audio" via your browser.

Sound Files

There are many kinds of sound files available, and, unfortunately, many need different players to hear them. You will also need to have a sound card to hear sound files such as music clips, stereo, and so on. However, your PC speaker can handle some speech and sound files.

Here is a list of the most common files and what players you will need to hear them.

DOS/Windows/Win95   For an extensive list of DOS and Windows file formats, see the Web page at

```
http://www.travelresource.com/form-pc.html
```

Table 10.3 summarizes the most important formats.

File Extension	What is it?	What can I play it on?
.AU	The most common sound format found on the Web. Commonly used by NeXT and UNIX computers.	Use Wplany to play these files.
.AVI	Microsoft's Video for Windows Audio Interleaved. Allows both audio and visual information.	Use Windows Media Player included in Windows to play these files.
.VOC	Creative Labs, Inc. VOiCe format for use with Soundblaster PC sound Card.	Use WPlany to play these files.
.WAV	Microsoft WAVeform format for use with Windows.	You can use WPlany to play these files, or use Windows native programs, such as Windows Media Player.

Table 10.3.   DOS/Windows/Win95 Sound File Formats

The Players   *WPlany* is a versatile sound player that plays AU, IFF, PC raw SND, VOC and WAV format files. You can get it from

```
ftp://ftp.ncsa.uiuc.edu/Mosiac/Windows/viewers/wplny12a.zip
```

Windows Media Player is the application included with Microsoft Windows. It's typically found in the Accessories group under the Program Manager.

Netscape's browser includes an audio player package, too.

For more information about audio players that can be used with browsers, visit one of the many mirror sites for *Stroud's Ultimate Winsock Apps Pages*. The primary sites for these pages, which are extremely useful for Windows users, can be found at

```
http://www.cwsapps.com
```

and

```
http://www.stroud.com
```

Macintosh Files   For a comprehensive listing of Macintosh sound file formats, see the Web page at

```
http://www.travelresource.com/form-mac.html
```

Table 10.4 summarizes the most important formats.

File Extension	What is it?	What can I play it on?
.AU	The most common sound format found on the Web. Binary.	Use Sound Player to play it.
.AIFF	A fairly common sound format. Binary.	Use Sound Player to hear these files.
.WAV	Windows Wave format. Binary.	You can use SoundApp to play .wav files.

Table 10.4: Macintosh Sound File Formats

The Players   *Sound Player* is a multipurpose sound program that can record and play back .au and aiff format sounds. You can find it at

```
http://wwwhost.ots.utexas.edu/mac/pub-mac-sound.html
```

SoundApp is small but will play most audio files. You can find it also at

```
http://wwwhost.ots.utexas.edu/Mac/pub-Mac-sound.html
```

There are many other players for both Macintosh and DOS/Windows. Read the documentation that came with your browser for more information.

Real Audio

Real Audio plays the sounds over your browser and your Internet link, as opposed to you downloading them and listening to them. Many radio shows, such as NPR's All Things Considered, also have their broadcasts available via Real Audio. Figure 10.17 shows the NPR archive of Real Audio information.

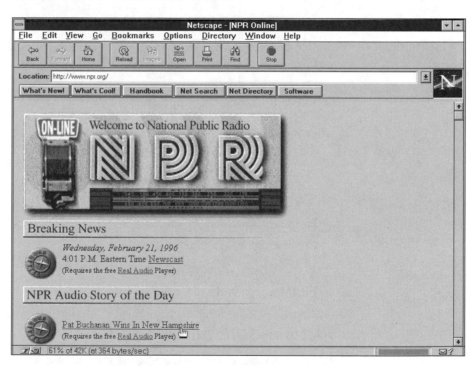

Figure 10.17. **The NPR Real Audio archive via Netscape.**

Real Audio requires that you have a player installed on your machine, and it has other system requirements. Most importantly, you must have a sound card installed on your system. Additionally, Real Audio sounds best over a faster Internet link. If you don't have at least a 28.8 modem,

it may sound like a slowed-down record. And, if there is sudden congestion on the Internet, slowing the packets coming from the server, your
sound may come out attenuated or choppy. But many people think Real
Audio is a tremendous breakthrough in live audio over the Net.

The player is available commercially; test versions are available on
the Net at

`http://www.realaudio.com`

The Real Audio FAQ is located at

`http://www.realaudio.com/help.html`

Real Audio is currently supported on these browsers:

Netscape Navigator

AIR Mosaic (Internet In a Box)

CompuServe connection using AIR Mosaic

Cello WWW Browser

EINet WinWeb

InternetMCI Navigator

NCSA Mosaic

Spyglass Mosaic and Enhanced Mosaic

Microsoft Internet Explorer

Booklink InternetWorks

Quarterdeck Mosaic

NetCruiser (version 2.0 or later)

NetManage Websurfer (version 4.6)

Pictures–Stills and Movies!

It's also possible to download and view a vast array of pictures over the
Internet, including movies. Not only are there static pictures (such as
weather maps, satellite images, stills from movies and TV), there are
also moving pictures available.

Like audio, video requires special helper applications or plug-ins to look
at most pictures. (Most browsers let you view GIFs and JPEGs right in
the browser, but you will need help to see others.) Again, here are the
most common formats and the players you will need to use with them.

DOS/Windows/Win95

Table 10.5 summarizes the most important image and video file formats for DOS/Windows/Win95.

File Extension	What is it?	What can I view it with?
.AVI	Microsoft's Video for Windows Audio Visual Interleaved. Allows both audio and visual information.	Windows Media Player (included in Windows)
.BMP	Microsoft Windows BitMaP format. BMP allows up to 16.7 million colors, but provides no built-in compression	Lview or LviewPro
.FLI, .FLC	Animation program. Popular for playing fractal animations on the Web.	Windows Media Player or AAplay
.JPG, .JPEG, .JIFF	Joint Photographic Experts Group, a 24-bit graphic format.	LView or WinJPEG
.MPG, .MPEG	MPEG (Moving Picture Experts Group) is the standard movie platform for the Net.	Mpegplay
.MOV, .QT, .MOVIE	Quicktime Movie format; Apple Macintosh native movie platform.	Quicktime for Windows
.TGA	TrueVision Targa files from the Amiga family of computers. This format is used as input to create other utilities, such as programs to generate fractals.	Use LView to view them.
.TIFF, .TIF	TIFF (Tagged Image File Format) is a very large high quality image format.	Use LView , or WinJPEG to view.

Table 10.5. **DOS/Windows/Win95 Image and Video File Formats**

The Players *AAplay* (The Autodesk Animation Player) not only provides a Windows-based application to play FLC/FLI animations, but it also extends the Windows Media Player to include these animation formats. You can find it at

`ftp://crusty.er.usgs.gov/pub/animation/fli/waaplay.zip.`

LView is an excellent freeware package for viewing multiple picture formats, including JPEG, BMP, GIF, TGA, etc. LView also provides a few image processing features and supports slide show viewing. Find it at:

`ftp://msdos.archive.umich.edu/msdos/windows/graphics/util/`

Mpegplay is a Windows Win32 application. It plays animations, including sound synchronization if your computer is configured with a Windows sound driver. Find it at

`ftp://princeton.edu:/pub/clk/pc/win3/mpegw32h.zip`

Quicktime for Windows by Apple Computer supplies both a player for QT animations, and a viewer for JPEG files. You'll find it at

`http://www.astro.nwu.edu/lentz/mac/qt/`

Windows Media Player is the application included with Microsoft Windows. It's generally found in the Accessories group under the Program Manager. *WinJPEG* handles multiple formats. It's available via anonymous FTP from

`ftp://ftp.cica.indiana.edu//pub/pc/win3/desktop/winjp265.zip`

Macintosh

Table 10.6 summarizes the most important Macintosh image and video file formats.

File Extension	What is it?	What can I view it with?
.JPG, .JPEG, .JFIF	JPEG/JFIF, a 24 bit graphic format. Binary.	JPEGView.
.MPG, .MPEG	MPEG, the standard movie platform for the Net. Binary.	Sparkle
.MOV, .QT, .MOVIE	QuickTime Movie, Apple Macintosh native movie platform Binary.	Sparkle, FastPlayer, MoviePlayer.
.TIFF, .TIF	TIFF is a very large high quality image format. Binary.	JPEGView

*Table 10.6. **Macintosh Image and Video File Formats***

The Players *JPEGView* is a freeware graphic program designed to read GIF, JPEG, TIFF, and PICT files. It runs fast and will dither nicely to any size of screen/color palette. Source site:

    http://www.med.cornell.edu/jpegview.html

Also:

    ftp://ftp.med.cornell.edu/pub/aarong/jpegview/

Sparkle is widely considered the best MPEG player for the Mac. You can play and convert between Quicktime and MPEG. Get it from

    ftp://ftp.utexas.edu/pub/mac/graphics/

New Stuff

On the Internet, new things happen quickly and interest in them proliferates even more quickly. We've explicitly mentioned the new audio and video applications and their uses exemplified by Real Audio and VDO-live (although these applications are not the *only* new audio and video applications on the Net).

And we've talked about animations within the Web. Some ways to do that include the applications in the presentation program *Astound* from Gold Disk:

    http://www.golddisk.com

This will support animated presentations, streaming to your computer from a server. Probably the hoped-for applications people are talking about most are those that may eventually be possible using Java™, a new language from Sun Microsystems:

    http://www/sun.com

To quote the Javasoft

    http://www.javasoft.com

page, "Java is a simple, object-oriented, distributed, interpreted, robust, secure, architecture-neutral, portable, high-performance, multithreaded, dynamic, buzzword-compliant, general-purpose programming language. Java supports programming for the Internet in the form of platform-independent Java applets." What Sun is trying to tell you is that Java is a language in which programmers can write small applications (applets) that can be downloaded (unless you stop them) onto your computer within a page written for a Java-"compliant" or "enabled" browser. The only Java-enabled browsers available today are Netscape Navigator 2.0 and Sun's HotJava. Hot Java is only available for the Windows NT 3.5 and Windows 95 platforms or for SPARC platforms running Solaris 2.2, 2.4, or 2.5. If you are running Netscape Navigator 2.0 and you don't want to execute Java applets, choose Options ➤ Security Preferences, and click on the box that says "Disable Java."

The Java language is interpreted (executed directly rather than from compiled program code) and will run on many types of computers ("architecture-neutral"). It's called Java to make people think of "live-liness, animation, speed, interactivity, and more."

Why are people excited? Well, because of the potential inherent in such an idea. The programmer can create programs that will run on your computer. Programs that will start automatically; programs that will run the same way on a number of different kinds of computers. Other people are not so excited. They are worried about security and viruses and turning programs loose on unsuspecting users. Probably both views are valid. We'll have to wait and see what wonderful ideas the creative people design and implement.

If you'd like to be among the people who are watching closely, go to the Javasoft page shown above and sign up for one of the mailing lists, or bookmark the page and visit it often. With new technology from one of the world's top technology companies, you can expect that the Java world will be changing fast.

Finding Things?

You still have to know where to start to find things on the Web, and it would be nice to be able to click on a "search" button and find things, wouldn't it? Well, we can't offer you that, but Chapter 12 offers the next best thing: an in-depth presentation of searching the World Wide Web (and the rest of cyberspace).

Now It's Time to Explore!

As we said at the beginning of this chapter, the Web is bringing the resources of the Internet to computer users at all levels of technical sophistication.

The Web is the fastest growing area on the Internet. More and more organizations are announcing more and more servers and pages each week. More and more, Web pages are becoming prime places to do advertising, marketing surveys, and similar kinds of outreach and publicity.

The NCSA What's New Page:

```
http://www.ncsa.uiuc.edu/SDG/Software/Mosaic/Docs/archive
-whats-new.html
```

gets bigger and bigger each week. The number of new Web servers each month is bigger than the number of new Gopher servers and new services that you can reach via Telnet and FTP, although those are all growing, too. The Web allows you to illustrate and describe, to teach and let interested people interact with the information an organization can provide. (In Chapter 20 you'll learn how to create a Web page for your organization.) The Web and the possibilities it presents have truly captured the imagination of many potential information providers.

Other terrific starting points include the What's New and What's Cool pages at Netscape

```
http://www.netscape.com
```

and the What's New page at Yahoo

```
http://www.yahoo.com
```

For a really eclectic start, go to one of the excellent search tools for the Net that you'll find in Chapter 12, and enter a single word like "book" and see all the wonderful things that come back for you to view.

With so many good client programs readily available and the servers relatively easy to install on many differing platforms, the World Wide Web is truly linking threads of information around the globe. Now it's time to start exploring it on your own.

CHAPTER 11

Going for Gopher

FEATURING

Chapter 11
Going for Gopher

LIKE the Web, Gopher is a set of services that let you connect to resources without having to know exactly where you are going ahead of time. Internet users have coined the term *gopherspace* to describe the whole set of computers with Gopher servers and the information they contain. Once you've connected to any Gopher site, the information at all of the sites is available to you, through a hierarchical system of menus. These menus are lists of pointers or links. If you choose to exercise a link, you are "transported" to the next menu until you are viewing a document or downloading a graphical image file, for example. The links may point you to other files on the Gopher server you're connected to, or to files stored on computers halfway around the world. The strength of gopherspace is that you, as a gopherspace-traveler, do not need to know where any of the files are stored.

Of course, if you do have an exact citation, Gopher clients (like most Web browsers) allow you to enter the address directly. And most Gopher clients also have a bookmark facility. Once you've created a bookmark, you can call it up at any time, and the stored link takes you directly to the specific place that you wanted to remember. For example, if you place a bookmark in the National Institute of Environmental Health Sciences Gopher server (gopher.niehs.nih.gov), every time you select that bookmark your client will open the Institute's Gopher page. This feature allows you to keep particularly useful Internet sites at your fingertips.

MASTER WORDS Gopher, like FTP, is beginning to merge with the World Wide Web (from the user's point of view, if not in a narrow technical sense). Since most Gopher resources can be accessed via the Web, most people use their Web browsers to get to gopherholes. This lets some really fine resources become available to more people.

What Gopher Does

Gopher was one of the most exciting developments in Internet tools to come along. Gopher allowed novice users to find many of the cool things we Internet fanatics rave about, without having to be a technical expert to do it. Gopher became one of the tools that let schools and educators find and use resources on the Internet, and because of its simple, text-oriented interface, it was usable on even very low-end workstations over slow links.

More than that, a Gopher server is easy to build and maintain, and many people and organizations found it easier to become Internet information providers.

Since the burst of development on the World Wide Web in the past year, however, most people are using Web browsers to access Gopher resources just as they access Web resources.

Gopher allows you to find and retrieve information using a hierarchy of menus and files. Your Gopher client connects to a Gopher server (like the Michigan State University Gopher illustrated in Figure 11.1) and, using the menu structure, displays another menu, a document or file, an index, or a connection to another remote application using Telnet. The Gopher protocol allows all the Gopher clients on the Internet to talk with all the other "registered" Gopher servers on the Internet. Each time you select another menu, Gopher connects to the linked server, retrieves the next menu level or the file wanted, and returns control to your local client. Gopher both uses Internet resources efficiently and allows you to find and use information dispersed throughout the world.

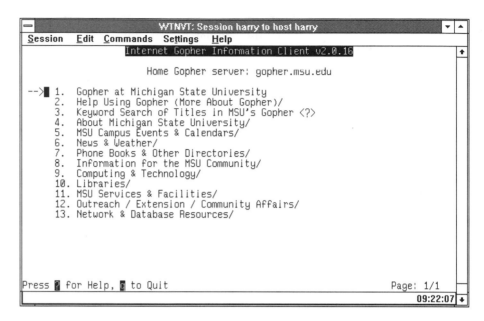

Figure 11.1.   The main Gopher menu at Michigan State University (gopher.msu.edu).

Gopherspace is the universe of Gopher servers connected to the Internet. Each server has a location (Internet address and port number) of its own and links to other Gopher servers. (A port number is just the equivalent of a telephone at which the Gopher server will listen for connection requests.) Most Gopher servers are registered with the Mother Gopher at the University of Minnesota. Its menu contains the option All The Gopher Servers In The World, which you can select to see a list of all the registered Gopher servers. With Gopher you can connect to each and every one of them, regardless of their physical location in the world. A Gopher server must be "up" to listen for your connection, however. Sometimes computers break down or Net connections are lost, and sometimes people just turn off their computers. When this happens, of course, you can't connect to the Gopher.

In general, gopherspace is organized geographically. For example, if you want to see information from South America, from a Gopher menu with links to other servers, choose

    Other gophers

    South America

Gopher will display a menu that gives you access to South American Gopher servers.

If you want to use a separate Gopher client rather than your Web browser, you can. Gopher clients have been written for most of the computing platforms that support the TCP/IP protocol suite. Some of these clients really take advantage of the available user interface. For example, TurboGopher offers the familiar Macintosh point-and-click interface, with buttons and menus. Others run on host computers and operate using the VT100 terminal emulation interface. Note that some Gopher objects (the type of files that Gopher can access) cannot be displayed on all clients. If you are attached as a VT100 terminal to a host computer, you will not be able to see the pictures or hear the audio that can be stored on a server and transmitted by choosing a particular Gopher menu item. But VT100 Gopher clients do serve to connect the user to information located all over the Internet, and they have the advantage that the network connections of many host systems are much better than those of most home systems. This means that you will be able to move large amounts of information to your site more quickly if you are using a Gopher client on a larger host system.

Many Gopher clients will also let you send material back to yourself or to anyone you choose by e-mail or file transfer, right from the Gopher session.

A Brief History of Gopher

Gopher was developed at the University of Minnesota to provide a better interface to distribute campus information for local users. As with many good ideas, the charm and simplicity of Gopher appealed to many people. Gopher servers and Gopher clients soon began to pop up all over the Internet. To find more information about Gopher development and to obtain program source code for Gopher servers and clients, you can use Gopher or FTP clients to connect to the computer called boombox.micro.umn.edu. Or you may use your Web client to connect via http, Gopher, or FTP protocols. This computer supports http, FTP, and Gopher access. You can Gopher there directly by entering boombox .micro.umn.edu with an "open a connection" command that you can find in most Gopher clients; or, from any Gopher, you can choose

```
Other gophers
North America
USA
Minnesota
University of Minnesota
```

This path, while not direct, demonstrates one of the easiest things to understand about navigating via Gopher—the ability to pilot around through many locations and still end up with something useful. Not all people find (or want to find) information in the same manner.

Finding Gopher Clients

If you have a host-dial account on a BBS or other service or if you have an Internet application suite like Netscape Navigator, Microsoft's Internet Explorer, Quarterdeck's Internet Suite, Woologong's Emissary, or Netcom's NetCruiser, you probably already have access to a Gopher client. If you have a VT100 style connection, type gopher at the main system prompt to call up your local Gopher client. Otherwise, you can try entering

```
gopher://scilibx.ucsc.edu
```

or

```
gopher://peg.cwis.uci.edu:7000
```

to reach two interesting Gophers. UC Santa Cruz has an excellent Gopher called InfoSlug that is well organized for easy research. UC Irvine has a super Internet Assistance Gopher called PEG (for Peripatetic Eclectic Gopher).

However, if you are working with TCP/IP-based software on your personal workstation, you may want to install a Gopher client on your workstation. As the originator of Gopher, the University of Minnesota maintains an excellent anonymous FTP site on the host named boom-box with the clients they support, as well as newly submitted clients from contributors in the worldwide Gopher community.

Most popular Gopher clients are capable of dealing with flat ASCII files, folders, and index searches under Gopher. Most clients are also capable of handling the common still-image format GIF (developed by CompuServe). Windows, Windows 95, and Macintosh clients have joined their cousins, the NeXT and Sun workstations, and can play sound (.SND or .WAV) files, which means they can play audio files delivered over the network.

Most of the clients come bundled with several files in an archive format appropriate to the computer and operating system you will be using them on. Most also have DOC or README files that assist in using the clients.

Windows Gopher Clients

There are several clients available for Windows. BCGopher, GophBook, and HGopher all need Windows 3.1 and WINSOCK.DLL. These clients have been tested using Windows 3.1, WINSOCK.DLL, and PCTCP software 2.2.

BCGopher

This client is available via FTP from Minnesota at

    boombox.micro.umn.edu

in /pub/gopher/Windows/bcg08b.exe, and some directions are available from the same site in /pub/gopher/Windows/bcg08b.txt. The file is a self-extracting archive.

GophBook

This client is available via FTP from Minnesota at `boombox.micro.umn.edu` in /pub/gopher/Windows/gophbook. Items in this Gopher client are displayed as pages in a book. GophBook can display images when used in conjunction with a Windows viewer. You can also play sound, and save and edit bookmarks.

HGopher

This client is available via FTP from

    lister.cc.ic.ac.uk

"in pub/wingopher as well as from the `boombox` site noted above. It uses a familiar Windows interface. In addition to the common features found in GophBook, HGopher can support user-specified "viewers" for displaying almost any type of document. The `lister` FTP site also includes several Windows viewers in the pub/wingopher/viewers directory.

Apple Macintosh Gopher Clients

Our favorite client for the Macintosh is Turbogopher, from the University of Minnesota. It is faster than earlier Macintosh clients, uses icons to distinguish document types, and opens multiple windows on screen as necessary. Turbogopher is capable of launching GIF viewers installed on your Mac. This client is also available from

    boombox.micro.umn.edu

in the /pub/gopher/Macintosh-TurboGopher directory.

Part
II

The Internet Toolkit

Other Types of Gopher Clients

Also at the boombox.micro.umn.edu site are clients for OS/2, DOS, MVS, Amiga, Windows NT, VMS, and VM/CMS operating system environments. You can see that one reason that people use Gopher to provide information is that there are clients for so many of the common computing systems in use today.

How to Use Gopher

To use Gopher from a UNIX host system Gopher client, type:

```
gopher
```

This command will connect you to the local or default Gopher server for your host. On the Netcom host systems, for example, this command is the same as entering

```
gopher gopher.netcom.com
```

The Netcom Gopher server will then display the top-level menu, as shown in Figure 11.2.

As an example, we will find and retrieve the local access numbers for Netcom's network. From the displayed menu, we see that the second menu entry is

```
Information about NETCOM
```

This looks like a reasonable place to find information about the access numbers, so we select the item (using the arrow keys) and press Enter. This connects the Gopher client to the Gopher server and requests a connection to the link specified by this menu entry.

When this connection is made, you'll see the menu shown in Figure 11.3.

From here, you can move your cursor to the Netcom Local Access Numbers entry and press the Enter key. Again, this connects the Gopher client to the Gopher server and requests a connection to the link specified. The server will then pass the specified file of access numbers to your client, which will display them on your screen (Figure 11.4).

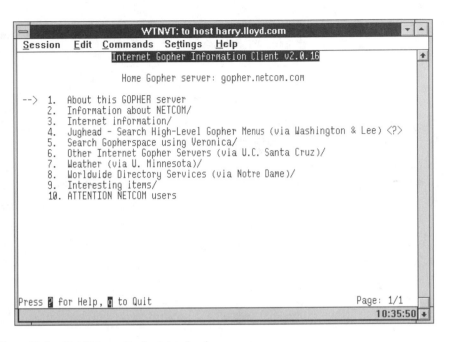

Figure 11.2. **The Netcom Gopher's top-level menu.**

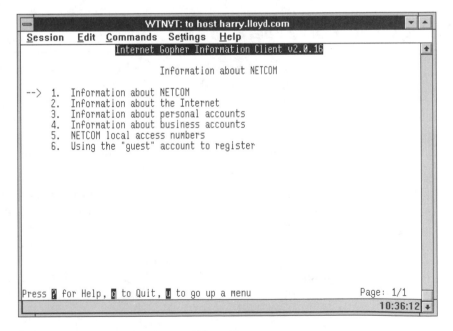

Figure 11.3. **The Information about Netcom menu.**

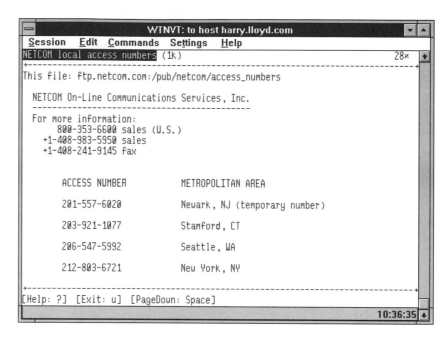

Figure 11.4. ***The Netcom access numbers located by our Gopher search.***

Things You Can Expect to Do

Gopher clients offer some other features besides connecting you to documents and other files. The most important of these is saving the item you've retrieved. Some clients move the desired files to a host system and you will need to download them to your local machine. Others save directly to the local machine. Some send them to you via your e-mail account. Again, you will need to consult the help files in your Gopher client software to see how it can best serve you.

Sometimes you don't really want the file itself, you just want to be able to get to this "gopherhole" again directly. Consider the electronic books stored in various servers on the Internet. Or the size of the CIA World Factbook, a reference work with information gathered about countries all over the world (see Chapter 22). You don't really need a personal copy of the material—you just need to get to it again promptly when you want. This is perhaps the most wonderful feature of gopherspace—the fact that multiple copies of the same work don't need to be made and yet many, many people can read the material. It is a magnificent saving in time, disk space, and resources.

To keep your own personal reference pointer to the Factbook, investigate the ability of your client to store "bookmarks." These are files that contain pointers that link information to a specific item in a specific Gopher server menu. Unfortunately, bookmarks work at the item level; there is not yet a way to go to exactly the line you were reading when you stopped reading.

In large documents, like the country entries in the CIA World Factbook, it is nice to be able to go quickly to a specific known point. Or to find whether a specific point is present in the file. To serve this function, many Gopher clients have a search capability. You select the Search option, enter the word or words you are looking for, and the Gopher client moves your cursor to the point in the document where that word appears.

For navigation within a menu and a server, Gopher uses the command Back or Up. The spatial metaphor refers to what you've done before arriving at your current point. If you choose this command, you will be returned to the last menu you viewed before this one. You can continue to choose Back until you reach the menu at which you entered gopherspace for this session. Sometimes this "gopherhole" is called "home." To go back to the previous spot, most Gopher clients use the left-arrow key.

What Kinds of Information Will I Find in Gopherspace?

Information in gopherspace can be any of the following:

another menu (sometimes represented by a folder icon)

a document, a graphic file, or a text file (sometimes represented by a document icon)

a search entry (sometimes represented by a magnifying glass icon)

a pointer to a text-based remote login (Telnet)

a pointer to a software gateway to another service (Usenet or FTP)

Veronica and Jughead

Veronica (Very Easy Rodent-Oriented Net-wide Index to Computer Archives) and Jughead are Gopher services that construct menus for you, based on "keywords" you enter. (As the names suggest, they're related to the Archie tool, which you'll learn about in Chapter 12.) To try either of these tools, bring up the main Veronica Gopher, at

```
gopher.scs.unr.edu
```

From the main menu, select either Veronica or Jughead. As in Figure 11.5, you'll be asked to enter the word or words you would like to find—the *search argument*. Veronica searches the menu titles of the Gopher servers that are known in gopherspace and constructs a personal menu showing the titles available for you to access. Figure 11.6 shows the "personal Gopher" displayed for the word *business*.

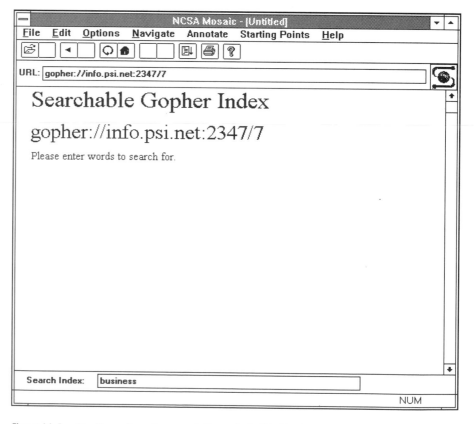

Figure 11.5. **Starting a Veronica search through the World Wide Web.**

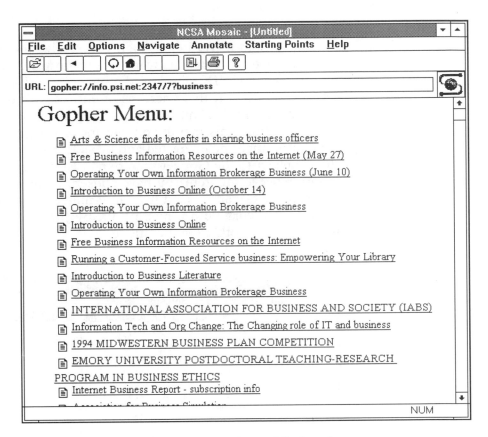

Figure 11.6. Results of a Veronica search on the word "business."

Jughead does much the same thing, but it looks only at the higher level Gopher menu titles rather than all the available menus on all levels. Jughead searches are occasionally restricted to searching the menus that appear in a particular Gopher. This service is offered by the particular Gopher server and must have been set up by the Gopher administrator or designer at the site. Once you have received the search results from your Veronica or Jughead search, you interact with the Jughead- or Veronica-built menu just the way you would with any other Gopher.

MASTER WORDS   Sometimes Jughead searches are called "Search Gopherspace by Top-Level Menus" rather than Jughead.

As an example of such a menu, from the Netcom Gopher, choose the Jughead search menu item. When you receive the prompt asking for your search term, enter the word **telecommunications**. At this writing, using the UNIX client on the Netcom host systems, this search returned a menu with 17 screens of entries with the word "telecommunications" in their menu title. (Figure 11.7 shows the first of these screens.) From this menu, you can move your cursor to an item in which you might be interested and press Enter. The Gopher client will then connect to the Gopher server and, using the link provided by the menu, retrieve the item you have chosen. If the item is a document, you can use e-mail to send it to an e-mail address or you can download it. You work with a menu built by Jughead the same way you would with any other Gopher menu.

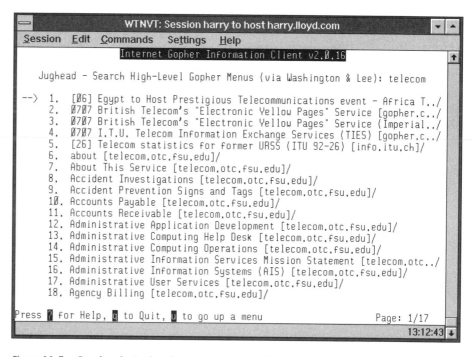

Figure 11.7. **Results of a Jughead search on the word "telecommunications."**

MASTER WORDS Many Gophers display pages that are not self-identifying. That is, you cannot tell by looking at the page where the information came from. Usually, that is not important. But if you see an announcement of a lecture you would like to attend, for example, it would be nice to know in which town, state, and country the lecture is being given. Most clients have a way to display the fully qualified name and address of the server from which information is being shown. Using the help screen (press "?" in most clients), you can discover how your client displays this information. In some clients it's called "technical info about this item or directory." In most line-mode clients, press ^ to show the fully qualified name. This name might help you locate the site from which the information is being displayed.

Taking Advantage of Geography

With its easy-to-use navigation tools and hierarchical structure, Gopher lends itself to browsing. This is particularly true if there's a geographical focus to your interest. If you want information about South America, for example, you might just wander through the

```
All the gophers in the World

South America
```

hierarchy. By selecting links that look promising, and using the Up and Back options, you can move around the globe, looking for information in a quick, but relatively unstructured, way. Sometimes, browsing in this manner will help you find information about a topic that you wouldn't have thought about, or whose specific category name you didn't know. Not to mention, of course, that it's fun!

CHAPTER 12

**Resource Discovery—
Finding Things
on the Internet**

FEATURING

Chapter 12

Resource Discovery—Finding Things on the Internet

THE Internet basic tools discussed in previous chapters—e-mail, FTP, Telnet, the Web, and Gopher—give you the necessary information to transfer files to your machine, to send and receive messages, to log in to a remote computer on which you have an account; and to use hierarchical menus or hypertext links to move around in Cyberspace. These are wonderful things to know, but if you want to find the address of a specific person to whom you want to send e-mail, what do you do? How do you know where a file you want to transfer might be found? How do you find a Web page if you don't know its URL or other pages it may be linked to? How can you find some specific services or Internet presence in which you are interested? This chapter attempts to address these questions.

In 1995, the problem of finding things on the Internet became vastly easier with the advent of searchable databases. The early ones, The Web Worm and the CUI indexes, were great boons. Then came Lycos and Yahoo and InfoSeek and … Corporate sponsorship (and the ability to run ads on these terribly popular sites) has helped these network search tools grow and become even more useful.

Today, you can find almost anything with these tools. Sometimes one of the older tools is faster, and in that instance we have given you instructions on how to use the old standby.

In this chapter, to avoid confusion (because you can do almost anything with a Web search tool), we've put all the Web search engines in one section, and refer you to that section if it applies elsewhere.

MASTER WORDS When you navigate the Internet, be sure to keep a notepad by your computer. This way you can note down the address or URL of interesting items; there's nothing worse than finding a gold mine and not being able to get back there again! Some Internet tool client programs, particularly for the navigation programs like Web browsers and Gopher (discussed in Chapters 10 and 11), provide a bookmark facility to store markers. These facilities let you leave a signpost for a page or Gopher menu where you think you'd like to come back again. When you use a bookmark, your computer makes the notes for you.

Finding People

It remains true that the very best method to discover the e-mail address of a particular person is to ask him or her. This method guarantees that you have found the preferred e-mail address for your proposed correspondent (some people have several e-mail addresses, and they use these addresses for different things).

It also confirms that your correspondent will actually participate in e-mail correspondence. Some people have e-mail addresses and don't use them. One sure sign of this is the response "Hmm, I don't really have that at my fingertips. I'll let my secretary get back to you with that information." (Glee actually heard a United States Representative say that to a roomful of constituents who had just listened to him speak on the virtues of "The Information Superhighway.") This example does illustrate the second-best method, though, which is to ask someone *else* who would know the address you need.

Occasionally, however, it is difficult or inconvenient to ask for an e-mail address. You may want to correspond with an expert in a field about which you need information. Or you may want to send e-mail to an address representing a functional position, rather than a specific person. In the first case, you'll want to choose methods of determining the exact e-mail address for a person. In the second case, you'll be looking more for a specific Internet domain to which to send your message.

MASTER WORDS Several of the Web search engines, in particular DejaNews and WhoWhere?, are good at finding people.

Let's take a really easy case. Suppose you want to send a message to the President of the United States giving your opinion about, say, a proposed executive position on taxation. This example is one of the "ask someone" variety. It's included in practically every book about the Internet and every basic e-mail training class; and virtually everyone who has used the Internet in the United States knows it. Address your e-mail to:

```
president@whitehouse.gov
```

But suppose for a moment that we are stuck at home without immediate access to our friends and colleagues who already know this information, so we will use a few Internet tools to identify the appropriate address.

Finger

Finger (introduced in Chapter 7's "Who Knows What about Me?" discussion) is an Internet standard tool that lets you "reach out and touch" a computer on the Internet with your "finger" to find out information about "accounts" that are registered on that host. Each Finger client (as you would expect) uses similar syntax to say "touch the account named *user* at the host computer *hostname*." For UNIX systems, the command looks like

```
finger user@hostname
```

Some hosts will return a list of all the accounts on the system if you send the command

```
finger @hostname
```

Note that in this case, you left the user ID part of the command blank.

If you try the command

```
finger clinton@whitehouse.gov
```

you will see one of the first problems with this particular facility. Not all sites support the command. Some sites choose not to support it for security reasons, not wanting everyone who can connect to the Internet and issue the command to be able to access a particular user or a user list at the site. Others make the same decision for considerations of privacy rather than security. So, in early 1996, you receive the message shown in Figure 12.1, to the effect that Finger is not supported for arbitrary addresses within the whitehouse.gov domain.

Figure 12.1. **Results from Fingering the White House.**

The message continues with the information that electronic mail may be sent to the addresses

    president@whitehouse.gov

and

    vice-president@whitehouse.gov

The command did tell us that we have the correct domain identifier, though. With that information we can use the Whois service to obtain more information about this domain.

On some systems, Finger will return more information than a simple association of user ID and "full name." Finger will display some information about the system associated with the domain in question and some information about the user. On UNIX systems in particular, Finger can be configured by the host administrator to display the user ID, the full name of the user, the last time the user was logged in to the system, whether mail is waiting, and the arrival time of the last

Part
II

The Internet Toolkit

received message. Figure 12.2 shows a Finger response with all of this information.

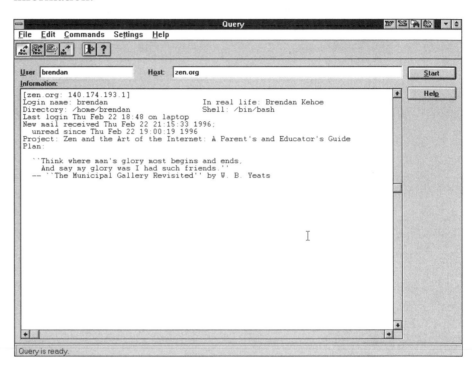

Figure 12.2.   A typical Finger response.

Some systems will respond to a blank user ID. Finger will then answer with a display of all the active users on that host system. Sometimes that response contains many users, and therefore, will be quite long. When you try this you may want to send (or "pipe" on a UNIX system) the results of your Finger command through a paging command like more, or you may want to send the results to a file. To "pipe" your answer through the more command, enter

    finger @*hostname* | more

To send the results to a file, enter

    finger @hostname > filename

Figure 12.3 shows the result of a Finger command.

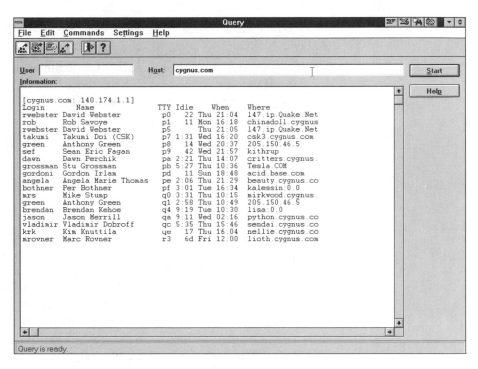

Figure 12.3.   Using Finger to see who is signed onto a large system.

From this discussion, you will no doubt have noticed that you need to have the name of the appropriate Internet host in order to use the Finger command to find a user on another system. On most systems if you just enter the command finger *userID*, you will only be looking on the system to which you are connected. Of course, the information you can retrieve about other users of your local host system can also be useful: Are they connected now (so you can perhaps try the Talk command, described in Chapter 15)? Have they read all their mail?

But let's say you want to find our friend, Sue Joiner, and someone told you only that she is working now for the Merit network. Finger won't yet be the appropriate tool to use. You need more information than you have now. You need to find out what host name would be appropriate to use. The Whois database is a good place to look for that information.

Whois—Searching for Registered Domains

The Whois service is a client/server program in which the client queries the Internet database of domains for information about particular domains. If you are logged on to a machine that supports Whois queries, you may get a response simply by entering

```
whois domain-identifier
```

at a command prompt. On some host systems, for example, if you enter

```
whois whitehouse
```

or

```
whois merit
```

the client program will check the nearest copy of the database (that is, nearest in network geography, not in physical geography) and return what information it can. If the server is not the "official" domain database, which is kept by the InterNIC, the information will be accompanied by a disclaimer stating that you might want to check the information with the official listing before you consider it valid. Normally, the only reasons to check the official data would be to determine if a domain had been assigned but not yet completely distributed throughout the domain name system, or to confirm an IP address before doing something that required an absolute IP address. If you were planning to register a domain name, you would want to make sure it had not already been used. With the acceptance of the domain name system and more and more implementations of it among TCP/IP software vendors, there are fewer and fewer reasons to need to know the IP address of a particular site. Although its usefulness to most Internet users might seem limited, Whois is pretty handy if you want to find the domain of a company to guess its Web site name or a host on which to issue a Finger command.

Many suites of TCP/IP software for your desktop come with a program that will do both Finger and Whois queries. To do Whois queries you will need to tell the program to search at the main Whois database at `rs.internic.net`.

At this writing, the `whitehouse` search returns the display shown in Figure 12.4. It shows that `whitehouse.gov` is the relevant domain. If you continue searching by entering `whitehouse.dom` as the argument to your Whois search, you'll find that there is a domain called `EOP.DOM`.

(We assume that EOP stands for Executive Office of the President.) Anyway, if you're interested, you can find out who the administrative and technical coordinators are for the Executive Office's IP network this way. The same is true of the merit.edu domain.

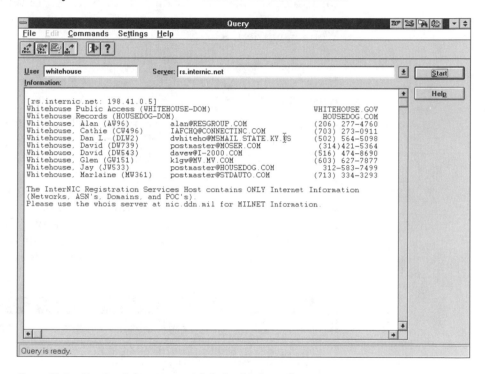

Figure 12.4. Results of the command "whois whitehouse."

The Whois database also contains information about a number of registered individuals. Unfortunately, the Whois database contains only the people who have voluntarily registered themselves. If you don't find an entry here for a particular person, all you know is that the person is not registered with the InterNIC. You'll need to look elsewhere for information that is missing. Most Internet users are not individually registered.

If you do not have direct access to the Whois database (by entering the command Whois at a command prompt or by using a whois function on your local system), you can use one of the public Whois servers by using Telnet to login to the remote server. The authoritative server is located at `rs.internic.net`. If you connect to this host via Telnet, you will receive instructions that will tell you how to search the Whois database.

If you prefer not to use Telnet, you can use one of the Internet navigator programs like Gopher or your favorite World Wide Web browser to connect to the InterNIC site. Gopher to `rs.internic.net`. Or, in the Web, enter the URL

```
http://rs.internic.net/rs-internic.html
```

If you scroll down the resulting page to "Registration Tools," you'll see a listing for Whois.

To find the appropriate domain for Sue Joiner takes a bit more work. A search for the word "joiner" returns some results, but none of them are Sue. She's not registered in the Whois registration database. So you need to search for "merit." If you enter a search for that word, as in Figure 12.5, you'll see a number of entries, some of which are names of people, some of which are names of domains. Since you are pretty sure that Sue is still in Michigan, you look among the entries for Merit Network and find the primary domain record for Merit. Now you can go on and use Netfind to find out if there is information about Sue in that domain.

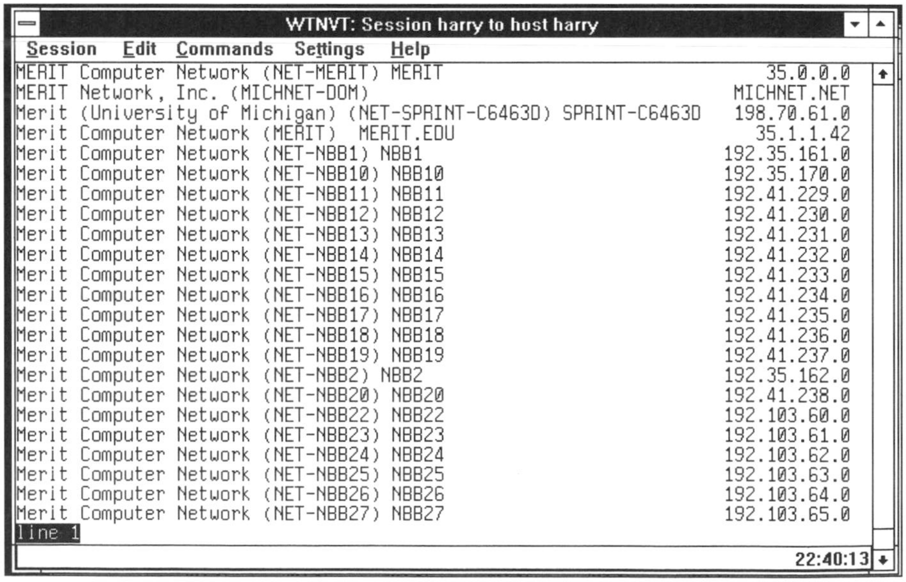

```
┌─────────────────────────────────────────────────────────────────────┐
│ ─               WTNVT: Session harry to host harry           ▼ ▲ │
├─────────────────────────────────────────────────────────────────────┤
│ Session   Edit  Commands  Settings   Help                           │
│ MERIT Computer Network (NET-MERIT) MERIT                35.0.0.0  ↑ │
│ MERIT Network, Inc. (MICHNET-DOM)                     MICHNET.NET    │
│ Merit (University of Michigan) (NET-SPRINT-C6463D) SPRINT-C6463D 198.70.61.0 │
│ Merit Computer Network (MERIT)  MERIT.EDU               35.1.1.42    │
│ Merit Computer Network (NET-NBB1) NBB1               192.35.161.0    │
│ Merit Computer Network (NET-NBB10) NBB10             192.35.170.0    │
│ Merit Computer Network (NET-NBB11) NBB11             192.41.229.0    │
│ Merit Computer Network (NET-NBB12) NBB12             192.41.230.0    │
│ Merit Computer Network (NET-NBB13) NBB13             192.41.231.0    │
│ Merit Computer Network (NET-NBB14) NBB14             192.41.232.0    │
│ Merit Computer Network (NET-NBB15) NBB15             192.41.233.0    │
│ Merit Computer Network (NET-NBB16) NBB16             192.41.234.0    │
│ Merit Computer Network (NET-NBB17) NBB17             192.41.235.0    │
│ Merit Computer Network (NET-NBB18) NBB18             192.41.236.0    │
│ Merit Computer Network (NET-NBB19) NBB19             192.41.237.0    │
│ Merit Computer Network (NET-NBB2) NBB2               192.35.162.0    │
│ Merit Computer Network (NET-NBB20) NBB20             192.41.238.0    │
│ Merit Computer Network (NET-NBB22) NBB22             192.103.60.0    │
│ Merit Computer Network (NET-NBB23) NBB23             192.103.61.0    │
│ Merit Computer Network (NET-NBB24) NBB24             192.103.62.0    │
│ Merit Computer Network (NET-NBB25) NBB25             192.103.63.0    │
│ Merit Computer Network (NET-NBB26) NBB26             192.103.64.0    │
│ Merit Computer Network (NET-NBB27) NBB27             192.103.65.0    │
│ line 1                                                               │
├─────────────────────────────────────────────────────────────────────┤
│                                                    22:40:13 ↓ │
└─────────────────────────────────────────────────────────────────────┘
```

Figure 12.5. **Results of "whois merit" command.**

Netfind

Netfind is another tool for finding individuals on the Net. The original Netfind server is located on the Internet host

```
bruno.cs.colorado.edu
```

To find whether this program is available on your host, enter the command `netfind` at the command prompt. If you receive an error message, like

```
Command invalid
```

or something similar, you know you'll need to look elsewhere for this service.

To use Netfind to find an e-mail address for a person, you will need two pieces of information about them—one distinguishing part of their name and one part of a domain in which you might expect to find them. Mike Schwartz of the University of Colorado began the development of Netfind with the idea that with these two pieces of information, it should be possible to determine possible (and then best-possible) e-mail addresses for people.

Let's continue with our example of Sue Joiner at Merit. On a system that is running Netfind, you would enter

```
netfind joiner merit
```

As Figure 12.6 shows, you will receive a message that tells you that too many possible hosts were found with *merit* as part of their domain name. The possible hosts will be displayed and you will be asked to pick not more than three from among the displayed names.

Let's pick the host `merit.edu`. As shown in Figure 12.7, we enter the number of that host listing at the prompt, and Netfind will continue processing. Using Finger among other tools, Netfind displays the information for Sue Joiner. By looking at the fully qualified domain name for the machine that Sue used to connect to merit.edu, Netfind recommends the e-mail address

```
smj@pony.merit.edu
```

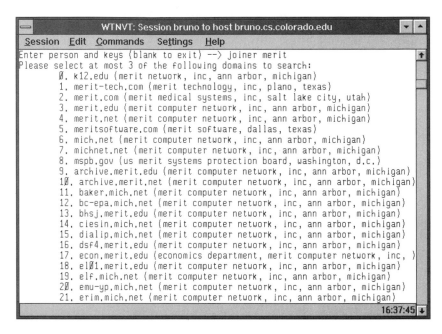

Figure 12.6. *Results of the command "netfind joiner merit."*

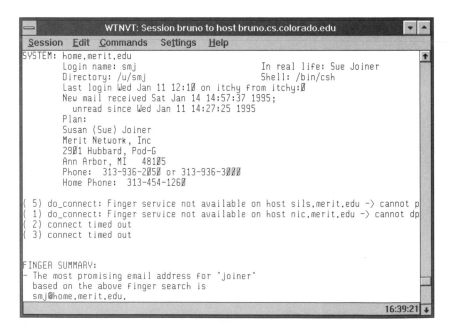

Figure 12.7. *Netfind yields Sue Joiners's whereabouts!*

TELNETTING TO NETFIND

If the host to which you are connected does not run Netfind, you can Telnet to one of the publicly accessible Netfind servers. The original server is at the University of Colorado. Telnet to `bruno.cs.colorado.edu`, as we've done here:

Log in as `netfind`. The server limits Netfind connections, so your connection may be refused (although the one shown here was successful). However, the server lists all other Netfind servers that can be used. Select one that is reasonable for you. Remember that sometimes servers that are geographically nearby may not be good choices. Consider how much activity there is likely to be in your time zone. It might be less load on the Internet as a whole to connect to a machine that is 9 or 10 hours away, because that computer is not as busy serving its local users. (If your geography is a little rusty, you can use Gopher to find the 'Local time' displays from around the world.)

Netfind will not find everybody who can receive e-mail via the Internet. For example, there is no way to inquire about the e-mail addresses of people who are connected to the Internet through an e-mail gateway. If your correspondent uses GEnie, for example, there is no way for Netfind to discover and recommend an address for that person. If your correspondent is in a location where the X.500 directory standard has been implemented, you can use the Gopher to X.500 address gateway or you can use the Paradise system directory.

Paradise

Paradise is a directory user agent (DUA) for an X.500 server that is located in the United Kingdom. A *user agent* is another name for a client program—just differing terminology for the same concept. In this case, the client program is an agent that consults the directory on behalf of the user (you). X.500 is an international standard for geographically hierarchical directories. The concept behind X.500 is the same as your telephone directory: you need to know the geographical location of the person you are trying to reach. Without that information, you don't know in what part of the directory to look. This is the same as needing to know the city in which your friend resides before you can consult the telephone directory for her telephone number.

X.500 is used much more in Europe than in the United States at this time. To use it, Telnet to

```
paradise.ulcc.ac.uk
```

and enter dua at the login prompt. You'll see the display shown in Figure 12.8.

The Paradise directory service helps you to find out information about people and the organizations they work for. The introductory material displayed when you connect reminds you that once you have provided information about a person's name and where they are based, the

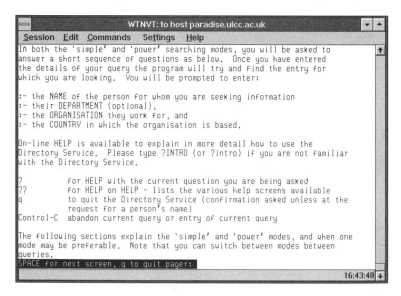

Figure 12.8. **The main Paradise instruction screen.**

Part
II

The Internet Toolkit

directory service will search various local and remote databases to try and find information about people with a name matching the one you have given.

Like all services of this kind, the directory service can, of course, only find entries for people who work for organizations that are participating in this pilot service. Paradise is a good place to look for the e-mail addresses of people who work for organizations concerned with international standards because the directory itself is an early implementation of the X.500 distributed directory standard.

CSO Phone Books

This brief list wouldn't be complete without mentioning the CSO phone books that are kept at some university Internet sites. CSO is another client (paired with the *ph* server) program named for its original developer, the Computing Services Organization of the University of Illinois. These are searchable databases that allow you to search by name, user ID, or department. The searchable fields vary with each implementation of the database. For universities, the academic department can be a search term. This field is not usually relevant if the organization is not an academic institution, and other fields may be used instead. A CSO phone book is frequently the faculty-staff directory for an institution. You can find the list of current servers relatively easily by Gophering to Notre Dame University in Indiana and choosing menu items that lead you to the World Wide "telephone" book list, as in Figure 12.9.

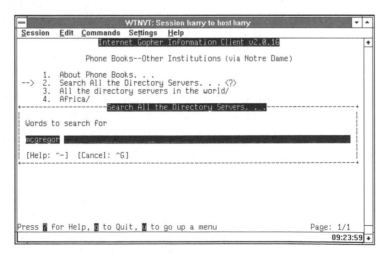

Figure 12.9.   A Gopher search of all the connected phone books.

The methods we've just described depend upon your knowing the site through which your correspondent is connected to the Internet. This is the same problem as trying to use the directory services provided by the telephone companies in the United States. If you know approximately where the person you want to reach lives, your chances of being able to discover their number are pretty good, unless they choose to be unlisted. Pretty much the same is true of directory services available on the Internet. While the Internet itself allows you to break the barriers of time zones and geographical location, the directories haven't caught up quite yet.

Switchboard and Other People Pages

More and more people-finding services are showing up on the Web. One that collects information from telephone book white pages and makes it available is "Switchboard" at

```
http://www.switchboard.com
```

You can enter just a last name or a first and last name and further specify a city to help narrow your search. If you have an unusual last name (like "Harrah", for example), it's interesting to see how many people of that name you can find. The version available in early March 1996 shows the names, addresses and phone numbers of anyone who has a listed telephone number. There are no e-mail addresses yet.

Susan Estrada, who was a founder of CERFNet, one of the original NSFNET Regional Networks, now operates a service called NetPages. There are yellow (business), and blue (survival guide) as well as white pages (people). You'll find that searchable service at

```
http://www.aldea.com
```

You can download portions of these pages to your printer, too. This directory has e-mail addresses and URL references. If the registered user chooses, a picture can be linked in, too.

Many local telephone companies provide telephone number information by dialing 411. There's one on the Net, too. You'll find it at

```
http://www.four11.com
```

There'll be new ones coming along, too. Look at them; try them out. See which one fits your needs. Some will help you find people's e-mail addresses, others telephone numbers. When you find one that works for you, be sure and register so that other people can find you.

Finding Stuff: Files, Articles, Pictures, and Libraries

The best thing about today's Internet is the enormous range of resources on it. The worst thing, of course, is that there's no coherent guide to those resources. Finding information can be a nightmare or a serendipitous delight. However, in the last year finding "stuff" on the Internet has become so much easier that school children are doing it on a daily basis from their school computer labs.

Web search engines have been developed that will help you hunt for research material on the Net. In past weeks we've looked up research on Arab tents, slipglazing as a ceramics decoration technique, and Renaissance music samples on-line.

These Web search engines all work in much the same way: Someone, either a staffer who spends all his or her time looking for cool things on the Net, or the creator of an Internet resource, enters the URL of a site into the search database. The categorizing software picks up key words and, when you make your search, brings up a list of sites where the search terms you gave it match. They all work with different search methods; while there are many overlapping sites in the larger databases, not every site is registered or categorized in every database. Therefore, it is worth your while to try more than one.

When you send your search term to the database, a program compares your term to all the entries in the database. The program builds a personal Web page, with appropriate links, which is displayed as a result of your search. You can then use this Web page to move to any (or all) of the pages whose references met your search criteria. If you would like to save the results of your search, you download or save the page to your computer.

 MASTER WORDS Netscape's browser has a button right on the main screen called *Net Search.* Click on it to find one of the most comprehensive lists of Web search engines out there. For those of you not using Netscape, the URL of this page is:

`http://home.netscape.com/home/internet-search.html`

One thing you will notice right away is that there are lots of ads on the search engines. This is to your advantage; these advertisers are gambling that while you are running a search, you might wander off to see their product. It seems to be working. The benefit to you is that their support helps keep these valuable search engines up-to-date while improving their technology all the time.

Some of the search engines have a limited free database and a more extensive database to which you can subscribe. You'll have to decide whether the increased database is worth subscribing to, with the world of free search engines on the Net.

Lycos

One of our favorite search engines is Lycos, developed by Carnegie-Mellon University (`http://www.lycos.com/`). This comprehensive index of the Internet finds what you need very quickly, usually in less than seconds, including text, pictures, audio, and videos. *PC World* rated Lycos best of the top 11 Internet search engines in late 1995, for quality of information and how well they matched your search terms to the results.

Most of the search engines work the same way as Lycos. We'll do a complete search here to show you how it works. For fun, let's search on a very noncomputer topic–sheep!

Figure 12.10 shows the Lycos opening screen. The Lycos big search engine for access to over three and a half million Web pages. Type the word or words you want to search for in the space provided. Lycos will hunt among the thousands of pages for those which match your search parameters most closely.

Lycos, like most search engines, will scale the retrieved documents according to how well they match your parameters. If you gave five keywords, and they all showed up in the document's keywords, the title, or in the text itself, the document would be a 1.000 match. If only one showed up, deep in the text, it would have a lower grade, perhaps 0.2. Generally, you have a good search result if the sites you find have 0.6 or better grading.

In Figure 12.11, we see that Lycos returns both a set of matches with the word "sheep" in the keywords, and also gives you summaries of the top 10 matches. You can either click on the key word in the list, or scroll down to see the top ten matches.

Figure 12.10.   The Lycos main screen gives you access to the big search engine and over 3.5 million Web pages.

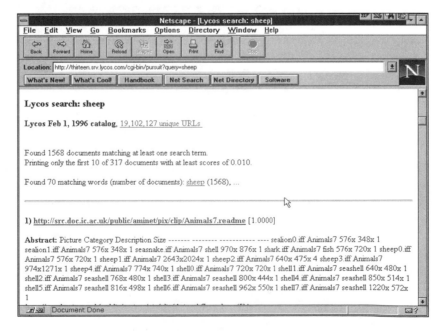

Figure 12.11.   Lots of sheep flock to join our search results!

Just for fun, we clicked on the keyword "sheephomepage"—after all, wouldn't you want to see what kind of a home page a sheep would build? Figure 12.12 shows what we found there.

Figure 12.12.   *Sheep Home page–How are Ewe?*

EINET Galaxy

Another distributed index organized by topic is the one at Galaxy, started at EINet within their Manufacturing Automation and Design Engineering project. EINET became TradeWave Corporation in 1995. According to their literature, "TradeWave" emphasizes their commitment to electronic commerce and enthusiasm for the coming wave of opportunities. TradeWave is a wholly-owned subsidiary of SunRiver Corporation.

Galaxy uses volunteer "editors" with particular expertise to construct pages that provide links to other pages. One reason that we like it is that there are lots of eclectic and unusual links archived here that don't always make it onto the bigger search engines. We also like the personal touch from the volunteer editors. Figure 12.13 shows how to start a search on Galaxy.

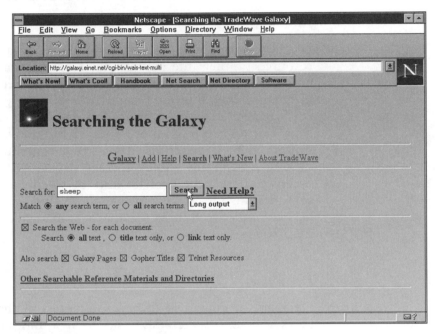

Figure 12.13.   **Searching for sheep on Galaxy.**

To try this Galaxy, navigate to

```
http://galaxy.einet.net/galaxy.html
```

Other Search Engines

There are many other search engines out there. We're listing as many as we can find; you will likely discover more.

AliWeb

AliWeb is a British search engine, sponsored by NEXOR, a company that specializes in providing electronic communication products and services worldwide. AliWeb was one of the early free search engines. Try it out at:

```
http://web.nexor.co.uk/public/aliweb/search/doc/form.html
```

Alta Vista

Digital Equipment Corporation developed Alta Vista as a way to find resources on their internal Intranet. Now they have made it available as a public search index, and as a product that other companies can use to index their own internal resources. Alta Vista gives both verbose and very compact search results. Digital claims that Alta Vista can help you find your way through more than 12 billion words on more than 21 million Web pages. It also provides a full-text index of more than 13,000 newsgroups. The full-text searching, instead of keywords, means you are more likely to find the word you are looking for in the search. It also means you are likely to find more irrelevant material, because if the word turns up anywhere in a page, Alta Vista will present that page to you. Try it out at:

```
http://altavista.digital.com/
```

DejaNews

DejaNews claims to be the world's largest publicly searchable Usenet news archive. It is certainly easier to look things up on DejaNews than to use the UNIX search facility, *grep,* at the main Usenet archive at MIT! DejaNews has very versatile search options to let you find articles by date, author, subject, and newsgroup. DejaNews is a particularly good resource for finding the e-mail address of a single individual on the Internet, particularly if you think that person has ever posted a news article. We look for the name of a friend in Figure 12.14, and the results show in Figure 12.15. (Be sure to use the AND option if you're looking up a "firstname lastname" pair.)

You can also access the Britannica Encyclopedia from the DejaNews Web page, although you will have to buy an account. See for yourself at:

```
http://www.dejanews.com/
```

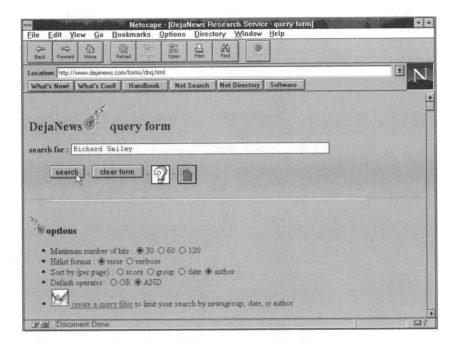

Figure 12.14. **Looking up a friend in the DejaNews database.**

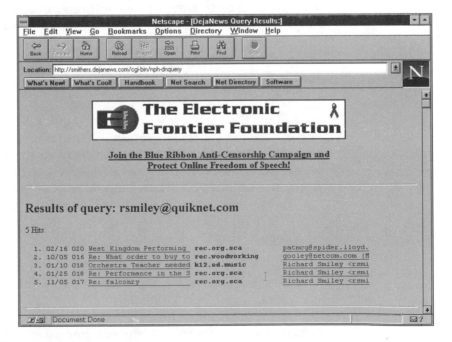

Figure 12.15. **The results of our search.**

Excite

Excite hunts for information by searching for concepts, not keywords. This means that you can type your query in the form of a phrase or near sentence. Excite's database contains what the company claims are more than 1.5 million Web pages, 50,000-plus Web page reviews written by journalists, the latest two weeks of Usenet news, and classifieds. The Excite staff also claims that their database is updated on a weekly basis. Excite also includes City.Net, news from Reuters, and an interactive cartoon. Try it at:

```
http://www.excite.com/
```

The Electric Library

The Electric Library lets you run comprehensive searches across an extensive database of full-text resources. According to their publicity information, any researcher can pose a question in plain English and launch a comprehensive, simultaneous search through more than 150 full-text newspapers, over 900 full-text magazines, two international news wires, two thousand classic books, hundreds of maps, thousands of photographs, as well as major works of literature and art. Electric Library is sponsored by Infonautics Corporation, and is a charged-for service. There are time or usage limitations, and subscribers pay a minimal monthly fee. There is a free trial available on the Web site at

```
http://www.elibrary.com/
```

InfoSeek

InfoSeek was the first truly commercial search engine. At first, you could do a free preview search, and could subscribe for access to the larger database. Now, apparently, sponsorship by Netscape and other companies, including the owner, Reuters, lets this resource be free to all on the Net. InfoSeek is a very good search engine, with access to Web pages, newsgroups, FAQs, and special reviews of sites. Check it out at

```
http://guide.infoseek.com/
```

Magellan

Magellan is the McKinley Group's Internet Guide, and is sponsored by Netcom. Magellan's big diff2erence is that it rates and reviews sites, including a vast collection of Web, FTP, and Gopher sites and Usenet newsgroups. You can browse Magellan's selected topics or search specific keywords or phrases. For parents and others concerned about appropriate material on the Internet, Magellan provides a green-light feature that indicates content deemed appropriate for general viewing. Try it out at:

```
http://www.mckinley.com/
```

Open Text Index

The Open Text Index searches every word of every Web page the company has indexed over 21 billion words and phrases. Most excitingly, OpenText is available in several foreign languages, including Japanese. The OpenText company, a Canadian Internet products company which sells, among other things, Intranet equipment, claims it's one of the largest indexes available. You can create queries of virtually any length, or focus in by searching only titles or links. Try it at

```
http://www.opentext.com
```

Shareware.com

Before the advent of Web search engines, we used to refer you to a tool called *archie* to look for public domain software, upgrades and trial modules, shareware, and so on. Now, we suggest you go right to Shareware.com. Since its advent, this site makes it simple to find software on the Internet. You can search over 170,000 files, and download them from shareware and corporate archives on the Internet. *Newsweek* magazine said, "shareware.com does for software what Yahoo did for finding Web sites." shareware.com is operated by a company called c|net, which has a really cool Web site of their own at

```
http://www.cnet.com
```

and they also run a TV show weekly, filmed in the center of their offices in San Francisco.

Try out this powerful search engine at

```
http://www.shareware.com/
```

WhoWhere?

WhoWhere? is a comprehensive White Pages service for locating people and organizations on the Net. WhoWhere? handles misspelled or incomplete names, and you can search by initials. You will get better results if you know where someone lives or where they might have an e-mail account. Figure 12.16 shows the results of a search for the same friend we hunted for in Figure 12.15. Try out WhoWhere? at

```
http://www.whowhere.com/
```

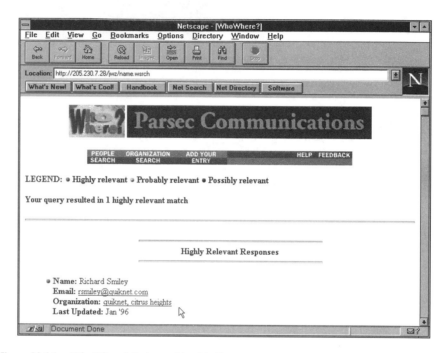

Figure 12.16. WhoWhere? finds our friend in Sacramento.

YAHOO!

Two bored Stanford University graduate students became entranced with the World Wide Web in late 1994, and started collecting an index of cool Web sites, and a searchable front end. By the middle of 1995, Yahoo had venture capital, full-time employees, and was one of the best ways to find things on the Web. They do check out every URL that's submitted to them, and filter for good quality content. Yahoo's excellent editors and Websurfers, along with sheer longevity, have allowed it to build a very useful, comprehensive cross-disciplinary index. Use it at:

    http://www.yahoo.com

> **MASTER WORDS**   Feeling jealous? Want to get your Web page listed on all these search engines so people can find you? Instead of submitting your URL to each one individually, try the free publicizing service at Scott Bannister's SubmitIt!, found at
>
>   http://www.submit-it.com/
>
> It's a one-stop shopping service. (If you haven't created your own Web page yet but have information you want to provide in that form, see Chapter 20, Building the Resource.)

Special Indexes

A number of specially constructed indexes that are available throughout the Internet are particularly helpful in finding things via Gopher and the Web. Many of these indexes are used as references throughout this book. The people who have constructed them have provided a service that is almost without parallel. It is efforts like these that show how effective a collaborative environment the Internet can be. Someone needed to provide a list that demonstrated many of the features of the Internet, or that gathered information about one specific topic, or that attempted to make a general survey of one corner of cyberspace. So here are a few of the famous efforts along with references to where you can find them and a word of thanks to the people behind the index.

The University of Geneva's W3 Catalog

The University of Geneva has developed a particularly useful catalog that collates information from around the World Wide Web and allows searching for words that may be associated with specific pages and services, as shown in Figure 12.17. This special meta-index of search pages lets you search lots of the engines we list above, plus many more. The sources include many of the descriptive services available through the Web; you may want to explore each of them when you are browsing. Each service brings another view of the Web. We find each perspective to have value. You'll need to explore to see which of them best fits your needs and interests. To use the catalog, use your Web browser to connect to

    http://cuiwww.unige.ch/meta-index.html

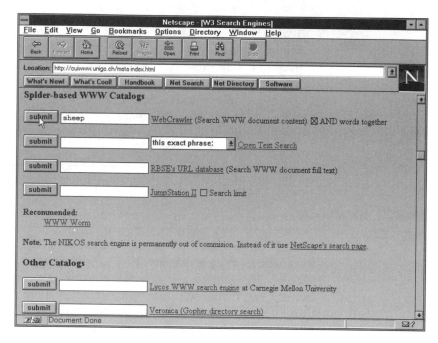

Figure 12.17.   Starting a search on the catalog.

Special Internet Connections

Special Internet Connections (AKA the Yanoff List) is one of the lists used to construct the W3 Catalog. It contains many resources of potential interest. Scott Yanoff compiles and updates it, and the list is posted frequently across the Net. It can be reached via anonymous FTP from the host

    csd4.csd.uwm.edu

(University of Wisconsin, Madison, Wisconsin) as well as via the Web at

    http://www.uwm.edu/Mirror.inet.srvices.html

Oliver McBryan's World Wide Web Worm

Oliver McBryan started the idea of a program that crawled around the World Wide Web collecting and indexing sites. This award-winning

Navigational Aid (Winner, Best of Web '94) is among the experimental search tools being built for the World Wide Web. The "Worm," located at

```
http://www.cs.colorado.edu/home/mcbryan/WWWW.html
```

and its companion, Oliver McBryan's "Mother of All Bulletin Boards," located at

```
http://wwwmbb.cs.colorado.edu/~mcbryan/bb/summary.html
```

represent two interesting approaches to finding things in the Web's truly distributed information base. The Worm searches for you by following links and looking for the search pattern you give it. Neither approach is ideal, because there is not yet a reasonable way to capture all the pages that might possibly be of interest to you. Great ideas, both of them. Explore and use them to your advantage.

The Virtual Reference Desk

As part of the University of California at Irvine's Campus Wide Information Service (CWIS), Cal Boyer of UCI's Office of Academic Computing has built an excellent Gopher that includes what he terms the Virtual Reference Desk. These references are a collection of valuable Gopher links you can use to access information about the Internet and how to use it from the Internet itself.

If you want to navigate here via the Web, the reference is

```
gopher://peg.cwis.uci.edu:7000/11//
VIRTUAL%20REFERENCE%20DESK
```

(The "%20" characters are the ASCII code for the space character. They are recorded this way because URLs can't contain internal spaces. And of course, we've broken this URL only because it won't all fit on a single typeset line. As always, enter it into your browser as one line.)

The Virtual Tourist

We can't leave navigational aids for the Web without a pointer to a very special tool: Brandon Plewe's "Virtual Tourist" page. This "index" is graphical and geographical. Go there to use your graphical Web browser to point and click your way around the world, starting from a world map. You can reach it at:

```
http://www.vtourist.com/webmap/
```

Collaborative Efforts at University of Michigan

This list of indexes should not be closed without reference to the fine work done in indexes being built and maintained by classes in the School of Information and Library Science at the University of Michigan. These topical and subject indexes cover the humanities and the sciences in specific subject areas and are made available through Gopher. There is a Web page as an entrance into the collection. Figure 12.18 shows the list of indexes available at the SILS database. To reach it, open the URL:

```
http://http2.sils.umich.edu/hp/Collaborativeprojects.html
```

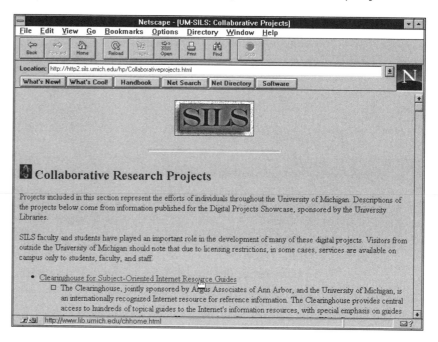

Figure 12.18.   The SILS indexes, available through the Web.

Lost at Sea? There's Help on the Way

Work is being done under the auspices of the Internet Engineering Task Force and similar bodies to consider the volatility of the information on the Internet and to build directories of material that include "self-identifying" and classifying attributes. At this writing, the expansion on the ideas from the Universal Resource Locators (URLs) and similar tagging mechanisms (generally called Uniform Resource Identifiers (URIs)) haven't been completed. Discussion includes concepts like Uniform Resource Names or Naming that would serve as an identifier like the International Standard Book or Serial Numbers for books and periodicals. As the ideas become more refined and as more ideas for directories are proposed, built, tested, and refined, the process of resource discovery will become more like driving the highway and less like trying to find a new sea route to India—"Beyond this point be dragons."

The Center for Networked Information Discovery and Retrieval (or CNIDR) is among the groups available to help discover and distribute appropriate tools. You can find more information about their activities via the Web at

```
http://kudzu.cnidr.org
```

Although the most common metaphor for the Internet is the "InfoBahn" or "Information Superhighway," looking for resources can make you feel more like a Renaissance seaman instead of the confident highway driver you probably are. The sea of resources is vast and ever-changing; the landmarks are sometimes distant, and sometimes seemingly not related to the landscape about you. You need to learn to navigate from point to point and to be willing to explore no matter where you come ashore.

CHAPTER

13

Usenet Newsgroups

Featuring

Chapter 13
Usenet Newsgroups

AFTER e-mail, Net News is the single largest information-sharing mechanism on the Internet. Net News is asynchronous, one-to-many communication—in other words, someone makes an article or message available, and anyone who is interested can read it whenever they like. The information can be authoritative or untrustworthy, detailed and official, or chatty (or catty!). News covers every conceivable category; if you don't find what you like, you can start a new group to talk about it.

Net News, *Usenet News*, and *News* are all names for the same concept: the broadcast of "posted" messages to a newsgroup. The original News software was developed for UNIX systems in 1979 by two graduate students at Duke University, as an early information-sharing and conferencing method. As good ideas on the Net tend to do, it spread like wildfire. Within a year, fifty UNIX sites, including Bell Labs, were participating.

Some newsgroups get hundreds of messages per day; some, only a few. Figure 13.1 shows what was available on a given day in the `misc.kids` newsgroup.

A News item looks much like an e-mail message; it has headers and a body of text. But News items are stored and handled by a different set of programs, and there are specialized *newsreaders*—programs to let you more easily handle the volume of news available. Newsreaders let you select what you want to read, discard what you don't want (or filter it out altogether before you even see it), and keep items in a single discussion or *thread* together.

```
WTNVT: Session harry to host 158.222.1.6
 Session  Edit  Commands  Settings  Help
misc.kids              794 articles
a Penelope Gaines    4  >fruit or veggie for first food?
  J Sullivan
  Lyen Hache
  Debra Ann Simms
b Penelope Gaines    1  >Kids out late
d MGW                7  Delta: No more kids meals
  Susan Engberson
  Steven M. Scharf
  n friedman
  Celia Modell
  John Mobley
  oremb@skydivskyl
e Valerie C. Bock    2  >Successful "Early" Potty Training (long)
  Kevran Day
f Mario Guerreiro    1  >she's a teenager now
-- Select threads (date order) -- Top 1% [>Z] --

                                                      16:17:52
```

Figure 13.1.   A typical News menu (from misc.kids).

 MASTER WORDS   Networks and host systems agree to accept News in certain groups and to feed postings to certain groups. They need not accept all possible newsgroups. This is particularly important for communities that include people such as young students or college students for whom some of the material in newsgroups is not appropriate. We have included an article on issues of censorship and college students as Appendix E.

There are over 16,000 newsgroups worldwide as of early 1996. New ones are added each day. The groups are arranged in hierarchies and subhierarchies roughly according to subject. The groups reflect the diversity of the Internet community. For example, fans of Robert Jordan, a writer of speculative fiction or sci-fi, can discuss his work in the newsgroup

    alt.fan.robert.jordan

soccer fans have

    rec.sport.soccer

and programmers can discuss particular technical points in compilers or networking protocols in groups with names like

    comp.infosystems.*

Part II

The Internet Toolkit

New Usenet users should look at the groups

```
news.newusers
```

or

```
news.newusers.announce
```

to find what's available.

Not all newsgroups are available in all countries. In the United States, for example, over one thousand foreign groups cannot be accessed.

A specialized kind of Net News is the commercial subscription service ClariNet, which broadcasts news from Associated Press (AP), Reuters, and/or United Press International (UPI) to its subscribers. You can read ClariNet if your News provider has paid to deliver it to you.

 WARNING ClariNet is a subscription service, and if you receive it, your provider has signed an agreement that they will not redistribute it. DO NOT pass along items from ClariNet in e-mail to your buddies.

Newsgroup Hierarchies

With thousands of newsgroups available, how do you find the ones you're interested in? Usenet newsgroups are organized into hierarchies, either by subject matter or geographically; and newsgroup names reflect this hierarchy. The first part of the name is the top-level hierarchy, the broadest category; and the following parts refer to more specific topics. For example, in the name

```
rec.sports.soccer
```

it's not hard to see that the specific topic of soccer is part of the broader category of sports, which is in turn part of the rec (recreational activities) hierarchy. The top-level subject hierarchies are as follows:

comp   Computer-related topics

news   News about the Usenet network itself and the News system

rec   Recreational subjects such as music, art, hobbies, etc.

sci   Science and engineering discussions

soc   Social groups and societal issues

talk   Random discussions

misc   Miscellaneous topics

alt   New groups that have not yet passed the newsgroup addition process or topics that do not fit into other categories

Almost all sites that take News carry the top-level hierarchies. When someone wants to begin a new newsgroup within one of these hierarchies, they submit a proposal to the Usenet community, in the group

```
news.announce.newgroups
```

A discussion period begins, followed by a formal vote. This process is designed to ensure that the new group will have enough users to remain active and will not waste network resources. The alternative (alt.) newsgroups are not governed by the formal evaluation process.

The names of the organizational and geographical hierarchies reflect the diversity of the organizations and geographical areas that are organized into the Usenet. Some of the hierarchies include:

de   for a group of systems in Germany

fj   for a group of systems in Japan

ba   for a group of systems in California's Bay Area

atl   for a group of systems in Atlanta, Georgia

umn   for a group of systems at the University of Minnesota

In addition, local organizations frequently have a local News hierarchy that runs only on their machines, and it is used to keep members of the organization in touch. Some large companies and universities have extensive internal hierarchies, including some that mirror topics on the larger News hierarchies, for internal discussion only. Figure 13.2 illustrates a posting on one such newsgroup.

```
═══════════════ WTNVT: Session harry to host harry.lloyd.com ═══════════ ▼ ▲
 Session   Edit   Commands   Settings   Help
cygnus.west (no posting) #1525 (0 + 2 more)                          [1]    ↑
From: brian@cygnus.com ("Brian R. Smith")
[1] Upcoming modem changes
Original-To: cygnus-west@cygnus.com, jmr@fusion.com,
+           cwpage@cygnus.com (Christopher W. Page),
+           cari@cygnus.com (Cari McAskill), tae@cygnus.com (Terri-Ann
+           Evans),
+           sac@cygnus.com (Steve Chamberlain)
Date: Mon Aug 22 15:50:26 PDT 1994
X-Mailer: ELM [version 2.4 PL23]
Content-Type: text
Content-Length: 593
Distribution: cygnus

For folks who use cygnus-west dialin modems:

Wednesday, August 24th, around, say, 4pm, I'll be changing the modems
on our portmaster from 7 bits/even parity (7E1) to 8 bits/no parity
(8N1).  This is mostly so that PPP will work, since PPP requires an 8
bit connection.

(Those of you who switched to using 903-0912, which I already switched
to 8N1, can switch back to using 903-0121 at that point.  Bill S.,
--MORE--(85%)
                                                              15:10:02  ↓
```

Figure 13.2. **A local newsgroup for staff information sharing.**

How Does It Work?

News is propagated, or distributed, cooperatively. Starting with a site with a full *feed* (all the possible newsgroups), other sites get this feed shipped over the Net to them daily. A full feed of the approximately 16,000 newsgroups that are distributed in the United States will take about 250 megabytes of file storage per day. In turn, these secondary sites may feed other sites downstream from them. Many sites get their News feed from a central News hub, which makes for efficient distribution.

Each site administrator can make the decision about what groups to receive. Many sites receive only the main groups (that is, everything but the alt. hierarchy). Others, because of site storage limitations or policies about personal use of computing resources (see Chapter 19), may get only certain specific groups.

News items are *expired* in order to keep the amount of file space consumed by this monster at a minimum. Most sites expire News items in 5–7 days. Some keep things around a little longer; some for only 48–72 hours. You'll notice that automatic expiration helps manage this large volume of information without too much work on the part of the News administrator.

A News message is called, in newsgroup jargon, a *posting* or an *article*. A posting and all its responses are called a *thread*. If you read a posting and want to post a reply, you will compose it in much the same way as writing an e-mail message. Once you send or post the message, it will appear instantly in the menu for that newsgroup hierarchy on your machine. Then it will go out to the Net to be gathered into the feed for your site, and will propagate across the rest of the sites receiving that group. It can take as long as a week for postings to show up at all the sites that get your group. This delay can make it difficult to keep track of which thread a given message was intended for. In response, News enthusiasts have developed both the social practice of "context quoting," as in e-mail, and newsreader software designed to sort and distribute mail.

Each News posting or article has "tags" that help the News software sort and distribute it. They are:

Subject:	The subject or title of the article.
From:	The author's name and electronic address.
Date:	The date posted.
Organization:	The organization from which the article was posted.
Keywords:	Important words chosen by the author, which allow some newsreaders to do keyword searching.
Summary:	A summary of the article, written by the author.
Newsgroups:	The newsgroups to which the article was posted.
Distribution:	An indication of how widely the article is distributed.

Your particular News software may not show or use all of these tags, but most newsreaders and posting software will let you edit them into your posting before you send it off. Tags have the format <tag>: <space> <word or words>. For example, an Organization tag might say:

```
Organization: Acme Properties, Inc. Coyote, Wyoming
```

Or a Newsgroup tag might look like this:

```
newsgroups: rec.org.sca, rec.food.historic
```

Later in this chapter you'll learn how to use these tags effectively in your own postings.

The Internet Toolkit **Part II**

Caveat Emptor

If you have seen a screaming headline like *"Local high-school student finds pornography on school computer,"* chances are the student (or his parents) was reading it on Net News. Among the posted items, it is possible to find material, including erotica, that may offend some people. All people who read News should be aware that such material exists and that *they can choose* whether to look at it.

On the Internet, there are all sorts of people posting all sorts of information and opinions. Some newsgroups contain material that is sexually explicit and potentially offensive to some adults and perhaps dangerous for children to see. This may not simply be what is called "soft pornography." You will find newsgroups and articles that explore (and illustrate, because systems on the Internet are not restricted to text) issues of bondage, sadomasochism, bestiality and many other sexually explicit topics.

There are also materials that offend people in other ways. There are discussion groups for every political point of view, for every possible lifestyle and belief system, and for many other topics to which some people (particularly parents of young children) wish to control access.

In general, sexually explicit discussion groups can be found in the alt.sex newsgroup hierarchy. You can also find a lot of new and interesting ideas being discussed in the alt. hierarchies, so you should not assume that all alt newsgroups are sexually oriented. Nor should you assume that all other groups are clear of any potentially offensive material. (For example, the group rec.arts.erotica is a moderated group for erotic fiction and poetry.) Appropriate caution should be taken.

You will also find discussions from people who are very angry at or pleased with other persons or groups, or the world in general. Do not be surprised if you find comments that are sexist, racist, or otherwise offensive. The Internet, particularly in the Usenet newsgroups, is a free-form exchange and there is little or no censorship other than the kind imposed by peer pressure. There have been instances where illegal files, such as child pornography, were posted to News. In cases like this, as many systems operators as possible are notified through the Net, and those files are removed. Attempts are usually made to prosecute the persons who post illegal materials.

If you are offended by a certain posting, you may send an e-mail (not a flame, as people do not respond positively to being attacked) to the person who posted the article explaining your point of view. You can post an article to the newsgroup explaining your point of view. You can decide not to read articles from that person anymore (and even never see another one if your news client has "kill" files). Everyone has a right to their own opinions as long as those opinions do not actually harm others. Actions that are harmful are generally against the law and lawful authorities should be informed.

WARNING   With the passage and enactment of the Telecommunications Reform Act of 1996 came the Communications Decency Act of 1995. This act made it illegal to "knowingly" make available "indecent" and "obscene" material to minors in the United States. At this time (late February 1996) there are two suits in United States courts intended to clarify or overturn the act. Judge Buckwalter of the 3rd District Court has issued a Temporary Restraining Order enjoining enforcement of the "indecency" provisions. The obscenity provision is still in force. (See Appendix G for an analysis of the Communications Decency Act by the law firm of Piper & Marbury, L. L. P.) A very real problem for Internet users is knowing where there might be minors or in what country the people are who might be viewing material that you post. There are several quite fine "Internet Citizen Empowerment" programs like *Surfwatch, Parental Guidance Inside, Cyberpatrol* and so on that each Internet user can install and run to prevent inadvertent and inappropriate images and words from being made available to minors.

In news.announce.newusers, you will find the periodic posting *A Guide to Social Newsgroups and Mailing Lists*, by Dave Taylor. This important and useful document describes the socially oriented newsgroups and some of the netiquette you will find useful for reading and posting to them.

We discuss policies for helping children who work on the Net in Chapter 18, on the K-12 presence on the Net.

Moderated or Unmoderated?

Although for the most part Usenet is a free-for-all, governed only by peer pressure and consensus, some newsgroups have decided to filter the content and tone of the group by the use of a mechanism called *moderation*.

Moderated newsgroups (and mailing lists, for that matter) have strict guidelines for content, following the topic, and tone (emotionality and flames are not tolerated). A single individual (in lower-traffic groups) or a group of people handle the moderation tasks. They are called, not surprisingly, the moderators.

Here's how moderated groups work: when you post an article to a moderated newsgroup, the message is intercepted by the News distribution software and sent to the moderator(s). The moderator will decide whether to allow the posting to be distributed further. Sometimes the moderator will add comments or further headers to show that the posting has been passed.

Moderators usually "rule" with an even hand. They will tolerate a little bit of horseplay, but topics seldom stray from the newsgroup's topic for more than a few postings (or a couple of days).

You can tell if a group you are reading is moderated by reading the headers carefully, looking for postings from the moderator. You should also read the FAQ for any newsgroup you are interested in participating in before leaping into the fray.

Reading News

Newsreader software exists for most computing environments. Most full-featured browser and integrated Internet applications programs include a newsreader. Those include Netscape's Navigator, Microsoft's Internet Explorer, Quarterdeck's Internet Suite, and Netcom's NetCruiser (included on the accompanying CD), as well as the software provided by the commercial online services like America Online, CompuServe, and Prodigy. Table 13.1 lists the most common public-domain or shareware programs and the sites where you can get them.

This list is derived from the Usenet News History and Sources FAQ written by Gene Spafford at Purdue. You'll find it at

```
http://www.cis.ohio-state.edu/hypertext/faq/usenet/
usenet/software/part1/faq.html
```

check there for the most current version.

Environment	Site	Reader	Comments
UNIX	ftp://ftp.academ.com	rn	/pub/rn
	ftp://ftp.uu.net	trn	/networking/news/readers/trn
	ftp://ftp.germany.eu.net No response	nn	/pub/news/news reader/unix/nn
	ftp://ftp.germany.eu.net	tin	/pub/news/news reader/unix/tin
VMS	ftp://kuhub.cc.ukans.edu	ANU-NEWS	
	ftp://ftp.arizona.edu	VMS/VNEWS	
VM/CMS	listserv@psuvm.psu.edu or listserv@psuvm.bitnet	NetNews	Send e-mail message with command "help" for list of commands
	ftp://ftp.uni-stuttgart.de	NNR	
MVS	ftp://ftp.uni-stuttgart.de	NNMVS	
Mac	ftp://ftp.apple.com	HyperNews	
	http://www.demon.co.uk/sw15	Newshopper	
	ftp://ftp.acns.nwu.edu	newswatcher	/pub/newswatcher
	ftp://ftp.ruc.dk	Nuntius	/pub/nuntius

*Table 13.1. **Guide to Usenet Newsreader Software.***

Environment	Site	Reader	Comments
MS-DOS	`ftp.utas.edu.au`	Trumpet	
MS-Windows	`ftp.utas.edu.au`	Wtrumpet	
	`ftp://ftp.forteinc.com` `http://www.forteinc.com`	Free Agent	
	`http://www.magi.com/` `~rdavies/qnews.html`	Qnews	
	`ftp://ftp.ksc.nasa.gov`	WinVN	/pub/win3.winvn
	`http://www.inlink.com/~tht/nx.html`	News Xpress	Various versions for Windows 3.1, NT, and 95
X-Windows	`ftp.x.org`	xrn	
	`export.lcs.mit.edu`	xvnews	
EMACS	Most GNU sites.	GNUS	For use with GNU EMACS editor.
	Most GNU sites.	GNEWS	For use with GNU EMACS editor.
OS/2	`ftp://ftp.germany.eu.net`	tin	/pub/news/news reader/os2/tin

Table 13.1. (continued) **Guide to Usenet Newsreader Software.**

rn and nn

With the simple UNIX newsreaders—rn (read news), nn (no news), and trn (threaded read news)—you can read News happily without anything more than a spacebar. But if you do that, you'll read every item in every group, and it can become pretty overwhelming pretty quickly.

With these three, you type the name of the reader at the UNIX system prompt, and follow the prompts. nn, tin, and trn have nice menu-based and configurable interfaces, which let you read the groups you want and the specific items you want without having to read everything. For example, Figure 13.3 shows how trn lets you select a newsgroup in which to explore. In Figure 13.4, an item from the rec.org.sca group has been selected.

 MASTER WORDS nn, tin, and trn all let you use the + symbol to display a listing of the available News articles. Display the list, select (by letter or number) the articles you want to read, and then, if you are pretty sure you won't want to come back and read something else, use the "c" command to mark everything else as read. This keeps the newsgroup manageable.

Enter **h** at almost any prompt to get a help menu. Typing **q**, or Shift-**q**, or Ctrl-**q**, will almost always get you back out to either the main News prompt or the system prompt.

There are other UNIX newsreaders: GNUS and GNEWS within EMACS. Both require knowledge of the complexities of the EMACS editor, and are not for the faint of heart or the beginning UNIX user.

 MASTER WORDS nn is a nice interface to use for several reasons, not least of all because if there are no new items, it tells you "No news is good news!" and automatically exits.

```
┌─                    WTNVT: Session harry to host harry              ▼ ╪
│ Session   Edit  Commands  Settings   Help
│harry-pat[~]>trn                                                        ▲
│Unread news in rec.org.sca                             78 articles
│Unread news in lloyd.news-stats                         9 articles
│Unread news in misc.kids                              164 articles
│Unread news in rec.music.early                         41 articles
│Unread news in alt.binaries.pictures.d                 25 articles
│etc.
│
│======  78 unread articles in rec.org.sca -- read now? [+ynq] █
│
│
│
│
│
│
│
│
│
│
│                                                          12:56:05 ▼
```

Figure 13.3. Entering trn from a system prompt.

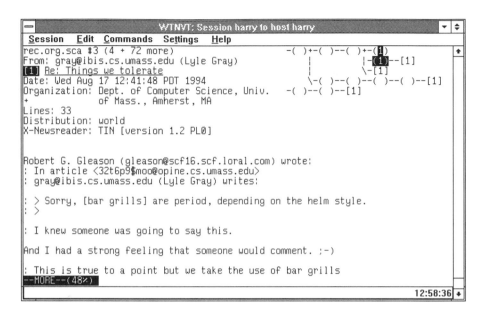

Figure 13.4.   Reading a News item (notice the quote from a previous message).

Workstation-Based Newsreaders

Many modern newsreaders use GUI clients, just like the Telnet and FTP clients we discussed in earlier chapters. These newsreaders make accessing and reading Net News even simpler.

When you install your client software, you will need to know a News server host to "point" your newsreader at. You'll be asked to supply the host name (and sometimes the IP address) of the News server. Ask your service provider for this information; there are very few public News servers available to nonsubscribers.

Subscribing to Groups

After you've installed your client, you'll need to subscribe to the newsgroups you are interested in. Usually you will double-click on the name of a group or drag it from the Unsubscribed list to the Subscribed list. Figure 13.5 shows this step using Trumpet, a popular newsreader. Unsubscribing from groups is just as easy.

Choosing Which Articles to Read

Once you pick a newsgroup to read, the names of the articles will appear in your window, as shown in Figure 13.6.

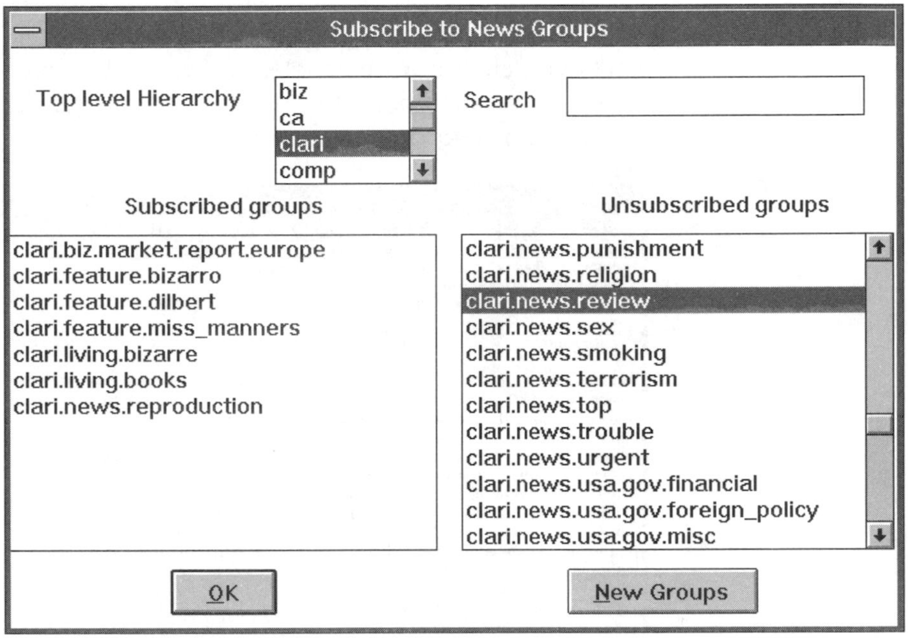

Subscribe to News Groups

Top level Hierarchy

| biz |
| ca |
| **clari** |
| comp |

Search [   ]

Subscribed groups

clari.biz.market.report.europe
clari.feature.bizarro
clari.feature.dilbert
clari.feature.miss_manners
clari.living.bizarre
clari.living.books
clari.news.reproduction

Unsubscribed groups

clari.news.punishment
clari.news.religion
clari.news.review
clari.news.sex
clari.news.smoking
clari.news.terrorism
clari.news.top
clari.news.trouble
clari.news.urgent
clari.news.usa.gov.financial
clari.news.usa.gov.foreign_policy
clari.news.usa.gov.misc

[O̲K]   [N̲ew Groups]

Figure 13.5.   Subscribing to newsgroups using Trumpet.

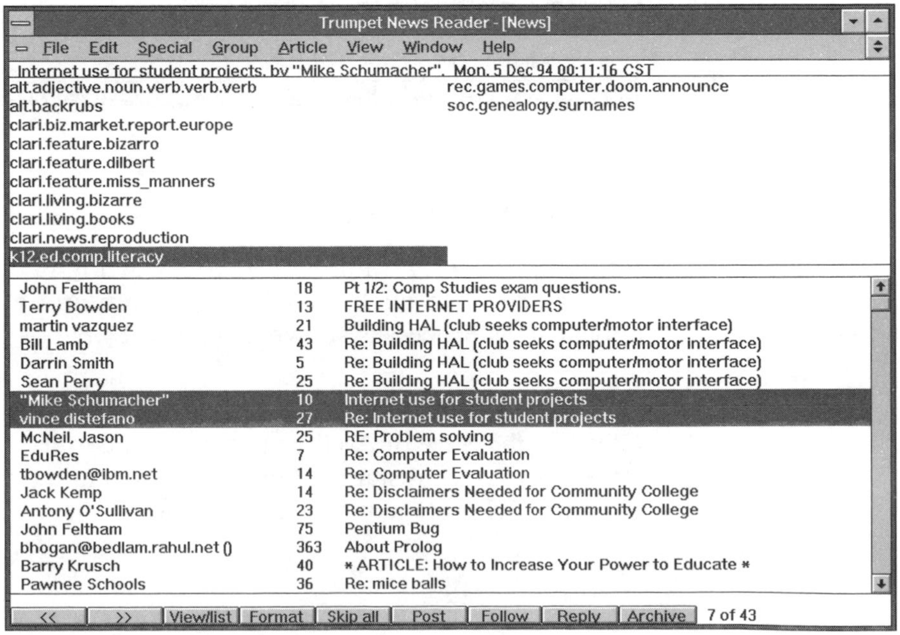

Trumpet News Reader - [News]

File   Edit   Special   Group   Article   View   Window   Help

Internet use for student projects, by "Mike Schumacher", Mon. 5 Dec 94 00:11:16 CST

alt.adjective.noun.verb.verb.verb	rec.games.computer.doom.announce
alt.backrubs	soc.genealogy.surnames
clari.biz.market.report.europe	
clari.feature.bizarro	
clari.feature.dilbert	
clari.feature.miss_manners	
clari.living.bizarre	
clari.living.books	
clari.news.reproduction	
k12.ed.comp.literacy	

John Feltham	18	Pt 1/2: Comp Studies exam questions.
Terry Bowden	13	FREE INTERNET PROVIDERS
martin vazquez	21	Building HAL (club seeks computer/motor interface)
Bill Lamb	43	Re: Building HAL (club seeks computer/motor interface)
Darrin Smith	5	Re: Building HAL (club seeks computer/motor interface)
Sean Perry	25	Re: Building HAL (club seeks computer/motor interface)
"Mike Schumacher"	10	Internet use for student projects
vince distefano	27	Re: Internet use for student projects
McNeil, Jason	25	RE: Problem solving
EduRes	7	Re: Computer Evaluation
tbowden@ibm.net	14	Re: Computer Evaluation
Jack Kemp	14	Re: Disclaimers Needed for Community College
Antony O'Sullivan	23	Re: Disclaimers Needed for Community College
John Feltham	75	Pentium Bug
bhogan@bedlam.rahul.net ()	363	About Prolog
Barry Krusch	40	✱ ARTICLE: How to Increase Your Power to Educate ✱
Pawnee Schools	36	Re: mice balls

[<<] [>>] [View/list] [Format] [Skip all] [Post] [Follow] [Reply] [Archive]   7 of 43

Figure 13.6.   Choosing articles to read.

Reading Articles

After you click on the article you want, the text will appear in a new window, as shown in Figure 13.7. You can scroll back and forth through this text at your leisure.

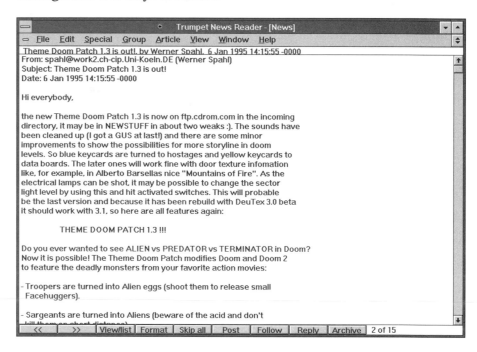

Figure 13.7.   **Reading an article in Trumpet.**

Replying to a Posting

Replying (posting a follow-up) to a posting is easy with GUI news-readers. You can click on a Reply button and a News template will appear. This process is shown in Figure 13.8.

Saving to a File

Click on the Save or Archive button or menu item to save an article to a file on your workstation. You will be prompted for the directory and file name. This stage is shown in Figure 13.9.

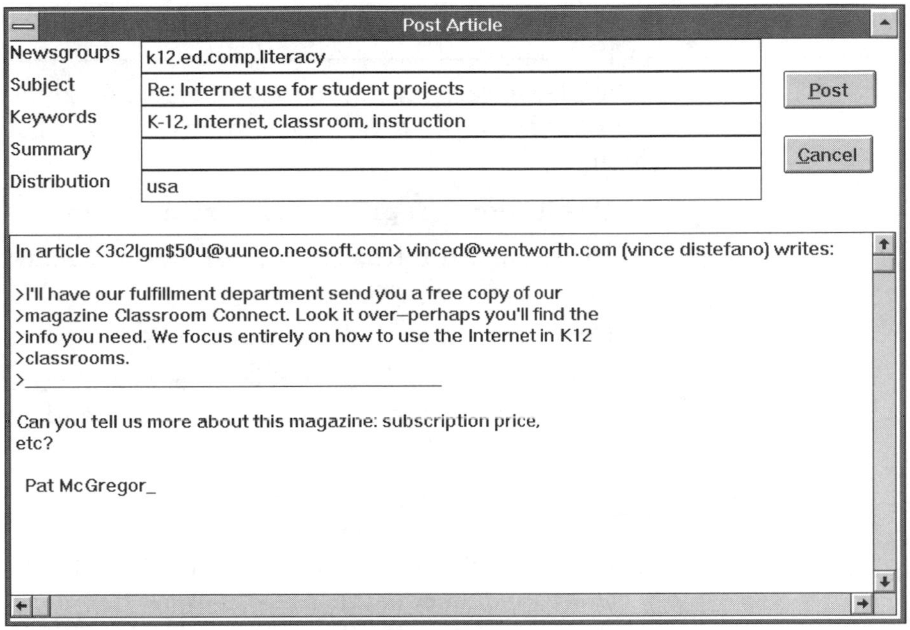

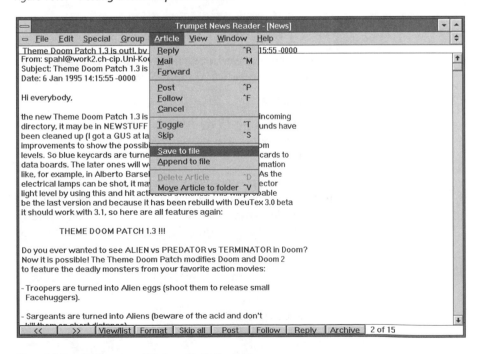

Figure 13.8. **Posting a follow-up to an article.**

Figure 13.9. **Saving an article to a file in Trumpet.**

Non-Text Files on News

The News mechanism is used to transfer all kinds of information. Not all of it is simple text. Other things you can get (or post) on News include:

Public domain programs in binary format.

Pictures and images of all sorts (including maps, satellite images, and clip art).

PostScript files of documents and other materials.

As you'll see in the next section, images and other binary files require special processing to get them out of News and into your computer.

 WARNING *Practice Safer Computing!* **Just as with any file you download, or any diskette you accept from anyone else, you must be cautious about loading any file into your workstation and running it without checking for viruses and other hostile agents. Always run your protection software; always check any file before you install and run it!**

Getting Images off the Net

The most comprehensive information available about getting pictures and other compiled binary information out of newsgroups is in the

`alt.binaries.pictures.d`

newsgroup. The FAQ for this group comes in three parts. The second and third parts are named `pictures-faq/part2` and `pictures-faq/part3`.

This FAQ is posted every other Monday to the `alt.binaries.pictures` newsgroups and to `news.answers`. It is also available by anonymous FTP or through e-mail by using the services available from at least two mail servers. For anonymous FTP access, you can look on

`rtfm.mit.edu in`

/pub/usenet/news.answers/pictures-faq in files "part1," "part2," or "part3," on

`ftp.cs.ruu.nl`

in /pub/NEWS.ANSWERS/pictures-faq for "part1," "part2," or "part3," or on

```
ftp.uu.net
```

in /usenet/news.answers/pictures-faq as the files "part1.Z," "part2.Z," or "part3.Z."

For e-mail access, send a message to `mail-server@rtfm.mit.edu`, with the single-sentence body

```
send usenet/news.answers/pictures-faq/part1
```

to get the first part,

```
send usenet/news.answers/pictures-faq/part2
```

for the second, and

```
send usenet/news.answers/pictures-faq/part3
```

for the third. You can also send e-mail to

```
mail-server@cs.ruu.nl
```

with

```
send NEWS.ANSWERS/pictures-faq/part1
send NEWS.ANSWERS/pictures-faq/part2
```

and/or

```
send NEWS.ANSWERS/pictures-faq/part3
```

in the body of the message.

Most people post to the `pictures` newsgroups in the UUencode encoding standard. This program, included with most implementations of UNIX, converts binary files into plain-text ASCII files, which can be handled by the mail system. In the past, you had to use the UUencode program yourself to convert the encoded files out of ASCII back into binary. In addition, the pictures are generally split into two or more articles in the newsgroup to keep the size of the posting small. Somehow, you have to recombine the parts of the pictures and also decode them. Luckily, some newsreaders have an "extract" capability that automatically decodes articles—this means you don't have to save the postings to a file and then decode them. On UNIX host systems, the `rn`, `nn`, and `trn` newsreaders can do this.

PICTURES ON EXHIBITION

The most common type of picture is the GIF format (which usually has the file suffix .GIF or .gif). GIF stands for Graphic Interchange Format. It is a standard format for images, developed by CompuServe to store pictures independent of the type of computer on which they originated. The GIF format includes Lempel-Ziv-Welch (LZW) compression, which makes the files fairly small. In early 1995, CompuServe announced that it will require a licensing fee from companies using the GIF format. GIFs are expected to become less available on the Net, in favor of the free JPEG format.

JPEG is another standardized image compression mechanism. JPEG stands for Joint Photographic Experts Group (the original name of the committee that wrote the standard). More and more JPEG-type pictures (.JPG or .jpg file suffix, usually) are getting posted to the Net. Some Net watchers claim that JPEG is destined to overtake GIF format in popularity, because it uses much less space to store the same picture. JPEG may well take over from GIF, but that will probably take a while to happen, as more people have GIF software and viewers, but lack the JPEG equivalents. Undoubtedly, and probably faster than we expect, JPEG utilities will spread to more home computers, but at this point, JPEG is still in its infancy.

The latest and greatest info about JPEG is included in the Tom Lane's "JPEG image compression: Frequently Asked Questions" (archive name is **jpeg-faq**), posted on a regular basis to the **alt.binaries.pictures.d**, **alt.graphics.pixutils**, **alt.binaries.pictures.erotica.d**, **alt.sex.pictures.d**, and **news.answers** newsgroups.

The newest and most fun picture format on the Net is MPEG, a format named for the Moving Pictures Experts Group. As the name implies, MPEG is movies on the Net. Some are extremely sophisticated; most are somewhat jerky, and the picture quality is somewhat poorer than with GIF or JPEG. However, it's a start. Most MPEG postings come in the form of movie loops. You'll need to have an MPEG viewer to see these movies.

Most PC and Macintosh FTP archives (Chapter 9 shows where to find a current list of anonymous FTP sites) have several shareware viewers for GIF, JPEG, and MPEG. Try them out and see which one works best for you.

Using Your Newsreader to Decode the Pictures

Select the articles you want to decode. You need to make sure you get the entire sequence of articles. Most people post picture sequences with subject lines that let you know which one in the sequence it is and how many you can expect; for example,

```
Mel Gibson as Hamlet JPEG part 1 of 24
Mel Gibson as Hamlet JPEG part 2 of 24
```

```
Mel Gibson as Hamlet JPEG part 3 of 24
Mel Gibson as Hamlet JPEG part 4 of 24
Mel Gibson as Hamlet JPEG part 5 of 24
Mel Gibson as Hamlet JPEG part 6 of 24
Mel Gibson as Hamlet JPEG part 7 of 24
Mel Gibson as Hamlet JPEG part 8 of 24
Mel Gibson as Hamlet JPEG part 9 of 24
```

and so on. Figure 13.10 shows a group of articles that make up a single picture selected.

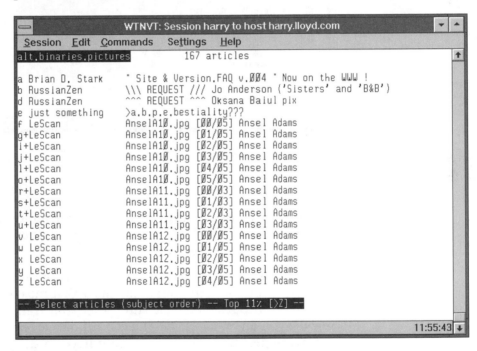

*Figure 13.10. **Selecting a group of files that make up a single picture.***

After you've chosen all the pictures you want to decode and display (or download), type this sequence:

```
:e
```

This command means "extract the selected items." Your newsreader will extract the articles, reconnect them into one file, and let you know what file they are stored in. Figure 13.11 shows the process of extracting the pictures we selected in Figure 13.10.

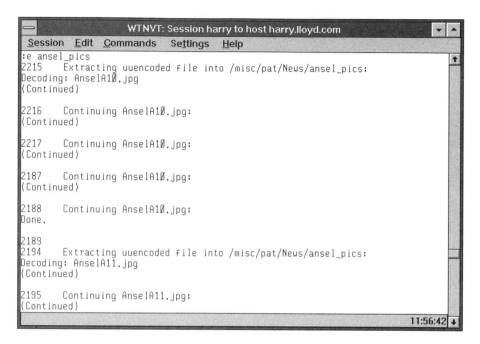

```
WTNVT: Session harry to host harry.lloyd.com
 Session   Edit   Commands   Settings   Help
:e ansel_pics
2215     Extracting uuencoded file into /misc/pat/News/ansel_pics:
Decoding: AnselA10.jpg
(Continued)

2216     Continuing AnselA10.jpg:
(Continued)

2217     Continuing AnselA10.jpg:
(Continued)

2187     Continuing AnselA10.jpg:
(Continued)

2188     Continuing AnselA10.jpg:
Done.

2189
2194     Extracting uuencoded file into /misc/pat/News/ansel_pics:
Decoding: AnselA11.jpg
(Continued)

2195     Continuing AnselA11.jpg:
(Continued)
                                                          11:56:42
```

Figure 13.11.   *Recombining and extracting the image.*

Viewing the Picture

You can view the picture on the most convenient machine for you. Sometimes this will be a remote host machine; sometime it will be your home or office computer.

If you're going to download the decoded picture file to a home machine, or move it around a network, remember that most decoded file outputs are stored in binary files. Be sure to set your transfer protocol accordingly. If you are moving the UUencoded data around, an ASCII transfer will work just fine, however. (You'll have to decode it eventually, of course.) For the UNIX system user, it can be more convenient to decode the image with a newsreader and then transfer it to the home machine.

MASTER WORDS   If you *don't* transfer the decoded file in binary mode, your transfer will appear to work just fine—*until* you attempt to view the picture. You'll get error messages and peculiar looking images, but not the pictures you want to see. Some FTP clients will warn you if the file appears to be binary and you're transferring in ASCII (or vice versa), but not all will. You'll need to remember.

Posting to News

There are two ways to post to News. One is to post a reply or response (or even a new item) while you are reading items. The exact command to do this varies: with line-mode readers usually it is **F** to follow-up (and include the quoted material) and **f** to follow-up without any preceding material (or to start a new thread). Graphic interface news-readers may have a button or pull-down menu to start this process.

The other way to post News is from the system prompt. In UNIX systems the tool you will use is likely to be the Pnews program. Other operating systems have other programs; you'll need to ask your local News junkies. Figure 13.12 shows the first steps in preparing to post a item from the Pnews program, Figure 13.13 shows a typical editing session for a News item, and Figure 13.14 shows the stage of actually posting the article.

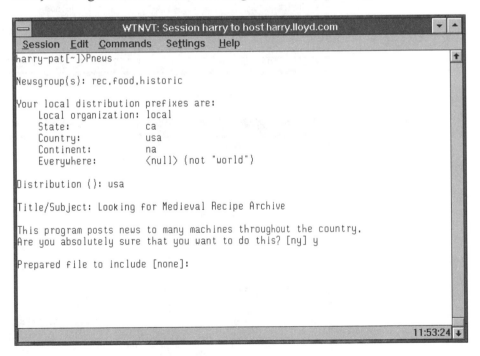

Figure 13.12. **Starting a News posting in Pnews.**

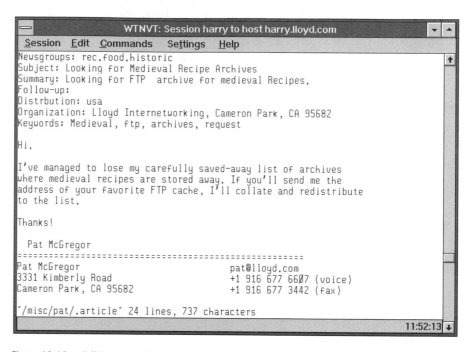

Figure 13.13. **Editing a posting.**

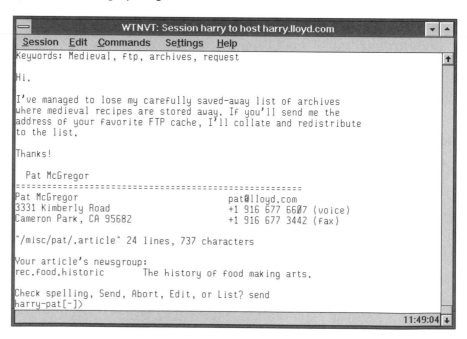

Figure 13.14. **Posting the article.**

The easiest way to prepare a News posting is to edit it in a file, separate from the News process itself. This lets you think carefully about what you are writing. You can save the posting which prompted your response to a file, edit in your response, and then post it.

To save a posting from a line-mode newsreader like tn, follow these steps:

1. Select and read the article you want.

2. At the command prompt at the bottom of the item, type the command

    :s filename

3. You will be prompted about whether you want to save this in mailbox format: enter **no**.

4. The file will be save in the News directory, with the filename you have entered.

   Figure 13.15 shows the step of saving a posting to a file using tn.

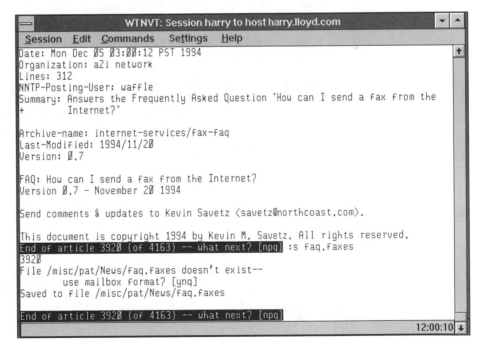

```
                    WTNVT: Session harry to host harry.lloyd.com
 Session  Edit  Commands   Settings   Help
Date: Mon Dec 05 03:00:12 PST 1994
Organization: a2i network
Lines: 312
NNTP-Posting-User: waffle
Summary: Answers the Frequently Asked Question "How can I send a fax from the
+        Internet?"

Archive-name: internet-services/fax-faq
Last-Modified: 1994/11/20
Version: 0.7

FAQ: How can I send a fax from the Internet?
Version 0.7 - November 20 1994

Send comments & updates to Kevin Savetz (savetz@northcoast.com).

This document is copyright 1994 by Kevin M. Savetz. All rights reserved.
End of article 3920 (of 4163) -- what next? [npq] :s faq.faxes
3920
File /misc/pat/News/faq.faxes doesn't exist--
        use mailbox format? [ynq]
Saved to file /misc/pat/News/faq.faxes

End of article 3920 (of 4163) -- what next? [npq]
                                                               12:00:10
```

Figure 13.15. **Saving an article to a file.**

With a GUI newsreader, saving a file is easier. You press the "Save File" button (or pull down a menu and click on the item) and you'll be presented with a dialog box asking you what filename you want to give it. Type in the name, and the article will be saved in that file.

The third way to save a posting is to select it (if your terminal emulator supports copy and paste for text on the screen) and copy the selection to a file.

Once you've edited your file to include the old posting, and the new information you want to add, you can post it to the newsgroup. You should remember to make sure that you've added more new material than you quote; most newsreader and posting software will keep you from posting anything that does not make significant additions to the information on the Net.

As part of posting to News, you'll usually be asked questions to help the posting software distribute your News properly, and to put the proper tags and headers on your posting.

When you post from a GUI newsreader, you click the "post" button or select the posting option from a pull-down menu. You'll be prompted for the filename you want to use for your posting. Figure 13.16 shows posting from the Trumpet newsreader software.

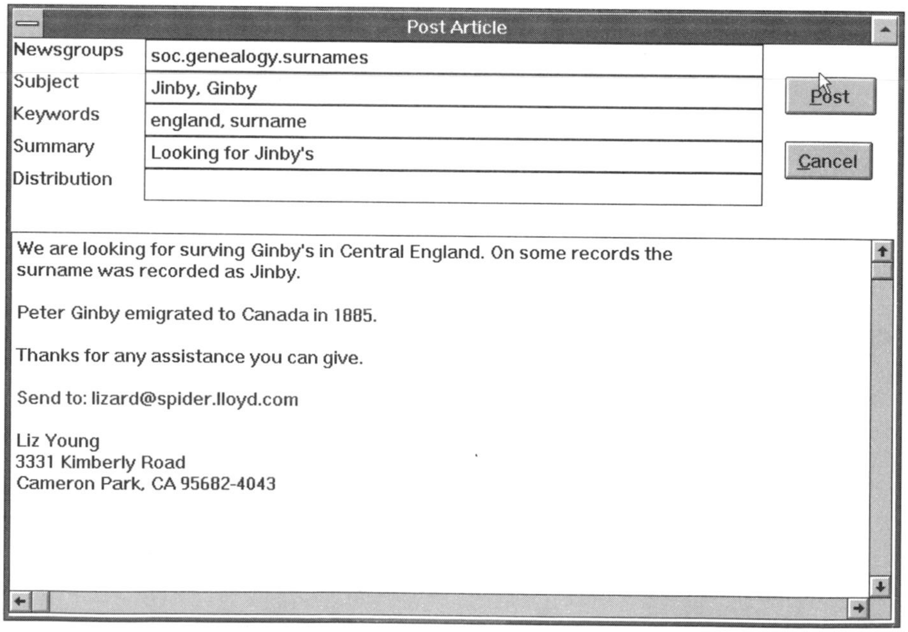

Figure 13.16. **Posting from Trumpet.**

MASTER WORDS   At the end of the editing process, you will be offered a chance to list or reread your article. *Do it!* Make sure you've said what you intended, and that you really want to say it publicly.

Appropriate Distribution, or "Who Cares?"

As unlimited as the Internet may seem, its resources are limited. With the vast amount of Usenet traffic that traverses the Net each day, it is expensive to post items of local interest to the whole world. Some articles (such as an announcement of a car for sale) are obviously not of interest to users at distant sites. In fact, you may get unpleasant responses from readers in far-away places if you post items meaningful only in your backyard. To help manage this, you can use the `Distribution:` line to limit where an article is sent. To attempt to limit distribution, add this line to the article header:

```
Distribution: area
```

You will be prompted (with an intimidating message about wasting Net resources) about distribution when you start a new posting. Take it seriously: think carefully about whether what you are posting adds anything to the conversation. If all works well, the distribution mechanism will keep your posting limited to the folks who are most likely to be interested in it.

MASTER WORDS   What do we mean by "*attempt* to limit distribution"? The News distribution hierarchy is supposed to ensure that geographic distributions—ba for the Bay Area, atl for Atlanta, or oh for Ohio, for example—stay in their geographic region. When you post a response or new item, you will be asked if you want to limit distribution. Unfortunately, because newsfeed software is not very efficient at screening out distribution codes (and because some systems administrators do not activate distribution filtering), it usually does not work. Be careful about posting items of local interest only to world-wide newsgroups.

Steering Responses to the Right Place

Sometimes you post to several groups but intend that follow-up discussion take place only in one group (it's easier for everyone to follow the discussion that way). Along with mentioning this in your article, you can get the News software to help you. Specify that follow-ups to your article are to go to a specific newsgroup by adding this line to the article header:

```
Followup-To: groupname
```

Replace *groupname* with the name of the group to which responses will be directed. If you want responses to come to you by e-mail, you can add the line

```
Followup-To: poster
```

Enter this line exactly as shown, including the word *poster*. All responses to your posting will be sent to you via e-mail, and will not be posted to News.

Organization Name

This tag shows what organization the machine you are posting from is affiliated with. Usually this is automatically filled in from a standard template placed on the system by the system's administrator.

However, you may sometimes want to change this. For example, if you are posting from your work machine to a newsgroup discussing, say, gay rights, you may not want your company or organization name on the posting. Edit the "Organization:" line to say which organization you want, or delete the line entirely.

Where's the Beef?—Making Your Content Count

You have an objective in posting to News: you want to distribute information. Other people have their own objectives, one of which is to waste as little time as possible reading News in order to glean the most possible information. The quality of your message and its content are important. Following are some guidelines that will help you get your message to its widest appropriate audience.

Flames

Practically everyone has heard of flames—wildly inappropriate, highly personal overreactions to something that someone else has said on the Internet. Some flames will be very vituperative and scurrilous.

But not all angry responses are flames. Consider the following (remember, '>' shows a previous message for context):

```
On Tuesday, Dennis wrote:
> Barbara Bush should have stayed at home and minded the
>puppies instead of pretending to know anything about
>literacy campaigning. We made no progress whatsoever during
>the Reagan-Bush years in stamping out illiteracy.

Dennis, that kind of statement makes me really mad.
Barbara Bush brought a visibility to the literacy problem
that we hadn't achieved in thirty years with conventional
attacks. What kind of evidence do you have??

Janet
```

Nothing inappropriate or offensive here. But if Janet had said:

```
Dennis, you are a sexist jerk. Any one who would
slam Mrs. Bush has got to be one of those stupid
Democrats. You probably learned to read from a cereal
box.

Janet
```

we could label Janet's response as a flame on Dennis. When Janet took the argument to the personal—when she said something unpleasant about Dennis, rather than disputing his ideas—then this became the match for a flame war.

This kind of behavior is discouraged. Some people will enter something like <flame on> to indicate that they are responding emotionally to a particular topic. Emotional responses are not discouraged, but attacks on people rather than ideas will in turn incur flames from others. These *flame wars* can be unpleasant—but they sometimes can turn a misunderstanding into a new understanding shared by the group. Flames can therefore be an interesting group process.

Some people enjoy causing flame wars. They respond with emotional or harassing statements in order to stir things up. One particularly obnoxious poster said to Pat, "I like a good flame war. The Internet is for those who are tough. If you can't take it, don't read News." Luckily, this sort of participant is rare, and becoming rarer as more people use newsgroups as widespread discussion groups and support groups.

One way to avoid a flame war is to ostracize the folks who are trying to stir one up. If, after several requests to stop the flaming a poster keeps it up, you can just ignore that person's postings.

KILL FILES

Most newsreader software has something called a "kill file" function. This lets you sort your incoming News items—to autoselect things you want to read, and reject things you don't. Kill files are great for ignoring people whose postings are obnoxious. Once you put them in your kill file, it is as if they disappeared off the Net. Check the man pages for your newsreader to find out how to create a kill file entry. Most newsreaders either respond to a Shift-K or have a pull-down menu item to let you select or deselect certain strings (letter patterns) in News headings. Here's a list of items marked for deletion in **trn**.

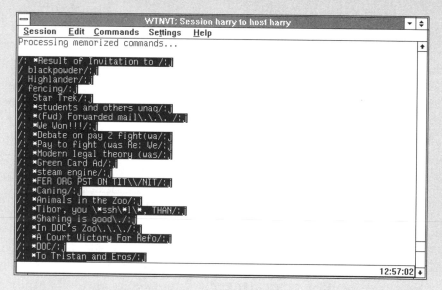

Chapter 7, which discusses "netiquette," includes a basic guide to appropriate behavior on newsgroups as well as mailing lists and other general Net citizenship. We suggest you read it, and any other related material you come across, if you are new to newsgroups.

Flames and FAQs

A good way to avoid being flamed if you're looking for specific information about something is to first see whether the answer to your question isn't already written down somewhere, perhaps in a FAQ (Frequently Asked Questions) document. Frequently asked questions are just that—questions that every newcomer to a subject (whether it's azaleas or C programming) asks. Old-timers get tired of answering the same questions over and over again, so they write down the answers and post them where any interested person can find them. FAQs are the subject of Chapter 14, but the important point here is that if there's a FAQ on your topic and you've ignored it, someone may tell you—perhaps unpleasantly—that you've wasted the entire group's time.

Brevity Is the Soul of Wit

Chuq von Rospach, a respected Net veteran, says, "Never say in ten words what you can say in fewer. Say it succinctly and it will have a greater impact. Remember that the longer you make your article, the fewer people will bother to read it."

Make Sorting Easier: The Subject Should Be Descriptive

Remember that time on the Internet costs something: either your money paid to your provider, money spent by your company; or the reader's time. Most people make decisions on what to read based on the subject line.

That line lets people with limited time quickly decide whether to read your article. Tell people exactly what you are talking about. A title like "Safe Kids" doesn't help as much as "Tips for Fire-Safe Children." Most people won't bother to read your item to find out what it's about; they expect the subject to tell them.

 MASTER WORDS   Chuq says, "Some computers truncate the length of the subject line to 40 characters, so keep your subjects short and to the point."

To Know You Is to Love You

There are over a million computers on the Net, and many of those have more than one person using them. It's unlikely that most of the people who read your postings know you personally. Most will come to know you only by your words—what you say and how well you say it. Your writing, your posting, and the quality of what you have to say represent you. Make sure your postings will not embarrass you. Before you send the posting out, check for:

spelling errors

clarity

civility (see *Flames* above)

context (and that you aren't quoting too much)

signature

This isn't to say you have to be an award-winning author to write on the Net. Most of us aren't. But you should make sure that your writing is clear, concise, and as mechanically correct as you can make it.

 MASTER WORDS   Not certain if your software is working? Want to see if the text or image file you just converted really goes over the Net? If you want to test something, *don't* use a Net-wide newsgroup! Messages with subjects that say "This is a test" are likely to provoke many irritated messages. Post those messages to `misc.test`. You'll also get a surprise back: many hosts that receive `misc.test` send back an automated response. You'll get messages from all over the globe.

Context, or What Are You Talking About?

Because it can take as long as a week for a posting to get to all the machines on the Net, helping your readers keep track of context is particularly important. Some of them may get your response before they get the original posting! When you follow up someone's article, it helps to summarize the parts of the article to which you're responding. This lets others spend time thinking about what you said rather than trying to remember what the original article said.

The easiest way to summarize what's gone before is to include appropriate quotes from the original article. Don't include the entire article, since it will irritate the people who have already seen it. Even if you're responding to the entire article, summarize only the major points you are discussing.

If you want to include points from more than one person, you should label their individual comments in some way. There are a couple of conventions for labeling. One is to put all the comments from the same person together:

```
Jennifer (wander@taliesen.com) said on Tuesday:
> We have six databases to consolidate. I think the best
> thing is to pick the one which is set up most efficiently,
> and then just trash the others.
<design criteria snipped>
> This will keep us from having to re-enter the data. I'm
> not interested in spending several weeks typing 30,000
> entries in again.

Christian (jfh@carlyle.edu) replied:
> None of them is particularly well-designed. It would be
```

```
> better to redesign from the ground up and then transfer
> all the information into the new database. We have money
> in the budget to pay for data entry personnel.
```

The other convention is to use the person's initials at the front of their comments to distinguish who is saying what:

```
Jennifer (wander@taliesen.com) and Christian
(jfh@carlyle.edu) are discussing what to do about the
databases:

>J: We have six databases to consolidate. I think the best
>J: thing is to pick the one which is set up most
>J: efficiently, and then just trash the others.

>C: None of them is particularly well-designed. It would be
>C: better to redesign from the ground up and then transfer
>C: all the information into the new database.

>J: This will keep us from having to re-enter the data. I'm
>J: not interested in spending several weeks typing 30,000
>J: entries in again.

>C: We have money in the budget to pay for data entry
>C: personnel.
```

Summarizing the discussion that came before does take thought and editing. It's worth it, however, to make sure that your information gets respect from those you are writing to.

Mail or News: How Best to Respond to a Posting?

Since so many of us read and respond on the Net, chances are that we all will know the right answer to some question. Often, someone will ask a question over Net News, and for a couple of weeks identical answers will clutter up the newsgroup. This is very irritating to everyone and can set off further clutter as irritated people send off snappish follow-ups telling people not to answer such questions on the Net. (You're right. It's not logical.)

You can help prevent such silliness. Before answering such a question, mark it to show up again in your newsgroup (in most readers the command will be **m** or a menu choice). Scan the rest of the day's items and see if someone else has answered it correctly. If so, don't duplicate the information. If you do want to respond, e-mail your answer to the person instead of posting a follow-up, and suggest that they summarize the answer or answers in a single posting (see next section). This way, only a single copy of the answers goes out, no matter how many folk answered the question.

If you post a question, please remind people to send you the answers by e-mail and offer to summarize them to the network.

Gathering In the Harvest

If you request information from the network, it's common courtesy to report your findings so that others can benefit as well. The best way of doing this is to take all the responses you receive and edit them into a single article that's posted to the places where you originally posted your question.

Take the time to strip headers, combine duplicate information, and write a short summary. Credit the information to the people who sent it to you (if you keep track of the original mail carefully, it is easy to do this).

Keep It Clean and Legal

The laws of the country in which you live (and possibly of every country where your article is received!) apply to your postings. Once something is posted onto the network, it effectively goes into the public domain. No matter how carefully you copyright your work, others may well copy it or post it elsewhere.

Additionally, remember that copying or retyping into a posting movie reviews, song lyrics, or anything else published under a copyright could cause you, or your company, to be held liable for damages, so consider carefully whether you want to use this material.

It may be legal to reproduce short extracts of a copyrighted work for critical or review purposes (it's hard to tell in today's uncertainly electronic copyright environment), but reproduction in whole is strictly and explicitly forbidden by US and international copyright law. Remember that people make their living by these words; if you steal them and give them away, the writer's ability to make a living may well be damaged.

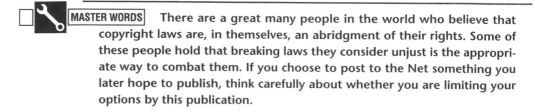

MASTER WORDS There are a great many people in the world who believe that copyright laws are, in themselves, an abridgment of their rights. Some of these people hold that breaking laws they consider unjust is the appropriate way to combat them. If you choose to post to the Net something you later hope to publish, think carefully about whether you are limiting your options by this publication.

Many people read News from company or organization machines. Most companies and organizations do not have official opinions on most of the topics represented in newsgroups. You should consider all opinions or statements made in News articles as the opinions of the person who wrote the article. They don't necessarily represent the opinions of that person's employer, of whoever owns the computer from which the message was posted, or of anyone involved with News or the underlying networks which comprise News.

At the same time, some people do respond to News as official representatives of their companies. You can take what they say as authoritative.

Legal precedents view posting on News as being similar to publishing your own books or magazines. You are legally responsible for the content of your postings. Don't post instructions for how to do some illegal act (such as jamming radar or obtaining cable TV service illegally); also don't ask how to do illegal acts by posting to the Net.

Authorities are particularly sensitive to pornographic material on the Net. In almost all jurisdictions, child pornography is illegal.

In Germany in late 1995, discussions with legal authorities caused CompuServe to block the reception of many newsgroups from their News servers worldwide until CompuServe could make blocking software available through their service. With the Communications Decency Act of 1995, there is uncertainty about what may be legal in the United States. Without trying to inhibit you in what you may want to say or do, we do point out that you may want to think twice about your legal position before posting such materials. Free speech mechanisms may not protect you, particularly in countries where free speech is an ideal to be discussed, not a right.

Don't Ruin the Ending!

On a lighter note, many newsgroups discuss movies, books, and other material. Some people like to talk about these items in detail, including plot information and (sigh) the endings. Lots of people don't want to know the endings or other surprise information: it really upsets them and may cause them not to see the film or read the book. Such information, in News jargon, is called a "*spoiler.*"

If you choose to post something that might spoil the surprise for other people, please mark your message with a warning so that they can skip the article. When you post a message with a spoiler in it, make sure the word "spoiler" is part of the Subject line. You can also insert blank spaces or empty lines before your entry. Some newsreaders will pause when they encounter the Ctrl-L key sequence. If you insert one in your text just above where you start to talk about the surprise material, the newsreader will pause and let folks stop reading the article at that point.

Being Young and/or Female on the Internet

There has been a great deal of publicity in the past few years about women feeling threatened on the Net, or of very young people feeling uncomfortable when approached by older correspondents. Anecdotes tell of women who started responding to a newsgroup, or participating in other kinds of exchanges (IRC, or MUDs), and who received unwanted sexual offers.

It's hard to say how threatening the Internet actually is. For many years, the Internet was almost exclusively a male domain, because so many men were in the professions that used or were exposed to the Net. But increasingly, women and children as well as men are coming to the Net to find or provide information, to exchange e-mail, and so on. The Internet is like the rest of the world. Some places in it are safer than others. Some places are more comfortable than others.

It's also true that there are a lot of immature males on the Net. Many users of social interaction groups (other than those limited to women only) on community bulletin boards and on college campuses tend to be young males, some of whom are not very socially adept. Why aren't there more women in these groups? Some theories point to social conditioning of women as a barrier to computing fluency.

When you add to this the feeling of safety that the Net's anonymity provides, it's easy to see why some men feel they can say *anything* to a woman, even a stranger, over this communication medium.

Sexual harassment aside, it's also true that some newsgroups have a more argumentative style than others, and that many women do not feel comfortable in the sort of rough-and-tumble give-and-take that occurs in these groups.

Obviously, both authors of this book work on the Net, and a great many other women do. Some women feel that only female-restricted conversation will help women new to networking gain the confidence they need; and so private mailing lists and other resources have been set up. Other women feel that the best armor is a slightly thicker skin and a willingness to speak up if you think a behavior is inappropriate. What we can say to you is this: The Internet is full of a great many people, most of whom have something valuable to offer. Not everyone knows how to offer that information in an appropriate way. Some learn; some don't. You have the choice, and the technology, and the policy backups, to keep these people from bothering you.

Protect Yourself

If you get e-mail or contacts in other ways from people you don't want to hear from, take these steps to protect yourself:

Tell the person you do not want any further contact of this nature. Be firm. (For example, you might say, "I do not wish to get any more mail with sexually explicit content in it from you.") Keep a copy of the correspondence, and a copy of your request, for evidence if it continues.

If the inappropriate contact does not stop, contact your systems administrator or postmaster, and the postmaster at the sender's host. To reach the postmaster, send to postmaster@*host*. All Internet sites are required to have a live human being reading and responding to mail addressed to "postmaster."

Compute smart. Find out how to use kill files, as discussed earlier in this chapter. Read headers, or use other ways (such as asking your local systems administrator or postmaster) to find out who is sending you the material.

Check to see if your personal information (available via Finger and other sources) has anything you do not want the world to see; fix any problems.

Use peer pressure. If a responder on a newsgroup is behaving inappropriately, ask your fellow Net citizens to either ignore the responder or let the responder know why they are unhappy.

Larry Magid wrote a series of tips called *Child Safety on the Information Highway.* You can find it at the Interactive Services Association Web site (http://www.isa.net) along with some other tips for where to find more information about using your Internet resource in a safe way.

The Internet is *your* resource, too. Don't let anyone drive you away from it.

Adding Emotional Bandwidth

When we speak, our tone of voice and facial expression may convey as much of our meaning as the words we use. In a brief, hastily written message, these connotations may be lost or blurred—Was that a joke? Is he really angry? Is she sad? Because of this lack of *emotional band-width* (we don't have full video and audio capability over the Net yet), people have invented ways to let the reader know how they are feeling.

Word Shorthand

We mentioned <flame on> as a signal that the poster was getting hot under the collar (and knew it). Other signals include:

<hug>	Sends a hug to the reader/readers
<smile>	The poster is smiling
<wink>	The poster is winking
<sigh>	Sadness, exasperation, resignation (must be read from context)

These are word signals. Other shorthand includes:

RTFM	Read the (fine) manual
IMHO	In my humble opinion
YMMV	Your mileage may vary (in other words, people's experiences differ)
ROTFL	Rolling on the floor laughing
TANSTAAFL	There ain't no such thing as a free lunch
<std.dis>	Insert standard disclaimer (that is, these are my opinions, not my employer's).

Smileys

Probably the best-known form of shorthand signal is the set of symbols called "emoticons" or "smileys." This is a simple smiley:

:-)

If you haven't ever seen one, turn the page sideways. The characters **:-)** should look like a simple "happy face" sort of figure. Here are some more:

:-(	Frown
:-o	Surprise (or shout)
:-|	Grim expression (or null face)

;-)	Wink
:-J	Wry smile (or licking lips, in some vernaculars)
<:-)	Spock-like raised eyebrows
:-P	Tongue in cheek

You may see people who have distinctive "smileys" in their postings, as well.

Signatures

As in e-mail, your *signature* is a standard text block that you append to any posting you send out. These are important, because some News software mangles your address so that people can't tell who you are or how to send a message to you in response to your posting (or e-mail). And also because, as discussed earlier, you might be stating your own opinions on your company/organization's machine. Most e-mail and News software has some way to set up an automatic process to append your signature. You can also read it in from a file (retyping it every time gets very wearisome).

Signature blocks are a source of both amusement and frustration for Net News readers. Some folks, particularly newbies, discover signature blocks and just go wild, including ASCII art (pictures made of standard characters), quotes, and the like, so that their signature blocks sometimes are longer than their postings!

The standard netiquette asks that you keep your signature block to four lines or less. A basic signature block includes:

Your name

Your e-mail address

Some people also include:

A phone number where strangers can call

A paper mail address

A fax phone number

Company or affiliation

And, of course, there are signature quotes.

 MASTER WORDS Interested in seeing a wild collection of signature quotes? Try Vicki's Signature Block page (`http://www.gulf.net/~vbraun/sigs/part1.html`) from your Web browser.

So, let's make up a good sample signature (called a *sig* in Internet lingo):

```
--------------------------------------------------------
Hilary St. Montain (hilary@everest.org) +1 901 555 1234 (v)
Explorer's Hut, Mt. Washington, NH 00000 +1 901 555 1222(f)

"On the mountain, there is only the rock, the summit, the
rope, and you."
```

(Some folks would quibble that the dashed line is part of the sig, and that it is therefore five lines long. YMMV.)

Trusted signatures and signatures that include a public encryption key are likely to be the next improvement in signatures. These will let you verify that the person whose signature is on the bottom of any message is really the person who they claim to be.

Do I Trust It?

Hundreds of thousands of words go out over News every day. Most of those words are the opinions of the people writing them. Some of those people are experts in their field; some are just folks who read newspapers and other newsgroups. Some postings contain verifiable facts, some contain rumors. How do you tell whether the information is authoritative?

Well, how do you tell at a cocktail party, a staff luncheon or meeting, or any other way that you get information? You depend on several things:

The speaker's sources

The speaker's credentials

The speaker's presentation

Your past history with the speaker's information

The same criteria can hold true in evaluating News postings. For example, suppose you see this posting:

```
John asked about how to get chickens to lay more eggs in
the winter. Increasing the hours the lights are on in
the hen house, keeping the temperature up (and reducing
drafts), and adding extra green bits to the food mixture
are all ways to stabilize egg production seasonally.
```

```
You can get more detailed information on this from your
local county extension agent. Look for them in the phone
book under your county government listings. There are
several publications out that have detailed instructions
on how to stabilize your egg production.
If you don't get good answers, please send me e-mail and
I'll try and help.

Martha Hart, Extension Poultry Specialist, Bucks County
(hart@ces.bucks.gov)
```

You can probably be sure that Martha knows her stuff. You judge her information to be trustworthy because:

Her language is professional and factual.

Her credentials are in the right field.

Her e-mail address looks legitimate (and it comes from a .gov domain, which means she is at least affiliated with the government).

She offers more information and further contacts.

By contrast, you might be suspicious of the quality of information in a posting like this:

```
Hey, John!
Somebody was talking the other day at a party about
this, and I think they said that you had to change the
lights and make sure the chickens are warm. You have to
do something with the food, too.
Maybe you need to buy a new rooster!

Pam
```

"Somebody said," "I was reading in the paper," "A book I once read," and other nebulous sources are what Internet cynics call "Standard Internet Sources." Some folks even quote these sources if they know their information is hearsay. Treat such information just as you would the same information in a conversation or paper letter.

 WARNING   We made this example up from remembered fragments of a talk on poultry farming. It may have no bearing on the realities of chicken farming. Standard Internet Sources apply! ;-)

CHAPTER 14

Just the FAQs, Ma'am—Nothing but the FAQs

*F*EATURING

Newsgroup-related FAQs

Topical FAQs

Business and commercial FAQs

The "peer review" process for FAQs

Finding FAQs via Usenet and other Internet tools

Chapter 14

Just the FAQs, Ma'am—Nothing but the FAQs

ONE of the hardest things about gathering information from public Internet sources is determining how authoritative the information is. Since anyone can post to newsgroups or put up an information server, how do you know what information to trust?

About the most public and most authoritative Usenet postings that can be found are the FAQs—lists of Frequently Asked Questions (and their answers).

In Chapter 2 we introduced a way of classifying types of communication on the Internet. According to that classification, FAQs are Type III communications—they are public, they come from many contributors and go to many recipients, and they are authoritative. They are published in the Internet manner: they are posted periodically (usually once a month) to the newsgroups that discuss their specific topics. FAQs also are found in the *.answers newsgroups. There are more than 500 FAQs available, and the list grows daily. There are FAQs about everything from specific computers and the programs that run on them, to the description of the Society for Creative Anachronism (SCA) illustrated in Figure 14.1, to a FAQ about Social Security Numbers. But what makes the information in a FAQ authoritative? As you'll see shortly, that comes from the collaborative process of producing the document.

The idea of collecting common information and distributing it is not new: any organization or group of people with common interests can do this by preparing a flyer or leaflet or even a book about their topic. But the difference between those items and FAQs on the Internet is accessibility, timeliness, and availability. For little or no charge in most instances, you can access the archives for a newsgroup or send e-mail to get a FAQ whenever you want, from anywhere in the world. The FAQ can be updated and new information distributed in less than a day. Fresh copies are always available: FAQs usually don't go out of print.

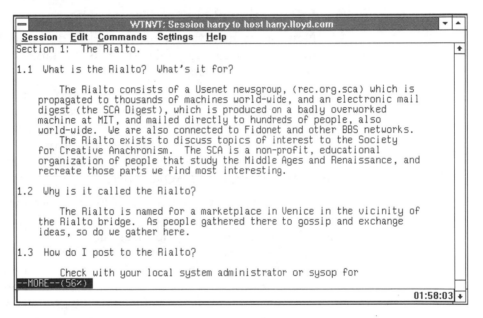

Figure 14.1. **The SCA FAQ as it appears in Usenet News.**

And the group putting out the FAQ doesn't need to spend money finding out what newspaper you read, or printing the FAQ, or mailing it to you. (As discussed in earlier chapters, there are costs associated with the Internet; nothing is free. But these costs generally are less to all concerned than the costs associated with print publication.)

Newsgroup-Related FAQs

FAQs frequently describe the charter (discussion rules) of a particular newsgroup. Other kinds of information you'll find include:

Rules about commercial postings (most commonly, the rule is that they are not allowed).

Suggestions for appropriate topics for discussion in the group.

Information about the format of postings.

Newcomer questions, such as "How do I find *X*?" (*X* being some item related to the topic, such as a shareware program if it's a computer newsgroup).

A moderated group will include information about how to post to the newsgroup—where the article should be sent and what criteria the moderator will use to judge how appropriate the posting is for the group. Usually there is only one FAQ per newsgroup, but some newsgroups have gathered extensive archives and make pointers to the archives available through the FAQ and periodic posting mechanism.

A good example of a thorough FAQ that pertains to a specific newsgroup is the one written by Diane Lin for the misc.kids newsgroup. Ms. Lin first describes the discussion topics accepted in this active group. She points people to discussions of newsgroup posting netiquette that can be read elsewhere, and she expands from the general netiquette rules to the specific ones used for misc.kids. Then she writes about "de-lurking"—introducing yourself to the group as a whole after you've read the group for a while. Misc.kids has a special "de-lurking" time where introductions of new readers are especially welcome.

The misc.kids FAQ contains further pointers for more information: to World Wide Web pages maintained by readers of misc.kids; to the e-mail addresses of specific people who have volunteered their expertise on particular topics like adoptive children, or car seats, or nannies; and to mailing lists that discuss special points.

Many of the newsgroups don't have a compiled FAQ. You may find that a group in which you are particularly interested lacks a FAQ. After you have participated in the newsgroup for a while, consider offering to compile a FAQ for the group yourself. You can learn a lot about the topic that way, and more about using the Internet effectively.

Who Knows All the FAQs?

FAQs are written by people like you—volunteers, from the community that reads a newsgroup, who want to offer their help to other members of their community. Frequently the FAQ development process goes like this:

1. Someone begins writing down information about a specific topic for personal use.

2. The writer posts it to the newsgroup and offers to accept comments on the work.

3. Readers from the newsgroup will offer suggestions for improvement of the work.

4. The author may accept and add to the work. Individual contributions are often specifically noted.

5. The community agrees that the work is complete and accurate within the scope defined by the community itself; the work is accepted as authoritative.

6. The writer/maintainer then keeps the authoritative copy and posts it to the group about once a month.

Legally, a FAQ about a newsgroup is generally the intellectual property of its writer/maintainer. (When you read FAQs, note their copyright notices. They range from extremely liberal to very restrictive.)

 MASTER WORDS Legally, publication on the Internet is a very slippery topic. If you have signed a contract with your employer concerning the rights to anything you produce on the job, you may need to discuss works published on the Internet with them.

Topical FAQs

Another type of FAQ is one that discusses a topic, not how to participate in a particular newsgroup. The meditation FAQ is an example of this type. This FAQ discusses meditation itself and presents answers to questions like: "What is meditation?"; "Should I meditate with my eyes open or closed?"; or "What is the best time of day to meditate?" Figure 14.2 shows the opening screen of the meditation FAQ.

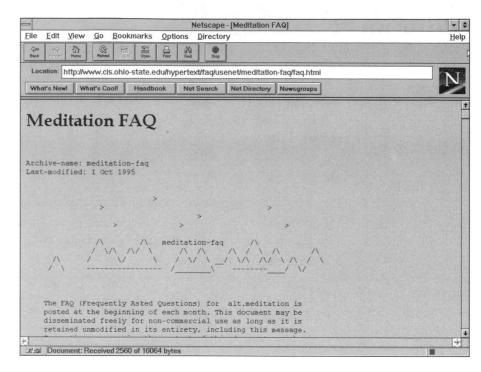

Figure 14.2.   The meditation FAQ.

More and more topical FAQs are becoming available on the Net, as shared expertise and information is being collected. Topical FAQs are generally validated in much the same way as newsgroup FAQs: that is, they are posted, the authors accept comments and make revisions, and then they are accepted. If the author is a recognized authority in the topic, the process may be shortened somewhat.

Business and Commercial FAQs

The FAQ format has become so useful and so widespread among Internet users that many other organizations besides newsgroups have started using them. Many software manufacturers prepare FAQs that you can get by sending to special e-mail addresses, or that are posted (if permissible) to newsgroups devoted to their product; computing consultants prepare them to give to users who ask about a common problem; a midwifery organization on the Net has a FAQ about becoming a midwife.

Keeping Up the Information

Maintaining a FAQ is relatively easy. As new information becomes available, the writer/maintainer simply adds it to the FAQ, amends the "date-last-changed" statement that every good FAQ should have, and posts the FAQ.

New information can come from nearly anywhere: printed material from a manufacturer or software house, the government, volunteer researchers, anecdotal histories, or testing results. Many FAQ maintainers attempt to confirm new information before adding it into the list. (As you might expect, some FAQs are likely to be more rigorously fact-checked than others. Consider the source—is the FAQ maintained by an advocacy group presenting its view of a controversial issue, for example, or by academic researchers summarizing current work in their discipline?)

Many FAQs have a summary section at the top where changes since the last posting are listed. Sometimes changes are listed with plus signs (for new information) and minuses (to show where information has been deleted). In some instances, these + and – symbols can be run through a text processor to update the old files automatically. In most instances, however, it's easier to discard the old one and keep the new one.

How Is a FAQ Different from a Book?

The publication process for a FAQ is quite different from that of the printed work—but it's a very common method of publication on the Net. The development process for a printed work (like this book, for example) goes something like this:

1. The author submits a proposal.

2. The author's proposal is accepted by the publisher, whose marketing staff has determined that there is sufficient interest in the subject matter for a book of the proposed scope to be published profitably.

3. A general outline and schedule are agreed upon.

4. The work is written and submitted to an editor. In the course of writing, the author may have circulated some or all parts of the work to colleagues for comment, but those people are not held responsible for the accuracy of its content.

5. Editors and technical editors amend or suggest amendments to the work. Technical editors attempt to verify the accuracy of all the information in the work, with varying degrees of thoroughness.

6. The manuscript is prepared for printing.

7. It is printed and sent through distribution channels.

    Early in the distribution stage, the work is sent to various publications in the field for review. Editors of these publications then send the work to reviewers whom they consider authoritative in the subject area. The reviewers then read and construct their comments for publication or broadcast. The authors and publishers of the work hope the reviewer's comments will be positive and in turn will encourage potential readers/consumers to purchase the work. The comments of the reviewers do not affect the content of the work itself—it's already written—but they can certainly affect its acceptance by the intended audience. Ultimately, no matter how much or how little the author and publisher may have done to verify the information, authoritativeness is bestowed (or not) after the actual publication—if the consensus of the reviewers is positive, then the work is considered authoritative. The ownership of the intellectual property of the work is dictated by the contract between the author and the publisher.

    With a FAQ, authoritativeness arises from the collaborative nature of the FAQ development process itself—the community has agreed that the work is good and true. If the community does not agree, the FAQ is rejected. If someone thinks the information wasn't helpful, or was wrong, not only are you likely to receive e-mail telling you your work was wrong, but your more opinionated fellow Net News readers will no doubt post an incisively worded critique of your work to related newsgroups.

    An important difference between the two types of publication, of course, is the significant financial investment behind the print publication of any work. Publishers employ people and use equipment to prepare a work for publication, to print it, to distribute it, to market it, and so on. If they are to recover these costs (and make a profit), a sufficient number of people need to buy the work. Many, if not most, books fail to earn a profit; a few "blockbusters" may account for most of the publisher's sales. In the case of the FAQ, there are no editing costs (because the editors work for free), the printing costs (if any) are borne by the reader, the distribution channel already exists as part of another service, and the marketing costs are nil, because the marketing is limited to a simple announcement.

All of this is intended only to show that the publication of a FAQ is a lot less complex than that of print publication, with significant benefits. Because the costs are so much less, the information can be updated much more frequently. Moreover, information that's of interest to an unprofitably small audience can be published in this way. On the other hand, the only recompense is the (usually unstated) appreciation of the information seeker who needed to know what is in the FAQ. Sometimes the information seekers will send you a brief e-mail of thanks if your information was helpful.

I'm Ready, Show Me the FAQs

You can find the FAQs in several places on the Internet. FAQs are available most easily to everyone with access to the full set of Internet tools, because you can use FTP, Gopher, and the Web to locate them. People who are restricted to e-mail access can get them, too. Here's a quick guide to locating them.

Using News Itself

Read the groups `news.announce.newusers` and `news.answers` (and any `*.answers` group). Watch the postings in any newsgroup you might read for an article labeled FAQ or Periodic Posting.

(We can't emphasize this one enough: `news.answers` is probably the single most interesting and useful newsgroup you'll ever read.)

Using the News Archive at MIT

Use FTP to connect to the server `rtfm.mit.edu`. You'll find the FAQs in the pub/usenet directory. Use the Get command in FTP to bring the FAQ to you.

Using the World Wide Web

Using your favorite Web browser, connect to

```
http://www.cis.ohio-state.edu/hypertext/faq/usenet/
```

You'll see the introductory page shown in Figure 14.3; the list itself follows on subsequent screens.

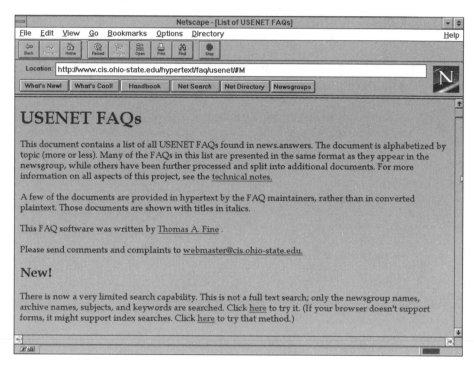

Figure 14.3. *The USENET FAQs page as seen through a Web browser.*

Using E-Mail

Send e-mail to `mail-server@rtfm.mit.edu`. The body of the message should look like this:

```
help
index
```

Do not add signature lines. The mail server will send further instructions in response to the command word *help* and a list of available files in response to the command word *index*.

Using Gopher

The FAQs are available at sol.csd.unb.ca. Once you get there, select Frequently Asked Questions Archives. Once there, you'll see a Gopher menu organized by higher level newsgroup hierarchy; select the hierarchy for the newsgroup whose FAQ you are interested in reading.

 WARNING If the FAQ you want has a file name ending with the characters ".Z", it means that the file has been compressed with the UNIX compression utility. To read the contents of the file, you will need to move the file to a UNIX machine where you can run an uncompression utility before you can read it. You'll find more about compression in Chapter 9's discussion of FTP.

CHAPTER 15

Instantaneous Personal Communication: IRC and Talk

FEATURING

Chapter 15

Instantaneous Personal Communication: IRC and Talk

ONE of the most exciting things about the Internet is how fast you can communicate with folks: sometimes we've exchanged more than twenty messages with people in England in the course of an hour! The communication is fast and fun.

The most personal and instantaneous methods of communication are Internet Relay Chat (IRC), its derivatives, and Talk. These facilities let you communicate with others right from the keyboard (and in some cases, using a microphone!). IRC lets you talk to many people at once, almost like a CB radio or cocktail party. Talk is more personal; it's just two people chatting together on screen. Even the keystroke corrections show up. Today's Graphical User Interface (GUI) IRC clients make using IRC easy and fun.

Internet Relay Chat: Keeping a Finger on the Pulse of the Internet

Popularly known throughout the Internet as IRC, Internet Relay Chat offers the ability to communicate interactively with many thousands of people around the world about nearly any subject imaginable. Unlike any other Internet service, IRC enables you to hold a spontaneous conversation, in real time, with a group of individuals who may never physically meet. Moreover, your conversation is transmitted using more than 125 interconnected servers, which means that you can talk with a wide variety of people from every interconnected country in the world at the same time.

But if you think Usenet newsgroups are anarchic, wait until you try IRC. When groups of individuals from widely disparate backgrounds come together in a physical meeting, the topics discussed are usually constrained by each participant's perception of what would be allowed or generally accepted by the other participants. In Internet Relay Chat, anarchy reigns.

In most cases there are no constraints on the topics that may be discussed. Topics range from the serious (an oft-mentioned example is the successful use of IRC to relay information into and out of Russia during the 1993 Boris Yeltsin coup; it was also used in the 1994 and 1995 earthquakes in California and Kobe, Japan), to the inevitable computer-speak, to the recreational topics of international society, such as sports, movies, books, gossip about the rich and famous, and political debate. Topics may be controversial or mainstream at the whim of the participants, and anyone can create a topic (known as a *channel* within IRC).

Those of us old enough to remember the 1970s may be reminded of the Citizen's Band (CB) radio phenomenon. But comparing Internet Relay Chat with CB radio reveals more differences than similarities. Like CB, Internet Relay Chat is spontaneous—you can enter IRC, choose an existing channel or create a new one, and begin talking. Yet IRC does not have the limitations of CB: whereas CB users must be geographically close because the medium is radio waves, IRC works over the Internet, a world-wide collection of thousands of interconnected computer networks. Participants in an IRC channel may be from Michigan, California, London, Moscow, Taipei, or virtually any location where Internet service is available. IRC topics and language are also not constrained by FCC regulation.

A striking similarity with CB is the fact that IRC has developed its own culture and etiquette. (Members of the CB subculture pretended to be truck drivers and often spoke in fake Southern accents. Everyone had a "handle"; Betty Ford's was "First Mama." If you disagreed with what someone said, you told them to "Lay down 'cuz yer tired." More seriously, an informal protocol arose so that people did not interrupt each other, recreational conversations did not interfere with actual truckers' business, and so on. As in other subcultures, this protocol was enforced by peer pressure.)

Similar cultural evolution has happened with IRC. Obnoxious characters are ignored or cut out of the conversation. Those who are dealing with serious topics (depression, abuse, and so on) receive support but not the sometimes raucous banter encountered in the less serious channels. Each person on an IRC channel has a "nickname," just like handles on CB, which lets them develop an online persona.

Learning (and if desired, becoming a part of) the IRC's culture is one of the more challenging and entertaining aspects of using this Internet service. Fortunately, documents are available from Internet Relay Chat experts that explain the workings of the IRC programs and provide a glimpse into its culture. (See "Accessing Internet Relay Chat" later in this chapter to locate the IRC Frequently Asked Questions.)

Internet Relay Chat has proven to be an effective tool during emergencies, natural disasters, and political upheavals. In addition to the Boris Yeltsin incident, IRC was used to convey current information during the 1991 Persian Gulf war, in several earthquakes, and during Hurricane Andrew. Because the IRC (and the underlying Internet) are carried over such widely distributed computers, information can arrive from areas where conventional communications may have failed. Also, since these current topics can be discussed in real time, with information coming in from different sources simultaneously, an IRC user can learn a great deal about a situation very rapidly.

Unfortunately, the *scroll rate* (the speed at which incoming text from IRC flows off the screen) can be incredible when many IRC users are "talking" (typing text) into an IRC channel. To solve this problem, IRC client programs usually have the capability to log all text from one or more channels into a file for later reading or to separate conversations into multiple windows. We'll talk about using this client software next.

Accessing Internet Relay Chat

Internet Relay Chat works as a client/server application, and the IRC servers are interconnected to form, from the user's perspective, one large service. Each IRC user must use a client program on their Internet host. You instruct the client to connect to at least one IRC server, preferably a server nearby to minimize network delays and inefficiencies. Internet Relay Chat clients are available for Microsoft

Windows-equipped PCs with Winsock support, the Macintosh, IBM mainframes running VM, most UNIX systems, and VMS with a TCP/IP package. IRC clients must run on a computer attached directly to the Internet.

Some of you will find that IRC is already installed and popular on the computer where you have a host account. Others may need to install an IRC client on your home computer, to run over your dial-up IP link. These steps will get you started, letting you collect the necessary software and documentation:

1. Obtain the latest Frequently Asked Questions (FAQ) files regarding IRC. These files are indispensable, as they contain updated information on how to configure the software and include the latest list of IRC servers that are publicly available for clients to connect to. FAQ files and documentation for IRC are available via the World Wide Web at

    ```
    http://www.funet.fi/~irc/
    ```
    and
    ```
    http://www.undernet.org/
    ```

2. On a UNIX or VMS host, try the `irc` command. If that command is not available, you'll need to obtain and build the IRC client. Personal computer users will also need to obtain the client. If the command does work, and a screen similar to Figure 15.1 appears, proceed to "Using Internet Relay Chat" below.

3. Use the list of IRC client sources in the Frequently Asked Questions file to obtain the appropriate client. A few widely used personal computer clients are suggested in "Commercial IRC Networks and Services" later in this chapter. UNIX system users will find that the ircII (the command is `irc` or `irc2`) client is most commonly used. The Frequently Asked Questions provide pointers to World Wide Web and anonymous FTP sites that contain easily accessed free or low-cost IRC client software.

4. Select an initial server you'll connect to. The Frequently Asked Questions files list a number of public servers that are useful to use. Later, by asking IRC server operators for leads on nearby servers, you may be able to find a server that is faster and less heavily used than the well-known public servers listed in the Frequently Asked Questions files. Most clients require the host name or IP address and the port number (usually 6667) of the IRC server.

5. Install the client software following the instructions in the README file provided with the software. When the client is started, a screen similar to Figure 15.1 should appear. If the connection to the server fails, try another from the public server list in the FAQ.

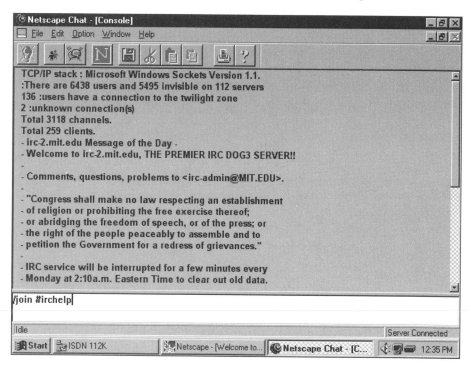

Figure 15.1. **Initial connection to IRC server** `irc-2.mit.edu` *using the Netscape Chat client with Microsoft Windows 95.*

Using Internet Relay Chat

Each IRC user has a nickname, a unique word they have chosen. Other IRC users may send private messages to the nickname, and users within channels refer to participants generally by their nickname. Nicknames must be unique and are not owned or permanently recorded in IRC. This means you choose your nickname each time you access the IRC. The nickname should be nine characters or less. IRC users often use a whimsical name, their first name, or some other unique word that has special meaning.

MASTER WORDS   When you want to access the IRC, you cannot take the same nickname as someone already online. You may need to change your nickname to something else. When you access IRC and are the first one there with your selected nickname, of course, other people will have to choose their nicknames so as not to conflict with yours.

Most IRC clients will prompt for a nickname, or the nickname may be specified on the command line or environment variable. For example, the UNIX ircII client accepts the command:

```
irc Annette irc-2.mit.edu
```

This command sets the nickname to "Annette" and connects to the IRC server `irc-2.mit.edu`. There may be other, more convenient methods of setting the nickname described in the client documentation.

Selecting and Creating Channels

Once you've connected to an Internet Relay Chat server and chosen a nickname, finding or creating a channel of interest is the next step. There are often over 1000 channels active on IRC, but most users find a selected few that are of interest and regularly use them. Listing channels the first time may be a mind-numbing experience, and it helps to have a small notepad handy to write down the names of channels that sound interesting for future use. The `/list` command will list all channels currently active within IRC. To look for the busiest channels, try `/list -min 10` to list channels with a minimum of 10 active users.

Again, recall that IRC is anarchic and freewheeling, so do not be surprised if some of the channels sound unsavory or are unconventional. Channel names that begin with a # are IRC-wide channels available to any IRC user. Channels beginning with & are available only from the current IRC server. You will almost always find at least one interesting IRC-wide channel (and often many more). Figure 15.2 includes a very small portion of the output of the `/list` command.

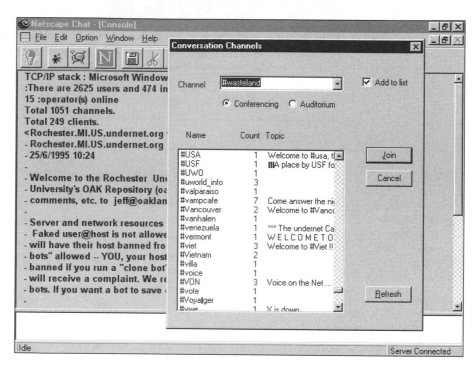

Figure 15.2.   A small portion of /list on the Undernet IRC network.

To access a channel, type /join *name*, where *name* is the channel's name. The command /join #sports would join the sports channel within IRC. If there is no channel of immediate interest, you can easily create a new channel. Type /join #name, where *name* is a word describing the channel's topic. For example, the command /join #karate would join the #karate channel if one existed in IRC; but if there was no such channel, the command would create one. You could then use the /topic command to add a short phrase describing your new channel:

    /topic Interested in Karate?

When IRC users use the /list command to list channels, the topic helps identify the channel as new, and it provides an insight into what you propose to discuss in the channel.

After you select or create a channel, any text you type will be sent to participants of the channel. (If you are the first one there, no one will answer you, of course.) IRC shows the user that typed each line of text in the channel. A typical dialog might look like Figure 15.3.

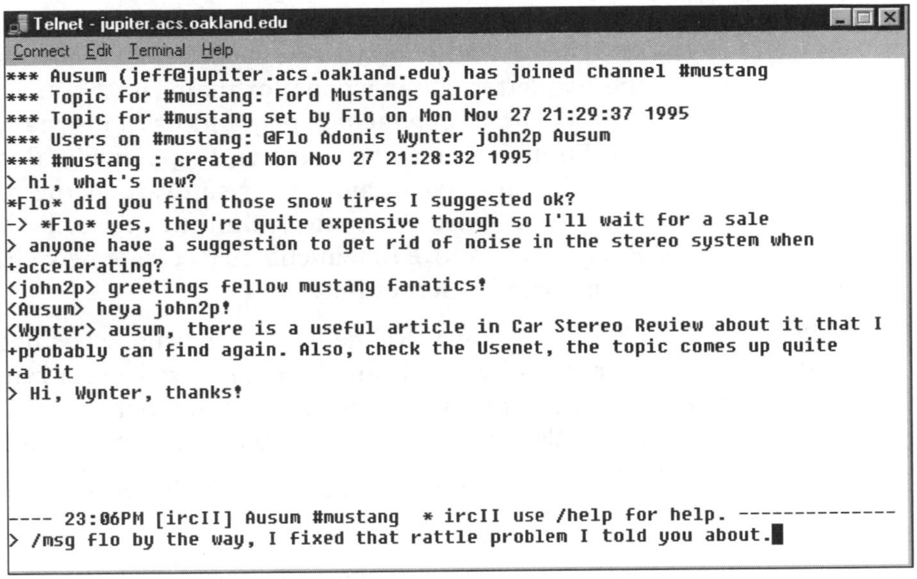

```
┌─ Telnet - jupiter.acs.oakland.edu ─────────────────── _ □ ✕ ─┐
│ Connect  Edit  Terminal  Help                                │
│ *** Ausum (jeff@jupiter.acs.oakland.edu) has joined channel #mustang │
│ *** Topic for #mustang: Ford Mustangs galore                 │
│ *** Topic for #mustang set by Flo on Mon Nov 27 21:29:37 1995 │
│ *** Users on #mustang: @Flo Adonis Wynter john2p Ausum        │
│ *** #mustang : created Mon Nov 27 21:28:32 1995              │
│ ▷ hi, what's new?                                            │
│ *Flo* did you find those snow tires I suggested ok?          │
│ ─▷ *Flo* yes, they're quite expensive though so I'll wait for a sale │
│ ▷ anyone have a suggestion to get rid of noise in the stereo system when │
│ +accelerating?                                               │
│ <john2p> greetings fellow mustang fanatics!                  │
│ <Ausum> heya john2p!                                         │
│ <Wynter> ausum, there is a useful article in Car Stereo Review about it that I │
│ +probably can find again. Also, check the Usenet, the topic comes up quite │
│ +a bit                                                       │
│ ▷ Hi, Wynter, thanks!                                        │
│                                                              │
│                                                              │
│                                                              │
│ ──── 23:06PM [ircII] Ausum #mustang  * ircII use /help for help. ─────────── │
│ ▷ /msg flo by the way, I fixed that rattle problem I told you about.█ │
└──────────────────────────────────────────────────────────────┘
```

Figure 15.3. *An IRC conversation in a quiet channel.*

The IRC nickname is shown in angle brackets (<>) when the typed message is directed to every participant in the channel. When the name is shown in asterisks (*), the message is private and is only seen by the recipient (in Figure 15.3, Flo sent a message to Ausum). Thus, both public (to all channel viewers) and private messages may be sent and read simultaneously while using IRC.

See "IRC Commands" for a summary of the commonly used commands within IRC, including those for sending private messages to other IRC users.

The Undernet and Other IRC Networks

Recognizing that the current Internet Relay Chat network (known as EFnet by IRC users) is overcrowded, a group of IRC server administrators came together within the past two years to create a new IRC network known as the Undernet. Still others have created other IRC networks, and the commercial Internet services have just begun forming their own networks.

Generally using the same software and servers, accessing the Undernet and the other derivative IRC networks just requires connecting to a different server. In the case of the Undernet, the server is usually known as *country*.undernet.org, where *country* is the two-letter country code for the nearest country with an Undernet server. The us.undernet.org and ca.undernet.org servers handle the United States and Canada, respectively. Because the Undernet uses the same client and server software as the rest of Internet Relay Chat, you'll use the same techniques described in "Using Internet Relay Chat" above to join channels, create new channels, and communicate over Undernet IRC.

These derivative IRC networks are usually less active than the frenetic EFnet, to be sure, but their improved organization, added services (such as Undernet's popular Channel Service that is used to moderate channels), and increased reliability are very popular.

The popular Yahoo World Wide Web index available at

    http://www.yahoo.com/

indexes the home pages of many of the derivative IRC networks (search for Internet Relay Chat). Some of the networks listed (including KidLink, a private youth IRC network used by K-12 students and teachers) are private but application instructions are included in the listings.

Commercial IRC Networks and Services

Commercial Internet services have realized the potential of IRC and are forming their own networks and coming up with new, intriguing ideas for Internet Relay Chat. Enterprising commercial organizations have brought to the table the ability to use the IRC for inexpensive or free voice "telephone" calls worldwide, better IRC client and server programs, and moderated conferencing tools. It is certain that further rapid evolution of IRC will be driven by these organizations.

Quarterdeck's Prospero Systems Research division:

    http://www.prospero.com

recently released the Global Chat client and Global Stage server programs. Global Chat is a free GUI IRC client that is both easy to use and powerful at the same time, and Global Stage enables organizations to set up private and public IRC servers for special events, technical support, or other purposes quickly and easily.

Netscape Chat from Netscape Communications:

```
http://www.netscape.com/comprod/chat_install.html
```

is gaining a loyal following. Similar to Global Chat, it offers a friendly interface to IRC. Netscape Chat tightly integrates into Netscape's popular Netscape Navigator World Wide Web browsing program and is easy to install and use. One reason for its popularity is its ability to integrate web and IRC so that you can send your chat partners a URL and they can immediately execute it.

As an alternative to the text-based conferencing that IRC clients and servers have typically provided, voice communications are now possible over IRC and other Internet services! Electric Magic (makers of a voice-over-the-Internet product for the Macintosh) has put up an index of free and commercial products at

```
http://www.emagic.com/netphone/othersites.html
```

Voice communication over the Internet, whether via IRC or another Internet service such as the World Wide Web, greatly expands the ability to use the Internet as a conference medium. Improved encoding, development of specialized IRC services for voice, and innovative users will keep this aspect of the Internet a hot spot of change.

Talk: Person to Person

Like IRC, Talk happens on screen and instantaneously. The `talk` command is supported on most UNIX hosts, and a great many LANs have an analogous command, sometimes called CHAT or WRITE. There is even a Macintosh TCP/IP client called "talk," which simply lets you talk to folks over the Net.

Talk is much less formal than IRC, if you can believe it, because it is simpler. Talk is just two people instead of an endless number. Talk can happen between two folks on the same host or between people on differing hosts. Pat, logged on at home, can talk to Glee, logged into a Netcom machine. If you know the person's address, you can attempt to talk to them.

You need two things to have a successful talk session: a terminal emulator running a VT100 (visual) terminal emulation (or a more advanced visual terminal), and the person's e-mail address.

Starting a Talk Session

To start a Talk session, generally you type the `talk` command and the person's address:

    talk jeff

or, if Jeff is on a different host than you are:

    talk jeff@jupiter.acs.oakland.edu

Jeff will hear a bell and see your Talk request on his screen, as in Figure 15.4.

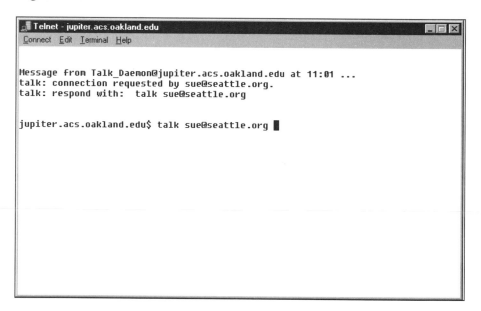

*Figure 15.4.   **Preparing to respond to a Talk request.***

> **MASTER WORDS**   Sometimes the e-mail address you have for someone is an alias. You will need to find out what their real login is and what machine they are working on. The easiest way to find this information is to have them start a Talk session with you. Then you will see on your screen exact instructions on how to respond.

If you try to initiate a Talk session with someone, your screen will divide in half and the Talk daemon will tell you that it's trying to reach your friend. If the person is on a different host, you will see a note that the daemon is trying to talk to a remote daemon as seen in Figure 15.5.

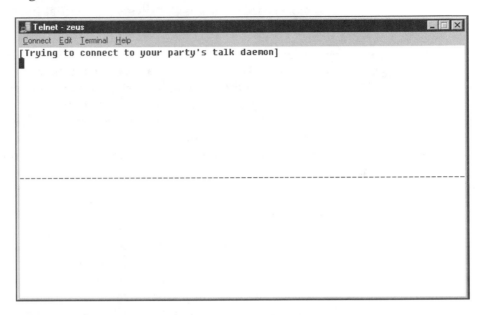

Figure 15.5. **What the person initiating the Talk session sees.**

While on your end you see a series of notes that your daemon is "Ringing your party again," your friend will get a series of requests, like the one shown earlier in Figure 15.4, accompanied by a bell sound. (If your friend should have her session set to reject Talk requests, or if she is not logged in, you'll get a message to that effect, and you'll go back to the regular system prompt.)

Once your friend has responded, and the connection is established, you can start typing, and your friend will see every keystroke—including the typos and the backspaces!

Don't Everyone Talk at Once!

One convention is that only one person writes at a time. In practice, you will frequently be writing at the same time. When that happens, you just pause and wait for the other person to continue.

Some folks end each "transmission" from their side with two carriage returns, to show that they have stopped "speaking" and the other person can go ahead.

People use Talk for everything from personal (and sometimes intimate) chat to quick business conversations. Since Talk is unmonitored and not recorded, it has the greatest potential for truly private conversation over the Net.

MASTER WORDS   "Unmonitored" is a relative term. No one is recording the Talk sessions on either host, in general. However, if someone happens to be monitoring the physical connection (for example, if they are attempting to troubleshoot a network problem, or if they are crackers attempting to catch passwords transmitted without encryption over the network) and catches your Talk session, it can be recorded—along with the hundreds of other transmissions going over that connection at the same time.

It might seem that using Talk demands someone's attention immediately, in a way that e-mail does not. It's true that a Talk request repeats endlessly (and somewhat obnoxiously) until the sender terminates it. But if you do not want to be bothered with Talk requests, you can set up your terminal session to refuse Talk connections (ask your systems administrator or other guru how to do this for your particular system). Courtesy says that if you initiate a Talk session with someone, and they tell you that it's not convenient right now (or that they do not want to talk to you at all), you terminate the connection and send your urgent communications (if any) via e-mail.

Figure 15.6 shows the beginning screen for a Talk session.

Your words will appear at the top of the screen, and your friend's at the bottom. At her end, things are reversed: her words are on top and yours on the bottom.

As the conversation goes on, you may type more than the 10 lines or so allotted to each party. If that happens, the Talk daemon will just scroll your lines back to the top of the screen, and you will overwrite your old conversation. This may take a little getting used to. Figure 15.7 shows the overlapping nature of a long-running Talk session.

Hanging Up

To end your Talk session, let your partner know you need to go, and then type Ctrl-C. This will close the session. Your words go off the screen and are gone, just like when you hang up from a telephone call.

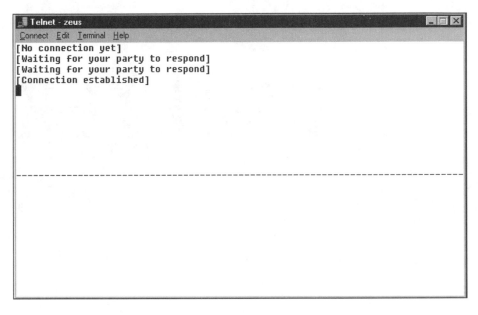

*Figure 15.6.   **Starting a Talk session.***

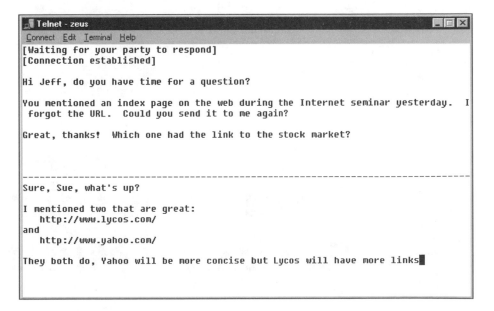

*Figure 15.7.   **A long-running Talk session.***

CHAPTER 16

Living Out Your Fantasies: MUDs

FEATURING

Chapter 16

Living Out Your Fantasies: MUDs

A *MUD* (Multiple User Dimension, Multiple User Dungeon, or Multiple User Dialog; also known as a MUSE, or Multiple User Simulated Environment) is a computer program in which many users interact. As the various interpretations of the acronym suggest, MUDs can take many forms, but most are fantasy games. Most are available via Telnet, but many are becoming available with WWW.

 MASTER WORDS MUD is the generic term for a whole range of interactive environments. Other names are MOOs, MUSHes, MUCKs, TinyMUDs, AberMUDs, and so on. The name varies depending on the software underlying the shared environment. In this chapter we use the term MUD unless a specific software is intended.

What's Special about a MUD?

In the late 70s and early 80s, many computer users enjoyed playing a game called Adventure, where they rambled through a cave, solving problems and interacting with various creatures in the cave. Many newer computer users have played Dungeons and Dragons or other fantasy role-playing games. MUDs combine several elements of each of these experiences.

In a MUD, you type commands to manipulate objects, make a general announcement, or whisper in a friend's ear. You read descriptions of your locale, and can wander at will, exploring your environs. There are rooms, or caves, or conference rooms. You can read papers. You can change your clothes, perform actions on other objects (jump on a table, break an egg, eat breakfast). All these actions and experiences are familiar to folks who've played games like Adventure or Zork on a computer.

However, when you played Adventure your friends were clustered around you in chairs, watching the screen and shouting suggestions about what to do next. No one was in the game with you. Every time you went through a certain part of the cave, everything behaved predictably.

Role-playing games, on the other hand, are ensemble expeditions. Random chance (the toss of a die or the whim of the game's "master" or "wizard") changes the behavior of both villains and friends. You can experience the action together, each from your individual viewpoints. It's a group experience, and has more similarity to the unpredictability of real life than a game of Adventure.

In a MUD, you have the on-screen descriptions, the typing of commands, and the manipulation of objects; all of which are familiar to the users of earlier text-based computer games. You also have dozens of other autonomous beings in the environment with you, real humans taking a role in your experience and interacting with you according to their personalities, abilities, and whim. You can flirt, dance, design a marketing program, hold a meeting, explore an adventure game, or just chat.

Across the world, hundreds of thousands of MUDders are doing just that. Figure 16.1 shows an internationally popular MUD, called the Imperial DikuMUD or, because of the host it originally ran on, "Supergirl." You can Telnet to the MUD at `imperial.cs.hut.fi` (or `130.233.40.66`), port 6969.

 MASTER WORDS Notice that for this MUD, we've given an IP address (`130.233.40.66`) as well as the equivalent domain name (`imperial.cs.hut.fi`). This practice is widespread in the MUD community. In the early days of MUDs in the US, most MUDding was restricted because of bandwidth problems, and so MUDders used hidden or frankly illegal resources to run their games. Even though many MUDs are now acceptable to the owners of the resources, the tradition of using IP addresses continues.

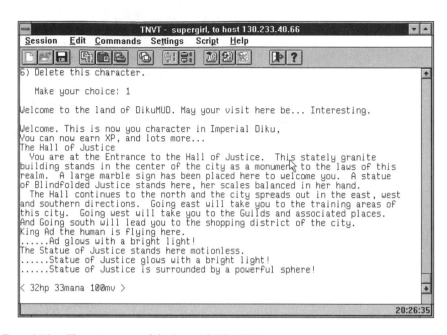

Figure 16.1.   The entry room of the Imperial DikuMUD.

A Short History of MUDs

Historically, MUDs derive from an artificial intelligence (AI) experiment by Richard Bartle and Roy Trubshaw at the University of Essex (England) in the early 1980s. MUD1, written in 1979–80, is generally accepted as the first MUD. One of the goals of the experiment was to see if a program could be developed that would respond to the actions of multiple users with appropriate environmental responses. For example, if you dropped a vase, could the program decide if it would break depending on what you were standing on, or random chance?

The name MUD was trademarked to the commercial MUD run by Bartle on British Telecom (the motto was: "You haven't *lived* 'til you've *died* on MUD!"). Like most other fascinating concepts, this one became popular with students, and many new and improved MUD-like programs sprang up on the European academic networks. Most of these had associated bulletin-board systems for social interaction. Because Usenet feeds were spotty and difficult to get in the UK, and the British JANET network (a cousin of the US BITNET) didn't support FTP or remote login via Telnet, the MUDs became major focal points for social interaction among hackers there before Internet connections became plentiful.

MUD variants crossed the Atlantic around 1988 and quickly gained popularity in the US; they became nuclei for large network communities with only loose ties to the traditional hacker community. A second wave of MUDs (TinyMUD and variants) arose; these games tended to emphasize social interaction, puzzles, and cooperative world-building as opposed to combat and competition.

Enter a New Reality

In a typical MUD, each user takes control of a computerized being (also sometimes called persona, incarnation, avatar, or character). You type commands and the affected users or objects respond. Your persona can walk around, chat with other characters, explore dangerous territory, solve riddles and puzzles, and even create your very own space. Many MUDs are live, role-playing games in which you assume a new identity and enter an alternate reality through your keyboard.

Each MUD has its own personality, which largely comes from the creator who developed its rules, laws of nature, and information databases. Some MUDs stress the social aspects of on-line communications—users frequently gather on-line to chat and join together to build new structures or even entire realms. Others are closer to "Dungeons and Dragons" and are filled with sorcerers, dragons and evil people out to keep you from completing your quest—through murder if necessary. Several have themes—such as a world based on the fantasy *Pern* series, or on the *Worlds of Amber* series.

Who Inhabits a MUD?

In all MUDs there are two types of character—NPCs (non-player characters, those that are computer generated and part of the landscape) and PCs (players). PCs can be split into two categories, mortals and immortals. Mortals are what you start out as, roaming the land, questing, killing, solving and dying. From gaming comes the term "running your character."

Immortals are those folks who have decided they want something more from the game. Immortals are basically housekeepers to the MUD, debugging, developing, moderating and above all helping out mortals with their numerous problems.

In the Imperial-style MUD, you are entering a typical role-playing environment. You equip yourself with items to prepare you to start an adventure, you gather companions, you learn magic spells and increase your skills and potentials. This is a magic-users world.

Other Kinds of MUDs

By contrast, the SchMOOze, a MOO (MUD, Object Oriented) sponsored by Canadian schools, recreates a school campus. Newcomers take beginning classes, go to seminars, explore the campus. Later in this chapter, you'll see how these very different MUDs handle similar operations.

The advantages of MUDs for conversation and communication have not been lost on the business and research worlds. Several firms have "virtual conference rooms"—really MUDs—where participants scattered across the globe can meet to talk, in the same way they would talk if they were all in the same room. The meeting planner can even develop agendas, AV displays (participants download GIFs and MPEGs to display on their own workstations), and so on, which the participants can manipulate and display for themselves.

The UM Library MOO

The School of Library Science (SILS) at the University of Michigan has developed an interactive session where you can talk to a reference librarian if you are having trouble finding something. The SILS MOO includes a reading room, reference sections, and a librarian's office where you talk to the Librarian on duty. Figure 16.2 shows the main entrance to the Library, and Figure 16.3 shows a conversation with a librarian.

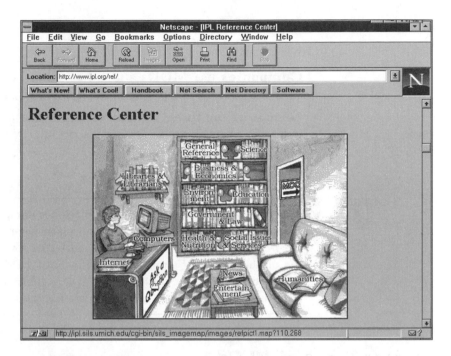

Figure 16.2. **The SILS Library MOO.**

Figure 16.3. **Talking to a reference librarian.**

Being Creative with MUDs

Other creative uses for MUDs are:

Companies use MUDs and other shared environment software similar to MUDs for brainstorming, creative development work.

Groups of far flung friends or family use MUDs as an alternate form of communication (especially popular with students).

Oklahoma State University uses a MUD for conversations among its varied systems administrators.

 WARNING　MUDding and other game playing is not acceptable behavior at many companies and institutions, particularly when players are connecting from shared labs or other public work space. One problem (besides the obvious waste of employee time) is that MUDders use up resources intended for study or business use. If in doubt, contact your systems administrator to see what the appropriate use rules are for your site.

Different Types of MUDs

Along with the original MUDs, there are a number of variants. Each has its own flavor, and the underlying basic game and databases of objects and commands are focused on or modified to reflect the flavor of the game. The four major variants are described below.

LPMUDs

LPMUDs are free-form MUDs. In these environments each room is an independent universe and may be created by different individuals. Each has its own rules and realities. Anything can happen. Most LPMUDs are puzzle-oriented or social rather than combat games. LPMUDs are the most sophisticated MUDs. LPMUDs have programming bases similar to the original MUDs, but each room is limited only by its creator's imagination.

TinyMUDs

TinyMUDs are an offshoot of LPMUDs, which use less disk space and frequently have a smaller number of rooms (although they are still quite extensive).

DikuMUDs

DikuMUDs are role-playing adventure games, based on the "kill, kill, kill" principle. Characters kill monsters and evil characters created by the gods, wizards, and other players. Killing off monsters lets characters gain status, experience, equipment, fame and (fake) money. DikuMUDs have many social-interaction commands, as well, and some have evolved into places where participants can go to chat and socialize with each other. DikuMUDs are usually based on one of three or four stock game and database setups. From these beginnings all have diverged into many individual flavors, some being distinctly non-Diku. All rooms tend to radiate from a central hall, which is usually called Midgaard. After that, the adventure begins.

AberMUDs

AberMUDs are much like DikuMUDs except that they are based on players killing (Pking) each other rather than monsters or other artificial denizens of the game. In essence, the players hunt one another. Some purists regard AberMUDs as true combat environment, because your opponents are real, and not computer generated.

MUSHes

All MUSHes are theme-based: for example, many are based on science fiction or fantasy books such as Frank Herbert's *Dune* or Anne McAffrey's *Pern* series. The creators of these games start off with a standard game program and database, and customize it to reflect the environment, customs, and characters from the books. In the *Dune* MUSHes, for example, they have imported the Houses Royal, Houses Major, and the Spacer's Guild, as well as the physics and the magic systems from Herbert's novels. Similarly, in one of the *Pern* MUDs, characters take on personas based on characters in that series: they become weyrwomen, dragon riders, holders, guild members, and goon. They interact in games designed around the geography and customs of the books. If you wish to be a dedicated player in one of these games, you will be assigned a character and role by the wizards or gods. Reading all the books about your theme-world is critical to your success there. Guests take minor roles and wander in and out of the action. Frequently the MUSH's creators will create a crisis, which the participants must resolve—in character.

Graphical MUDs

Graphical MUDs at this time are still a very rare and finicky breed, most needing some level of technical competence to use. The best sources of up-to-date information are the Usenet groups, specifically `rec.games.mud.misc`, `rec.games.mud.admin` and the MUD FAQs posted bimonthly on these groups. Clients for these MUDs are even rarer. Check the list of clients commonly available. One good client for graphical MUDs is Pueblo, for WinNT and Win95 (a version for Win3.x will be available soon). Pueblo, from Chaco Communications, adds the ability to view 2D (GIF, JPEG, BMP) and 3D graphics (VRML), listen to music (MIDI, WAV) and view both plain text and hypertext (HTML). Expect a lot of rough edges in graphical MUDs, as these are extremely new. For further details check out Pueblo's home page:

```
http://www.chaco.com/pueblo
```

How Do I Connect to a MUD?

There are several ways to hook yourself up to a MUD. We'll start with Telnet.

Telnet

You can use Telnet once you know the MUD's network address and port number. If, for instance, we knew that PernMUSH was at the network address `cesium.clock.org` at port 4201, we could type:

```
telnet cesium.clock.org 4201
```

On some VMS systems you will need to type:

```
telnet cesium.clock.org/port=4201
```

And you arrive in a new reality!

 MASTER WORDS   If you get back an error message like "host unknown," you'll need to use the IP address rather than the domain address. Most MUD directories have both the domain name and IP address listed.

If you're using Telnet on a VMS system, you may need to make sure that your terminal has "newlines" turned on. If it doesn't, the MUD's output will scroll across the screen without any carriage returns, making it very difficult to decipher and interact with.

MUD Clients

Telnet is a low-tech and unpleasant way to connect to most MUDs, since it doesn't handle text wrapping. Even worse, if someone speaks to you and you are typing at the same time, your lines will become horribly intermingled, making it hard to see what you're typing and hard to keep track of what's going around you in the MUD. A better way to connect is via client software. MUD client programs provide:

Access or transport to the MUD

Pre-formatted macros that let you change MUDs conveniently

Macros to "gag" (suppress) or highlight certain MUD output.

Most clients use BSD UNIX, although many are written to compile and run under System V (SysV) UNIX and other variants. Other operating systems for which there are MUD clients include VMS with either MultiNet or Wollongong networking, Macintosh, and IBM's VM. Lately reliable clients for Windows have emerged, although for DOS there are very few.

Where Do I Find Clients?

 MASTER WORDS   The following list of clients came from the MUD FAQ, and the commentary is taken from the contributors to that list. (Because this commentary was originally written for experienced MUDders, it's pretty terse. The accompanying glossary will help to clarify the more cryptic terminology.) You should use a Web search or index , like InfoSeek or Yahoo, or Veronica within Gopher (see Chapter 11) to look for the latest versions of these clients.

According to experienced players, TinyTalk, TinyFugue and TinTin varieties are among the easiest to learn; Tcltt and VT are more professional. Some of these clients have more features than others, and some require a fair degree of computer and programming experience to use. Since many MUDders write their own clients, this list can never be complete. Your best bet is to try out a couple, and ask more experienced folk for their recommendations.

In this list, Windows, Windows95 WindowsNT and DOS clients appear first, followed by Macintosh, and then UNIX, VMS, and miscellaneous clients.

Part
II

The Internet Toolkit

GLOSSARY OF CLIENT TERMS

Here's what those cryptic terms on the MUD list mean:

Auto-login: The client automatically logs into the game for you.

Hiliting: The client allows boldface or other emphasis to be applied to some text (often particular types of output, such as whispers, or particular players).

Regexp: The client lets you use UNIX-style regular expressions to select text to highlight.

Gag: The client allows some text to be suppressed. The choice of what to suppress is often similar to hiliting (players or regular expressions).

Macros: The client allows new commands to be defined.

Logging: The client allows output from the MUD to be recorded in a file.

Cyberportals: The client supports special MUD features that can automatically reconnect you to another MUD server.

Screen mode: The client supports some sort of screen mode (beyond simply scrolling) on some terminals.

Triggers: Events that occur when certain actions on the MUD occur (for example, waving when a player enters the room); the client supports these automatically.

Programmability: The client allows you to customize it to some extent.

File and command uploading: The client supports using FTP or similar Internet tools from within the MUD. This allows you to download files (such as graphics) from other players, and to read mail and do other activities from within the game.

Multiple connections: The client lets you connect to the same game more than once, so that you can (for example) run more than one character or persona at a time.

Command history or *history buffers:* The client keeps a listing of the commands you have issued, so that you can keep track of what you have done, or go back and repeat sequences.

To see how these features are implemented in a particular client, you'll need to read that program's documentation.

 WARNING   Some clients enable you to login multiple characters and control them as one. But be warned, some MUDs have a very strict one-at-a-time policy. So before you start having fun with multiple characters, check with the maintainers of the MUD.

Microsoft Windows and DOS-Based Clients

VWMud   Runs on MS Windows using WinSock. Features include macros and triggers. You can find the program at:

```
ftp://ftp.microserve.com/pub/msdos/winsock/vwmud110.zip
```

WinWorld   Runs on MS Windows using WinSock. You can find the program at:

```
ftp://ftp.mgl.ca/pub/winworld
```

MUTT   Runs on MS Windows using WinSock. Latest version is 01I or above. MUTT stands for Multi-User Trivial Terminal. Features include scripting, multiple connections, triggers, macros, logging, etc. You can find the program at:

```
ftp://caisr2.cwru.edu/pub/mud
```

or

```
ftp://ftp.graphcomp.com/pub/msw/mutt
```

MudWin   Runs on MS Windows using WinSock. Features include command history, simple macros, and logging. You can find the program at:

```
ftp://ftp.microserve.com/pub/msdos/winsock
```

MUDSock   Runs on MS Windows using WinSock. Works mainly with TinyMUCK, but should work with other MUDs. The program is still in beta, which means there may be bugs. You can find the program at

```
http://www.cyberspy.com/~jfurlong/links.html
```

or

```
http://www.umn.edu/nlhome/m279/fayxx001
```

WinTin   Port of TinTin-III to MS Windows 3.1x. Works only with some TCP/IP stacks (specifically, it **does** work with Microsoft's tcp-ip32, but does not work with Trumpet). You can find the program at:

```
ftp://ftp.cs.cmu.edu/afs/cs/user/johnmil/ftp
```

MUDCaller   Runs under MS-DOS. Latest version is 2.50 or above. Requires an Ethernet card, and uses the Crynwr Packet drivers. Does NOT work with a modem. (If you Telnet in MS-DOS, you can probably use this.) Features include multiple connections, triggers, command-line history, scrollback, logging, macros, and separate input and output windows. You can find the program at:

```
ftp://ftp.tcp.com/pub/mud/Clients
```

or

```
ftp://ftp.math.okstate.edu/pub/muds/clients/misc
```

Windows95 and WindowsNT-Based Clients

Pueblo   Runs on MS Windows95 and Windows NT using WinSock. Latest version is 0.90. Features full support for hypertext (HTML), 3D graphics (VRML), 2D graphics (GIF and JPEG), audio (MIDI and WAV). Brings up a complete hierarchy of active MUDs. You can find the program at:

```
http://adobe.chaco.com/pueblo/
```

NTTinTin   Port of TinTin-III to Windows NT. You can find the program at:

```
ftp://ftp.cs.cmu.edu:/afs/cs/user/johnmil/ftp
```

Macintosh-Based Clients

MUDDweller   Runs on any Macintosh. Latest version is 1.2 or above. Connects to a MUD through either the communications toolbox or by MacTCP. Usable for both LPMUDs and TinyMUD-style MUDs. Current features include multiple connections, a command history, and a built-in MTP client for LPMUDs. You can find the program at any of these sites:

```
ftp://rudolf.ethz.ch/pub/mud
ftp://mac.archive.umich.edu/mac/util/comm
ftp://ftp.tcp.com/pub/mud/Clients
```

Mudling   Runs on any Macintosh. Latest version is 0.9b26 or above. Features include multiple connections, triggers, macros, command line history, separate input and output windows, and a rudimentary mapping system. You can find the program at:

```
ftp://imv.aau.dk:/pub/Mudling
```

or

```
ftp://ftp.math.okstate.edu/pub/muds/clients/misc
```

BSD-Based Clients

TinyTalk Tiny Talk runs on BSD or SysV. Latest version is 1.1.7GEW. Designed primarily for TinyMUD-style MUDs. Features include line-editing, command history, hiliting (whispers, pages, and users), gag, auto-login, simple macros, logging, and cyberportals. You can find the program at any of these sites:

```
ftp://ftp.math.okstate.edu/pub/muds/clients/UnixClients
ftp://parcftp.xerox.com/pub/MOO/clients
ftp://ftp.tcp.com/pub/mud/Clients
```

TinyFugue Runs on BSD or SysV. Latest version is 3.2beta4 or above. Also called 'tf'. Designed primarily for TinyMUD-style MUDs, although will run on LPMUDs and Dikus. Features include regexp hilites and gags, auto-login, macros, line editing, screen mode, triggers, cyberportals, logging, file and command uploading, shells, and multiple connections. You can find the program at:

```
ftp://ftp.math.okstate.edu/pub/muds/clients/UnixClients/tf
```

or

```
ftp://ftp.tcp.com/pub/mud/Clients
```

TclTT Runs on BSD. Latest version is 0.9 or above. Designed primarily for TinyMUD-style MUDs. Features include regexp hilites, regexp gags, logging, auto-login, partial file uploading, triggers, and programmability. You can find the program at:

```
ftp://ftp.white.toronto.edu/pub/muds/tcltt
```

or

```
ftp://ftp.math.okstate.edu/pub/muds/clients/UnixClients
```

VT Runs on BSD or SysV. Latest version is 2.15 or above. Must have vt102 capabilities. Usable for all types of MUDs. Features include a C-like extension language (VTC) and a simple windowing system. You can find the program at:

```
ftp://ftp.math.okstate.edu/pub/muds/clients/vt
```

or

```
ftp://ftp.tcp.com/pub/mud/Clients
```

LPTalk Runs on BSD or SysV. Latest version is 1.2.1. Designed primarily for LPMUDs. Features include hiliting, gags, auto-login, simple macros, logging. You can find the program at:

```
ftp://ftp.math.okstate.edu/pub/muds/clients/UnixClients
```

SayWat   Runs on BSD. Latest version is 0.30beta. Designed primarily for TinyMUD-style MUDs. Features include regexp hilites, regexp gags, macros, triggers, logging, cyberportals, rudimentary xterm support, command line history, multiple connections, and file uploading.

You can find the program at:

```
ftp://ftp.math.okstate.edu/pub/muds/clients/UnixClients
```

PMF   Runs on BSD. Latest version is 1.13.1 or above. Usable for both LPMUDs and TinyMUD-style MUDs. Features include line editing, auto-login, macros, triggers, gags, logging, file uploads, X-window interface, and ability to do Sparc sounds. You can find the program at:

```
ftp://ftp.lysator.liu.se/pub/lpmud/clients
```

or

```
ftp://ftp.math.okstate.edu/pub/muds/clients/UnixClients
```

TinTin   Runs on BSD. Latest version is 2.0. Designed primarily for Dikus. Features include macros, triggers, tick-counter features, and multiple connections. You can find the program at:

```
ftp://ftp.math.okstate.edu/pub/muds/clients/UnixClients
```

TinTin++   Runs on BSD or SysV. Latest version is 1.5pl5. Derived and improved from TinTin. Additional features include variables, faster triggers, and a split screen mode. You can find the program at:

```
ftp://ftp.princeton.edu/pub/tintin++/dist
```

or

```
ftp://ftp.math.okstate.edu/pub/muds/clients/UnixClients
```

TUsh   Runs on BSD or SysV. Latest version is 1.74. Features include hiliting, triggers, aliasing, history buffer, and screen mode. You can find the program at:

```
ftp://ftp.math.okstate.edu/pub/muds/clients/UnixClients
```

LPmudr   Runs on BSD or SysV. Latest version is 2.7 or above. Designed primarily for LPMUDs. Features include line editing, command history, auto-login and logging. You can find the program at:

```
ftp://ftp.math.okstate.edu/pub/muds/clients/UnixClients
```

VMS-Based Clients

tfVMS   VMS version of TinyFugue (see above). Uses Wollongong networking. Latest version is 1.0b2. You can find the program at:

```
ftp://ftp.math.okstate.edu/pub/muds/clients/VMSClients
```

TINT   Runs on VMS with MultiNet networking. Latest version is 2.2. Designed primarily for TinyMUD-style MUDs. Features include hiliting (whispers, pages, users), gags, file uploading, simple macros, screen mode. See also TINTw. You can find the program at:

```
ftp://ftp.math.okstate.edu/pub/muds/clients/VMSClients
```

TINTw   Runs on VMS with Wollongong networking. See TINT. You can find the program at:

```
ftp://ftp.math.okstate.edu/pub/muds/clients/VMSClients
```

or

```
ftp://ftp.tcp.com/pub/mud/Clients
```

FooTalk   Runs on VMS with MultiNet networking and BSD UNIX. Primarily designed for TinyMUD-style MUDs. Features include screen mode and it is programmability. You can find the program at:

```
ftp://ftp.math.okstate.edu/pub/muds/clients/VMSClients
```

IBM VM-Based Clients

REXXTALK   Runs on IBM VM. Latest version is 2.1. Designed primarily for TinyMUD-style MUDs. Features include screen mode, logging, macros, triggers, hilites, gags, and auto-login. Allows some IBM VM programs to be run while connected to a foreign host, such as TELL and MAIL. You can find the program at:

```
ftp://ftp.math.okstate.edu/pub/muds/clients/misc
```

RXLPTalk   Runs on IBM VM, and anything that uses REXX. Partially derivative of REXXTALK. Latest version is 6.0. Designed for use with LPMUDs. Features include hilites, gags, logging, macros, and multiple connections. You can find the program at any of these sites:

```
ftp://ftp.math.okstate.edu/pub/muds/clients/misc/
ftp://ftp.math.okstate.edu/pub/muds/clients/misc/
ftp://ftp.math.okstate.edu/pub/muds/clients/misc/
```

Connecting to MUDs via the Web

Many MUDs are now available from WWW clients, which often use a Telnet intermediary to get you to the MUD.

One of the best entry points to MUDs via the Web is via the Lysator machine at

    http://www.lysator.liu.se:7500/mud/main.html

Figure 16.4 shows the main listing for MUDs on the Lysator Web page.

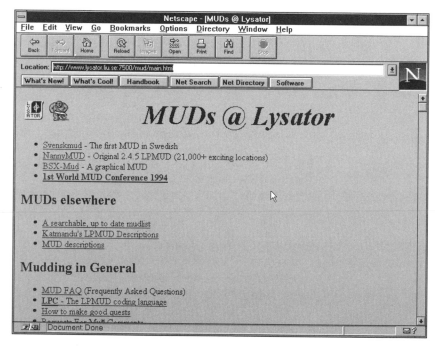

Figure 16.4.   A listing of MUDs available via the Web.

Other entry points are available. One of the most comprehensive is at:

    gopher://spinaltap.micro.umn.edu/11/fun/Games/MUDs/Links

You can also look for MUDs using the various WWW search engines discussed in Chapter 12.

Mud Resources on the Web

There are some fun resources related to MUDs on the World-Wide Web:

MU*s: An Introduction to MUDs, MOOs, etc.   This site has a good general introduction to various MUD and MUD-like games. The MUD FAQ is also available from this page.

```
http://www.vuw.ac.nz/who/Jamie.Norrish/mud/mud.html
```

The MUD Archive   Lauren P. Burka has compiled an excellent Web page with lots of documents related to MUDs and MUDding.

```
http://www.ccs.neu.edu/home/lpb/muddex.html
```

The Cardiff Internet VR pages   The pages focus mainly on MOOs.

```
http://arachnid.cs.cf.ac.uk/User/Andrew.Wilson/VR/vr.html
```

Educational VR sites   Sponsored by the Technology Training department at the University of Geneva, this page focuses on educational MUDs and other online resources.

```
http://tecfa.unige.ch/edu-comp/WWW-VL/eduVR-page.html
```

Once You're In, What Do You Do?

Watch and learn is the first rule for MUDding, unless you have an experienced player sitting at your shoulder telling you what to do. Carefully read the login screens and instructions for new users, and find out how to get help.

In a role-playing MUD, and for many people in social MUDs, the character is the thing. You'll want to create a character you enjoy playing, and in which you can comfortably interact with the people around you. Some MUDs allow you to create your own character, and others require you to send off for an assigned role via e-mail. If you have to send off for one, send one e-mail request and then wait for the Powers That Be to reply.

In the examples below, we have Telnetted to the MUD on a plain Telnet client. The examples from Gizmo (`gizmo.bchs.uh.edu`, port 6969; formally called Imperial Omega, also known as Ronin) show how the MUD looks to an experienced player who has set several options on; the examples from the Imperial are for a new player.

Stepping into the MUD

The first steps, then, are these:

Connect to the MUD and register. You can usually register as a guest to try things out; many MUDs let you give yourself a persona name to help you feel comfortable. Figure 16.5 shows the registration procedure for the Imperial, which is pretty standard.

Read the opening screens carefully. They will give you something of the flavor of the game, and they will show you where important information can be found. Figure 16.6 shows the opening screen in the RoninMUD.

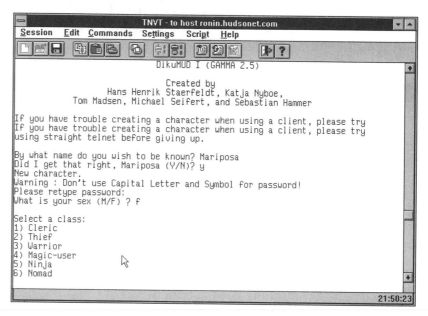

Figure 16.5. **Registering in the Gizmo DikuMUD.**

Type *help,* read the instructions and directions, and make sure you understand them. Keep asking questions until it's clear how each instruction or command works. Figure 16.7 shows the help screen in RoninMUD.

Read the current news (type *news*), because it will tell you about policies, changes, and the like. It's also a lot of fun! Figure 16.8 shows the news on the Imperial.

Read the policy statement (type *policy*). This will tell you the restrictions and agreements the game operates under. It's important to know and agree to these policies. Figure 16.9 shows the policy statement for the Imperial.

Some MUDs have a newcomer's guide, to help you get started. Reading it will prevent stumbling around and feeling frustrated while you're getting started. Instructions for finding it will usually be somewhere in one of the documents you've already read. Figure 16.10 shows the newbie guide for the Imperial.

Practice using the commands you've learned to get comfortable with the movement in the game. Figures 16.11–14 show commands and movements in the Gizmo.

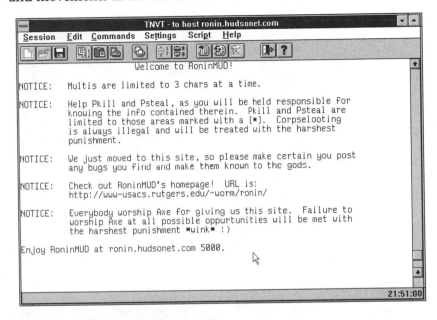

Figure 16.6. **The RoninMUD opening screen.**

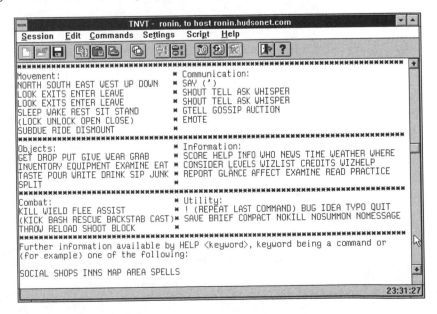

Figure 16.7. **Getting help in Gizmo.**

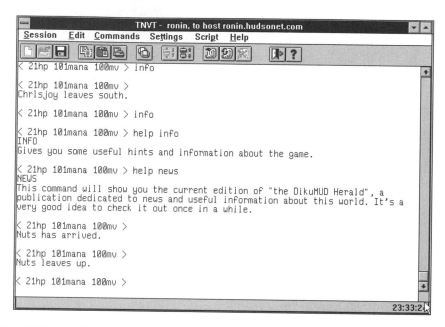

*Figure 16.8. **Reading the news.***

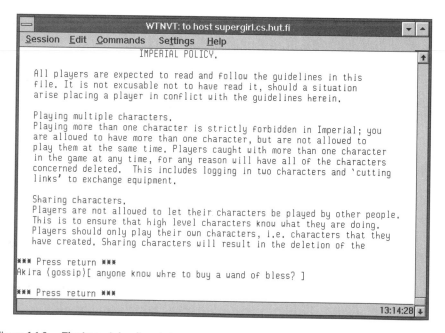

*Figure 16.9. **The Imperial policy statement.***

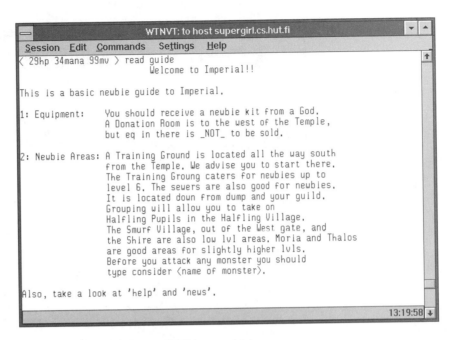

Figure 16.10.   **The newcomer's guide at the Imperial.**

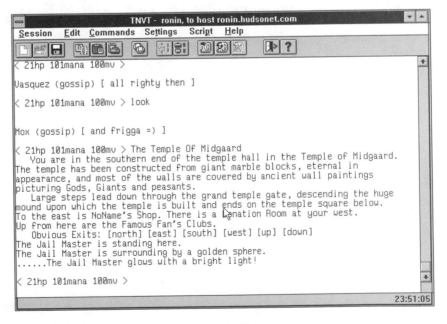

Figure 16.11.   **Beginning a series of movements in Gizmo.**

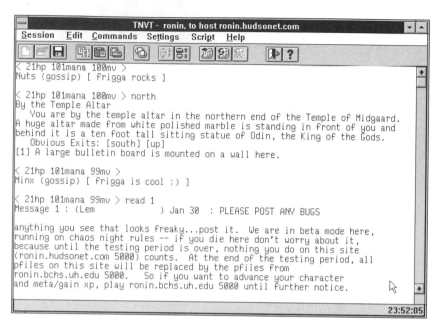

Figure 16.12. Movement through Gizmo, part 2.

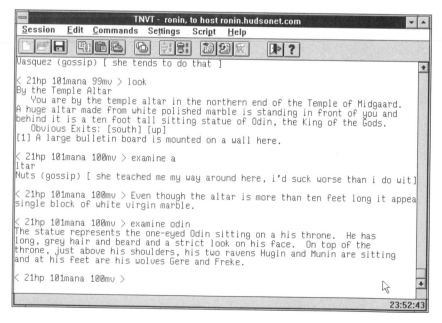

Figure 16.13. Movement through Gizmo, part 3.

The Internet Toolkit

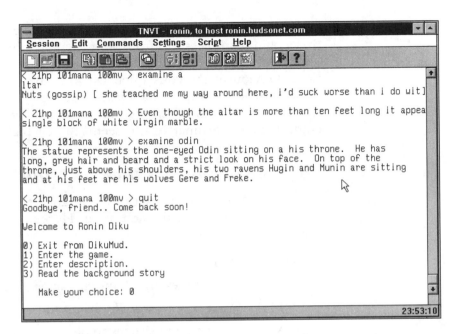

```
                TNVT - ronin, to host ronin.hudsonet.com
Session   Edit   Commands   Settings   Script   Help

< 21hp 101mana 100mv > examine a
ltar
Nuts (gossip) [ she teached me my way around here, i'd suck worse than i do wit]

< 21hp 101mana 100mv > Even though the altar is more than ten feet long it appea
single block of white virgin marble.

< 21hp 101mana 100mv > examine odin
The statue represents the one-eyed Odin sitting on a his throne.  He has
long, grey hair and beard and a strict look on his face.  On top of the
throne, just above his shoulders, his two ravens Hugin and Munin are sitting
and at his feet are his wolves Gere and Freke.

< 21hp 101mana 100mv > quit
Goodbye, friend.. Come back soon!

Welcome to Ronin Diku

0) Exit from DikuMud.
1) Enter the game.
2) Enter description.
3) Read the background story

   Make your choice: 0
                                                           23:53:10
```

*Figure 16.14. **Exiting Gizmo.***

Why Not Jump Right In?

Jennifer "Moira" Smith (jds@math.okstate.edu), editor of the MUD FAQ, says, "Some people are easily annoyed when other people clearly have no idea what they are doing, even if they were recently in that position themselves. It'll be much easier for you to cope without some fella saying things you don't understand to you and possibly killing you. However, many MUD players are helpful, and asking them, 'Excuse me, are you busy? I'm a brand new player, and I have a question,' will often work just fine."

Feeling Secure

Unless you are perpetually a guest, you will want to create a password for your character on every MUD you play on. Choose that password as carefully as you would one for your host system: there are MUD crackers who enjoy trying to break into other people's MUD accounts. **Never** use the same password as the one you use on your host system! Changing it regularly might be a good idea, as well.

Why would anyone want to break into your account? Posing as you, they could send messages from your account which would be traced to you, or simply get all your characters into weird and unpleasant situations. Obviously, the consequences would be less serious than if they broke into your company databases, but if they crack your MUD password, hackers could then try that same password on your company computers. Unfortunately, this seems to be a high calling for them.

Common Commands Used on MUDs

Most MUDs have a core set of commands that players use to move around and interact with each other. Here are a few to help you get started:

Command	Action
say X	Sometimes "X". Your character speaks the word X.
look	Your character looks around.
go X	Your character goes to point X.
home	Takes your character home (in TinyMUDs).
help	Displays a help document.
news	Displays important things the creator wants you to know.
who	Lists all the other characters in the MUD at that time.

Some MUDs allow you to alter certain things in the database, by using commands prefixed with "@": @describe, @name, @dig, and @link allow you to expand the universe, change it, or even, perhaps, @destroy it.

Most MUDs have documentation on-line, although better documentation can be gotten via FTP from other sites. Standard sites to check are

    ftp://ftp.tcp.com (128.111.72.60)

and

    ftp://ftp.math.okstate.edu

in the directory /pub/muds/misc.

Asking for Help

According to real MUD veterans, the most dangerous time for a budding MUDder is when you think you know what's going on. That's when you are most annoying (and, in adventure MUDs, possibly most likely to be killed by players you've annoyed). You can, however, ask for help nicely. Immortals (also called wizards) are usually helpful; if you know that someone is a wizard, you can usually ask them a question, as long as you make sure they're not busy first. Also, players who have been logged on for a long time (which you can check using the who command) are often helpful. In combat MUDs, ask relatively high-level characters. But remember, the quickest way to annoy people on a MUD is to constantly pester and whine at them. If you do this you can expect to be *shunned*, or ignored by all.

SchMOOze University: A Different Kind of MUD

Clearly, the social atmosphere of the adventure or combat MUDs we've looked at so far is not for everyone. If you'd rather not worry about getting killed for annoying someone, take heart.

Schools in Canada and the US have taken the MUD concept and created an interactive campus. SchMOOze University is an experiment in bringing the K–12 environment to the MUD world.

MASTER WORDS SchMOOze is a MOO—MUD, Object-Oriented. This means that the underlying programs are object-oriented (like C++), rather than using older programming styles (like Fortran). This lets the programmer build modules or sections of the code and interconnect them more flexibly. In practice, players should see few differences deriving from this programming style. SchMOOze U differs from combat-style MUDs in its content and purpose rather than its programming techniques.

Schmooze U has a different flavor than the combat-oriented Imperial MUD; Figure 16.15 shows the opening screen. It also has a map of the campus to help you get oriented; Figure 16.16 shows this map. Even the news has a different flavor at SchMOOze U, as you can see in Figure 16.17. And instead of reading a newcomer's guide, participants go to a beginning class to get their feet on the ground at the U.

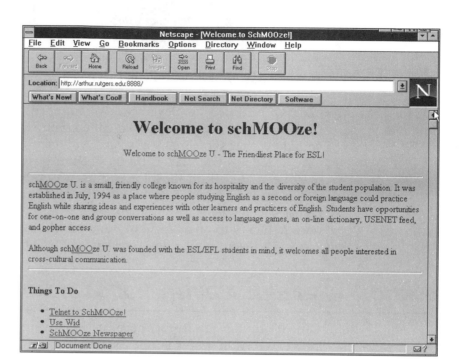

Figure 16.15.   The SchMOOze University opening screen.

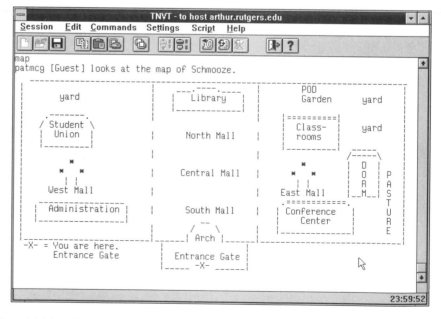

Figure 16.16.   The SchMOOze U map.

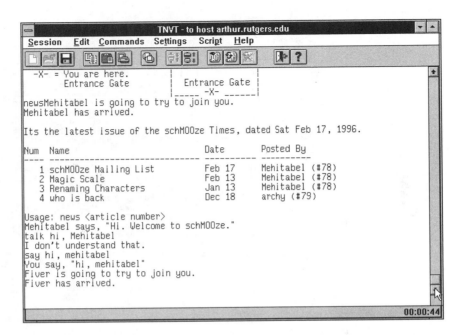

Figure 16.17. **The news at SchMOOze U.**

Julie Falsetti, who teaches English as a Second Language at Hunter College (City University of New York) and calls her persona Mehitabel, created SchMOOze U as a forum for ESL students to practice their English and for other interested people to help them. In Figures 16.18 and 16.19, you can see part of a typical exchange.

Visiting SchMOOze U

With a Web browser, you can visit the SchMOOze U home page at this URL:

```
http://schmooze.hunter.cuny.edu:8888
```

There you can learn more about the game and current players, and you can click on Use Wid (WWW Interaction Device) to explore your surroundings a little. To participate as a player or guest, however, you'll need a Telnet helper application configured with your Web browser.

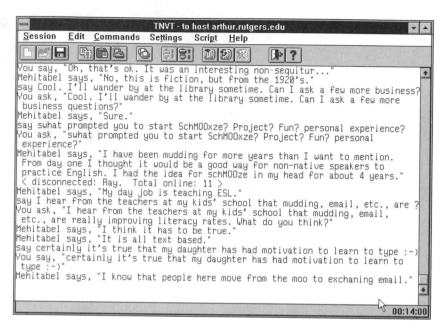

Figure 16.18.   Mehitabel describes the founding of SchMOOze U.

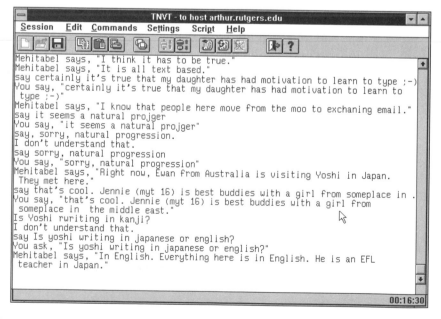

Figure 16.19.   SchMOOze U is a global activity.

Talking about MUDs in Newsgroups

People talk about almost everything in Usenet newsgroups, so it's not surprising that there are several newsgroups associated with MUDs. You can check out any of the following:

Newsgroup	Discussion topic
rec.games.mud.admin	Postings pertaining to the administrative side of MUDs.
rec.games.mud.announce	Moderated group, for announcements of MUDs opening, closing, moving, partying, and so on.
rec.games.mud.diku	Postings pertaining to DikuMUDs.
rec.games.mud.lp	Postings pertaining to LPMUDs.
rec.games.mud.misc	Miscellaneous postings.
rec.games.mud.tiny	Postings pertaining to the Tiny family of MUDs.
alt.games.mud	More miscellaneous postings, unmoderated.

As always, post your news appropriately. If you want to post something to Usenet, please do it in the group where it best belongs—no posts about TinyMUSH in the Diku group, no questions about an LPMUD in the Tiny group, and so on.

MUD Lore

The MUD Frequently Asked Questions list, compiled by Jennifer Smith, gives not only a lot of useful basic information, but also a vivid sense of what it's like to interact with MUDs and MUDders. Following are some extracts, including a glossary.

You can find the MUD FAQ at:

    http://www.lysator.liu.se:7500/mud/faq/faq1.html

or

    http://www.ccs.neu.edu/home/lpb/muds/ashne.faq.new

How Do I Start My Own MUD?

After you've grown proficient at conquering the worlds of others, you will be tempted to define and rule your own world for others to conquer. To do this you will need to pick server software. You'll have to figure out how to compile it and get it running, and you'll need to know how to keep it running, which usually involves some programming skills, generally in C, and a good deal of time. Of course, you also need to be well versed in the ways and commands of that particular MUD server, and you'll probably need help running the place from a few of your friends.

Don't forget that you'll have to have a computer system to run it on, and the resources with which to run it. Most MUDs use anywhere from 5 to 90 megabytes of disk space, and memory usage can be anything from 1 to 35 megabytes. A good rule of thumb is to first ask around for specifics on that server; average MUDs need around 25 megabytes of disk space for everything, and about 10 megabytes of memory, although the exact numbers vary widely.

If you don't *explicitly own* the machine you're thinking about right now, you had better get the permission of the machine owner before you bring up a MUD on his computer. MUDs are not extremely processing-consumptive, but they do use up some computing power. You wouldn't want people plugging in their appliances into the outlets of your home without your permission or knowledge, would you?

MUD Glossary

Here are some of the most important definitions from the FAQ list.

bot A *bot* is a computer program that logs into a MUD and pretends to be a human being. Some of them, like Julia, are pretty clever—legend has it that Julia's fooled people into believing that she's human. Others have less functionality. Bots are generally frowned upon; ask the administrators of the MUD if you can run them.

clueless newbie A *newbie* is someone who has only recently begun to participate in some kind of activity. When we're born, we're all life-newbies until we get experience under our belts (or diapers). You're a clueless newbie until you've got the hang of MUDding, basically.

cyborg A *cyborg* is defined as "part man, part machine." In the MUD world, this means that your client is doing some of the work for you.

For instance, you can set up many clients to automatically greet anyone entering the room. You can also set up clients to respond to certain phrases (or "triggers"). Of course, this can have disastrous consequences. If Player_A sets his client up to say Hi every time Player_B says Hi, and Player_B does likewise, their clients will frantically scream Hi at each other over and over until they manage to escape. Needless to say, runaway automation is very heavily frowned upon by anyone who sees it. If you program your client to do anything special, first make sure that it cannot go berserk and overload the MUD.

dino   A *dino* is someone who has been around for a very long time (the word is an abbreviation for "dinosaur"). These people tend to reminisce nostalgically about dead or nonexistent MUDs that were especially fun or interesting.

furry   A *furry* is an anthropomorphic intelligent animal. If you've ever seen Zoobilee Zoo on The Learning Channel, you know what I mean. Furries are not unique to MUDdom—they originated in comics, and can usually be found at comic or animation conventions and the like. Generally, any MUD character that has fur and is cute is deemed a furry. Most furries hang out on FurryMUCK, naturally.

HAVEN   On many TinyMUDs, there are several "flags" associated with each room. The HAVEN flag is probably the most famous one. In rooms where the HAVEN flag is set, no character may kill another. (See "player killing" below.)

log   Certain client programs allow *logs* to be kept off the screen. A time-worn and somewhat unfriendly trick is to entice someone into having TinySex with you, log the proceedings, and post them to rec .games.mud—and have a good laugh at the other person's expense. Logs are useful for recording interesting or useful information or conversations, as well.

Maving   Mav is a famous TinyMUDder who sometimes accidentally left a colon on the front of a whisper, thus directing private messages to the whole room. The meaning of the verb has changed to include making any say/whisper/page/pose typing confusion.

net lag   The Internet is made up of thousands of interconnected networks. Between your computer and the computer that houses the MUD, there may be up to 30 gateways and links connecting them over serial lines, high-speed modems, leased lines, satellite uplinks, etc. If one of these gateways or lines crashes, is suddenly overloaded, or gets routing confused, you may notice a long period of lag time between your input and the MUD's reception of that input. Computers that are (logistically) nearer to the computer running the MUD are less susceptible to net lag. Another source of lag occurs when the computer that hosts the MUD is overloaded. When net lag happens, it is best to just patiently wait for it to pass.

player killing   Can you kill (permanently) another player's persona? The answer to this question varies widely. On most combat-oriented MUDs, such as LPMUD and Diku, player killing is taken quite seriously. On others, it's encouraged. On most TinyMUDs, as there is little or no combat system, player killing is sometimes employed as a means of showing irritation at another player, or merely to show emphasis of something said (usually, it means "and I really mean it!"). It's best to find out the rules of the MUD you're on, and play by them.

spam   Spamming, derived from a famous Monty Python sketch, is the flooding of the MUD with information (such as repeated very long "say" commands). Unintentional spamming, such as what happens when you walk away from your computer screen for a few minutes, then return to find several screenfuls of text waiting to scroll by, or when you change huge quantities of equipment you are wearing, is just a source of irritation. Intentional spamming, such as when you repeat very long "say" commands many times, or quote /usr/dict/ words at someone, is usually frowned on, and can get you in trouble with the MUD administration.

TinySex   TinySex is the act of performing MUD actions to imitate having sex with another character, usually consensually, sometimes with one hand on the keyboard, sometimes with two. Basically, it's speed-writing interactive erotica. Realize that the other party is not obligated to be anything like he/she says, and in fact may be playing a joke on you (see *log*, above).

Wizard or *God*   Gods are the people who own the database, the administrators. In most MUDs, wizards are barely distinguishable from gods—they're just barely one step down from the God of the MUD. An LPMUD wizard is a player who has "won" the game, and is now able to create new sections of the game. Wizards are very powerful, but they don't have the right to do whatever they want to you; they must still follow their own set of rules, or face the wrath of the gods. Gods can do whatever they want to whomever they want whenever they want—it's their MUD. If you don't like how a god acts or lets his wizards act toward the players, your best recourse is to simply stop playing that MUD, and play another.

A more appropriate name for wizards would probably be "janitor," since they tend to have to put up with responsibilities and difficulties (without pay) that nobody else would be expected to handle. Remember, they're human beings on the other side of the wire. Respect them for their generosity.

Time Spent, or Time Wasted?

College officials and K–12 educators have stated publicly in some areas that MUDs, like other computer games, are a waste of time. Certainly those folks who've learned to do programming and database design in order to create their own MUDs would disagree. Most regular visitors to MUDs would agree that they are, like many other forms of netsurfing, highly addictive. Jennifer Smith says in the MUD FAQ: "The jury is still out on whether MUDding is 'just a game' or 'an extension of real life with game-like qualities.' You shouldn't do anything that you wouldn't do in real life, even if the world is a fantasy world. The important thing to remember is that it's the fantasy world of possibly hundreds of people, and not just yours in particular. There's a human being on the other side of each and every computer screen! Always remember that you may meet these other people some day, and they may break your nose. People who treat others badly gradually build up bad reputations and eventually receive the NO FUN Stamp of Disapproval."

Finding a MUD

You should check out the most recent list of MUDs, which is available online. Most MUDs are available via Telnet, but many are becoming available with WWW. The online list is the most authoritative list of MUDs available; it may not contain every MUD (not all are publicly advertised, and some MUDs may be unavailable from time to time). However, this list should provide you with a solid entrance into the many worlds available via MUDs.

You can find the whole list of MUDS via the Web at:

```
http://shsibm.shh.fi/mud/docs.html
```

Becoming an Information Provider

CHAPTER 17

Should My Organization Be "On" the Net?

FEATURING

Chapter 17

Should My Organization Be "On" the Net?

I**N** Parts I and II, we talked about how individuals can use the Internet to find information and exchange ideas. Now we're going to turn our attention to businesses, government agencies, and other organizations. This chapter is addressed to those of you—managers, executives, and administrators—who must decide whether to connect your organization to the Net.

Broadly speaking, businesses and other organizations can use Internet technology in two ways. Any organization can benefit from an external Internet presence, using e-mail, maintaining Web pages or FTP sites, and so on. Larger businesses can also use Internet technology internally, creating an internal "intranet," bringing all the advantages of the Net to internal communication and enhancing productivity. The focus of this chapter is on external connections, but you'll also see how many of the concepts discussed apply to intranets.

You've heard all the hype about fast communication, easy access to information, and hidden treasures on the Net. You've also heard about the horror stories: crackers breaking into company data, employees storing pornography on accounting machines, and so on. How do you balance the potential for good against the headaches?

Certainly, getting an Internet connection, either by buying host accounts or biting the bullet and getting your whole company wired up, is an expensive proposition. You need to invest that money wisely.

And, once you've gotten connected, how do you make smart business decisions about that asset: who will use it, how will it be supported, and how will it enhance your service to your clients or customers?

Let's walk through these issues one by one.

WHAT IS AN INTRANET?

Many of you may have seen the word "intranet" on the covers of magazines and on the news. An "intranet" is an "internal internet"—a network for your company that runs on IP protocols. You may already have an "intranet" if your various LAN components, such as Novell or Banyan, talk to each other via a TCP/IP link.

An intranet differs from a conventional LAN in two ways: it links more than one kind of networking technology using the Internet protocols, TCP/IP; and it uses afirewall to keep the larger Internet out of your internal information resources.

A firewall is a computer or several computers that sit between your network and the greater Internet. Using filtering and specialized routing, as well as rules you decide upon, firewalls keep out people who don't have permission to access your resources internally. You, on the other hand, can access all the resources of the general Internet (unless some policy prevents you).

In some ways, the word "intranet" is a portmanteau word which logically combines the concepts in "internal internet between business sites." Going deeper, we see that an intranet uses not only the protocols for transport but the tools for collaboration, information dissemination, and resource sharing that the Internet offers. Internal Web servers, FTP archives, newsgroups, and other resources become the way your employees get their work done.

"The intranet" is expected to become the hottest new use of Internet technology in 1996–97. Certainly growth within companies is projected to equal the growth of the general Internet in the time period 1994–1995.

Several companies specializing in intranet services have case studies on the Net, so you can get an idea how you might use Internet technology internally. We offer these profiles with the warning that they are sales literature intended to sell certain products: take them with a grain of salt.

Netscape

Netscape offers lots of products to help you build an intranet. To that end, they also have quite a few case studies. Check them out at

```
http://home.netscape.com/misc/hp_promo/nsatwork/atwork.html
```

OpenText

The OpenText company not only has a terrific search engine on the Web, they'll be happy to sell you one to use internally, or several other internal server products. They, too, have customer profiles available at

```
http://www.opentext.com/livelink/otm_ll_test.html
```

Continued on next page

Part III

Becoming an Information Provider

Attachmate

Do you have "legacy apps" that you fear will never be convertible to Internet applications? Attachmate is developing solutions for just this problem. Look at their list of customer profiles at

    `http://www.attachmate.com`

More info?

If you're interested in exploring the concept of intranets further, go to any of the search engines we told you about in Chapter 12 and enter the term as a search query. You'll likely find more than you expected!

What Are the Benefits?

There is one most important question that a planner needs to be able to answer when considering an Internet connection—What do you want to accomplish?

You want to communicate, internally and externally, more efficiently.

You want to access resources quickly and for the least possible cost.

You want to find up-to-date information on your product's marketplace—for example, what your competition is doing, what your customers want, and the business and government environment.

You want to deliver information and support to your clients in the most cost effective, quickest, and most efficient manner.

As a business, governmental agency, or nonprofit organization, presumably you want the same things anyone wants from a potential information and communications service. Let's look at an Internet connection the same way you look at any other corporate investment decision. You want to use your investment wisely:

To reduce unnecessary expenditures.

To improve productivity of your staff.

To improve relations with your customers (including funding agencies and boards of directors).

To improve the speed and accuracy of your agency's communications.

Assuredly these are laudable goals. Now let's see how the Internet can help your organization meet them.

Reduce Unnecessary Expenditures

Joel Maloff (joel@maloff.com) of The Maloff Company, a telecommunications consulting firm based in Dexter, MI, cites a study stating that more than 35 percent of most business long distance costs are for sending faxes. So, let's compare the cost of an e-mail message to that of a fax.

If the fax were a formal one, it would cost about the same as a business letter to produce. The outright and hidden costs of business letters are very high:

The time of your professional and clerical staff to compose it.

The time to enter it.

The time to proofread and correct it.

The time to print it out, copy it, and file it (using paper, disk files, or both).

The amortized costs of the computer used for word processing.

The cost of the paper you print it on.

The cost of delivering it, using either US Mail or a courier service.

These are the production costs, and they can really add up! With a fax, the only difference is that for the delivery expense, you replace the postage or express courier charges with those of the telephone line toll charges and the amortized cost of the facsimile machine itself.

How could the Internet improve the cost picture? Look at these savings:

No printing or stationery costs.

Fax delivery long distance charges should be compared to the amortized or direct costs of the e-mail transmission over the Internet, that is, the telephone and networking costs.

Reduced clerical costs: most professionals compose and correct their own e-mail correspondence, but clerical staff is often used to print and transmit faxes.

The costs for filing and saving what was written would be incurred as part of the e-mail costs.

In addition, if an e-mail system already exists for internal or departmental use, the composition, proofreading, and storage costs could be amortized over a larger body of work.

We're sure that you can see how such calculations go. In order to present a well-documented case, of course, you need to be able to identify all the cost components of how you are doing things now and compare them with how you might do things with an Internet connection.

How about comparing delivery, though? Because we are more familiar with faxes, we tend to trust them more: common wisdom says they are more reliable, and you're using telephone lines in each case. Let's compare the typical e-mail delivery to a fax delivery.

Faxes can fail to go through because:

> The phone line is busy on either end.

> The fax machine was not turned on.

> The receiving fax had no paper.

> The receiving fax misprinted the message and the message needed to be resent.

Lots of things can go wrong with faxes. By contrast, e-mail generally has these advantages:

> It transmits faster: most e-mail messages travel at line speeds of at least 14.4 kbps, and many go at the T1 rate or higher.

> It monitors itself if it needs to be retransmitted.

> It doesn't end up on the floor or in the wrong person's mailbox for days.

Can facsimiles be better than e-mail? Realistically, there are only two points where faxes would provide improved communication. The first is if the sending or receiving e-mail system is not capable of handling image files and images are needed in the communication. The second is if the person or organization you want to send e-mail to doesn't have e-mail.

Phone Bill Blues

Let's suppose you have an office in England and an office in Atlanta. Your sales people talk regularly to coordinate shipments; the ten members of your staff may make at least five long-distance phone calls, lasting 20 minutes or more, to London a day. Your long-distance charges alone will be over $3000 a month, according to a cost estimate by a Southern Bell sales representative.

With Internet host accounts, your charges for those ten people, and all the e-mail traffic they send back and forth, would (in general) be less than $750 per month, computed on an average cost of $50 to $75 per person per month quoted by four Internet service providers.

With a direct link into your company LANs in both sites, after startup costs your phone bill for the phone line that links you into the Internet would be less than $1500, and *all the other advantages of the Internet come with it.*

One-Stop Shopping

If your organization is using information from several different dial-up information providers like Dialog or Dow/Jones, you will likely be able to consolidate your dial-up services in one Internet provider. This would allow you to concentrate your energy on interacting with the data and not with the method of acquiring the data. You would use your Internet connection (dial or dedicated) to reach the Internet itself. Then you would Telnet or use a Web browser to access the desired information services. Note that your contractual relationship with these services remains. You will still need to pay for the services that you use. There is nothing about the data access using the Internet that changes your relationship with the information provider.

Destroy Fewer Trees

Using e-mail instead of a photocopier to pass along announcements, memos, company-wide policies, and the whole range of items to be communicated can save thousands of dollars a year in paper, toner, maintenance, and replacement costs, not to mention the administrative staff time involved. No one has to stand at the photocopier, sort, and deliver the papers, either.

MASTER WORDS Using e-mail for company announcements needs to be monitored carefully. It's easier to send junk mail via e-mail than by photocopying and distributing paper leaflets. In addition, some folks type and send e-mail without really thinking carefully about what they are saying. One vice president at a Fortune 500 company sent out a memo during the 1994 elections that many employees took as instructions on how to vote. So be sure and think before you type!

Improve the Productivity of Your Staff

Faster access to information about new products and techniques can make a big difference in applying new methods for improving anyone's professional activities. News from professional colleagues can travel the Internet much faster than via the conventional methods of letters and papers given at conferences. And the news can get to more people at the same time.

Let's take a relatively recent example: During July 1994, the eyes and telescopes of the earth's astronomers were turned to the planet Jupiter to observe the pieces of the comet Shoemaker-Levy 9 strike the planet. Interest in the telescopic images photographed from the Hubble Telescope was so great among the Internet community at large that the common sites for astronomical images were swamped with requests. And those requests were from the amateur community!

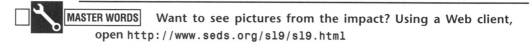

MASTER WORDS   Want to see pictures from the impact? Using a Web client, open `http://www.seds.org/sl9/sl9.html`

The professional astronomers had set up private mailing lists that cited specific observations from each observatory. As the world turned in its diurnal rotation, different observatories would have views in turn. Some had views obstructed by cloud layers. Others had quite clear views. As each group in turn recorded its successes and failures and shared them with their colleagues, the groups that followed in the viewing pattern were able to modify the settings of their observations. One scientist remarked that without these communications, their observatory would have completely missed the excitement; they had been looking in the wrong part of the light spectrum. Information from another observatory allowed them time to change their settings before Jupiter rose in their night sky.

What about Regular Folk?

Yes, you say, but these people are scientists. They are used to collaborative efforts. That's how they work even without something like the Internet. Quite so. Let's think about how other people can become more productive doing research on the Net. Here are two examples from the real world:

In mid-1995, people who use Microsoft's Word product discovered that a virus was spreading in a new way, and it affected only Word documents. The virus travels in the macros and templates that you make up for your documents. Within two days of the discovery, several clean-up processes and templates were available on the Net, both from Microsoft and from other people. As the folks creating the macro viruses became more proficient, more macro viruses were developed. Each time, cures were available within hours of the discovery. Some of us, luckily, got copies of the cures installed before we got hit by copies of the macro viruses!

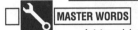 **Want to find out more? Check out Microsoft's Web site, at** `http://www.microsoft.com`

For another example: Thousands of people use Intuit's tax-return programs to prepare their taxes. In 1995, the programs for preparing the 1994 taxes had a problem with certain calculations. Most folks found this out via newsgroups where Intuit employees were discussing the problems and how to get around it. Even most national news outlets found the story online and then "broke" it in print and other media.

These are two famous examples, but there are less flashy examples that could affect you tomorrow.

Say a spreadsheet program is malfunctioning in your environment. Your network administrator sends an e-mail describing the problem to the customer support people for that product. They return a message saying that they know about the bug and have placed a patch (or fix) for it on their FTP server. Your administrator can then go and get the new program code, install the fix, and have your spreadsheet users up and running quite quickly.

Here's another type of research: Let's say that you are interested in determining the appropriate standards for a potential development project your company is preparing for possible purchase by a government agency. You can go to a library, look up the citations for the documents containing those standards, and then write the agency to ask for a copy of the relevant documents. Or you can use the Internet to connect with The Document Center

`http://www.service.com/doccenter`

and contract with them to supply you with the relevant documents much more quickly.

Or suppose you want to see whether the name of the product you're going to market clashes with other products. You might check out their Web page, as we have done with the Tangram Web page (illustrated in Figure 17.1).

Figure 17.1.   The Tangram Financial information page.

Document sharing and collaborative work are enhanced by the Internet. For example, if you already have an internal e-mail system, you probably know that a document can be electronically circulated among your staff for comments much more easily than if the author had to print, photocopy, and distribute it by hand. An Internet connection lets you take the process a step further and circulate documents outside your organization. The author can put it in an FTP archive, Web page, or Gopher server, and then send an e-mail to the appropriate people telling them where to find it and what sort of feedback he needs.

WARNING   Access to e-mail doesn't make people read and return documents faster if they are prone to leave them on their desk and forget them. You may still have to nag people to read and comment on documents, even with e-mail and document sharing. But at least it's easier to nag!

Quantity and Quality Time

Say a customer sends in a critical problem report via e-mail at 6 PM one evening. One of your staff checks her mail from home, and is able to set a fix for the client in motion over the network, including having a report back in the client's mailbox the next morning, and a shipping order cut to go out as soon as the courier service can get there in the morning.

One major Chicago newspaper discovered in the early 1990s that when they allowed their staffers to call in from home, the number of column inches produced increased by 16% over the next four months.

A side benefit to having Net access, particularly if your staffers can access your system from home, is that they can work from home even during domestic crises like chicken pox, broken cars, and visiting mothers-in-law.

Interoperability

It's a common problem: Let's say your accounting department bought their computer equipment from IBM, and your sales department bought theirs from Apple. They can't easily share documents, e-mail, or files.

Using Internet technology internally can provide you the ability to share these items between and among different e-mail systems. Your accounting department can send spreadsheet files via e-mail or transfer them using FTP to your sales department. Using interoperability software or hardware, you can link those departments and cut down on duplication of effort.

Improve Relations with Your Customers

What's the most difficult thing to do well in business? We think it's providing enough information to keep your customers happy.

Providing Information to Your Customer

As most of us know, getting and providing technical support for computer software and hardware can be a frustrating process for all concerned. If you've been on the consumer end, you've probably spent a lot of time listening to annoying elevator music, waiting for someone to field your call (or staring at your screen, waiting for an e-mail response).

Frequently the information that you needed is a simple fact, or something that should be in the company's literature. Internet information publishing provides a way to get that information into your customer's hands with fewer phone calls and happier customers.

Please note that this concept is not original: many, many technology companies provide customer communications using Internet publishing mechanisms. Offices of the United States federal government, like the Census Bureau, for example, have also been publishing information via the Internet for some time, and, because they now have a mandate to do so, all of them will be on line in the near future. More and more local and state offices are doing so, too.

Sometimes the information is relatively simple: agendas of meetings that are required by law to be published before the meeting happens; hours and telephone numbers of city offices, and so on. Sometimes the information provided is more complex: information about how to file an application for a specific type of permit, or even the application itself.

With a Web page that handles the form for you, most people can complete it online easily. And, if the computer system checks the data as you enter it, you can file a complete and accurate form without hassles, follow-up phone calls, or resubmitted of forms. Everybody wins: you don't have to go to the permit office, the permit people have fewer walk-in applicants to interrupt their work flow, and the application itself is more complete the first time it is turned in.

Improve the Speed and Accuracy of Your Communications

The permit application is a good example for this theme, too. If the application form is available on-line, the agency has, in effect, provided the necessary information immediately.

Or let's say that you suddenly have a job open in your organization. What could be quicker than to have your human resources agent post that job description to an appropriate newsgroup or job bulletin board where people who have the skills you need might see it? If you also suggest that qualified applicants e-mail their materials to you, you may have a pool of qualified applicants very quickly from a very broad base of potential candidates. You'll be able to respond to them with your questions via e-mail or the telephone that very day.

MASTER WORDS Recently, a call went out for proposals for multimedia projects for educators. Within two days, over 900 completed proposals were submitted—via e-mail. And when the organization asked for resumes for a coordinator for the project, close to 500 resumes flooded into their mailbox in just a few hours.

This actually happened for Pat. A former employer posted a job opening to the Net early one morning. Pat was living in Michigan, looking for opportunities in California. By 11:30 AM Michigan time (within an hour of the posting), Pat had e-mailed her resume and faxed some additional materials to the company. By 2 PM Michigan time, she had a confirmed interview. All this was done by telephone and e-mail. (By the way, she got the job.)

 WARNING If you're going to post a job announcement to the Net, make sure you've informed the people in your organization who might be affected by it. You don't want the job posting to reach the internal audience via an outside third party. If this happens, your quick, accurate communication can turn the affected department into a shambles even quicker than you will receive appropriate responses.

How Can We Use It?

Back in Chapter 2 we outlined different types of communications and showed how the various Internet applications and tools correspond to those types. Now that you've had a closer look at those tools, let's go through those communication types and see how you can use the Internet to achieve certain types of communications that are appropriate and necessary for business and government organizations.

Interactive/Simultaneous Communications

Interactive and simultaneous uses of the Internet are not as common as the asynchronous communications. For many users, one of the most convenient features of the Internet is that communication *doesn't* have to be simultaneous—you can send e-mail for someone to read at their convenience, you can download a file at midnight, or you can communicate with someone in a different time zone.

Interactive communications have the same limitations as do telephone conversations: they are costly and they require people to be in a specific place at a specific time. If someone in California wishes to communicate with someone in France, for example, they have a lot of arranging to do ahead of time. Nonetheless, there are some valuable ways that businesses and other organizations can use the Internet's interactive/simultaneous tools.

Talk

Talk, discussed in Chapter 15, is the Internet tool to use for *Type I,* private, individual-to-individual communications that may be authoritative. It is best for the type of message that need never be saved: "Please bring home some milk, dear" is an important (and probably authoritative) message, but it need not be saved for posterity. Don't use Talk for anything that needs to be kept for organizational records.

Why not simply use the phone? It can be less expensive to use Talk than to use the telephone. Telephone calls from business telephones are expensive. Figure 17.2 shows a Talk session in progress.

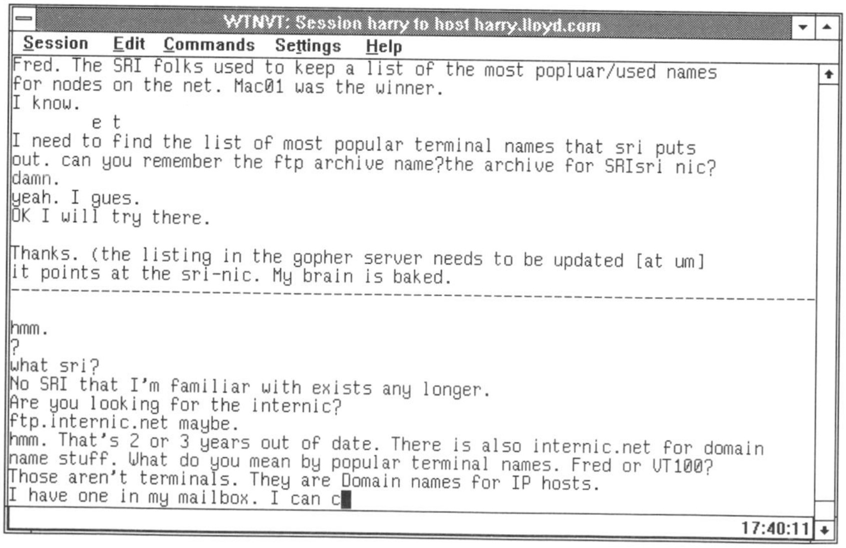

```
┌─────────────────────────────────────────────────────────────────┐
│ ═      WTNVT: Session harry to host harry.lloyd.com      ▼ ▲ │
├─────────────────────────────────────────────────────────────────┤
│ Session  Edit  Commands  Settings   Help                          │
│ Fred. The SRI folks used to keep a list of the most popluar/used names │
│ for nodes on the net. Mac01 was the winner.                       │
│ I know.                                                            │
│        e t                                                         │
│ I need to find the list of most popular terminal names that sri puts │
│ out. can you remember the ftp archive name?the archive for SRIsri nic? │
│ damn.                                                              │
│ yeah. I gues.                                                      │
│ OK I will try there.                                               │
│                                                                    │
│ Thanks. (the listing in the gopher server needs to be updated [at um] │
│ it points at the sri-nic. My brain is baked.                      │
│ -----------------------------------------------------------------  │
│                                                                    │
│ hmm.                                                               │
│ ?                                                                  │
│ what sri?                                                          │
│ No SRI that I'm familiar with exists any longer.                  │
│ Are you looking for the internic?                                  │
│ ftp.internic.net maybe.                                            │
│ hmm. That's 2 or 3 years out of date. There is also internic.net for domain │
│ name stuff. What do you mean by popular terminal names. Fred or VT100? │
│ Those aren't terminals. They are Domain names for IP hosts.        │
│ I have one in my mailbox. I can c█                                 │
│                                                      │ 17:40:11 │↓ │
└─────────────────────────────────────────────────────────────────┘
```

Figure 17.2.   A Talk session in operation.

IRC and MUDs

These are the Internet tools to use for *Type II* communications: public, many-contributors-to-many-recipients, and nonauthoritative. IRC is discussed in Chapter 15 and MUDs are discussed in Chapter 16. While it's true that many MUDs specialize in slaying dragons and wielding swords, the idea of a shared world or environment can have more serious applications.

Training is a good example of this. You need to train a group of people; they should be working interactively (research has shown that people learn more effectively if they are actively engaged in the process); and someone (the trainer) needs to manage their communications and the environment in which they're working.

What to do? Have a multiuser shared environment designed to handle your training case. Instead of dragons and swords, you have your specific business case included: your products, competitor's tactics, and so on. You can then provide the training environment to many people, geographically dispersed or not, at the same time, keeping participants on the topics to be discussed and learned. The dragons you slay could be those of your competition.

IRC on internal networks has been used by several computer hardware development companies for conversation among geographically widespread engineers and programmers. It's the equivalent of a meeting without the travel time. Participants preferred IRC over a telephone conference call. You can always tell who was talking in IRC because each comment is labeled with the name of the "talker," no one was ever "inaudible," and participants had easy access to online information.

Audio/Video Conferencing

Audio/Video conferencing on the Internet isn't quite ready for "prime time" at this writing, although it's getting closer than it was when we wrote the first edition of this book in 1994. When it is implemented, it will be *Type III* communication—that is, it will be public, with many-contributors-to-many-recipients, and it may be authoritative.

As the technology improves, it may be possible to use the Internet to deploy this type of service in a relatively low-cost manner to anywhere that can be reached by the Internet. The advantages are obvious: being able to televise a complicated or unusual medical procedure would be a wonderful way to reach medical professionals who want to keep their skills up-to-date. Traveling to meetings is expensive, yet the benefits of hearing from and seeing colleagues in similar positions in other organizations are again well-documented. Much that is useful comes from the interchange of information and ideas among colleagues.

As the technology becomes less expensive and more widely deployed, the communication itself will become less formal. It will be easier to use, and more people will know how to use it and have access to it. When that happens, you will get the Internet equivalent of the gossip in the hallways at conferences; and everybody knows that that's where the *real* action is, anyway.

Broadcast Messages on Systems and Networks

These are not very exciting, but they represent the *Type IV* communications: they are public, published contributions to many recipients, and they are authoritative. When you are logged into a host system, and a message warning you about possible system instability is transmitted, you do believe it and act accordingly. This type of message is completely irrelevant to you if you are not connected to that system at that time.

One building facilities manager uses broadcast messages over the various networks in the building to send notices of impending fire drills, cars with lights on, and other time-critical information. This was the fastest way to reach most of the people in the many different companies housed in the building.

Non-Simultaneous Communications

Asynchronous communication is where the Internet excels. The sender and the recipient need not be connected at the same time, and they may not even know one another. In particular, to distribute a published work on the Internet you don't need to know someone's address. The recipient comes to find the information. It's the best kind of direct mail advertising or announcing: the people who are interested read your material; the people who aren't interested don't read it. And you haven't wasted any material resources to provide the information to your audience.

E-Mail

E-mail (discussed in Chapter 8) remains the most used feature on the Internet. It's *Type I* communication: private, individual-to-individual, and possibly authoritative. In this category you find the responses to questions about your products: what does it do? where can I obtain it? what does it cost? what are the terms and conditions for a customer to use it? These questions can be directed to a specific person to answer, or to a specific mailbox (like Support or Accounting). You can designate a person to answer or have a programmed answer (prepared e-mail auto-responses) and then forward it to a specific person or group for action. Figure 17.3 shows a typical customer request for information.

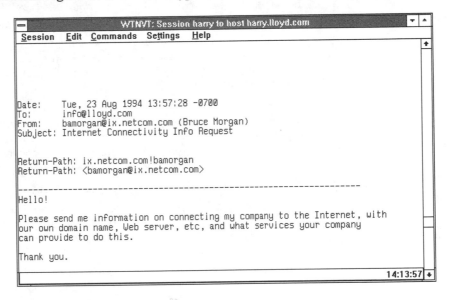

```
┌─────────────────────────────────────────────────────────────────┐
│ ▬         WTNVT: Session harry to host harry.lloyd.com      ▼ ▲ │
├─────────────────────────────────────────────────────────────────┤
│ Session   Edit  Commands  Settings   Help                      ↑ │
│                                                                   │
│                                                                   │
│                                                                   │
│ Date:     Tue, 23 Aug 1994 13:57:28 -0700                        │
│ To:       info@lloyd.com                                          │
│ From:     bamorgan@ix.netcom.com (Bruce Morgan)                   │
│ Subject:  Internet Connectivity Info Request                      │
│                                                                   │
│ Return-Path: ix.netcom.com!bamorgan                               │
│ Return-Path: <bamorgan@ix.netcom.com>                             │
│                                                                   │
│ ------------------------------------------------------------      │
│ Hello!                                                            │
│                                                                   │
│ Please send me information on connecting my company to the Internet, with │
│ our own domain name, Web server, etc, and what services your company │
│ can provide to do this.                                           │
│                                                                   │
│ Thank you.                                                        │
│                                                      14:13:57  ↓ │
└─────────────────────────────────────────────────────────────────┘
```

Figure 17.3. A typical customer inquiry via e-mail.

MASTER WORDS The most common address for folks to try if they don't know how to reach you is info@*youraddress* (for example, info@lloyd.com). If you place an auto-response at this address, people can get a summary of your services without someone having to answer all the e-mail personally—another savings in staff time.

AUTORESPONSE FILES IN E-MAIL

One of the best uses of e-mail technology is to send an automated responses back to people who send messages to your company. A quick acknowledgment of e-mail, just as with regular mail, satisfies the customer that her message has actually been received and is in the pipeline. It also gives you two benefits: you can send them more information about your company, and you can give your staff some breathing room to answer the mail at a more convenient moment, confident that the client has received an acknowledgment of the original mail.

Setting up your e-mail to send an autoresponse is fairly easy on typical UNIX systems, using the capabilities of the *alias database*. Here's how it works:

Usually, `sales` or `info` is the alias for a group of folks who handle such mail. You can add a command to the alias database entry which says to the e-mail system, "Deliver this message to these folks, but also send a copy to this UNIX program." The program, called a *script file*, will use the e-mail system to reply with a prepared file, sent to the sender of the original e-mail.

Usually, the alias database has permissions set so that only the systems administrator can modify it, and setting up the script file is something best left to either that person or someone else who is UNIX-literate. But you, or your marketing people, can (and should) write the response itself. It can look something like this, the response sent when someone sends e-mail to `info@widget.com`:

```
Thanks for contacting The Widget Company!

We have received your e-mail message, and it has been passed
on to our Sales staff. We usually answer e-mail within two
days during the business week, and sometimes during the
weekends, as well!

The Widget Company is the leading manufacturer of Widgets
and equipment for Widget support and upkeep. In business
since 1867, we pride ourselves on the quality not only of
our Widgets, but on the service you, our customers, get when
you become a member of the Widget family.

If you are contacting us about an order for our new model 27
automated Widgetwasher, we need to ask for your patience. We
knew this was a good product, but you have been ordering
them in unanticipated quantities! As a result, deliveries
are running approximately 10 days behind. We are currently
filling orders placed by September 23, 1996.

We have added additional shifts to our manufacturing plant
to catch up with the demand. We expect to be back on top of
our normal 2-day order turnaround by November 10, 1996.
```

> Our new Web pages now contain full-color images of our 1996-7 catalog. Point your Web browser at http://www.widget.com/ to see it. Or, call 1-800-WIDGETS to get a free copy sent to you via regular mail.
>
> Again, thanks for contacting the Widget Company. Our Sales staff will respond in detail to your e-mail in the next day or two.

Make sure the file for this autoresponse is in a directory where your sales staff can easily edit and update it, so that information stays current. You'll probably want to make sure its permissions are set so that only the folks you want to edit the file have access to it; otherwise, you might send out something surprising!

FTP

Making files available for transfer via FTP (discussed in Chapter 9) is another form of nonsimultaneous communication. The files you "put up" can be something relatively simple like a list of telephone numbers for various functions in your organization, or a list that describes the products offered. Or, you can use an FTP archive to provide document sharing between sites, including word processing files, spreadsheets, film clips, slide shows, and so on.

With Web Browsers becoming more and more common, you can even use your Web site to link into your FTP archive, making your customers even happier.

MASTER WORDS Not everyone has PostScript or other specialized software designed to view new formats that aren't widely used yet. Luckily, it is possible to distribute information with attached readers so that the people "picking up" the information have the ability to read/view it, but doing so makes the operation more complex for the information consumer. Unless you can provide self-extracting files, which more-or-less set themselves up for your intended audience, you will need to leave instructions that sometimes folks have trouble following. Once you are at that point, it's time to open a technical support department.

Figure 17.4 shows files being downloaded from the FTP site that Microsoft maintains for distributing information and some kinds of software. Here, we are selecting from the /deskapps (desktop applications) directory.

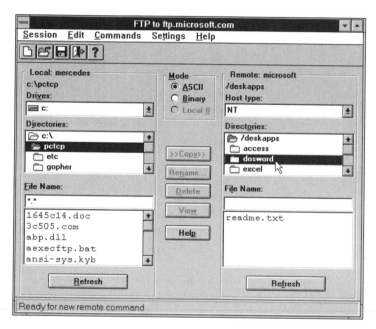

Figure 17.4.   **Retrieving FTP files.**

Finger

Another way of making information about your organization available to anyone who wants it is to place it in a file accessible by Finger, discussed in Chapter 9. This type of communication is suitable for relatively simple information, such as hours of operation or simple product literature.

Figure 17.5 shows the information that Cygnus Support makes available via Finger.

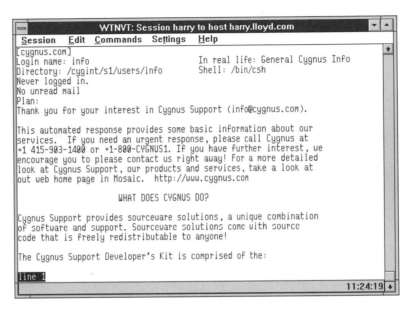

Figure 17.5. **Response from fingering info@cygnus.com.**

SETTING UP A FINGER INFORMATION FILE

You can easily set up information files for your clients and others to access using the Finger utility. (These instructions are for those on standard UNIX systems. If you're on another operating system, consult with your systems administrator to work out the exact details: the general principles hold.)

You (or your systems administrator) should set up a user named `sales` or `info` or any other name you want people to be able to access information from.

Then, on this user's account, create a `.plan` file with the information you want to distribute.

In this file, which should be no more than 24 lines long (if you want it to display as one screenful of information), you can put relevant and interesting information about your company. Remember to include access information, so that neophyte Net users can figure out how to reach you.

A sample file for `sales@widget.com` might look like this:

    Thanks for contacting The Widget Company!

    You surprised us!

Continued on next page

```
We knew our new model 27 automated Widgetwasher was a good
product, but you have been ordering them in unanticipated
quantities! As a result, deliveries are running
approximately 10 days behind. We are currently filling
orders placed by September 23, 1996.

We have added additional shifts to our manufacturing plant
to catch up with the demand. We expect to be back on top of
our normal 2-day order turnaround by November 10, 1996.

Our new Web pages now contain full-color images of our 1996-
97 catalog. Point your Web browser at http://www.widget.com/
to see it. Or call 1-800-WIDGETS to get a free copy sent to
you via regular mail.
```

Make sure permissions for this file are set correctly so that others may write to it without having to sign on as user `sales`, so that you can quickly and easily edit the information and keep it up to date.

You will also need to make sure that your systems administrator has set up the *finger daemon* correctly so that `.plan` files on your system can be shown to those outside your local network. Be sure to warn company staff before you enable this feature, if it's currently disabled.

Usenet

Still another Internet tool for making your information available to people, no matter what time of day they want it, is Usenet. As discussed in Chapter 12, Usenet newsgroups may be either moderated or unmoderated.

Unmoderated Mailing Lists and Usenet Newsgroups

These are examples of *Type II* communications—public, many-contributors-to-many-recipients, and nonauthoritative. For our purposes there are no real differences between newsgroups and mailing lists in this context. In the appropriate newsgroups and mailing lists you can announce enhancements to your product lines, ask for help, find people who might like to work for you, and so on. They are the Internet's equivalent of the grocery store bulletin board; and as with most public bulletin boards, there is likely to be more information and data than you will want to know about. If you want to reach people in the insurance industry in Omaha, Nebraska, you will post in a different place than if you want to reach people in aircraft jet maintenance in Orlando, Florida. These lists and newsgroups can be good places for you to get information, too, of course. The unmoderated nature of these media make them nonauthoritative, but after "lurking" for awhile you will know some of the "Net-personalities" of that particular Net arena and decide whether you believe what they say. Figure 17.6 shows a newsgroup discussion about midwifery and childbirth.

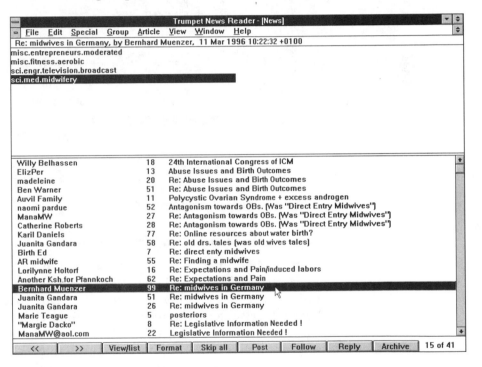

Figure 17.6.   A newsgroup listing about midwifery.

Another excellent way to use the News software is to set up in-house newsgroups, which can only be read by your staff. This lets you have good discussions while taking advantage of the information sorting available with news, and still keep your conversations private. Figure 17.7 shows an example.

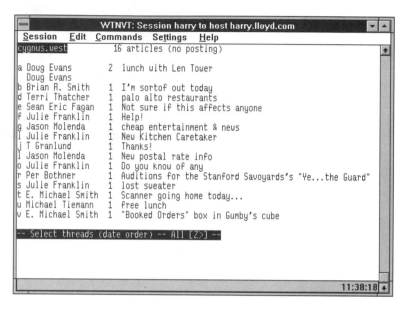

```
┌─────────────────────────────────────────────────────────────────────┐
│ ─         WTNVT: Session harry to host harry.lloyd.com        ▼ ▲    │
├─────────────────────────────────────────────────────────────────────┤
│ Session   Edit   Commands   Settings   Help                          │
├─────────────────────────────────────────────────────────────────────┤
│cygnus.west            16 articles (no posting)                    ↑  │
│                                                                      │
│a Doug Evans        2  lunch with Len Tower                           │
│  Doug Evans                                                          │
│b Brian A. Smith    1  I'm sortof out today                           │
│d Terri Thatcher    1  palo alto restaurants                          │
│e Sean Eric Fagan   1  Not sure if this affects anyone                │
│f Julie Franklin    1  Help!                                          │
│g Jason Molenda     1  cheap entertainment & news                     │
│i Julie Franklin    1  New Kitchen Caretaker                          │
│j T Granlund        1  Thanks!                                        │
│l Jason Molenda     1  New postal rate info                           │
│o Julie Franklin    1  Do you know of any                             │
│r Per Bothner       1  Auditions for the Stanford Savoyards's "Ye...the Guard"│
│s Julie Franklin    1  lost sweater                                   │
│t E. Michael Smith  1  Scanner going home today...                    │
│u Michael Tiemann   1  free lunch                                     │
│v E. Michael Smith  1  "Booked Orders" box in Gumby's cube            │
│                                                                      │
│ -- Select threads (date order) -- All [Z>] --                        │
│                                                                      │
│                                                           11:38:18 ↓ │
└─────────────────────────────────────────────────────────────────────┘
```

*Figure 17.7.   **An in-house newsgroup menu.***

Moderated Mailing Lists and Usenet Newsgroups

These tools are more difficult to use as communications media than the unrestricted groups. They offer *Type III* communications: public, many-contributors-to-many-recipients, and possibly authoritative. Their authority depends directly upon their charter and the trustworthiness of the moderator. If the moderator is devoted to the charter of the group, everything posted to the list or group will meet the "contract." Less literal moderators may actually provide a better arena in which to hold discussions, because articles or e-mail messages that are slightly off-topic might be interesting to the group as a whole and improve the value of the group.

Judicious moderators will usually let such topics be introduced in order not to appear dictatorial or have the group be too rigid. Generally, we believe the free flow of information and data will produce better results. The only place where this is not appropriate is the *.announce newsgroups. These groups are strictly moderated to include appropriate announcements only.

This ensures that the readers will know exactly what to expect from the articles posted to these groups. These groups are used (usually) to announce meetings of interest to the readers. If the group is ba.announce, for example, the announcements are restricted to concerts, readings, meetings of general interest to the people living in the San Francisco Bay Area.

If the mailing list is PACS-L (illustrated in Figure 17.8), which discusses issues related to public access in libraries, the announcements and discussion will range slightly wider since there are many issues related to the public access of information. The readers of the list discuss copyright law, and networking CD-ROMs on LANs, and conferences of interest to people who work in information provision, libraries, the development of library systems, and so on. The wide range of material discussed contributes to the value of the list.

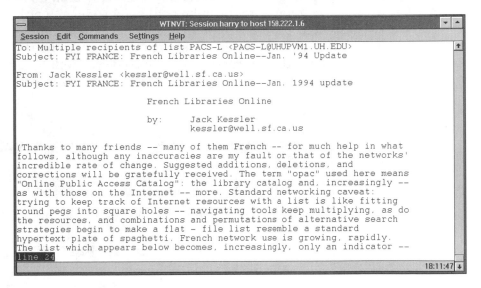

Figure 17.8. **A PACS-L mailing.**

Internet Publications

Internet publications are the final type of communication we will discuss. These are *Type IV*: public, one-source-to-many-recipients, and authoritative. The category includes Web pages, Gopher documents, corporate/organizational files placed for FTP and Finger, and search-able databases made available to Internet users.

These products or services might be made available without charge, by giving your customers special access codes or passwords, or they might be available by purchasing access to the product or service. The resource list-ings we provide in the chapters on government, business, education, and general resources discuss many of these publications in detail. Look at them to get ideas on how you can publish your information on the Net.

How you choose to use the Internet as a publishing mechanism again depends on the results you want to achieve.

Web Pages

As discussed in Chapter 10, using Web pages allows you to display color graphics, animation, and sound as well as explanatory text. As such, Web pages are more like brochures than anything you can produce using other Internet tools. You can present materials about your organization's products and services in an attractive and easy-to-use manner that can be read by anyone with access to a Web browser client program. Not all clients have the ability to see all the features, but as long as the Web page designer keeps the different clients in mind, the information can be conveyed well for any possible information consumer. Figure 17.9 shows the Web page for the Computer Literacy bookstores:

```
http://www.clbooks.com/index.html
```

Figure 17.9.   The Computer Literacy Bookshops "home page" on the Web.

Hundreds of thousands of businesses are on the Web these days. One of the fastest-growing uses of Web pages is for customer service. For example, you can order photocopying supplies from Xerox via their Web page. Figure 17.10 shows the various supplies you can order from the Xerox Web site.

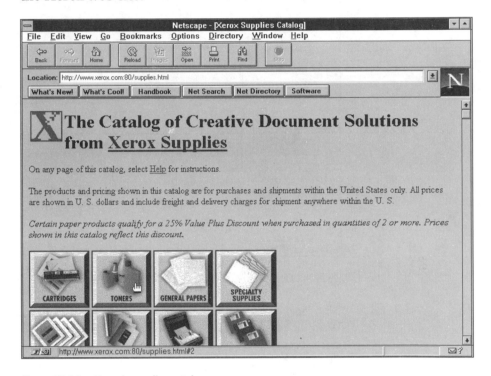

Figure 17.10.   Xerox's supplies catalog page.

With the advent of secure browsers, you can send information with relative confidence of its security. In addition, you can create semi-private areas on your Web site, where your customers can check out their orders, see new discount pricing, even have a customized page where their name is displayed and the page itself only has information of interest to them, all triggered by entering their name and password.

Figure 17.11 shows the order form at the Dilbert Store, where you can buy Dilbert cartoon-related items.

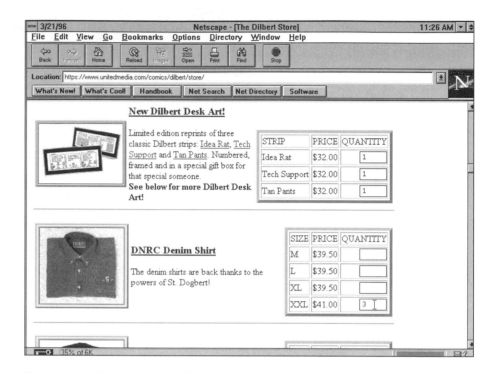

Figure 17.11. *Shopping at the Dilbert Store using a secure browser.*

The best way to come up with new ideas about what you can do on a Web site is to cruise the Net and look at ideas. One site may spark your creativity or give a good idea about something you can do. Go out and browse!

 MASTER WORDS   Want to get your Web site advertised in all the search engines? Check out the submission site at

    `http://204.52.210.13/infolink/listem.htm`

This site has a comprehensive listing of the submission services that have sprung up. These services are automated sites where you can choose which search engine to send your URLs to.

Gopher

Gopher, discussed in Chapter 11, allows quick and concise displays of hierarchical information. Its strength lies in the ability of associated services like Veronica and Jughead to build information menus from all of gopherspace.

Unfortunately, that's also its weakness for the information publisher. Because people can jump to your carefully designed menu item from anywhere, they may not see where it fits in the larger context of your menu hierarchy. This can make delivery of a total impression slightly more difficult.

It's as if when you mailed out literature about your company, the binder came open and the chapters were disarranged. The recipient might read the chapter on your manufacturing processes, then the one on your charitable contributions, and so on. Your carefully arranged marketing story would no longer be in the order you had planned, and so the impact would be different.

Many Tools Make Light Work

As you've just seen, the Internet's tools can be used in virtually limitless ways to find information for your organization, to make information about it available to the public, and to share information within your organization. The possibilities are limited only by your imagination. Of course, to make the most effective use of these tools, you'll need a good systems administrator (and possibly an Internet consultant) who can set up your system so that anyone inside or outside your organization can easily find the information they need.

INTERNETWORKING CONSULTANTS

Selecting a consultant should be the same sort of process as selecting an employee. You'll need to work well with your consultant, being able to communicate your needs. The consultant should give you options about how to use internetworking to meet your needs.

You can probably find knowledgeable people among your personal community to help you. Maybe someone will help you for little or no money or will barter their services for yours. When you make this kind of arrangement, make sure that both parties understand the terms of the arrangement so there are no hard feelings later. Professional consultants will provide contracts and expected due dates. These may be better suited to your needs. In any case, always ask for and check the references of any consultant.

Continued on next page

Part III

Becoming an Information Provider

There are many people and organizations that can provide consulting for you and your organization in making your information available over the Internet. We have no special way to identify all of them. A number of consultants have registered with the CommerceNet registry of consultants. CommerceNet is supplying the directory space and makes quite clear that the list is made of those consultants who listed themselves. CommerceNet is not in a position to recommend specific consultants. The CommerceNet directory is available on the Web, at

```
http://www.commerce.net/directories/consultants/consultants.html
```

Here are a few people and firms that we know will do a good job for you. This short, alphabetical list is a completely biased one, made up of people we know and like to work with. It's by no means complete. Browse their Web pages or contact them to see if you can find a consultant that you will feel comfortable working with.

Consultants	Contact Info:
Bunyip Information Systems	`http://services.bunyip.com`
Intuitive Systems	`http://www.intuitive.com`
Lloyd Internetworking	`http://www.lloyd.com`
Liberty Hill Cyberwerks	`http://www.cyberwerks.com`
ManyMedia	`http://www.manymedia.com`
SmartPages	`http://www.smartpages.com`
TNT Media	`http://www.tntmedia.com`

How Should We Use It?

By this question we mean not "which applications should we use to accomplish our goals" but "what conduct is acceptable?" The Internet is a strange part of cyberspace. Historically, it has developed through the academic and research community, and appears to be "free" to many students, faculty, and staff; and because of this, Internet users have been profoundly ambivalent about commercial activities on the Net. On one hand, Internet users—like everyone else—want to find out about products and services of interest to them; on the other hand, they want to preserve a medium of communication that is not dominated by commercial interests.

The easiest way to discuss this love-hate relationship is through anecdotes and examples. The clearest of these come from the Usenet newsgroups, where (at this writing) product advertisements are mostly not welcome. We emphasize the word *mostly,* because there are places where this intention is ignored continually by the posters and the readers.

Personal Classifieds or Yard Sales

The `misc.forsale` newsgroup is one where the fine distinctions seem clearer to the person who has been reading the newsgroup for awhile than to the person who has only recently come to the Internet. It's intended to be used by individuals occasionally selling items they don't need anymore, not by ongoing retail businesses. Netcom receives several complaints a week about postings to the group that are not considered appropriate, because of the sensitivity to commercial versus noncommercial use.

`Misc.forsale` is a widely dispersed garage sale. This means that while some people do occasionally post commercial advertisements for large numbers of (for example) hard disk drives for specific types of computers, the average seller has one piece of equipment or a book or a musical instrument that is no longer needed and is going to be turned into cash. The owner posts an article to `misc.forsale` and perhaps also the local supermarket bulletin board and maybe has a "real" garage sale rather than a virtual one. The user who wants to buy uses e-mail to negotiate a price, delivery method, and form of payment. When the price is agreed upon, a check is sent (usually) and the merchandise is shipped to the purchaser. Most people who purchase products this way are pleased that they have acquired something they wanted for not too much work and not too much expense—as in real garage sales, the prices charged in `misc.forsale` are much less than the retail price for the equivalent new product.

For example, Glee was pleased to find a set of German language lessons with both the manual and two CDs when she wanted to acquire some German quickly prior to a trip to Germany. The product description and price were posted. She sent an e-mail message indicating interest. The seller replied with a postal address. She sent a check. He sent the materials. Both parties were happy: the seller got rid of the materials and received money; Glee got the materials for a fair (that is, below retail) price.

There are occasions when you send the check and the seller does not provide your product or service. You do have a few recourses should that happen. The one most frequently used is to post far and wide about the person who cheated. Be sure to read the FAQ called "HOW TO POST/BUY/SELL on MISC.FORSALE." before you participate.

For a more detailed discussion of buying and selling products and services on the Net, see Chapter 21.

New Product Announcements

Announcements offering information about a new product or service are generally tolerated (if not welcomed) in the Usenet newsgroups as long as two basic conditions are met:

1. The announcement is posted to a group that actually discusses something related to the product or service, and

2. The material posted is simply an announcement, not an advertisement.

The second condition is somewhat subjective—"beauty in the eye of the beholder." In the Internet environment, an announcement is regarded as "too much marketing fluff" if it contains a large number of adjectives and adverbs designed to enhance the nouns. The more adjectives, the more complaints that will be received by your Internet access provider about your posting. Most providers will discuss the complaints they receive with you, so you will know about them.

Bad Karma on the Net

The most famous recent case of inappropriate posting to the newsgroups is that of the so-called "Green Card Lawyers." A husband-and-wife law firm posted a message to thousands of newsgroups offering their services in immigration information to foreign nationals residing in the United States. The posting was blatantly commercial. It was posted to practically every newsgroup that is widely distributed throughout the United States. It was read by many people who were really angry about the misuse of the newsgroups.

The angry readers "mail-bombed" the original poster with nasty e-mail messages. So many messages were received that the mail server for their Internet provider was overwhelmed and was taken out of service. Posting to a large number of groups like this is clearly done on purpose. A person might choose to do it once and be surprised about the vehemence of the reaction to the posting. After seeing that reaction, most posters begin to understand that posting to inappropriate newsgroups is not appreciated.

The first problem with this posting was not its content: it was that it was scattered indiscriminately across every newsgroup, including many where it was clearly not in line with the charter of the group. This is the first thing that made newsgroup readers angry.

Then they got angrier: the posters said they were not sorry for posting to inappropriate groups and that they intended to do it again. Furthermore, the posters stated their intention of opening an advertising business that would repeat their actions and said that they would be happy to do it again on behalf of other people, if they were paid a fee, since there was no law forbidding this activity.

At this point, Netcom (one of the providers with whom the poster had an account) decided to terminate the account. Another provider, PSI, worked out an agreement with the posters that was intended to keep them from continuing the behavior. Many articles were written and posted to mailing lists and newsgroups throughout the Internet and in print media as well.

In our opinion there were several things that made people feel so strongly about this case. One was the attitude of the posters. They seemed to take pride in throwing the culture of the Internet community back in our faces. Anytime one's culture is directly attacked, the reaction is loud and fast—reprisal! Also, the posters seem to believe that because a thing is not illegal, it is okay to do.

Many things in our culture are not illegal (at least, not in every jurisdiction) but they are taboo. Let's consider the example of changing clothes in the laundromat: not in the restroom, but out next to the dryer. Not only would most of us not do it, we probably wouldn't sell tickets to see others doing it, or charge money to sell the tickets for others.

The "Green Card Lawyers" not only put up their ads in the wrong place, they claimed that they were going to start selling tickets to others to do the same thing.

It seems that the posters were more interested in challenging the culture, the nonexistent law, and the remediation process than they were in enlarging their business. They do claim, however, that the advertisement was quite successful.

Their example sparked a few more forays into posting indiscriminately to large numbers of newsgroups. One clever wordsmith declared that his posting was not against netiquette and therefore appropriate because he was giving away a product in a contest. No doubt this explanation would have sounded better to his access provider had he done a better job of matching the product one could win in the contest to the newsgroups to which he posted the contest advertisement. But he didn't, lots of people complained to his access provider, and he became another person with whom the Usenet posting rules were discussed in great detail.

The bottom line here is that you can't get your message out on the Net by ignoring the culture. If your postings are complained about to your service provider, your provider may well refuse you access.

Ads on Your Web Page

There is one place where advertising is socially acceptable and, in fact, works almost exactly the same way it works in other venues, and that's on Web pages.

You advertise your product on your Web space just as you would in print or on TV.

Or, you sell advertising space on your Web site to a company or concern that agrees to support your expenses in maintaining the Web site in return for a prominent location and permanent link to *their* Web information.

The difference that makes Web space advertising more palatable than commercial information in Usenet news groups is that folks have to come to your site to see the ads. Your ads don't intrude on their space. In other words, they have to ask for the information. It's not like junk mail in your mailbox.

Ethics and Legalities

The central point of doing business in cyberspace is the same as doing business in physical space. If you represent yourself, your company, and your product or service well to the people who will be interested in knowing about it; provide the service or product ethically—good value at a fair price, for example—chances are you will do reasonably well. (Unless you have a product or service that no one wants, of course.) Conducting such a business requires knowledge of your market or audience, the applicable laws, and the ethics involved in your communities (the physical/cultural one in real space and the one in cyberspace).

Legal Issues

If something is illegal, it is illegal. It remains illegal in cyberspace. Being on a network does not change the action. If you do, or are suspected of doing, something that is illegal—selling child pornography, for example—your access provider probably will cooperate with the appropriate governmental bodies to capture you and put you away.

Geographic boundaries may not protect you. In late 1994, bulletin board owners in Milpitas, California, were convicted by a Tennessee court for distributing obscene materials. *Under the laws of Tennessee,* the material was obscene by Tennessee community standards. A Tennessee user had dialed into the bulletin board in California. The Tennessee prosecutors successfully argued that this brought the California computer system and its owners into Tennessee's jurisdiction.

You should remember that special laws concerning business in cyberspace aren't there yet. Most law in the United States is based upon case law—that is, precedent cases. There aren't a lot of precedents in this area yet. And once the data or information crosses an international border, whatever laws there are become different.

The laws concerning computer crime and networking are changing as we write. Neither of us are qualified to give you legal advice. If you need legal assistance, talk to an attorney.

International Issues

There aren't a lot of global laws. There are some treaties and international agreements, but they are not always signed by all relevant governments.

One of the most interesting assumptions that most Americans make is that their right to free speech is guaranteed. Making some reference to that right is actually guaranteed to cause a lot of amused comments from people from other countries who contribute to the Internet's mailing lists and newsgroups.

Trademarks

If you decide to operate a service on the Internet, you will lose the rights to the name of your service once any part of it crosses an international border, if you don't trademark the name in all the appropriate countries. To do that for the ten largest countries in terms of available Internet access was estimated in 1994 to cost about $300,000 (more recent figures are not available, but the costs are unlikely to have decreased). This puts trademarking outside the reach of most start-up companies.

Export Restrictions

Certain kinds of products, notably security software with encryption, cannot legally be exported to some countries. Current government regulation takes the stance that if you have a public FTP archive with a restricted product available in it, you are *de facto* exporting it to restricted countries. This regulation and its interpretation are being argued hotly, but the law could conceivably apply to other things, such as catalog images in Web pages (some countries restrict images of naked or semi-naked people, birth control information, and so on), game or software demos, and the like.

 MASTER WORDS   For more information about export restrictions and the principles behind these restrictions, please see John Gillmore's writings in the Electronic Frontier Foundation archive available at `gopher.eff.org` or look for discussions in the `comp.protocols.kerberos` newsgroup.

Management Issues

We've talked about things you can do with the Internet either to obtain or to provide information that will be to your advantage as a governmental organization or a business. There are some lessons to be learned from the access providers, too. These things involve policies for internal use, resource management, and security.

Developing Appropriate Use Policies

Early use of the Internet in the research and education community sparked the development of "appropriate use" policies. This term is used to describe what sort of information is allowed to be carried on a network. The policy was developed to do two things: protect the government funding agency from being accused of providing subsidies to commercial services, and to provide a clear description of appropriate traffic so that inappropriate traffic could be kept off the network.

All network developers should have some sort of appropriate use policy. If the purpose of your network is to carry messages regarding work from one employee to another, say so. That way, when you find someone playing *Doom* on your network, or running an archive of pictures or sounds on the disk drives that are owned by your organization, you have a clear statement of why you are going to stop that action. Appropriate use policies don't need to be complex or difficult to understand. In fact, they will be best if they aren't. A good collection of policies can be found at

```
http://www.eff.org
```

sponsored by the Electronic Frontier Foundation. This group was founded to address the complex issues of the rights provided by the United States Constitution in the global information economy.

Chapter 19 is a complete discussion of appropriate use policies, and we include there some sample policies. In this section we summarize the most important issues.

Clear Guidelines for Employees

One thing you will need to make clear to your employees is what you *will* allow them to do with their accounts.

Many of your employees will be interested in mailing lists that are not work-related. Will you allow them to read those lists on your organization's time? Will you allow them to read those lists using your organization's equipment? On their own time? Perhaps you will let them read things of personal interest during their lunch hours or coffee breaks (much as you allow reading a novel or magazine during breaks). Will you instead suggest that these people get personal accounts with an Internet access provider?

 MASTER WORDS   You probably already have policies concerning the use of company computers, printers, fax machines, photocopiers, and telephones. Coordinate your new Internet policies with the ones you already have.

Can your employees FTP personal material to their work machines, and then print it off on your printers? Will you let them put personal material up to be collected via FTP or other means?

Are your employees allowed to post to nonwork-related newsgroups, such as `misc.kids`, or `rec.arts.startrek`, from a user ID that points to your company? If they do post, do they need to put a disclaimer on the posting? (Something like: "This posting does not represent the policies of Automation International, or their affiliates.")

Will you let your staff put up personal Web pages, containing pointers to organizations they are affiliated with? Or to put up an organizational resource using your machines?

Some Internet service providers do their *pro bono* work by serving the Web pages of nonprofit organizations; for instance, see the pages at

```
http://www.intac.com/PubService/Service.html
```

Many university sites provide Web space to their students, faculty, and staff. Because of issues of academic freedom, the Web spaces are not usually moderated. Organizational policies concerning personal use vary as widely as the organizations themselves. Cygnus Software is very different from the United States Department of Defense.

Another issue to consider is use of the company *connection* to contact other machines. For example, Pat's contract with Cygnus required that she not work on this book over their Internet connection. Her contract said that anything she created on Cygnus equipment must be shared with Cygnus: the management took that to mean the wires that make up the Internet connection, as well. So Pat did not Telnet home to work on her home computer from a work machine, even during nonworking hours.

(Cygnus participates in the GNU software distribution license. That is, they believe that you should give freely of your artistic creations, including software, without restriction. This book, along with other items Pat has written, would have fallen under that agreement.)

Many employees these days consider free (unrestricted) network access to be one of the perks of working for a company with Internet access. Obviously, you need to take that into consideration when you make your policies (just as you consider use of the phone and photocopy machine). Be sure to spell out your policies clearly so that everyone knows what to expect. If you are not yet connected, take the opportunity to develop your policies before your connection is installed. Then you can talk about the policies during training. If you are already connected, make certain your policies are covered during new employee orientation.

Appropriate Use Policies and Employee Privacy Rights

As a manager or as an employee, you should be familiar with the laws in your state regarding computers and employee privacy; and managers should formulate and implement their appropriate use policies accordingly. Recent cases have tended toward the point of view that *unless you tell them otherwise,* from the beginning of their employment or from the beginning of the time computer access is given to them, your employees have what is called a "reasonable expectation of privacy" concerning their computer transactions.

This means that unless you tell *every* employee when they join the company about your appropriate use policies, they have the right to expect that their e-mail is private. If it is your company or organization's policy that no private e-mail transactions should take place on the system, then you need to make sure that policy is well explained and broadly available.

Most employees assume that no one will go snooping in their computer files—the same assumption they make about their desk drawers. Unless you make it clear that you regularly check personal files (and, for that matter, desk drawers and lockers), your employees are considered by law to reasonably expect that their file space, unless they permit it to be readable by others, is safe from snooping.

 MASTER WORDS If your organization does not have a policy in place regarding appropriate Internet use, and there is a conflict with an employee over it, mediation agencies, union management, and courts tend to look at your other policies for guidance in computer issues. Therefore, if you allow people to have private materials (books, letters, and so on) in their desks or lockers, the courts are likely to generalize that policy to include computer files. It's important to consider your policies and put them in place as soon as you put in the phone line that links you to the Internet.

How Many Years of E-Mail Do You Have?

Archiving of system files is another issue related to privacy and employee rights. Some systems administrators make routine backups of their system every night (this is, actually, a Good Thing!), but those backups include the e-mail that is on the system, either incoming or in mailboxes, at the time.

Some backups are stored for years—one university recently announced that it had file backups for the past 25 years in their archives.

The problem for you, as a manager, is one of privacy and archives. Suppose you suspect an employee of giving away trade secrets. Should you ask the systems administrator to search all the file backups looking through all this person's e-mail? Or suppose an employee leaves the organization. What happens to all his electronic archive files? Can you just randomly search through them, or do you need to have a good reason?

Again, look to your policies on paper and other resources to give you guidance, as well as checking with the computer crime bureau in your state.

Resource Management and Planning for Growth

Resource management, like the other topics we've discussed in this chapter, has two faces; your organization may be accessing the Internet both as a consumer and as a provider.

Use, Like Work, Grows to Fill the Resources Allotted

On the consumer side are those folks who are using your computing resources. For each and every person for whom you are managing Internet access, you need to maintain a data pipe wide enough to provide access to the kinds of services that person will need to carry out his or her responsibilities effectively.

Some of your people will need very little: access to their e-mail messages will do it. These folks will not stress your resources at all. Other people, like marketing research staff, or library staff, or legal representatives, people who gather information as part of their daily tasks, will stress your resources. These people will need full Internet access to use the navigation programs, to transfer large sets of statistical data from repositories, to use search engines like WAIS to find particular cases or citations in registers and court opinions. They will need fast IP-based or direct connections, rather than slower host-dial pipes. How do you figure out what you need?

Make a census of your employees to see how many of each type of consumer you have; this will help you plan. Make certain that you allow room for growth. Initially, people don't believe they will use the network for much of anything, but their use grows, sometimes exponentially. Measuring your network usage will allow you to (maybe) keep one step ahead of the growth curve.

Don't Outgrow Your Resource

If you are an information provider, you need to try to estimate the size and type of your audience. If you are providing statistical data, for example, and the data will be desired by many, many people, you will need a larger computer to use as a server than if you are simply providing a small number of e-mail messages as automatic bounce-backs to marketing inquiries.

Providing FTP directories is not difficult, and the personnel requirements for maintaining them are pretty low; however, transferring large files by FTP requires more network bandwith than delivery by Gopher or a short menu. You will need to plan not only for a fast network connection, but a computer with more memory and a faster CPU. If you need to restrict access, you can set up systems that refuse more than a set number of connections at one time. Limiting the number of simultaneous connections and being aware of the resources taken by the delivery method you have implemented will give you a controlled environment. You will need to keep track of the connections that you refuse, however, so that you can choose to expand the possible number of connections at an appropriate time for your organization.

A WWW site with forms, graphics that change regularly (some firms change their graphics *at least* twice every 24 hours), updated customer information, and other material which brings the customer back needs a fast link, a server with lots of CPU power, and so on. You'll need staff dedicated to both administration and content.

This has necessarily been a general discussion of resource management issues. To plan specifically for your network resources now and in the future, you will spend your investment dollars wisely by either hiring a qualified full-time employee or contracting with an Internet consulting firm.

Security

There are two kinds of security related to your Internet installation: protecting your organization from outsiders and protecting it from insiders.

Smart Defense

In a way, defending yourself from outsiders is easier. Sensitive data about your organization should be kept off the server that is connected to the Internet. The Internet is a very open environment. The most frequently used operating systems in the Internet are variations of UNIX, which is (from a security perspective) a very open system. If you want something to be private, the Internet is not a good place for it *at this time*.

There is a lot of very interesting work being done on data encryption technologies, on private keys, on trusted signatures, on access authorizations. These technologies will become more mature and more trusted in the next several years.

This does not mean that you can't be on the Internet if you have private data. It means that *data* shouldn't be connected to the Internet. Many installations use a firewall to protect their internal networks from unwanted intrusions. *Firewalls* are so named because they protect what is behind them from being burned, just like steel firewalls in your offices protect your file cabinets from being burned in a fire.

Usually, access through firewalls is limited to e-mail because a computer—the firewall machine—can act as a gateway between the internal and external networks. A well-known example of such an installation is the firewall that protects Intel. Intel has one of the largest internal networks in the world (it's hard to know who exactly has the largest, because those statistics are proprietary). It is possible to send e-mail into, and out of, the Intel internal network. But there are almost no places where any Intel servers are actually connected to the Internet itself. And most Intel employees who use the Internet have personal accounts outside the Intel systems in order to do so.

Trouble from Within

The largest danger to any internal network and server system comes from the people who have access to it internally. Even if the people aren't malicious, they can cause havoc. Many really bright computer users (called hackers in some circles; don't confuse them with crackers, whose motivation is explicitly destructive) feel that anything they can explore or do they should be allowed to do. If they make a mistake—even an innocent error—you can have real problems.

What kind of steps should you take? To start with, access to system-privileged accounts should be severely restricted. All changes should be logged. Careful backups of the systems should be taken and at least one cycle of backup tape stored off-site. Care should always be taken in training people about security concerns. This means teaching all your staff how to protect their own data, as well as making sure your systems administrators are trustworthy.

Getting Help with Security

It's better to build security in from the ground up. When planning your installation, you might want to have a security audit done. Many Internet consulting firms will check your installations for possible security gaps, which you can then plug yourself or hire them to fix. The goal is to find the gaps so that you can plug them before information about your organization leaks out all over the world.

Much more information about security can be found in RFC 1244, the Site Security Handbook by Paul Holbrook and Joyce K. Reynolds. You can get it at any of many RFC archvies, including

```
http://www.research.digital.com/nsl/org/WebGuide.html
```

An additional site for information about security is the Computer Operations, Audit, and Security Technology (COAST) Security Archive at Purdue University in Indiana. It contains software, standards, tools, and other material dealing with everything from access control and authentication, to security tools and social impacts. The COAST address is

```
http://www.cs.purdue.edu/coast/coast.html
```

There are several mailing lists that discuss security issues. One of the better ones is

```
firewalls@greatcircle.com
```

To sign up for this list, send to

```
firewalls-request@greatcircle.com
```

One of your best resources for system security is a savvy and ethical systems administrator. This person is worth her (or his) weight in gold.

Don't skimp on the salary for this person when you are installing a network for your company that costs—and can save—you thousands of dollars a year.

Training

Once you decide to get an Internet connection, how do you teach your staff to make the best use of it?

Perhaps you have an employee (the one who talked you into taking this leap) who can do beginning seminars and training. Peer-to-peer training is very powerful, and you'll be amazed at the number of folk on your staff who pop up with Internet knowledge.

Alternately, you can hire a consulting firm to come and do training. Sometimes this training is included along with the price of your connection from your Internet provider. Certainly they are the place to start when looking for a consulting firm to do training.

In general, you need to make sure your employees know the following by the time they finish their beginning course in NetSurfing:

What the Internet is and why you are connected to it.

What benefits they, and their clients or customers, will get from this connection.

How to use the network client software you have installed: e-mail at least, and whatever others you plan to use.

How to connect to the Net from their workstations.

How to explore the Net to learn more.

What your policies are concerning Net use and access.

Whom to call for help.

Conclusion: The Picture Is Pretty Bright

Because there are so many serious issues to consider when starting to do business on the Net, it can sound very daunting. Luckily, many other folks have taken this step before you, and resources for business and governmental use are springing up all over the Net. In Chapter 22, we present an annotated list of these resources, how to reach them, and what they can do for you.

In addition, you'll find that your customers and staff in general get pretty excited about using the Net. Perhaps e-mail will be the trigger, or using the Web (a lot of novices get hooked on the Net by using the Web). Once they do, you'll find that they are thinking up new and better ways to use the Net to help your business or organization.

Part
III

Becoming an
Information Provider

CHAPTER 18

The K–12
Internet Presence

FEATURING

Benefits and consequences of being networked

Strategies for getting funded

Technical planning
(before the equipment goes in)

Determining who
will have access to network components

"Cyberporn" and censorship

Training and maintenance

Chapter 18

The K–12 Internet Presence

THE Internet is an unparalleled resource for education. (Unparalleled aside from the teachers and students, that is!) Connectivity gives a school access to curriculum development tools, graphics, teaching associations, support groups, and even Net pen-pals for the students. The K–12 (Kindergarten to 12th grade) presence on the Net is perhaps one of the fastest growing. Twenty-five years ago, we began to see the first library catalogs online. Several years later, teachers began talking to one another over the Net via e-mail and mailing lists. At conferences, teachers who had Net connections through local colleges, bulletin boards, or other sources would huddle together to try and figure out how to use this resource. Then schools began to get grants for inter- and intra-school networks. But it wasn't until the late 1980s that colleges and universities, in partnership with schools, businesses, and network-savvy parents, began to get the schools linked to the greater Internet.

In this chapter (along with the resource lists in Chapters 24 and 25 and the technical guidelines in Appendix D), the K–12 educator and student will find ways to enrich their classrooms by using the resources of the network. They will also find ways to share their knowledge with other students and teachers. Parents interested in bringing the Internet to local schools will find valuable source materials here, too.

 MASTER WORDS   The Internet was once a treasure trove for computer enthusiasts only, but today's Internet has resources for science, math, art, music, writing; you name it, and you can find it online. And thanks to the modern browser tools for the Web and for Gophers, today's Internet resources are available to even the most computer-shy.

Benefits and Consequences of Being Networked

Just as with any other organization, being linked to the Internet gets you immediate access to a vast pool of resources. K–12 schools are the fastest growing new category of connected organizations. More and more organizations, connectivity providers, and other networked entities are recognizing that the K–12 crowd are a growing audience, and are providing more and more Web pages, Gopher servers, and other online resources for educators. To cope with this wealth of material, folks looking for K–12 resources need to be particularly savvy about using all the tools to find their specialty resources.

Additionally, more and more of you are talking to each other. Starting with the FidoNet-based K12Net project some years ago, teachers have taken to the nets to talk to each other in droves. Not only are teachers talking, but students are conversing, using IRC, doing collective projects, and so on.

Schools have particular problems associated with being connected, as do other public entities that have general access to the Net. Some of the material on the Net may not be appropriate for children to see or participate in. Parents have concerns about reading material, news groups with inappropriate images and material, games versus education, and so on. In some ways, for teachers, access to the Internet is just another ball in the juggling act they have always performed.

Schools can also find a ready-made audience for information they can provide, however. Some of those folks and some of their interests include:

Everyone:

1. Homework assignments
2. Conference schedules
3. School year schedule (including vacations, sports, meetings, etc.)
4. Menus
5. Policy information
6. District election information
7. Class and bell schedules
8. E-mail to teachers, administrators, school board, each other, etc.

9. Bus schedules

10. District contact information

11. Staff information (perhaps pictures!)

12. Newsletters

13. Student works, including art work, audio clips, movies, and so on

Parents:

1. Registration information

2. PTA and other organizational information

Students:

1. Test results (password guarded, of course)

2. Library research materials

3. Social resources (IRCs, MUDs, mailing lists, newsgroups)

Teachers:

1. Sub lists

2. New policy information

3. Job postings

4. Curriculum resources

5. Staff conferencing and information sharing

School boards and district officials:

1. Student databases

2. Meetings schedules and agendas

3. Funding and other election materials

The potential list goes on and on. Schools could begin to reach out to their districts in ways that would allow for faster updating of information, more ecologically sound distribution, and technical training and literacy for students.

 MASTER WORDS   Want to make sure folks begin to use the electronic resource instead of more traditional ways of distributing information? Distribute some interesting pieces of information *only* via e-mail or other distribution on the Net. Give your potential audience a chance to join you online.

Special Educational Advantages

Schools, particularly K–12 public institutions, are very well placed to take advantage of networking. Here are some reasons:

Schools hold our future in the form of our children. Parents, employers, and other groups are interested in seeing that schools get access to resources which help increase our future national productivity.

Much of the legislation for networking infrastructure in the United States has special sections for making sure the K–12 education system is included in the connection strategies.

Corporations are interested in getting into partnerships with K–12 schools in order to take advantage of tax and public relation benefits for such partnerships.

School-related vendors (such as publishers of textbooks, curriculum materials, and so on) are putting special education resources on the Net to attract business from school districts.

Because schools are not required to link to commercial providers, they can take advantage of government-subsidized network infrastructure.

Some telephone service providers have funded special programs to connect K–12 schools to the Internet. Contact your providers to see if they have such a program.

Granting agencies such as the National Science Foundation have grant competitions for K–12 networking projects.

Higher education institutions, particularly those running mid-level or regional networks, have both a mission-related objective to connect K–12 institutions and a financial objective. (Hooking up schools can bring in grants and other funding, which benefits their entire infrastructure.)

Strategies for Getting Funding

Networks do cost money. In order to be connected, you will need to find the resources to fund equipment, design expertise, and ongoing staffing. No individual can do it alone; cooperation is essential. How will you—parents, teachers, administrators—achieve it?

Step One: Find Out What You Can Do with a Network

The first thing you need to do in order to start building a people-network to support a school networking strategy is find out what you can do with it. Reading this book will help. Visit, write, or otherwise contact any of the school districts we mention (or that you know about from other sources) to find out how they are using the network. Call meetings of parents to find out what they want to do, and want the schools to do for their children. Contact your state Board of Education to see what the computing resources are at the state level. Most states have a commission or task-force working on this very problem (and it never hurts to get your input in as early in the game as possible).

One of the best places to look for other schools on the Net is at Gleason Sackmannn's SENDIT K-12 home page, at

```
http://www.sendit.nodak.edu
```

 WARNING Like most of the other resources in this book, K-12 Web site home pages change with lightning speed. We expect the URLs to remain stable: the picture you see in the book may not match today's picture on the actual site.

Student and Classroom Examples

Here are some examples of projects undertaken by schools and collections of schools, to help you think about what you might do with a school network or network access. (Many of these examples came from the EDUCOM study on K–12 Networking, which was partially funded by IBM. Others came from Gleason Sackmann's Net-Happenings news group, the K12-NET project, the NCSA and CERN education pages, and from the MichNet K–12 project. Some projects are described in the participants' own words; other descriptions are from published accounts.) You can find further examples, such as the New South Polar Times electronic newsletter, described in Chapters 24 and 25.

Hunter Lake Elementary School, Reno, Nevada Hunter Lake Elementary School is a good example of a typical school Web site. They have pictures of current happenings, class projects, a new playground structure, and copies of the school newsletter. Much of the site is student authored. You can check this site at

```
http://www.unr.edu/hunterlake/index.html
```

In Figure 18.1, you see the opening page of the site after a recent press conference held at the school.

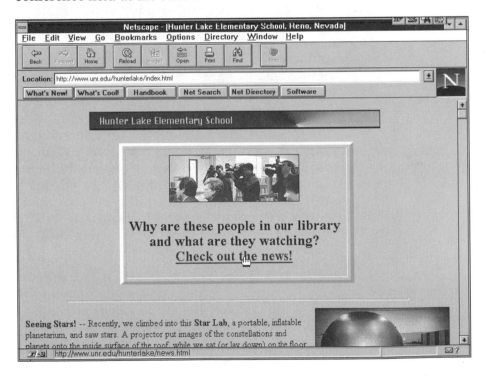

Figure 18.1. **The Hunter Elementary School Home page, showing reporters at a recent press conference.**

Learning through Collaborative Visualization (CoVis) Traditionally, K–12 science education has consisted of teaching well-established facts. This approach bears little or no resemblance to the question-centered, collaborative practice of real scientists. Through the use of advanced technologies, the CoVis Project is attempting to transform science learning to better resemble the authentic practice of science. And, perhaps as importantly, this teaching method can be more exciting for students, motivating them to learn the fundamentals and go on to their own explorations.

In the first-ever educational use of wideband ISDN networks, CoVis (sponsored by Northwestern University) enables high school students to join with other students at remote locations in collaborative work groups. Also through these networks, students communicate with university researchers and other scientific experts.

Participating students study atmospheric and environmental sciences—including topics in meteorology and climatology—through project-based activities. Using state-of-the-art scientific visualization software, specially modified to be appropriate to a learning environment, students have access to the same research tools and data sets used by leading-edge scientists in the field.

The CoVis Project provides students with a "collaboratory" workbench that includes desktop video teleconferencing; shared software environments for remote, real-time collaboration; access to the resources of the Internet; a "Software/Collaboratory" notebook (a multimedia scientist's notebook); and "CoVis Software" (scientific visualization software). In addition to providing new technology, the project is working closely with teachers at the participating schools to develop new curricula and new pedagogical approaches that take advantage of project-based science learning.

Figure 18.2 shows the home Web page for the CoVis project:

```
http://www.covis.nwu.edu/
```

Walpole, Massachusetts   Here's how Bruce Goldberg, in his article "Restructuring and Technology: Part One" described one of the earliest Internet classroom projects:

"Why are there fewer pets in a certain small Louisiana town than there are in Walpole, Massachusetts? Mrs. Griffith's fourth grade class sits in deep thought. They had already gathered the data, talked about classifying it, and through their telecommunications network, compared the findings with their Louisiana counterparts.

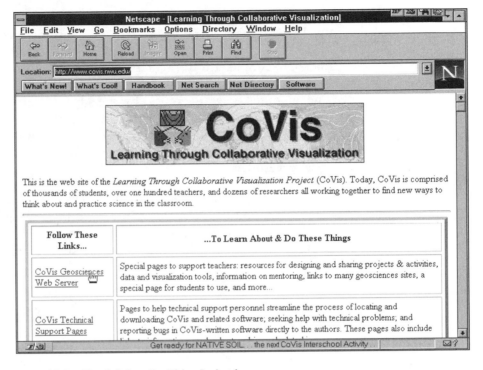

Figure 18.2. **The Collaborative Vision Project home page.**

"Hands soon shot up. One thinks the difference has to do with climate. Another that parental attitudes are more restrictive. Still another thinks the Louisiana town might be poorer. 'I know,' shouts Joshua, a student classified as learning-disabled. 'I bet it has nothing at all to do with that stuff. I bet that school is in a place where there's government housing, and that the kids can't have any pets.'

"Mrs. Griffith and the rest of the class seem stunned. Not only had no one thought of this as a possible (and plausible) explanation, but no one had expected Joshua to think of it.

"The students got busy. At Joshua's lead, they contacted their Louisiana counterparts, and much to everyone's amazement, discovered that Joshua had been right. The Louisiana town does have a large proportion of its population housed in government housing, and yes, there are very explicit restrictions against owning pets.

"No one looks at Joshua the same way anymore. Especially Joshua. Buoyed by his success, he begins assuming a more assertive role in his small team."

Lincoln, Nebraska   Kids in the Lincoln, Nebraska School District set up the Kids' Travel Agency as part of a summer school project. Using CMS School-Net, they sent a survey only to kids, requesting information such as their favorite restaurants, motels, and historical attractions. Several classes from San Diego, California, responded. These students were excited by the idea of being able to tell "land-bound" students about Sea World, the Pacific Ocean, and Disneyland. The Lincoln students eagerly read, edited, and processed the data, then developed information packets from a kid's perspective for each area surveyed.

Stuyvesant High School, New York   Stuyvesant has several sets of curriculum material on the Net. One of the most interesting is from the archaeology class, which is a senior science elective. The class is taught by Mrs. Dietz, who also compiled the "class packet" (textbook), which is used extensively throughout the term.

The archeology class information is informal, informative, and translatable to other settings and classrooms. Even a description of the final class project is available on the Net.

See for yourself what Mrs. Dietz and her students are doing by going to:

```
http://www.stuy.edu/sc/arch/arch.htm
```

Figure 18.3 shows the Archeology page.

Binghamton, New York   The Electronic Field Trip (described in the US Congressional Office of Technology Assessment report *Linking for Learning: A New Course for Education,* November, 1989) is an inexpensive way to put students in isolated areas in contact with professionals in a variety of fields. Field trips included "visits" to the local mayor, social activists, steel mill workers, international students in Australia, Alaska, and England, and musicians.

One electronic field trip was scheduled with a rock musician. Only those students interested enough to do background research were allowed to participate. The school's music teacher, telecommunications coordinator, and librarian guided the research. After two weeks of preparation, an enthusiastic audience of eight students, a mix of aspiring musicians, college-bound students, and kids with no stated future plans, communicated for over an hour.

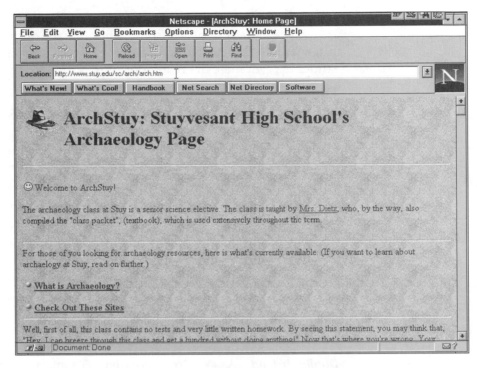

Figure 18.3. Mrs. Dietz's archeology project at Stuyvesant High School.

Afterward, the students proudly talked about the project. One commented, "We would like to talk to another musician who has not made it big and compare the interviews." Another student regretted the lack of reporting from the local paper: "If this had been a local football game, they would have given it two columns of reporting."

The students' hard work paid off in many ways. They learned how to organize their thoughts on paper and to think on their feet, how to work together as a team, and how to plan; and they learned more about a career to which some of them aspire.

By the end of 1995, over 15,000 students have participated in electronic field trips.

Hillside Elementary, Cottage Grove, Minnesota Students at Hillside Elementary School in Cottage Grove, Minnesota are creating many pages of information on their World Wide Web server:

```
http://hillside.coled.umn.edu/
```

This is a joint project with the University of Minnesota College of Education. Their goal is "to incorporate use of the resources on the Internet into the curriculum of elementary school students and to have students participate in creating resources that are on the Internet."

During the 1995–1996 school year, innovative teacher Chris Collins has been working in cooperation with Sharry Lammers and her sixth grade class to:

Publish student work

Access information and conduct research

Communicate and share ideas

Collaborate

There are now home pages for grades 1–5 on the site, as well. Mrs. Weyland's third grade class:

```
http://hammer.sowashco.k12.mn.us
```

is studying holidays and customs, and is collecting links to other student pages on the same topics. You can see in Figure 18.4 a story that Marissa wrote about her last birthday.

Dublin, Ireland   As an extracurricular activity, students in the Dalkey School Project in the suburbs of Dublin, Ireland, found pen-pals in the United States and Canada. Initially, the objectives were to share student writing and learn a little more about other cultures. This pen-pal project has opened up a new world to these students.

From the KidSPHERE distribution list:

```
kidsphere@vms.cis.pitt.edu
```

contacts were made with other children from several locations in the United States, including Aurora, Colorado; Charlottesville, Virginia; Franklinville, New York; and Tallahassee, Florida; and from British Columbia, Canada. Students' tele-letters often contained information about themselves, their families, schools, and neighborhoods.

The students have begun to understand the nature and operation of the network, and have become very interested in people in distant places and how they live, primarily because they have been able to make friends so easily over the network. The students' keyboarding, editing, and word-processing skills have also improved.

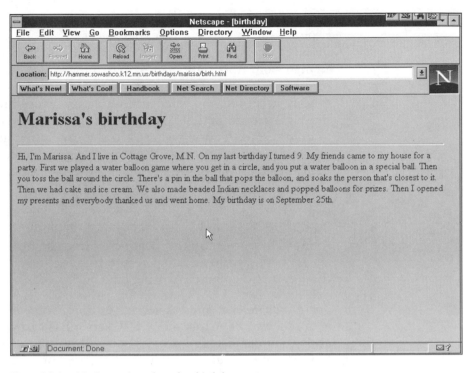

Figure 18.4.   **Marissa writes about her birthday party.**

Toronto, Canada   "What a wonderful learning experience it has been. It has given me a new perspective on learning and learning how to learn. With other writers of the world, we have all responded and contributed to one another. I see this as something that has changed my life. Education shouldn't always be within classroom walls."

This is what one 12th grade student (quoted in *DISTED Electronic Journal*. March 1990) wrote about her English class after telecommunications technology projects had been introduced into the curriculum. Students, teachers, and writers throughout Canada, the United States, and the world correspond, and the students' work is critiqued by the professionals. The "Writers in Electronic Residence" program of the Riverdale Collegiate Institute in Toronto is supported by the College of Education at Simon Fraser University, and forms the basis of these language-based studies.

Students' works, primarily poetry and short fiction, are posted in electronic conference areas established for their use. The students are in control of the media before them, and they use those media to broaden their classroom experiences. The "Electro-Poets" project involved a class in Toronto, one in British Columbia, and a poet also in British Columbia. During this four-month project, over 200 pages of original writing and comments were generated by the students. They readily accepted the telecommunications activities as part of their daily classroom activity. Another project, "New-Voices," involved a poet, a science-fiction writer, and a short-fiction author, and schools in Ontario and British Columbia. A third project, "Wired Writer," connects ten schools and one author from a past project.

These language-based telecommunications projects have inspired students to develop language appropriate to the activity, and they offer direct and personal access to computer activities that are relevant today. These telecommunications projects increased the students' access to the world and, as a result, bring to the classroom experiences that meet and enhance existing curricular needs.

The Armadillo Web Site   A service of Rice University and the Houston area schools, the Armadillo WWW server has many area school projects and resources listed. This site started as one of the first educational Gopher sites. Many student and teacher projects all over Texas are collected on the server.

One such project is student papers about the Buffalo Bayou outside of Houston. The Armadillo WWW server is available at the URL

```
http://riceinfo.rice.edu/armadillo/
```

Figure 18.5 shows a paper about the history of the Buffalo area from a Houston area classroom.

Roxboro, North Carolina   A Global Grocery List has been posted on FrEdMail's IDEAS bulletin board by the Person County Schools in North Carolina. Students ask for the local price in local currency of specific quantities of 14 items. To date, students from Michigan, Illinois, California, North Carolina, and England have responded.

The Person County School students expect to use the data in other classroom projects including math, social studies, and science to study economics in the marketplace. Data are periodically compiled and posted to the IDEAS bulletin board for other classes who may wish to access the information.

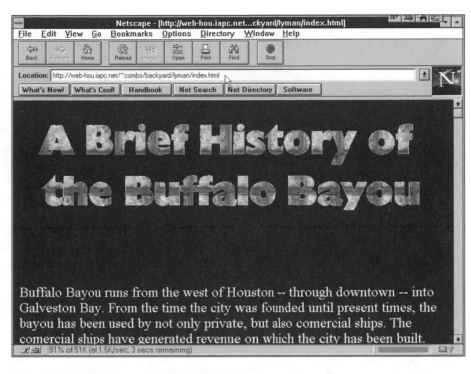

Figure 18.5.   A student paper on the Buffalo Bayou.

FrEdMail (Free Education Mail) was founded by Al Rodgers to connect students and teachers, originally via modem-to-modem connections. Later, the project was helped onto the Internet by CERFNet, a regional mid-level network located in southern California. Mr. Rodgers's ideas for simple, shared projects "connected" many students throughout the United States and led to further projects like the Global Schoolhouse Project, funded by the National Science Foundation and many other sponsors. The Global Schoolhouse Project is described in Chapter 23 and located on the Web at

```
http://k12.cnidr.org
```

Alconbury, England   Peanut Butter and JAM—food for thought. JAM (Junior Atlantic Monthly) is one of several online projects of the Department of Defense Dependents Schools (DoDDS) Stars and Stripes Bulletin Board System at Alconbury Elementary School. JAM, a student-generated magazine, contains classroom work from students in grades 4–6. A special K–3 section, called Peanut Butter, is being planned.

The magazine includes all types of creative writing, including short stories, poetry, essays, and interviews. A schedule of topics for each issue is posted on the bulletin board, as JAM hopes to integrate with current classroom curriculum. Submissions are uploaded to a special area on the bulletin board and editing is performed by editorial groups, located at various schools, as part of their language arts curriculum. Rejected articles are returned to the author with comments or explanations. Final works are uploaded to the bulletin board for publication and distribution.

Tallahassee, Florida   Learning-disabled students at Rickards High School now have a bulletin board message area they can call their own. Knowing the educational value of being able to communicate with others around the world, the Leon County Schools in Tallahassee, Florida, established an electronic bulletin board at Rickards High School, available to those in the Tallahassee area with a computer and a modem. (For information on getting an account, contact the school at 904-488-1783.)

Initially, communication in the Special Students message area is limited to other Rickards High School students, as an intermediate step for those overwhelmed by the variety of message areas. Reading and writing skills are reinforced as messages are exchanged. Deaf and blind students have joined the fun through the use of adaptive devices on their computers.

When these students are ready to advance, they may join several projects that were developed for the bulletin board, including Alien Visit, where a teacher, parent, or other adult logs on and poses as an alien, asking questions on various topics; writing their own surveys and collecting data; writing and reading messages in foreign languages; establishing a county-wide magazine by and for students about their school's activities; and the online serial novel, where one class composes a section and posts it on the bulletin board for another class to continue.

Barriers of academic ability have broken down and a challenging and motivating curriculum has been provided for students, thanks to the foresight of the administrators in the Leon County School System.

Ralph Bunche Elementary School Ralph Bunche School, in New York City's Harlem, which houses third through sixth graders, has exceptional access to computers and other high-technology equipment. Figure 18.6 shows how one student describes the school. You can explore the site at

```
http://mac94.ralphbunche.rbs.edu/
```

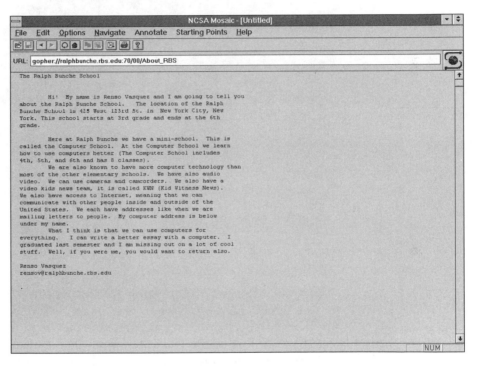

Figure 18.6. ***Renso Vasquez describes the Ralph Bunche School. (use old figure)***

One unusual project on the Bunche Web site combines pictures and stories. Students write stories about pictures and then post them on the server. Figure 18.7 shows one picture and the story it inspired. (This story demonstrates one of the "hidden" capabilities of the Net—helping to make the "haves," who have traditionally been the majority of Net users, aware of the realities of life for disadvantaged people.)

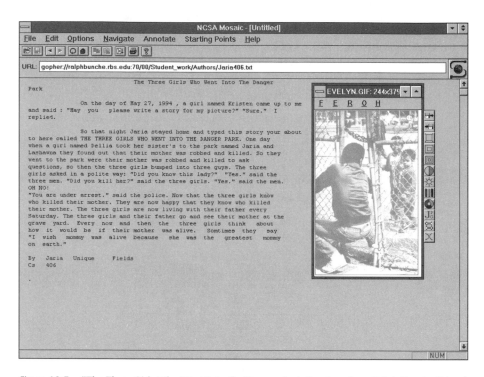

Figure 18.7.   "The Three Girls Who Went into the Danger Park," a story from Ralph Bunche School.

Ann Arbor, Michigan   Motivating students is often a concern for teachers at the K–12 level. So you can imagine the satisfaction it gives a high school teacher when students ask to give up their own lunch periods to go online or inquire about what they can read over the summer to increase their knowledge about international politics.

These exciting things are happening with students involved in Interactive Communications & Simulations (ICS), a program linking students around the world in an interactive, collaborative learning environment. In partnership with the University of Michigan, which provides the conferencing software, high schools and middle schools all over the United States are expanding their classrooms to include students of different cultures and backgrounds.

ICS has two types of programs, Communications Exercises (Earth Odysseys and International Poetry Guild) and Simulation Exercises (Environmental Decisions, Arab-Israeli Conflict, and United States Constitution). In Earth Odysseys students travel vicariously by conversing, via networked computers, with travelers on unusual expeditions.

The Simulations Exercises involve role-playing, where the students act as real-life characters such as prominent world leaders.

For information, contact ICS by e-mail at

`info@ics.soc.umich.edu`

or by phone at 313-763-6716.

Global Education: New Zealand and Colorado   In the K12-NET newsgroup `k12.ed.science`, an enthusiastic student from New Zealand described his attempt to study the effect of the earth's rotation on the way toilets flush. His conclusion, that water drains clockwise in the southern hemisphere, and counter-clockwise in the northern hemisphere, received a very detailed response from a correspondent at the University of Colorado in Boulder, who described the relevant scientific principle (the Coriolis force) in detail, and told him how to set up a scientifically verifiable experiment.

Physics Challenge   High school physics students in Oregon, California, Maryland, and Nova Scotia attempted to replicate Eratosthenes' experiment to measure the size of the earth by measuring the length of a shadow cast by a stick at "true" noon on three successive Mondays in October 1991, posting their data, and performing the necessary calculations in the "Physics Challenge" IRC channel. Their calculations were accurate to within 7%. Their reports were posted on the `k12.ed.science` newsgroup.

Global Warming Study   Students at all levels on K12-NET have participated in the "CO2 Challenge" project to reduce carbon dioxide in the environment. Led by Marshall Gilmore of Earth Kids Net, students have tackled the issue of global warming with "Quick Facts" questions and answers as well as a number of environmental projects. More recently, students have been participating in the "Global Environmental Watch." The Global Village News project solicits local news items from the student participants, and expects them to analyze the feature stories for local and regional differences in news reporting.

Special Needs   A handicapped K12-NET system operator in the United Kingdom led a discussion of problems faced by those with special needs, and an important conclusion emerged from this topic— telecommunications networks are significant equalizers because the participants are evaluated by their contributions rather than their appearance, race, or ethnic background. It is this aspect of networking which offers the most significant opportunity to effect social change. Students who telecommunicate with their fellow students around the world are less likely to accept the stereotypes fostered by their communities and governments. Differences in the age of participants are similarly diffused in an environment which applauds eloquence and depth of expression. Teachers in rural schools can expand their gifted students' horizons by giving them access to K12Net and appropriate peers to stimulate their intellectual and artistic creativity.

Other Schools on the Net

There are literally hundreds of other K–12 projects on the Net. Three good resources for your own exploration are:

The Best of K12 on the Net, sponsored by the University of Illinois at Champaign-Urbana:

```
http://www.mste.uiuc.edu/k12/k12.html
```

Janice's Outpost, sponsored by CNIDR (Clearinghouse for Networked Information Discovery and Retrieval, see Chapter 24):

```
http://k12.cnidr.org/janice_k12/k12menu.html
```

Figure 18.8 shows the Janice's Outpost home page.

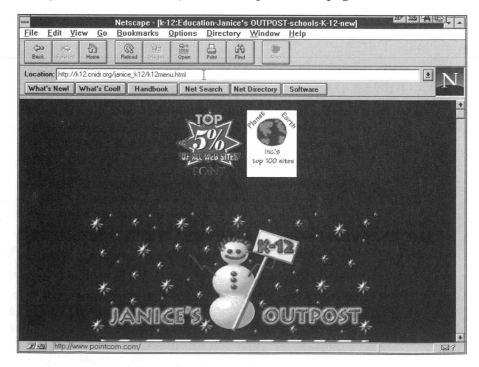

Figure 18.8.　Janice's Outpost at CNIDR.

Special Education Collections

Many organizations now have special Web pages and other Internet resources for educators, providing links to education resources. Some of the best are listed here to help you discover more resources for educators and students.

NASA Education Resources NASA provides, as part of the High Performance Computing initiatives, a vast number of resources for teachers, including curriculum modules, access to databases and indices, and papers and other articles to help teachers better educate their students with the help of the Internet. There are lists of school and community resources available through the NASA server:

```
http://quest.arc.nasa.gov/
```

BBN Education Pages Bolt, Beranek, and Newman (BBN), one of the oldest network information providers (they began providing user information in the days of the ARPANET) has a special education server, located at

```
gopher://copernicus.bbn.com:70/11/k12
```

K12 Best From Minnesota comes a selected and varied listing of K–12 resources on the Internet, for both students and teachers:

```
gopher://informns.k12.mn.us:70/11/best-k12
```

Figure 18.9 shows the first of many pages of directory listings about Bosnia and the conflict in Eastern Europe.

Merit Network Merit/MichNet provides resources for educators and a number of case studies of K–12 experiences using networking technology:

```
http://www.merit.edu
```

Figure 18.10 shows a list of Merit K-12 initiatives, including a toll-free dialup program for Michigan Schools.

Learning Resource Project University of Illinois at Champaign-Urbana (UIUC) has collected a tremendous number of invaluable resources for educators. Check out the server at

```
http://www.ed.uiuc.edu/
```

Figure 18.11 shows the main index for the project.

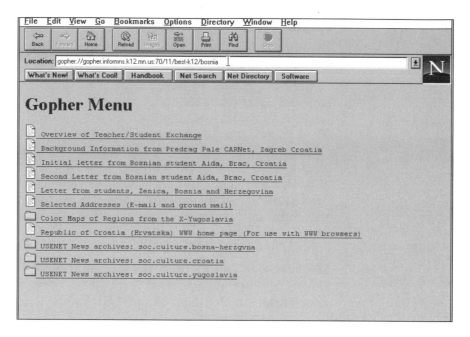

Figure 18.9. *The K-12 Best Bosnia resources*

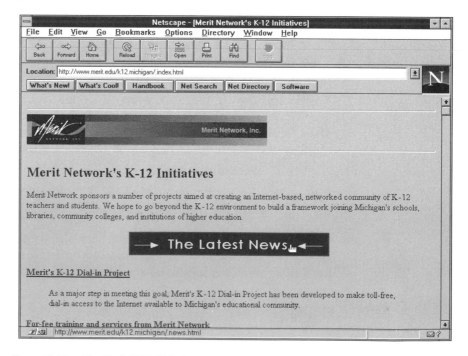

Figure 18.10. *The Merit K-12 Web Site*

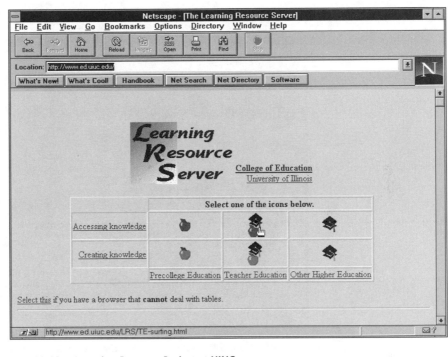

Figure 18.11.   **Learning Resource Project at UIUC.**

The Computing Teacher   *Computing Teacher* magazine has been providing expertise and education for teachers struggling to use new technology in their classrooms for several years now. Judi Harris, whose articles have helped teachers learn to mine the Internet, has now provided some of those articles online via the UIUC server. You can find out more about *Computing Teacher* by calling 800-336-5191, or via e-mail at

    iste@oregon.uoregon.edu

Harris's articles are available online at

    http://www.ed.uiuc.edu/Mining/Overview.html

Web66   Web66 is a ground-breaking project sponsored as part of the Hillsdale, MN, computing project described earlier, to assist teachers in creating their own network resources. Just as Route 66 helped shape the development of the United States, Web66 wants to help shape the Internet to come. Figure 18.12 shows the Web66 home page, located at

    http://web66.coled.umn.edu/

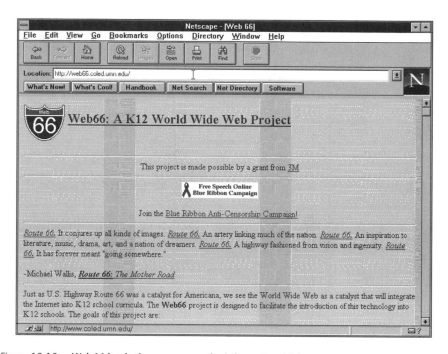

Figure 18.12. **Web66 leads the way across the information highway.**

SuperQuest for Teachers SuperQuest helps teachers sharpen their Internet skills and learn to translate those skills into the classroom to enrich their resources. The Web server for SuperQuest is available through the UIUC server, at

```
http://www.ncsa.uiuc.edu/Pubs/Exhibits/SC93/
SC93Education.html
```

Figure 18.13 shows the SuperQuest introductory page.

New York State Education Department Gopher Server Looking for curriculum information in the arts, humanities, sciences, math, social studies? Looking for information on the newest standards for teaching students with disabilities? The New York State Education Gopher has unparalleled resources for teachers. The server is available at

```
gopher://unix5.nysed.gov/
```

Figure 18.14 shows the description of the purpose of the service.

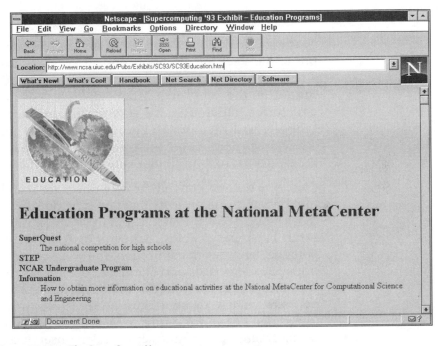

Figure 18.13. The SuperQuest Home page.

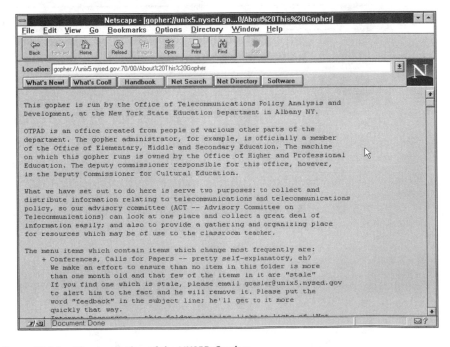

Figure 18.14. The description of the NYSED Gopher.

Step Two: Convince Others

Many network consulting firms and network providers say that the impetus for getting a school connected comes from two main sources: a teacher or group of teachers who have decided that they want their school on the Net; or a school district that has come to the same conclusion. Obviously, it's easy for one teacher or one parent or one school board member to have an individual connection to the Net. The harder part is convincing others, especially those with money in their pockets, to help fund a network connection.

Once you've found out all the cool things that can be done with the Net, think about some projects that could be done in your area, particularly those which address visible issues in your community. Gather about you some like-minded folks. Schedule a series of discussions about the potential for network connection. You will need to make formal presentations to local boards and chambers of commerce, one-on-one sessions with local leaders and money folk. Talk to the PTA. Invite guest speakers, particularly teachers and administrators who have successfully integrated networking into their schools, to come and speak to your teachers' unions, training seminars or "inservices," and so on.

 MASTER WORDS   If you can arrange to get continuing education credit for these workshops, so much the better. Your audience of teachers and administrators will jump.

Step Three: Pull Together a Proposal

Once it looks as though you are developing momentum, get a group together to write a formal proposal for a networking strategy in your school, town, district or unified district—whatever size seems right to your planning group. Contact your regional network providers; the phone company; LAN software and hardware vendors; corporate partners. The bigger the coalition backing the proposal, the better your chances of success.

Really successful proposals vary from district to district. We can only give you general guidelines on what's likely to be successful; you'll need to create your own with your specialized knowledge about your community.

You're more likely to succeed if your proposal:

Has technical input—someone or some group who really know what they're talking about.

Has a staged implementation plan that will allow spending to happen over a series of years rather than in a lump sum.

Includes funding proposals that are researched and realistic. Partnerships, donations, and matching programs that have buy-in are all better than bake-sales or airy guesses.

Includes a grant opportunity or other funding model from outside sources (but don't forget to talk about what to do when the grant runs out).

Has references to successful programs modeled similarly to yours.

Is timed so that it can be considered carefully. This means you need to get someone on your team who understands the proposal and budgeting cycle in your community or district.

Builds on computer infrastructure that is already in place or in the pipeline.

Can be included in a scheduled renovation, remodeling, or new building project rather than requiring extensive physical plant modifications. New phone systems or switches, cable installations, or new buildings are good opportunities to get a computer network in place.

Good politics say that after your proposal is prepared but before it is formally submitted is the time to start garnering wider support for it. Hold focus groups, public meetings, and coffees to talk to parents, businesses, and other taxpayer groups. Present your "draft" proposal, and see how it flies. If it meets with a storm of protest, the time may not be right for a formal proposal. Rework it until it seems to meet the needs of your community.

When your proposal has a head of steam and people are excited about it, get their support for the formal approval process. Start a mailing list: notify people about public hearings, votes, and so on. Invite people to come and speak in favor of the proposal at citizen's comment sessions, and encourage them to write to whoever is making the decision.

If you are working on a millage proposal (that is, one involving a tax increase), once your ideas get acceptance at the school board level, you become partners with those officials in the campaign for public acceptance. Get your mailing list together, and get those folks out to help campaign for the proposal.

From this point on, turning your proposal into reality is an exercise in local politics in your area. Find a savvy local person who knows this process, and recruit them to help get your school network in place.

 MASTER WORDS Looking for a place where you can see what people who've been in your position have done? Check out

http://www.cosn.org/EPIE.html

for a report entitled "Practical, Universal Networking for Learning in Schools and Homes," sponsored by the Coalition for School Networking.

Funding Models

There are many models for funding school projects. We list three of the most common—you may find that a different model works best, or a blend of these three.

District Budgets and Millage Elections

Getting the taxpayers to foot the bill is perhaps one of the hardest ways to fund a networking strategy, but it can be one of the more reliable. Convincing your district that networking is a serious objective, and getting a networking strategy in place so that it shows up on the budget, can only happen successfully when coalitions of parents, teachers, students, local government, and local business have been formed.

Partnerships

Partnerships with computer software or equipment manufacturers or vendors are a fun way to get at least part of your network together. Usually such partnerships involve some outlay on the school's part, with a large donation of time and materials from the donor. Sometimes that donation comes with expertise in setting up the network; sometimes it doesn't. If you get a partnership going, make sure you also recruit a network designer or consultant to work with your school to make sure that what you get really solves your problems.

Potential partners might include:

Network software vendors and manufacturers (Novell, Banyan, and so on)

Regional network providers

Telephone companies

Cable companies

Power utilities

Hardware vendors (both the local computing stores and the big guys)

Big local employers

Chambers of Commerce

One good source for potential partnership information is a local network provider. Usually they are well-informed about initiatives from the government, vendors, and other sources. They can help leverage an expressed interest into a coalition or partnership.

Remember that once the network gets built you'll need ongoing funding to help maintain and upgrade it.

Parent or Teacher-Driven Fund-Raisers (Private Donation)

These campaigns are the easiest to propose, and the hardest to make fund a computing initiative for the long term. Since computing initiatives can cost well into the tens of thousands for start-up, and have ongoing maintenance costs that include staff payrolls and equipment upgrades, this is an uphill fight unless you have a district populated with deep pockets.

But raising your own seed money, matching funds, or start-up funds can be an important part of a larger funding initiative.

Obviously, selling candy bars is not likely to fund a computer lab unless your kids are really good salespeople. But some other ideas, garnered from anecdotes from successful initiatives, include:

Scrip sales in conjunction with local merchants.

"Worker" services (watch child labor laws!) where residents can contract for lawn work, housework, and other services on a regular or one-shot basis.

Grocery-store campaigns (people buy a tag or card for a donation, which the store passes along to the school).

Series of yard sales, auctions, book sales, and raffles.

MICROSOFT & MCI PUT SCHOOLS ON THE WEB

In early March, 1996, Microsoft Corporation and MCI Communications Corporation jointly announced one of those partnership arrangements which may prove a boon for schools wanting to create a Web site but without the resources to have their own server.

MCI and Microsoft created a program that makes it possible for every school in the country to establish its presence on the World Wide Web.

As part of the Microsoft/MCI Schools on the Web, MCI will make available 10 megabytes (MB) of space on the Global Schoolhouse (GSH) Web site to every school that wants to put up information about its activities and programs, but doesn't have a server or a local Internet service provider.

If the school already has an Internet presence, it can still list its sites on the GSH Schools on the Web registry. That makes it possible for Internet users anywhere to look up information on schools across the country.

As part of the initiative, every school that creates new Web pages or registers existing sites through the GSH Web site is eligible for technology grants totaling $100,000 for software, hardware, training, or support for their classrooms or schools.

Microsoft is also making available its new Internet Jump Start CD for Educators. The disk contains Microsoft products and tools to help the school set up its own Web server, explore the Internet, and build a new or enhance an existing Web site.

Microsoft operates a K-12 Web site that contains resources for educators, including the complete content of Microsoft's Teacher's Activity Guides for all of the company's multimedia education titles. Those include Encarta Multimedia Encyclopedia, Scholastic's The Magic School Bus series, and the Encarta World Atlas. Teachers can also access the Global Schoolhouse Web site to evaluate lesson plans and teaching strategies that have been contributed by teachers and schools across the country.

The Global Schoolhouse is at

```
http://www.gsh.org
```

To obtain the Microsoft Internet Jump Start CD, contact Microsoft at 800-426-9400.

Technical Planning

Appendix D presents an excellent paper, by Joan Gargano and David Wasley of the ISN Working Group, on planning your school network. It covers hardware, wiring, software, and suggested protocols. We recommend you study it carefully as you work out your proposal for your school network.

Plan before the Equipment Goes In

When you get your plans for the physical network together (or perhaps while the funding drive is ongoing), you should also be planning for the management and policy issues for your network. Things you need to consider include:

How will you deal with your employees?

What policies do you want to set in place concerning who can get access to your network?

How will you deal with student access to the Net?

How will you accomplish training of staff and students?

Who will manage your resource?

Schools Are Also Businesses

If you are hoping to get your school on the network, you should realize that your school is also a business—you have a budget, and customers to serve, and you need to get the best possible advice about getting connected to the network.

If you have not already read the chapters on getting connected (Chapter 4) and businesses on the Net (Chapter 17), you should do so. There we talk about your options for connections, legal aspects of being on the Net, staffing, finding someone to help you design your Net, and so on.

One advantage that schools have over other businesses, however, is that you have a community of parents who want to see the best for their children. School districts can frequently find parents (or parents with connections) who have expertise in networking, computing strategies, electrical wiring and contracting, and many of the other skills you will need on hand to plan and execute your network. Even if you can't get the work done completely free, you can often get volunteer assistance in all phases of network planning, implementation, and ongoing management and maintenance.

You will also need to look at the realities of having your employees have Net access. All the same policy dilemmas that other businesses and organizations have to resolve need to be resolved for employees of schools, as well. Chapter 19 discusses "appropriate use" policies in detail.

If you currently have policies for your employees concerning use of school resources for private use, look to them for guidance for your electronic appropriate use policies as well. In addition, the Electronic Freedom Foundation is an excellent resource for education policies. In their FTP archives

    ftp.eff.org

they have a wide collection of education policies and critiques on those policies, as well as recent legislation and other decisions and criteria that may help determine your policies.

Policies for Students as Well as Staff

In general, the more you can treat your students, parents, and staff similarly in access policies, the easier to administer and less subject to challenge your policies will be. As general policy, computer media should be treated the same as other media. In K–12 settings, teachers and administrators should have the same privacy rights to their computer files as they have to their paper files. Policies for searches of student's computer files should be similar to those for searches of student's lockers. Outside computer material should be selected in the same way as library materials. Students should have exactly the same freedom of expression in computer media as they have in paper media.

 MASTER WORDS   An excellent source of K–12 appropriate use policies is Rice University's education Gopher. Using a Gopher client, go to `riceinfo`
`.rice.edu` Using a Web browser open the URL `gopher://riceinfo.rice`
`.edu:1170/11/More/Acceptable`. If you are writing new staff policies to deal with the electronic age, be sure to include your staff in the writing process. You'll get better compliance if you have staff input from the beginning.

THE BREVARD COUNTY, FLORIDA, ACCEPTABLE USE POLICY

Here is the text of the Brevard County, Florida, policy on access and use of the network. It's a fairly typical policy, and covers a number of important issues. We include it (and similar policies) as examples to help you create your own policies.

APPLICATION FOR ACCOUNT

DIRECTIONS: Copy the following for use in applying for an account for your students. Edit the areas marked Name Name High School (NNHS) to reflect the name of your own school. Change each of the (NNHS) to reflect your school. Be sure that everybody who signs the contract has read the application and understands the terms.

Send a copy of both signed forms to:

Kevin Barry
Florida Institute of Technology
Academic & Research Computing Services
150 University Boulevard
Melbourne, FL 32901-6988

The user account will be assigned after the application forms are received.

APPLICATION FOR ACCOUNT AND TERMS
AND CONDITIONS FOR USE OF INTERNET

Please read the following carefully before signing this document. This is a legally binding document.

Internet access is now available to students and teachers in the Brevard County School District. The access is being offered as part of a collaborative research project involving Name Name High School (NNHS), Florida Institute of Technology, and the US Department of Education. We are very pleased to bring this access to Brevard County and believe the Internet offers vast, diverse and unique resources to both students and teachers. Our goal in providing this service to teachers and students is to promote educational excellence in the Brevard County Schools by facilitating resource sharing, innovation and communication.

The Internet is an electronic highway connecting thousands of computers all over the world and millions of individual subscribers. Students and teachers have access to

1. electronic mail communication with people all over the world;

2. information and news from NASA as well as the opportunity to correspond with the scientists at NASA and other research institutions;

3. public domain and shareware of all types;

4. discussion groups on a plethora of topics ranging from Chinese culture to the environment to music to politics;

Continued on next page

5. access to many University Library Catalogs, the Library of Congress, CARL and ERIC.

With access to computers and people all over the world also comes the availability of material that may not be considered to be of educational value in the context of the school setting. (NNHS) and Florida Institute of Technology have taken available precautions to restrict access to controversial materials. However, on a global network it is impossible to control all materials and an industrious user may discover controversial information. We [(NNHS) and Florida Institute of Technology] firmly believe that the valuable information and interaction available on this worldwide network far outweighs the possibility that users may procure material that is not consistent with the educational goals of this Project.

Internet access is coordinated through a complex association of government agencies, and regional and state networks. In addition, the smooth operation of the network relies upon the proper conduct of the end users who must adhere to strict guidelines. These guidelines are provided here so that you are aware of the responsibilities you are about to acquire. In general this requires efficient, ethical and legal utilization of the network resources. If a (NNHS) user violates any of these provisions, his or her account will be terminated and future access could possibly be denied. The signature(s) at the end of this document is (are) legally binding and indicates the party (parties) who signed has (have) read the terms and conditions carefully and understand(s) their significance.

Internet—Terms and Conditions

1. *Acceptable Use*—The purpose of NSFNET, which is the backbone network to the Internet, is to support research and education in and among academic institutions in the US by providing access to unique resources and the opportunity for collaborative work. The use of your account must be in support of education and research and consistent with the educational objectives of the Brevard County School District. Use of other organization's network or computing resources must comply with the rules appropriate for that network. Transmission of any material in violation of any US or state regulation is prohibited. This includes, but is not limited to: copyrighted material, threatening or obscene material, or material protected by trade secret. Use for commercial activities by for-profit institutions is generally not acceptable. Use for product advertisement or political lobbying is also prohibited.

2. *Privileges*—The use of Internet is a privilege, not a right, and inappropriate use will result in a cancellation of those privileges. (Each student who receives an account will be part of a discussion with a (NNHS) faculty member pertaining to the proper use of the network.) The system administrators will deem what is inappropriate use and their decision is final. Also, the system administrators may close an account at any time as required. The administration, faculty, and staff of (NNHS) may request the system administrator to deny, revoke, or suspend specific user accounts.

3. *Netiquette*—You are expected to abide by the generally accepted rules of network etiquette. These include (but are not limited to) the following:

   a. Be polite. Do not get abusive in your messages to others.

   b. Use appropriate language. Do not swear, use vulgarities or any other inappropriate language. Illegal activities are strictly forbidden.

   c. Do not reveal your personal address or phone numbers of students or colleagues.

   d. Note that electronic mail (e-mail) is not guaranteed to be private. People who operate the system do have access to all mail. Messages relating to or in support of illegal activities may be reported to the authorities.

   e. Do not use the network in such a way that you would disrupt the use of the network by other users.

   f. All communications and information accessible via the network should be assumed to be private property.

4. NNHS and Florida Institute of Technology make no warranties of any kind, whether expressed or implied, for the service they are providing. NNHS and Florida Institute of Technology will not be responsible for any damages you suffer. This includes loss of data resulting from delays, nondeliveries, misdeliveries, or service interruptions caused by its own negligence or your errors or omissions. Use of any information obtained via NNHS or Florida Institute of Technology is at your own risk. NNHS and Florida Institute of Technology specifically deny any responsibility for the accuracy or quality of information obtained through its services.

5. *Security*—Security on any computer system is a high priority, especially when the system involves many users. If you feel you can identify a security problem on Internet, you must notify a system administrator or e-mail barry@sci-ed.fit.edu. Do not demonstrate the problem to other users. Do not use another individual's account without written permission from that individual. Attempts to log in to Internet as a system administrator will result in cancellation of user privileges. Any user identified as a security risk or having a history of problems with other computer systems may be denied access to Internet.

6. *Vandalism*—Vandalism will result in cancellation of privileges. Vandalism is defined as any malicious attempt to harm or destroy data of another user, Internet, or any of the above listed agencies or other networks that are connected to the NSFNET Internet backbone. This includes, but is not limited to, the uploading or creation of computer viruses.

7. *Updating Your User Information*—Internet may occasionally require new registration and account information from you to continue the service. You must notify Internet of any changes in your account information (address, etc). Currently, there are no user fees for this service.

Continued on next page

8. *Exception of Terms and Condition*—All terms and conditions as stated in this document are applicable to the Brevard County School District, the Florida Institute of Technology, in addition to NSFNET. These terms and conditions reflect the entire agreement of the parties and supersedes all prior oral or written agreements and understandings of the parties. These terms and conditions shall be governed and interpreted in accordance with the laws of the State of Florida, and the United States of America.

I understand and will abide by the above Terms and Conditions for Internet. I further understand that any violation of the regulations above is unethical and may constitute a criminal offense. Should I commit any violation, my access privileges may be revoked, and school disciplinary action and/or appropriate legal action may be taken.

User Signature:_____ Date: ___ / ___ / ___

****

PARENT OR GUARDIAN (If you are under the age of 18 a parent or guardian must also read and sign this agreement.)

As the parent or guardian of this student I have read the Terms and Conditions for Internet access. I understand that this access is designed for educational purposes and (NNHS) and Florida Institute of Technology have taken available precautions to eliminate controversial material. However, I also recognize it is impossible for (NNHS) and Florida Institute of Technology to restrict access to all controversial materials and I will not hold them responsible for materials acquired on the network. Further, I accept full responsibility for supervision if and when my child's use is not in a school setting. I hereby give permission to issue an account for my child and certify that the information contained on this form is correct.

Parent or Guardian (please print): _____

Signature: _____ Date: ___ / ___ / ___

****

SPONSORING TEACHER (Must be signed if the applicant is a student). I have read the Terms and Conditions and agree to promote this agreement with the student. Because the student may use the network for individual work or in the context of another class, I cannot be held responsible for the student use of the network. As the sponsoring teacher I do agree to instruct the student on acceptable use of the network and proper network etiquette.

Teacher's Name (please print): _____

Teacher's Signature: _____ Date: ___ / ___ / ___

****

Part
III

Becoming an
Information Provider

APPLICATION PORTION OF DOCUMENT

User's Full Name (please print): _____

Home Address: _____

Home Phone: _____ Work Phone: _____

I am a.....

____ (NNHS) student and will graduate in _____.

____ (NNHS) teacher, teaching _____ in grade _____.

____ (NNHS) staff working as a _____.

____ Brevard County School District community member.

When your account is established you will be notified of your logon name and user password. Thank you for your interest and support of this exciting new resource in the Brevard County Schools.

Who Should Get Access?

You will notice in the Brevard County policy that local members of the community can apply for access to the network. Other schools have allowed access to members of other schools, alumni of the school, local government members, senior citizens, and other special groups.

You may or may not want to allow access by persons not related to the school. Advantages include:

You may be able to charge for such access, helping to fund school-related computing projects.

You gain support in the community for your computer and networking projects, particularly when the community becomes dependent on your project for their access.

Your students will gain a wider experience of the world by exchanging views and information with other members of the local community.

Your students gain credibility with the members of the local community by their responsible and appropriate use of computing resources.

Students and community members can exchange expertise.

However, there can be disadvantages, as well:

Your students are bound by codes of behavior and at least minimal habit to follow the guidelines set down by the school authorities. Outsiders may not have such restrictions.

It is harder ethically (because of First Amendment issues) to justify monitoring non-school-related users for inappropriate use, including the storage of pirated software, inappropriate materials, and other problematic items.

It is even harder to prevent outsiders from sharing these materials with your students once they are stored on your own system.

If you allow general access by the community, you will need to allocate technical, administrative, and clerical resources to manage the accounts.

The new computing decency laws, enacted as part of the Communications Act of 1996, may place you in the position of an Internet provider if you allow outside access. You may be in the position of being required to monitor your community members for appropriate, indecent, or obscene speech.

You will need to make your own decisions about allowing outsiders access to your system. One strategy is to get the system up and running first, and then allow access slowly, if at all. This lets you get some experience under your belt before opening this new can of worms.

Bill of Rights for Students and Institutions in Cyberspace

One item that might help when thinking about appropriate use for students and staff alike is the *Bill of Rights and Responsibilities for the Electronic Community of Learners*. The Bill was begun as part of EDU-COM's Educational Uses of Information Technology program. EDUCOM is a consortium of around 600 colleges and universities focusing on the use of computers and telecommunications. EDUCOM leaders worked with leaders from the American Association for Higher Education (AAHE) in order to reach out to educational leaders across campus and in school districts.

The exciting thing about the *Bill of Rights* is that it covers all aspects of good policy-making for educational institutions: personal responsibility, security, institutional responsibility, training, and legal issues.

BILL OF RIGHTS AND RESPONSIBILITIES FOR THE ELECTRONIC COMMUNITY OF LEARNERS

PREAMBLE

In order to protect the rights and recognize the responsibilities of individuals and institutions, we, the members of the educational community, propose this Bill of Rights and Responsibilities for the Electronic Community of Learners. These principles are based on a recognition that the electronic community is a complex subsystem of the educational community founded on the values espoused by that community. As new technology modifies the system and further empowers individuals, new values and responsibilities will change this culture. As technology assumes an integral role in education and lifelong learning, technological empowerment of individuals and organizations becomes a requirement and right for students, faculty, staff, and institutions, bringing with it new levels of responsibility that individuals and institutions have to themselves and to other members of the educational community.

ARTICLE I: INDIVIDUAL RIGHTS

The original Bill of Rights explicitly recognized that all individuals have certain fundamental rights as members of the national community. In the same way, the citizens of the electronic community of learners have fundamental rights that empower them.

Section 1.

A citizen's access to computing and information resources shall not be denied or removed without just cause.

Section 2.

The right to access includes the right to appropriate training and tools required to effect access.

Continued on next page

Section 3.

All citizens shall have the right to be informed about personal information that is being and has been collected about them, and have the right to review and correct that information. Personal information about a citizen shall not be used for other than the expressed purpose of its collection without the explicit permission of that citizen.

Section 4.

The constitutional concept of freedom of speech applies to citizens of electronic communities.

Section 5.

All citizens of the electronic community of learners have ownership rights over their own intellectual works.

ARTICLE II: INDIVIDUAL RESPONSIBILITIES

Just as certain rights are given to each citizen of the electronic community of learners, each citizen is held accountable for his or her actions. The interplay of rights and responsibilities within each individual and within the community engenders the trust and intellectual freedom that form the heart of our society. This trust and freedom are grounded on each person's developing the skills necessary to be an active and contributing citizen of the electronic community. These skills include an awareness and knowledge about information technology and the uses of information and an understanding of the roles in the electronic community of learners.

Section 1.

It shall be each citizen's personal responsibility to actively pursue needed resources: to recognize when information is needed, and to be able to find, evaluate, and effectively use information.

Section 2.

It shall be each citizen's personal responsibility to recognize (attribute) and honor the intellectual property of others.

Section 3.

Since the electronic community of learners is based upon the integrity and authenticity of information, it shall be each citizen's personal responsibility to be aware of the potential for and possible effects of manipulating electronic information: to understand the fungible nature of electronic information; and to verify the integrity and authenticity, and assure the security of information that he or she compiles or uses.

Section 4.

Each citizen, as a member of the electronic community of learners, is responsible to all other citizens in that community: to respect and value the rights of privacy for all; to recognize and respect the diversity of the population and opinion in the community; to behave ethically; and to comply with legal restrictions regarding the use of information resources.

Section 5.

Each citizen, as a member of the electronic community of learners, is responsible to the community as a whole to understand what information technology resources are available, to recognize that the members of the community share them, and to refrain from acts that waste resources or prevent others from using them.

ARTICLE III: RIGHTS OF EDUCATIONAL INSTITUTIONS

Educational institutions have legal standing similar to that of individuals. Our society depends upon educational institutions to educate our citizens and advance the development of knowledge. However, in order to survive, educational institutions must attract financial and human resources. Therefore, society must grant these institutions the rights to the electronic resources and information necessary to accomplish their goals.

Section 1.

The access of an educational institution to computing and information resources shall not be denied or removed without just cause.

Section 2.

Educational institutions in the electronic community of learners have ownership rights over the intellectual works they create.

Section 3.

Each educational institution has the authority to allocate resources in accordance with its unique institutional mission.

ARTICLE IV: INSTITUTIONAL RESPONSIBILITIES

Just as certain rights are assured to educational institutions in the electronic community of learners, so too each is held accountable for the appropriate exercise of those rights to foster the values of society and to carry out each institution's mission. This interplay of rights and responsibilities within the community fosters the creation and maintenance of an environment wherein trust and intellectual freedom are the foundation for individual and institutional growth and success.

Continued on next page

Part
III

Becoming an
Information Provider

Section 1.

The institutional members of the electronic community of learners have a responsibility to provide all members of their community with legally acquired computer resources (hardware, software, networks, databases, etc.) in all instances where access to or use of the resources is an integral part of active participation in the electronic community of learners.

Section 2.

Institutions have a responsibility to develop, implement, and maintain security procedures to insure the integrity of individual and institutional files.

Section 3.

The institution shall treat electronically stored information as confidential. The institution shall treat all personal files as confidential, examining or disclosing the contents only when authorized by the owner of the information, approved by the appropriate institutional official, or required by local, state or federal law.

Section 4.

Institutions in the electronic community of learners shall train and support faculty, staff, and students to effectively use information technology. Training includes skills to use the resources, to be aware of the existence of data repositories and techniques for using them, and to understand the ethical and legal uses of the resources.

August 1995

The Lady or the Tiger: Dealing with Student Access Problems

Welcome to the nightmare:

> *"Cool, man! Did you see the naked pictures Tom has?"*
>
> *"Joey's passing out copies of a really hot story he found."*
>
> *"Suzy programmed the Macintosh so it says 'F**K Me' when you turn it on."*
>
> *"I was mudding and someone tried to get me to tell him where I lived, and told me he was masturbating while he typed."*

The issue of access to age-appropriate material and contact with potentially abusive people is not limited to electronic media. Librarians, school security specialists, and every parent has faced these issues.

They become more volatile when the computer networks are involved, perhaps because of the vast availability of materials of all kinds, the difficulty in monitoring and controlling appropriate access and contact, the general uncertainty and computer-phobia of the uninformed citizen, the tendency of the press to blow any network-related incident out of proportion, and the personal liberty and censorship issues involved.

Carl M. Kadie, attorney for the Electronic Freedom Foundation, has said this about access policies:

"If you fear that students will access material on the Net that you would rather they not, you have two practical choices:

"Try to set up your system so they can only access material you approve of. (This is analogous to keeping them on the school grounds.)

"Warn parents that the school has no control on what is available on the Net (This is analogous to having the parents sign releases for field trips.)

"A high school has no legal (or moral) way to stop a Net site, say, at U. of Houston or 'U. of Finland' from making age-inappropriate material available to all. (This is analogous to not being able to make the U. of Houston library remove *Playboy* for fear that high schoolers might access it.) "

Donald Perkins, who set up the Armadillo Gopher system we cited earlier, says:

"I think the main problem will be how to use the Net with kids appropriately and let parents know that the Net is being used by the kids and that some sort of monitoring and discussion of the appropriate use of this resource must occur. And here I am puzzled and a bit concerned, because we live in a litigious society. And often excuses are sought for not moving into new realms."

What about Cyberporn?

Few people can have missed the lurid cover of *Time* magazine on July 3, 1995, which featured a stunned child in the light of a computer screen. That same week, *Newsweek* (in a more sedate, studied way) featured the "danger" to our children in their magazine, as well.

The national media play about "Cyberporn" made most local newscasts and local talk shows, as well.

What didn't get much airplay is the fact that the study on which *Time* based its article, and which generated much of this hysteria, was a carefully crafted "hit" piece that misled more than it informed. *Time* bought the rights to publish excerpts from the paper, which later appeared in the non-juried (and non-peer-reviewed) *Georgetown Law Review.*

Carnegie-Mellon undergraduate Martin Rimm reported that on those Usenet newsgroups where digitized images are transmitted, 83.5% of the images are pornographic. The biggest demand, he reported, is for "deviant" pictures, rather than straight heterosexual material and, according to Time, "Trading in sexually explicit imagery is now 'one of the largest (if not the largest) recreational applications of users of computer networks.' "

Time for Truth?

What *Time* didn't report came in fast and furious on the Internet and, somewhat later, in the news media.

First, let's talk about the report itself and its researcher. According to Brock Meeks in *CyberWire*, Rimm collected his data in an unusual way. Rimm contacted the operators of adults-only BBSs (not connected to the Internet—these BBSs were subscription services only) and offered to analyze the contents of pornographic literature and images in order to help the operators better market their wares. After analysis, Rimm was able to show the BBS operators which imagery (both verbal and pictorial) were most attractive and sold best.

Then he turned around and used the same data for his undergraduate explorations of "Marketing Pornography on the Information Super-highway," and apparently surprised those folks he'd been dealing with by using the data he'd collected in a different way.

Let's examine some of the problems with the facts as reported in *Time* and in other news media.

Rimm studied adults-only BBSs, not the Internet itself. Most of the BBSs he investigated are not connected to the Net, and their customers do not fit the average demographics of the Internet user community.

Rimm's study equates USENET news with all of the Internet. USENET is popular, but the other popular services (e-mail, FTP, and WWW) have much more traffic and many more pictures, including scientific data and studies, medical information, and so on.

It describes the "average" Internet user as being mostly interested in pornography and salacious imagery, including pedophilia. But Rimm only studied the customers of adults-only BBSs, which is a *group self-selected* for their interest in erotic material.

Unfortunately, the refutations of Rimm's work (and of *Time*'s gaudy coverage) did not get as much press as the articles themselves. Some of the best sources of information about the controversy are, not surprisingly, on the Net itself. You can browse the Internet to find some really interesting and thoughtful material about the report, about *Time*, and about Rimm himself.

NPR's John McChesney, a respected technology reporter, interviewed both Rimm and his main critic, Donna Hoffman, on *All Things Considered* the evening of July 11. You can check out a RealAudio version of the interview from NPR's Web server at

```
http://www.npr.org
```

(The actual interview is stored on the RealAudio Web server, but you can easily get there from NPR's page. You'll need to download the RealAudio software, but it's worth it.)

McChesney's report is described in the RealAudio Archive.

Perhaps the best collection of critiques of the *Time* article, including one from the lead writer on the *Time* story, is at

```
http://www.soci.niu.edu/~cudigest/rimm/rimm.html
```

You can also check the HotWired online magazine site, at

```
http://www.hotwired.com/special/pornscare/
transcript.html
```

Here you will find Brock Meeks' *CyberWire* dispatches about his conversations with Rimm, Hoffman and Novak's minute dissection, Rimm's responses, and many more thoughtful pieces from folks on both sides of the controversy.

Parents, teachers, and others can also watch for more information on the media and the Internet by subscribing to the newsgroup

```
alt.internet.media-response
```

Is There Any Good Here?

Suprisingly, there may be. The backlash of publicity about porn on the Net has kicked off a surge of companies and organizations marketing ways that parents, schools, and organizations can police what is accessed from their computers.

The Interactive Services Association's **Project Open** is a new consumer education project, including parental empowerment. Founding members include America Online, AT&T, CompuServe, Microsoft, Netcom, and Prodigy (and many others may join in the next few months). Their Web page helps parents and teachers find out how to better work with their children and students to have a more successful online experience:

```
http://www.isa.net/project-open
```

Open Market has just announced the formation of a new organization, **PICC** (Partners for Identifying Content in Cyberspace). PICC was established to accelerate the adoption of a new content classification solution developed by Open Market, Inc. of Cambridge, MA. This is a proposal to the Internet Engineering Task Force (IETF) to develop a standard that will indicate content of material posted on the Internet and particularly the World Wide Web to be identified with a descriptive and numeric tag in the protocol header.

Content posted on the Web can be categorized according to the organization defining the tag, by category (or attribute) and by numeric tag (i.e. Dewey/Math/322.23, eWorld/Adult/443.34, Chrysler/Saturn Launch/2003, etc.), which could then be used by a proxy server, a browser, an online service provider (AOL, Prodigy, CompuServe, etc.), or a general Internet service provider to retrieve, index, or filter content according to the content's classification.

You can check out PICC's proposal at

```
http://www.openmarket.com/picc/picc.html
```

PICC is a direct response to Speaker's Gingrich's challenge to find technology to let us control our own computers.

An IETF working group has proposed a similar standard, in **the KidSafe Browser** concept, using "KidCode: Naming Conventions for Protecting Children on the World Wide Web and Elsewhere on the Internet Without Censorship."

The proposal is intended to be complementary to the "blacklist" approach taken by several software manufacturers, and it also provides hooks for the kinds of ratings authorities considered by PICC.

However, its main function is to provide a URL naming convention by which a lot of the intended goals can be achieved with minimal effort.

The IETF proposal can be viewed at

```
ftp://ftp.fv.com/pub/nsb/draft-fv-kidcode-00.txt
```

Monitoring Software

There are many companies making software to help you keep control of your child's "Tube Time" on the Internet. Several sources include:

Cyber Patrol An Internet filter that works with all 16/32-bit browsers, newsreaders, and chat clients, from AOL to Microsoft Internet Explorer. The company claims to have the most comprehensive list of sites that should be blocked, and the software includes comprehensive time and budget management functions to help you manage your family's online budget. Cyber Patrol also is compliant with the PICS standard. Contact:

Microsystems Software, Inc.

(508) 879-9000

http://www.cyberpatrol.com/

CYBERsitter A Windows 3.1x and Windows 95 application designed to filter and block adult-oriented material, including both graphics and language, from Internet newsgroups, chat areas, World Wide Web pages and e-mail. The software is available for stand-alone PCs and networks.

CYBERsitter is extremely flexible in its operation, giving the parent or other concerned individual the ability to limit their children's access to objectionable material on the Internet. Parents can choose to block, block and alert, or simply alert them when access is attempted to these areas. Contact:

Solid Oak Software, Inc.

(800) 388-2761

http://www.solidoak.com/cybersit.html

The Internet Filter A program that monitors, filters, analyzes, and logs Internet access. There are both free versions and commercial versions of the Internet Filter. You are free to use, copy, and distribute the free version (version Zero) in its unmodified form. The free version includes a preset, unchangeable configuration, support for any Windows 3.1*x* system, and silent Installation. Contact:

Turner Investigations, Research and Communication

(604) 733-5095

`http://www.xmission.com/~seer/jdksoftware/netfilt.html`

iScreen This program is extremely customizable, and declares itself "First Amendment Friendly." It uses a technique called "can see" filtering, which lets objectionable content be defined by customers.

Furthermore, the SafeSites database is rated by educated employees, most of whom are parents, who insure rating accuracy based on site context, not just terminology. Contact:

NewView

(415) 299-9016

`http://www.newview.com/`

Net Shepherd This program allows the setup of individual, password-protected accounts that restrict Web browser software to Web sites and documents with a specific rating.

All individual accounts as well as Web site/document ratings are controlled through a supervisor (master) account. As a supervisor, the user can surf the Internet and assign ratings to any Web site. The default scale of Net Shepherd is a G through X system, but Net Shepherd will accommodate custom rating scales as well.

Net Shepherd also gives a supervisor account the option to subscribe to Ratings Services—custom ratings databases housed on Net Shepherd's server. Contact:

Net Shepherd Inc.

(403) 250-5310

`http://www.shepherd.net/`

NetNanny A Canadian offering; hence the name. NetNanny compares the characters entered at the keyboard against a customer-developed list of URLs and keywords. If a violation occurs, NetNanny locks the keyboard and prohibits the user from unlocking it. A parent or other responsible person must type in a password to reset the program.

One of the pluses of the NetNanny software is that the manager of the system (whether a parent or a teacher) can select what's appropriate and what's not. This takes care of problems of differing standards in differing environments. It also takes care of the nagging problem that not every "danger" on the Net is related to sex: some parents worry more about their credit cards and online shopping than they do about "dirty pictures." The database is encrypted after modification and can't be accessed without a password. Contact

Net Nanny Ltd.

(800) 340-7177

`http://web20.mindlink.net/netnanny/`

SafeSurf   An "online organization that assists and educates parents and concerned citizens in protecting children on the Internet," and is "dedicated to creating a safe cyber-playground for children by the time school resumes in September." They have developed a rating system that is "simple to implement and provides a solid solution to the issue without censorship." More information about their rating system is at their Web site:

`http://www.safesurf.com/index.html`

The implementation of their rating system is that you mark your Web pages as "kid friendly" by including a special HTML comment at the top of each page. With this, they promise that "all the children of the world will benefit and the Internet will forever be safe from censorship." SafeSurf favors voluntary ratings systems.

Contact:

Wendy Simpson, President

SafeSurf

`SafeSurf@aol.com`

16032 Sherman Way #58

Van Nuys, CA 91406

(818) 902-9390.

SurfWatch   An American firm that has had a lot of publicity in the wake of the *Time* story and the ongoing legislative efforts (such as the Communications Decency Act, discussed in Appendix G). SurfWatch's software is a combination of client software (installs in your TCP/IP stack) and a subscription service to their "list of appropriate sites" to block.

Unfortunately, SurfWatch's database and list of keywords is not user-modifiable, and they have not released a public list of what they are blocking and what the keywords are. Given the diversity of opinion of what's appropriate and what's not, this is a major problem. (One NetWit suggested that SurfWatch could make as much money forming a second company to market their database as "Hot sites to cruise online!")

Contact them at:

SurfWatch Software

105 Fremont Avenue, Suite F

Los Altos, California 94022,

415-948-9500

 Fax 415-948-9577

E-mail

   `info@surfwatch.com`

Their Web site is at

   `http://www.surfwatch.com/`

and a demo is available at

   `http://www.surfwatch.com/surfwatch/demo.html`

SurfWatch's demo site shows you what your child will see if they attempt to access an inappropriate site.

 MASTER WORDS   Thanks to Judi Clark of ManyMedia, Inc., for information on the various software packages and organizations online. Thanks also to Brendan Kehoe, Rory O'Connell, and a host of other Internet writers and reporters.

Is Censorship Possible in the Networks?

Parents and politicians, when asked about this problem, sometimes say, "Just don't let children get to the bad stuff." Accustomed to technological wizardry, they expect that restricting access to the Internet ought to be as simple as guarding the money in a bank or locking the final exams away. But reading any newspaper will tell you that even these security precautions can be circumvented. Can the Internet be censored?

Howard Rheingold, author of *The Virtual Community,* said in the *San Francisco Examiner* (April 6, 1994):

"It's not hard to imagine Jesse Helms standing before the US Senate, holding up an X-rated image downloaded from the Internet, raging indignantly about 'public funds for porno highways.'

"As the public begins to realize that communications technology is exposing them to an unlimited array of words and images, including some they might find thoroughly repulsive, the clamor for censorship and government regulation of the electronic highway is sure to begin.

"But it would be a mistake to let traffic cops start pulling people over on the highway.

"Yes, we have to think about ways of protecting our children and our society from the easy availability of every kind of abhorrent information imaginable. But the 'censor the Net' approach is not just morally misguided. It's becoming technically impossible. As Net pioneer John Gilmore is often quoted: 'The Net interprets censorship as damage and routes around it.'

"The Net's technological foundation was built to withstand nuclear attack. The RAND Corporation designed the network to be a thoroughly decentralized command-and-control and communications system, one that would be less vulnerable to intercontinental missiles than a system commanded by a centralized headquarters."

Let's suppose that your school decides not to provide the `alt.sex` news hierarchy in your news service, to prevent your middle-school students from reading the potentially offensive materials on that group. Will that keep the students from reading them? Probably not—they could use the Veronica search engine to find the locations where the groups are archived and read the stories over a Gopher server.

What should you do? What kind of policies and procedures can you put in place to keep students, parents, and school personnel happy?

Discussion, Argument, and Consensus

The best way to come up with a comprehensive policy that stands some chance of being acceptable to everyone is to get input on the policy from all the affected parties. Get a committee together that includes students, parents, local clergy, school board administrators, legal experts, teachers, and so on.

One excellent technique to help hammer out a good policy is to get everyone grounded in the same information. You might pass out articles and relevant policies, and have people report on each article or policy at your meetings, explaining the issues covered and the solutions discussed. As you do this, the members of your committee will (we hope!) start to discuss how they feel about the issues, how it affects your local situation, and other important concepts.

You'll undoubtedly have heated meetings. With luck, your committee will be committed enough to the needs of the community and to the process itself to be able to get through the tough times. Listen carefully to each other and to the underlying beliefs and needs that cause the hot words.

Make sure someone writes down anything that sounds like consensus or strong agreement on general principles. When you're done talking about the articles and background information, you should have a good list of principles to start forging into a policy.

Once it's drafted, send it out for comment as widely as you can. Unfortunately, some of your squeakiest wheels won't respond now: they'll holler when they find their child downloading pictures from *Wicked Lady* onto Dad's work machine. But you'll be on higher moral ground if you can prove you have community support for the policy you've developed.

Obviously, no policy is going to satisfy everyone. The religious fundamentalists and the Libertarians can't agree on most other issues in your community, and you're unlikely to get them both to be satisfied with any policy that is agreeable to the middle ground. But if you can keep 90% happy, you'll have done well.

Remember to keep one guiding principle in mind: Treat computer media the same way you do other media. Do you have a policy on plagiarism? Are *Catcher in the Rye, Huckleberry Finn, Little Black Sambo,* and *Sons and Lovers* in your school library? What do you do when Nazi or other hate literature appears on campus? Do you restrict the rights of student editors of the campus newspaper concerning newspaper content?

Responsibility and Agreements

Every user of your system, from the kindergartners learning their ABC's to the secretary in the School Board office, must be aware of the rules and responsibilities before they use the network. Anyone who can't be made to understand the limits under which they must operate should not use your computing resources, including the network. Make your users sign an application that includes the appropriate use policy, and make sure the student's parents sign it, too (the Brevard County, Florida, document presented earlier is a good example of such a combined policy/application).

Experienced principals say that making sure the parents understand the basic ground rules, and that they are aware of the potential (limited or otherwise) for encountering difficult materials and situations, is critical to the success of any policy. Not only will the parents be your allies when and if an infraction or incident occurs, but by requiring them to sign the application as well as the student, you make them equally responsible for enforcing the policy.

You know best how to enforce the policy for your community: remember the principle we discussed above, and treat infractions of the computing policy the same way you do infractions of other rules. But do enforce it. If you don't, the students won't respect it (and you may be legally liable for other problems).

Protecting Children by Educating Them

Unfortunately, it's not always a nice world, even in cyberspace. Students may well encounter nasty e-mail, harassing or abusive adults, even truly sick individuals on the Net. Parents should have the right, and the ability, to control the massive information-flow into the home, to exclude things they don't want their children to see. But sooner or later, most children will be exposed to everything parents have shielded them from, and then all they will have left to deal with these shocking sights and sounds is the moral fiber that both parents and teachers have helped them cultivate. The rules for protecting them in cyberspace are similar to those you have taught them about existing in the physical world:

You don't have to answer e-mail from anyone unless you know them.

If anybody asks whether you are home alone, or says anything that makes you feel funny about answering, then just don't answer until you speak to a trusted adult.

Be politely but firmly skeptical about anything you see or hear on the Net.

Don't be afraid to reject anything—images, sounds, or text communications—that repels or frightens you.

Develop and respect your own sense of your personal boundaries. You have a right to defend those boundaries physically and socially.

People sometimes lie: they aren't always who they present themselves to be in e-mail, news, and other contexts.

Predators exist. You don't have to be a victim.

Keep personal information private.

Confide in a parent, teacher, or other trusted adult if something doesn't seem right.

Damage Control

What do you—teachers, administrators, parents—do if an incident occurs?

Virginia Rezmierski, who wrote the article in Appendix E about Internet censorship and college students, has handled many incidents at the University of Michigan with tact and good sense. We feel that some of the principles she uses in handling problems are worthy of wide distribution.

Be sure your system is as secure as possible.

Handle problems promptly. Don't let little problems grow into big ones.

Handle problems privately. Respect the privacy of both the perpetrator and (if there is one) the victim.

Handle problems appropriately according to your established procedures. Minor infractions should have minimal repercussions, major ones greater repercussions.

Make sure that the solution you choose allows the student to learn and grow as much as possible within the context of the problem itself.

There are some things you cannot allow on your system: child pornography and pirated software, for example, can create a liability for you as the system owner. You will, of course, have made that clear in your policy and in your training for users, and you will need to remove any such material from your system promptly. (Some experts advise saving it to tape if evidence in any legal action becomes necessary.)

If necessary, call in the computer crime experts with your local or state law enforcement agencies for assistance.

FURTHER RESOURCES FOR K–12 POLICIES

The Electronic Frontier Foundation maintains the Computers and Academic Freedom Archive, including documents related to K–12 education, in its pub/ academic directory. Carl Kadie of the EFF provides an annotated list of these resources, including complete instructions for downloading them. This list is available at this site:

```
http://www.eff.org/archives.html
```

Training

Training for users will include not only how to find and use the Internet, but ethical and social policy information as well. A good basic curriculum would include all the topics included in this book, as well as a good grounding in the local policies for your school network and regional network provider.

There are many training service companies for educators today: your regional provider will be able to point you to training providers in your area. Additionally, look for training services that offer continuing education credits for training sessions, so that teachers will be able to continue to accrue these important points as well as become more Internet-literate. Continuing education credits are an added incentive for attending training courses.

You will most likely want to designate one or more teachers per site to have more extensive training in network topics, so that they can become trainers and troubleshooters for others at your school, and assist in designing curriculum modules for your students.

Maintaining the Network

You will be best served by hiring at least one staff person exclusively to manage and maintain your system. Attempting to add system maintenance and management to the tasks already assigned to teaching or administrative staff is likely to result in less efficiency in both areas.

Some schools have had good success using high school and older middle-school students to help manage their networks and computer resources. The kids are excited about the project, usually very skilled, and in many instances this privilege can be used as extra credit or as a reward for exceptional leadership or scholarship.

Other resources for network management are parents, college interns, local network consultants, or the computing specialists for your district.

Order out of Chaos

As in the rest of the networked world, the rise of K–12 networking started slowly. Ten years ago navigating the Internet was a trip for the most intrepid: both the tools and the technology required patience and specialized expertise, and the rewards for the K–12 teacher were slight. Today, with the advent of the two great user-friendly tools, the World Wide Web and Gopher servers, teachers are taking firm hold of this resource and using it to enrich their classrooms.

In fact, getting classrooms connected to the Internet has become a national goal. On March 9, 1996, NetDay, thousands of educators, network vendors, and even President Clinton and Vice President Gore rolled up their sleeves to pull wire and install computers, routers, and other equipment in hundreds of schools across the country. With this kind of national attention and focus, we can expect to see more resources, more aids for classroom development and distance learning, and even more fun things to do as we move into the 21st Century.

CHAPTER 19

Rules, Policies, and Other Mutual Agreements

FEATURING

Chapter 19

Rules, Policies, and Other Mutual Agreements

A *policy* is a course of action designed to influence and determine decisions and actions. According to the American Heritage dictionary, both *policy* and *police* are derived from the Greek word *polis* or city. This makes sense, doesn't it? What we are talking about is our own behavior in the larger Internet community.

In this chapter, we'll consider why formal Acceptable Use Policies (AUPs) are necessary, whom they serve, and what kinds of activities they should cover. At the end of the chapter, you'll find two examples of complete Acceptable Use Policies. The first is from the University of Michigan, and the second is from the commercial Internet directory service Four11.

This chapter is addressed primarily to those of you who are responsible for managing your organization's Internet resources and for defining policies about the use of those resources. You should also read this if you're not a manager but an employee working under an Acceptable Use Policy (or without the benefit of any clearly defined policy). It will help you understand why such policies are not merely arbitrary, bureaucratic restrictions; and it may motivate you to urge your organization's management to define its policies more consistently or more realistically. Similarly, if you have an individual account with an Internet service provider, this chapter will provide some context for your provider's policies.

Before we begin, a few general words of advice:

Keep Your Goals Clear: In order for your policy to address all the relevant issues effectively, you need to be clear about what you are trying to do:

▶ Are you trying to protect yourself from legal action?

▶ Are you trying to protect your organization's resources from being misused?

▶ Are you trying to stretch limited resources and not let any one person or activity grab more than a "fair share" of them?

▶ Are you trying to protect your staff from harassment by others?

In most cases the answer will be "all of the above." You'll be able to write much better policies if you define your goals first.

Ask Your Lawyers: While you are developing your policies, make sure your lawyers check them for legality and validity, particularly with regard to copyright issues and employee rights. The authors of this book aren't lawyers. Don't just follow our advice; get some good advice from people who know the law, human resources policies, and how your company policies can make best use of both.

Make Your AUP Accessible: Make sure you tell your user community what the policies are. Keep them where they can be referred to.

Why Do We Need Policies?

Formal policies make some people quite uncomfortable and strike others as overkill. Others, of course, think there ought to be more rules, particularly rules that inhibit actions they don't like.

In the Internet community, rules and laws are generally regarded with trepidation. After all, people have been getting by with pretty few rules and not too much trouble on the Internet for some time now. You'll often hear Internet users say something like this:

"Why should we need to include rules—Isn't that an invasion of privacy? Or at least against the kind of academic freedom that a lot of people on the Internet enjoy? What about just depending on people to be responsible— shouldn't that be enough? Besides, the Internet is a free-wheeling place and if someone from your organization steps out of line, no doubt they will be

flamed, chagrined, and enlightened; and they won't make that particular mistake again. That's the Internet way."

Most of us would like to live in the kind of world where "Net-police" aren't needed and the only rule would be "do unto others as you would have them do unto you." Unfortunately, we don't live in such a world. For example, what if one of your employees posts a copyrighted, unreleased version of some software where others can retrieve it? What if that retrieval space is on one of your computers? This is clearly a violation of someone's copyright. What are you, the manager of this space, going to do? Do you want to figure out your position on intellectual property only when you get a threatening letter or phone call from the copyright holder's lawyer? The alternative is better: get your ducks all in line *before* it happens, so that you know exactly what to do next.

What's a good yardstick to tell if you need policies? If there is more than one of you on your staff, you probably need policies. And even if you are a one-person business or organization, we'd argue that you should have some clear delineation between resources for your personal use and those for use in the name of your organization or company. Policies, particularly written policies, can help you allocate resources and expenses for tax purposes, for example. There's nothing quite like the idea of an IRS audit to make us all think we should be better about our policies and our record-keeping.

Policies are similar to contracts in that they protect all the parties involved, not just the owners. Well-written policies will help people to understand the possible results of their actions. They might prevent the thoughtless act by someone that can hurt themselves or others. Well-written policies explain what *can* happen and then what *will* happen if the policy is not followed. This gives all parties the opportunity to understand each other's positions. And finally, well-written policies outline a process of appeal that allows the person who committed the violation of the policy a chance to explain his/her actions. Well-written policies should provide for due process—not just summary judgments.

For example, even though some tech-support people and moderators joke about shooting users in the kneecaps for posting inappropriate articles to scores of newsgroups, in fact the Netcom process for Usenet abuse is to warn the user via e-mail that a complaint was received and explain the policy. At this point most people say "oh, I didn't understand,

I'm sorry" or something similar. The persistent abusers are warned again. If they continue, Netcom places their accounts on hold until they are talked to in person. If at this point, they promise to "be good," Netcom releases the hold. It's only after several (and continued), deliberate actions on the part of the user to ignore the policy that Netcom actually closes an account. This policy can be a pain for the enforcers as well as for the people who have to read the inappropriate articles and then complain to Netcom. But it does allow the abuser plenty of chances to change behavior. Since changed behavior is the desired outcome, Netcom finds that this policy usually works. And just as a service like Netcom wants to hold onto its customers, your organization presumably wants to hold onto its employees.

Who Is Served by an AUP?

If you are an employer or provider of network services, policies best serve you and your users by being explicit, clear-cut, fair, and well advertised. We recommend that you avoid using "Guidelines," which are statements of reasonable and prudent behavior for the users and the organization; they state your intent but do not, usually, describe actions and consequences. Good policies, for the most part, detail the expected behavior and the consequences of undesirable behavior.

As a user, you are best served by reading and understanding the Appropriate Use Policies of your network provider and any network segments your traffic crosses. Don't sign up with a network provider if you do not intend to abide by their policies: there are many providers available, some with more lenient policies and some with more restrictive policies. You should ask to see the policies that affect you and be certain you can abide by them before you sign on the dotted line. If your network provider (or your employer, for that matter) is reluctant to show you copies of policies before you sign up, you should take care in your dealings with them.

What Should Your Policy Cover?

Here are some of the topics you'll want to think about in formulating your Acceptable Use Policy. We say *think about* because every Internet site is different. Except for a really obvious policy like "no illegal stuff on our computers," there probably isn't an item on this list for which every site will have the same policy.

Actions by Individuals

First, let's talk about policies concerning the things individual people do: e-mail, chat programs (like Talk), IRC, and FTP storage.

Personal Messages

Are your employees allowed to send and receive personal messages at an e-mail address at your organization's Internet site? If so, can the employees read personal messages when they arrive (most Internet e-mail is delivered continually, not in a batch at a specific time) or need the mail wait until lunch or break-time or after work? If they may not receive e-mail, can you effectively police this? As parents who are quite experienced in children sneaking things by us, we'd recommend against making an unenforceable policy.

Talk, IRC, MUDs?

Will you be running a Talk program? An Internet Relay Chat server? Will you allow connections to an IRC server during work hours from your equipment? Will you be running a multiuser program like a MUD to deliver training and information about your organization? If you answer "yes" to any of these questions, you'll need to state your position about their use for personal message traffic. We've noted in Chapter 14 that Talk can be really convenient to check in with one's spouse, roommates, and so on. It's much quicker than a telephone call.

What's Your Telephone Policy?

Your organization's policy about personal use of e-mail and Talk facilities should be derived from its policies on personal telephone use, although the two may not be exactly the same. Many organizations state that a few personal calls from time to time are fine, especially when there are family emergencies. However, personal long-distance calls are expected to be paid for. Usually this is a cost-of-resource issue—the organization doesn't want to incur expensive long-distance telephone bills unnecessarily. Interestingly enough, the Internet can shine here because the rates for Internet traffic are not usually based upon number of packets nor the distance the packets travel, so the motivation to forbid long-distance traffic isn't there.

To think about how your employee's e-mail and other personal message traffic can affect your organization you need to consider the resources they are using: intellectual effort, time, and network bandwidth. You probably should be most concerned about the time and intellectual effort employees might spend on personal communications.

"I Spy" or Reasonable Caution?

When creating policies concerning employee use of your systems, you must clearly address the privacy of employee e-mail and stored files. It's really important that everyone is clear on this one. Internet e-mail can inadvertently be read by someone not intended to see it for a number of reasons that have nothing to do with monitoring employee actions: for example, when someone prints out a message at a public printer.

We generally recommend that no one say anything in electronic mail that they wouldn't want to share with their mothers, but we *all* break that rule from time to time. Neither author would complain about our supervisors in a private message, for example. But if you do complain about someone and the e-mail gets forwarded to the person about whom you were complaining because you didn't think about what you were doing, you'll be embarrassed. Being embarrassed can be difficult, but it is not at all the same thing as having your e-mail monitored and your thoughts reported.

Your employees deserve to know if you are going to be monitoring their e-mail, just as they should know if you are monitoring their telephone calls. Sometimes it may be appropriate to monitor mail (when you are training people to answer e-mail for the organization, for example). If you are doing that, tell the people involved. Otherwise, people really do believe their e-mail conversations are private. No doubt this assumption has something to do with the fact that we interact only with a computer keyboard and screen. After all, there's no other person involved. It's unfair to let your employees continue to have this impression if you intend to monitor their mail.

We can think of one exception to this "rule." If you have a case where you are cooperating with a law enforcement agency, you should, of course, under the advice of your attorneys and within the bounds of the law, follow their instructions on whether or not to let people know they are being monitored.

For much more complete discussion of issues surrounding privacy and electronic messages, see the Electronic Frontier Foundation archives, available by the following means:

World Wide Web:

    www.eff.org

Gopher:

gopher.eff.org

FTP:

ftp.eff.org

EFF staff members analyze and write extensively on issues of freedom and privacy in cyberspace. Their archives contain these writings as well as a complete copy of the Electronic Communications Privacy Act (ECPA) of 1986, and an extensive collection of terms and conditions-of-use statements and critiques of those statements. EFF and Computer Professionals for Social Responsibility (CPSR) are excellent sources for information about privacy issues.

Reading Newsgroups or Mailing Lists That Aren't Work-Related

Newsgroup reading can use a lot of time, too. Trade magazines are common in many fields now—magazines devoted to specific types of computing, for example, or to a specific type of medicine. Reading newsgroups or mailing lists that are related to the thrust of your organization is like reading these trade magazines. However, reading newsgroups or mailing lists that aren't directly related to work is more akin to reading magazines for pleasure. Some people like to read scientific journals for pleasure. Others like to read magazines devoted to the entertainment industry. If your organization is devoted to neither of these topics, reading either *Science* or *People* is probably something that shouldn't be done on your organization's time. If you agree, you will most likely want to say that reading rec.art.books or rec.sport.soccer or even alt.adjective.noun.verb.verb.verb, while interesting and certainly not evil, is something best not done during working hours.

Another area of concern involves the content of files—graphic image—that can be found on newsgroups such as alt.sex.binaries and others. These images may be offensive to people who have not initiated the download or display. In certain cases, using some of these graphic images as screen backgrounds or causing them to be printed to public printers has been deemed to be sexual harassment. We'd recommend that you state very clearly any policies you have about this type of material.

MASTER WORDS In California, and in several other states, this is not merely a matter of company policy; it's illegal. In California, for example, sexual harassment violates the Fair Employment and Housing Act and is specifically defined to include "displaying of sexually suggestive objects or pictures, cartoons, or posters." Arguably that would include displaying these images on a computer screen. Potentially it would include pictures from even museum and classical collections such as LeWebMuseum. Recently in one California town an art exhibit in a public office building that included nudes was canceled at the last minute on the grounds that it would have created an "offensive work environment" for employees there. The point is that even images clearly not intended for sexual gratification could illegally offend somebody. See Appendix E for a discussion of how these issues can arise in an educational context.

Passing around Copyrighted Material

There are hundreds of news services on the Internet today, from Dow Jones to *PC Week* magazine. There are articles, tidbits, and whole Web pages that people will want to pass along. It's not a good idea. Many of these services have explicit prohibitions against redistribution electronically, especially to company-wide mailing lists or onto company news or BBS systems. Be diligent about educating your staff about these documents. Never forward an article yourself without being clear about the copyright status; if there is a copyright statement allowing distribution, be sure and include it prominently.

Game Playing on Your Organization's Time or Equipment

Unless you are in the business of designing, implementing, and/or testing games, it is hard to make a case for allowing employees to play games on your time or using your equipment. You could, of course, state that if the equipment is not needed for work-related activities during nonworking hours, and its use will not endanger the equipment itself, then using the equipment for playing games is permitted.

Non-Organization Business on Your Organization's Time or Equipment

Should employees be allowed to use your Internet connection, and company time, to do work for some other organization they're affiliated with? Given our strong stand on games, you may wonder why we even ask you to think about this topic. The answer doesn't seem quite as clear-cut to us. What will your policy be on using your organization's connection to find information for a nonprofit organization for which your company provides volunteers? What if it's the United Way and your company provides a lot of volunteers and donations? What if it is for an organization that is teaching literacy and/or language to some of your employees? What if the effort is in the name of a school that your organization has "adopted?" What if it's for a school attended by the children of some of your employees? Or a church, mosque, or synagogue attended by some of your employees? These are uses that you might well choose to allow.

No matter what your policy is on these issues, you should explicitly spell it out in your employee handbook. It should be in the same area as your policy about using company resources (even during the employee's nonwork hours) to run a for-profit business or to support political campaigns. This policy should parallel similar policies about use of the organization's libraries, copy machines, and the like.

Reasonable Care in Retrieving, Downloading, and Installing Documents or Programs

Throughout this book we've talked about the Internet as a place where you can find wonderful software and documents that will help you with research, provide new insights into recent discoveries, and give you useful tools to help you manage your software archive. By acquiring these materials, employees can certainly benefit your organization. Unfortunately, there are also some risks involved. Some files arc illegally made available for downloading. You need to be careful about copyright and licensing issues just as with software you buy on a diskette. Moreover, some files may have viruses.

When you evolve your policies to cover these issues, think about the next four considerations in your discussions and writing sessions.

Where Is the Information From? Don't believe everything you can retrieve on the Internet just because it is on the Internet. Use the same criteria you would for other published materials. If the information or software comes from a recognized and announced archive site, it's more likely to be authoritative than if it comes from a file belonging to someone you (or your contacts) have never heard of. Do notice that we said "recognized and announced." Many individuals—Scott Yanoff and John December are two of the best-known examples—have given a lot to the Internet in their efforts to gather and make available information, and their work is indeed authoritative.

Run Virus Checkers   If you download files, make sure that you run virus checkers on them. Make sure that this is not only a paper policy, but one that actually is implemented. If you buy software from other sources, run virus checkers on that software, too.

Understand and Enforce Copyright and Licenses   Copyright is another issue that must be addressed for all information and software in your organization, but the availability of materials for downloading from the Internet makes it especially important to include in your Appropriate Use Policy. We suggest designating someone to serve as the "responsible party" for software. (In a large organization, you may need to assign this responsibility to one person in each department or division.) This person would be responsible for knowing what software is on each computer in your organization and for making sure that all the copyright and licenses for each piece of software are in order, that your organization can account for each installation, and that there is adequate documentation of the appropriate licensing kept for each copy of the software. It is easier to manage this if your policy also says that no software that is not owned by or licensed to the organization can be placed on organization systems or networks. This means that employees should not place their personal software on your systems. If an employee needs a specific piece of software to perform a task, the organization should purchase the software if it's going to be placed on one of your systems.

We have heard of disgruntled former employees "blowing the whistle" on organizations that weren't careful about their software licenses. The Software Publishers Association will visit and ask for an audit. You wouldn't want to fail such an audit.

Shareware is a special case of licensing. Usually you can download the software from a recognized archive. The terms and conditions suggest that you evaluate the software. If you continue to use it, you are asked to pay a fee. The fees are quite small and it might be tempting to disregard them. Don't. The entire concept of shareware depends on people paying their fair share. The developers don't get rich but are compensated somewhat for their work. It's a nice exchange.

Is the Information or Program Work-Related?   If an employee downloads something from the Internet that isn't work-related, we'd recommend you not let it stay on your systems. One approach might be to let people download material, put it on diskette, and take the diskette to other some other machine (not at work) to run. In this case, you've provided the Internet connection that made the download possible. Again, explicit mention of your policy is best.

Consuming Bandwidth Resources

So far we've talked about how an individual's activities on the Internet can consume resources such as time and put the organization at risk of legal violations and "viral infections." It's also possible for one person's use of the Internet to impede the work of others. For example, if your connection to the Internet is low-bandwidth and is shared by many, someone transferring large quantities of information will prevent others from transferring information themselves. (As discussed in Chapter 4, *bandwidth* is a measure of the capacity of your physical connection—the telephone wires, satellite links, and so on—to carry information. You can think of the bandwidth available to you as a pipeline of a fixed size.)

You can expect that people will find more and more uses for Internet usage as time goes on. There'll be more organizations with whom you work that will get connected, and you will want to exchange messages with them. You'll want to look at more information from other people's information servers. You'll want to put more information on your servers, and more people will want to view that information.

With your own usage expected to grow, you will want to save some room for growth, even if it seems that you've obtained a connection with plenty of room for growth. This means that you will need to develop policies about how the bandwidth is used. Image and sound data files can carry much useful information, but they are also large files and therefore consume more bandwidth than, say, text files. As in a water pipeline, if the pipeline is busy, you can't pour more down it.

Viewing those large radar/weather map images or viewing the beautiful Impressionistic paintings displayed at the Louvre Museum in Paris is very enjoyable and fun. It's educational. It's impressive. It's probably not work-related.

Official Voice or Personal Voice?

One of the common practices in the Internet is to apply a "signature" of three or four lines to a posting to a public e-mail list or to a newsgroup. The signature is a text file that's appended to every message sent from a particular account. In its purpose, it resembles the way you sign a letter. If the account from which you are sending the posting or article is an organizational one, it is considered good netiquette to identify the organization. You might include an e-mail address where you can be reached and in some cases you might want to include a telephone number or postal address.

A good candidate for a policy about posting to public e-mail lists or Usenet newsgroups by your employees or from accounts within your organization is a statement about what to include in the signature file. If the posting is not "official" and the signature file includes some information identifying the signer as being part of your organization, you should have the signer include a disclaimer. (This needn't be elaborate; Glee's is simply "in her own write.") Conversely, if the posting is "official," that information should be included in the signature, too. Make sure that everyone who will be posting knows your e-mail software's method for creating a signature.

Multiple Mailing Lists

A final shared-resource issue is mailing lists. If your mail machines handle and distribute a large number of mailing lists, you will affect the performance of your systems. Your list server takes a single piece of e-mail and mails it to the entire list. As long as the lists are in support of the organization's goals, no one should complain too much. However, if you allow other unofficial mailing lists to be managed by your mailing list handler, you may run into more difficult conflicts among the users who wish to share the same resource.

Actions by or for the Organization

We've spent a lot of time trying to demonstrate how an organization can have an "Internet presence" to provide information about itself, and to shape an image for Internet citizens to see. Once you've made the commitment to do that, it's pretty important to make sure that the image you present is the one you intend. This means you need clear policies about who can post the official positions for the organization.

You'll need your own terms and conditions of use for the information prepared, owned, and shared by the organization.

Who Can Post Official Company Material?

An effective method for many organizations is the check-off process. This means that for *anything* that goes into accessible cyberspace in the name of your organization, you should have a responsible person or persons review the posted material for spelling, avoiding offensive language, or whatever is important for your organization. These folks should agree to both the information content and the appropriateness of its placement. It's never a good idea to "surprise" the officers of your organization with a wonderful new feature that has to be retracted with much embarrassment and hard feelings by all.

While you are designing the check-off process, try to keep it simple. If you involve too many people or departments you lose the ability to get information out immediately—one of the real benefits of information dissemination over the Internet.

Disclaimers, We All Hate Them

In our litigious society disclaimers have become one of those "facts of life." You should include a disclaimer in the Web page, the Gopher space, the FTP directory, and in any other Internet-accessible resource stating the terms and conditions for the use of information owned or provided by your organization. You need something that states that you can't be held responsible if people use the information and they are harmed by it. Again, to have the type of disclaimer that best protects you, it is essential to consult with attorneys that represent your organization and are knowledgeable about your circumstances.

Do develop a set of terms and conditions and policies about use. We've included two general ones at the end of the chapter as examples. They contrast nicely because they are for totally different internetworked communities: a university and a commercial online service. The one for the University of Michigan addresses the issues of shared resources based on an underlying sense of community and individual responsibility. The one from Four11 is very different. It tries to explicitly outline the contractual responsibility between the two parties—Four11 and the user. Both have paragraphs and ideas that we believe are well stated. If you are developing policies for a small business, you will probably want to state your policies in terms more like the Four11 policy. You have some sort of contractual or similar relationship with both your customers or clients and your employees. You'll want to spell out the responsibilities each has and brings. If you are a nonprofit or community organization, you may want to develop your policies more like the ones from the University of Michigan. You will be talking about shared responsibilities and shared (and probably limited) resources. Again, starting from a statement of your own goals will help you determine which type of policies are best for you.

What Goes into a Policy, Anyway?

Policies don't need to be complicated. They really only must contain a statement about the desired (or conversely, the undesired) behavior and what consequences may be suffered if the policy is not followed. Each policy should contain the following sections.

I. Background

This section might be necessary if you think that the audience might not understand why a policy on Internet use is necessary. Here you can explain what problems the policy is intended to address. You'll be the best judge of when you need this section and when you don't, because you know your audience best. The desired outcome is that you don't have to explain the policy in the heat of some moment. All who read it should understand what the policy addresses.

II. The Policy Itself

Be sure to relate the policy stated here to other policies for your organization. Everyone potentially affected by your Internet use policy needs to understand where it fits among all the policies of the organization.

Make sure that the policy is clearly stated and that the consequences of not following the policy are outlined. Include any appeal processes. Action and consequences are the heart of good policy development. If you are clear about what should be done and what will happen if it isn't, not only will you usually get the desired behavior, but you will also save yourself a lot of grief when someone doesn't choose to follow the policies.

Coordinate your Internet policy with other policies. If, for example, you have a policy about written memos, any policy about e-mail should relate to that policy as well as to any policies about other electronic information delivery or use of electronic resources, and so on. Include those other policies in the electronic one, or incorporate the electronic policy into the other policies. When you have policies that are hard to find, people trip over them (that is, they find out about them only when they have inadvertently broken a rule) and they are resentful.

Glee notes that the Standard Practice Guide, the large collection of policies made available to managers at the University of Michigan, helped her transition into management in that environment. It covered everything from the organization of the University itself (it's always a puzzle to figure out how the administrative part of a large institution is shaped), to the sick-leave policies, to the policies about use of computing resources. It's presented in a large binder, organized chronologically within a relatively wide organizational scheme. It has an index as well as a table of contents to let you find things quickly. The guide is kept available in all departments and it's easy to find and refer to when you have a question. We recommend similar access to policy information.

III. Policy Interpretations

In this section include any hypothetical examples that you may want to add to your policy to demonstrate what you mean. If you decide to include this section in your policy, make sure that your examples are clear and understandable. It won't help at all if you make things "muddier" with your interpretative examples.

State here exactly what you want people to do or not to do. We believe that stating policies positively is better from a motivational viewpoint.

This section is where you should list the variations you can think of. If you give examples, make sure it's clear that they *are* examples. If you don't do this, you will end up with a "letter of the law" person who will try the old "But the policy doesn't say I can't do <fill in some closely related thing that is almost but not quite what you said>" ploy. This section is a good place for a "standard disclaimer" that says that you are covering typical cases, not exhaustively listing all possible types of similar behavior.

IV. Procedures

The final section should state exactly what steps will be taken if the policy is invoked. This section should include a chronology of expected actions.

Netcom's Usenet newsgroup abuse policy, for example, states that there is a set of steps that are to be taken and lists the order in which they are to be done. If the steps are followed in the proper order, *and* the abuser does not comply with the request to stop, Netcom will terminate the account. While this isn't pleasant for anyone involved, it is clear what will happen.

Two Sample Policies

Now that you've seen what appropriate use policies in general should cover, consider two very different examples of specific policies. The first, from the University of Michigan, is highly detailed and explains every point. The second, from the commercial online directory service Four11, takes the opposite approach and consists of only six simple rules.

THE UNIVERSITY OF MICHIGAN APPROPRIATE USE POLICY AND GUIDELINES FOR ADMINISTRATION

This is the base policy for appropriate use at the University of Michigan, and the addendum which was issued in September 1995. The complete set of guidelines for the University of Michigan are available at

    http://www.umich.edu/~wwwitd/policies/

Policy: Proper Use of Information Resources, Information Technology, and Networks at the University of Michigan

Section: General University Policies and Procedures

Number: Standard Practice Guide 601.7

Date Issued: 25 May 1990

Issued by: Provost and Vice President for Academic Affairs

Applies To: All Employees

Continued on next page

I. Policy

It is the policy of the University to maintain access for its community to local, national, and international sources of information and to provide an atmosphere that encourages access to knowledge and sharing of information.

It is the policy of the University that information resources will be used by members of its community with respect for the public trust through which they have been provided and in accordance with policy and regulations established from time to time by the University and its operating units.

In accordance with the above policies, the University works to create an intellectual environment in which students, staff, and faculty may feel free to create and to collaborate with colleagues both at the University of Michigan and at other institutions, without fear that the products of their intellectual efforts will be violated, violated by misrepresentation, tampering, destruction and/or theft.

Access to the information resource infrastructure both within the University and beyond the campus, sharing of information, and security of the intellectual products of the community, all require that each and every user accept responsibility to protect the rights of the community. Any member of the University community who, without authorization, accesses, uses, destroys, alters, dismantles or disfigures the University information technologies, properties or facilities, including those owned by third parties, thereby threatens the atmosphere of increased access and sharing of information, threatens the security within which members of the community may create intellectual products and maintain records, and in light of the University's policy in this area, has engaged in unethical and unacceptable conduct. Access to the networks and to the information technology environment at the University of Michigan is a privilege and must be treated as such by all users of these systems.

To ensure the existence of this information resource environment, members of the University community will take actions, in concert with State and Federal agencies and other interested parties, to identify and to set up technical and procedural mechanisms to make the information technology environment at the University of Michigan and its internal and external networks resistant to disruption.

In the final analysis, the health and well-being of this resource is the responsibility of its users who must all guard against abuses which disrupt and/or threaten the long-term viability of the systems at the University of Michigan and those beyond the University. The University requires that members of its community act in accordance with these responsibilities, this policy, relevant laws and contractual obligations, and the highest standard of ethics.

II REGULATIONS

Though not exhaustive, the following material defines the University's position regarding several general issues in this area.*

The University characterizes as unethical and unacceptable, and just cause for taking disciplinary action up to and including non- reappointment, discharge, dismissal, and/or legal action, any activity through which an individual:

(a) violates such matters as University or third party copyright or patent protection and authorizations, as well as license agreements and other contracts,

(b) interferes with the intended use of the information resources,

(c) seeks to gain or gains unauthorized access to information resources,

(d) without authorization, destroys, alters, dismantles, disfigures, prevents rightful access to or otherwise interferes with the integrity of computer-based information and/or information resources,

(e) without authorization invades the privacy of individuals or entities that are creators, authors, users, or subjects of the information resources.

This policy is applicable to any member of the University community, whether at the University or elsewhere, and refers to all information resources whether individually controlled, or shared, stand alone or networked. Individual units within the University may define "conditions of use" for facilities under their control. These statements must be consistent with this overall policy but may provide additional detail, guidelines and/or restrictions.

Where such "conditions of use" exist, enforcement mechanisms defined therein shall apply. Where no enforcement mechanism exists, the enforcement mechanism defined in the Information Technology Division Responsible Use statement shall prevail. Disciplinary action, if any, for faculty and staff shall be consistent with the University Standard Practice Guides and the Bylaws of the Regents of the University. Where use of external networks is involved, policies governing such use also are applicable and must be adhered to.

*Information resources in this document are meant to include any information in electronic or audiovisual format or any hardware or software that make possible the storage and use of such information. As example, included in this definition are electronic mail, local databases, externally accessed databases, CD-ROM, motion picture film, recorded magnetic media, photographs, and digitized information such as the content of MIRLYN.

Guidelines for the Administration of the Proper Use Policy of the University of Michigan: Responsible Use of Technology Resources

September 1995

"The Proper Use of Information Resources, Information Technology, and Networks at the University of Michigan" (Standard Practice Guide 601.7) applies to any member of the University community, whether at the University or elsewhere, and refers to all information resources, whether individually controlled or shared, stand alone or networked.

Continued on next page

To assist the community in the administration of the Proper Use policy, these guidelines specify the responsibilities each member of the UM community agrees to assume by his or her use of campus technology resources. It stands as the base set of guidelines for use of resources offered by all service providers (1) across campus, including the Information Technology Division, the Computer Aided Engineering Network, Medical Campus Information Technology, and others.

Service providers may supplement this document with more unit-specific guidelines for their users, but unit-specific guidelines do not supersede this document or the Proper Use policy.

The University of Michigan provides information technology resources to a large number and variety of users-faculty, staff, students, and outside clients. As members of the University of Michigan community, and in accordance with the Proper Use policy, all users have the responsibility to use those services in an effective, efficient, ethical, and legal manner. Ethical and legal standards that apply to information technology resources derive directly from standards of common sense and common decency that apply to the use of any shared resource. The campus computing community depends first upon the spirit of mutual respect and cooperation that has been fostered at the University of Michigan to resolve differences and ameliorate problems that arise from time to time.

These guidelines are published in that spirit. Their purpose is to specify user responsibilities in accordance with the Proper Use policy and to promote the ethical, legal, and secure use of computing resources for the protection of all members of the University of Michigan computing community. The University extends membership in this community to its students and employees with the stipulation that they be good citizens, and that they contribute to creating and maintaining an open community of responsible users.

Appropriate and Responsible Use

Central to appropriate and responsible use is the stipulation that, in general, computing resources shall be used in a manner consistent with the instructional, public service, research, and administrative objectives of the University. Use should also be consistent with the specific objectives of the project or task for which such use was authorized. All uses inconsistent with these objectives are considered to be inappropriate use and may jeopardize further access to services.

You should be aware that although service providers provide and preserve security of files, account numbers, authorization codes, and passwords, security can be breached through actions or causes beyond their reasonable control. You are urged, therefore, to safeguard your data, personal information, passwords and authorization codes, and confidential data; to take full advantage of file security mechanisms built into the computing systems; to choose your passwords wisely and to change them periodically; and to follow the security policies and procedures established to control access to and use of administrative data.

User Responsibilities

When you use the University of Michigan's computing services, you accept the following specific responsibilities:

1. To respect the privacy of other users; for example, you shall not intentionally seek information on, obtain copies of, or modify files, tapes, or passwords belonging to other users or the University, shall not represent others, unless authorized to do so explicitly by those users, nor shall you divulge sensitive personal data to which you have access concerning faculty, staff, or students without explicit authorization to do so.

2. To respect the rights of other users; for example, you shall comply with all University policies regarding sexual, racial, and other forms of harassment. The University of Michigan is committed to being a racially, ethnically, and religiously heterogeneous community.

3. To respect the legal protection provided by copyright and licensing of programs and data; for example, you shall not make copies of a licensed computer program to avoid paying additional license fees or to share with other users.

4. To respect the intended usage of resources; for example, you shall use only the unique name and password, funds, transactions, data, and processes assigned to you by service providers, faculty, unit heads, or project directors for the purposes specified, and shall not access or use other unique names and passwords, funds, transactions, data, or processes unless explicitly authorized to do so by the appropriate authority.

5. To respect the intended usage of systems for electronic exchange (such as e-mail, IRC, Usenet News, World Wide Web, etc.); for example, you shall not send forged electronic mail, mail that will intimidate or harass other users, chain messages that can interfere with the efficiency of the system, or promotional mail for profit-making purposes. Also, you shall not break into another user's electronic mailbox or read someone else's electronic mail without his/her permission.

6. To respect the integrity of the system or network; for example, you shall not intentionally develop or use programs, transactions, data, or processes that harass other users or infiltrate the system or damage or alter the software or data components of a system. Alterations to any system or network software or data component shall be made only under specific instructions from authorized faculty, unit heads, project directors, or management staff.

7. To respect the financial structure of a computing or networking system; for example, you shall not intentionally develop or use any unauthorized mechanisms to alter or avoid charges levied by the University for computing, network, and data processing services.

8. To adhere to all general University policies and procedures including, but not limited to, policies on proper use of information resources, information technology, and networks; acquisition, use, and disposal of University-owned computer

Continued on next page

equipment; use of telecommunications equipment; ethical and legal use of software; and ethical and legal use of administrative data.

Service Provider Responsibilities

All service providers have the responsibility to offer service in the most efficient manner while considering the needs of the total user community. At certain times, the process of carrying out these responsibilities may require special actions or intervention by service provider staff. At all other times, staff have no special rights above and beyond those of other users; they are required to follow the same policies and conditions of use that other users must follow. Every effort shall be made to ensure that persons in positions of trust do not misuse computing resources or data or take advantage of their positions to access information not required in the performance of their duties.

Service providers are not responsible for policing user activity. However, when they become aware of violations, either through the normal course of duty or by a complaint, it is their responsibility to initiate an investigation. At the same time, in order to forestall an immediate threat to the security of a system or its users, service providers may suspend access to the unique name(s) involved in the violation while the incident is being investigated. They may also take other actions to preserve the state of files and other information relevant to an investigation. Service providers will act in accordance with existing policy governing privacy of user information by seeking permission to examine the content of e-mail and other private files. In instances where user permission cannot be obtained and the content of files or e-mail may jeopardize the security of systems, safety of users, or ability of the University or its constituent parts to conduct necessary business, service providers must obtain authorization from a higher administrative authority to examine content.

Violations of Guidelines

Violations of any of the above guidelines are certainly unethical and may be violations of University policy or criminal offenses. You are expected to report information you may have concerning instances in which the above guidelines have been or are being violated. In accordance with established University practices, policies, and procedures, confirmation of inappropriate use of University of Michigan technology resources may result in termination of access, disciplinary review, expulsion, termination of employment, legal action, or other disciplinary action. Service providers will, when necessary, work with other University offices such as the Judicial Advisor, the Department of Public Safety and Security, schools and colleges disciplinary councils, the Office of the General Counsel, and others in the resolution of problems. Other Responsible Use Guidelines for Specific Services.

Additional responsible use guidelines applying to the use of networks and telecommunications services and administrative data processing systems and services can be found in GOpherBLUE and the Standard Practice Guide. Also, other external networks to which the University of Michigan maintains connections (e.g., BITNET) have established acceptable use standards (see GOpherBLUE). It is your responsibility to adhere to the standards of such networks. The University cannot and will not extend any protection to you should you violate the policies of an external network.

Reporting Incidents

In general, reports about violations of these guidelines should be directed to the administrative school, college, or unit for the system involved.

At the College of Engineering, contact CAEN Security by sending e-mail to security@engin.umich.edu or calling 763-4910.

For services provided by ITD, contact the ITD User Advocate by sending e-mail to itdua@umich.edu or calling 763-8940.

If possible, please forward a copy of any information relevant to the incident you are reporting.

If it isn't clear where to report the problem, you may send it to the ITD User Advocate. The Advocate will redirect the incident to the appropriate person(s) for action or will handle it directly.

Further Information

These guidelines and the University's Proper Use policy are available online. On the Web, use the URL: `http://www.umich.edu/` and then choose "Information Technology". In GOpherBLUE, select "Information Technology Policies and Guidelines" from the GOpherBLUE main menu.

(1) "Service provider" is used to mean a University department or unit that is providing some kind of information technology service (mail, file service, computational cycles, statistical analysis, etc.) to other users within that unit, and/or to others outside of it, on a sustained basis.

THE FOUR11 APPROPRIATE USE POLICY

The Four11 White Page Directory is an online service where Internet users can register their Internet addresses (e-mail and Web) and look for other Internet users. Free basic access, which includes a free listing and free searching, is provided to help ensure they reach their goal of creating an all-inclusive Internet white pages. The directory is funded by a combination of membership upgrades and sponsors.

Continued on next page

Here is their Appropriate Use Policy:

FOUR11 ACCEPTABLE USE POLICY

Four11 Directory Services are offered by Four11 Corp subject to rules governing the use of these systems and related services. By subscribing to and using Four11 Directory Services, you agree to abide by this Acceptable Use Policy and applicable rules.

1. You agree to use your own name and other personal information.

2. You agree not to use the system for any illegal purpose.

3. You agree not to use the directory to contact persons in ways they find objectionable.

4. You agree not to copy information from the database for commercial purposes and/or financial gain.

5. Four11 reserves the right to terminate a user's access to the system.

6. Four11 makes no warranties.

If you have any concerns or legal questions, please read our FAQ.

© 1994, 1995, 1996 Four11 Corp., All Rights Reserved

CHAPTER 20

Building the Resource

FEATURING

Chapter 20
Building the Resource

OK. You have decided that you have information you want to share. Next you need to determine the best design for your networked information system—what tools might work best for you and how to present information using them. In this chapter we discuss three relatively simple ways to provide information via the Internet—FTP, Gopher, and WWW. These methods are not mutually exclusive. You can choose to use one, two, or all three of them at the same time. We'll discuss these tools in order of their complexity (from the provider's point of view); an FTP site is the simplest to create, and a Web site is the most complex.

This chapter is intended more for the designer of the information structure than for the information systems administrator who will construct the technical configuration for the information server and will maintain that server. We do include notes about how to locate, install, and use specific server and client programs. These notes are intended simply to get a systems administrator started with these programs. More information about the server programs will be found at the Internet site that provides those programs. For example, John Franks of Northwestern University provides a server program called GN, which is capable of presenting information to both http and Gopher clients. The complete documentation for the server is located at the same address on the Internet as the server code itself. When you are ready to begin detailed implementation planning, you should read the documentation provided.

Let Client/Server Be Your Servant

FTP, Gopher, and the Web all use the client/server computing model, which (as you learned in Chapter 1) divides the various tasks between two pieces of software—a client program and a server program. In making your information available for access by one of these tools, you are designing your information server. It will "serve" (or send) your information over the Internet to anyone who has a client program that can request it (and who also has appropriate permissions, of course). In theory, this means that to get the servers working, you don't really have to worry about all the commands, programs, computers, and connections the user will rely on to seek and display the information. That is taken care of by the client software.

Practically, however, you should test your information presentation with as many different clients as you can. Not all clients are created equally. You may find that your presentation works really well in Lynx, but not in Cello (even though both are WWW clients). Then you will need to change your presentation until it looks fine using both clients.

The Systems Development Process

Designers of information systems have models that help them design and implement systems. These models are sets of steps that help to prevent some (but not all) mistakes in building information systems. The specifications and the steps we list don't need to take a long time to produce, nor do they need to be very formal in all cases. But if you take the time to do a bit of planning, we believe you will save time in the long run—you won't need to "re"-implement because someone didn't like what you produced. We like the development model that has these phases:

Functional Specifications: A written plan that outlines what information you are trying to convey and to which intended audience. A good place to begin is an inventory of the information you want to dispense. The types (and forms) of your information may dictate the tools you will want to use. For instance, if most of the information you have to present is in the form of graphical images, or if your information includes sound files, you probably will want to use the Web. If the information you have doesn't include graphical images, you may want to add images to your information. Again, you'll need to think about who your audience may be and how best to reach them. If you expect that your audience will not be able to use Web browsers but will have access to an FTP client, you will want to provide an FTP server instead of a Web server. The information gathering and analysis that you will do for a functional specification will help you decide what tools will best suit your needs. If you have any constraints (for example, what kind of computer you must use, or when the project should be complete), they should be included explicitly in your plan. It is also a good idea to include a section that describes any assumptions you are making. If you expressly state your assumptions, you may be able to prevent later misunderstandings. When everyone who has a "stake" in the system has agreed to your description, you'll have "buy-in" for your project.

Detailed Specifications: This is the stage at which you expand on your functional specification to describe what server software you have chosen and exactly how the information you are serving will be updated. The analysis that leads to writing these specifications is the important step. The specifications themselves are simply the documentation of your decisions.

Implementation: You may not believe this now, but this is the easy part. In this step you obtain the server software and documentation, install it on your chosen server hardware, and then configure the software and hardware to work properly in your environment. You obtain copies of the information you are going to present and store it on the server. Of course, "you" here can mean one person or a team of people working together. Implementation should include trying out all the client software you can to make certain that your information is presented well in as many different clients as possible.

Testing: In this phase, the specifications are compared to the system as implemented. When the system and the specifications don't match, you'll need someone to decide which gets changed. Sometimes the specifications need to be changed because of something you learned in implementation. In other cases, the implementors erred and the system will need to be changed.

Deployment: Announce your service. Accept congratulations. Prepare your plan for periodic review of your information service, because the systems development process is a continuing one.

Design Considerations

Presenting information via FTP, Gopher, and/or WWW is relatively easy for those with a little technical skill. This ease of implementation has both its good points and its bad points. Ease of implementation enables your organization to make information available quickly, for instance. However, because many organizations don't yet know about or have firm policies about Internet information and presentation (and because a person with technical skills rather than presentation skills may have done the implementation), not all information presentations are well designed. Here we've tried to list some things to keep in mind while designing and implementing your own information exposition so that your ideas can be conveyed effectively.

Keep Your Information Presentation Simple and Clean

In any design, leaving space between and among the words and images helps the reader/viewer to "receive" the messages much easier.

For an FTP space, this means grouping similar files together within a single directory. Collect similar directories together to provide an "Information Tree" that your viewer can follow. Provide an Index or Readme file at each level of your information to describe the contents of each directory. Provide a "terms and conditions statement" that informs your viewers of their responsibilities as well as yours.

For a linking Gopher menu (one that leads to other menus as opposed to one that is a document or downloadable image file), keeping your presentation simple means keeping your Gopher menu titles short but descriptive. For most Gopher menus, keep the number of items on the menu to 15 or fewer so that the viewer can reasonably choose an appropriate item. Figure 20.1 shows the top-level menu for the Netcom Gopher server. You can see that it is easy to choose among these menu items.

If you are linking to an item that's not on your own server, include this information in your menu item. A parenthetical statement of source (for example, "from Notre Dame") is fine. The wonderful Internet Assistance section of the University of California at Irvine's PEG (Peripatetic, Eclectic Gopher) Gopher breaks the "don't put too many items on the menu" rule very successfully (see Figure 20.2). Cal Boyer has built a valuable entry point to many information sources about the Internet. When you are building a comprehensive resource you won't necessarily want to divide your information into smaller sections, making deeper information trees. Note that Boyer does indicate in his menu titles when the information is from another location.

For a linking Web page (one that leads to other pages as opposed to one that is a document or downloadable image file), keeping it simple means including plenty of "white space" around your information.

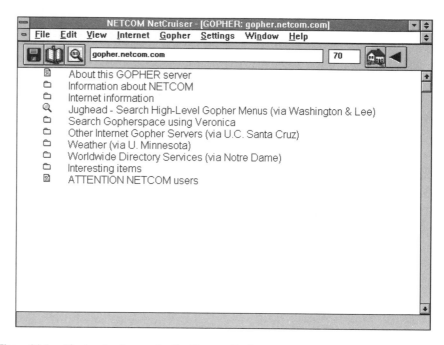

Figure 20.1.   The top-level menu for the Netcom Gopher server.

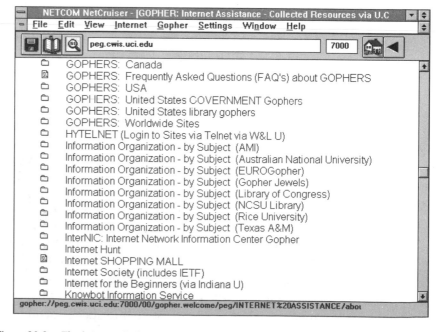

Figure 20.2.   The Internet Assistance section of the PEG Gopher.

Allow for Users Who Cannot View Graphics

Remember that many people (at least for the next several years) are looking at your design with computers that may not be able to display graphics; there may also be people who have chosen to turn off the automatic download of them (as Glee does) so that the display of the Web page does not take anywhere near as long. Use the graphics to illustrate, not necessarily to inform—or make parallel implementations for those with graphics and those without.

Allow for the User's Choice of Fonts

Remember that you can't count on everyone choosing the same default fonts for the headings and text in their Web browser, and that not every Web browser allows the page to override the client's settings. Don't count on the particular look of a font. If the font choice is very important to you, make the font part of a displayable graphic image, rather than part of the text.

MASTER WORDS   To make a displayable graphic of your text, use a drawing or desktop publishing program. Enter the text in the work area, use the tools of the program to select the appropriate font, font size, and any emphasis characteristics like bold or italics. Make the complete image the appropriate size and shape for your Web page. Save your image in GIF or JPG format. Transfer your image to a computer and directory that can be accessed by your http daemon program. Then include a link to the image (and any alternate text for nongraphical browsers) in your hypertext document.

Test, Test, and Test Again

Test your design and implementation on all the clients and platforms that you know about. Of course, not every designer and implementor has access to several kinds of Internet accounts or different computer systems (like both a Macintosh and a DOS computer) or to different types of Web browsers or Gopher clients. First, test using all the ways you can. Then do the next thing, ask your friends to help. You can also ask people who are on a mailing list or newsgroup in which you participate to test for you and report back. This kind of "early release" testing is the best way to get good feedback from people who have different types of connections. Many of your fellow Internauts will be happy to help you.

Ask an Outsider to "Test-Drive" Your Information

Your "guinea pig" should be someone unfamiliar with your product, service, or organization. If it isn't clear to your tester why something is there, take it out. This type of testing can be done by people anywhere on the Internet, but you might want to be in the same room with your early testers so that you see and hear their first reactions. Make sure any questions your tester might have about your organization, products, or services are clearly answered. And remember to listen to their comments. Their reactions should cause you to modify your design and/or implementation before you release them to the world at large.

Think about the Next Generation of Information Dispensers

As object-oriented systems become more prevalent and allow specific players/viewers to be shipped with the data and information, there will be more rather than fewer things to think about when you design for the user. Will what you are designing now lead to an improved design in the future?

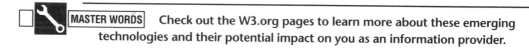

MASTER WORDS Check out the W3.org pages to learn more about these emerging technologies and their potential impact on you as an information provider.

A Design Rule

You have probably noticed that we don't usually state our ideas in terms of rules. Partly that's because we believe in people choosing their own rules (at least for rules of reference) and partly it's because we both like (and approve of) lots of options for people. There is one rule that you must follow, however. *Don't put anything up on your information server that you don't have permission to distribute.* This means any information whose copyright you or your organization does not own should not be distributed via your information service. There is no difference between an FTP space, a Gopher server, or a Web page and any other publishing mechanism in the eyes of the law. Stealing someone's intellectual property (whether it is a graphic image, a sound file, a document, or a software program) is against United States law. You can be prosecuted.

In the United States, you also may not distribute child pornography (via electronic or any other means). Other jurisdictions may have other laws that can apply to what is and is not legal to distribute.

United States laws with regard to electronic information are not extensive yet. There is much work to be done. Fortunately, with the help of the publishing mechanism of the Internet itself, you can (and should) keep up by watching and reading the materials stored at the Electronic Frontier Foundation

```
http://www.eff.org
```

As more agencies of government (United States and others) come online, there will be more attention given to laws about what is and is not legal to distribute.

Who Is (or Should Be) Your Audience?

As we've noted before, the people who use and cruise the Internet are quite varied. They could be geographically located in any place in the world where one can obtain telephone service. They could speak or read almost any language (although today there are more connections in English-speaking countries). They could be any age (elementary school children to respected elders). They could have any kind of equipment from very old 1200 baud modems and green-on-black screens to many-colored displays directly attached to a very high speed connection. You will need to decide whether you are going to try to reach *all* the users on the Internet as your audience, or to target a specific subset. As you work on your information presentation, you will want to keep your audience in mind.

Figure 20.3 shows the DernWeb page of Daniel P. Dern, Internet Pundit, Curmudgeon, (and friend). This page is designed so that all the information is equally available to anyone regardless of the type of terminal and Web browser. Actually, if you visit Daniel's page and take the link marked "Don't Click Here if you are using Netscape," you'll find interesting information about lots of other browsers.

As a contrast, let's look at the home page for the online magazine *HotWired*. Here the designers have chosen to target their audience to those with faster connections and with good graphical browsers. Figure 20.4 illustrates the kind of presentation that is possible if you target the higher-end audience. Although there is an alternate textual interface, this site is not really designed for use without a graphical browser. The folks at *HotWired* believe that more and more people will get better and better connections to the Internet, and they design for the audience they want to have. These are the two extremes; you'll want to figure out where your server should fit on the scale of what is possible.

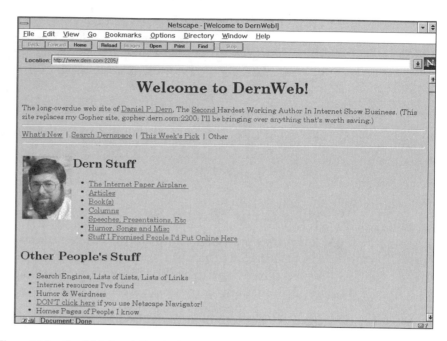

Figure 20.3.   Daniel P. Dern's DernWeb page.

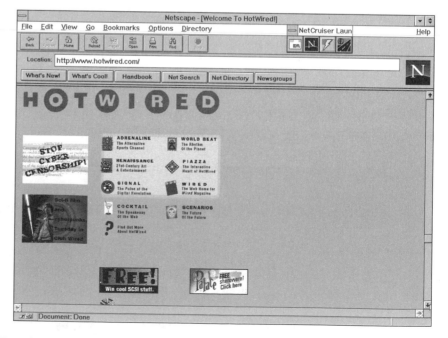

Figure 20.4.   The Web home page for the online magazine HotWired.

Choosing and Connecting Your Server

Once you have delineated the information you wish to serve and the audience you wish to reach, you will have a preliminary idea of the type of server software you will wish to operate. The other important factor in a good information service on the Internet is the speed and connectivity of the server hardware itself.

If you have the ability to specify new hardware and Internet connections, you will want to try to get a high-bandwidth connection and you will want to run a fast computer. (This is the same as you want to do as an Internet information consumer.) The processor speed and connection bandwidth will affect how quickly users can access your information and how many can access it simultaneously.

Must You Use UNIX?

Many of the Internet tools are written in UNIX. UNIX is a complex and rich environment, and most UNIX implementations include native TCP/IP implementations; this makes it relatively easy for programs written for one implementation to be moved (or "ported") from one UNIX environment to another. These facts explain why there are so many server programs written for the UNIX environment. Because many of the tools were written as part of grants where the funding was public funds, and because of the cooperative nature of the Internet, many of these server programs are in the public domain and easily accessible for you to use on your own computer. If your site already has expertise running a UNIX environment, a UNIX information server is probably the best choice. Such server environments typically come with an FTP daemon that can be configured to serve information. The http and Gopher daemons can be obtained from the Internet and configured to serve information. Then you are ready to begin structuring your information as you designed.

 MASTER WORDS   *Daemons* are the programs that listen for requests coming in to a server from the Internet. They are usually started when your computer is turned on. When a request arrives, the daemon "reads" the request and acts on it. For example, if an anonymous FTP request comes in, the daemon connects the request to the "anonymous" account, making the directory tree (all the information that the account is permitted to view, write, or execute) available to the connected user.

Even if your site does not have experience running a UNIX environment, you may still want to use a UNIX server because of the availability of specific tools. There are an increasing number of relatively inexpensive UNIX servers ($10,000 to $15,000 or so, including both the hardware and the software) that can provide a base system from which to grow. When you are evaluating server packages, make certain to include configuration and management software so that you can effectively manage your server.

It is possible to run Web and Gopher servers on higher-end Macintosh and PC platforms. These platforms are suitable for schools and nonprofit organizations that do not expect a lot of network traffic. One of the resources we list, the Prince Edward Island Crafts Council, uses a pretty small server. If you connect to that resource:

```
http://www.crafts-council.pe.ca
```

you can see the results. On a PC you can choose from among several operating environments, such as Microsoft Windows, Microsoft Windows NT or Windows 95, or a few UNIX implementations.

The speed of your operating environment is not the only consideration. You'll want to connect your server to as fast a network connection as you can reasonably afford. The lowest-speed connection from which you can provide information is a dedicated 14.4 Kbps connection. With the compression algorithms that are built into these modems, you can achieve higher transfer rates. Compression will be used if both your modem and the modem used by your Internet service provider can use the same transfer protocols, so this is not something you would have to think about after making sure that you and your provider "speak" the same protocols. 28.8 Kbps modems are becoming more common. Again, with compression, these can transmit at higher speeds. Some Internet service providers can connect you using ISDN connections. This technology makes it possible to move multiple data streams through a conventional telephone line. ISDN is considerably faster than a 14.4 or 28.8 modem, but it requires synchronous communications processing that can be expensive to add to a computer (for both ends of the connection).

Without going to ISDN, the next level, 56 Kbps, provides a significant jump in speed (and cost). Here you will need a router (a special-purpose computer that moves packets off of and on to the Internet from your site) and special purpose connection equipment called CSUs/DSUs. The equipment is more expensive, as is the price your Internet service provider will charge you. Internet Distribution Services has one of their servers connected at this speed. Go to Internet Distribution Services

`http://www.service.com`

to see this type of link.

Finally, if you will want to provide a large number of big graphics files, a lot of sound files, and/or a lot of motion picture files, you'll want to have a server connected at the T1 rate. The MCA server, located at

`http://www.mca.com`

is an example of a site that offers sound and movie clips. Figure 20.5 shows the top of the MCA Web page.

MASTER WORDS   Remember that the connection of your server to the Internet is only one part of the service equation: the connection of your potential customers is an important part of their perception of your service.

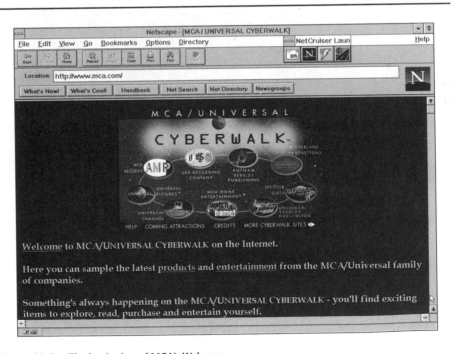

*Figure 20.5.   **The beginning of MCA's Web page.***

Now that we've covered some of the criteria for good design and service, you should be ready to think about which kind of presentation will work best for your information.

Providing Information via FTP

FTP is the most basic form of Net communication. People have been using it for years to move data, images, and information between specific points. FTP's strength is the efficient transfer of data between two connected computers. In Chapter 9 you learned how to find and retrieve files from FTP servers that others have provided. Here we discuss how to set up your own FTP server. If you'd like more information about the underlying FTP protocol itself, you'll find it in RFC 959. Figure 20.6 shows the Web version of RFC 959 as done by Tim Berners-Lee, the "father" of the World Wide Web.

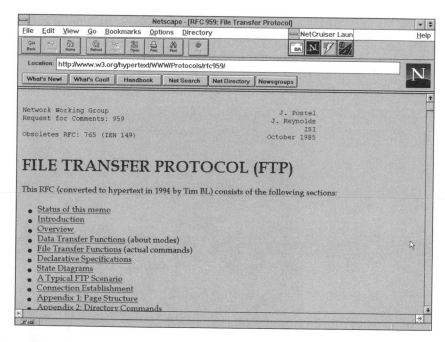

Figure 20.6.   RFC 959 as it appears on the Web.

What You'll Need

In order to create your own FTP server (or "FTP space"), you will need, in addition to a computer capable of running FTP and connected to the Internet, the following:

Information you want to provide. The design work of an FTP space is organizing the information in some reasonable manner (similar files in the same directory, for example). Of course, "reasonable" is in the eye of the beholder. It's a good idea to show your design schema to someone else before you implement it. Testing your design this way can save you time and effort if your design isn't clear to someone else.

A plan for security. File permissions must be established to restrict users to read from or write to specific files within specific directories.

The authority to set up a user account (usually either "anonymous" or "FTP") using standard procedures for setting up a new user. This authority resides with a systems administrator for your system.

The authority to create directories within the appropriate user account. If you have the password for the account you can do this.

The FTP daemon (ftpd) should be started each time the system is started. You should be able to find more information about ftpd on your system by entering the command man ftpd at the command prompt.

The following additional items are also valuable:

Readme or Index files in each directory to tell your users what they can expect to find in your FTP space. An index usually contains the name of each file in the directory and a short description of the contents of the file.

Terms-and-conditions statements. Your organization's legal staff might require you to add such statements. Or maybe you'll want to add copyright and service mark information for your organization's products and services. Figure 20.7 shows an example of such a terms-and-conditions statement. Here Netcom reminds the user that the FTP archive is provided as a service to Netcom customers and that all risks are borne by the user. There is also a warning that access to the Netcom FTP archive is logged.

You can choose to "log" or record the address of each user who accesses your FTP space. Logging is a good idea. With logging you can have some idea who has been visiting. Furthermore, you can run statistical processing programs on the logged information. These programs can give you an idea of the type of user by domain, or the times of day when your FTP space is the busiest, and the like. Reviewing the logs can help you improve your service.

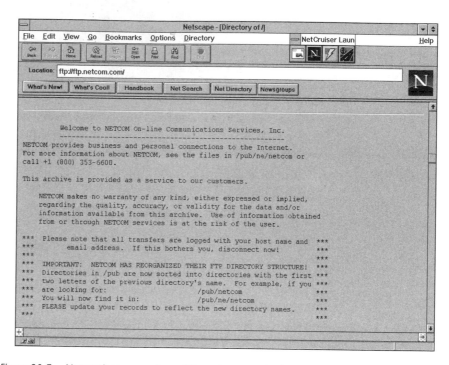

Figure 20.7. Netcom's terms-and-conditions statement for its FTP archive.

Anonymous FTP

Recall from Chapter 9 that with FTP you can make your files accessible to anyone who has an Internet connection, or you can restrict access so that specific login names are required. The first option is known as anonymous FTP (because anyone can log in using the account anonymous), and it's the method used by most organizations that publish files to be copied by FTP.

The strength of anonymous FTP lies not only in the fact that every user has access to the files you've chosen to make available in this way, but also in the fact that the informed Internet user can guess to look for such access given the name of any particular domain.

Remember the Domain Naming System we talked about in Chapter 3? You can use that system to set up an address for your site that anyone who's interested can easily find. For example, suppose a Macintosh user wants to see what information (and perhaps software enhancements) Apple Computer provides for anonymous FTP. She could reasonably guess that the domain name would be apple.com, and attach to ftp .apple.com.

If your site already has a domain name, you should have the computer (or host) for your FTP space configured with the name ftp.*your.domain*. If you don't have a domain name yet, you'll need to work with your Internet service provider to have one assigned and registered. This is usually part of connecting your server or network to the Internet. After your domain name is assigned, you should have the host computer where you will be running the FTP service configured to respond to the name ftp.*your.domain*.

Helping Users Find Your Files

Once users have found your FTP site, they also need to find specific files within your directory structure. You can make that task easier for them by following a few simple conventions. The first convention is to place the available files in a directory named /pub/. This name usually denotes that the directory is public. Members of the public may only be able to read files in the directory, not write to them, but anyone who can access the computer system using the account anonymous can read from the directory.

If the files you're making available are executable programs, it's conventional to group them into subdirectories by platform or operating system. Put your Macintosh programs in a directory named /mac/; your DOS programs in /msdos/, /pcdos/, /dos/, or /pc/; your Windows (version 3 or later) in /win3/; and your Windows 95 programs in a directory named /win95/. Similarly, your UNIX software might go into directories named, for example, /sun/ or /bsd/; or you might place them all in a directory named /bin/. A directory named /doc/ is a good place to put documentation.

Within each directory, it's a good idea to place a text file called something like 00index or 00Readme or Readme or Index to describe the contents of the directory. (The zeroes at the beginning of the file name cause the item to appear first in an alphabetical directory listing.)

Besides listing and describing available files, your Readme files should describe the terms and conditions of use for the available files. Both items should carry the date they were last changed. This helps the user determine whether the information is current.

In very active FTP spaces, some publishers also make available a file that describes any recent changes to the FTP space—additions, enhancements, deletions, and so on. Figure 20.8 shows the Readme file from the Oakland University Oak archive.

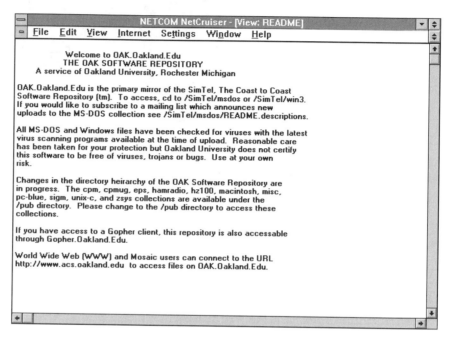

Figure 20.8. The Readme file from Oakland University's Oak archive.

Usually Readme files are text files that can be displayed easily. Sometimes the more complex files are arranged in reverse chronological order. That is, there will be a heading at the top of the file with the date of the last changes to the directory. Following the date will be a short paragraph describing the changes. Then there is a line with the date of the previous change followed by its descriptive paragraph, and so on. Each time there is a change, the maintainer inserts a date and descriptive paragraph at the top of the file. Such a file provides the user with a brief history of the development of the space—a very nice feature indeed.

An anonymous FTP space can be a convenient place for people to leave files for your organization, too. For example, suppose your business is having some work done by an outside consultant. If that consultant is connected to the Internet, drafts of the consultant's work or reports might be left in your FTP directory for review. This is both quicker and less expensive than using a courier service.

If you expect that people will be leaving documents, information, or programs on your computer, for simple security you should set up a separate directory (usually called /incoming/) for them to use. That way, you can set the permissions on the files that you want people to transfer to read-only. The directory where you want people to leave things for you must have its permissions set to write. Otherwise the person who is trying to store a file on your computer will have that transmission refused. Usually, you won't want people to have write access to your complete FTP space. Including an /incoming/ directory and designating it as the only directory within the anonymous account to have write access will take care of that problem.

Security for Incoming Files

You should be aware of a potential misuse of /incoming FTP directories—as a "drop point" for software pirates. In 1994, someone left 60 MB of copyrighted software in an /incoming directory of one of the more popular archives on the Internet. The software pirate then "announced" the action to many by telling people about the directory, and these people told others. The software was distributed throughout the Internet.

There is a program available for UNIX systems at the archive at Washington University in St. Louis:

```
wuarchive.wustl.edu
```

that offers a solution. It sets up a process so that materials dropped into /incoming by an anonymous user will have the permissions set to another account resident on that computer system. This will stop someone from using your anonymous FTP space as a transshipment point for files. There may be similar programs for non-UNIX systems, or you may wish to have something similar written for your system.

Who's Playing in Your Space?

Many FTP daemons offer the ability to log transactions. This is a very nice feature if you want to track access to your FTP space. You can either write a small program to process the log and produce reports that tell you what files are more popular, or you can search for such a program on the Internet. This is the kind of feedback that you don't often get just by making material available.

If you are going to log transactions, it is usually good netiquette to tell people so. You can put this announcement in the Readme file you have placed in your directory for people to read.

Again, Washington University in St. Louis (`wuarchive.wustl.edu`) has some very good logging software for keeping track of who's been connecting to your FTP server and taking and leaving materials. The directory /wuarchive-ftpd/ has the entire `wuarchive` FTP server and associated software available for downloading.

Dos and Don'ts for Providing Anonymous FTP

Do make an index file (and keep it up to date).

Do make any terms and conditions clear.

Do structure the directories so that people can find things: keep related things together and name them clearly.

Do make a special directory for people to leave files for you.

Do use archive management software that changes permissions on incoming files so that no one can use it as a transfer point for stolen software. This protects you.

Don't forget to keep copies of your information in some other electronic form (on another disk, on a tape, on diskette, etc.) in case your disk fails.

Providing Information via Gopher

The best reasons to publish your information via Gopher are its ease of use, its ease of implementation, and the near-ubiquity of simple clients. Pretty much anyone who is connected to the Internet has access to a simple Gopher client.

Gopher is very popular. There are thousands of servers around the globe. If you add one, you'll be part of an interconnected network of *information*, not just a network of computers. The servers (assuming you choose to announce your Gopher server to the world for other Gophers to link to) can provide access to vast quantities of information in a simple-to-learn format. And you can use it to connect to other services through several "gateway" Gophers or links—Telnet or e-mail or telephone directories. Also, of course, it's fun.

If It's So Easy...

Why doesn't everyone use it? Well, some people don't like the fact that all the servers are connected to one another in such an unstructured way. They find this especially confusing because the design of the menus makes Gopher appear structured. Also, there really isn't a good way of conveying enough information in a menu item. The indexing is a little wacky (there is no good way to eliminate duplicate entries, for example), and the presentation of the search results as a menu with little or no hint as to where the menu item resides can be really confusing.

What You'll Need

In order to create your own Gopher server (or "gopherhole"), you need the following:

Gopher server software that will work in your computing environment or the ability to add information to a Gopher server being managed by someone else. Suitable Gopher servers can be found from the University of Minnesota team

    boombox.micro.umn.edu

or the GN server from John Frank at Northwestern University

    http://hopf.math.nwu.edu:70/

The examples in this section were taken from the GN server.

Files of text, images, or information that you want to serve. The best design document for a Gopher server is an outline (Gopher is hierarchical, so an outline best mirrors the organization of your Gopher server) organized in some reasonable manner (similar files on the same menu, for example).

File permissions established to allow users to read from specific files within specific directories pointed to by the menu structure. If you neglect to make the files readable, people will be able to select the menu item but not to see the actual file.

You'll also find the following items valuable:

Readme or Index files in each directory. A good place for these is usually at the top of the menu for that directory.

A link from the top-level menu to a gopherspace search server (Veronica) so that your clients can find materials that are not on your server.

Terms-and-conditions statements. Your organization's legal staff might require you to add such statements. Or maybe you'll want to add copyright and service mark information for your organization's products and services.

A facility that allows your user to search either the directory contents or the file contents of the information contained within your Gopher server.

Logging and statistical processing of the logs so you have some idea who has been visiting.

Copies of the public domain and commercial Gopher clients for as many of the computing platforms as possible, so that you'll be able to test your design and implementation. At least obtain the major ones for the most common platforms: Macintosh, DOS, and UNIX systems.

Getting and Installing the GN Server

Rather than taking the time and space to rewrite the excellent documentation that accompanies John Frank's GN Gopher, we'll just point you to the code and the documentation and give you enough to get started. You can use your Web browser or your Gopher client to read the documentation or to download the software. The URL is

```
http://hopf.math.nwu.edu:70/
```

or

```
gopher://hopf.math.nwu.edu
```

Or you can use anonymous FTP to connect to

```
ftp.acns.nwu.edu
```

In the pub/gn directory you will find the latest copy of the GN code in a ".tar.gz" file. Transfer the file using binary mode. Uncompress the code, configure the server as specified in the documentation, compile it, and install it. After you have installed the server, you will need to add GN to your `inetd` configuration tables. (Inetd is the process that controls a lot of the UNIX networking processes.) Then, you are ready to create the data directories and put the information into them.

A Few Implementation Details

While the focus of this chapter is on designing information presentation, it is helpful to know a few things about implementation details because they may affect what you are able to do as well as how it is done. (If the next few paragraphs of information are more than you want to know about implementing Gopher menus, please feel free to skip this part and go on to more design issues.)

Gopher clients read and act on two kinds of files that they obtain from a Gopher server as a result of a Gopher request: the file that builds and displays the Gopher menu (the links file) and the file that transmits the information that the viewer wants, no matter what format (image or text, for instance) the information is in (the item itself). The links file is read by the client program and used to display the menu for the user. When a particular item is selected, the Gopher client uses the data stored with the menu name in the links file to construct the next Gopher request. If the item requested is another menu, another links file is fetched and another Gopher menu is constructed and displayed. If the item requested is the last point on the information tree, the item is fetched and displayed or stored.

You need a links file on your server for each menu that you want to present. A links file is created by processing a file that contains lines of text with specific "command" words that tell your Gopher server what to do with the information stored on that line. Figure 20.1, earlier in this chapter, shows the relatively simple top-level menu that makes the gopher.netcom.com Gopher. The links file was built from command word data fed to a program called *mkcache*. This program creates the links file that the server returns as a Gopher request result. Compare the menu presented to the file that produced it (shown on the following pages), and you can see what we mean.

Giving the User Choices

The top-level menu in the Netcom Gopher offers the user a small number of items that can be easily read. The choices that are presented are sufficiently different that the user can quickly decide what path is appropriate for the task at hand.

If the user chooses the first or last item, a text file is presented. That file is stored in the current directory. The name of the file appears in the Path= statement.

If the second, third, or ninth choice is selected, Gopher presents another menu, stored in the directory referenced by the path statement. Gopher changes its pointers to the new directory, and displays the file named Menu in that new directory. The menu file will appear similar to this one, except, of course, that it will point to other files and links.

If the fourth, fifth, sixth, seventh, or eighth choice is selected, the server connects to the host listed in the Host= statement and presents the menu item listed in the Path= statement. Notice that you can specify more than one level of menu from the linked Gopher. Each slash (/) in the path statement represents a level in the linked menu. For example, the statement

```
Path=1/The World/Other Internet Gopher Servers
```

presents the menu (type=1) linked by the "The World" menu and within that menu the Other Internet Gopher Servers menu from the host scilibx.ucsc.edu. When the user selects Other Internet Gopher Servers from the Netcom Gopher menu, the next menu that is presented comes from the University of California, Santa Cruz (UCSC) server. Specifically, it comes from the The World selection in that server's top-level menu and then from the Other Internet... selection within the next menu. This way you can link material to your Gopher that your clients might find very useful, no matter what menu level the material may have in some other Gopher.

BEHIND THE NETCOM GOPHER MENU

```
# This is the top-level menu for the NETCOM gopher.
# Comments are in italics.
Name=About this GOPHER server
Path=0/about.server
Type=0
# This section provides a pointer to a file within the
# same directory as this links file.

Name=Information about NETCOM
Path=1s/guest
Type=1
# This section provides a pointer to another directory on
# the same computer system as this links file.

Name=Internet information
Path=1s/internet-info
Type=1
# This section provides a pointer to another directory on
# the same computer as this links file.

Name=Jughead - Search High-Level Gopher Menus (via Washington &
Lee)
Path=
Type=7
Host=liberty.uc.wlu.edu
```

```
Port=3002
# This section provides a pointer to a search service on
# another computer system.

Name=Search Gopherspace using Veronica
Path=1/veronica
Type=1
Host=veronica.scs.unr.edu
Port=70
# This section provides a pointer menu that points
# to a search service on another computer system.

Name=Other Internet Gopher Servers (via U.C. Santa Cruz)
Path=1/The World/Other Internet Gopher Servers
Host=scilibx.ucsc.edu
Port=70
# This section provides a pointer to a menu on another
# computer system.

Name=Weather (via U. Minnesota)
Path=1/Weather
Host=ashpool.micro.umn.edu
Port=70
# This section provides a pointer to a menu on another
# computer system.

Name=Worldwide Directory Services (via Notre Dame)
Path=1/Non-Notre Dame Information Sources/Phone Books—Other
Institutions
Host=gopher.nd.edu
port=70
# This section provides a pointer to a menu on another
# computer system.

Name=Interesting items
Path=1/interesting-items
Type=1
# This section provides a pointer to a menu on the same
# computer system as this links file.

Name=ATTENTION NETCOM users
Path=0/netcom.notice
Type=0
# This section provides a pointer to a file in the same
# directory as this links file.
```

The Structure of a Gopher Menu Entry

From the example, you can see that entries in a Gopher menu file have a common structure:

Comments can be liberally sprinkled throughout the menu. If you add them, someone coming along after you may be able to understand what you intended. You identify a comment by putting a "#" in the first character of the field.

Each menu item has a `Name=` statement. The words following the equal sign will be displayed on the screen for the user to select.

Each menu item has a `Path=` statement. This statement contains the type of the data, followed by a slash (/) character and then the path name for linked entry. The path may include multiple levels of a Gopher directory hierarchy, if the pointer is to a linked Gopher.

That's all you really need, if all the items you are going to link are stored on the same computer with your server. However, if you are linking in menus from Gopher servers on other computers, you will need `Type=`, `Host=`, and `Port=` fields. These fields tell your server what remote computer (the "host") to connect to; what TCP/IP "port" to connect to, and what information it must ask for when it gets the connection to the remote computer.

One of the Gopher information types is "menu." This tells the server that the information that will be displayed is another list of links that the user may choose. When the host statement is not present, the menu will be found in the path specified on the current host. This is how you link in menus that are lower in your hierarchy of design.

Build Your Next-Level Menus

Once you have coded your top-level menu, you know exactly how to code the rest of your information. Simply follow the design that you outlined, making sure that you store your menu, image, and data files in the appropriate directory for your menu in order to link them in. Then you just repeat the process until you're done.

GOPHER FILE TYPES

Gopher servers can serve a number of different kinds of file types. To do this successfully, the server must have information about what kind of file any particular file is—so that the user's client will not try to send an ASCII text file through a graphical viewer, for example. Or so it won't try to send a search through a sound file. Here are the file types that you'll need to know to set up your menus so that Gopher can process them as you intended:

0   Plain or HTML text. The server will transmit the contents of the file as it is stored. The client will display it. If the file type has a Z appended to it, it is compressed (type=0Z). The Gopher server will automatically uncompress it before handing it to a client.

1   The menu. This type defines the contents as a set of links to other files. The server transmits it as text. The client presents it as the next set of choices for the user.

2   A link to the CSO telephone book servers. Gopher passes this on to the CSO servers. The server transmits it as stored. The data is simply a URL.

3   An error message from the server.

4   Binary files processed by the Macintosh Binhex program. Transmitted as text files.

5   DOS .exe files. Binary files.

6   UUencoded files. Transmitted as text files.

7   A menu that invokes special processing within the server—for example, searches of the Gopher menus.

8   A link to the Telnet protocol: Gopher passes this on to Telnet. Not all clients implement this link.

9   Binary files. If the file type has a Z appended to it, it is compressed (type=9Z). The Gopher server will automatically uncompress it before handing it to a client.

I   Binary image files. If the file type has a Z appended to it, it is compressed (type=IZ). The Gopher server will automatically uncompress it before handing it to a client.

s   Binary sound files. If the file type has a Z appended to it, it is compressed (type=sZ). The Gopher server will automatically uncompress it before handing it to a client.

Public vs. Private Gopherholes

If you want to limit access to your information to specific people or groups of people, you may do so. The GN Gopher is very flexible and you can set your server up to allow the "world" into much of your Gopher and yet allow a restricted set of domains or addresses to access material intended only for that group. This feature allows you to present both private and public information from the same Gopher.

Peering into Gopherspace

There are several Gopher design techniques that you can use to help your users find things within your gopherspace.

The first and simplest is to include a file within each directory that lists what the user can expect to find linked to each menu item. The hardest thing about this technique is to remember to change the text when you change the menus. One way to leave yourself a reminder is to use the comment field within the menu. Include a comment that says

```
# Description of menu items—remember to update!
```

or something similar.

The second method is to provide a search capability. Searching in Gopher causes the servers to build a new menu display, with any file that contains the search term listed as an entry. With the GN server, there are two methods you can use to do this.

The Simple Search

The first is a simple search that works really well if you keep the number of files to less than 100 or so and the files are not very large. To build the simple search mechanism, you add two menu entries to your Gopher menu. The first entry tells the server that you are providing searching:

```
Path=1s/directory path and file name
```

Adding the "s" to the type code gives the server permission to run searches on the files in the named directory.

Then you add another menu entry:

```
Path=7g/directory path and file name
```

This tells the server that the directory may be searched with a UNIX "grep-like" search. The "7" tells the server "search." The "g" tells the server "grep-like." Grep is the "regular expression" search, which is rather complicated and really beyond the scope of this book. Generally, simple requests—for example, using a single word or word part as a search argument—will return results that are useful.

Providing Efficient Service

If you have really large files, you may want to store them in compressed format. The servers are capable of keeping documents in compressed format and uncompressing them only when it is time to transfer them to a client process. To do that you need only compress the files that you want to serve, and add a pointer to the decompression program that you'd like to use in the configuration file set up when you install your Gopher server. When you set up your menu, add a letter "Z" to the path type field to tell the server that the named file is compressed and instruct the server to uncompress it when required.

You can even give your users a choice with compressed files—just put in two menu items for the same file, one with the "Z" added to the path type and one without it. The user who chose the second option would have the compressed file moved to his/her computer system and would uncompress it at that site. People might want to do this if the files are particularly large. Obviously, larger files take longer to transfer than smaller files, and sometimes time connected to the network is of more concern than work performed on the local computer. Whoever does it, uncompression/expansion is done only once. If you choose to compress, you'll want to add information somewhere about what compression program you used. Remember, compression programs are not all compatible with each other; one program may not be able to expand another program's output.

Think about the User's Needs

When you design your Gopher menus, think about the information needs of the users who will most often access it. The Netcom Gopher, for example, serves (usually) as an entry point into the larger Internet gopherspace. The UCSC Gopher, by contrast, is serving information about its locality, and it's a focal point for a very specific geographical and institutional location. Its top-level menus are designed to serve the students, faculty, and staff of the University of California, Santa Cruz. These are of less interest to subscribers to Netcom, so the links are best made directly to the lower level to be useful for most Netcom users.

Check the Links

Once you have constructed your Gopher, you'll need to test it. Make sure that each and every link works—that is, that it jumps to the server you intended and to the file or menu you intended. You'll also need to make sure that you do a "link" audit periodically. Gophers move their holes. Files move from Gopher to Gopher. Servers shut down, or move domains, or...

Over time you'll want to modify the links to point to new and interesting places to visit, to improve the information you provide about your organization, or to remove links to places that disappeared from cyberspace.

Dos and Don'ts for Gopherhole Diggers

Do make an outline. Since Gopher uses hierarchies, outlines are a most effective design tool.

Do make sure your file permissions are set properly so that they can be read by the intended readers and not written to by people who shouldn't be writing to them.

Don't put too many items on a single menu. Make the hierarchies deeper if you can, instead. This makes choosing among the items on the list easier for the user.

Do make explicit the difference between links to data on your server and to data elsewhere on the Net. You need to make it clear that you aren't responsible for all the information accessible through your server.

Do put in a disclaimer that holds your organization harmless from incorrect information received via your server.

Do point to the gateway servers if your system doesn't provide complete access to all the services available on the Internet. You can let people use WAIS, X.500 directories, time-of-day around the world, and so on from within your Gopher server.

Don't point to FTP access if your system also provides FTP. Using Gopher to serve FTP files is not a good use of resources. Direct use of FTP is much more efficient.

Do check your Gopher links to see if they still point to what you thought. A good program to do this is go4check, a Perl utility that will help automate your link audit.

Do review your text files every four or five weeks. Periodic checking prevents possible embarrassment.

Do spell-check your menus.

Do have someone other than the person who designed it look at the menu structure. Maybe it only makes sense to the designer.

Don't forget to keep copies of your link files and data on another disk, a tape, or diskette, in case your disk fails.

Don't install your server or the files (images or information) that you want to serve on an account owned by a person. If you do, you will need to find that person each time you want to enhance your server. Make the "owner" of the directories an account named for the function (for example, you might name the account "gopher-master" or "support").

Do read the documentation provided by the server software's authors. It contains valuable information that will improve your ability to do a good design and provide a good service.

Providing Information via the World Wide Web

The Web may be the most popular technology since the Swiss Army knife. And it is being used for just about as many things as that little knife with all the built-in clippers, screwdrivers, and so on.

We think the reason for the popularity is that the Web best combines all the things we like about slick magazines with the ability to jump around from page to page with little effort. It's pretty; it's useful; it's amusing. How can you miss?

People respond to Web pages in much the same way as they respond to magazines. Web page designers need to consider their audiences much more than the designer of a Gopher menu or an FTP space. For example, compare the pages shown in Figures 20.9 and 20.10. The Web page for Intel, the manufacturer of processor, communications and networking, and semiconductor products:

```
http://www.intel.com
```

says something totally different than the Web page for the Rolling Stones:

```
http://www.stones.com
```

Figure 20.9.   *The Web page for Intel.*

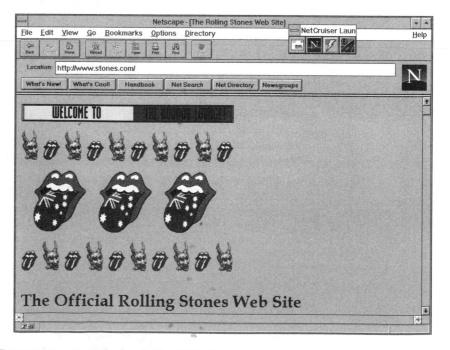

Figure 20.10.   *The Web page for the Rolling Stones.*

Clearly these services are aimed at different audiences—or the same audience at different times. Both pages are very effective. They convey image, attitude, information, and provoke specific behavior in response to that image, attitude, and information. Even if the same person who would buy a Voodoo Lounge tour t-shirt might also purchase a piece of equipment from Intel, they would not do so for the same reasons; so the presentation for each is entirely appropriate.

A Web "page" is actually a multimedia presentation. It can include sound and images and motion pictures as well as text.

An effective presentation should have something in it that will capture the attention of the visual learner, the aural learner, *and* the kinesthetic learner—those who learn by seeing, those who learn by listening, and those who learn by doing and touching. World Wide Web is the first application that allows the Internet information service implementor to do all of those things in the same environment.

In presenting information, we all try to give our audience a clear understanding of what we want them to know, to feel, and to do with the information we have conveyed. Using text, images, and sometimes sound in a Web page, we can do that and have our message delivered quickly down the hall, across the street, or across several time zones, to people who ask to see it. This makes the Web a presentation-builder's dream tool.

What You'll Need

To create your own information Web, you'll need all of the following:

An http server. If you are going to run your own system, suitable server programs can be found at both the NCSA

```
ftp.ncsa.uiuc.edu
```

and World Wide Web Consortium—W3C

```
ftp.w3.org
```

public domain sites.

Information you want to serve organized in some reasonable manner. If you want to display existing text files, you should add HTML coding so that http clients can display the text properly. Images need to be stored in .GIF, .JPEG (.JPG), or .MPEG (.MPG) format. Sound files need to be in .AU format for many clients.

(Sometimes .WAV or .AIFF formats can work, too—this difference depends on the client. Some clients will allow the addition of helper applications that will enable the user/viewer to see/hear/view portions of a page that could not ordinarily be viewed. A readily recognized helper application is Adobe's Acrobat document viewer.)

File permissions established so that users can only read from or write to specific files within specific directories. If you plan on having users enter data into fill-in-the-blank forms, you'll need to set up data space to receive the information they enter. If you don't plan on that, you can restrict the directories that contain your information to read-only for all but the account that is allowed to add, change, or remove information for your organization.

You may also want to include or have available these items:

Graphical images like the symbol that represents your organization, or some image that highlights the topics covered on the page.

Terms and conditions and/or disclaimer statements. Your organization's legal staff might require you to add such statements. Or maybe you'll want to add copyright and service mark information for your organization's products and services.

A link from the top-level menu to a Web space search server so your clients can find materials that are not on your server.

Logging and statistical processing of the logs so you have some idea who has been visiting.

For testing your pages, you'll need access to the public domain and commercial Web browser clients for as many of the computing platforms as possible. At least obtain the major ones for the most common platforms: Macintosh, DOS, and UNIX systems.

Maybe You Want More?

There are additional things you can do with a Web site, like add chat with perhaps Global Chat from Prospero Systems Research

```
http://www.prospero.com
```

or streaming audio with perhaps the RealAudio servers and clients from

```
http://www.realaudio.com
```

or video conferencing with perhaps CU-SeeMe from Cornell University

```
http://cu-seeme.cornell.edu/
```

Those aren't the only possibilities either. There's WebTalk from Quarterdeck:

```
http://www.qdeck.com/qdeck/products/webtalk/
```

where you and a friend can talk, or Internet Phone and Internet Wave, an audio-on-demand product, from VocalTec

```
http://www.vocaltec.com/
```

There's VDOLive

```
http://www.vdolive.com
```

for Live Video at relatively low speeds, and the animation techniques demonstrated at the Micro Movie MiniMultiple:

```
http://www.teleport.com/~cooler/MMMM/MMMM.html
```

where you can learn about the last thing we'll mention here, backgrounds.

This can't really be a book about all the things you can do effectively (or ineffectively but with a great deal of flash) using all the techniques and helper applications that have been invented for the Web. Nor is this the place for you to learn about VRML (Virtual Reality Modeling Language), an emerging technology for three-dimensional information and entertainment. What follows is a list of the basics and a few pointers to places like the World Wide Web Consortium and the Yahoo Index of Web-related items on the Net

```
http://www.yahoo.com/Computers_and_Internet/Internet/
World_Wide_Web/
```

that'll help you find more. Once again we recommend that you use the tool itself to provide yourself with the latest and greatest information on the topics about which you are most concerned.

Dos and Don'ts for Web Spinners

Do try to make your page visually interesting—remember your audience! Use the facilities within HTML to provide a visually pleasing as well as useful page. Provide plenty of white space, for example. Use spacing to make the anchor links obvious. Provide visual cues like horizontal bars to separate different types of information on the same Web page.

Don't try to put too much on one page. Some clients don't handle scrolling around in a large page very well. If you must put a very large batch of text on one page, put in within-page index links, so that the user can jump to a specific part of the page.

Remember that really large graphics take a long time to transmit, and many graphical clients allow you to turn off the automatic display of "in-line" graphics (those designed to be displayed immediately on the page rather than to be fetched and displayed by themselves). If they have to wait a long time, people may choose not to view your graphics. Design your in-line images so that they are informative and attractive but are respectful of people's time and patience. You want most people to view the images, not to turn them off because they are a pain to wait for. Another good idea is to construct images that are more horizontal than vertical. This will allow them to load faster because screens are "written" left to right, and then top to bottom. You get more "mileage" from a horizontal image. Furthermore, if you choose a smaller color palette (8-bit rather than 16, for example) you will use fewer bits for the same size image.

Don't use too many images, either. Fetching each image requires a separate action across the network. If you use too many, users will either turn off automatic image display or halt displaying your page before it is finished being fetched. Neither result is what you wanted when you designed the page.

Do include descriptive paragraphs that accompany each linked "anchor" on your page.

Do include a judicious mix of things to do, things to see, and things to know in your own information as well as in the information that you link in from other points around the Web.

Do include an address block at the end of your page. This section should include the e-mail address to which page visitors should send their questions. It can also include the date the page was last changed. This is a nice way to tell people how current the information on the page is.

Do include a disclaimer stating that your organization is not responsible for incorrect information received via your server. Everyone needs to understand that not all of the information to which your Web page points is under your control. One suggestion from Tim Berners-Lee, the original WWW developer, is to put your disclaimer on a page that is pointed to by an anchor in the address block.

Do point to the gateway servers if your system doesn't provide complete access to all the Internet services. You can let people use WAIS, X.500 directories, time of day around the world, and so on from within your Web page.

Do make sure your file permissions are set properly so that they can be read by the intended readers and not written to by people who shouldn't be writing to them.

Do check your Web links to see if they still point to what you thought.

Do review your pages every four or five weeks. Periodic checking prevents possible embarrassment.

Do spell-check your pages, even the headings! And especially check the words in your images. Reversed signs or misspellings, particularly in things like the name of your organization, will be quite embarrassing.

Do have someone other than the person who designed it look at the page. Maybe it only makes sense to the designer.

 MASTER WORDS As the Web grows in importance as a communication medium, a new computer profession is emerging—the Web site designer. If you want to leave the implementation to someone else, check the list of information publishers on the accompanying CD or the ads in your local computer weekly. But one of the most interesting sources of this new service comes from a very old tradition indeed. The Benedictine order has been creating illuminated manuscripts since the sixth century; and the *New York Times* (March 17, 1996) reports that the Christ in the Desert monastery in the Sangre de Cristo mountains of New Mexico is now supplementing its income by creating hand-lettered, illuminated home pages for its Web clients. "The hand lettering is done on canvas, and the illuminations are scanned into the computers before being incorporated into the Web pages" reports the *Times*. Of course, the monastery had to add a few more solar panels to power the computers, and buy a telephone. You can check out their work at

http://www.technet.nm.org/pax.html

Code by Example

Figure 20.11 shows Glee's Web page, a very simple Web page that includes a few photographs as well as links to other Web pages. The accompanying listing shows the HTML code that produced the page. Looking at the code, you can see the elements needed to produce a simple, yet informative set of links.

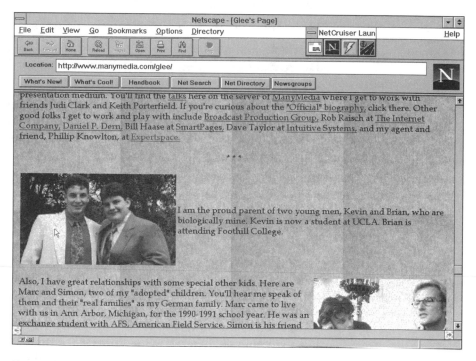

Figure 20.11.   Glee's Web page—midview.

GLEE'S WEB PAGE

```
<HTML><HEAD><TITLE>Glee's Page</TITLE></HEAD>

<BODY background="backg.jpg">

<H1>Glee Harrah Cady</H1>

<P><IMG src="gleesm.gif" alt="[Glee's portrait]"> Hi. Thanks for
stopping by. </P>

<P>This page is a very personal page and is about friends and
family and my theory that, really, the Internet allows one to have
```

the most amazing extended family — one that you can choose for yourself — experts to help you with your problems or loved ones to help you over tough spots in your life and to share your joy with the grand times. My friend and co-author, <A href="http://www.lloyd.com/~patmcg">Pat McGregor,</A> wrote a <A href="http://www.lloyd.com/~patmcg/dec95.htm">great webpiece</A> on family and relationships which expresses this very well. I hope that you will enjoy it. Some of my tough spots in the past few years have included losing my beloved husband, Frank, to cancer. Pat is able to write about this better than I can right now, because I am still too close to it. I do plan to add some of Frank's wonderful poems to this set of pages because I wish you all could have known him.</P>

<P>Life is what happens to you when you are trying to implement Plan B, right?</P>

<P>My life is net-centered at this time — I expect that this, too, will change with time. The music parts (I play the flute, but not often enough any more) and the cooking parts are at a lower ebb and I can't seem to get really interested in the garden as much as I used to be. I continue my love of the historical novels of <A href="http://www.almac.co.uk/business_park/thin/dunnett.htm">Dorothy Dunnett,</A> who has just published <I>To Lie With Lions</I>, the 6th book in her House of Niccolo series. It's not even available in the States yet, but our extended family of Dunnetworkers found copies at a bookstore in Belgium and we bought out the place. Isn't networking wonderful? I did manage to read a Ross Thomas thriller called <I>Ah, Treachery</I> which I recommend to all who love sardonic wit. For a wonderful book of essays, I recommend <A href="http://www.sfgate.com/columnists/carroll">San Francisco Chronicle columnist Jon Carroll's</A> <I>Near Life Experiences</I>. I plan to give a lot of them as gifts this coming holiday season.</P>

<center><p>* * *</P></center>

<P>I work at <A href="http://www.netcom.com">NETCOM,</A> an Internet Service Provider where I try to help people see/hear/feel how they could benefit by using the Internet (and the larger <A href="http://www.tic.com/mids/midshome.html">Matrix</A> as named by John Quarterman and Smoot-Carl Mitchell) to achieve their own goals. In doing that, I give lots of talks. Some of them, I give using the web as a presentation medium. You'll find the <A href="gtalks.html">talks</A> here on the server of <A href="http://www.manymedia.com">ManyMedia</A> where I get to work with friends Judi Clark and Keith Porterfield. If you're curious about the <A href="biopg.html">"Official" biography,</A> click there. Other good folks I get to work and

play with include <A href="http://www.bpgnet.com">Broadcast
Production Group,</A> Rob Raisch at <A href="http://www
.internet.com">The Internet Company,</A> <A href="http://www
.dern.com:2205/dernweb.html">Daniel P. Dern,</A> Bill Haase at
<A href="http://www.smartpages.com">SmartPages,</A> Dave
Taylor at <A href="http://www.intuitive.com">Intuitive
Systems,</A> and my agent and friend, Phillip Knowlton, at <A
href="http://www.expertspace.com/expertspace">Expertspace.</A>
</P>

<p>* * *</P>

<table border=0>

<tr>

<td align=right>

<IMG src="boys.gif" alt="[Kevin and Brian Cady, 1994]"
align="Top"></td>

<td align=left>

I am the proud parent of two young men, Kevin and Brian, who are
biologically mine. Kevin is now a student at UCLA. Brian is
attending Foothill College. </td>

</tr>

</table>

<P><IMG ALIGN=RIGHT src="marsim.gif" alt="[Marc and Simon,
1994]" align="Top">

<P>Also, I have great relationships with some special other
kids. Here are Marc and Simon, two of my "adopted" children.
You'll hear me speak of them and their "real families" as my
German family. Marc came to live with us in Ann Arbor, Michigan,
for the 1990-1991 school year. He was an exchange student with
<A href="http://www.vcnet.com/afs/">AFS,</A> American Field
Service. Simon is his friend from pre-school. Simon came to
Milford, Michigan, that same year via <A href="http://csbh
.mhv.net/~yfu/welcome.html">YFU</A>, Youth for Understanding. We
benefited from them both. This picture was taken last October on
a quick weekend trip through Munich that I got to make on my way
home from a talk I gave in Israel. Simon is a student at the
journalism school in Munich. Marc takes classes in acting,
voice, and music in between appearing in a television series for
German television and appearing on stage.

<P><A href="http://www-personal.umich.edu/~mdushane/index
.html">Mike Dushane</A> is the first of my "kids" to have his
own page. He's now a student at the University of Michigan.

<P>You can send me a note at <A href="mailto:glee@netcom
.com">glee@netcom.com.</A> </P> </BODY> </HTML>

The HTML code includes a title statement; a background image that some browsers can display; an opening image; a first-level heading with Glee's name; and text with links and images. The links provide jumps to Pat's page and the pages of other friends. Most of those pages are not stored on this same server. The images used are all on the same server and, in fact, within the same directory. Therefore the image SRC statements do not include full path names. There are links that jump to other pages in the same directory (`biopg.html` and `gtalks.html`). There's a pointer to the main page at the server itself (`www.manymedia.com`). Unlike many pages of this type, there is not an address block, nor a jump back to the top of the page. This is not a very formal page; it simply concludes a with "mailto" link so that people can send e-mail to Glee.

It does illustrate some interesting tricks for formatting, though. Look at the simple centered line of three asterisks. Put in between some paragraphs, the line serves to visually break up the page without an extra download for another image or the intrusion of the horizontal rule that HTML gives you. Also, look at how the placement of the images and text shown in Figure 20.11 was accomplished. The first image is placed within a table. The image is aligned right within the table data. The text is aligned left within the table data. This provides pleasant spacing. The next image is aligned right and the explanatory text flows around the image.

This page does not include examples of all the things you can do with a Web page, of course. It leaves out structured and unstructured and/or bulleted lists. It leaves out connections via other protocols than http and FTP. Remember that Web browsing clients can use the Gopher protocol, too. And many Web clients can use the Usenet and Telnet protocols, as well as process input from the user by using forms. If you use forms, you will need underlying programs to process the input in addition to the HTML code that provides the input areas on the displayed page.

You can adapt this code to reflect your organization's needs. If you do, be sure to follow the "Web etiquette" hints shown in Figure 20.12, by Tim Berners-Lee of the W3 Consortium team

```
http://www.w3.org/pub/WWW/Provider/Etiquette.html
```

and read the other Web pages that you can find by taking a jump to the Web developer's page developed by Barry R. Greene

```
http://oneworld.wa.com/htmldev/devpage/dev-page.html
```

Then you'll soon be spinning Web pages with the rest of us.

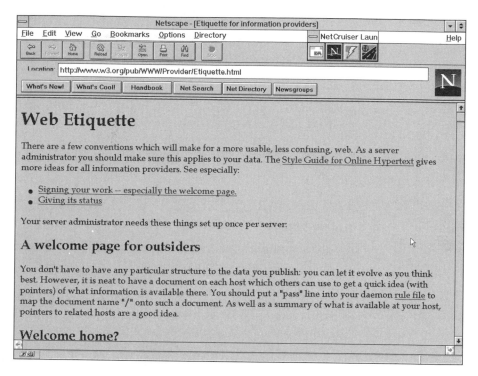

Figure 20.12.   Web etiquette hints from W3.org.

Opening the Door to the World

Whether you're working with FTP, Gopher, or the Web, once you've got your server running, and your data formatted and ready, you need to let people on the Internet know you are receiving requests.

If your server contains data of particular interest to a specific community of users, be sure to announce it to any mailing lists or newsgroups that specialize in that subject.

Send an announcement of your new server to the net-happenings mailing list maintained by Gleason Sackmann. The number of announcements that are made each day is now so large that Mr. Sackmann prefers to accept submissions via the Web-form found at

http://www.gi.net/NET/input.html

although e-mail to

net-happenings@dsmail.internic.net

will be accepted. Include the type of resource it is (WWW; Gopher; or Telnet/FTP). Note that Net-Happenings announcements can include new books, new training courses, and all kinds of resources in which Internet users will be interested.

Announcing Your New FTP Site

For new FTP sites, if you wish your files to be included in the Archie indexes, you'll need to send e-mail to

```
archie-admin@bunyip.com
```

You should include the fully qualified domain name of your FTP server and the root directory from which you are making information available. For example, Netcom might send this message:

```
Files for indexing will be found in the /pub directory
of ftp.netcom.com.
```

Announcing Your New Gopher Server

For new Gophers, you need to:

1. Send e-mail to gopher@boombox.micro.umn.edu with the following items in the body of the message:

   ▶ The name of your server.

   ▶ The host name on which the server is running.

   ▶ The port number (70 is assumed).

   ▶ The administrative contact.

   ▶ A selector string (the menu name to be used in other people's Gopher menus to point to your server).

2. Post an announcement to the comp.infosystems.announce news-group. This is a moderated group.

   If you do not announce your server, people will still be able to access it directly by giving the appropriate server name (complete domain address) and the appropriate port number. However, other Gopher server designers won't necessarily know about your server and won't be able to point their servers to yours. Also, the Gopher indexing services only gather data from those servers that are announced via the "mother" Gopher at the University of Minnesota. Clearly, there are real disadvantages to going it alone.

Announcing Your Web Server

To announce your new Web server to the rest of the Internet, you need to:

1. Register with the World Wide Web Consortium (W3.Org) the following information (if you have a Web browser that supports forms, you can simply fill in the form found at

   ```
   http://www.w3.org/hypertext/DataSources/WWW/
   Geographical_generation/new.html
   ```

   The form includes:

   ▶ The title under which you wish your service to be referenced.

   ▶ The location—country, state.

   ▶ A summary (2–3 lines) of what your server provides.

   ▶ The URL of the entry point you would like. (Include the relevant port number if you are using another port. Port 70 is the common port for Gopher, port 80 is the common port for http, and port 21 is the common port for FTP.)

   ▶ If the information is officially mandated and representative of your organization, you should say so. In general, it is assumed that, unless you specifically say otherwise, the information is "hosted" by the organization that owns the domain rather than being the "product" of that organization.

2. Send e-mail to `whats-new@ncsa.uiuc.edu`. These folks like the e-mail to be in HTML format so they can just drop your announcement into the "what's new" page.

3. Post an announcement to the `comp.infosystems.www.announce` newsgroup. This is a moderated group.

4. Investigate the various other indexes and listings that might be appropriate to list your resource.

   ▶ First, read carefully the pages that you use to help you navigate the Internet. If you habitually use Yahoo or Lycos or Magellan, probably the people who will want to know about your resource will look at those sites, too. The sites themselves may tell you how to submit your resource for their attention.

▶ You can even use the directories listed above (particularly Yahoo) to find announcement services. Either use the Search function from the main Yahoo page and enter the word **announcement** in the search box, or choose WWW from the Computers and Internet/Internet topic list and then choose Announcement Services. These services (some free and some for-fee) will help you announce your new Web site across the Net. Yahoo lists services like The Postmaster

```
http://www.netcreations.com/postmaster/
```

and Submit It

```
http://www.submit-it.com/
```

that help you find places to list your resource by providing forms for you to fill out.

▶ Good netiquette should tell you that misrepresenting your resource or listing in places that don't generally list the type of resource you have created is not a good idea. Much of the value of these directories and listings comes from our ability to trust the information they give to all us users.

What Next? Feedback from the Community

Well, you won't get to sit back and admire your work for very long. Get ready for visitors!

If you put an e-mail address on your Web or Gopher server, make sure it is working, because the traffic will rise dramatically from the first day. You'll need to prepare procedures for answering the mail, for reviewing what's on your server, and for adding new things to your server. You'll get lots of comments for improving your services. Some you'll like and want to implement. Some will be from people who were pleased to receive your information. It's really nice to get those!

Don't forget to watch the logs of traffic. You can look at them to see which pages and menus are being used the most. You may want to rearrange your pages and menus based on how others actually use them.

Internet Resources

CHAPTER 21

Buying, Selling, and Supporting Products and Services

FEATURING

Chapter 21

Buying, Selling, and Supporting Products and Services

I N previous chapters we have discussed how to cruise around using various Internet applications and tools to find people and information, to play, to listen, to be entertained. We've also talked about how you can effectively provide information about yourself and/or your organization. And we've talked about Netiquette and appropriate usage of Internet services as part of the global Internet community. In this chapter we are going to build on that information to consider the exchange of money for products or services using the Internet as a transmission medium.

If you're planning to buy products and services over the Net, be aware that there will be people who are honest and very helpful like many of your local merchants. There will also be "confidence men" who will try to defraud you. The ability to use a computer does not confer honesty upon your potential trading partner. When you visit a "real" store you can use the "look and feel" of the store to help you determine if the site represents a credible and creditable business. It's harder to do that when you are visiting a "virtual store." This means not that you shouldn't buy and sell over the Net (in fact, we recommend it!) However, you should keep your eyes open and be aware that fraud is possible.

MASTER WORDS   The most important thing we can say to you about trade on the Internet is that the Internet is not an extension or virtual representation of the world we live in, it *is* the world we live in with all the benefits, problems, and complications of our world.

When you are setting up shop, you'll need to remember that your Internet transactions are subject to the same laws, regulation, and taxation as if you were buying or selling from a storefront in your geographical location. If you're selling, you'll need the appropriate business licenses, and you'll need to collect and pay the appropriate taxes. Neglecting these "implementation details" will doom your enterprise, and you may even face criminal charges.

 MASTER WORDS   **std.disclaimer:** The information in this chapter is current as of early 1996. Electronic commerce initiatives are among the most fluid of the ever-changing Internet. What we write today may well no longer be true when you read this. Thus, in this space we're going to provide a lot of pointers to places on the Internet where you can check for more up-to-date information. That's a real advantage of the Internet.

Buying and Selling

"Things" for sale on the Internet can be either tangible, deliverable items or intangible (but still deliverable) ideas. They can be for sale by individuals or by corporate entities. They can be new (like new automobiles or, more commonly, new computers) or used (where computers are even more common), or perhaps "pre-owned" like houses. Probably the distinguishing characteristic of sales transactions is how formal or informal they are.

Psst! Wanna Buy a Bike?

Informal sales are those that take place in "The World's Largest Garage Sale," also known as the `misc.forsale` newsgroup and any of its regional newsgroups, e.g. `ba.misc.forsale` (San Francisco Bay Area) or `wi.madison.forsale` (Madison, WI area). The newsgroups hold articles that describe single or small-quantity items, usually used, that are owned by individuals who want to sell them. A description of the item is published. Price and delivery terms are described. If you are interested in buying the item, you send e-mail or send postal mail or speak on the telephone with the owner for any further information you may need or want. Then, if you still want it, the two of you agree upon a price and arrangements for delivery of the item. Both of you gain.

Remember that point about delivery. The buyer and the seller need to figure out how to move that item from one location to another.

This transaction is like selling/buying, say, a used exercise bicycle in the local classified ads. You read a posting about it. You decide whether you want it. The seller decides whether she will accept your check for payment. If she wants the space occupied by the bike badly enough, she's likely to accept a lower offer and your check, even if she doesn't know much about you. If she's only mildly concerned about selling it, she may ask that you pay by money order or one of the electronic cash mechanisms discussed later in this chapter. She may even take bids on it, if it turns out to be a popular item. This protects her monetary interest in the bike.

MASTER WORDS   Speaking of classified advertisements: you might check with your preferred print publication and see if their advertisements are carried as part of their on-line presence. If so, you might be able to get double duty from your ad insertion. See the classifieds at *The San Jose Mercury News* at `http://www.sjmercury.com` on the Web. Just think how many more people may see your ad for that exercise bike!

Again, `misc.forsale` and the other newsgroups are intended to be for single-item sales. If you consistently and persistently post long lists of items for sale to these newsgroups (or to others whose charters and FAQs do not explicitly permit such postings), you will be considered a newsgroup abuser. People who read the newsgroups may complain to you and to your service provider about your newsgroup abuse. Many service providers will, upon investigation, point out to you that you are, indeed, abusing the network and suspend your account or your posting privileges.

Posting to newsgroups is a privilege, not a right.

Send Your Sweetie Some Flowers?

More formal transactions take place when you shop at one of the many "Internet Shopping Malls" that now abound on the Net. These shopping opportunities are organized collections of items for sale. You'll usually find about the same assortment of different types of products and services that you would find in a "real" shopping mall. In fact, a number of "real" shopping malls, like the Stanford Shopping Center and the Aloha Tower Marketplace, have "cyber-replicas" on the Net. (Usually you won't be able to buy products from a real mall's Internet Web site, but you will be able to find information about it.)

TEN MALLS FOR BROWSING

The Internet Mall

http://www.internet-mall.com/index.html

This set of pages has grown from an original list that was sent via e-mail and FTP into a biggish site on the Web itself. Dave Taylor, who maintains the site, has a background that many people envy: programmer and designer extraordinaire. Worth visiting. Be sure and take the links that lead you to Dave's other interesting stuff.

InterAge

http://www.interage.co.il/menu.html

Now these pages are interesting because they are both similar to what you'll find elsewhere (twenty general categories of merchandise from business listings to fashion) and totally different (they're done in Israel). Some links here are to Israeli products from Israeli companies. Others are linked to other parts of the globe. We've included the site here to demonstrate the borderless nature of information about products.

The World Wide Web Pavilion

http://www.catalog.com/tsw/Pavilion/pavbiz.html

This mall includes one of the better Art Gallery collections on the Internet. It's difficult to sell things electronically unless you can see or feel what they are. Here you can look at the art that you might want to own.

NSTN's CyberMall

http://www.nstn.ca/commerce.html

NSTN is Canadian and includes a view of commerce from North of the Border. Just as if you traveled to Nova Scotia and found that the stores in the malls differed, you find that difference reflected here. While you're visiting, admire the Inuit art in the signs.

Stanford Shopping Center

```
http://netmedia.com/ims/ssc/ssc.html
```

Aloha Tower Marketplace

```
http://www.alohatower.com/atm/
```

These two are malls in the real as well as the virtual world. The map and photos of the Stanford Shopping Center are informative and pleasing to the eye. The pages from the Aloha Tower Marketplace make you want to visit in the flesh and try out some of the wonderful food mentioned. Of course, the photos of the beach and the fish help a lot, too.

Shopping2000

```
http://www.shopping2000.com/
```

Shopping 2000 offers you products you will recognize from companies that you know. Frequently, there will be special offers and discounts. The selection is large, you can window shop, and ordering is easy. For ordering, you can choose to use a secured browser or use their 800 number. You can also order a catalog.

Internet Shopping Network

```
http://www.internet.net/
```

This is perhaps the best known of the significant shopping sites on the Net. Here, the Internet Shopping Network folks have gathered together products and presented them in a way that makes shopping easy for the viewer. You'll find suggestions for current holiday presents, directories for easy browsing, specials, and a powerful, easy-to-use search facility. Several name brand merchants are represented here, too.

The Branch Mall

```
http://branch.com/
```

The Branch Mall is considered the "first" mall on the Web. Branch Mall and its member florist, Grant's, are written about frequently when commerce on the Net is discussed because of the success enjoyed by the two together. Note that Grant's includes a reminder service. You can make sure that the people from whom you would like to get flowers are reminded of your special occasion.

The All-Internet Shopping Directory

```
http://www.webcom.com/~tbrown/
```

This site includes a Top Shopping Site Directory, rated for ease of use, good design for customer services, etc. There are topical headings like Books within Arts and Entertainment, etc. The autopilot (or guided) tour is a good way to learn your way around at first.

Internet Mall listings

```
http://www.opse.com/mallistings/
```

If the ones listed here didn't provide that exact match to the mall you were looking for, you might try here and jump to the links you haven't already tried. If you still haven't fulfilled that gotta-shop craving, you should try the search services for the words "shopping" or "mall." Be prepared for the answers to be different every day.

But I Don't Like Malls

Of course, just as in your real-life shopping, you need not go to a mall. You can go directly to a store that sells the product you want to buy. To go directly to a shop, use one of the many excellent directories available on the Net. Yahoo and Galaxy can help you. You can also use one of the search services to look directly through full-text searches for an item that isn't easily described in a simple word or two. An index like Yahoo or Galaxy excels with the single term like "flowers." A search service like Alta Vista or Open Text would be better if you wanted to search for "tropical flowers." For many searches, a combination works well. Start with Yahoo and the search term "flowers." Then move on to Open Text and from the initial Open Text search result, refine your search (narrow it) by adding more terms to describe exactly what kind of flowers you'd like to find.

The screen shots included here show that process. First we started with Yahoo (Figure 21.1) by entering the term **flowers** into the search dialog box. The search returned (on this day) 165 matches. Some of

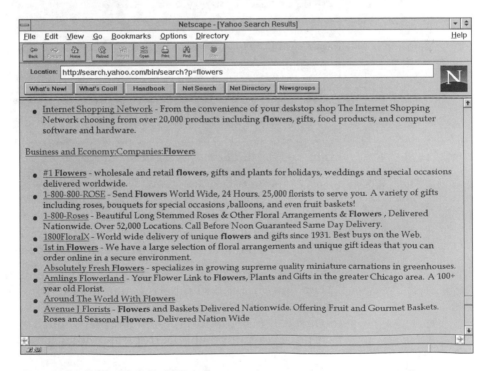

Figure 21.1. ***Yahoo result for "flowers."***

them were descriptions of photographs of flowers. Some of them were writings and research about flowers. The illustration shows a middle part of the first 25 matches—the part that displayed flower sellers.

Then, we clicked on the Open Text button at the bottom of the Yahoo display. Yahoo passed the search term to Open Text, which reported a result of 8860 pages that contained the word *flowers* (Figure 21.2).

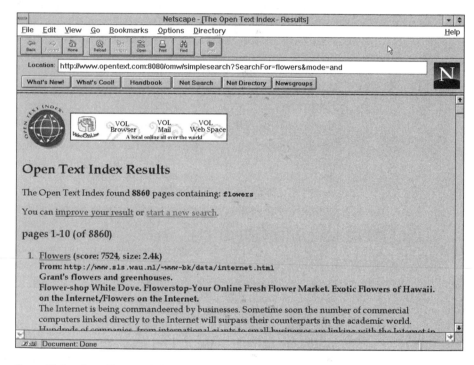

Figure 21.2. **Open Text result for "flowers."**

Then we choose "Improve your result" from the top of the Open Text page. This choice presents another page (Figure 21.3) where you can add to your search terms to make them more specific.

Adding the term "tropical" to flowers and including the search directive "near" lowered the number of matching entries from 8860 to 158. This is closer to the number we started with in Yahoo, but you'll notice the first entry (Figure 21.4) looks like pretty much what we wanted in the first place—a store that sells tropical flowers.

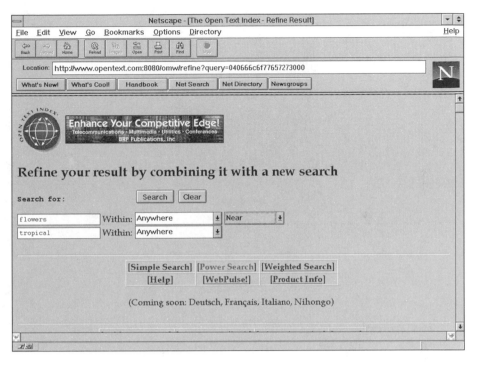

Figure 21.3. **Open Text search refinement: add "tropical."**

So let's visit and see what happens. Figure 21.5 shows the entryway to Tropical Flowers by Charles. We next choose "Aloha Bouquets and Ordering Information."

Finally, we can pick and choose what to send to our friends. Figure 21.6 shows the top of the order form. This business gives you two methods of paying for your purchase: credit card via secure transmission, and postal mail of money order or cashier's check. (As you'll see, other businesses may offer other payment methods.)We've picked the item we want—the "Small Aloha Bouquet." Once we send that page, we get back a confirming page (Figure 21.7), which gives the total that we've accrued in this transaction, asks for some information about us (telephone numbers, names, ship-to addresses, and credit card information) and lets us submit the order.

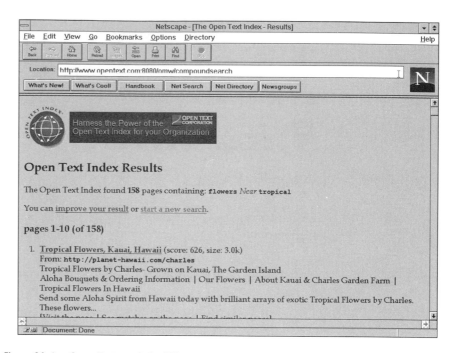

Figure 21.4. *Open Text result for "Flowers near Tropical."*

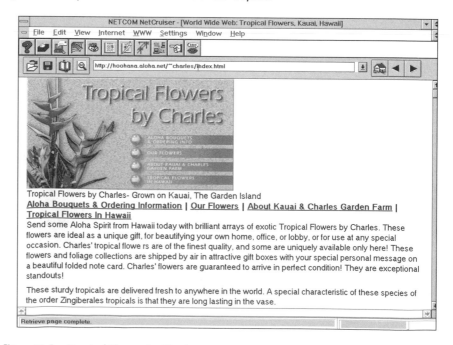

Figure 21.5. *Tropical Flowers by Charles.*

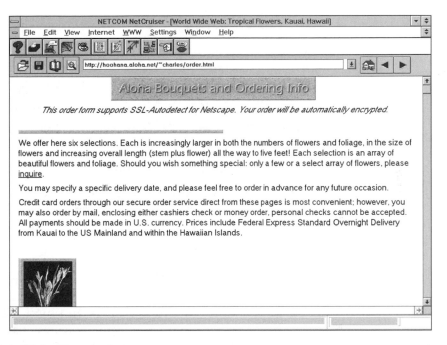

Figure 21.6. **The order form.**

Figure 21.7. **The confirmation form.**

So, How Can I Pay for Things?

As in any commercial transaction, there are several ways you can provide payment for things you acquire over the Net (assuming that you have the money to pay for your purchases, of course :-)).

For the simple, informal case where you are buying from a fellow, private Net-citizen, you can arrange to send a personal check. Or if you are close geographically, you can arrange to meet and exchange cash for goods.

For more formal purchases you can:

Send your Credit Card number (encrypted or not) across the Net, via e-mail or via a form on a Web page. See Cybercash:

    http://www.cybercash.com

and First Virtual

    http://www.fv.com

Send a bank check. You can do this in several ways. With postal mail you simply write the check and mail it as usual. You can also send it via telephone or computer, where a service writes the check for you; for example, there is OnLine Check at

    http://www.onlinecheck.com

Or you can write a check and send it via the Net; for example, using NetChex at

    http://www.netchex.com

Send money or money equivalents (digital cash) via the Net. See the services offered by Cybercash, Ecash:

    http://www.digicash.com

and First Virtual.

Select your purchase from information on the Net, but give your credit card number over the telephone, take them your money, or send it via postal service—keeping the financial part of the transaction off the Internet.

Commit your organization via purchase order to a purchase (usually done using EDI—Electronic Data Interchange software and services). True EDI services are outside the scope of this book.

In other words, your choices are the same as for other types of purchases, with the addition of a few services that are Net-specific.

SENSIBLE MONETARY BEHAVIOR AND THE NET

There is a lot of fear about financial fraud via the Net, particularly in relation to un-identified people taking your credit card numbers and charging up large amounts to your card without your knowledge.

This fear is partly reasonable (because you can't *see* the person with whom you may be transacting business) and partly unreasonable (because the same state-ment is true of some person at the other end of some telephone call to a catalog order department that you may be making).

In the cases that we know about where charges appeared on cards unexpectedly, the card numbers were obtained from the garbage cans of restaurants and drug stores where the cards had been used.

You have certain protections with your credit cards that are part of each account you have. Make certain that you understand those protections. Often they include the ability to stop payment; the ability to reduce your losses to a certain amount in the event of fraud; and the ability to get your money returned if the product is defective. These are part of the advantages of having credit cards in the first place.

You also have certain responsibilities: Don't give your number out indiscrimi-nately, don't recite your number at pay telephones, etc. Use secure payment methods when you can. If you can't and you want to purchase an item, think about who is getting the number and what you know about them. If they appear to be a legitimate business, you should be fine.

Internet service providers usually keep their networks physically secure (so that packet sniffers, etc. can't be put on their networks). Systems administrators, who could possibly see what is in a packet traversing the network, don't really have the time or the inclination to be watching all those packets for credit card numbers. Your greatest risk of having someone find your credit card numbers will probably come from accidentally leaving your card where an unscrupulous person can find and use it.

Reasonable care should prevail in *every* transaction you make on your credit cards. Your credit card companies provide the information about using cards intelligently. You'll find it with your bills or on the Net. Try

```
http://www.visa.com
```
and
```
http://www.mastercard.com
```

It's also important to note that the choices you have for your Internet purchases are changing rapidly. There are working groups of banks and financial transaction companies, service providers, and software developers that are inventing new mechanisms to improve the stability and integrity of purchasing via the Net. New announcements are made each week. If you just want to buy things and not be bothered, all you have to do is follow the directions on the order forms provided by the company from whom you are making your purchase. But if you are curious about the discussions and inner workings of the groups, you can frequently follow them on the Net, too. Here are some interesting Web sites on those topics:

Mastercard:

http://www.mastercard.com

VISA:

http://www.visa.com

The Financial Services Technology Consortium:

http://www.llnl.gov:80/fstc/about.shtml

Automated Transaction Services:

http://www.calypso.com/ats/

Security First Network Bank:

http://www.sfnb.com

Interactive Services Association:

http://www.isa.Net

To see how the various payment options work, go to:

First Virtual:

http://www.fv.com

and their client **Reuter's Money Network** at

http://www.moneynet.com

Royal Copenhagen's Georg Jensen Jewelry:

http://dis.dk/royal/index.html

This site also uses Ecash:

http://www.digicash.com

Virtual Vineyards:

http://www.virtualvin.com/vvdata/352724056/to-order.html

This site lets you pay by credit card or Cybercash at

http://www.cybercash.com

I've Got a Great Idea for a Product!

And I want to sell it on the Net. What do I do next?

Well, the first thing to do in developing your new business for the Net is the same sort of thing you'd do for a non-Net business. There's fabulous information about getting a new business off the ground available from the United States Small Business Administration. Go to their Web site at

```
http://www.sbaonline.sba.gov
```

and choose "Starting your business" from the very first Web page. You'll find great resources: books, papers, hints, ways to talk over your idea with experienced people from the Service Corps of Retired Executives and with people from the SBA itself. You'll find hints on financing your business. You'll find a complete workshop on developing your business plan that'll help you refine your ideas so that your business will have a greater chance of success. And you'll find shareware computer programs that'll help you make sure you've got all your ducks lined up.

Developing a business plan will help you determine if your idea is one that fits the Net of today or the near future. If you are planning on selling a product, will your potential customers be on the Net already? Or will you need to bring them to the Net? The demographic picture of the Net is a wee bit hazy. This is the nicest way we can think of to say that you can find a statistical survey to prove just about any point about the Net today. There are surveys that show the percentage of women users to be either high or low; that show that the average user fits in some demographic category or another. You can find the surveys by using one of the index services. Mostly you'll see that you'll really need to think through how you will find your market on the Net.

Once you've decided to take the plunge, you should add to your business plan any information you can get about the law. This too, is changing. Here are some sites where you can check the latest information about cyberspace and the law.

Electronic Commerce Law at

```
http://www.intermarket.com:80/ecl/
```

This is the Information Technology Division, Section of Science and Technology, American Bar Association, along with the CyberNotary® Committee at

```
http://www.intermarket.com:80/ecl/notary.html
```

Part IV

Internet Resources

The ABA's list of their Current Publications on Science and Technology at

```
http://www.abanet.org/scitech/scitechpubs.html
```

A List of European Legal Sites from The Centre for Commercial Law at

```
http://www.link.org
```

United States Patent and Trademark Office at

```
http://www.uspto.gov
```

The American Marketing Association at

```
http://www.ama.org/
```

and a list of Public Relations Agencies at

```
http://www.webcom.com/impulse/prlist.html
```

may be of help when you are ready to launch your business.

Choices for Operating

Once you've got your product or service organized and your business plan written, you'll need to figure out how best to process orders and accept money.

Processing orders can be done via the Web using forms, cgi-scripts, and interaction with your customer. A good example to look at for a pattern is the site for Virtual Vineyards

```
http://www.virtualvin.com
```

where the order form makes it easy by having the shipping and handling rates calculated for the consumer. As in all commercial design, a good design goal is to make it as easy as possible for your customer to buy. We recommend that you spend a lot of time looking at the design of other sites to see what you think works and what you think doesn't; then apply those judgments to your site design.

Accepting Your Customer's Money

The information supplied about forms of payment for buying through the Net earlier in this chapter can be used to help you figure out what you want to do for selling. Investigate the various financial services with an eye toward what they can provide to merchants and at what cost. See which best fits your needs.

If you have an international business in mind, you may want to look at an organization like Octagon Technology Group at

```
http://www.otginc.com
```

This company offers services that enable you to sell internationally: distribution, language translation, and jurisdictional information as well as Web presence building, etc. There are probably other companies that provide similar services.

Remember that you need to observe appropriate law in your business. Make sure you know what regulations apply to you. As has been said about many other things: ignorance is not an adequate defense.

Sold! Now What?

Once you've sold and delivered your product or service to your customer, you'll want to make sure your customer is satisfied with your product and has the kind of experience that'll make your product one that she recommends to others. Here are some of the most important points (some of this information appears in slightly different form in a chapter Glee is contributing to Daniel P. Dern's upcoming *Internet Business Handbook*).

Internet-based customer service can be a highly visible, high technology, high advantage, and relatively low-cost activity when Internet delivery is used to supplement or replace the extant services performed by multiple departments in a business. We mean that customer service includes all the many activities involved in interacting with your customer community. This usually means:

Responding to requests for information about your organization and/or your products and services.

Taking orders from your customers and responding to inquiries from your customers about the status of their orders.

Addressing problems your customers may be having with *using* your product or service.

In today's customer-focused organization, prompt, efficient customer service is of paramount importance. To your customer, your customer service organization *IS* your organization. It reflects your company's image as well as presenting information and solving problems.

Customer service departments have always been quick to explore and adopt new technologies to help improve the timeliness, quality, and cost-effectiveness of their activities. Within the past decade, for example, we have seen customer service departments implement 1-800 and 1-900 numbers, faxback, interactive voice response (IVR), training videos, CD-ROM, Bulletin Board Systems (BBSs), and dedicated topical areas (e.g. SIGs and Forums) on national on-line services.

As increasing numbers of companies are discovering, the Internet can join these tools as an access/delivery tool for customer service.

Here we discuss how to use the Internet as an additional customer service tool and why that might be good for your organization. The Internet should be just another delivery mechanism for communication between your organization and your customers, one that complements your other delivery mechanisms: the 800 number, the facsimile transmission (fax), the telephone, the telex, or the postal and courier delivery services. You may be able to replace some of these delivery mechanisms with Internet services.

To use the Internet effectively requires developing policies and procedures that fit in with your current customer service delivery methodologies.

MASTER WORDS   Good Customer Service will usually result from Good Customer Communication.

Using the Net for "Custom" Communications

In today's customer-focused business environment, all of us are concerned about our ability to retain our customers. Most of us believe that excellent customer service is an important avenue to use for keeping our customers. Business consultants like Tom Peters, first in his *In Search of Excellence* and then in his subsequent works, have demonstrated the importance of each and every customer to our companies' continued financial health. We each want to use effectively any and all tools available that might help us; and such tools are in the Internet Basic Toolkit. You can use them to improve your ability to deliver service to your customers. Good use of the tools makes it possible to quickly respond to your customers' queries. As so many of today's businesses are service-oriented, rather than product-oriented (our services *ARE* the products), it has become more and more important to deliver the right service to the customer as quickly and efficiently as possible.

With Internet publishing tools like the World Wide Web, FTP, and Gopher, you can provide information that the customers can retrieve themselves at their convenience. The entry costs for implementing Internet-based customer service procedures are relatively low. You might be able to offset some of the money spent on telephone, printing, and/or facsimile transmission services if you replace or supplement some of those activities with uses of Internet tools.

The potential risks are low; in fact, the only one I can think of is annoying your customer by not replying "promptly" enough to his or her query. This makes delivery over the Internet a "win-win" action, where you provide better service (your customer wins) with little extra expense (your organization wins.)

Companies using the Internet for customer service range from computer and technology vendors such as Microsoft, IBM, Xerox, and Novell to banks (Wells Fargo) and credit cards (Visa). Arguably, government agencies, nonprofit organizations, and others are all also using the Internet for "customer service" in the widest sense of the term; for example, the Department of Agriculture's Extension Service, the Department of Commerce, the University of Pennsylvania's Oncology Department, and the Internal Revenue Service. The Electronic Frontier Foundation, the Internet Society, and the Computer Professionals for Social Responsibility all have member services pages in their Web and Gopher sites.

The four basic benefits you can get by using the Internet are:

Your customer receives improved responsiveness: E-mail provides you a tool to respond personally and quickly to each query. Gopher and WWW provide you tools to let customers find their own answers.

Your customer receives improved service: Prompt answers are good. Clear, concise, and consistent statements are even better. You can use Internet tools to deliver standard and approved company communications, thus improving the quality of your communication.

You receive a more efficient customer service staff: Having standardized communications makes it relatively easy for the customer service staff to respond quickly, thus allowing more queries to be answered in less time.

You receive happier customers, which encourages repeat business: Your customer is more likely to return if you have satisfied his or her concern. Measuring customer satisfaction cannot be the province of this chapter, but anecdotal evidence hints that technical support telephone calls transferred to e-mail improved the ability of the support group to give prompt and accurate answers that were less liable to misinterpretation by the customer. Misinterpreted answers from Customer Support staff cause not only unhappy customers, but repeat customers (at least to the Support lines). *This* kind of repeat business shouldn't happen. The desired outcome of any interaction with your customer is to make sure that the customer will be glad to interact with your organization again.

The expense for adding an e-mail service to an existing e-mail system is negligible. You will need to train your customer service staff; prepare work areas where Internet-attached workstations are available; and spend some of your customer service management time and effort in preparing standardized answers to common customer queries as well as to preparing procedures for developing answers to not-so-common queries. The operating costs for an e-mail response system are less than for a typed business letter. The expense of the postage itself pales in comparison to the considerable expense of getting the letter onto your business letterhead.

The incremental expense for publishing descriptions of products and/ or making available corporate information over the Internet is small if your company already has an Internet information server. Again, information order fulfillment is much easier if the customer supplies both the request and the delivery mechanism. And you don't even have to print as many copies of your product literature!

A Quick List of Customer Support Ideas

Use FAQs to describe your products and services and how to contact your billing and/or fulfillment departments. Distribute your FAQs via e-mail, FTP, and the Web.

Use e-mail to "functional addresses" like support@YourCompany.com or accounting@YourCompany.com to direct messages from your customers to the right place in your organization. This works well even if the organization is just you. E-mail is simple and quick, and you can develop "standardized" answers that explain things to your customers in terms they understand.

Use private newsgroups to enable your customers to ask questions and to let you (or your other customers) answer them in a timely manner—newsgroups are fast.

Use mailing lists for similar things. If you have multiple products, keep a mailing list of the customers for each of your products. Make announcements of new features this way. Or if you need to do a recall, you can reach your customers this way quickly and inexpensively.

FTP can be used to distribute changes to your products (if your products happen to be software) or to distribute updated manuals.

Gopher and WWW continue to be the preferred places to distribute information that you want to reach potential customers as well as current customers. Here's were you want to put announcements of new products and changes in your business.

Legal Concerns

Any customer service organization has concerns about legal operation and legal responsibility for its actions. An Internet-based customer service organization is no different. Internet-based customer services have additional concerns that must be discussed with your organization's legal staff, however:

Intellectual property law: If your organization publishes information over the Internet, you will want to consider the implications of copyright law. Right now, the copyright law is broken many, many times per day on the Internet. Generally, the lawbreaker is not malicious, but people routinely send the intellectual property of another off to a friend or colleague using e-mail and they don't even think about the implications of what they are doing. Several very popular newspaper columnists (particularly Dave Barry and Miss Manners) have had their copyrighted works spread like ripples in a pond when a stone is tossed into the water. If you have intellectual property about which you are particularly concerned, you will probably not want to put it on the Internet until the law and its recourse become more clear and more able to be enforced.

Many of the nicer graphical Web pages contain copyright statements that are intended to protect both the images and the text contained therein. Look at the statement at

```
http://www.hp.com
```

or

```
http://www.sun.com
```

for examples from Hewlett-Packard and Sun Microsystems.

Indemnity: You will want to include some sort of statement somewhere among your customer services information that indemnifies you and your organization in case someone is harmed by the use of, or the inaccuracy of the information. Once more, you will want to discuss this issue with your legal advisors. The ability of a user of your information to be harmed is probably not any different than if the information were published on paper. However, if you provide the ability to download or transfer files to another computer system from your customer service unit, you will want to explicitly state something about the contents of the files and the accuracy of them. If you guarantee their quality, then there is no problem.

Be particularly careful to display a good disclaimer if you allow people other than those in your control (employed by you or contracted to you) to place files on your server for transfer to others. Also, if you, as a service to your customers, provide links to other information servers, you will want your disclaimer to point out that you can't be responsible for the material that is not under your control.

If you provide a method of sharing ideas among your customer community (Usenet or mailing lists, etc.), you will want to think a bit about libel law and your potential indemnity. Your legal advisors will be able to advise you. A recent case held that information service providers are more like booksellers (that is, not necessarily responsible for the content of the books in the bookstore) than they are like authors. With the Internet tradition of the "flame" message, you might want to think about making clear rules about what is acceptable to you (and your legal advisors) within your customer service environment. This does assume that your customer service employees are not posting or mailing libelous material over your organization's name. You may well be responsible for the actions of your employees. Again, consult your legal advisors.

Jurisdiction: Finally, you will want to consult with your legal advisors about the laws of your governmental jurisdiction as they might affect doing business electronically. The Internet is global but local laws do apply. Some jurisdictions, for example, require specific legal terminology on purchase orders. If the terminology is required to be printed on the back of the "form" and there is no "form" (or back of the form), you might not be able to implement the acceptance of purchase orders over the Internet as part of your customer services.

A Final Concern: Security

You will want to give careful consideration to security for your customer services system. This means that if you allow your customer to log in to your systems, they should have explicit user IDs and passwords, or they should be in a controlled environment (like using an approved client program that attaches to your server). Unless your service is one that provides a programming or computing environment for others, your customers should not be allowed to roam around your computing environment without restriction.

Other prudent security measures include strict controls over file permissions (a file permission determines who can read, write and/or execute the contents of a file)—how they are implemented, by what criteria, and by whom. Security is best served by letting "outsiders" into your system only via the appropriate client software, such as Gopher or Web browsers, or FTP clients—not by Telnet. This client software can have appropriate permissions applied that will keep unauthorized people out of areas where they do not belong.

On the Internet there is a certain fringe set of users who revel in breaking into other computing systems and leaving messages so that systems administrators will know they have been broken into. Usually the intrusions are not malicious, but you must expect that it will happen to your site. Be prepared. Conduct regular security audits (along with your content audits) to check the walls.

22

General Resources
for Internet Masters

FEATURING

General resources

E-mail mailing lists

Newsgroups

Online archives

Professional or special-interest groups

Chapter 22

General Resources for Internet Masters

YOU'LL remember we said at the beginning of the book that there were too many fun things going on with the Net for any one person to be able to know and use all of them. But here are some useful, interesting, or just plain fun things that we think everyone ought to know about.

Many of our favorite resources have been documented in the chapters devoted to individual Internet tools. We have tried not to duplicate those references here.

Be sure to check the other "Resources" chapters as well as this one; our categories necessarily overlap a little, and you may find items of interest in those chapters, too.

General Resources

There are so many general sites and resources on the Net that not only would a book about them be bigger than this one is now, it would never catch up to the new changes. So we'll give you some of our favorites and things we've found most useful.

Project OPEN

Project OPEN—the Online Public Education Network—is an educational organization that hopes to "Make the Net Work for You." Formed by several commercial online and Internet service providers under the auspices of the Interactive Services Association, Project OPEN focuses on four basic points: parental empowerment, intellectual property, privacy, and consumer protection. In conjunction with the National Consumers League, Project OPEN and the ISA provide a site that includes pointers to Internet and online service site selection programs, guidelines for consumers using online investment services, and links to other sites for more information. You can also download the Project OPEN brochure or request that one be sent to you. Figure 22.1 shows the Project OPEN home page.

WWW:

```
http://www.isa.net/project-open
```

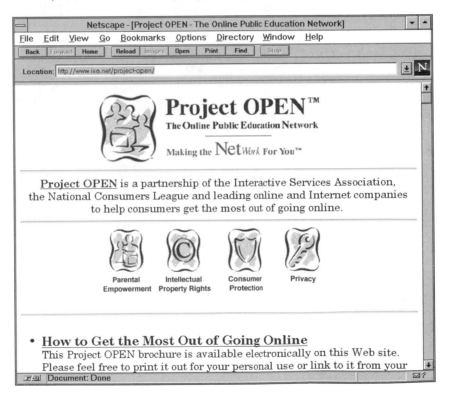

Figure 22.1. **The home page for Project OPEN.**

National Fraud Information Center

The National Consumers League, in conjunction with the US Federal Trade Commission and The National Association of Attorneys General, has founded the National Fraud Information Center. Here you can report suspected telemarketing and Internet scams. Figure 22.2 shows their home page.

WWW:

```
http://nfic.inter.net/nfic
```

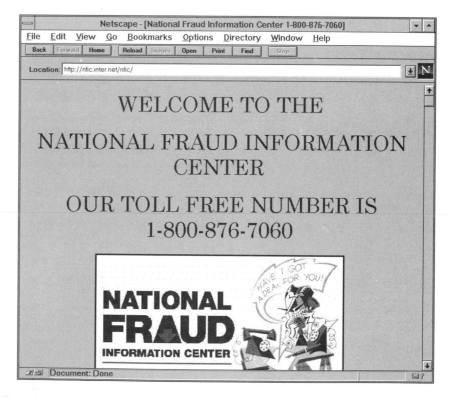

Figure 22.2.   The home page for the National Fraud Information Center.

The Federal Trade Commission

The FTC maintains its own Web site, of course. Here you can join a discussion about privacy, find out the latest information on hearings, locate commission documents, and find pointers to still more sites that will help you be a wiser consumer.

WWW:

```
http://www.ftc.gov
```

Voters Telecommunications Watch

This site, along with the EFF site at

```
http://www.eff.org
```

and the Center for Democracy and Technology

```
http://www.cdt.org
```

are among the best of the sites to gather information about issues on the Internet. Decidedly individualistic, VTW follows the issues and how they are treated, discussed, and legislation enacted about them in the United States. It includes a bill watch, a congressional directory service, and a number of FAQs about parental empowerment, the Communications Decency Act, and "The Citizens Guide to the Internet." Figure 22.3 shows the VTW home page.

WWW:

```
http://www.vtw.org
```

Grant-Getter's Guide to the Internet

A Gopher resource that serves as a major entry point for grant-finding on the Internet. The Federal Register, FEDIX, MOLIS, Fedworld, and others can be accessed from this one site. The Guide itself is a nice bibliography of grant sources on the Internet.

Gopher:

```
gopher://gopher.uidaho.edu
```

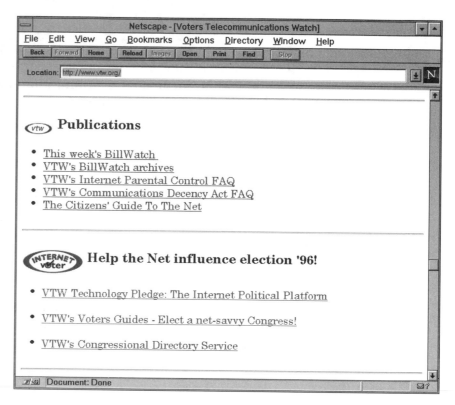

Figure 22.3.   *The home page for VTW.ORG.*

News and Views

The following Web sites help you keep up with the latest news around the globe—from the people who are practiced in bringing it to you, the news gathering force of the journalistic community. There are many newspapers on the Net, here we show just a few.

CNN Interactive

Now you can stay glued to your computer tube as well as your TV screen and get the latest news from CNN.

Figure 22.4 shows the CNN Interactive home page.

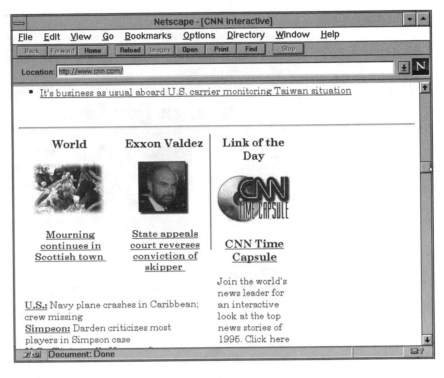

Figure 22.4.   The home page for CNN Interactive.

The New York Times on the Web

The *New York Times* online site has most of their articles as well as background information on sources, etc. You'll need to register but there is no extra fee involved at this time. Look for the crossword puzzles.

Figure 22.5 shows the *Times* home page.

WWW:

http://www.nytimes.com

Mercury Center: The San Jose Mercury News

This newspaper from the heart of Silicon Valley has a service, called Mercury Center, that allows you to read the first paragraph or so of the news story. You must be a subscriber to their online service to read the remainder of the story. Subscription services are available online.

WWW:

http://www.sjmercury.com

Figure 22.6 shows the Mercury News home page.

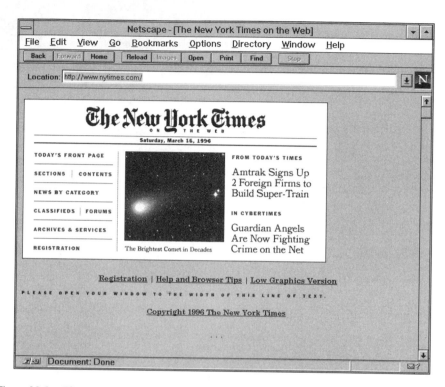

Figure 22.5.   *The New York Times on the Web home page.*

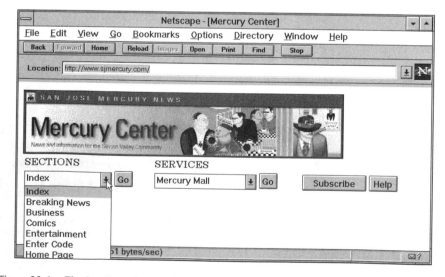

Figure 22.6.   *The San Jose Mercury News home page.*

SFGate: The San Francisco Chronice and the San Francisco Examiner

A service of the *San Francisco Chronicle* and the *San Francisco Examiner*, The Gate changes its look twice a day (morning and evening editions). Additional news is added throughout the day. A particular delight of this service is access to the *Chronicle* and *Examiner* columnists. Figure 22.7 shows the home page.

WWW:

http://www.sfgate.com

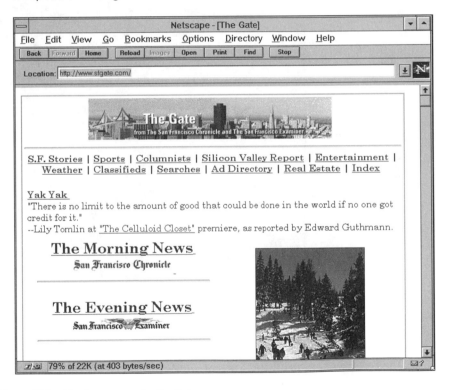

Figure 22.7. **The home page for the Gate.**

USA Today

The online version of *USA Today*. Look particularly at the "Web Traveler." An excellent resource for quick hits on topics of immediate interest. Like other newspapers, this site changes frequently, so frequently that you can hit "reload" every two minutes during big basketball tournaments to get the latest scores in the Sports section. Figure 22.8 shows the home page.

WWW:

```
http://www.usatoday.com
```

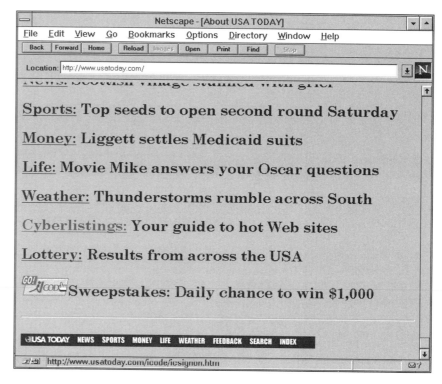

Figure 22.8. The USA Today home page.

Voice of America News

Despite the end of the Cold War, the Voice of America still broadcasts its news services all over the world. The main focus is on international news, and the sports reporting is mainly about soccer. The time lag is minimal—five minutes from when the report is released by VOA central—making this a very timely and useful resource. You can connect to VOA Audio and hear the broadcasts, too.

Gopher:

```
gopher://gopher.voa.gov
```

Inter@ctive Week

Inter@ctive Week is a "trade" publication—a magazine directed to the people who are building, managing, designing the networks and the Internet sites that we all use. The publication has an important online component, too. You may not be able to subscribe to the print publication (it's a restricted publication, intended for those in the industry), but you can see what the industry is reading at this Web site. *Inter@ctive Week* is a publication of Ziff Davis. Figure 22.9 shows the home page.

Figure 22.9. **The home page for Inter@ctive Week.**

WWW:

    http://www.interactive-week.com/~intweek

Other Ziff publications can be found at

    http://www.zdnet.com

Libraries and Reference Information

The Internet is a convenient place to look for lots of general reference resources. Here are a few really useful ones.

American Memory Project

The American Memory Project, from the Library of Congress, contains sound recordings, prints, and photographs. Primary source materials and archival materials relating to American culture are available through the library's Web server. There are photographs from the Civil War, Documentation from the Constitutional Convention, 600 portraits from the Matthew Brady studio, sound recordings from the presidential election of 1920, and an exhibit of the works of Carl Van Vechten, photographer of American celebrities, artists, and literary figures. The Library of Congress' American Memory Web pages can be reached via

WWW:

```
http://lcweb2.loc.gov/ammem/ammemhome.html
```

Michigan Electronic Library

An electronic public library from the libraries of the state of Michigan, The Library of Michigan, the Merit Network, and University of Michigan Library's MLINK program. It's arranged by broad subject categories: business and economics; computers and technology; education; entertainment and recreation; environment; government and politics; health and nutrition; humanities; libraries and information science; Michigan; news services, newsletters and journals; a reference desk; science; social issues and social services; and the Internet and its other resources. This service is one of the best starting points for new Internet users and has subject collections in great depth for experienced users. One of the better reference desks on the Internet.

WWW:

```
http://mlink.hh.lib.umich.edu/
```

CARL

The Colorado Alliance of Research Libraries (CARL) offers much more than just an online library catalog of Colorado academic, public, and special libraries. The CARL UnCover document delivery service is open to the public, offering a keyword index to over 17,000 periodicals (magazines and journals). Journal Graphics will mail or fax television news transcripts in their archives. You must have a credit card or deposit account with CARL.

Telnet:

```
telnet:database.carl.org
```

for more information. This address is also the entry point for accessing many of the library catalogs supported by CARL Systems. In this service, you pay for the articles that you wish sent to you.

LC Marvel

The main Gopher server at the Library of Congress, LC Marvel, contains an enormous amount of information not only about the Library of Congress itself, but also about the US government. Library of Congress publications, the Center for the Book, Services to the Blind and Physically Handicapped, Reading Rooms, the American Folklife Center, the Asian Collection, Geography and Maps, and the On-line Business Center are only a few of the areas covered by this Gopher. Although it's sometimes hard to move through because of the incredible amount of information, this Gopher is worth delving into. A hierarchical menu tree file of what's available is helpful.

Gopher:

```
gopher://marvel.loc.gov
```

The Internet Law Library

A part of the information gathered for the US House of Representatives is available as the Internet Law Library, illustrated in Figure 22.10. You'll find links there to federal, state, and international laws and treaties.

WWW:

```
http://www.pls.com:8001
```

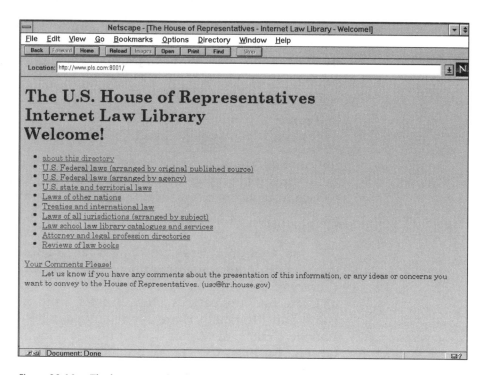

Figure 22.10.   The home page for the Internet Law Library.

1990 Census Data

Census Data from the US government is of great importance to almost every business, institution, nonprofit and other organizations for planning and implementing new products, programs, services and marketing. Since much of the government's data is now being released in machine-readable format (and in some cases *only* in machine-readable format), and since that information is in the public domain, a number of depository libraries have found the Internet to be an ideal method of disseminating this data. The State of Michigan, for example, has organized a Web site with Michigan's data. Other sites include ones such as Beaver County, Pennsylvania's, and, of course, the Web site from the Census Bureau, itself.

WWW:

```
http://mic1.dmb.state.mi.us/michome/mic.htm
http://www.co.beaver.pa.us/
http://www.census.gov
```

A Hypertext Dictionary

The Hypertext Webster Interface, illustrated in Figure 22.11, is an online dictionary. Enter the word about which you'd like more information in the space provided, and submit your entry. The definition will be returned to you. Each word in the definition may be linked to other words in the hypertext dictionary, so that if any of those aren't known to you, you can simply click and look that word up, also. And, the dictionary is linked into a thesaurus, the entries of which are also hyperlinked to more definitions. An excellent tool.

WWW:

http://c.gp.cs.cmu.edu:5103/prog/webster

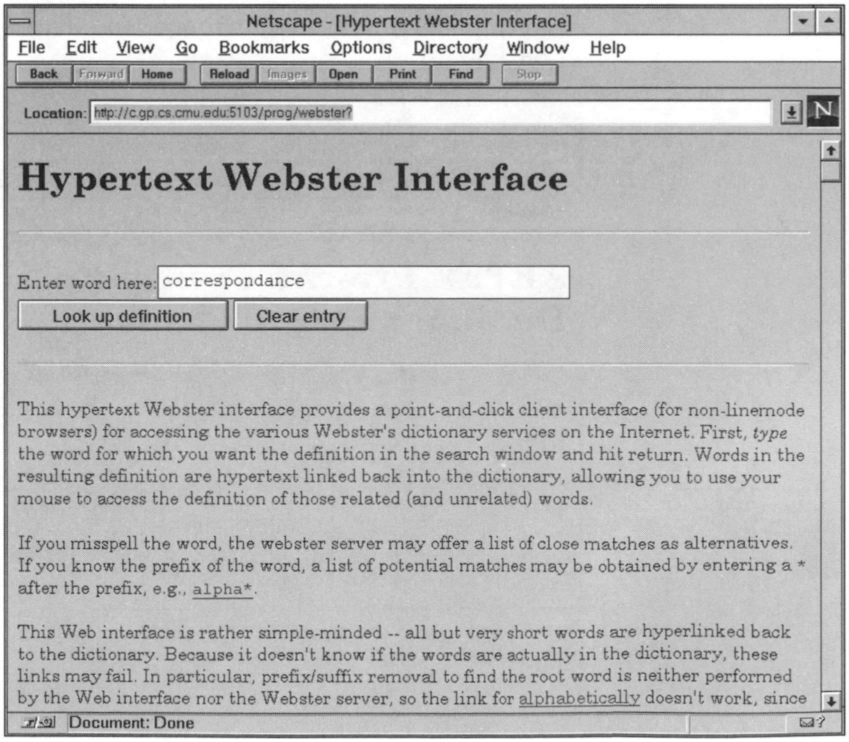

Figure 22.11. The Hypertext Webster Interface home page.

A French-English Dictionary

English-to-French and French-to-English, what more could one want? Here a site at the University of Chicago provides easy-to-use forms that will get you from one language to another. The dictionary, illustrated in Figure 22.12, is part of the Project for American and French Research on the Treasury of the French Language (the ARTFL Project). You can find out more about the project at

WWW:

> http://humanities.uchicago.edu/ARTFL.html

The dictionary can be found at

WWW:

> http://humanities.uchicago.edu/forms_unrest/
> FR-ENG.html

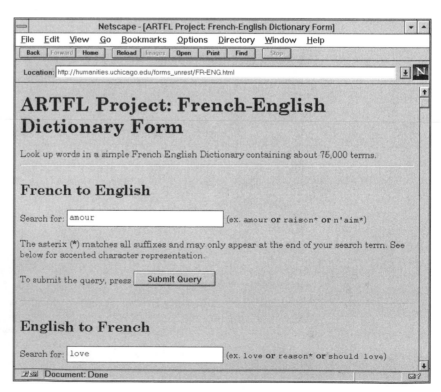

Figure 22.12.   *The ARTFL Project home page, a French-English dictionary.*

Zip Code Lookup

The US Postal Service has provided a great lookup service, illustrated in Figure 22.13, so that you can get those cards and letters to the right place. If you have an address (street or mailing), a city name and the state, you can enter those into this page. You'll get back the correct ZIP + Four postal code so that your letter or package will arrive promptly.

WWW:

http://www.usps.gov/ncsc/lookups/welcome.html

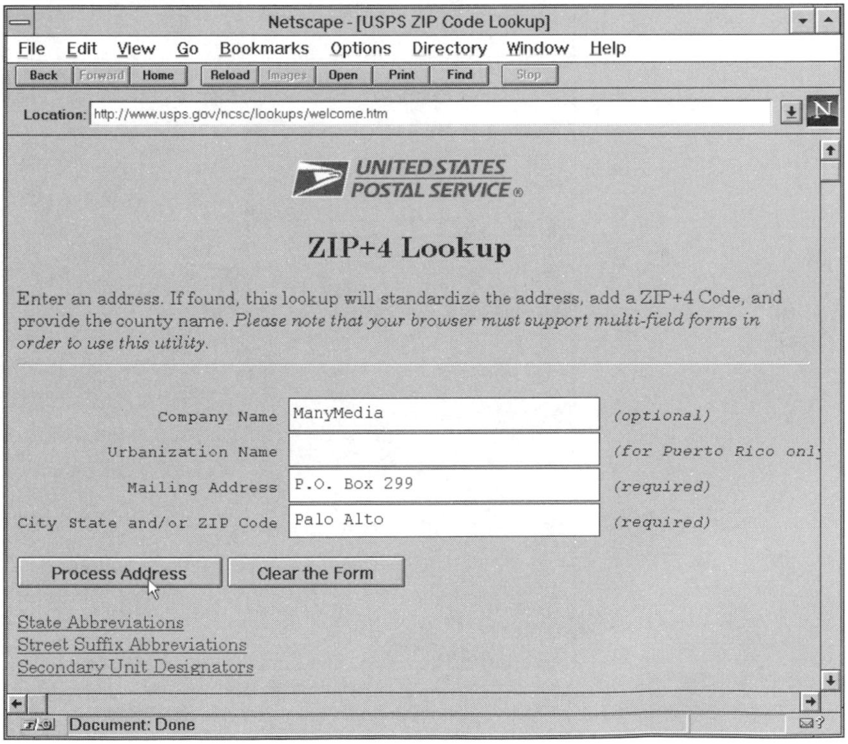

Figure 22.13. The US Postal Service ZIP+4 Lookup home page.

Calendar

If you need to know the specific day of the week on which a certain event happened, this calendar is for you. You enter the month and the year, and the formatted calendar is displayed for you, as illustrated in Figure 22.14.

WWW:

> http://www.cmf.nrl.navy.mil/calendar

Figure 22.14.   **Looking up January 1974 in the Calendar.**

Time—Anywhere

If you need to know whether it's too late to call your family or friends in Germany, here's the site to help you. If you select either the time zone or a city near your point of interest, the correct day of the week, month, day of the month, time of day, time zone, and year will be displayed. Figure 22.15 shows a typical view.

WWW:

http://www.bsdi.com/date

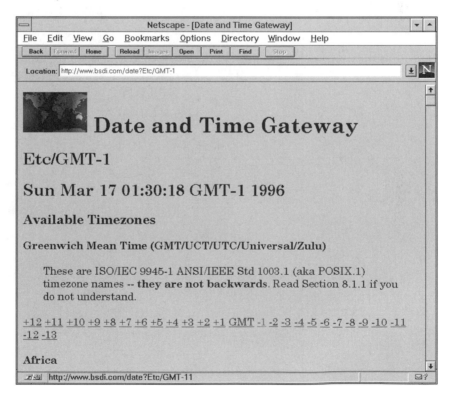

Figure 22.15.   The Date and Time Gateway.

CIA World Fact Book

The US federal government's externally focused intelligence agency has long been known for its excellent documents describing all the parts of the world. Each year, the CIA produces another "World Fact Book." You can find the 1995 edition (Illustrated in Figure 22.16) online at the CIA's Web site. Earlier versions are available around the Net, too.

WWW:

```
http://www.odci.gov/cia/publications
```

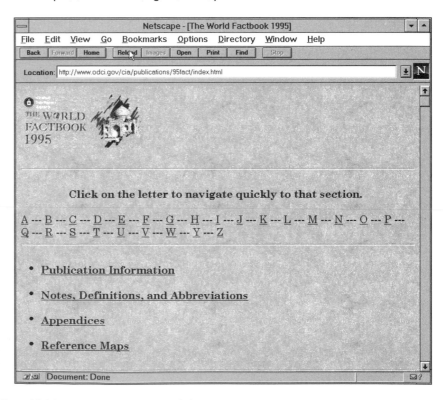

Figure 22.16.   ***The CIA World Factbook for 1995.***

Rehabilitation Information Center

The National Rehabilitation Information Center provides resources to disabled persons and their families via the Web. Some of their full-text online materials include resources for stroke victims and their families, and resources for those who have suffered spinal cord injuries and brain trauma, as well as a valuable publication on modifying your home so that it works better for your disabled person.

WWW:

```
http://www.cais.net/naric/
```

NCSA Mosaic Home Page

The home of Mosaic, the University of Illinois at Champaign-Urbana's Supercomputing Center is "the" place to get information about the Mosaic client for the World Wide Web. Mosaic is only one of many WWW clients and browsers, but it made the greatest initial impact on the use of the Web. Their home page includes a Mosaic demo, What's New on the Web, Web security information, e-mail addresses for help with Mosaic, and connections to FTP sites for the various Mosaic clients available.

WWW:

```
http://www.ncsa.uiuc.edu/
http://www.ncsa.uiuc.edu/General/NCSAExhibits.html
```

(This the URL for a wonderful set of science exhibits hosted at NCSA.)

```
http://skydive.ncsa.uiuc.edu
```

(This is the address for the Virtual Federal Agency, working to facilitate interagency cooperation.)

Sporting Sites

In the past year or so, the Web sites produced by fans of particular sports have been somewhat eclipsed by the introduction of the professionally designed, implemented, and maintained sports sites. Two of the best that cover many sports are

WWW:

```
http://espnet.sportszone.com
http://www.sportsnetwork.com
```

We're sure that you'll find different pages that are especially good for the sport (or team) you love to play (or watch).

Internet Resources Meta-Index

A hypertext bibliography of tools for finding information on the Internet, such as the World Wide Web Worm, The Clearinghouse for Subject-Oriented Internet Resource Guides, The NCSA Mosaic What's New page, the Central Index of WWW servers at CERN, and more. A good starting place for new Web users.

WWW:

```
http://www.ncsa.uiuc.edu/SDG/Software/Mosaic/
MetaIndex.html
```

Xerox Map Viewer

The Xerox Palo Alto Research Center (PARC) is providing the PARC Web Map Viewer as an experiment in dynamic information retrieval. Maps of the world and the United States can be requested using a WWW client such as Mosaic. Embedded hypertext links allow you to pan, zoom or change the level of detail. Map data (all of which is public domain) is from the CIA World Data Bank II with higher-resolution US data provided by the USGS 1:2,000,000-Scale Digital Line Graph Data. Though not as sophisticated as using some of the commercially available Graphical Imaging System (GIS) software, this is an important move toward easy-to-use GIS on the Internet. A Best of the Web '94 winner for both Technical Merit and Best Use of Interaction, as well as the winner of many other awards. Figure 22.17 shows the opening Web page, and Figure 22.18 shows the view after clicking on a point in northern California.

WWW:

```
http://pubweb.parc.xerox.com/map/
```

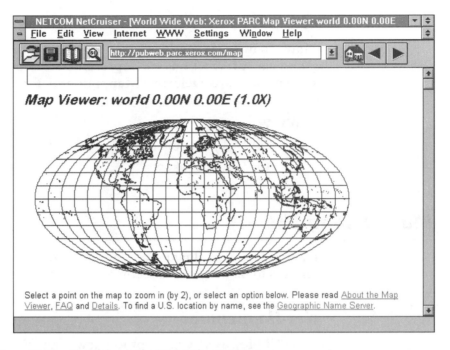

Figure 22.17. **The Globe via the PARC Web map viewer.**

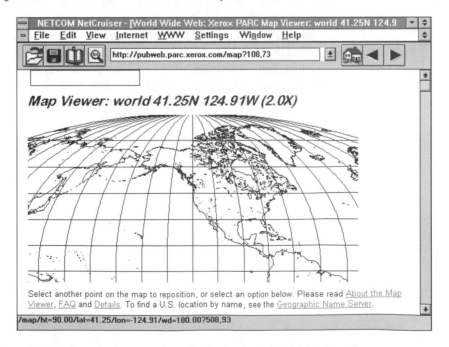

Figure 22.18. **Zooming in on northern California via the PARC Web map viewer.**

Mapping Information

Many companies that produce information products based on geographical information are represented on the Internet. Two well known ones are Delorme Mapping and Etak Incorporated. These companies (and many others) demonstrate their products via the Web.

WWW:

```
http://www.delorme.com/
http://www.etak.com
```

E-Mail Mailing Lists

Here are some mailing lists to join if you'd like announcements of new services to be delivered directly to your e-mail in-box.

Net-Happenings

"The" list for users who want to know *everything* that's new on the Net and that's happening to the Net. List owner Gleason Sackmann forwards thousands of bytes of information a day to keep up with the ever-changing Internet environment. This list has a digest option that will allow you to receive the postings in big gulps rather than dribs and drabs; but be warned, even in Digest form it generates a large amount of mail. This list is essential to Gopher or Web administrators and others who serve as the Internet expert for their community. To subscribe, send a subscription message to:

```
majordomo@lists.internic.net
```

and include either

```
subscribe net-happenings
```

or

```
subscribe net-happenings-digest
```

in the body of your message, depending upon which you'd like to receive.

You can also read Net-Happenings via the Web at

WWW:

```
http://www.gi.net/NET
```

and

WWW:

```
http://www.gi.net/NEWSLETTER/
```

for the newsletters.

GopherJewels

This mailing list sends out a small amount of daily traffic on interesting Gopher finds. Usually there are no more than five messages per day. This list is perfect for those who'd like to see what's good and new in gopherspace or who are maintaining a Gopher server that includes outside resources. To subscribe, send a message to:

```
listproc@einet.net
```

GopherJewels-Talk

Since the GopherJewels list is limited to postings about interesting Gopher sites, GopherJewels-Talk supplies a place for people to ask questions about Gopher or discuss issues. It's mainly for Internet neophytes who are looking for a friendly place to pose a Gopher question and not get flamed by the "experts." To subscribe, send a message to:

```
listproc@einet.net
```

NEWNIR-L

Announcements of new Network Information Retrieval services and OPACs (On-line Public Access Catalogs) are made here and include WWW, Gopher or WAIS servers and CWISes. Another high-traffic list like Net-Happenings, but without the extra "information technology" postings. To subscribe:

```
listserv@itocsivm.bitnet
```

or

```
listserv%itocsivm.bitnet@icineca.cineca.it
```

New-List Mailing List

New-List is an announcement service for new mailing lists on the Internet and BITnet. To subscribe:

```
listserv@ndsuvm1.nodak.edu
```

ASSESS List

ASSESS—Assessment in Higher Education. Assessment methodology is not just relevant to higher education situations; it can also be transferred to other learning environments. Topics in the past have included teacher effectiveness, TQM (Total Quality Management), surveys, and portfolio assessment. Subscribe to:

```
listserv@ukcc.bitnet
```

or

```
listserv@ukcc.uky.edu
```

COM-PRIV

A heavy-traffic list that discusses the commercialization/privatization of the Internet. This is a hot issue right now, with the big communications corporations wanting part of the pie and the "old culture" of the Internet wanting things to remain the same. A good place to find out who's doing what on which front. To subscribe, send e-mail to:

```
com-priv-request@psi.com
```

Searching for mailing lists

There are several sites that can help you find a mailing list in which you might be interested. Try them all, because they are each a little different. You will receive a larger number of possibilities if you enter a single word, or part of a word.

WWW:

```
http://www.liszt.com/
http://www.lsoft.com
http://www.nova.edu/Inter-Links/cgi-bin/news-lists.pl
```

Newsgroups

As discussed in Chapter 13, there are literally thousands of Usenet newsgroups. Here are a few of the most useful and interesting. (Thanks to Dave Taylor for the descriptions from his FAQ about social newsgroups.)

comp.infosystems.announce

This is where new Internet services and tools are announced. Be sure to look periodically for corrections. Many service providers get excited and jump the gun, leaving out pertinent information.

comp.infosystems.gopher

This newsgroup focuses mainly on the technology behind Gopher and announcements of new Gopher servers. However, there are better ways to find out about new Gopher servers if you aren't interested in the technological talk. (See GopherJewels and Net-Happenings under "Discussion Lists," later in this chapter.)

comp.infosystems.www.users

This heavy-traffic group discusses ways to use the World Wide Web and new Web servers and services.

comp.society.privacy

This group discusses privacy and networking subjects such as credit card information and bank accounts on the Internet, how to make an anonymous posting on the Internet, e-mail privacy cases, and phone taps.

soc.couples

Being in a short- or long-term relationship offers much in the way of joy, pleasure, and emotional satisfaction, but it also offers the chance for major arguments and other problems. This is where you can talk about the relationship you're in with others who are also in relationships.

soc.feminism

This is a moderated newsgroup for the discussion of feminist issues. Both men and women are encouraged to post to it, and discussion is not limited to the pro-feminist viewpoint. This group differs from soc.women (see below) in that moderation keeps out the flames and inappropriate cross-posts. In addition, there are subjects appropriate for soc.women but not soc.feminism (for example, the sporadic "where do I find comfortable shoes?" discussion that turns up in soc.women or discussions of women's health that aren't related to policy).

soc.men

This group discusses similar issues to soc.women (see below), but from the male perspective. Topics include equal rights, child support, custody of children, relationships, and so on. In addition, there are often topics specific to men including shaving in the shower, post-workout skin care, and similar. Both men and women are active participants in this group.

soc.motss

While the Usenet community is pretty open-minded, many social groups tend to be populated primarily by heterosexuals. Soc.motss (Members of the Same Sex) is where people who are lesbian, gay, bisexual, or just interested and sympathetic can share conversation about relationships, dating, travel, and the like. Discussion of the validity or appropriateness of homosexuality is inappropriate, however, and will not be appreciated.

soc.singles

Of all the things that people seem to have in common, perhaps the most common thread of all is the bouts of being single, and the hunting and searching for relationships that this implies. This group is a forum for all discussions even vaguely related to either being single or the quest for a relationship. Indeed, it has been likened to an electronic cocktail party, where people have known each other (electronically, usually) for years. There are also a number of people in relationships who share their thoughts, as well as a high level of aggression between some of the contributors.

soc.women

Soc.women is an unmoderated group that discusses similar issues to soc.men, but from the female perspective. Topics include equal rights, child support, custody of children, relationships and so on. In addition, there are often topics specific to women including shaving legs, finding comfortable shoes, and so on. Both men and women are active participants in this group.

Support Groups

In the `alt.support`, `misc.health`, and `alt.psychology` Usenet hierarchies, you'll find a variety of online support groups. For example:

Depression and mood disorders	`alt.support.depression`
Eating disorders (anorexia, bulimia, etc.)	`alt.support.eating-disord`
Learning disabilities (dyslexia, etc.)	`alt.support.learning-disab`
Stopping or quitting smoking	`alt.support.stop-smoking`
Stuttering and other speaking difficulties	`alt.support.stuttering`
Other support topics and questions	`alt.support`
Diabetes, hypoglycemia	`misc.health.diabetes`
General discussion of AIDS and HIV	`misc.health.aids`
General help with psychological problems	`alt.psychology.help`

Archives

Archive is the general name given to any authoritative or at least well-maintained site that stores interesting articles, programs, or texts from newsgroups for long periods. Searching Internet archives can be as interesting as searching the archives at a major research library. These are sites you can "mine" for historical treasure—even though the history is relatively recent.

CERT Security Archives

The Computer Emergency Response Team is the group responsible for tracking and fixing security problems on the Internet. When problems are reported to the group, it responds to the Internet community by issuing CERT Advisories that detail the problem and the solutions. Being able to access these advisories is important to any and all system administrators on the Internet.

Gopher:

```
gopher://gopher.systems.cit.princeton.edu
```

then choose Production ➤ workstations ➤ security ➤ cert from the menus.

FTP:

```
ftp://cert.org/pub/cert_advisories
```

Electronic Frontier Foundation

The Electronic Frontier Foundation (EFF) is an organization formed in 1990 to ensure that the First Amendment rights and the principles of the US Constitution are protected as we move into the new technologies. They also support people waging legal battles in this new area and offer materials to help support community building and equal access to electronic information. They maintain a large archive of documents related to legal cases in this area, news releases, articles of interest, recent and proposed legislation, materials for online activists, electronic publications, and information alerts.

Gopher:

```
gopher://gopher.eff.org
```

FTP:

```
ftp.eff.org
```

WWW:

```
http://www.eff.org/
```

CICNet Electronic Journals Collection

The CIC universities (the Big Ten plus the University of Chicago and Notre Dame) oversee the CICNet Electronic Journal Collection and the CICNet E-Serials Archive. You'll want to read about the collection policies so you'll know what is in the collection. CICNet is the regional education and research network in the Great Lakes region of the United States.

An interesting aspect of CICNet is that it is an activity of the Committee on Institutional Cooperation (CIC), where the universities have been working together for more than 30 years. In the About file, CIC notes that they focus on FTP site-available journals and are less aggressive about e-mail journals. The CICNet journal archive is an important resource as librarians and publishers struggle over the issue of maintaining records in an electronic environment. A Subject arrangement provides more access than the usual list of titles. Like the Research Libraries of its member institutions, CICNet and its Networked Information Resources Committee have developed collection policies for this archive. The more formal collection has pages that allow you to browse by title or by topic via the Web. The E-Serials archive has a Gopher interface.

Part IV

Internet Resources

Gopher:

```
gopher://gopher.cic.net:2000/11/e-serials/archive
```

for the E-Serials archive.

WWW:

```
http://ejournals.cic.net/
```

for the managed CIC Electronic Journals collection.

MERIT Internet Archives

The MERIT Organization managed the NSFnet (the former principal US backbone of the Internet). In that capacity, MERIT kept statistics in its Gopher and FTP services. These statistics, still available at the sites below, are useful for charting the growth of the backbone and of particular services on the network until the network was retired in 1995. Unfortunately, there is no single place like MERIT for the statistics to be gathered today.

WWW:

```
http://nic.merit.edu
```

Gopher:

```
gopher://nic.merit.edu:70/1/.nsf-info
```

FTP:

```
ftp://nic.merit.edu
```

MERIT/University of Michigan Software Archives

A large body of public-domain, freeware, shareware and licensed software (the licensed software is *not* available by anonymous FTP) with Macintosh software by far the best represented. Atari, MS-DOS and Apple II files are also maintained to a lesser degree. This site is mirrored in many places around the world.

Gopher:

```
gopher://nic.merit.edu/1/.software-archives
```

FTP:

```
ftp://mac.archive.umich.edu
ftp://msdos.archive.umich.edu
ftp://atari.archive.umich.edu
ftp://apple2.archive.umich.edu.
```

Other US mirror sites:

```
ftp://wuarchive.wustl.edu (mirrors)
ftp://grind.isca.uiowa.edu (mac/umich)
ftp://archive.orst.edu (pub/mirrors).
```

Privacy Rights Clearinghouse

A Bulletin Board System (BBS) with a good collection of fact sheets, legislation, resources and press releases on issues relating to privacy. Some materials are available in both Spanish and English. There is a Web page that describes the clearinghouse, and a Gopher server. You can also reach the clearinghouse via Telnet.

WWW:

```
http://www.seamless.com/talf/ftc/priv.html
```

Gopher:

```
gopher://gopher.acusd.edu
```

then choose USD Campus-Wide Information System ➤ Privacy Rights Clearinghouse from the menus.

Telnet:

```
telnet:teetod.acusd.edu
```

and log in as `privacy`.

Professional or Special Interest Groups (SIGs)

Special Interest Groups and societies have long been a way to meet other people with similar interests and share resources. Here's a short list of those that might interest you in seeking more that you can contribute to, as well as gain from, your time on the Internet.

Internet Society (ISOC)

The Internet Society is an international organization that seeks to facilitate the collaborative means by which the Internet is run. Thousands of organizations are part of the Internet, and those organizations are eligible to participate through an institutional membership. Individuals may also be members. A journal, an annual meeting, workshops, and symposia are sponsored by this group.

WWW:

```
http://www.isoc.org
```

You can join the Society yourself via the forms on this site. For surface mail contact, write to:

The Internet Society Secretariat

12020 Sunrise Valley Drive, Suite 210

Reston, VA 22091

Americans Communicating Electronically (ACE)

Membership of ACE is very broad and includes individuals and private and government organizations wishing to promote interaction between any and all information providing bodies. To join yourself, fill out the entry form.

WWW:

```
http://www.sbaonline.sba.gov/ace/guide96.html
http://www.sbaonline.sba.gov/ace/signup.html
```

Other Goodies

Finally, here are a few interesting items that didn't fit well into other categories. We hope you'll enjoy them.

Pizza on the Internet

First in California... you can order your pizza via the Internet. Pizza Hut has debuted PizzaNet, a way for hungry cybernauts to get their nutrition with one hand while surfing with the other! You need to be in the Santa Cruz area and have a WWW client to place an order.

WWW:

```
http://pizzahut.com
```

We wonder if it gets cold over the Internet...

WWW Virtual Library

A hypertext document links you to Internet collections of resources on various topics in WWW, Gopher and FTP. The list is not comprehensive, and is organized (we think) by keyword as opposed to a classification scheme of some type. Consider this a good place to start a research project. Alphabetical by keyword.

WWW:

```
http://www.w3.org/pub/DataSources/bySubject/
Overview.html
```

Clearinghouse of Subject-Oriented Internet Guides

The University of Michigan Library and the School of Information and Library Studies began the clearinghouse as a joint project to help make librarians and students more aware of the wealth of Internet resources for reference and collection development work. It now houses bibliographies of Internet sources from people all over the world and serves as the major site for Internet subject bibliographies. More are added regularly and most are updated by their authors at least annually.

WWW:

```
http://www.lib.umich.edu/chhome.html
```

ARL Directory of Electronic Journals and Newsletters on the Internet

The fifth edition of a printed work begun by Diane Kovacs and now produced by the Association of Research Libraries with a team including Ann Okerson, editor. For each journal or newsletter you'll find a description of the item and subscription information. Information about the printed and Gopher editions can be found on the Web at:

WWW:

```
http://arl.cni.org/pubscat/publist.html
```

Gopher:

```
gopher://arl.cni.org/11/scomm/edir
```

Part
IV

Internet Resources

Direct from Pueblo

The US Consumer Information Center (you know, the one in Pueblo, Colorado) is online via a Bulletin Board Service, the Web and Gopher. From the Web site, you can download the 1996 Consumers Resource Handbook.

BBS:

202-208-7679

WWW:

```
http://www.pueblo.gsa.gov/
```

Gopher:

```
gopher.gsa.gov
```

then choose Consumer Information Center (cic).

disABILITY Information and Resources

There is a short but comprehensive list of Internet resources on disabilities made available by Jim Lubin. You can find out more about resources and about Jim himself by going to

WWW:

```
http://www.eskimo.com/~jlubin/disabled.html
```

CHAPTER 23

Government and Business Resources

FEATURING

General resources

E-mail mailing lists

Newsgroups

Professional or special-interest groups

Web pages

Chapter 23

Government and Business Resources

THIS listing of resources that are especially interesting for businesses is not exhaustive, but it does detail some of the more interesting ones available. For each resource there is a description and an address where you can find it, whether by Gopher, the Web, or by using Telnet to connect to the service.

Many of the general resources listed in Chapter 22 are also pertinent to businesses.

General Resources

Because the interests of business people are as far-ranging as the myriad businesses that can exist, this list of general resources is pretty far-ranging, too. We have included mostly United States government sources, because we live in the United States. The US government, however, is by no means the only government providing information via the Internet, so we've included some pointers to government information outside the US. And no list of government resources would be complete without a note that you can send e-mail to the president and vice president of the United States quite simply. Their addresses are president@whitehouse.gov and vice.president@whitehouse.gov. Mike Harris, the premier of Ontario province in Canada, can also be reached via e-mail. His address is premier@gov.on.ca.

EDGAR Dissemination Project

The EDGAR dissemination project makes available electronic corporate filings with the US Securities and Exchange Commission. Indexes are listed by company name and are updated daily. Users should note that not all corporations' files are public. This service evolved from an experimental service on the Internet that became so popular that demand for the data helped form this newer service. By mid-1996 all registrants will become subject to electronic filing requirements and you'll be able to find all those filings here. This service is of particular interest to businesses and investors who used to subscribe to another service to get copies of these reports.

WWW:

    http://www.sec.gov/edgarhp.htm

The EDGAR project was an early success story of Ralph Nader's Taxpayer Asset Project (TAP). Jamie Love with TAP is an active advocate of each and every citizen having reasonable access to the information gathered in the name of the citizenry. You can find the archives from the project at

WWW:

    http://cpsr.org/pub/taxpayer_assets

The White House

The Executive Branch of the United States government now has an Internet entry point beginning at the White House. Figure 23.1 shows the picture index that you will see with a graphical Web browser. From here you can take a virtual tour of Washington, DC, see pictures of the "First Family," and move to other sources of federal information. Clicking on the portion of the picture (or choosing from the textual index) "the Executive Branch" will present you with choices for "the President's Cabinet" (Figure 23.2) and "the Independent Federal Agencies and Commissions" (Figure 23.3).

This entry point provides "one-stop" shopping for information from the top down. If you have trouble remembering which particular agency goes with which cabinet department, an index to federal sources of information is available on the "Executive Branch" Web page. Or, from that same page, if you remember where the office is geographically, you can use a map of Washington, DC, to locate your information source.

WWW:

    http://www.whitehouse.gov

Part
IV

Internet Resources

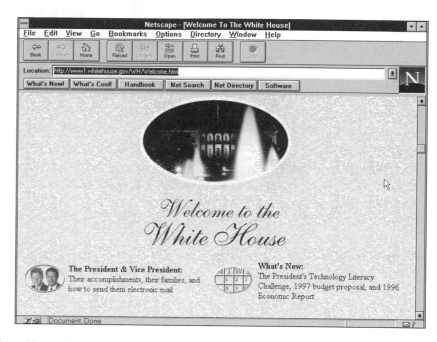

Figure 23.1.   **The Web page for the White House.**

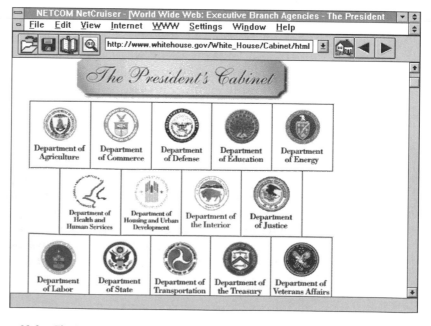

Figure 23.2.   **The Web page for the President's Cabinet.**

Figure 23.3. The Web page for Independent Federal Agencies and Commissions.

STAT-USA

The Department of Commerce includes among its information providers the Economics and Statistics Administration. This service provides economic, business, and social/environmental information from more than fifty federal sources. This service was built around the popular National Trade Data Bank (NTDB). STAT-USA provides data using the Web, Gopher, and FTP. The access is free for most data. Some cost recovery fees are charged for more recent data being served by the Web. The STAT-USA FTP site shown in Figure 23.4 contains data for which there are no access charges.

Gopher:

    gopher.stat-usa.gov

FTP:

    ftp.stat-usa.gov

WWW:

    http://www.stat-usa.gov

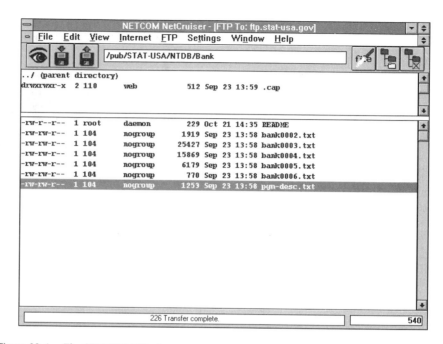

Figure 23.4. The STAT-USA FTP site.

SBA Online

The Small Business Administration provides another extremely useful federal information site. From their Web pages you can find information about, for example, financing businesses and about export arrangements. Figure 23.5 shows the graphical entry point to this information.

WWW:

    http://www.sbaonline.sba.gov

Canadian Federal Government Open Government Pilot

The federal government of Canada is also sponsoring a project to make its information more widely available via the Internet. Because of the long distances and sparse population of Canada, they've chosen to distribute their information across the country by keeping copies of the information at "mirror sites." This allows Canadians (and other interested people, too, of course) reasonable access to the sites. Figure 23.6

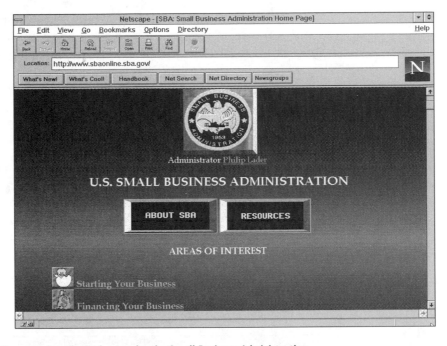

Figure 23.5. The Web page for the Small Business Administration.

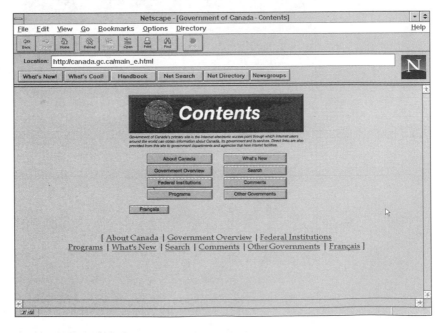

Figure 23.6. The Web page for Canada's Government.

shows a section of the entry Web page, with the bilingual entry points to the House of Commons and the Canadian Senate. From this page you can also find entries for the federal departments and agencies.

WWW:

```
http://www.gc.ca/
```

Her Majesty's Information

It's not just North American countries that are making their national information available. Figure 23.7 shows an entry point for the United Kingdom. These pages are being developed by the Government Centre for Information Systems, also known as the CCTA Government Information Service. They are responsible for stimulating and promoting effective use of information systems in support of efficient delivery of business objectives and improved quality of services by the public sector.

WWW:

```
http://www.open.gov.uk/
```

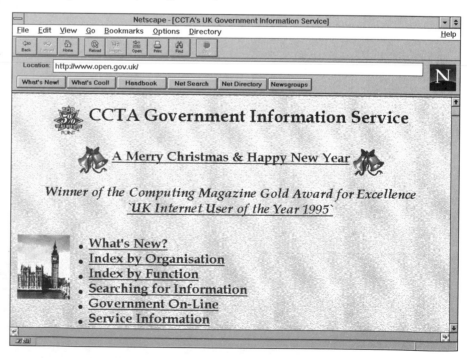

Figure 23.7.   The Web page for the UK's Government Centre for Information Systems.

South Dakota

Government information on the Internet isn't limited to that from national governments. South Dakota provides an entry point (shown in Figure 23.8) with its most famous landmark, Mount Rushmore, featured prominently. Click around the mountain for information about tourist locations, business opportunities, and education located within the boundaries of this Plains State.

WWW:

    http://www.state.sd.us

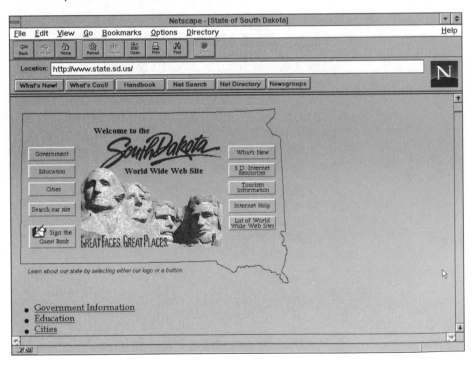

Figure 23.8. **The Web page for the State of South Dakota.**

Fedworld

Fedworld is a bulletin board system from the National Technical Information Service. Some of the $70 billion in scientific and technical research is represented here in the form of downloadable files or publications one can purchase from NTIS. Almost every scientific field you can think of has a research report here. The NTIS publications catalog can be downloaded here also, and online ordering is available. Fedworld also offers a gateway to other federal services such as federal job openings.

Telnet:

```
fedworld.gov
```

Log in as "new" if you haven't used the system before.

WWW:

```
http://www.fedworld.gov/
```

FEDIX and MOLIS

The Federal Information Exchange provides online information about agency grants, scholarships, procurement notices, and minority opportunities from the US federal government. MOLIS, which is a part of FEDIX, gives information about historically black colleges and universities and Hispanic-serving institutions and universities, including research centers, scholarships and fellowships, statistics, faculty profiles, and enrollment figures.

Telnet:

```
fedix.fie.com
```

Gopher:

```
gopher.fie.com
```

WWW:

```
http://web.fie.com/
```

US Department of Agriculture

Export statistics and research reports on agricultural products, situation and outlook reports, and other information about agriculture in the United States is made available full-text from the USDA. The Foreign Agricultural Service provides this information, which is of particular importance to exporters and agribusiness.

WWW:

```
http://www.usda.gov:8000/fas/fas-programs-services-
resources/fas-services/fasservices.html
```

Commerce Business Daily

The US Department of Commerce's Commerce Business Daily is available on the Internet full-text (for a fee), and the government bids notices are provided here free. Members of the Community of Science (who register and identify themselves) may access the information without an additional fee. Some Internet access providers include a subscription to the Commerce Business Daily information as part of their services. Ask your Internet access provider if they do so.

WWW:

```
http://cos.gdb.org/repos/cbd/cbd-intro.html
```

Economic Bulletin Board

The US Department of Commerce's Bulletin Board comes in two versions on the Internet. The data provided by the Department of Commerce is from the horse's mouth, but the offerings are for fee— you'll need to subscribe but then you can search the databases online. The University of Michigan Library's Documents Center downloads a number of the files from the EBB daily and makes it available on Gopher. The EBB provides an incredible amount of data on economic indicators, business statistics, employment, industry statistics, and summary text files for the economic indicators. It's also a good source for currency exchange information. Many of the files are in compressed format, and all but the text files are tabular. The help files are very well written and definitely needed for this source. You have to visit to see what's actually there because there's too much to list.

WWW:

```
http://www.stat-usa.gov/BEN/Brochures/ebb.html
```

Gopher:

```
gopher://una.hh.lib.umich.edu
```

FTP:

```
una.hh.lib.umich.edu (/bin)
```

EconData

A huge number of economic time series—over two hundred thousand—are mounted by the University of Maryland and updated from the Economic Bulletin Board three to four days after they're released. You need to use the help files before downloading because the procedure gets complicated.

Gopher:

```
info.umd.edu
```

FTP:

```
info.umd.edu
```

Then choose Educational_Resources ➤ Economic Data from the menus.

Economic Development Information Network

An interactive service from the Pennsylvania State Data Center that allows the user to retrieve data for any state about business, capital resources, government, income, labor force, economic development, agriculture, and international trade. A nice feature is the Economic Development Directory, which allows the user to construct a search for an agency or organization.

Telnet:

```
psuvm.psu.edu, port 23
```

(This is a tn3270 site.)

Gopher:

```
psuvm.psu.edu
```

Community Idea Net

A Gopher resource from Sunsite at the University of North Carolina that "disseminates ideas about making governments more effective." This is a project of UNC's Leadership Information Archives. Descriptions of projects, contact persons, and information on teenagers, insect pests, highways, budgets, immigrants, farming, graffiti, and more.

Gopher:

```
gopher://sunsite.unc.edu/00/sunsite.d/politics.d/idean
et.d/CINet_Briefly
```

Catalog of Federal Domestic Assistance

Each year the federal government of the US issues a new edition of this guide to grants and monies available to states, groups, and individuals from most government agencies and projects. From food stamps to information technology to building projects, this searchable version of the CFDA is an important contribution to the Internet.

Gopher:

```
gopher://solar.rtd.utk.edu:70
```

Then choose Federal ➤ CFDA.

E-Mail Special Interest Lists

Sometimes, rather than seeking information via your own actions, you'd like some person or organization to let you know when they are doing something you might find interesting. Special-purpose mailing lists serve that purpose. If you subscribe to one of those listed here, you'll receive messages in your e-mail. When you read them, you can forward them to other people (respecting the intellectual property rights of others, of course), save them for future reference, reply solely to the author, or take part in a list-wide discussion of the matter at hand by replying to the list. Mailing lists are a good way to discuss ideas with other people who have similar interests.

BIZ-WIRE

This moderated list is for the discussion of business and the creation of businesses. Announcements and press releases are welcome.

E-Mail:

```
listserv@ais.net
```

In the body of your message, include:

```
subscribe biz-wire (your real name)
```

econ-dev

This list is for people who want to share information about economic development. The people who sponsor the list are professionals who help grow businesses in Colorado, and they share an interest in economic and systems theory.

E-Mail:

```
majordomo@lists.csn.net
```

In the body of your message, include:

```
subscribe econ-dev (your email address)
```

WWW-Marketing

This list discusses using the Web for marketing and sales.

E-Mail:

```
majordomo@aros.net
```

In the body of your message, include:

```
subscribe www-marketing (your email address)
```

Newsgroups

Here are some of the more useful Usenet newsgroups for business users. These newsgroups are a few of the many available via newsfeed. The groups not covered here include newsgroup hierarchies for specific companies like Digital Equipment Corporation or Oracle. If you are interested in the products and services of these corporations, you'll want to investigate reading the groups in those hierarchies.

In addition, you may want to subscribe to an Internet access service that includes the ClariNet news service. The ClariNet news includes extensive business feeds.

ClariNet is a specific, commercial service that provides "real" news through the avenue of Usenet news feeds. ClariNet News includes many, many newsgroups in it's "biz" hierarchy. They include groups like

```
clari.biz.industry.construction
clari.biz.industry.dry_goods
clari.biz.industry.energy
clari.biz.market.commodities
clari.biz.market.dow
clari.biz.mergers
```

The information you receive in these newsgroups comes from the business and market press and is distributed by Associated Press,Reuters, and similar agencies that have associations with ClariNet.

Some Internet Service providers have arrangements with ClariNet to "feed" the ClariNet news to their subscribers. An easy way to find out if your provider does this is to look in your provider's list of active newsgroups for any group that begins with the letters "clari." Information about ClariNet itself is available via the Web.

WWW:

```
http://www.clarinet.com
```

alt.business

This is one of the sections for business in Usenet, but generally it contains advertisements.

biz.books.technical

This newsgroup announces new books that may be useful to business computer users.

biz.comp.services

This newsgroup announces and discusses Internet services available to commercial businesses.

biz.software

This newsgroup has lots of advertisements for business software but also is a place to ask about software before you invest.

biz.comp.hardware

Mostly ads but some discussion of computer hardware suitable for business use.

biz.comp.software

Sporadic questions surrounded mostly by advertisements for business software.

biz.general

Anything goes on this business-oriented newsgroup as a topic of conversation or solicitation.

biz.job.offered

Not comprehensive, but still a source worth checking out for computing jobs.

biz.misc

Takes up where `biz.general` leaves off.

Professional or Special-Interest Groups (SIGs)

Among the many groups and organizations presenting information or a "presence" on the Internet are those organized around a specific theme. We've included some that you might be interested in here. Also, there are contact points for some organizations that aren't on the Internet but may be of interest anyway.

Center for Civic Networking

CCN/CIVICNET is an organization devoted to helping shape policies for the emerging national information infrastructure and a national vision to include civic networking. For information contact Miles Fidelman:

E-Mail:

(mfidelman@world.std.com)

The Center also provides a Web page at:

WWW:

http://www.civic.net:2401

Data Processing Management Association

Founded in 1951 as the National Machine Accountants Association, this 24,000-member organization includes educators, managerial personnel, staff and individuals associated with the management of information resources. An online network, professional certifications and courses, research projects and on-site managerial seminars are available to members. Publications include a monthly newspaper called *Inside DPMA*. They also hold an annual International Computer Conference and Business Exposition.

WWW:

WWW: http://negaduck.cc.vt.edu/DPMA

For membership information contact:

DPMA

505 Busse Hwy.

Park Ridge, IL 60068

708-825-8124

E-Mail:

70430.352@compuserve.com

International Association for Computer Information Systems

The membership of IACIS consists of individuals and organizations of educators and computer professionals at all levels of educational institutions. Publications include a quarterly *Journal of Computer Information Systems* and a periodic newsletter. For membership information contact:

Dr. Susan Haugen

Dept. of Accountancy

University of Wisconsin—Eau Claire

Eau Claire, WI 54702

715-836-2952

World Wide Web Pages

Finally, we list some interesting starting points that haven't been mentioned elsewhere. These pages will connect you to even more interesting sites. Remember that the best place to get information about what's on the Web is the Web itself. So from pages like these, and others you may find that reflect your own interests, you can discover even more interesting information.

Commercial Use (of the Net) Strategies Home Page

A copyrighted article by Andrew Dinsdale that provides information and advice for companies looking to use the Internet as an information, telecommunications, or marketing network. Topics covered include how to get connected, security concerns, impact on employees, government action on the national information infrastructure, and other issues of concern to businesses. Obviously of great use to businesses both large and small.

WWW:

```
http://pass.wayne.edu/business.html
```

Direct Marketing World

Mainsail Marketing Information, Inc. has made available this electronic directory of the direct marketing industry. They include industry professionals, mailing lists, information about direct marketing, jobs wanted, and jobs offered.

WWW:

```
http://www.dmworld.com
```

The Company Corporation

The Company Corporation is the largest on-line incorporation service in the world. Especially useful to small businesses thinking of incorporating.

WWW:

```
http://incorporate.com/tcc/home.html
```

The Definitive Internet Career Guide

If starting your own company isn't what you want to do, finding a new job or rethinking your career can be begun with the resources developed by the Oakland University Placement Office. They've built a comprehensive index to job and career pages from across the Net.

WWW:

```
http://phoenix.placement.oakland.edu/career/internet.htm
```

INFORUM

The Center for Global Communications, a research institute at the University of Japan, has gathered together information from varying sources about Japan and mounted it on this WWW server. Their primary aim is to lessen the friction between Japan and its trading partners and offer more timely information from literature that is often difficult to locate outside Japan. This is an important resource for people doing business with Japan or seeking information about Japan.

WWW:

```
http://www.glocom.ac.jp:80/Inforum/
```

These Web pages are presented in either Japanese or English.

The Latest News

For the very latest in news about business and industry around the globe there are many choices on the Net. Here are some of the most read/viewed sources of information in print and in the broadcast media. You'll see that they, too, have branched out to the Web as a place to reach their audiences. You'll find USA Today's Money section at

WWW:

```
http://www.usatoday.com/money/mfront.htm
```

and CNN Financial Network at

WWW:

```
http://cnnfn.com
```

The *Financial Times* offers highlights of today's paper plus information about additional services offered by The Financial Times Group. Specific stories about Europe, Asia/Pacific, The Americas, and Technology as well as the News in Brief.

WWW:

```
http://www.usa.ft.com
```

or

```
http://www.ft.com
```

Industry Net Daily presents online news source for developments in manufacturing, industrial engineering, industrial automation, computers, and communications.

WWW:

```
http://www.industry.net/daily
```

CHAPTER

24

K–12 Education Resources

FEATURING

General resources

E-mail mailing lists

Newsgroups

Professional or special-interest groups

Chapter 24

K–12 Education Resources

IN this list we present some of the more helpful aids to kindergarten through 12th grade (K–12) educators–and education–that are available on the Internet. As with all the lists presented in this book, because of the ever-changing nature of the Internet itself (so many new sites are coming on each week), the list can't be complete. The Internet can provide access to resources that might not otherwise be readily accessible to you.

If you haven't already read Chapter 12, "Resource Discovery—Finding Things on the Internet," go back and read it now. The search engines and discovery tools discussed there are your best resources for finding what you want and need, from curriculum resources to newsletters and mailing lists.

This chapter is addressed primarily to educators, rather than students or parents. It will help you get in touch with other teachers who are working on Internet projects you may be planning or implementing; and it will direct you to various sources of information and forums for discussion of particular educational issues. Many of the projects discussed in Chapter 25, "Resources for Kids," are also educational; although the focus in that chapter is on the students' own activities, educators will see further examples of what can be done. Anyone interested K–12 education and the Internet should also read Chapter 18, "The K–12 Internet Presence," which discusses the issues involved in getting a school or school district online, and Appendix D, "K–12 Internetworking Guidelines," an Internet Engineering Task Force document that presents detailed technical information.

Some of the resources listed here also pertain to adult education or higher education.

MASTER WORDS   Many of the resources listed in this chapter and the next will point you to other resources. Be sure to check out these links; they might lead you to serendipitous discovery of *exactly* what you need to use in your class tomorrow or next week. This discovery process is one of the great joys of Internet exploration.

General Internet Resources

Here are some general resources that are designed to provide curriculum assistance to teachers. Emphasis is placed on information about programs themselves and the hints and advice that the researchers in the field have gathered.

University of Minnesota's Web66 Project

We talked about Web66 briefly in Chapter 18; we can't recommend strongly enough that you get familiar with this great resource and its offerings. Here's how the Web66 project at the University of Minnesota describes itself in its home page:

"Just as US Highway Route 66 was a catalyst for Americana, we see the World Wide Web as a catalyst that will integrate the Internet into K–12 school curriculums. The University of Minnesota is beginning project Web66 to facilitate the introduction of this technology into K–12 schools. The goals of this project are:

1. To help K–12 educators learn how to set up their own Internet servers.

2. To link K–12 WWW servers and the educators and students at those schools.

3. To help K–12 educators find and use K–12 appropriate resources on the World Wide Web."

WWW:

    http://web66.coled.umn.edu

Figure 24.1 shows the Web 66 home page. Figure 24. 2 shows the Web 66 educational site cookbook, which has detailed instructions on setting up a Web site at your own school.

Part IV

Internet Resources

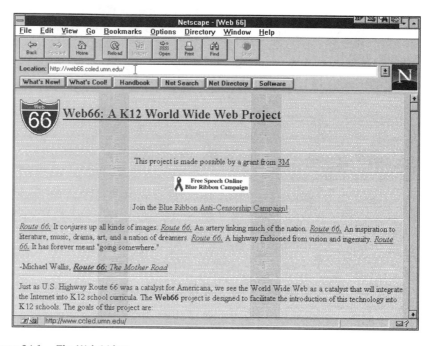

Figure 24.1.   *The Web66 home page.*

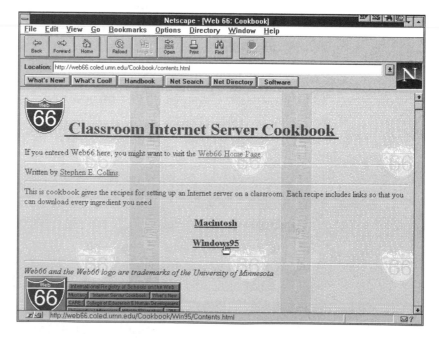

Figure 24.2.   *The Web66 Educator's cookbook page.*

Gleason Sackmann's HotList of K–12 Schools

Gleason Sackmann is himself one of the great resources of the Internet. Besides being the moderator for the InterNIC-sponsored Net-Happenings list and newsgroup, he has built a wonderful Web site with links to all the K–12 schools that are currently on the Internet. New schools go up monthly, so you'll want to visit often.

WWW:

```
http://www.sendit.nodak.edu/k12
```

Figure 24.3 shows that nearly every state now has K–12 schools on the Internet.

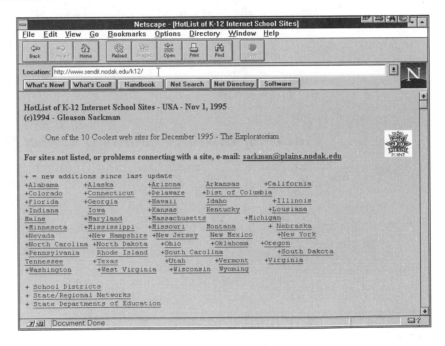

Figure 24.3. **Gleason Sackmann's list of K–12 connected sites.**

Electronic School

The Electronic School, sponsored by the National Association of School Boards, has many articles and resources for teachers, including some e-mail learning modules. You can access old issues of this online magazine, or browse the current edition. Every edition includes pointers on using computers and networking in your classroom. Figure 24.4 shows a recent edition, where the hot topic is whether teachers or techies should manage the school network. Stop by and see what's there for you.

WWW:

```
http://www.access.digex.net/~nsbamags/e-school.html
```

K–12 Library of Resources

Internet education resources are arranged in a meaningful manner for educators in this Gopher. Although most are accessible from other sites, this site from the New York State Education Department is by far one of the best collections of K–12 resources.

Gopher:

```
gopher://unix5.nysed.gov
```

Figure 24.5 shows the top-level menu of this valuable Gopher (using the Gopher+ client).

National Distance Learning Center (NDLC)

The National Distance Learning Center is a centralized electronic information source for distance learning programs and resources. Whether you are a program producer or a user of distance learning, the NDLC will assist you in distributing and accessing available courseware. The database is searchable by keyword.

WWW:

```
http://www.occ.uky.edu/
```

National Center on Adult Literacy/Litnet

This is the major center for information on literacy at the US and international levels. Research, the development of programs, curricula, and the use of new technologies are all areas that receive a good deal of attention. If you have a need in the area of literacy, the answer is likely to be here.

WWW:

```
http://litserver.literacy.upenn.edu/
```

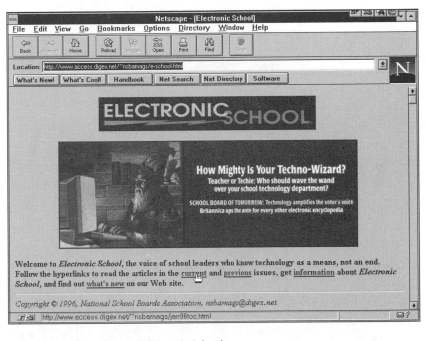

Figure 24.4.   A recent edition of Electronic School.

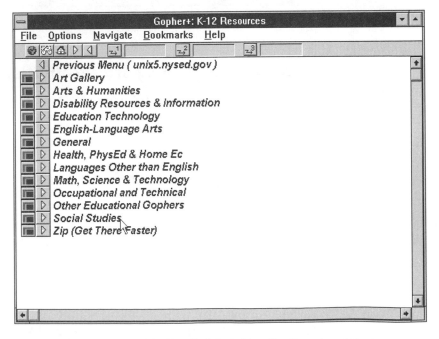

Figure 24.5.   The main menu of the New York State Education Department Gopher.

Figure 24.6 contains information about the NCAL's various publications and how to order them.

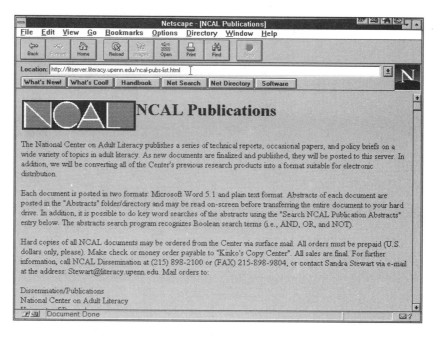

Figure 24.6.   The NCAL publication page.

EASI Site for People with Disabilities

A Web site devoted to information technology and its access by persons with disabilities has been established by EASI: Equal Access to Software and Information.

EASI is an affiliate of the American Association for Higher Education, and its mission is to serve as a resource to the higher education community by providing information and guidance in the area of access-to-information technologies by individuals with disabilities. EASI stays informed about developments and advancements within the adaptive computer technology field and spreads that information to colleges, universities, K–12 schools, libraries, and into the workplace.

EASI's information has special areas devoted to problems related to science, engineering, and math for persons with disabilities, library access for patrons with disabilities and also an area devoted to back issues of the electronic journal, *Information Technology and Disabilities*. It also offers e-mail workshops in the field of adaptive computing.

For further information write either:

Dick Banks, `rbanks@uwstout.edu` or Norman Coombs `nrcgsh@rit.edu`

or see the Web site at

`http://www.rit.edu/~easi`

National Consortium for Environmental Education and Training (NCEET)

NCEET describes itself as a clearinghouse for environmental education (EE) information and aims its services at K–12 educators including teachers, curriculum planners, and information specialists. To
reach this audience, it produces and gathers EE information in all
formats and offers access to electronic resources through a Gopher,
EE-Link, as well as a Web page.

WWW:

`http://www.nceet.snre.umich.edu`

Figure 24.7 shows the Web page.

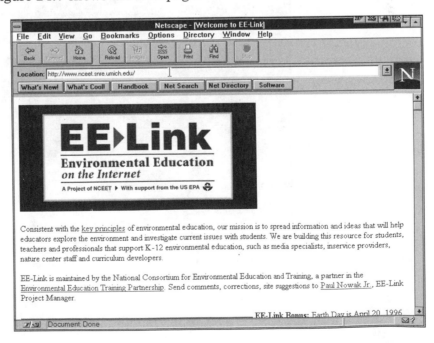

Figure 24.7.   The National Consortium for Environmental Training and Education Web page.

United States Department of Education (USDE)

This is a gold mine of information for educators, ranging from software programs to statistics, to research and school improvement programs. There are resources for all areas of education. The USDE provides connections to all of the ERIC Clearinghouses and has a Web site that includes a teacher's guide to the Department, a researcher's guide to the Department, and a valuable list of pointers to other educational sites on the Web. The full text of the 1995 edition of *Educational Programs That Work*, the National Diffusion Network's directory of programs and facilitators, is available through the US Department of Education's Web server.

WWW:

    http://www.ed.gov

Figure 24.8 shows the USDE home page. Figure 24.9 shows a list of program areas in which the USDE provides information.

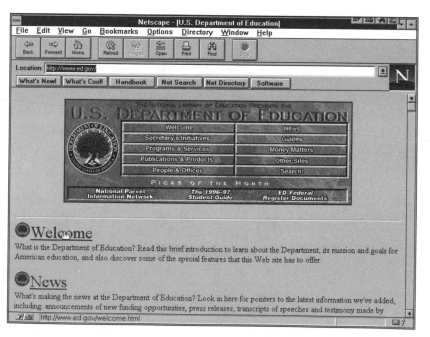

Figure 24.8. The USDE home page.

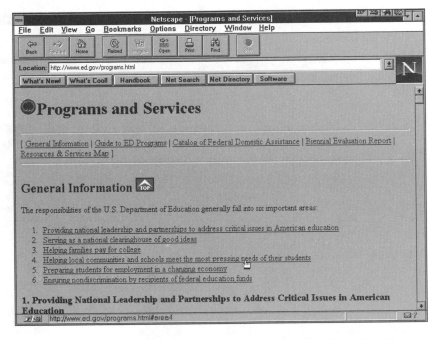

Figure 24.9. Here are some of the many areas in which the USDE provides information.

Clearinghouse for Networked Information Discovery and Retrieval (CNIDR)

CNIDR is a cooperative effort between the National Science Foundation (NSF) and MCNC, Information Technologies Division. These folks gather information about network retrieval tools, and they share those tools and the technology widely. Part of their efforts include the continuing support of FreeWAIS, the public domain version of the WAIS software, and the Global Schoolhouse project. You'll find their list of educational Web sites on many Web pages dedicated to education. You can find out more about all their efforts on the Web itself:

WWW:

```
http://kudzu.cnidr.org
```

Figure 24.10 shows the top of the CNIDR home page. Take the jump labeled "CNIDR Projects" to find out about specific projects like the Global Schoolhouse.

Part IV

Internet Resources

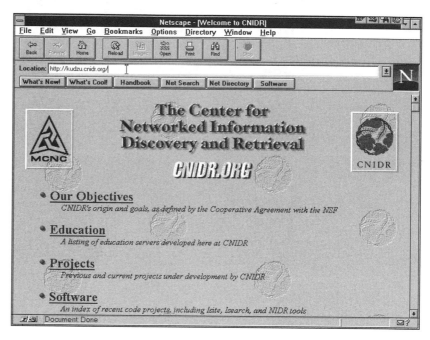

Figure 24.10.   **The beginning of the Clearinghouse for Networked Information Discovery and Retrieval home page.**

Corporation for Public Broadcasting EdWeb

Usually when you think of the Corporation for Public Broadcasting, you think of Bert and Ernie and Big Bird, or maybe Mystery or Masterpiece Theatre. Well, CPB is on the Internet, too. Andy Carvin of CPB has one of the more interesting sites on the Web. It's called EdWeb—Exploring Technology and School Reform. EdWeb explores the worlds of educational reform and information technology. With EdWeb, you can hunt down on-line educational resources around the world, learn about trends in education policy and information infrastructure development, examine success stories of computers in the classroom, and much, much more. EdWeb is a dynamic work-in-progress, and numerous changes and additions occur on a regular basis. EdWeb is also hosted by CNIDR.

WWW:

http://k12.cnidr.org:90

Indiana Department of Education

Along with information about the state's Department of Education, Indiana also offers a Professional Education Employee Referral Service (PEER). Job openings in Indiana, DOE openings, sample resumes, and resumes from licensed education professionals make this a nice one-stop-shopping resource for the state; it will also be useful to educators outside Indiana.

Gopher:

```
gopher://ideanet.doe.state.in.us
```

Michigan Department of Education

The state of Michigan compiles statistics on every school in the state, including teacher/student ratio, teacher salaries, enrollment figures, and scores on standardized tests. This resource also provides information about state grants to schools, school districts and teachers, and about classroom resources and educational technology. Figure 24.11

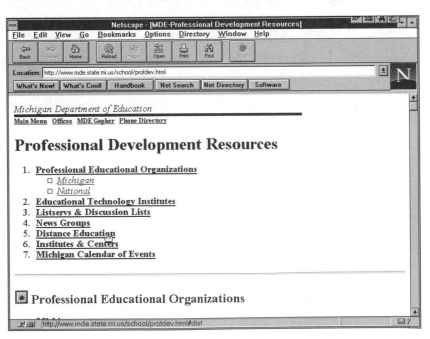

Figure 24.11. Professional development opportunities, both in Michigan and nationwide.

illustrates the various professional development opportunities that the MDE keeps track of.

WWW:

```
http://www.mde.state.mi.us/
```

Missouri Department of Elementary and Secondary Education

This department of the State of Missouri is constructing an education support tool for Missouri students, teachers, parents, administrators, and others interested in improving educational effectiveness. This resource contains Missouri school laws and legislation, school rules and regulations, and facts about the public schools in Missouri.

Gopher:

```
gopher://services.dese.state.mo.us
```

A similar effort for higher education in Missouri can be found at

```
gopher://dp.mocbhe.gov
```

InSITE (Information Network of the Society for Instructional Technology and Teacher Education)

The mission statement for InSITE describes the project as "a World Wide Web resource dedicated to exploring ways in which theInternet can be used both to benefit teacher education programs at colleges and universities around the world and to support K–12 staff development technology initiatives."

WWW:

```
http://teach.virginia.edu/insite
```

Figure 24.12 shows the Web page.

Texas Education Network (TENET)

TENET Web's purpose is to enable educators and students to move information across the barriers of time and space and to explore an evolving technology that is breaking down the isolation of the classroom. Figure 24.13 shows the home page for *TENET Connections*, the online magazine for the Texas Education network.

WWW:

```
http://www.tenet.edu
```

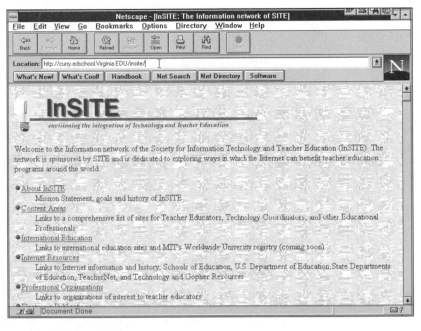

Figure 24.12. **The InSITE (Information Network of the Society for Instructional Technology and Teacher Education) Web page.**

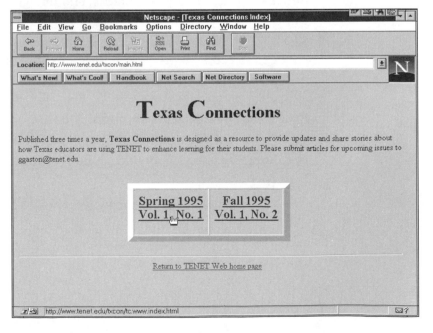

Figure 24.13. **The TENET Connections *home page.***

North Dakota's SENDIT Project

In North Dakota, K–12 educators and students have plugged into computer BBS-type networking that also gives them access to the Internet, thanks to SENDIT, a telecommunications network connected to the Internet via the North Dakota Higher Education Computer TCP/IP Network. Since 1995, SENDIT has also developed a WWW-based access point to much of its information, thus making SENDIT available to the world-wide educational community.

Developed by the North Dakota State University School of Education and Computer Center for use by school districts across the state of North Dakota, SENDIT is funded by the Educational Telecommunications Council (ETC).

SENDIT offers access to over 70 forums that focus on specific topics of interest to its members. They include topics for both teachers and students such as: Junior Chat, Senior Chat, English, Mathematics, Educational Technology, TAG-L, EduTech, Kidsnet, and more.

SENDIT also offers K12Net, an educational BBS network consisting of more than 300 bulletin boards located in schools around the globe, and distributed via the FidoNet network. K12Net offers chat areas, curriculum areas, classroom project areas, and foreign language areas, to name but a few.

SENDIT provides access to classroom projects, electronic mail services, lesson plans, discussion groups, newsletters/magazines/journals, access to on-line library catalogs, interlibrary loan services, and Internet tools such as Gopher and the World Wide Web.

Resources for curriculum modules based on the 1996 election are featured in Figure 24.14.

For more information about SENDIT, visit the Web site:

WWW:

```
http://www.sendit.nodak.edu/
```

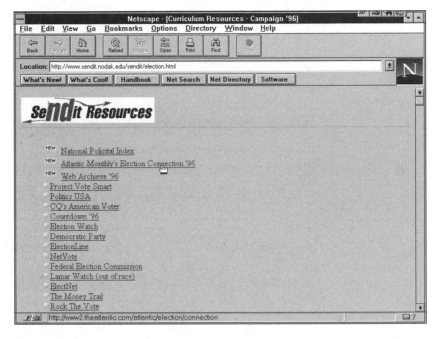

Figure 24.14.   The SENDIT 1996 campaign resource list.

Deaf Education Resource Archive

Information for teachers and parents of deaf students from Kent State University. Information includes education resources, the Americans with Disabilities Act, exemplary programs, addresses and contacts and much more. A well-packed site.

Gopher:

```
gopher://gopher.educ.kent.edu/11/edgophers/special/
deafed
```

Deaf Education Resources
from Ontario Institute for Studies in Education

This is another good resource on deaf education and does not duplicate the materials at Kent State's Deaf Education Resource Archive. Many text files cover the history of deaf education, social issues surrounding deafness, children's needs, American Sign Language, services to the deaf, legal issues, resources for educators, and other online resources.

Gopher:

```
gopher://porpoise.oise.on.ca
```

National Center for Research on Teacher Learning

This site at Michigan State University focuses on leadership for teacher learning. It contains issue papers, craft papers, conference reports, research reports and abstracts of their technical publications. Figure 24.15 shows the Gopher listing of all the publications available through NCRTL.

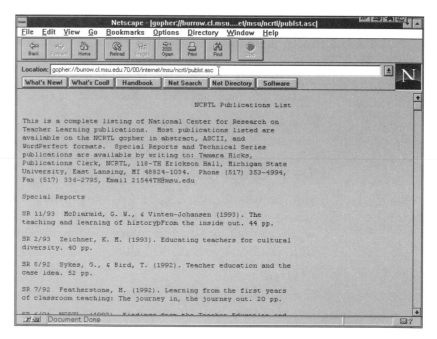

Figure 24.15.   A complete list of publications on teacher learning.

Gopher:

```
gopher://burrow.cl.msu.edu:70/11/internet/msu/ncrtl
```

North Central Regional Education Laboratory (NCREL)

NCREL provides papers and other resources on issues they consider critical to education in the North Central region, but certainly of interest to other areas of the United States as well. NCREL's programs include: Curriculum, Instruction & Assessment; Early Childhood and Family Education; Evaluation; Midwest Consortium for Mathematics and Science Education; Midwest Regional Center for Drug-Free Schools & Communities; Professional Development; Regional Policy Information Center; and Rural Education and Urban Education. Each program makes contributions to the site. Figure 24.16 shows the NCREL program "Pathways to School Improvement."

WWW:

http://www.ncrel.org/ncrel/sdrs/pathwayg.htm

Figure 24.16. *"Pathways to School Improvement."*

Other regional educational laboratories also provide information on the Internet. The Northwest Regional Educational Laboratory (NWREL) is at:

WWW:

http://www.nwrel.org

CICNet Education Gopher

CIC includes the Big Ten universities plus the University of Chicago and Notre Dame. They have banded together to share resources via CICNet. Their list of special projects includes rural access to the Internet, Native American projects, and Pioneering Partners, which links schools in Ohio, Michigan, and Kentucky. Figure 24.17 shows a list of CICNet's projects, from their home page.

Among other resources, CICNet houses one of the largest collections of electronic journals in the world in two separate collections: the CIC Electronic Journals Collection, a fully-managed collection of scholarly e-journals; and the original E-serials Archive with 880 Internet-published electronic serials.

WWW:

http://www.cic.net

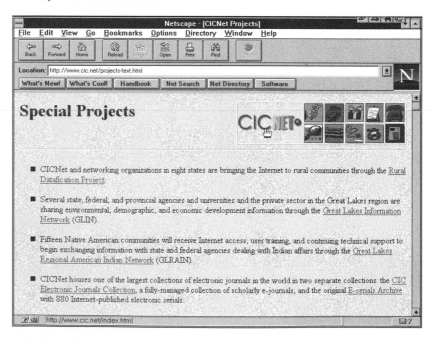

Figure 24.17. **CICNet's projects for interconnecting various communities.**

Consortium for School Networking (CoSN)

This is both a Web site with numerous K–12 resources and an organization that includes all types of groups and individuals willing to take on a leadership role for K–12 education. CoSN keeps up-to-date on issues surrounding the National Information Infrastructure and is helping to expand K–12 resources on the Net. Membership information is available at the page.

WWW:

> http://www.cosn.org

One of the good resources at this site is an excellent paper on practical approaches to getting your school networked, published jointly by The Center for Information, Technology & Society and The Educational Products Information Exchange Institute (EPIE). The table of contents for this paper is shown in Figure 24.18. You can get it at:

WWW:

> http://www.cosn.org/EPIE.html

COSN also sponsors an excellent discussion list for teachers. Subscribe at

E-mail:

> COSNDISC-request@list.cren.net

Part
IV

Internet Resources

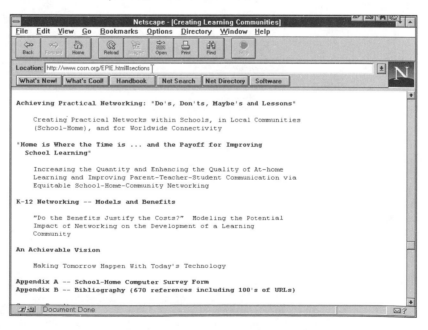

Figure 24.18.   The EPIE School Networking paper Table of Contents.

EDNET Guide to Usenet Newsgroups

A large guide with brief descriptions of each group related to education including K 12, higher education, media centers and specialists, and many more.

FTP:

> nic.umass.edu

and go to the pub/ednet directory.

The Children, Youth, and Family Consortium

The Children, Youth, and Family Consortium was established in fall 1991 in an effort to bring together the varied competencies of the University of Minnesota and the vital resources of Minnesota's communities to enhance the ability of individuals and organizations to address critical health, education, and social policy concerns in ways that improve the well-being of Minnesota children, youth, and families. Their Web site contains excellent information on helping families function better, including an electronic newsletter, information on the role of fathers in families, and a vast collection of articles in their Gopher archives. Information from the Adoption database is shown in Figure 24.19.

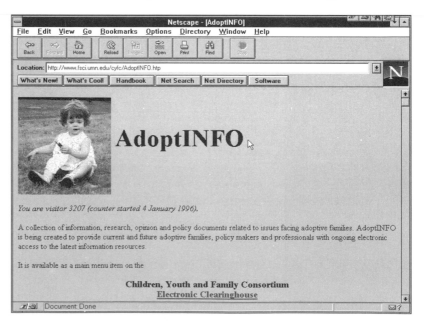

Figure 24.19. **The adoption information database.**

WWW:

```
http://www.fsci.umn.edu/cyfc/
```

Center for Talented Youth (CTY)

Formally established at Johns Hopkins University in 1979, the Institute for the Academic Advancement of Youth (IAAY) is dedicated to identifying young people with exceptional intellectual abilities and offering them accelerated academic programs specially suited to their own individual rates of learning. IAAY's original mission has grown to reach a broader student base, giving youth the opportunity to explore fully their individual academic abilities. CTY Academic Programs support and nurture academic talent by providing motivated, academically talented students with a chance to study at a pace or depth appropriate for their abilities.

Qualified students, generally between 7 and 16, choose from a wide range of courses in the humanities, mathematics, and sciences held at six sites in the United States. CTY Academic Program staff specifically design these courses to be challenging and exciting.

Information is provided about CTY's acclaimed summer programs as well as resource materials for parents and teachers. Figure 24.20 shows the 1996 summer program for young students (7–15).

WWW:

```
http://www.jhu.edu:80/~gifted/
```

National Center for Education Statistics (NCES)

Statistics on education are maintained constantly but seem to take forever to get released. The National Center for Education Statistics (NCES) collects these statistics and makes them available through their Gopher (a branch of the US Department of Education Gopher). They also provide statistics and analyses from their own studies in elementary and secondary education, post-secondary education, assessment, vocational education, and libraries.

Gopher:

```
gopher://gopher.ed.gov
```

Then choose Education Research, Improvement, and Statistics (OERI & NCES) from the menu.

Part
IV

Internet Resources

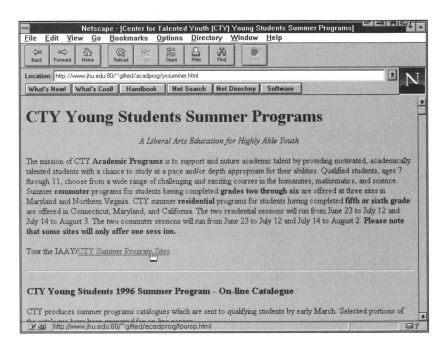

Figure 24.20.   *The CTY Young Students summer programs.*

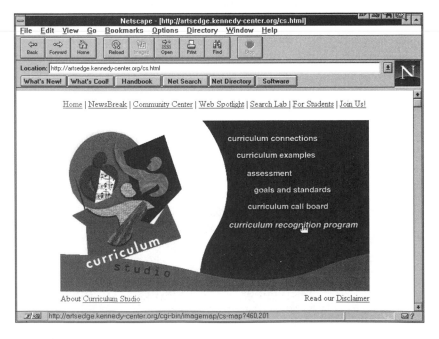

Figure 24.21.   *The ArtsEdge Curriculum Studio.*

Edupage (Electronic Journal)

EDUCOM supplies this three-times-weekly electronic newsletter, which digests news about information technology. It's a global newsletter, now translated into French, German, Hebrew, Italian, Hungarian, and Portuguese (and more languages are on the way). Figure 24.22 shows the Hungarian version.

*Figure 24.22.   **EduPage is available in Magyar!***

Some nice features of Edupage are its list of stories at the beginning of the file and its easy-to-read style. Current issues and archives are available via

WWW:

    http://www.educom.edu/web/edupage.html/

AskERIC Virtual Library

The Educational Resources Information Center (ERIC) has long been a provider of education-related resources. The ERIC indexes *Research in Education* and *Current Index to Journals in Education* have been standards in libraries for over thirty years. ERIC is federally funded by the US Department of Education and also supports the ERIC Clearinghouses, which provide varying levels of service to people in the field of education. The AskERIC Virtual Library has lesson plans, ERIC Digests (great short essays by professionals on "hot topics"), ERIC publications, reference tools, Internet guides and directories, government information, and archives for education-related discussion lists on Usenet. Of special interest to educators and media specialists, it's also a great resource for parents.

WWW:

http://ericir.sunsite.syr.edu/

The Scholastic Internet Center

Scholastic, Inc. has been a leading publisher in the field of education; most of us remember their paperback children's books, which we would purchase through our schools. The Scholastic Internet Center provides a catalog and ordering mechanism for those books plus hundreds of other educational books and materials listed in their Ultimate Education Store Directory. The Ultimate Learning Libraries provide curriculum-based lesson plans, activity guides, and research and resource materials. For some materials, the full text is present on-line; for other sources catalog entries are presented. The Center also offers electronic newsletters and the Scholastic Network, an interactive online service for students and teachers. Educators and parents should find this service useful. Figure 24.23 shows the Nutrition curriculum available from Scholastic Network.

WWW:

http://scholastic.com

Figure 24.23. Nutrition is an important curriculum topic for K–12.

Academe This Week

Academe This Week is an online portion of the *Chronicle of Higher Education*. You'll find job postings, a table of contents, events in academe, portions of the statistical almanac, best-selling books on college campuses, and more from this standard resource.

Gopher:
```
gopher://chronicle.merit.edu
```

Big Sky Telegraph

The great state of Montana provides low-cost access to their version of a freenet, one that has already gathered quite a reputation in education circles. You can have twenty minutes of free time as a visitor, but only $50 a year makes you a subscriber. Many of the forums concern education, and there is one especially for rural education issues. There are lots of curriculum ideas, a list of teachers and resource persons, and online classes.

Telnet:

```
telnet:bigsky.bigsky.dillon.mt.us
```

NCSA's "Incomplete Guide"

Incomplete Guide to the Internet and Other Telecommunications Opportunities Especially for Teachers and Students, K–12, from the National Center for Supercomputing Applications, is a resource guide and manual for students and teachers at all levels of Internet use.

FTP:

```
ftp.zaphod.ncsa.uiuc.edu
```

or

```
ftp.ncsa.uiuc.edu
```

then choose Education ➤ Education_Resources ➤ Incomplete_Guide from the menus.

Grant-Getter's Guide to the Internet

A Gopher resource that serves as a major entry point for grant-finding on the Internet. The Federal Register, Fedix, Molis, Fedworld and others can be accessed from this one site. The Guide itself is a nice bibliography of grant sources on the Internet.

Gopher:

```
gopher://gopher.uidaho.edu
```

then choose Science Research and Grant Information ➤ Grant Information.

Figure 24.24 shows the Gopher menu.

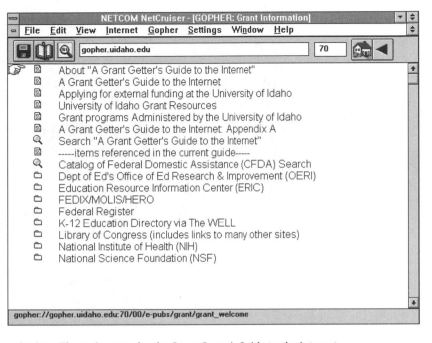

Figure 24.24. The main menu for the Grant Getter's Guide to the Internet.

San Francisco State University (SFSU) Department of Instructional Technologies WWW Server

The Department of Instructional Technologies at SFSU now has a World Wide Web server. You'll find information, educational tech resources, K–12 educator resources, and a great collection of links to job listings.

WWW:

    http://www.itec.sfsu.edu/

Figure 24.25 shows this "friendly little pothole on the information superhighway."

Part
IV

Internet Resources

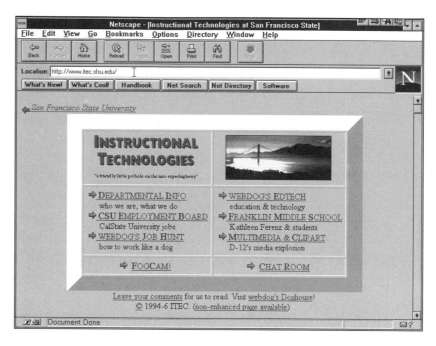

Figure 24.25. The SFSU Department of Instructional Technologies home Web page.

World Wide Web Virtual Library Education Page

Journals, lectures and tutorials, books, software, major education sites and networks, and specialized sources in education are hypertextually linked on this page. Though a large amount of data is linked, this list is a "good start."

WWW:

> http://life.anu.edu.au/education/library.html

Whole Frog Project

Only it's not whole anymore after you go through this interactive dissection! The Lawrence Berkeley Laboratory Imaging and Distributing Computing Group has taken the basic junior-high science project high-tech. The dissection is performed at the major organ level, and views can be generated from many different angles. You have got to see this!

WWW:

> http://george.lbl.gov/ITG.hm.pg.docs/dissect/info.html

Figure 24.26 shows the frog's skeleton.

This project has been translated into several languages by volunteer translators. If you can help by translating it into another language, the group would love to hear from you.

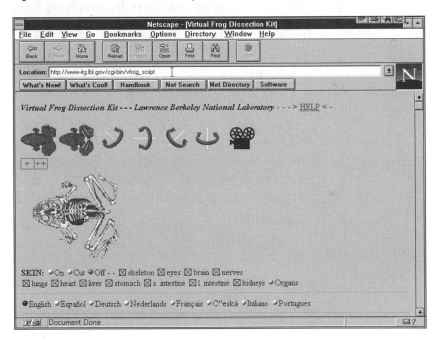

Figure 24.26. **The Whole Frog Project.**

Learning Research and Development Center (LRDC)

The LRDC at the University of Pittsburgh is a national center for education research. Descriptions of its projects, programs, scientists, departments and services are available on their Web page along with connections to other related Internet organizations and resources.

WWW:

> http://www.lrdc.pitt.edu

E-Mail Special Interest Lists

If you subscribe to these lists, you'll be a part of the current discussions taking place on the Internet about education. Here's the place to begin your own contributions.

National Information Infrastructure Teacher Forum

Teachers talking to each other about networking and teaching using networks. Subscribe at

E-mail:

```
NII-TEACH-REQUEST@WAIS.COM
```

Access E-mail Student Exchange

ESE provides an opportunity for students to correspond with other children from around the world by e-mail! Teachers can help their students do research, get pen-pals, compare classrooms. For a description, see

WWW:

```
http://fox.nstn.ca/~velmont
```

KIDSPHERE

Teachers, parents, software and curriculum developers, and others interested in education meet to discuss K–12 issues on this list. New network services, emerging networks, computer interfaces for children's use, and national and international collaborative projects are just some of the topics discussed. To subscribe:

E-mail Address:

```
kidsphere-request@vms.cis.pitt.edu
```

A spinoff list for children to use is called KIDS. To subscribe to KIDS:

E-mail Address:

```
joinkids@vms.cis.pitt.edu
```

Communet

Communet is *the* list for community networking advocates and anyone interested in community building. (As discussed in Chapter 18, building a network of community support is an essential part of creating and implementing a school district's Internet presence.) This list is very active and you'll receive a lot of messages, but we think you'll find it worthwhile. To subscribe:

E-mail Address:

```
listserv@uvmvm.uvm.edu
```

Daily Report Card of National Education Goals Panel

A good-sized daily electronic newsletter that analyzes education news in light of the goals set for US schools. Announcements of new services, innovative projects, and Washington news are some examples of topics covered. The newsletter tends to be technology-oriented. To subscribe to the digest version (a digest is sent once daily):

E-mail Address:

```
listserv@gwuvm.gwu.edu
```

The body of the message should be:

```
subscribe edpol-d your name.
```

Network News

An online newsletter focusing on library and information resources on the Internet. Updates the information found in *A Guide to Internet/Bitnet*. To subscribe:

E-mail Address:

```
listserv@vm1.nodak.edu
```

AAESA-L

AAESA-L is an open, unmoderated discussion list on the topic of Educational Service Agencies (ESAs) throughout North America. Discussion topics include such items as ESA problems and their resolution, new ESA ventures, ESA resources, and ESA futures. AAESA-L is for all ESA staff, their member districts, and anyone interested in sharing their ideas and comments to ESAs; it's open to the world. To subscribe:

E-mail Address:

```
mailserv@admin.aces.k12.ct.us
```

Other Lists

ACSOFT-L

Discussion of educational software.

E-mail Address:

```
listserv@ wustl.edu
```

ADLTED-L

Canada-based adult education list.

E-mail Address:

```
listserv@ureginal.uregina.ca
```

AEDNET

Discussion of adult education.

E-mail Address:

```
listserv@suvm.syr.edu
```

AI-ED

Artificial Intelligence in education.

E-mail Address:

```
AI-ED-REQUEST@SUN.COM
```

ALTLEARN

Discussion of alternative approaches to learning.

E-mail Address:

```
listserv@sjuvm.stjohns.edu
```

BGEDU-L

Educator's forum on reform.

E-mail Address:

```
bgedu-l@ukcc.uky.edu
```

BIOPI-L

Biology and education.

E-mail Address:

listserv@ksuvm.ksu.edu

CNEDUC-L

Computer networking in education.

E-mail Address:

listserv@tamvm1.tamu.edu

COSNDISC

CoSN (Consortium for School Networking; see the entry earlier in this chapter) discussion list.

E-mail Address:

listproc@yukon.cren.org

CTI-L

Discussion of computers in teaching.

E-mail Address:

listserv@irlearn.ucd.ie

CPI-L

List concerning the College Preparatory Initiative.

E-mail Address:

listserv@cunyvm.bitnet

CURRICUL

Discussion of curriculum development.

E-mail Address:

listserv@saturn.rowan.edu

DEOS-L

List of the American Center for the Study of Distance Education.

E-mail Address:

listserv@psuvm.bitnet

DISTED

Discussion of distance education.

E-mail Address:

```
listserv@uwavm.bitnet
```

ECENET

Early childhood education list.

E-mail Address:

```
listserv@uiucvmd.bitnet
```

EDNET

Discussion of education and networking.

E-mail Address:

```
listserv@nic.umass.edu
```

EDPOL

Education policy discussion.

E-mail Address:

```
listproc@wais.com
```

EDPOLYAN

Educational policy analysis.

E-mail Address:

```
listserv@asuvm.inre.asu.edu
```

EDPOLYAR

Educational policy analysis archive.

E-mail Address:

```
listserv@asuvm.inre.asu.edu
```

EDSYLE

Discussion of educational styles.

E-mail Address:

```
listserv@sjuvm.stjohns.edu
```

EDTECH

Education and technology list.

> **E-mail Address:**
>
> listserv@msu.edu

EDUPAGE

EDUCOM's news update.

> **E-mail Address:**
>
> edupage@educom.edu

ED2000-PILOT

Discussion of technological reform in education.

> **E-mail Address:**
>
> mailbase@mailbase.ac.uk

EDUCAI-L

Discussion of artificial intelligence in education.

> **E-mail Address:**
>
> listserv@wvnvm.wvnet.edu

ELED-L

Elementary Education list.

> **E-mail Address:**
>
> listserv@ksuvm.bitnet

EUITLIST

Educational uses of information technology.

> **E-mail Address:**
>
> euitlist@bitnic.educom.edu

HORIZONS

Adult Education journal.

> **E-mail Address:**
>
> listserv@alpha.acast.nova.edu

ICU-L

Discussion of research on computers in education.

E-mail Address:

```
listserv@ubvm.cc.buffalo.edu
```

IECC

International E-Mail Classroom Connection. Cultural exchange.

E-mail Address:

```
iecc-request@stolaf.edu
```

INFED-L

Broad discussion of computers in the classroom.

E-mail Address:

```
listserv@ccsun.unicamp.br
```

ITTE

Discussion on information technology and teacher education.

E-mail Address:

```
listserv@deakin.oz.au
```

JEI-L

Discussion of technology (especially CD-ROM) in K–12.

E-mail Address:

```
listserv@umdd.umd.edu
```

JTE-L

Journal of Technology in Education.

E-mail Address:

```
listserv@vtvm1.cc.vt.edu
```

KIDCAFE

Kid's discussion group.

E-mail Address:

```
listserv@vm1.nodak.edu
```

KIDS-ACT

Activity projects for kids.

E-mail Address:

`listserv@vm1.nodak.edu`

K12ADMIN

Discussions concerning educational administration.

E-mail Address:

`listserv@suvm.syr.edu`

LM_NET

Library media specialist information exchange.

E-mail Address:

`LM_NET@suvm.syr.edu`

MEDIA-L

Discussion of media in education.

E-mail Address:

`listserv@bingvmb.cc.binghamton.edu`

MMEDIA-L

Discussion of multimedia education.

E-mail Address:

`listserv@vmtecmex.bitnet`

MSPROJ

Discussion of the Annenberg/CPB Math-Science Project.

E-mail Address:

`listserv@msu.bitnet`

MULTI-L

Discussion of multilingual education.

E-mail Address:

`listserv@barilvm.bitnet`

NCPRSE-L

Discussion of science education reform.

E-mail Address:

```
listserv@ecuvm1.bitnet
```

NEWEDU-L

Discussion of new patterns in education.

E-mail Address:

```
listserv@uhccvm.uhcc.hawaii.edu
```

NLA

National Literacy Advocacy list.

E-mail Address:

```
majordomo@world.std.com
```

SCHOOL-L

Discussion of primary and secondary school issues.

E-mail Address:

```
listserv@irlearn.ucd.ie
```

SIGTEL-L

Discussion of telecommunications in education.

E-mail Address:

```
SIGTEL-L@unmvma.unm.edu
```

STLHE-L

Teaching and learning in higher education list.

E-mail Address:

```
listserv@unbvm1.csd.unb.ca
```

SUSIG

Discussion of math education.

E-mail Address:

```
listserv@miamiu.bitnet
```

TEACHEFT

Discussion of teaching effectiveness.

E-mail Address:

listserv@wcupa.edu

UKERA-L

Dialog on education reform policy making. Similar to BGEDU-L.

E-mail Address:

UKERA-L@ukcc.uky.edu

VOCNET

Vocational Education discussion.

E-mail Address:

listserv@cmsa.berkley.edu

Newsgroups

Usenet newsgroups (discussed in Chapter 13) offer another way to participate in discussions of education. Some people prefer to use their newsreaders (the client software that presents the news on your computer) to help them organize their reading into specific topic lines. Using a newsreader to pick and choose among the messages on a topic can be a handy way to browse through a lot of messages quickly. If the name of a newsgroup begins with the letters bit.listserv, it's a *gateway*, presenting the traffic on a mailing list copied into a newsgroup. You can choose which way you'd like to follow the discussion topics. Newsgroups that begin with k12 have been sent through a gateway from FidoNet, which is a direct computer-to-computer network widely used in the teaching community. (Before access to the Internet became widely available, teachers and educators used their computers to set up this network, where each computer owner would call another computer and pass on files and messages with specific FidoNet software. This cooperation is rather like the "telephone tree" that is used by parents to pass messages from a teacher to all the parents in a classroom, for example.)

alt.education.distance

Distance learning is becoming a hot topic with the use of technologies like satellite downlinks and online courses. The `alt.education.distance` newsgroup has professionals and end users discussing new technologies, concerns and experiences.

bit.listserv.edpolyan

A BITNET discussion list that allows discussion about education issues between professionals and students.

bit.listserv.edtech

A moderated LISTSERV redistributed on Usenet for the discussion of educational technology.

comp.edu

For teachers of computer science and those interested in computer literacy.

k12.ed.art

A discussion group for K–12 art education.

k12.ed.comp.literacy

A discussion group for K–12 computer literacy.

k12.ed.math

A discussion group for K–12 mathematics education.

k12.ed.music

A discussion group for K–12 music and performing arts education.

k12.ed.science

A discussion group for K–12 science education.

k12.soc-studies

A discussion group for K–12 social studies and history education.

k12.ed.special

A discussion group for K–12 education of students with disabilities and special needs.

k12.ed.tag

A discussion group for K–12 education of talented and gifted students.

k12.ed.tech

A discussion group for K–12 industrial arts education.

k12.lang.art

A discussion group for K–12 language arts education.

Professional or Special-Interest Groups (SIGs)

Again, we call to your attention some groups that provide special information or special emphasis on using internetworking. You may want to participate in some of these groups.

Center for Civic Networking

CCN/CIVICNET is an organization devoted to helping shape policies for the emerging national information infrastructure and a national

vision to include civic networking. For information contact Miles
Fidelman:

E-mail Address:

```
mfidelman@world.std.com
```

The Center's archives are part of the EFF archives:

FTP:

```
FTP://ftp.eff.org/pub/Groups/CCN
```

Association for Educational
Communications and Technology (AECT)

An international professional association dedicated to "the improvement of instruction through the utilization of media and technology."
Publications and job announcements are just two of the resources in
the AECT Gopher. Membership information is also available on the
Web site.

WWW:

```
http://www.aect.org/
```

Special-Interest Group for University
and College Computing Services (SIGUUCS)

A special-interest group of the Association for Computing Machinery,
SIGUCCS looks at all aspects of university and college computing
from training to supercomputer sites. A quarterly newsletter and an
annual conference are offered. Membership is for individuals. Contact:

Russell S. Vaught

Center for Academic Computing

229 Computer Bldg.

University Park, PA 16802

814-863-0421

Information about ACM and all its special-interest groups can be
found on the World Wide Web, too.

WWW:

```
http://www.acm.org
```

Coalition for Networked Information (CNI)

The Coalition for Networked Information is a joint project of the Association of Research Libraries (ARL), CAUSE, and EDUCOM. Their work "promotes the creation of and access to information resources in networked environments in order to enrich scholarship and to enhance intellectual productivity." Membership is limited to organizations and institutions; however, the CNI Gopher server is available to the public and includes a good deal of helpful information about the coalition, its members, and their work.

Gopher:

```
gopher://gopher.cni.org
```

CNI also sponsors a number of mailing lists, and you can find the descriptions on their site.

International Association for Computer Information Systems (IACIS)

The membership of IACIS includes individuals and organizations of educators and computer professionals at all levels of educational institutions. Publications include a quarterly *Journal Of Computer Information Systems* and a periodic newsletter. For membership information contact:

Dr. Susan Haugen,

Dept. of Accountancy

University of Wisconsin—Eau Claire

Eau Claire, WI 54702

(715) 836-2952

International Society for Technology in Education (ISTE)

This organization is for individuals interested in using technology to improve education. ISTE promotes the use of standards and communication between international policy-formers and professionals.

Publications include *Computing Teacher, Journal of Research on Computing in Education*, and *Update*. For membership information contact:

Maia S. Howes

University of Oregon

1787 Agate Street

Eugene, OR 97403

(503)346-4414.

E-mail Address:

iste@oregon.uoregon.edu

WWW:

http://isteonline.uoregon.edu/

Special-Interest Group for Computer Science Education

Another SIG of the Association for Computing Machinery. SIG CSE supports computer science educators at the secondary, associate, undergraduate and graduate degree levels. Publications include the *SIGSCE Bulletin*, and SIG CSE holds an annual meeting and symposium. For membership information contact:

Nell B. Dale

Computer Sciences Dept

University of Texas at Austin

Austin, TX 78712

(512)471-9539

CHAPTER 25

Resources for Kids

FEATURING

General resources and indexes

Educational projects and resources

Mailing lists

Newsgroups

And other interesting resources

Chapter 25
Resources for Kids

THIS listing of resources that are especially interesting for kids is not exhaustive, but it does detail some of the best available. With each resource you'll see how to find it, whether by Gopher, the Web, or by Telnetting to the service. We have attempted to find educational and fun resources, as well as game archives of various sorts.

You will need to be the judge of the fitness of various resources for your child's emotional and educational needs. We have not included any material that we know to be especially violent or in other ways objectionable, but your family's values and needs may vary.

Many of the general resources listed in Chapter 22 are also interesting for kids. Likewise, many parents should also look at the educational resources presented in Chapter 24. Obviously, the categories we've used to group resources into this chapter and the previous one overlap to a considerable extent. The difference is primarily one of emphasis. Chapter 24 focuses on resources for educators, and includes many examples of classroom activities. This chapter focuses on activities that kids can try out (both inside and outside the classroom); it also includes general fun sites and some resources of interest to parents and teachers. Many of the Web sites and other projects we cover offer material both for educators and for kids; these could have been listed in either chapter.

General Resources and Indexes

Brendan's List for Kids

Brendan Kehoe, author of *Zen and the Art of the Internet,* has turned his impressive knowledge of the Internet to compiling a resources list for kids. Figure 25.1 shows an index of kid's books, book reviews, and writings about books by kids. Brendan lists educational resources, pages for kids by kids, and just plain silliness, all rated "G." Find it at

WWW:

```
http://www.zen.org/~brendan
```

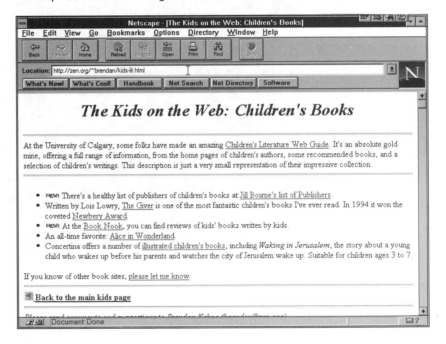

Figure 25.1. Brendan's collection of kids' books online.

Part
IV

Internet Resources

Sybex Internet for Kids Pages

A companion to the Sybex book *Internet for Kids,* these Web pages let kids try out sites and explore a new range of Internet resources. Figure 25.2 shows the 4Kids home page (designed by Glee, by the way).

WWW:

    http://www.sybex.com/i4kids.html

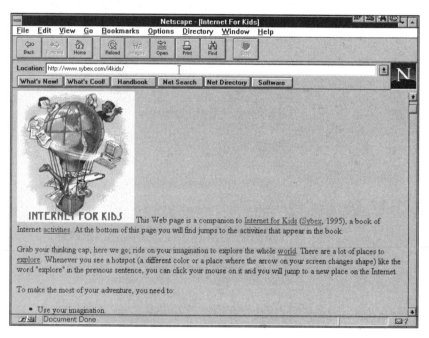

*Figure 25.2.   **The Internet for Kids companion pages.***

Uncle Bob's Kids Page

Without a doubt, Bob Allison has the largest and most eclectic annotated index of Kid's resources on the Net. His home page for kids is shown in Figure 25.3. With cheerful graphics and a parent's eye for good resources, he has been collecting and updating this page for almost four years.

WWW:

`http://gagme.wwa.com:80/~boba/kids.html`

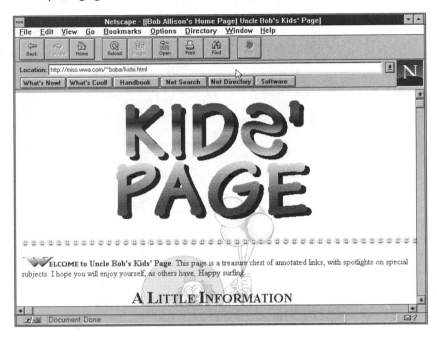

Figure 25.3. **Bob Allison's page for kids.**

Educational Projects and Resources

More and more people are moving onto the Internet more and more items of interest to kids. They are doing this for the same reason that other information providers are adding resources to the Internet: the Net provides a quick, efficient, and sometimes colorful and graphically interesting way to share ideas. Some of the more interesting projects being added are intended to share human as well as intellectual resources—they are projects that "connect" scientists or mathematicians or artists with kids. Here are a few of those types of projects as well as others that we hope you'll find fun.

Cyberspace Middle School

Middle school, yuck! Everybody knows middle school is the worst! Here's one you might want to go to—and go back to again and again. It includes student resources, interesting projects for teachers, and "Surf City," a great jumping-off point to surf the World Wide Web.

WWW:

`http://www.scri.fsu.edu`

From there, choose SCRI Special Projects. Figure 25.4 shows the Web page.

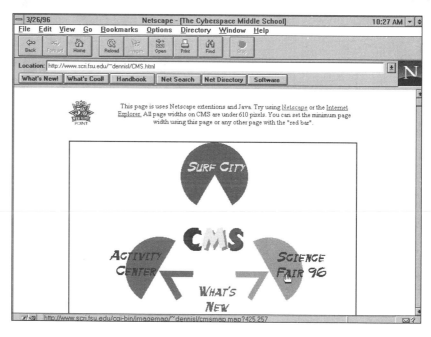

Figure 25.4. **The Web page for Cyberspace Middle School.**

Project Jason

Dr. Robert Ballard, the exploring scientist who led the expedition to investigate the *RMS Titanic*, leads another type of expeditionary force—that of students throughout North America, Bermuda, and Britain, on virtual voyages to remote parts of the world, which he calls Project Jason. The students are in their classrooms, helped by teachers who have been given lesson plans and curricula targeted to these specific voyages. The students assist the scientists, who are actually present in the remote sites. The students can operate some of the equipment remotely and talk with the scientists who are doing the physical as well as intellectual work. You can visit past Jason expeditions and find out more about upcoming work on the Web.

WWW:

```
http://seawifs.gsfc.nasa.gov/JASON/JASON.html
```

Figure 25.5 shows a part of the 1995 expeditionary description.

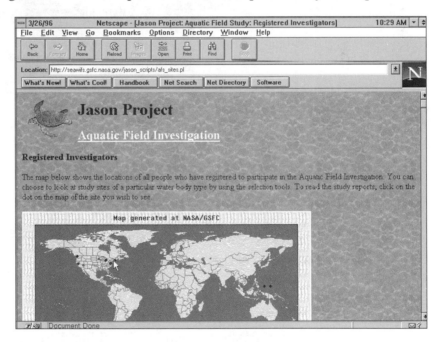

Figure 25.5.   The Web page for the Jason Project.

The New South Polar Times Project

This project gives us a newsletter from the Amundsen-Scott South Pole Station. Lt. Tom Jacobs writes a biweekly newsletter named after the first newsletter to be written at the South Pole. And Deakin University in Australia houses the newsletter on the project's Web pages. You can read the latest version as well as find out more about the South Pole and things like blizzards via the Web.

WWW:

`http://139.132.40.31/NSPT/NSPThomePage.html`

Figure 25.6 shows the current version of the *Times*.

Figure 25.6.   The New South Polar Times.

Explorer

Tired of trekking around the world in the cold? How about exploring mathematics? The University of Kansas contributes a site that develops and dispenses mathematics teaching programs. Figure 25.7 shows an example from one of these programs. To use them, you'll need a Macintosh computer running System 7.1 or later, MacTCP, and Clarisworks 2.0. The software is intended to be used in classrooms. Download the software via the Web.

WWW:

`http://unite.tisl.ukans.edu`

Figure 25.7.   Explorer, from the University of Kansas.

Canada's SchoolNet

Industry and Science Canada sponsors this Gopher, which provides students from preschool through grade 12 with fun and educational projects, ideas and network resources. A SchoolNet MOO and the full text of experiments and just plain fun things to do are here for non-Canadians, too.

Gopher:

    gopher.schoolnet.carleton.ca

Figure 25.8 shows the introduction to the MOO.

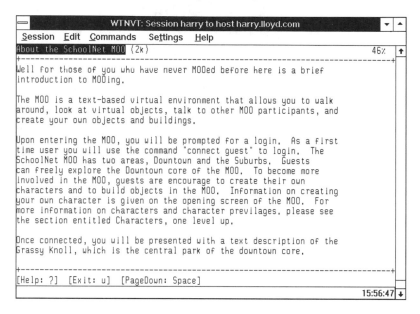

Figure 25.8.   The SchoolNet MOO.

WhaleNet

WhaleNet uses statistics gathered from whale watches to educate students. Students, teachers, and the Whale Conservation Institute collect and compile data on a BBS. Curricula and other classroom supports are available and described in the "about" files. Figure 25.9 shows information about participating in Whalenet, taken from the CICNet Gopher.

Gopher:

```
gopher.cic.net
```

Then choose the menu path Other CICNet Projects and Gopher Servers ➤ K thru 12-Gopher ➤ Classroom Activities and Projects ➤ Whalenet.

The Global Schoolhouse Project

The National Science Foundation sponsors this project, which provides examples of student and teacher publishing on the Web. The Global Schoolhouse project features partner schools, profiles of student participants, and the like. The home page is featured in Figure 25.10. You can reach this project by both the Web and Gopher.

```
http://k12.cnidr.org/gsh/gshwelcome.html
```

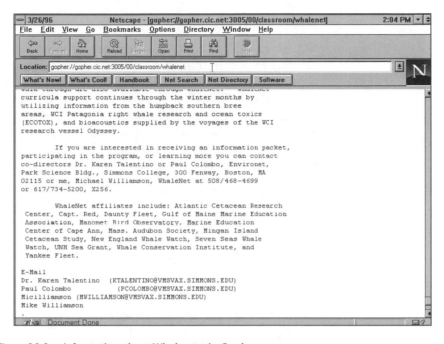

Figure 25.9.   *Information about Whalenet, via Gopher.*

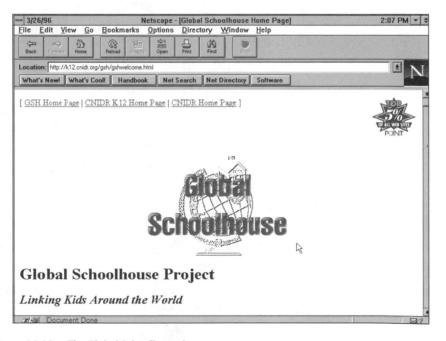

Figure 25.10.   *The Global Schoolhouse home page.*

Ask Prof. Maths

Mathematics students and teachers are encouraged to ask questions related to mathematics and math education, and the professor will send a response. Address queries to the e-mail address shown below and in the subject line indicate K–5 or 6–9 grade levels. State your question, some background to it, your name, grade level, your e-mail address and whether you're a teacher or a student. Archives can be found via FTP. The archive and the e-mail service are hosted at Saint Bonaventure University's Electronic Archives.

E-Mail Address:

maths@sbu.edu

Ask Mr. Science

Like Prof. Maths, Mr. Science will take on any challenge a student can pose in any field of science. Answers are usually posted within 48 hours; please send no more than five at a time.

E-Mail Address:

apscichs@radford.vak12ed.edu

Your questions will be answered courtesy of the Virginia Department of Education.

Weather Underground

PC-Meter reported in March 1996 that this site is among the top seven visited on the Internet, and no wonder. *Everybody* wants to know what the weather's going to be like. Interested in today's weather in your town? Information on hurricanes or earthquakes? Special classroom weather projects? The University of Michigan shares with you the National Weather Service's answers.

WWW:

http://groundhog.sprl.umich.edu/Weather_Underground.html

Follow the prompts.

Figure 25.11 shows the WeatherNet radar images page. Click on your city and see the weather radar, updated hourly! Figure 25.12 shows the color radar picture for Milwaukee, Wisconsin.

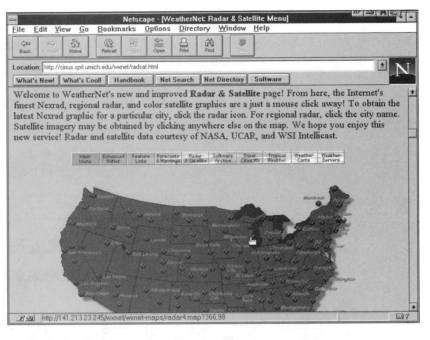

Figure 25.11. **You can get radar images for your city with WeatherNet.**

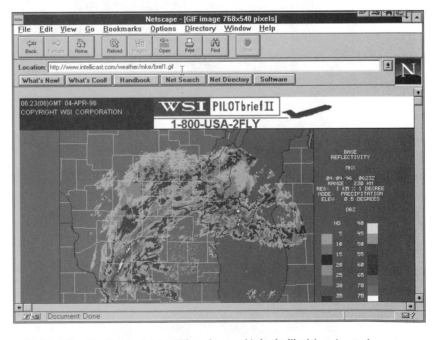

Figure 25.12. **The Weather radar for Milwaukee, and it looks like it's going to be wet.**

Alex: A Catalog of Electronic Texts

Need to check something in Shakespeare but don't have all the plays? Library Closed? Check Alex for the full text.

Alex uses Gopher to find and retrieve the full text of over 700 texts on the Internet taken from Project Gutenberg, Wiretap, the Online Book Initiative, Eris at Virginia Tech, the English server at Carnegie-Mellon University and the online portion of the Oxford Text Archive. Users can search by author and title. Figure 25.13 shows a browse for authors, in this case those with last names beginning with *I*.

Gopher:

```
gopher://gopher.rsl.ox.ac.uk/11/lib-corn/hunter
```

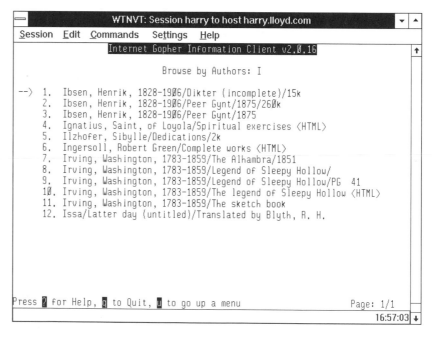

Figure 25.13.   Searching for authors by first initial in Alex.

The Alfred Wegener Institute for Polar and Marine Research

The AWI is a German national research center for polar and marine research, and as such has collected huge amounts of data related to Global Change research. Figure 25.14 shows information about the Neumeyer Antarctic Research Center.

WWW:

http://www.awi-bremerhaven.de

Direct any problems, comments, or ideas to:

E-Mail Address:

webmaster@awi-bremerhaven.de

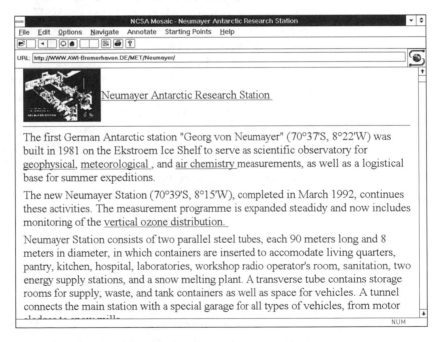

Figure 25.14. **The Neumeyer Antarctic Research Center, including diagram of the station.**

iMpulse Magazine

A comprehensive journal of music news, reviews, information, and opinion. It's delivered via Internet e-mail and published monthly. Recent topics have included Lollapalooza, new CDs, copyright issues on the Net, and Kaleidospace. To subscribe to iMpulse:

E-Mail Address:

iMpulse@dsigroup.com

In the Subject line, type **SUBSCRIBE IMPULSE**.

Remote Tele-Excavation via the Web

An interdisciplinary team at the University of Southern California is pleased to announce Mercury Site, a WWW server that allows users to tele-operate a robot arm over the Net. Users view the environment surrounding the arm via a sequence of live images taken by a CCD camera mounted on a commercial robot arm. The robot is positioned over a terrain filled with sand; a pneumatic system, also mounted on the robot, allows users to direct short bursts of compressed air into the sand at selected points. Thus users can "excavate" regions within the sand by positioning the arm, delivering a burst of air, and viewing the newly cleared region. Figure 25.15 shows instructions for new users of the excavation materials. To operate the robot you'll need a WWW client that handles forms. Have a blast.

WWW:

http://www.usc.edu/dept/raiders/

AgriGator

AgriGator is the Web server operated by the Institute of Food and Agricultural Sciences (IFAS) at the University of Florida (UF). In addition to providing information about UF, the IFAS, and different types of "Gators," it provides an extensive list of agricultural resources in Florida and worldwide. Other topics are also available (biotechnology, space, weather, environment and the "funny farm") and new ones are still under development and will be added later. Come visit the AgriGator swamp as it is being built. Figure 25.16 shows some of the agricultural information about Florida.

WWW:

http://WWW.IFAS.UFL.EDU/WWW/AGATOR_HOME.HTM

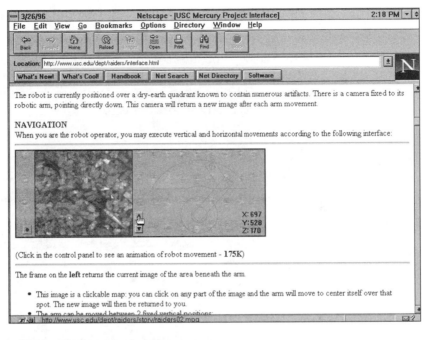

Figure 25.15.   The Excavator in action.

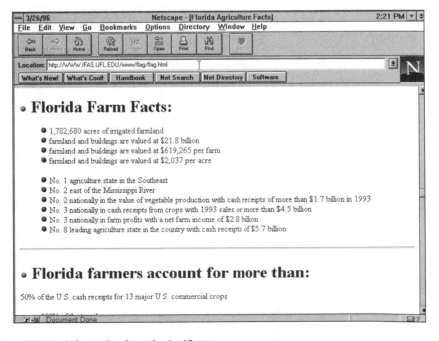

Figure 25.16.   Information from the AgriGator.

Egyptian Items

At the University of Memphis, the Institute of Egyptian Art and Archaeology operates a Web server that includes an exhibit of some of the Egyptian antiquities residing at the Institute and a short tour of Egypt. In Figure 25.17, you can see a perfectly preserved loaf of bread, and learn what it was used for (besides eating).

WWW:

    http://www.memst.edu/egypt/main.html

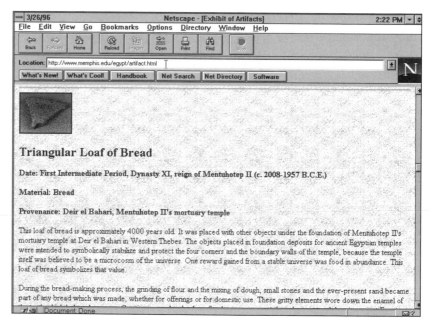

Figure 25.17. **The Institute of Egyptian Art and Archeology Web server.**

Aviation/Aerospace Newspaper

The Avion Online is Embry-Riddle Aeronautical University's weekly college newspaper specializing in coverage of aerospace activity, such as the space shuttle, and aviation topics like the Lockheed/Martin merger. Avion is the first Aviation/Aerospace newspaper to be available on the Internet.

WWW:

    http://avion.db.erau.edu

Army Handbooks

The US Army Area Handbooks provide a great deal of information about a country's culture, land, economy, and people. They are often found missing from library shelves, but they are on the Internet. You'll find information about Egypt, China, and more. Figure 25.18 shows an excerpt from the guide on Somalia.

Gopher:

```
gopher://UMSLVMA.UMSL.EDU/11/LIBRARY/GOVDOCS/ARMYAHBS
```

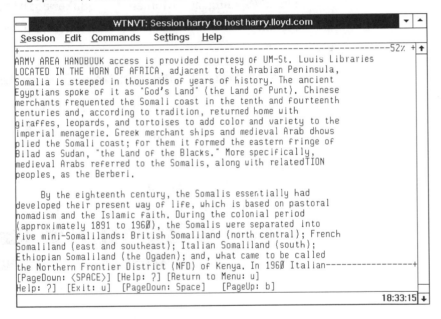

Figure 25.18. US Army Handbook on Somalia.

Earthquake Info

Want to find out what was shaking in the night? Use Finger to get information about recent earthquake activity for different regions from the following sites.

Area Served	Finger Address
The world	spyder@dmc.iris.washington.edu
The United States	quake@gldfs.cr.usgs.gov
Washington and Oregon	quake@geophys.washington.edu

Area Served	Finger Address
Alaska	quake@fm.gi.alaska.edu
Southern California	quake@scec2.gps.caltech.edu
Eastern Missouri and Southern Illinois	quake@slueas.slu.edu
Nevada and eastern California	quake@seismo.unr.edu
Northern California	quake@andreas.wr.usgs.gov
Utah, Wyoming, and Montana	quake@eqinfo.seis.utah.edu
Hawaii	quake@tako.wr.usgs.gov

NASA Network Information Center Gopher

This Gopher server provides one-stop access to resources at more than a dozen NASA information centers. Figure 25.19 shows a list of scientific resources available from NASA.

Gopher:

> gopher:naic.nasa.gov

then choose NASA Center NIC Information.

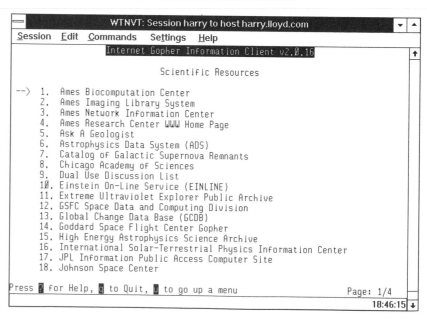

Figure 25.19.   Scientific resources on the NASA Network Information Center Gopher.

Kidlink

The Kidlink Gopher provides a large amount of information about the KIDS-*nn* (fill in a year) projects. Many of the things a kid can do via the Internet are accessible or described here. A rich resource for classroom teachers.

Gopher:

```
kids.ccit.duq.edu
```

RFC 1578: FYI on Questions and Answers

Subtitled "Answers to Commonly Asked 'Primary and Secondary School Internet User' Questions," this is an important FAQ for educators and students who are interested in finding Internet resources. It's available from the Directory and Database Services part of the InterNIC.

WWW:

```
http://ds.internic.net/rfc/rfc1578.txt/
```

Part IV

NCSU Library of Historical Documents

Got a history term paper due? Too nasty out to go to the library? North Carolina State University's Library provides the full text of dozens of historic government documents from the time of independence to the present day.

WWW:

```
http://www.lib.ncsu.edu/
```

Internet Resources

Wiretap

Wiretap is an amazing catalog of electronic texts, including a wide variety of government press releases, full-texts of books and journals, a large accumulation of laws, treaties, and other assorted legal and historical documents. You can access Wiretap via the Web, as shown in Figure 25.20, but they recommend that you use Gopher to search the texts themselves.

WWW:

```
http://wiretap.spies.com
```

or

Gopher:

```
gopher://wiretap.spies.com
```

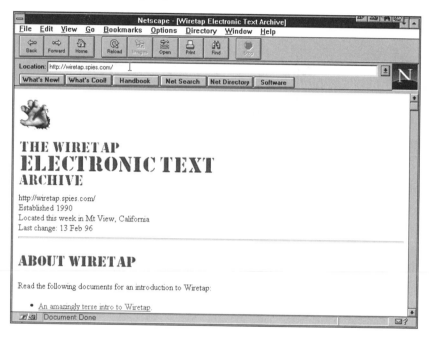

Figure 25.20.   The Wiretap Electronic Archive home page.

Movies!

All right, enough about homework. Want to find out about a movie that's showing? Want to view clips or artwork, or just neat things about your favorite movie? Lots of movie information is available online.

Web 500 Movie Index

WEB 500's survey of the top 500 Web sites (divided among 20 categories) will help you locate the sites that are shaping the WWW and changing the way we do business, inform you about the hot happenings in Web development and the new technologies being incorporated, and point you in the right direction in your search for information on the WWW. Their movie listings have some of the best from both movie producers and folks who have collected movie links. Be sure to put

WWW:

```
http://www.web500.com
```

in your bookmark file.

BuenaVista Home page

Disney's cousins have a flare for both movies and Web sites. Figure 25.21 shows a promo for *Celtic Pride,* a film released in April 1996: their home page has lots of information, video clips, sound clips, and other goodies about past and upcoming flicks.

WWW:

```
http://www.wdp.com/MoviePlex/HomePage.html
```

Figure 25.21. **The promo page for Celtic Pride,** *from BuenaVista.*

BIZ, The Entertainment Cybernetwork

TV, Movies, you name it, you can find information about it here. Sponsored by Time-Warner, this site has broad entertainment industry news and resources ranging from film, video, radio and TV to music, multimedia, and publishing. Although there are no adult-only pictures here, not all movies listed here are G-Rated.

WWW:

```
http://pathfinder.com/@@L@ekgrMxXwEAQL@x/bizmag/
```

Batman Forever

One of our favorite sites is Batman Forever. Even though the movie's been in rental video for quite some time now, the new material and riddles go on and on. Check it out at:

WWW:

```
http://www.batmanforever.com
```

Figure 25.22 shows the home page, which has really neat animation.

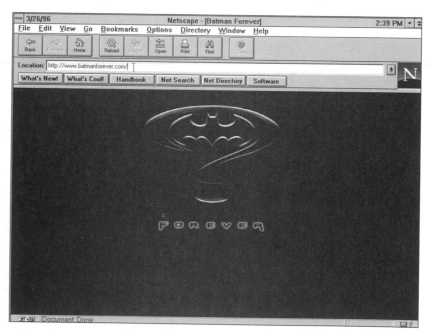

Figure 25.22. **The Batman Forever home page.**

Disney Flicks

Find the latest release schedule. Watch a promotional trailer. Download clip art. Disney has it all, at

WWW:

```
http://www.disney.com/
```

Figure 25.23 lets you see some of the kinds of things Disney shares on the Net.

Figure 25.23. **The Disney home page.**

Paramount Pictures

Paramount had one of the first media sites on the Web. As Figure 25.24 shows, their home page represents their studio gates. For those of you interested in movies, the Braveheart site is really spectacular.

WWW:

```
http://www.paramount.com/
```

Figure 25.24.   **The Paramount Virtual Front Gates.**

However, for those of you who are Star Trek: Voyager fans, a trip to the Voyager site is worthwhile. Newcomers to Voyager register in the sickbay. Here you can listen to the holographic doctor or watch a video clip. The introductory information will help you configure your browser to best take advantage of the page, including a list of video and audio helper software.

TV

The Big Eye on the Net

CBS has a cool site with daily tips and information on getting e-mail, schedules, etc. When you click on the "You're ON" image, you get a listing of the CBS schedule and show information, just in case your subscription to *TV Guide* has expired. Each of the other icons has detailed information on the shows featured.

WWW:

    http://www.cbs.com/

PBS

As part of their mission to inform, PBS has reached out into the Web in a big way. They have information on most of their big series (NOVA, Sesame Street, Masterpiece theater, McNeil-Lehrer) at their Web site, as well as lots of cool things to buy. Check it out and find out whether the Tsarina lives, and what Winton Marsalis thinks about music.

WWW:

```
http://www.pbs.org
```

FOX

The FOX Network has some amazing stuff on their Web site, including hot information about X-Files and many of their other new shows. Warning, however: this is a graphics intensive site, so you may want to open the URL, and then go make some popcorn while you wait for it to load. There are loads of character biographies, show plot lines, and other information for the avid X-files fan or even just a confused watcher.

WWW:

```
http://www.foxnetwork.com
```

FOX has information on kids' shows, sports, and adult entertainment. The URL to go straight to the X Files is

WWW:

```
http://www.delphi.com/xf_sd_ad/
```

Discovery Channel

Highlighted in *Electronic Entertainment* for October 1995, the Discovery Channel has really eye-catching graphics, and takes advantage of the latest Web technologies. The story on Corals is fascinating, with lots of great clips from the show. You can register with the Smart Viewer section, shown in Figure 25.25, to get e-mail information about upcoming features.

WWW:

```
http://www.discovery.com
```

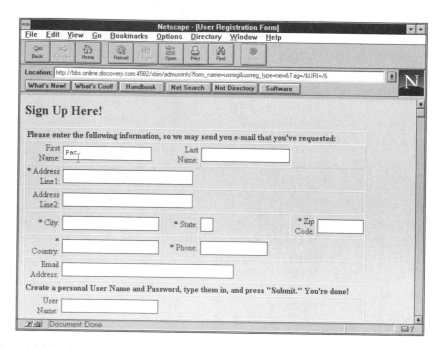

Figure 25.25.   Fill out a form for custom Discovery Channel info.

Nickelodeon

At this unofficial Nickelodeon home page, learn a little about the television network just for kids. You can even send e-mail to Nick at Nite. Also get guides to the Nickelodeon shows "Clarissa Explains It All," "The Adventures of Pete and Pete," and "Rugrats." Figure 25.26 shows the RugRats guide.

WWW:

```
http://www.ee.surrey.ac.uk/Contrib/Entertainment/
nickelodeon.html
```

Ventana Media guide for Kids

Ventana Media has created a very nice Web index for kids, shown in Figure 25.27. There are many Web pages linked to TV shows, from cartoons like *Mighty Morphin Power Rangers* to *Sesame Street*. They make a big effort to keep their links in the "G" and "PG" range, as well.

WWW:

```
http://www.vmedia.com/books/wwww_2nd/sec7/index.htm
```

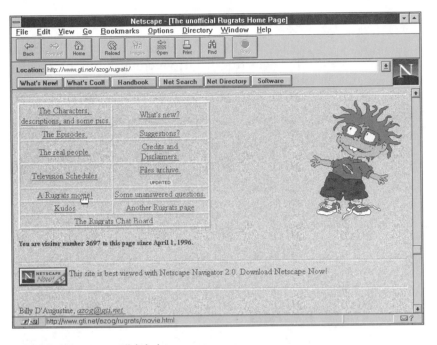

Figure 25.26. **Rugrats on Nickelodeon.**

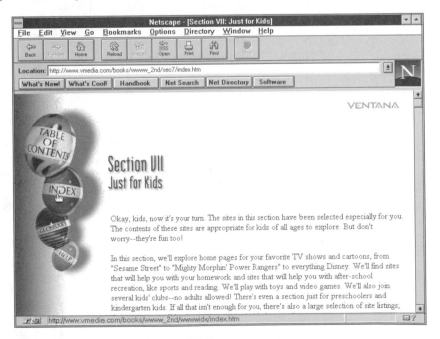

Figure 25.27. **The Ventana Media Just for Kids home page.**

Jay Jay the Jet Plane

Jay Jay the Jet Plane stars in an all new video series for preschoolers. This colorful Web site includes a bedtime story to read and see online and a coloring book of pictures to print on your printer. See the pages for activities and how to order the products.

WWW:

```
http://www.jayjay.com/
```

KidsWeb

KidsWeb is a huge digital library for the kids. Arts, sciences, social studies, sports, and more.

WWW:

```
http://www.npac.syr.edu/textbook/kidsweb
```

NetPets

The NetPets Virtual Gallery of Nature and Wildlife is a rotating exhibit of beautiful images of nature and animals. Figure 25.28 shows the "Bad Dog!" page, where kids can add their own stories about naughty things their dogs have done. It also has really a really cute Web animation of a puppy. Take a look at

WWW:

```
http://columbia.digiweb.com/~netpets/gallery/canvas.html
```

Yuckiest Site on the Internet

OK. You've seen the book, now here's the Web site. Brought to you by New Jersey Online, this site is packed full of gross scientific stuff for kids and families to explore. Presented by real scientists at the Liberty Science Center. Figure 25.29 shows a recent offering: Cockroach World!

WWW:

```
http://www.nj.com/yucky/
```

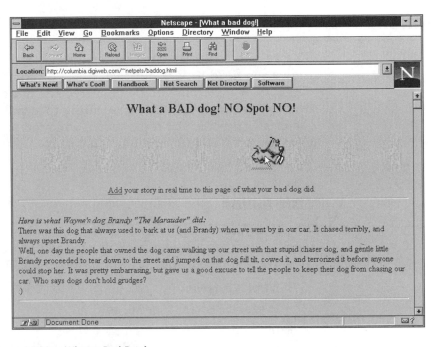

*Figure 25.28.   **What a Bad Dog!***

Figure 25.29.   Cockroach World, from the Liberty Science Center.

Mailing Lists

The resources we've listed so far fall generally into the category of things you need to seek out each time you want to use them. Another category of materials can be delivered to your e-mail box (your front door on the Internet). By subscribing to a mailing list, you can read materials on particular topics when you read your e-mail. And, unlike Gopher and Web information, you can contribute, too, by replying to the message.

Fish-Junior

The Fish-Junior mailing list is a way for students to communicate with marine scientists. Students of all ages and all countries are welcome. To subscribe send a standard subscription message to:

E-Mail Address:

    listserv@searn.sunet.se

or to

    listserv@searn.bitnet

Remember not to add a Subject line, and to enter

    subscribe fish-junior *yourfirstname yourlastname*

in the body of your e-mail message.

KidCafe

Children ages 10–15 from all over the world are invited to join this chat list and learn more about each other and their cultures. Adults may read but not post. Send a standard subscription message to:

E-Mail Address:

    listserv@vm1.nodak.edu

or

    listserv@ndsuvm1

THIS JUST IN

A tasty weekly collection of strange news from a California tech publisher. One issue told of a New Jersey man fined for "needlessly" killing an animal—a rat! Another story concerned a Venezuela teen who, needing a spot to relieve himself, somehow went into a lion's pen: "Perez struggled both to live and to get his pants up; a friend helped by hitting the lion with a brick. And that brick came from ... where?" To subscribe, send e-mail to:

E-Mail Address:

`listserv@netcom.com`

The Subject line should be `Ignored`; and the body of the message should read `Subscribe This-Just-In`.

Newsgroups

Newsgroups are something like mailing lists in that you have to subscribe to them and you may choose to participate in the discussions. But they're something like published information in Gopher or the World Wide Web, too, because they're broadcast to a lot of people around the world. One of the fun things to do in a newsgroup is to practice a language that you've been studying in school. You can find newsgroups where you can correspond (in public, of course) with students in Germany, for example. Try the `k12.lang.german` group. You'll meet some great people.

Chat/Discussion Newsgroups

K–12 students and teachers can discuss topics of interest in the appropriate `k12.chat` newsgroups.

Kindergartners through fifth grade: `k12.chat.elementary`

Sixth graders through eighth graders: `k12.chat.junior`

Freshmen through seniors: `k12.chat.senior`

Teachers at all levels: `k12.chat.teacher`

Other Interesting Things

Here are a few more items of interest to kids, their parents, and their teachers.

Personalized Children's Books

Personalized children's books make the child the star of his or her own story, and thus help to build self-esteem and interest in reading. "Personalized For You" features the titles of the Hefty Publishing Company, the largest and oldest publisher of personalized children's books. Figure 25.30 shows general information about the books.

WWW:

http://personalized4u.com/

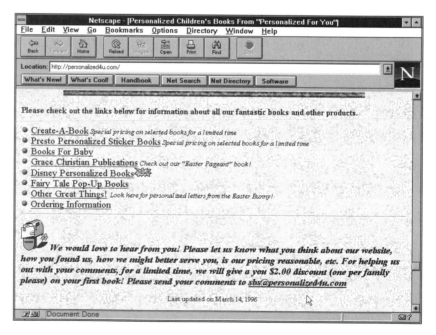

Figure 25.30.   *Types of personalized books available from Hefty Books.*

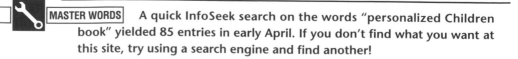

MASTER WORDS   A quick InfoSeek search on the words "personalized Children book" yielded 85 entries in early April. If you don't find what you want at this site, try using a search engine and find another!

Cookie Servers

Cookie servers don't really serve cookies, of course. They are databases of funny quotes and sayings. The name comes from the idea of the "fortune" cookies that are served in Chinese restaurants in the United States. The sayings are a time-honored Internet tradition and you'll see .sig (e-mail signature) files with cookie sayings built into them. Each time you Telnet to a cookie server, the server sends back a different saying. Be sure and include the port numbers!

Telnet:

astro.temple.edu

(port 12345)

or

Telnet:

129.32.1.100

or (for Star Trek quotes)

Telnet:

149.132.2.11

(port 10250)

Fun Fingers

With the Finger command, kids of all ages can find information that people have provided for fun (or their idea of fun, anyway), such as the status of drink and candy machines at various universities:

finger info or drink or graph@drink.csh.rit.edu

finger coke@cs.cmu.edu

or

finger coke@xcf.berkeley.edu

finger pepsi or cocacola@columbia.edu

finger coke@ucc.gu.uwa.edu.au

Weekly Trivia:

finger cyndiw@magnus1.com

or

finger cyndiw@198.242.50.4

Sports on the Web

Sports lovers can cruise the Internet at length with a multitude of sports information services available. Figure 25.31 shows the ESPN Interactive Zone, where you can find Interviews and Chat sites.

WWW:

> http://espnet.sportszone.com

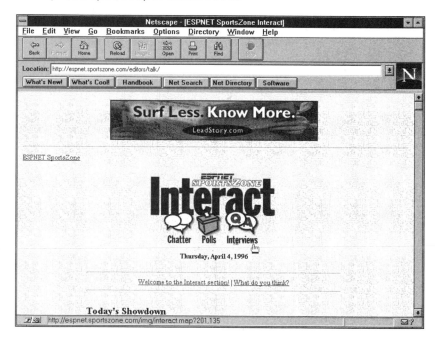

Figure 25.31. **The ESPN Interactive Zone.**

There are other sports servers available, at:

WWW:

> http://tns-www.lcs.mit.edu/vs/vssportsbrowser.html
>
> http://www.rsn.com/
>
> http://www.cs.fsu.edu/projects/group12/title.html

Sports Schedules

Here are some fun servers at the University of Colorado. You use Telnet to connect to a specific port number and you can see information about the National Basketball Association, the National Hockey League, the National Football League, or Major League Baseball. This is handy if you want to plan an outing to a game on a specific day, for example. Once you are connected to the server with the specific information you need, you can enter a date, for example 1/19, and see the schedule for that day for that sport. If you pick a day that isn't within the "season" for the sport, the servers will tell you that, too. If you follow a specific team, you can enter a code for that team. Or if you want to know only about a specific division within the particular league, you can enter a code for that, too. And if you just press the ENTER key, the servers will display the games for "today". Enter "help" for a complete set of instructions as well as a list of all the teams and leagues for that sport.

Enter the command **quit** to exit the service.

In addition to the Colorado Telnet sites listed below, you can also Finger copi@oddjob.uchicago.edu for sports schedules.

NBA

Telnet to culine.colorado.edu, port 859 or to the IP address 128.138.129.170, port 859.

NHL

Telnet to culine.colorado.edu, port 860 or to the IP address 128.138.129.170, port 860.

Major League Baseball

Telnet to culine.colorado.edu, port 862, or to the IP address 128.138.129.170, port 862.

NFL

Telnet to culine.colorado.edu, port 863 or to the IP address 128.138.129.170, port 863.

Part
IV

Internet Resources

National Hockey League Info

Extensive National Hockey League information is summarized on a new home page, including the latest NHL scores, the present league standings, team records against each other, the 1993, 1994. and 1995 Stanley Cup Playoff matchups broken down game-by-game, and the leading scorers. Current information, in early 1996, was for the 1995-96 season. Plans are to keep the HTML files updated automatically with the use of two FORTRAN programs that take as their input game scores and the names of players who have registered goals or assists. In addition, you can also get the history of matchups in the Stanley Cup finals, and NHL awards like the Rookie of the Year Award or the Most Valuable Player Award. Figure 25.32 shows the NHL Home page.

WWW:

`http://maxwell.uhh.hawaii.edu/hockey/hockey.html`

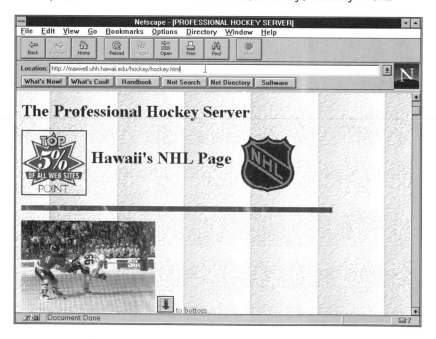

*Figure 25.32.   **The National Hockey League home page.***

The Games Domain

This Web server offers the largest collection of games-related connecting points on the Internet. This site contains over 140 links to various FAQs, walk-throughs, pointers to FTP sites, home pages, host sites for interactive environments, information documents, and much more! Figure 25.33 shows the result of a search for games related to music. There are also game reviews via the Web version of *GameBytes* magazine.

WWW:

    `http://www.gamesdomain.com/`

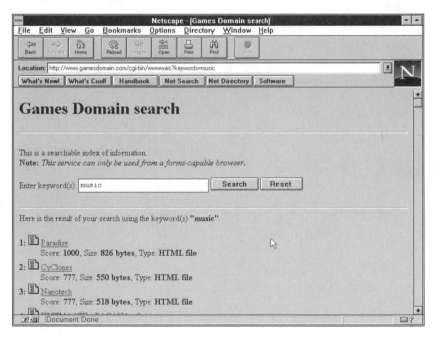

Figure 25.33.   *Results of a search for music games at the Games Domain.*

Glossary

PART

V

An Internet User's Glossary

WE'VE tried to include here every term that you might want to look up while reading this book. However, not all of the words in this glossary appear in the book. Some are included because you will come across them as you continue to explore the Internet; others are here because they're fun, and certainly one of the benefits of Internet communication is that it's fun.

In the following definitions, any term that appears in *italic* type is defined as a separate entry elsewhere in this glossary. Also note that acronyms are widely used in Internet terminology; and in most cases you are more likely to encounter the abbreviated form of a term than the spelled-out form. Therefore, except in the rare cases where the longer form is more commonly used, we have alphabetized and cross-referenced such terms under the acronym form.

Acknowledgments: Parts of this glossary come from the Internet Engineering Task Force (IETF) Network Working Group and their document RFC 1392. That document was edited by G. Malkin at Xylogics and T. LaQuey Parker of Cisco. Their acknowledgments include the User Glossary Working Group of the User Services Area of the Internet Engineering Task Force, and Jon Postel for his definitive definition of "datagram." Brendan Kehoe, noted Internet author, contributed ideas. Information also came to us from the glossaries compiled by the user services staffs at the University of Michigan; Merit, Inc.; and Netcom. Special thanks go to Laura Bollettino, Mark Davis-Craig, and Christine Wendt of the University of Michigan; Howard Chu, formerly of Lloyd Internetworking; and Jennifer Tifft of Sybase, Inc.

:-)

This peculiar-looking symbol is one of the ways a person can portray emotions in the low-*bandwidth* medium of computer-mediated communication—by using "smiley faces." There are literally hundreds of such symbols. This particular example expresses "happiness." Don't see it? Tilt your head to the left 90 degrees. Smiles are also used to denote sarcasm. See also *emoticon*. (Thanks to Brendan Kehoe.)

.plan

A plan file on a UNIX system is one that can be read by users on- and off-system using the *Finger* program (if the systems administrator has set up the system to allow it). It has the filename extension .plan and usually contains some information you want people to know about you, such as name, preferred e-mail address, and business phone. Some plan files also include information about the user's interests. Some systems administrators do not permit remote fingering of plan files for security or privacy reasons.

ACK (acknowledgment)

A response sent to confirm receipt of a message. See also *NAK (negative acknowledgment)*.

ACL (access control list)

A list of services available on a network, each with a list of the hosts permitted to use the service. Many network security systems operate by allowing selective use of services. An access control list is the usual means by which access to services is permitted or denied.

Acrobat

A proprietary document representation from Adobe that allows a formatted document to be represented the same (complete with all formatting) on a number of different computing platforms. Another program that does this is Farallon's Replica.

address

The unique identifier for a specific location on a network. There are several types of addresses in common use within the Internet. Ones that you may use are *e-mail address* (e.g. glee@netcom.com); *IP*, internet or Internet address, (e.g. 35.1.1.42).

Part V

Glossary

address mask

A pattern of numbers used to identify which parts of an *IP address* correspond to the network, *subnet*, and *host* portions of the address. This mask is often referred to as the *subnet mask*.

AD (administrative domain)

A collection of hosts and routers, and the interconnecting network(s), managed by a single administrative authority. See also *domain*.

agent

In the *client-server computing* model, the part of the system that performs information preparation and exchange on behalf of a *client* or *server application*. For example, in some database searches, the agent lets you ask questions in a format that is comfortable to you, and reformats the question as a strictly defined search argument for the database.

alias

A name, usually short and easy to remember, that is translated into another name, usually long and difficult to remember. In networking, aliases are frequently used to associate a service with a logical name, rather than with a particular computer or machine address. Aliases are also used to reroute mail and service requests from one computer to another; this allows the system or network management to change the computer providing the services when needed without affecting users, or to keep the underlying architecture hidden. Aliases are also used to indicate the service available from the host: for example, www.weather .org, gopher.msu.edu, or ftp.netcom.com. See also *mail alias*.

alias database

The group of public aliases on an e-mail system. Aliases include group names, nicknames, and services, such as "sales" or "support," that allow mail to be redirected inside the e-mail system.

anchor

An anchor is a place, identified by words, sounds, or images, in a *hypertext* document (Web page) that holds the linked *URL* identifying a linked location. When you select the anchor, the URL is read by your browser *client* and the linked hypertext document is fetched and then displayed. The URL in the anchor can be a link to another spot on the same page, to another document, or to a specific place in another document. Also called *hotspot*.

anonymous FTP

Anonymous *FTP (File Transfer Protocol)* allows a user to retrieve (and sometimes deposit) documents, files, programs, and other archived data from archives in the Internet without having to establish a *user ID* and *password* on the computer that contains the archive. Many, but not all, computers used as FTP *archive sites* allow anonymous access. By using the special user ID anonymous and the password guest, you can have limited access to publicly accessible files on the remote system. Many systems now request the user's e-mail address as a password, in order to have better access tracking.

ANSI (American National Standards Institute)

This organization is responsible for approving US standards in many fields, including computers and communications. Standards approved by this organization are often called ANSI standards (for example, ANSI C is the version of the C language approved by ANSI). ANSI is a member of *ISO (International Organization for Standardization)*.

API (Application Program Interface)

In general, a definition of all the functions that an operating system provides to application programs for performing tasks such as file management and displaying information on the screen, and of how the application should use those functions. In networking, an API also defines the method by which applications can take advantage of network features.

AppleTalk

A proprietary networking protocol of the Apple Computer Corporation used to connect computers to one another.

application

A program that performs a function directly for a user. *FTP*, *e-mail* and *Telnet clients* are examples of network applications. DOS, Windows, MacOS, and *UNIX* are examples of operating systems, on which applications run.

Part V

Glossary

Archie

A system to automatically gather, index and serve archive information on the Internet. The initial implementation of Archie provided an indexed directory of filenames from *anonymous FTP* archives on the Internet. Later versions provide other collections of information. See also *archive site, Gopher, Prospero, Wide Area Information Servers*.

archive site

A computer that provides access to a collection of files across the Internet. An *anonymous FTP* archive site, for example, provides access to this material via the FTP protocol. See also *Archie, Gopher, Prospero, WAIS (Wide Area Information Servers)*.

ARP (Address Resolution Protocol)

A method used to determine the low-level physical network hardware address that corresponds to the high-level *IP address* for a given *host*. It is defined in RFC 826.

ARPA (Advanced Research Projects Agency)

An agency of the US Department of Defense, responsible for the development of new technology for use by the military. ARPA was responsible for funding much of the development of the Internet we know today, including the Berkeley version of *UNIX* and *TCP/IP*.

ARPANET
(Advanced Research Projects Agency Network)

A network funded by *ARPA* (formerly DARPA). It served as the basis for early networking research in the 1960s, as well as the central *backbone* during the development of the Internet. The ARPANET's architecture consisted of individual *packet-switching* computers interconnected by leased lines.

ASCII
(American Standard Code for Information Interchange)

A standard character-to-number encoding widely used in the computer industry. Plain text, Postscript files, and BinHex files are among the types of data transferred in ASCII format. Spreadsheets, compiled programs, and graphics are transferred across the Net in *binary* format. In addition, the computer community has extended the ASCII character set to allow for the transmission of control and other characters within the data being transferred. This change allowed for high speed, "8-bit clean" data transmission, essential for the development of workstation *TCP/IP* applications. This lets users turn their home computers into Internet hosts. See also *EBCDIC*.

at-sign (@)

The at-sign (@) is the separator for most *e-mail addresses*; it separates the *user ID* from the *domain name* of the mail computer. See also *bang path, UUCP*.

ATM (Asynchronous Transfer Mode)

A method for the dynamic allocation of bandwidth using a fixed-size *packet* (called a cell). ATM is also known as "fast packet." ATM technology is used in high-traffic networks and in places where networks interconnect.

AUP (Acceptable Use Policy or Appropriate Use Policy)

Many networks, both the larger *transit* and regional networks as well as company networks and public BBSes, have policies that restrict the uses to which the network or computing facility may be put. A well-known example is NSFNET's AUP, which did not allow commercial use. Enforcement of AUPs varies with the network and systems administrator. See also *National Science Foundation*.

authentication

The verification of the identity of a person or process. The most common authentication process most users experience is the login challenge, which requests a valid login ID and a *password*. PIN numbers, "carding," and the famous military checkpoint challenge "Friend or foe?" are all examples of authentication in everyday life. See also *authorization*.

authorization

The granting of privilege based on identity. Authorization is a partner to authentication in computer networking, where your access to services is based on your identity, and an authentication procedure guarantees that you are who you say you are. See also *authentication, Kerberos, password*.

backbone

The top level in a hierarchical network. *Stub networks* and *transit networks* that connect to the same backbone are guaranteed to be interconnected. Backbone networks usually run at a higher speed, and with a larger *bandwidth*, than the networks that branch off of them.

bandwidth

Technically, the difference in Hertz (Hz) between the highest and lowest frequencies of a transmission channel. However, as typically used, it refers to the amount of data that can be sent through a given communications circuit. People are now also beginning to consider the amount of information in human interactions, such as expressions (smiles, frowns) and other body language that cannot be sent over electronic channels such as *e-mail* and *Usenet* news, and metaphorically describe electronic transactions as being "low in emotional bandwidth."

bang path

From the *UNIX* jargon: a "bang" is an exclamation point (!). A series of computer names used to direct electronic mail from one user to another, typically by specifying an explicit *UUCP* path through which the mail is to be routed. UUCP mail pathways looks like this, with the user name last: `andros!mailrus!jabberwock!cs-wisc!susan`. See also *at-sign, e-mail address, mail path, splat*.

baseband

A transmission medium through which digital signals are sent without complicated frequency shifting. In general, only one communication channel is available at any given time. *Ethernet* is an example of a baseband network. See also *broadband*.

bastion host

See *firewall*.

BBS (Bulletin Board System)

A computer (with associated software), that typically provides electronic messaging services, archives of files, and any other services or activities of interest to the bulletin board system's operator. Although BBSes were traditionally the domain of hobbyists and accessible only by using a modem, an increasing number of BBSes are connected directly to the Internet, and many are currently operated by government, educational, and research institutions. See also *e-mail, Internet, MUD, Usenet.*

bcnu

Be Seein' You.

binary

"It's all ones and zeros." Computers store information in the form of on/off electrical impulses, which correspond to the binary (base 2) digits 0 and 1. Files can be transferred over the Internet in either binary or *ASCII* (text) format. A binary file is one that contains any nonprintable characters; such as compiled programs, graphics files, word-processing and spreadsheet files, audio files, and so on. See also *FTP.*

BIND (Berkeley Internet Name Domain)

Implementation of a *DNS server* developed and distributed by the University of California at Berkeley. Many Internet hosts run BIND, and it is the ancestor of many commercial BIND implementations.

bit

*BI*nary digi*T*. A unit of data. There are usually eight bits in a byte. There are eight bits in one ASCII character. See also *kilobit, megabit.*

BITNET

A largely academic computer network that provides interactive electronic mail, interactive conversation, and file transfer services, using a *store-and-forward* protocol, based on IBM Network Job Entry protocols. BITNET-II encapsulates the BITNET protocol within IP packets and depends on the Internet to route them. See also *spooling.*

BOF (Birds Of a Feather)

A Birds Of a Feather (flocking together) is an informally structured, common-interest discussion group. It is formed, often ad hoc, to consider a specific issue and, therefore, has a narrow focus. BOFs are often held during long breaks or after the main sessions at computer and technology-related conferences; the term is spreading to more mainstream events.

Part
V

Glossary

bookmark

A collection of *Web URLs*, each stored at user request by a *Gopher* or Web *browser client*. Also called *hotlist*.

bounce

The return of a piece of mail because of an error in its delivery.

bounce-o-gram

A message from an automated mailer telling you that mail has bounced.

bridge

A device that forwards traffic between network segments. These segments would have a common network layer address. *AppleTalk* networks and *Ethernet* networks sometimes use bridges. See also *gateway*, *router*.

broadband

A transmission medium capable of supporting a wide range of frequencies. It can carry multiple signals by dividing the total capacity of the medium into multiple, independent bandwidth channels, where each channel operates only on a specific range of frequencies. Traditional cable television services operate on a broadband service. See also *baseband*.

broadcast

A special type of *multicast packet* that all *nodes* on the network are always willing to receive.

broadcast storm

An incorrect *packet broadcast* onto a network that causes multiple *hosts* to respond all at once, typically with equally incorrect packets; this causes the storm to grow exponentially. A broadcast storm can bring down a network in moments, usually from overloading of the *routers* and other packet handling equipment.

brouter

A device that *bridges* some packets and *routes* other packets. The bridge/route decision is based on configuration information.

browser

World Wide Web and *Gopher* services are accessed using *client* software called browsers, because they let you drift from link to link without having to have a purposeful search. Browsers encourage discovery by serendipity, hence the name.

BSD (Berkeley Software Distribution)

An implementation of the *UNIX* operating system and its utilities developed and distributed by the University of California at Berkeley. "BSD" is usually preceded by the version number of the distribution, for example, "4.3 BSD" is version 4.3 of the Berkeley UNIX distribution. Many Internet hosts run BSD software, and it is the ancestor of many commercial UNIX implementations.

btw

By The Way.

CCIRN (Coordinating Committee for Intercontinental Research Networks)

A committee that includes the United States Federal Networking Council *(FNC)* and its counterparts in North America and Europe. Co-chaired by the executive directors of the FNC and the European Association of Research Networks *(RARE)*, the CCIRN provides a forum for cooperative planning among the principal North American and European research networking bodies. These bodies are the principal planning and organizing bodies that plan the political and funding growth of the world-wide networks, as opposed to the IETF, which plans the technological growth.

CCITT (Comite Consultatif International de Telegraphique)

This organization is part of the United Nations International Telecommunications Union (ITU) and is responsible for making technical recommendations about telephone and data communications systems. Every four years CCITT holds plenary sessions where they adopt new standards; the most recent was in 1992.

CERT (Computer Emergency Response Team)

The CERT was formed by DARPA in November 1988 in response to the needs exhibited during the Internet *worm* incident, where a program

Part
V

Glossary

sent out on the Internet by a college student used security loopholes in networked computers to replicate itself, send itself on to other computers, and disable critical functions on the affected computers. The CERT charter is to work with the Internet community to facilitate its response to computer security events involving Internet hosts, to take proactive steps to raise the community's awareness of computer security issues, and to conduct research targeted at improving the security of existing systems. CERT products and services include 24-hour technical assistance for responding to computer security incidents, product vulnerability assistance, technical documents, and tutorials. In addition, the team maintains a number of mailing lists (including one for CERT Advisories), and provides an anonymous FTP server, at cert.org, where security-related documents and tools are archived. The CERT may be reached by e-mail at cert@cert.org and by telephone at +1-412-268-7090 (24-hour hotline). See also *Advanced Research Projects Agency.*

checksum

A method of verifying the accuracy of transmitted data, a checksum is a computed value calculated from the contents of a packet. This value is sent along with the packet when it is transmitted. The receiving system computes a new checksum (using the same algorithm as the transmitting end used) based upon the received data and compares this value to the one sent with the packet. If the two values are the same, the receiver has a high degree of confidence that the data was received correctly.

CIDR (Classless Internet Domain Routing)

A routing protocol for working with multiple Class C addresses.

circuit switching

A communications paradigm in which a dedicated communication path is established between two hosts, and on which all packets travel. The telephone system is an example of a circuit-switched network. See also *connection-oriented, connectionless, packet-switching.*

CIX (Commercial Internet eXchange)

The Commercial Internet eXchange is an association of Internet providers in the United States. CIX members have agreed to carry the commercial traffic of each member network. The CIX was formed to provide routing for commercial Internet traffic during the time that the NSFNET AUP (Acceptable Use Policy) specifically forbade purely commercial traffic. For more information, see the CIX *Gopher* and *Web* servers at `cix.org`.

client

In *client-server computing*, the "front-end" program that the user runs to connect with, and request information from, the *server* program. For most of the common Internet tools, many different client programs are available, designed to work in DOS, Windows, Macintosh, and UNIX environments. See also *Archie, WAIS, WWW.*

client-server computing

The model or scheme underlying practically all programs running on the Internet (as well as other network and database software). In this design, the work of an application (such as *FTP* or *Gopher*) is divided up between two programs—the *client* (or front end) and the *server* (or back end). The client program handles the work of connecting to the server and requesting files or information, and the server handles the work of finding and "serving up" the information (or of providing some other service, such as directing print jobs to a printer). See also *Archie, client, FTP, Gopher, server, DNS, NFS, WAIS, WWW.*

clipboard

In Macintosh, Windows, and OS/2 *applications*, a temporary storing area for cut or copied information. The clipboard holds the information until you cut or copy another selection to it or you exit from your environment.

congestion

Congestion occurs when the load exceeds the capacity of a data communication path. You may be experiencing congestion when any of the following happens: you get a busy signal when you dial into a modem pool; the response from the server or host you are trying to reach is slow; you get an error message telling you that no ports are available for the service or host you want to use.

connection-oriented

Describes a data communication method in which communication proceeds through three well-defined phases: connection establishment, data transfer, connection release. *TCP* is a connection-oriented proto-col. See also *circuit switching, connectionless, packet switching.*

connectionless

Describes a data communication method in which communication occurs between hosts with no previous setup. Packets between two hosts may take different routes, as each is independent of the other. See also *circuit switching, connection-oriented, packet switching.*

cracker

An individual who attempts to access computer systems without authorization. These individuals are often malicious, as opposed to *hackers* (who see themselves as benevolent explorers), and have many means at their disposal for breaking into a system. See also *CERT, Trojan horse, virus, worm.*

CREN
(Corporation for Research and Educational Networking)

This organization was formed in October 1989, when *BITNET* and CSNET (Computer + Science NETwork) were combined under one administrative authority. CSNET is no longer operational, but CREN still runs BITNET.

CSLIP

Serial Line Internet Protocol with compressed headers. See also *PPP (Point-to-Point Protocol), SLIP (Serial Line Internet Protocol).*

cursor

The symbol on your display screen that represents your logical posi-tion. The cursor can be either an arrow, a hand, a vertical bar, an hour-glass, or some other symbol. The symbol represents places where you can click your mouse. It may point to a link where you can click to jump to new information. In a *hypermedia* document, it may represent a place where you provide input from the keyboard. If material may be inserted or replaced, it will be inserted or replaced from this point. If you may select material, the selection will start from this point. The hourglass is usually shown when your client is working on the function that you have selected. It tells you that, even though the screen may not have changed, your request has been recognized and is being processed.

CWIS (Campus Wide Information System)

A CWIS makes information and services publicly available on campus via kiosks (information stations named for the familiar circular bulletin boards with posters stapled to them), and it makes interactive computing available via kiosks, interactive computing systems, and campus networks. They are usually found on college campuses, although some K-12 school systems are beginning to develop CWISes. Services routinely include directory information, calendars, bulletin boards, and databases.

cyberspace

Cyber comes from the 50s term "cybernetics," which is used to describe the science of computers. *Space* harkens to the 60s terms "inner space," "head space," and so on. Cyberspace is a term coined by either computer hackers or science fiction writers (both claim credit) to describe the virtual geography of the Internet. The term first appeared in print in William Gibson's 1984 fantasy novel *Neuromancer* to describe the "world" of computers and the society that gathers around them.

datagram

A self-contained, independent entity of data carrying sufficient information to be routed from the source to the destination computer without reliance on earlier exchanges between the source and destination computers and the transporting network. This entity has given rise to several joking and serious other sorts of communications: a *bounce-o-gram*, for example, is a message from an automated mailer telling you mail has bounced. A *nastygram* is a message, usually in *e-mail* but sometimes in *Usenet* news, that has unpleasant contents. See also *frame*, *packet*. [Term coined by J. Postel]

DCA

See *DISA (Defense Information Systems Agency)*.

DCE (Distributed Computing Environment)

In our current computing environment of heterogeneous computers, network architectures, and protocols, some standards had to be created for conventions to allow users of these varied computers to be able to function on remote systems. These standards define user interfaces, the way data will be formatted so that systems with differing internal structures will be able to process it, and other methods of *interoperability*. The goal is that the user will never have to know and negotiate the differences between systems. The DCE standards are promoted and controlled by the Open Software Foundation (OSF), a consortium led by Digital, IBM, and Hewlett Packard.

DDN (Defense Data Network)

A global communications network serving the US Department of Defense and composed of the MILNET, other portions of the Internet, and the classified networks that are not part of the Internet. The DDN is used to connect military installations and is managed by the Defense Information Systems Agency. See also *DISA (Defense Information Systems Agency)*.

DDN NIC (Defense Data Network Network Information Center)

Often called "the NIC." The DDN NIC's primary responsibilities are assigning Internet network addresses and Autonomous System numbers, administering of the root domain, and providing information and support services to the DDN. It is also a primary repository for *RFCs*.

default route

An entry in a *routing table*, used to direct packets addressed to networks not explicitly listed in the routing table. See also *static route*.

DEK (Data Encryption Key)

Used for the *encryption* of message text and for the computation of message integrity checks (signatures).

DES (Data Encryption Standard)

A popular, standard *encryption* scheme.

dialup

A temporary, as opposed to dedicated, connection between computers established over a standard phone line.

DISA (Defense Information Systems Agency)

Formerly called the Defense Communications Agency (DCA), this is the government agency responsible for managing the DDN portion of the Internet, including the MILNET. Currently, DISA administers the DDN, and supports the user assistance services of the *DDN NIC*. See also *DDN (Defense Data Network)*.

distributed database

A collection of several different data repositories that looks like a single database to the user. A prime example in the Internet is the *Domain Name System*.

DNS (Domain Name System)

The set of conventions for naming *host* computers on the Internet and the directory service for looking up names. Each host name corresponds to an *IP address*. The DNS is defined in STD 13, RFCs 1034 and 1035. See also *FQDN (Fully Qualified Domain Name)*.

DNS server

A computer that translates the *domain name* of another computer into an *IP address*, and vice versa, upon request. Most DNS servers maintain a large database of such correspondences, which is refreshed on a regular (at most daily) basis. Usually the request for translation comes from another computer, which needs the IP address for routing purposes.

domain

A named collection of network *hosts*. Some important domains are: .COM (commercial), .EDU (educational), .NET (network operations), .GOV (US government), and .MIL (US military). Most countries also have individual domains; for example, .US (United States), .UK (United Kingdom), .AU (Australia). See also *AD (Administrative Domain)*, *DNS (Domain Name System)*.

domain name

The human-language name of a computer on the Internet, as opposed to its more computer-friendly numeric *IP address*. For example, hermes .merit.edu is a domain name or address, and 42.1.1.6 is an IP address.

dot address (dotted decimal notation)

Dot address refers to the common notation for IP addresses of the form A.B.C.D; where each letter represents, in decimal, one byte of a four-byte IP address. See also *IP address*.

dynamic adaptive routing

Automatic rerouting of traffic based on a sensing and analysis of current actual network conditions.

EARN (European Academic and Research Network)

A network connecting European academic and research institutions with electronic mail and file transfer services using the *BITNET* protocol.

EBCDIC (Extended Binary Coded Decimal Interchange Code)

A standard character-to-number encoding used primarily by IBM computer systems. Most Internet hosts use *ASCII* encoding; however, you may encounter EBCDIC if you transfer data via tape or other physical media to or from a large IBM installation. Additionally, while most systems translate EBCDIC to ASCII during *FTP* or other electronic transmission, some older computers in non-US countries may still have files stored in EBCDIC.

e-mail (electronic mail)

A system whereby a computer user can exchange messages with other computer users (or groups of users) via a communications network. Electronic mail is one of the most popular uses of the Internet.

e-mail address

The domain-based or UUCP address that is used to send electronic mail to a specified destination. For example, one of the authors' addresses is `pat@lloyd.com`. See also *bang path, mail path, UUCP (Unix-to-Unix CoPy)*.

emoticon

A word, constructed from the EMOT part of emotion and ICON, intended to describe the symbols used in electronic communication to convey emotional tone. An emoticon, e.g., :-) for a smile, helps people understand when you are joking.

encapsulation

The technique used by layered protocols in which a *layer* adds header information to the protocol data unit (*PDU*) from the layer above. As an example, in Internet terminology, a *packet* would contain a header from the physical layer, followed by a header from the network layer (*IP*), followed by a header from the transport layer (*TCP*), followed by the application protocol data. For more information about layers, consult works about the *OSI* Reference Model.

encryption

The manipulation of a *packet*'s data in order to prevent any but the intended recipient from reading that data. There are many types of data encryption, and they are the basis of network security. See also *DES (Data Encryption Standard), Kerberos*.

Ethernet

A 10 Mbps standard for LANs, initially developed by Xerox, and later refined by Digital, Intel and Xerox. All hosts are connected to a coaxial cable, where they contend for network access using a Carrier Sense Multiple Access with Collision Detection (CSMA/CD) paradigm. See also *LAN (Local Area Network), token ring*.

Eudora

A proprietary *e-mail* program from the Qualcomm Corporation.

FAQ

Frequently Asked Question; that is, a document containing answers to a set of such questions. Many newsgroups put out these FAQ documents so that each new person does not ask the same questions; many computer product companies, as well as organizations that distribute information or do business over the Internet, have begun creating FAQs for their product, service, or information. Many FAQs are stored in an *anonymous FTP* archive, and many are broadcast across interested *mailing lists* at least once per month. See also *Flame, RTFM*.

fast packet

See ATM (Asynchronous Transfer Mode).

FDDI (Fiber Distributed Data Interface)

A high-speed (100 Mbps) LAN standard. The underlying medium is fiber optics. See also *LAN (Local Area Network), token ring*.

file transfer

The copying of a file from one computer to another over a computer network. See also *FTP (File Transfer Protocol)*, *Kermit*.

Finger

A program that displays information about a particular user, or all users, logged on the local system or on a remote system. It typically shows full name, last login time, idle time, terminal line, and terminal location (where applicable). It may also display any . *plan* and .project files left by the user.

firewall

A hardware device (or collection of devices) that is placed between two networks. One network is considered to be inside the organization (safe) and the other is considered to be outside the organization (not safe). All traffic, both from the inside and outside, must pass through this device. The firewall limits access to authorized users and systems by filtering packets as they come in based on the source or destination address, as well as an application's *TCP/IP* port. On the Internet, firewall, "bastion host," and "secure Internet connection" are synonymous.

FIX (Federal Internet Exchange)

A FIX is a connection point between the US governmental internets and the Internet. See also *CIX*.

flame

A strong opinion and/or criticism of something, usually in a deliberately insulting tone, in an electronic mail message or news posting. Flaming is frowned upon in polite Internet society. It is common to precede a flame with an indication of pending fire (such as "FLAME ON!"). "Flame Wars" occur when people start flaming other people for flaming when they shouldn't have. They can also start when a new reader in a *newsgroup* asks a question that older readers have answered many times, and that has been incorporated into a Frequently Asked Questions list. A warning to new users: some folk enjoy flame wars and deliberately try to provoke one. See also *e-mail*, *FAQ*, *kill file*.

FNC (Federal Networking Council)

The coordinating group of representatives from those federal agencies involved in the development and use of federal networking, especially those networks using TCP/IP and the Internet. Current members include representatives from DOD, DOE, DARPA, NSF, NASA, and HHS. See also *DARPA (Defense Advanced Research Projects Agency)*, *National Science Foundation*.

forms-capable browser

A *WWW (World Wide Web) browser* that allows users to "fill in the blanks" in questionnaires and other user-response items. Most *GUI* browsers are forms-capable, as are some of the line-mode browsers.

forwarding

Passing *e-mail* from one mailbox to another, particularly when the user is not reading mail regularly on the first system. Some users with accounts on many computers prefer to read mail on only one of them (for convenience, better user interface, cost, or other reasons), and so have all their mail forwarded to that account. Forwarding is also used to have mail come to a well-known public name (such as `info@host`, `postmaster@host`, or `help@host`) without the need for a specific separate mailbox for that name. See also *alias*.

FQDN (Fully Qualified Domain Name)

The FQDN is the full name of a *host* computer on the Internet, rather than just its host name. For example, `xrayf` is a host name and `xrayf.ge.com` is an FQDN. The host named `xrayf` is located within the institutional domain `.ge` (General Electric), which is within the top-level domain `.com` (commercial institutions). An FQDN corresponds to an *IP address*, but this correspondence is not fixed. If the service provided by `xrayf` is moved to a different computer, the administrator will be able to reassign the FQDN to the new computer's IP address. See also *host name*, *Domain Name System*.

fragment

A piece of a *packet*. When a router is forwarding an IP packet to a network that has a maximum packet size smaller than the packet being forwarded, it is forced to break up that packet into multiple fragments. These fragments will be reassembled by the IP layer at the destination host.

fragmentation

The IP process in which a *packet* is broken into smaller pieces to fit the requirements of a physical network over which the packet must pass. See also *reassembly*.

frame

A frame is an encapsulating *packet* that contains the header and trailer information required by the physical medium. That is, information or data packets are encapsulated to become frames. See also *datagram, encapsulation*.

Also, the ability to describe a particular set of coordinates in a hyper-media document that will contain the display of another hypermedia document. This is a "*netscapism*."

frame-capable browser

A *World Wide Web browser* that allows the independent display of multiple resources (from possibly multiple sources) on the same *Web page* (within a "frame").

freenet

A community-based bulletin board system with *e-mail*, information services, interactive communications, and conferencing. Freenets are funded and operated by individuals and volunteers—in one sense, like public television. They are part of the National Public Telecomputing Network (NPTN), an organization based in Cleveland, Ohio, devoted to making computer telecommunication and networking services as freely available as public libraries. See also *BBS (Bulletin Board System)*.

FTP (File Transfer Protocol)

A protocol that allows a user on one host to access, and copy files to and from, another host over a network. Also, FTP is usually the name of the program the user invokes to execute the protocol. It is defined in STD 9, RFC 959. See also *anonymous FTP, archive*.

FYI (For Your Information)

A subseries of *RFCs (Requests For Comments)* that are not technical standards or descriptions of protocols. FYIs convey general information about topics related to *TCP/IP* or the Internet. See also *STD*.

gateway

The term "router" is now used in place of the original definition of "gateway." Currently, a gateway is a communications device/program that passes data between networks having similar functions but dissimilar implementations. This should not be confused with a protocol converter, which allows dissimilar protocols (for example, DECnet and AppleTalk) to pass data between them. See also *mail gateway, router, protocol converter.*

Gopher

A menu-based program for retrieving information from resources across the Internet. Gopher uses a simple protocol that allows a single Gopher client to access information from any accessible Gopher server, providing the user with a single menu of information. Menu topics may lead to hierarchically organized subtopics. Public domain versions of the client and server are available. See also *Archie, archive site, Prospero, WAIS (Wide Area Information Servers).*

gopherspace

Depending on context, the term refers either to the whole collection of documents available from *Gopher servers,* or to what's available based on the menu selections you've already made in your *client.*

GUI (Graphical User Interface)

A GUI is a software "front end" that lets the user use pictures and "point-and-click" technology to access the software application. Many modern Internet clients are based on GUI principles and technology. See also *browser, World Wide Web, Gopher.*

hacker

Among programmers, a person who delights in having an intimate understanding of the internal workings of a computer system or network. The term is often misused in a pejorative context, where *cracker* would be the correct term. Hackers take joy in accomplishing difficult tasks ("hacking out" a working program, for example) and learning more and more about networking and computer systems.

handshaking

See negotiation.

Part
V

Glossary

hardware address

Particularly on *AppleTalk* and *Ethernet* networks, each computer has an address specific to the technology itself. These hardware addresses are mapped to the assigned *IP addresses*, and sometimes *domain addresses* as well.

header

The portion of a *packet*, preceding the actual data, containing source and destination addresses, error checking, and other fields. A header is also the part of an *e-mail* message or a Usenet news article that precedes the body of a message and contains, among other things, the message originator, date, and time.

hierarchical routing

The complex problem of *routing* on large networks can be simplified by reducing the size of the networks. This is accomplished by breaking a network into a hierarchy of networks, where each level is responsible for its own routing. The Internet has, basically, three levels: the backbones (such as the Netcom or Sprint backbones), the mid-level or *transit networks* (such as CICNet, or NorthWestNet), and the *stub networks* (such as The Little Garden Network Collective in San Francisco, or other small local networks). The backbones know how to route between the mid-levels, the mid-levels know how to route between the sites, and each site knows how to route internally.

HIPPI (High Performance Parallel Interface)

An emerging ANSI standard that extends the computer bus over fairly short distances at speeds of 800 and 1600 Mbps. HIPPI is often used in a computer room to connect a supercomputer to routers, frame buffers, mass-storage peripherals, and other computers. This allows for faster transmission of data (or faster interactions in an interactive session like Telnet) between the computer and the network. See also *ANSI (American National Standards Institute)*.

home page

A home page is, in *WorldWideWeb* terms, the base *hypermedia* document for an individual or organization. From this page there may be other pages of information or resources listed. The home page is generally what appears when you point a Web *browser* at http://www.*organization*/ (whatever address is signified by *organization*). See also *WWW*.

hop

A term used in routing. A path to a destination on a network is a series of hops, through routers, away from the origin.

host

A computer that allows users to communicate with other host computers on a network. Individual users communicate by using application programs, such as *e-mail*, *Telnet* and *FTP*. In some contexts, and in some philosophies of the way the Internet should work, the host itself is less important than the servers that run on it. For example, *Web* and *Gopher* servers distribute data to users without requiring the user to know which host the server is located on. See also *server*.

host address

See *internet address*.

host name

The domain name given to a computer. For example, `nic.ddn.mil`, `www.eff.org`, and `terminator.um.cc.umich.edu` are all host names. The terms "host name" and "*FQDN (Fully Qualified Domain Name)*" are interchangeable in most contexts; host name is a more informal term.

host number

See *internet address*, *IP address*.

hotlist

A stored collection of *URL*s that can be accessed by your *browser client* for easy use. Sometimes called *bookmarks*.

hotspots

The places in a Web document that are the entry points linking a page to another page via *URL*s. Hotspots look different than other words or pictures on a *Web page*. They may be a different color, or followed by a bracketed number, or underlined. Their appearance differs based on the client being used. You click on the hotspot or enter the number of the hotspot to invoke the link. See also *anchor*, *link*, *WWW*.

HTML (Hyper Text Markup Language)

The language used to "mark up" hypertext and hypermedia documents and then stored with those documents on a World Wide Web *server* and transmitted upon request to a Web browser *client* to be displayed. HTML is an application of SGML (Standard Generalized Markup Language), an ISO standard for defining the structure and managing the contents of any digital document.

HTTP (HyperText Transport Protocol)

The underlying protocol that supports the linking and transfer of *hypermedia* documents that make up the Web.

hypermedia

Hypermedia is a superset of *hypertext* that includes images and sounds.

hypertext

An interconnected web of textual information. *Anchored* links within the document can point to other places within that document or within other documents. Hypertext is text that points to other text and allows you to jump around in the text without necessarily reading it in a specific order.

I-D (Internet-Draft)

Internet-Drafts are working documents of the *IETF*, its Areas, and its Working Groups. As the name implies, Internet-Drafts are draft documents. They are valid for a maximum of six months and may be updated, replaced, or made obsolete by other documents at any time. Very often, I-Ds are precursors to *RFCs*.

IAB (Internet Architecture Board)

The technical body that oversees the development of the Internet suite of protocols. It has two task forces: the *IETF* and the *IRTF*. "IAB" previously stood for Internet Activities Board.

IEEE

Institute of Electrical and Electronics Engineers. The IEEE is one of the bodies that create and distribute standards for network protocols, interoperability, and hardware compliance, all of which allow for smooth operation of networks. In addition, many computer professionals belong to the IEEE and subscribe to its standards of professional behavior and ethics.

IESG (Internet Engineering Steering Group)

The IESG is composed of the *IETF* Area Directors and the IETF Chair. It provides the first technical review of Internet standards and is responsible for day-to-day management of the IETF.

IETF (Internet Engineering Task Force)

The IETF is a large, open community of network designers, operators, vendors, and researchers whose purpose is to coordinate the operation, management and evolution of the Internet, and to resolve short-range and mid-range *protocol* and architectural issues. It is a major source of proposals for protocol standards that are submitted to the IAB for final approval. The IETF meets three times a year and extensive minutes are included in the IETF Proceedings. To subscribe to the mailing list that carries IETF announcements, send e-mail to ietf-announce-request@cnri.reston.va.us. See also *Internet*, *IAB (Internet Architecture Board)*.

IINREN (Interagency Interim National Research and Education Network)

An evolving operating network system. Near term (through 1996) research and development activities will provide for the smooth evolution of this networking infrastructure into the future gigabit NREN.

imho

In My Humble Opinion; often actually means IMNSHO, for In My Not-So-Humble Opinion. :-)

internet

A collection of networks interconnected with routers. "Small-i" internets are often used to refer to collections of LANs, metropolitan or campus networks, or other regional networks. See also *network*.

Internet

The "Capital-I" Internet is the conglomeration of all the "small-i" *internets* connected together in the world. It is a three-level hierarchy composed of *backbone networks* (for example, UUNET, MILNET),

Part V

Glossary

mid-level networks (CICNet, NYSERNet), and *stub* networks. The Internet uses numerous protocols to ensure that all of its parts work together.

internet address

An IP address that uniquely identifies a node on an internet. An Internet address (capital "I") uniquely identifies a node on the Internet. See also *internet, Internet, IP address*.

Internet Explorer

A proprietary *Web browser* from Microsoft Corporation.

internet number

See *internet address*.

Internet Registry

The Internet Registry assigns *Internet addresses*, registers unique *domain names*, keeps the main *whois* database, and performs other registry and organizational tasks to allow the smooth running of the Internet. Its address on the Web is `http://rs.internic.net`.

Internet Research Steering Group

The IRSG is the "governing body" of the *IRTF (Internet Research Task Force)*.

Internet Society

The Internet Society (ISOC) is a nonprofit, professional membership organization that facilitates and supports the technical evolution of the Internet. It stimulates interest in and educates the scientific and academic communities, industry, and the public about the technology, uses and applications of the Internet, and promotes the development of new applications for the system. The Society provides a forum for discussion and collaboration in the operation and use of the global Internet infrastructure. The Internet Society publishes a quarterly newsletter, the *Internet Society News*, and holds an annual conference, INET. The development of Internet technical standards takes place under the auspices of the Internet Society with substantial support from the Corporation for National Research Initiatives under a cooperative agreement with the US Federal Government. [Source: V. Cerf]

interoperability

The ability of software and hardware from different vendors, and using different operating systems, to communicate meaningfully. Interoperability is a feature that anyone researching hardware and software to build or add onto an existing network should look for. The goal of most Internet *standards* and *protocols* is the smooth interaction and transmission of data between heterogeneous networks, which we also call interoperability.

intranet

The name given to the internetworked connection of local area networks within a specific organization; the internet within the Intel Corporation, for example.

IP (Internet Protocol)

The Internet Protocol, defined in STD 5, RFC 791, is the network layer for the TCP/IP Protocol Suite. It is a *connectionless*, best-effort *packet-switching* protocol. ("Best-effort" means that each *packet* is separately evaluated to find the best route available at that moment for sending the packet. Routes have formulas assigned to determine which is the most efficient for any given packet.)

IP address

The 32-bit address defined by the Internet Protocol in STD 5, RFC 791. It is usually represented in dotted decimal notation. For example, an IP address looks like this: 127.0.0.1, while a domain name looks like this: `spider.lloyd.com`.

IRC (Internet Relay Chat)

A world-wide "party line" protocol that allows users to converse with each other in real time. IRC is structured as a network of servers, each of which accepts connections from client programs, one per user. Some schools and organizations have disabled IRC on their computers and networks because of congestion problems or organizational policies about appropriate use. IRC had world-wide notice during the Persian Gulf war, when citizens on their computers in Tel Aviv during the bombing raids were describing the events as they happened over IRC to listeners around the world. See also *Talk*.

IRTF (Internet Research Task Force)

The IRTF is chartered by the Internet Architecture Board (*IAB*) to consider long-term Internet issues from a theoretical point of view. It has Research Groups, similar to *IETF* Working Groups, that are each assigned to discuss different research topics. Multicast audio/video conferencing and *privacy-enhanced mail* are examples of technologies that have emerged from IRTF Research Groups.

ISDN (Integrated Services Digital Network)

An emerging technology that (while having been around for years) is just beginning to be offered to the consumer by the telephone carriers of the world. ISDN combines voice and digital network services in a single medium, making it possible to offer customers digital data services as well as voice connections through a single "wire." The standards that define ISDN are specified by *CCITT*. If you are interested in finding out whether ISDN is available in your area, you may need to contact a local university or other large Internet site, or ask for the Data Marketing division at your local phone company. Many residential marketing customer agents at local phone companies are not fully briefed on ISDN.

ISO (International Organization for Standardization)

A voluntary, nontreaty organization founded in 1946, which is responsible for creating international standards in many areas, including computers and communications. Its members are the national standards organizations of the 89 member countries, including ANSI for the US. See also *ANSI (American National Standards Institute)*, *OSI (Open Systems Interconnection)*.

ISO Development Environment (ISODE)

Pronounced eye-so-dee-eee. Software that allows OSI services to use a TCP/IP network. See also OSI *(Open Systems Interconnection)*, *TCP/IP Protocol Suite*.

Java

A proprietary language from Sun Microsystems that enables executable programs to be downloaded and run via client Web browsers without explicitly asking the client computer's user for permission. Unless you turn off Java, you have given your permission for others to run programs on your computer.

The authors of this book caution you to weigh the benefits of Java (some of its features may be quite enticing) against the disadvantages of giving permission for unknown other persons to run programs on your computer.

KA9Q

An implementation of TCP/IP and associated protocols for amateur packet radio systems. KA9Q is most popular with users of home computers: KA9Q implementations for computers rather than radios run on many varieties of computers (including Atari and Apple II) to allow them to function as stand-alone Internet-connected workstations. "KA9Q" is the Amateur Radio call sign of the original author, Phil Karns. See also *TCP/IP Protocol Suite*.

Kerberos

Named after the three-headed watchdog of Hades in Greek and Roman mythology, Kerberos is a security system developed by MIT's Project Athena and others on the Net. It is based on symmetric key cryptography; you give your login and password to a trusted agent on your local computer, who authenticates your identity to the services you wish to use on another computer. See also *authentication, authorization, encryption, password*.

Kermit

A popular file transfer protocol developed by Columbia University. Because Kermit runs in most operating environments, it provides an easy method of file transfer. Kermit is *not* the same as FTP. See also *File Transfer Protocol*.

kill file

An automatically processed database of names, user IDs, topics, and so on, from whom or about which you do not wish to see e-mail or news postings. Kill files are useful to trim your information processing time down to something manageable, or to prevent you from seeing mail or postings from people who persist in behavior with which you do not agree. Kill files can be used to screen out messages from people who may be harassing you. See also *flame, news*.

Part V

Glossary

kilobit

One thousand bits. The kilobit is a convenient unit of data for talking about transmission speeds over computer networks. A 56-kilobit line, for example, can transmit 56,000 bits per second. A *T1* line, by comparison, can transmit 1,544,000 bits per second. Kilobits per second is abbreviated Kbps. See also *bit, megabit*.

Knowbot

An experimental directory service. See also *white pages,WHOIS, X.500*.

LAN (Local Area Network)

A data network intended to serve an area of only a few square kilometers or less. LANs usually serve either a single building or a group of closely located buildings. Because the network is known to cover only a small area, optimizations can be made in the network signal protocols that permit data rates up to 100 Mbps. Popular LAN software includes Novell NetWare and Banyan Vines.

LATA

Local Area Telephone Authority. Most states are divided into several LATAs. Knowing which LATA you are in will help you evaluate service offerings from your local "telco" and Internet providers, because calls (via either dial or dedicated connections) that cross LATA boundaries are more expensive than those that do not.

layer

Communication networks for computers may be organized as a set of more or less independent *protocols*, each in a different layer (also called "level"). The lowest layer governs direct host-to-host communication between the hardware at different hosts; the highest consists of user applications. Each layer builds on the layer beneath it. For each layer, programs at different hosts use protocols appropriate to the layer to communicate with each other. TCP/IP has five layers of protocols; OSI has seven. The advantage of using different layers of protocols is that the methods of passing information from one layer to another are specified clearly as part of the protocol suite, and changes within a protocol layer are prevented from affecting the other layers. This greatly simplifies the task of designing and maintaining communication programs. See also *OSI (Open Systems Interconnection), TCP/IP protocol suite*.

link

The place in a *hypermedia* document that signals a connection to another hypermedia document. A link may be an image, text, or sound. See also *anchor, hotspot.*

listserv

An automated *mailing list* distribution system (server) originally designed for the BITNET/EARN network. Listserver programs now also run on UNIX and other operating systems.

Lurking

In a mailing list or Usenet newsgroup, listening without responding publicly. As the name implies, this activity is considered somewhat antisocial, but it allows beginners to get a feel for the flavor and response patterns of the participants of the group, and also lets them get up to speed on the history of the group. See also *e-mail, FAQ, mailing list, Usenet.*

mail alias

A name for one computer that handles mail, but which points to another computer. For example, harold@saxon.org may be a mail alias for thane@danelaw.ac.uk. The university system accepts mail addressed to saxon.org and routes it to the correct user mailbox. Mail aliases are used in many situations, including assistance when one computer is down and mail needs to be spooled at another computer or when a domain name has been registered but no computers or physical network exist yet that correspond to that domain name. See also *alias, forwarding.*

mail bridge

A mail *gateway* that forwards *electronic mail* between two or more networks while ensuring that the messages it forwards meet certain administrative criteria. A mail bridge is simply a specialized form of mail gateway that enforces an administrative policy with regard to what mail it forwards. For example, SprintNet e-mail users cannot receive e-mail that originates from CompuServe.

mail exploder

Part of an *e-mail* delivery system that allows a message to be delivered to a list of addresses. Mail exploders are used to implement *mailing lists*. Users send messages to a single address, and the mail exploder takes care of delivery to the individual mailboxes in the list. Some systems administrators prefer to receive mailing list mail at a local exploder address on their system, and to have a local mailing list to which users can subscribe, rather than having each user subscribe to the various mailing lists separately. This helps control the amount of disk space used by copies of e-mail, and it can also prevent problems that would occur if the user's ID changes locally or the account terminates on the host. See also *e-mail address*.

mail gateway

A computer that connects two or more electronic mail systems (possibly dissimilar) and transfers messages between them. Sometimes the mapping and translation can be quite complex, and it generally requires a *store-and-forward* scheme whereby the message is received from one system completely before it is transmitted to the next system, after suitable translations. Some mail gateways also have the capability to select which messages will be allowed through, either on political or technical grounds. See also *e-mail (electronic mail)*, *mail bridge*.

mail path

A series of computer names used to direct electronic mail from one user to another. This system of e-mail addressing has been used primarily in UUCP networks, which are trying to eliminate its use altogether. See also *bang path, e-mail address, UUCP (Unix-to-Unix CoPy)*.

mail server

A program that distributes files or information in response to requests sent via *e-mail*. Internet examples include Almanac and netlib. Mail servers have also been used in *BITNET* to provide *FTP*-like services.

mailing list

A list of *e-mail addresses*, used by a *mail exploder*, to forward messages to groups of people. Generally, a mailing list is used to discuss a particular set of topics. If a mailing list is moderated, messages sent to the list are actually sent to a *moderator* who determines whether to send the messages on to everyone else. Requests to subscribe to, or leave, a mailing list should ALWAYS be sent to the list's "-request" address (for example, `ietf-request@cnri.reston.va.us` for the IETF mailing list).

megabit

One million bits. See also *bit, kilobit, TI*.

mh

A common UNIX mail client.

mid-level network

Mid-level networks (a.k.a. regionals) make up the second level of the Internet hierarchy. They are the *transit networks* that connect the *stub networks* to the *backbone* networks. NYSERNet, CERFNet, and SESQUINET are examples of mid-level networks.

MIME (Multipurpose Internet Mail Extensions)

An extension to Internet *e-mail* that provides the ability to transfer nontextual data, such as graphics, audio, and fax. Most common e-mail clients, such as *Pine, mh,* and *Eudora*, have at least simple MIME capabilities. It is defined in RFC 1341. See also *ASCII, binary*.

mirror

Just as a mirror reflects accurately the image portrayed in it, an "*FTP* archive mirror" contains all the contents of an original *archive* site (typically because the original site is heavily use). Mirror sites are updated on a regular basis to maintain congruency with the original site.

moderator(s)

A person, or small group of people, who manage moderated *mailing lists* and *newsgroups*. Moderators are responsible for determining which submissions are passed on to the list or newsgroup. The message must meet the standards the group has established for itself for topicality, civility of speech, and noncommercial content. See also *e-mail (electronic mail), Usenet, FAQ (Frequently Asked Questions)*.

MOO

MUD, object-oriented. A MUD that incorporates the ability to describe and manipulate objects in its command language.

MUD (Multi-User Dungeon)

Adventure or role-playing games or simulations (such as political campaigns, conferences, or creativity exercises) played on the Internet. Devotees call them "text-based virtual reality adventures." The games can feature fantasy combat, booby traps and magic. Players interact in real time and can change the "world" in the game as they play it. Most MUDs are based on the Telnet protocol. MUDs can be an excellent interaction and learning tool, as advanced "wizards" must learn to program the underlying structures in order to create their own realities, but the popularity of the game can cause resource problems for network administrators. See also *congestion, MOO, Telnet*.

multicast

A packet with a special destination address, which multiple nodes on the network may be willing to receive. See also *broadcast, broadcast storm*.

multihomed host

A *host* that has more than one connection to a network. The host may send and receive data over any of the links but will not route traffic for other nodes. See also *router*.

NAK (Negative Acknowledgment)

Response to receipt of a corrupted packet of information. See also *ACK (Acknowledgment)*.

name resolution

The process of mapping a name into its corresponding *IP address*. See also: *DNS (Domain Name System)*.

namespace

A commonly distributed set of names in which all names are unique.

nastygram

An unpleasant message, usually *e-mail* but sometimes in a *Usenet newsgroup*. Usually nastygrams come from a human being who is in a bad mood, but some folks refer to automated warning messages as nastygrams, as well.

NSF (National Science Foundation)

The US government agency whose purpose is to promote the advancement of science. NSF funds science researchers, scientific projects, and infrastructure to improve the quality of scientific research. The NSFNET, funded by NSF, was an essential part of academic and research communications. It was a high-speed hierarchical network. NSFNET also had connections out of the US to Canada, Mexico, Europe, and the Pacific Rim. The NSFNET has been retired and its network connections converted to a new model of multiple Network Access Points (NAPs).

negotiation

Just as diplomats negotiate terms of a settlement or treaty, so computers running Internet protocols negotiate with other computers running IP. These negotiations allow the computers to make sure they are communicating at the same speed, with the same processes, and that the information they exchange will be packaged so that each can properly direct the data to the intended destination. This process is also called handshaking, particularly when speaking of modems connecting to one another.

netiquette

A pun on "etiquette" referring to proper behavior on a network. There currently is no "Emily Post" of the Internet. There is, however, Emily Postnews. Look for this *periodic posting* in the answers newsgroups.

Netnews

See Usenet.

Netscape

The short name given to Netscape Navigator, a proprietary Web browser program from Netscape Communications Corporation.

netscapisms

Extensions made to *HTML* that extend beyond the HTML standard. These extensions give the Web browser, Netscape, a competitive advantage in the market. Some developers use the term pejoratively to describe what are seen as an attempt to subvert the cooperative development processes that characterized the early Internet. Others rush to use the new tools right away, without regard for whether end-users can receive and process hypermedia that is not standard.

network

A data communications system that interconnects several computer systems. A network may be composed of any combination of local area networks, metropolitan area networks, wide area networks.

network address

The network portion of an *IP address*. For a class A network, the network address is the first byte of the IP address. For a class B network, the network address is the first two bytes of the IP address. For a class C network, the network address is the first three bytes of the IP address. In each case, the remainder is the *host address*. In the Internet, assigned network addresses are globally unique.

network node

A machine, usually a computer, on the Internet. Routers, workstations, and modems are all nodes. Some nodes are at endpoints of a piece of the network, some are way stations or entry points.

network number

See *IP address*, *network address*.

newsgroup

A set of topically related articles distributed by the Usenet news mechanism. Newsgroup topics range from philosophy to health support groups to computer-intrinsics. There are over 9000 newsgroups worldwide, with over 6000 available to users in the United States. The term also refers to the group of people who read and respond to the above; sometimes these groups become friendly and close-knit as a result of their discussions.

newsreader

A client program that reads *Usenet* news.

NFS (Network File System)

A protocol developed by Sun Microsystems, and defined in RFC 1094, that allows a computer system to access files over a network as if they were on its local disks. This protocol has been incorporated in products by more than two hundred companies, and is now a de facto Internet standard.

NIST (National Institute of Standards and Technology)

The United States governmental body that provides assistance in developing standards. Formerly the National Bureau of Standards.

NNTP (Network News Transfer Protocol)

A protocol, defined in RFC 977, for the distribution, inquiry, retrieval, and posting of news articles. See also *Usenet*.

NOC (Network Operations Center)

A location from which the operation of a network or internet is monitored. Additionally, this center usually serves as a clearinghouse for connectivity problems and efforts to resolve those problems.

node

An addressable device attached to a computer network. See also *host*, *router*.

NTP (Network Time Protocol)

A protocol that assures accurate local time-keeping with reference to radio and atomic clocks located on the Internet. This protocol is capable of synchronizing distributed clocks within milliseconds over long time periods. It is defined in STD 12, RFC 1119.

octet

8 bits. In networking, this term is sometimes used instead of "byte," because some systems have bytes that are not 8 bits long.

OSI (Open Systems Interconnection)

A suite of *protocols*, designed by *ISO* committees, to be the international standard computer network architecture.

OSI Reference Model

A seven-layer structure designed to describe computer network architectures and the way that data passes through them. The lowest levels handle the physical media and transmission characteristics of the network. The highest levels handle the user applications and data transmission. This model (sometimes referred to as the "seven-layer model") was developed by the ISO in 1978 to clearly define the interfaces in multivendor networks, and to provide users of those networks with conceptual guidelines in the construction of such networks. See also *ISO (International Organization for Standardization)*.

packet

The unit of data sent across a network. "Packet" is a generic term used to describe a unit of data at all levels of the protocol stack, but it is most correctly used to describe application data units. Users of commercial networks should be careful to determine whether their pricing model includes a cost-per-packet; some do, and large file transfers, because of the number of packets involved, should be done at the least expensive (and least congested) time.

packet switching

A communications paradigm in which *packets* (messages) are individually routed between *hosts*, with no previously established communication path. See also *circuit switching, connection-oriented, connectionless*.

password

A secret key that you have chosen (or that is assigned to you by a systems administrator or key distribution program) and that you type every time you log into your system or services. Along with your valid login ID, this constitutes the two parts of your *authentication* process on most systems. See also *authorization*.

periodic posting

An article posted to a *Usenet newsgroup* on a regular schedule, for example, every four weeks.

Pine

A proprietary *e-mail* client from the University of Washington. There are Pine clients for several types of operating systems.

PING (Packet INternet Groper)

A program used to test whether a destination can be reached, by sending it an ICMP echo request and waiting for a reply. The term is used as a verb: "Ping host X to see if it is up!" Early tricksters on the ARPANET used to try to crash network gateways by overwhelming them with automated pinging; repeated pinging is also used as a test of network robustness today.

POP (Point Of Presence)

A site where there exists a collection of telecommunications equipment, usually digital leased lines and multi-protocol routers. Many network providers have modem pools in areas where they have POPs. Sometimes network providers have their equipment co-located with telephone company POPs.

POP (Post Office Protocol)

A protocol designed to allow single-user *hosts* to read mail from a *server*. There are three versions: POP, POP2, and POP3. Later versions are NOT compatible with earlier versions. See also *e-mail (electronic mail)*.

port

Your computer has a physical port into which you plug things; in *TCP/IP*, ports are also values defined in the protocol. For example, most computers that accept Telnet sessions create a port "23" to accept Telnet transmissions. When a packet comes in with the Telnet request, it will carry a request for port 23. Each application has a unique port number associated with it.

postmaster

The person responsible for taking care of *e-mail* problems, answering queries about users, and other related work at an e-mail *server* site. By agreement between sites, codified in the RFCs for e-mail, any site that has e-mail connectivity must have a human being who answers mail addressed to postmaster@host. Many postmasters are also handling security questions and systems ethics questions.

PPP (Point-to-Point Protocol)

The Point-to-Point Protocol, defined in RFC 1171, provides a method for transmitting *packets* over serial point-to-point links. PPP, like *SLIP*, allows dial-up users to connect their home computers to the Internet as peer hosts.

Privacy Enhanced Mail (PEM)

Internet e-mail that provides confidentiality, *authentication* and message integrity using various *encryption* methods. See also *e-mail (electronic mail)*.

Prospero

A distributed file system that provides the user with the ability to create multiple views of a single collection of files distributed across the Internet. Prospero provides a file naming system, and file access is provided by existing access methods (for example, *anonymous FTP* and *NFS*). The Prospero *protocol* is also used for communication between clients and servers in the Archie system. See also *Archie, archive site, Gopher, WAIS (Wide Area Information Servers)*.

protocol

A formal description of message formats and the rules two or more computers must follow to exchange those messages. Protocols can describe low-level details of computer-to-computer interfaces (for example, the order in which the bits from a byte are set across a wire), or high-level exchanges between application programs (for example, the way in which two programs transfer a file across the Internet).

protocol converter

A device or program that translates between different *protocols* that serve similar functions (for example, between TCP and TP4).

Protocol Data Unit (PDU)

What international standards committees call a *packet*.

protocol stack

A layered set of *protocols* that work together to provide a set of network functions. Most Internet networks use a TCP/IP stack. Also, the lower-level software that is used to connect your Internet applications to the network; usually called the "stack." See also *layer*.

PTT (Postal Telegraph and Telephone)

Outside the USA, PTT refers to a telephone service provider (usually a monopoly) in a particular country.

queue

A backup of packets awaiting processing. See also *spool*.

QuickTime

A proprietary movie program and graphic format from Apple Computer Corporation.

RARE (Reseaux Associes pour la Recherche Européenne)

European association of research networks.

RBOC

Regional Bell Operating Company.

Real Audio

A proprietary sound transmission format from Progressive Networks, Inc.

reassembly

The *IP* process in which a previously fragmented packet is reassembled before being passed to the transport layer. See also *fragmentation*.

regional

See mid-level network.

repeater

A device that propagates electrical signals from one cable to another. See also *bridge, gateway, router*.

RFC (Request For Comments)

The document series, begun in 1969, that describes the Internet suite of protocols and related experiments. The name comes from bureaucrat-speak, as do its government procurement cousins RFQ (Request For Quote) and RFP (Request For Purchase). Not all (in fact very few) RFCs describe Internet standards, but all Internet standards are written up as RFCs. The RFC series of documents is unusual in that the proposed protocols are forwarded by the Internet research and development community, acting on their own behalf, as opposed to the formally reviewed and standardized protocols that are promoted by organizations such as CCITT and ANSI. See also *FYI, STD*.

RFC 822

The Internet standard format for *e-mail* message *headers*.

RIPE (Reseaux IP Européenne)

A collaboration between European networks that use the *TCP/IP protocol suite*.

rlogin (remote login)

A *protocol* that allows operating on a remote computer over a computer network, as though locally attached. rlogin is an early Berkeley protocol, like rcp. It is used in some security programs (such as *Kerberos*); security precautions must be taken to prevent unauthorized use of the system via rlogin. See also *Telnet*.

route

The path that network traffic takes from its source to its destination. Also, a possible path from a given host to another host or destination.

router

A device that forwards traffic between networks, using information from the *network layer* and from routing tables. Some routers are "dedicated," meaning that they do nothing but shuffle traffic; some are also used for other purposes, including file storage. See also *bridge, gateway*.

routing

The process of selecting the correct interface and next *hop* for a packet being forwarded.

routing domain

A set of *routers* exchanging routing information within an *AD (administrative domain)*.

routing table

A table or database of routing paths and decision variables that allows a *router* to send packets on to the correct destination. Routing tables are maintained by both humans and computers.

RTFM

Read the "Fine" Manual. An acronym used to admonish neophyte users of a computer system to consult published sources of information (such as *FAQs*) first, before requesting the attention of someone whose time (or patience) may be limited. The popularity of this idiom can be considered a measure of the Internet's explosive growth.

RTT (Round-Trip Time)

A measure of the current delay on a network. It measures the time it takes a packet or other bit of information to reach the destination and the acknowledgment to return to the sender.

search engine

Any program that searches. In the Internet sense, a program that searches among a database of Internet sites or information.

server

In *client-server computing*, the "back-end" program from which a *client* program requests information or other resources. The server handles the work of locating and extracting the information. The term is also often used to refer to the computer running a server program, particularly if it is used only for that purpose (as, for example, a "print server" in a LAN). The various Internet *addresses* cited throughout this book as sources of information or files are the locations of computers running server programs for *applications* such as *FTP* or *Gopher*. See also *client, DNS (Domain Name System), NFS (Network File System)*.

Shareware

Shareware is software whose creator or author stores it on the network for access by anyone to try out. Once you decide you want to continue using the software, it is ethically correct to pay the shareware fee. Once you do, you will receive any updates to the software and/or manuals.

SIG

Special Interest Group.

signature

The three- or four-line message at the bottom of an *e-mail* message or a *Usenet* article that identifies the sender. Large signatures (over five lines) are generally frowned upon. These files usually have the file-name extension .sig or .signature. With many newsreaders and some e-mail clients this file is automatically appended to the sender's messages or postings. See also *e-mail (electronic mail)*, *Usenet*.

SLIP (Serial Line IP)

A protocol used to run *IP* over serial lines, such as telephone circuits or RS-232 cables, interconnecting two systems. SLIP is defined in RFC 1055. SLIP, along with *PPP*, is one of two popular protocols that allow home computer users to connect their computers to the Internet as peer hosts. SLIP and PPP encapsulate *TCP/IP packets* for transmission over phone lines.

SMDS (Switched Multimegabit Data Service)

An emerging high-speed datagram-based public data network service developed by Bellcore and expected to be widely used by telephone companies as the basis for their data networks. See also *ISDN*.

SMTP (Simple Mail Transfer Protocol)

A protocol, defined in STD 10, RFC 821, used to transfer electronic mail between computers. It is a server-to-server protocol, so other protocols are used to access the messages. See also *e-mail (electronic mail)*, *POP (Post Office Protocol)*, *RFC 822*.

snail mail

A pejorative term referring to the Postal Service to contrast with *e-mail*. Sometimes people use the term "earth mail" instead.

SNMP (Simple Network Management Protocol)

The Internet standard protocol, defined in STD 15, RFC 1157, developed to manage nodes on an IP network. It is currently possible to manage wiring hubs, computers, jukeboxes (multiple CD management hardware), etc.

splat

A colloquial name for the asterisk (*), which is used in UNIX and DOS file names as a wild-card, that can be read out quickly over the phone or shouted across an office without fear of misunderstanding.

spool, spooling

A *spool* is a storage area where e-mail, print jobs, and some other service requests are stored until they can be sent on to their destinations. *Spooling* is the act of storing up such messages or jobs. Items may be spooled for any of several reasons: most commonly if the destination *host* is down or for some reason not accepting transmissions, or (particularly in print jobs) the receiving printer has not finished printing a job or jobs ahead of the spooled job. *BITNET* traffic is often spooled if the next node on the line cannot accept it for any reason. For a long time, the story goes, disruptions in the phone lines between France and Israel because of the Gulf War made it faster for the French to send a tape with BITNET messages stored on them to Israel for redistribution than to wait for the phone lines to stay stable long enough to transmit all the messages spooled up and waiting.

standard

The explicit, approved rules under which a particular act is conducted. An Internet standard is the written, documented culmination of the cooperative standards development process. It is begun with a proposal. It is tested and documented to become an Internet Draft. From I-D stage, it passes to full Internet standard status. Appendix C contains information about Internet Standards, their naming conventions, and what they are called. See also *Internet Draft, (RFC) Request for Comments*.

static route, static routing

A table or database of destinations and pathways used to route *packets* to the correct destination. These tables are not dynamically updated by other computers in response to changing network operating conditions. For example, they cannot be automatically updated if a network portion goes down or if the router they want to send to is not functioning. As such, they are prone to problems if the network changes or is not functioning correctly. See also *routing, routing table*.

STD

A subseries of RFCs that specify Internet standards. The official list of Internet standards is in STD 1. See also *FYI (For Your Information), RFC (Request For Comments)*.

Part
V

Glossary

store-and-forward

A method of transmitting data where all the information is transmitted from one computer to another before any information is passed along to the next host in line. Packet transmission methods ship each packet as it comes along, choosing the best path for each individual packet, rather than using a fixed routing and time for an entire set of data. See also *BITNET.*

stream-oriented

Describes a type of transport service that allows its client to send data in a continuous stream. The transport service will guarantee that all data will be delivered to the other end in the same order as sent and without duplicates. See also *TCP (Transmission Control Protocol).*

stub network

A stub network only carries packets to and from local hosts. Even if it has paths to more than one other network, it does not carry traffic for other networks. See also *backbone, transit network.*

subnet

A portion of a network (which may be physically independent from the rest of the network) that shares a network address with other portions of the network and is distinguished by a *subnet address.* A subnet is to a network what a network is to an internet. See also *internet, network.*

subnet address

The subnet portion of an *IP* address. In a subnetted network, the *host* portion of an IP address is split into a subnet portion and a host portion using an address (subnet) mask. See also *address mask, IP address, network address, Internet address.*

subnet mask

See *address mask.*

subnet number

See *subnet address.*

T1

An AT&T term for a digital carrier facility used to transmit a signal at 1.544 megabits per second. The fiber links between many network nodes run at T1 speed; in some areas, you can get T1 service into your local home or office.

T3

A term for a digital carrier facility used to transmit a signal at 44.746 megabits per second. The NSFNET backbone fiber runs at T3 speed.

Talk

A protocol that allows two people on remote computers to communicate in a real-time fashion. See also *IRC (Internet Relay Chat)*.

TCP (Transmission Control Protocol)

An Internet Standard transport layer protocol defined in STD 7, RFC 793. It is *connection-oriented* and *stream-oriented*. See also *layer*.

TCP/IP Protocol Suite

Transmission Control Protocol over Internet Protocol. This is a common shorthand that refers to the suite of transport and application protocols that runs over the Internet. TCP/IP is the set of rules which makes the whole shebang run smoothly. See also *IP, TCP, FTP, Telnet, SMTP, SNMP*.

TELENET

A public *packet-switched* network using the CCITT X.25 protocols. It should not be confused with *Telnet*. In the United States the network is called SprintNet. Telenet/SprintNet has recently entered the *IP* networking market, and is beginning to offer IP dialup and direct connections.

Telnet

Telnet is the Internet standard protocol for remote terminal connection service. It is defined in STD 8, RFC 854 and extended with options by many other *RFCs*. See also *rlogin*.

terminal emulator

A program that allows a computer to emulate a particular type of terminal, in order to communicate with a remote host computer that is programmed to work with terminals of that type.

terminal server

A device that connects many terminals to a LAN through one network connection. A terminal server can also connect many network users to its asynchronous ports for dial-out capabilities and printer access. See also *LAN (Local Area Network)*.

TIA

Thanks In Advance.

TLA (Three Letter Acronym)

A tribute to the use of acronyms in the computer field.

TN3270

A variant of the Telnet program that allows one to attach to IBM mainframes and use the mainframe as if using a 3270 or similar terminal. IBM 3270 terminals (and *terminal emulators*) are noted for having full-screen displays, instead of line-oriented displays, and frequently have fixed fields or cells in the display where information can be entered and updated. Several popular library catalog interfaces work best with TN3270 emulators.

token ring

A type of *LAN* with nodes wired into a ring. Each node constantly passes a control message (token) on to the next; whichever node has the token can send a message. Often, the term "Token Ring" is used to refer specifically to the IEEE 802.5 token ring standard, which is the most common type of token ring.

topology

A network topology shows the computers and the links between them. A network layer must stay abreast of the current network topology to be able to route packets to their final destination.

transceiver

Transmitter-receiver. The physical device that connects a host inter-face to a local area network, such as *Ethernet*. Ethernet transceivers contain electronics that apply signals to the cable and sense collisions between packets and other conditions on the circuit.

transit network

A transit network passes traffic between networks in addition to carry-ing traffic for its own hosts. It must have paths to at least two other networks. See also *AUPs, backbone, stub network*.

Trojan horse

A computer program that carries within itself a means to allow the creator of the program access to the system using it. See also *virus, worm*.

TTFN

Ta-Ta For Now.

tunnelling

Tunnelling refers to *encapsulation* of protocol A within protocol B, such that B treats A, and its data, as if it were its own. Tunnelling is used to get data between *administrative domains* that use a protocol not supported by the Internet, and to make pseudo-connections in connectionless protocol systems like the Internet. For example, recent experiments in AppleTalk tunnelling have allowed users on one university campus to access services on another campus directly from their own Macs, with the services showing up in the pull-down menus, and being accessed as transparently as local services. See also *protocol*.

twisted-pair

A type of cable in which pairs of conductors are twisted together to produce certain electrical properties. Most recently, *Ethernet* run over twisted-pair wiring has proved an inexpensive method to wire up schools, campuses, and other clustered buildings.

UNIX

A powerful, complex operating system designed and originally imple-mented within Bell Labs. It is used in many Internetworking environ-ments because 1) there are public domain versions that are free or very inexpensive to license; 2) most versions have many of the TCP/IP protocol implementations built in; 3) many of the computers used to provide server machines are shipped with UNIX as the operating system; and 4) because of the first three factors, UNIX is frequently taught in academic computer science classes (creating more people who know how to use it).

urban legend

A story, which may have started with a grain of truth, that has been embroidered and retold until it has passed into the realm of myth. Urban legends never die, they just end up on the Internet! Some legends that periodically make their rounds include "The Infamous Modem Tax," "Craig Shergold/Brain Tumor/Get Well Cards," and "The $250 Cookie Recipe." There are also urban legends about computer systems and networks themselves.

URL (Uniform Resource Locater)

The standardized location of a particular Internet resource. The URL consists of the access *protocol*, the *host name*, and the complete directory path of the file.

Usenet

A collection of thousands of topically named newsgroups, the computers that run the protocols, and the people who read and submit Usenet news. Not all Internet hosts subscribe to Usenet and not all Usenet hosts are on the Internet. See also *NNTP (Network News Transfer Protocol)*, *UUCP (Unix-to-Unix CoPy)*.

user ID

An account name or login name.

UTC (Universal Time Coordinated)

Greenwich Mean Time.

UUCP (Unix-to-Unix CoPy)

Initially, a program run under the UNIX operating system that allowed one UNIX system to send files to another UNIX system via dial-up phone lines. Today, the term is more commonly used to describe the large international network that uses the UUCP protocol to pass news and electronic mail. See also *e-mail (electronic mail)*, *Usenet*.

virtual circuit

A network service that provides *connection-oriented* service regardless of the underlying network structure.

virtual reality

A term used to describe the appearance of three-dimensions in a computer interface. Often contrasted with hypertext, which certainly has only two dimensions.

virus

A program that replicates itself on computer systems by incorporating itself into other programs that are shared among computer systems. See also *Trojan horse, worm.*

VRML (Virtual Reality Markup Language)

A language that enables the display of three-dimensional images on a two-dimensional computer screen. As in other client/server applications, information from the server drives the client; in this case to let the end user "fly through" a building rendition, for example.

W3

See WWW (World Wide Web).

WAIS (Wide Area Information Servers)

A distributed information service that offers simple natural-language input, indexed searching for fast retrieval, and a "relevance feedback" mechanism that allows the results of initial searches to influence future searches. Public domain implementations are available. See also *Archie, Gopher, Prospero.*

WAN (Wide Area Network)

A network, usually constructed with serial lines, that covers a large geographic area. See also *LAN (Local Area Network).*

Web

The most commonly used shorthand name for the *World Wide Web.*

webcrawler

A program (like a virus) that travels around the Internet and gathers information.

WebCrawler

The proprietary search engine operated by America Online.

Web page

Using a *World Wide Web browser,* you can access "pages" of information placed on the network for your perusal by other people, companies, and organization. A page may include graphics, text, sounds, and movies.

white pages

The Internet supports several databases that contain basic information about users, such as e-mail addresses, telephone numbers, and postal addresses. These databases can be searched to get information about particular individuals. Because they serve a function akin to the telephone book, these databases are often referred to as "white pages." See also *WHOIS.*

WHOIS

An Internet program that allows users to query a database of people and other Internet entities, such as domains, networks, and hosts, kept at the NIC. The information for people shows a person's company name, address, phone number and e-mail address. See also *white pages.*

worm

A computer program that replicates itself and is self-propagating. Worms, as opposed to viruses, are meant to spawn in network environments. The Internet worm of November 1988 is perhaps the most famous; it successfully propagated itself on over 6000 systems across the Internet. See also *Trojan horse, virus.*

WRT

With Respect To, With Regard To.

WWW (World Wide Web)

A *hypermedia*-based, distributed information system created by researchers at CERN in Switzerland. Users may create, edit or browse *hypertext* documents. Pointers to the many clients and servers are found at `http://www.w3.org`.

WYSIWYG

What You See Is What You Get

zip

The file extension given to a particular kind of compressed file. To use a file with this extension you will need to "unzip" it with a decompression program.

Appendix A

Hobbes' Internet Timeline v2.4a

by Robert Hobbes Zakon

Internet Evangelist

The MITRE Corporation

Hobbes' Internet Timeline Copyright ©1993-6 by Robert H Zakon. Used with permission. Permission is granted for use of this document in whole or in part for noncommercial purposes as long as appropriate credit is given to the author/maintainer. A copy of the material the *Timeline* appears in is appreciated. For commercial uses, please contact the author first :

hobbes@hobbes.mitre.org

The author wishes to acknowledge the Internet Society for hosting this document, and the many Net folks who have contributed suggestions.

Contributors to *Hobbes' Internet Timeline* have their initials next to the contributed items in the form (:zzz:) and are:

ad1 - Arnaud Dufour (arnaud.dufour@hec.unil.ch)

amk - Alex McKenzie (mckenzie@bbn.com)

ec1 - Eric Carroll (eric@enfm.utcc.utoronto.ca)

esr - Eric S. Raymond (esr@locke.ccil.org)

feg - Farrell E. Gerbode (farrell@is.rice.edu)

gck - Gary C. Kessler (kumquat@hill.com)

glg - Gail L. Grant (grant@openmarket.com)

gmc - Grant McCall (g.mccall@unsw.edu.au)

jg1 - Jim Gaynor (gaynor@agvax.ag.ohio.state.edu)

mpc - Mellisa P. Chase (pc@mitre.org)

ph1 - Peter Hoffman (`hoffman@ece.nps.navy.mil`)

rab - Roger A. Bielefeld (`rab@hal.cwru.edu`)

sc1 - Susan Calcari (`susanc@is.internic.net`)

sk2 - Stan Kulikowski (`stankuli@uwf.bitnet`)

vgc - Vinton Cerf (`vcerf@isoc.org`)

zby - Zenel Batagelj (`zenel.batagelj@uni-lj.si`)

The online version of this document is available at:

`http://info.isoc.org/guest/zakon/Internet/History/HIT.html`

Please send comments or corrections to

`hobbes@hobbes.mitre.org`.

Authors' note: In addition to periodic updates, the online version includes a number of charts not reproduced here, *Hobbes' Internet Timeline FAQ,* and more extensive information about the sources used to compile the *Timeline.* The online version is also a hypertext document, containing links to other Web pages in many items.

1950s

1957

USSR launches Sputnik, first artificial earth satellite. In response, US forms the Advanced Research Projects Agency (ARPA) within the Department of Defense (DoD) to establish US lead in science and technology applicable to the military (:amk:)

1960s

1962

Paul Baran, RAND: "On Distributed Communications Networks" Packet-switching (PS) networks; no single outage point.

1965

ARPA sponsors study on "cooperative network of time-sharing computers."

TX-2 at MIT Lincoln Lab and Q-32 at Systems Development Corporation (Santa Monica, CA) are directly linked (without packet switches).

1967

ACM Symposium on Operating Principles

Plan presented for a packet-switching network.

First design paper on ARPANET published by Lawrence G. Roberts

National Physical Laboratory (NPL) in Middlesex, England develops NPL Data Network under D. W. Davies.

1968

PS-network presented to the Advanced Research Projects Agency (ARPA).

1969

ARPANET commissioned by DoD for research into networking

First node at UCLA [Network Measurements Center - SDS SIGMA 7:SEX] and soon after at:

> Stanford Research Institute (SRI)
>
> University of California at Santa Barbara
>
> University of Utah

Use of Information Message Processors (IMP) [Honeywell 516 minicomputer with 12K of memory] developed by Bolt Beranek and Newman, Inc. (BBN).

First Request for Comment (RFC): "Host Software" by Steve Crocker

1970s

Store-and-forward networks: used electronic mail technology and extended it to conferencing.

1970

ALOHAnet developed by Norman Abrahamson, University of Hawaii (:sk2:). Connected to the ARPANET in 1972.

ARPANET hosts start using Network Control Protocol (NCP).

1971

15 nodes (23 hosts): UCLA, SRI, UCSB, University of Utah, BBN, MIT, RAND, SDC, Harvard, Lincoln Lab, Stanford, UIU(C), CWRU, CMU, NASA/Ames

1972

International Conference on Computer Communications with demonstration of ARPANET between 40 machines and the Terminal Interface Processor (TIP) organized by Bob Kahn.

InterNetworking Working Group (INWG) created to address need for establishing agreed-upon protocols. Chairman: Vinton Cerf.

Ray Tomlinson of BBN invents e-mail program to send messages across a distributed network (:amk:).

Telnet specification (RFC 318)

1973

First international connections to the ARPANET: University College of London (England) and Royal Radar Establishment (Norway).

Bob Metcalfe's Harvard PhD Thesis outlines idea for Ethernet (:amk:).

Bob Kahn poses Internet problem, starts internetting research program at ARPA.

Vinton Cerf sketches gateway architecture in March on back of envelope in hotel lobby in San Francisco (:vgc:).

Cerf and Kahn present basic Internet ideas at INWG in September at University of Sussex, Brighton, UK (:vgc:).

File Transfer specification (RFC 454)

1974

Vint Cerf and Bob Kahn publish "A Protocol for Packet Network Internetworking," which specified in detail the design of a Transmission Control Program (TCP) (:amk:).

BBN opens Telenet, the first public packet data service (a commercial version of ARPANET) (:sk2:).

1975

Operational management of Internet transferred to DCA (now DISA).

"Jargon File," by Raphael Finkel at SAIL, first released (:esr:).

1976

Elizabeth, Queen of the United Kingdom, sends out an e-mail (various Net folks have e-mailed dates ranging from 1971 to 1978; 1976 was the most often submitted and the only one found in print).

UUCP (Unix-to-Unix CoPy) developed at AT&T Bell Labs and distributed with UNIX one year later.

1977

THEORYNET created at University of Wisconsin, providing electronic mail to over 100 researchers in computer science (using a locally developed e-mail system and TELENET for access to server).

Mail specification (RFC 733)

Tymshare launches Tymnet.

First demonstration of ARPANET/Packet Radio Net/SATNET operation of Internet protocols with BBN-supplied gateways in July (:vgc:).

1979

Meeting between University of Wisconsin, DARPA, NSF, and computer scientists from many universities to establish a Computer Science Department research computer network (organized by Larry Landweber).

Usenet established using UUCP between Duke and UNC by Tom Truscott and Steve Bellovin. All original groups under net.* hierarchy.

First MUD, named MUD1, by Richard Bartle and Roy Trubshaw at University of Essex.

ARPA establishes the Internet Configuration Control Board (ICCB).

Packet Radio Network (PRNET) experiment starts with DARPA funding. Most communications take place between mobile vans. ARPANET connection via SRI.

1980s

1981

BITNET, the "Because It's Time NETwork":

> Started as a cooperative network at the City University of New York, with the first connection to Yale (:feg:).

> Original acronym stood for 'There' instead of 'Time' in reference to the free NJE protocols provided with the IBM systems.

> Provides electronic mail and listserv servers to distribute information, as well as file transfers.

CSNET (Computer Science NETwork) built by UCAR and BBN through seed money granted by NSF to provide networking services (especially e-mail) to university scientists with no access to ARPANET. CSNET later becomes known as the Computer and Science Network. (:amk, lhl:)

Minitel (Teletel) is deployed across France by France Telecom.

1982

DCA and ARPA establish the Transmission Control Protocol (TCP) and Internet Protocol (IP), as the protocol suite, commonly known as TCP/IP, for ARPANET. (:vgc:)

> This leads to one of the first definitions of an "internet" as a connected set of networks, specifically those using TCP/IP, and "Internet" as connected TCP/IP internets.

> DoD declares TCP/IP suite to be standard for DoD (:vgc:)

EUnet (European UNIX Network) is created by EUUG to provide e-mail and USENET services. (:glg:) Original connections between the Netherlands, Denmark, Sweden, and UK.

External Gateway Protocol (RFC 827) specification. EGP is used for gateways between networks.

1983

Name server developed at University of Wisconsin, no longer requiring users to know the exact path to other systems.

Cutover from NCP to TCP/IP (1 January)

CSNET / ARPANET gateway put in place.

ARPANET split into ARPANET and MILNET; the latter became integrated with the Defense Data Network created the previous year.

Desktop workstations come into being; many with Berkeley UNIX, which includes IP networking software.

Need switches from having a single, large time-sharing computer connected to Internet per site, to connection of an entire local network.

Internet Activities Board (IAB) established, replacing ICCB.

Berkeley releases 4.2BSD incorporating TCP/IP (:mpc:)

EARN (European Academic and Research Network) established. Very similar to the way BITNET works with a gateway funded by IBM.

FidoNet developed by Tom Jennings.

1984

Domain Name Server (DNS) introduced.

Number of hosts breaks 1000.

JUNET (Japan Unix Network) established using UUCP.

JANET (Joint Academic Network) established in the UK using the Coloured Book protocols; previously SERCnet.

Moderated newsgroups introduced on USENET (mod.*).

Neuromancer written by William Gibson

1985

Whole Earth 'Lectronic Link (WELL) started.

1986

NSFNET created (backbone speed of 56Kbps)

NSF establishes five supercomputing centers to provide high-computing power for all (JVNC@Princeton, PSC@Pittsburgh, SDSC@UCSD, NCSA@UIUC, Theory Center@Cornell). This allows an explosion of connections, especially from universities.

The first Freenet (Cleveland) comes on-line under the auspices of the Society for Public Access Computing (SoPAC). Later Freenet program management assumed by the National Public Telecomputing Network (NPTN) in 1989 (:sk2,rab:).

Network News Transfer Protocol (NNTP) designed to enhance Usenet news performance over TCP/IP.

Mail Exchanger (MX) records, developed by Craig Partridge, allow non-IP network hosts to have domain addresses.

The great Usenet name change; moderated newsgroups changed in 1987.

BARRNET (Bay Area Regional Research Network) established using high-speed links. Operational in 1987.

1987

NSF signs a cooperative agreement to manage the NSFNET backbone with Merit Network, Inc. (IBM and MCI involvement was through an agreement with Merit.) Merit, IBM, and MCI later founded ANS.

UUNET is founded with Usenix funds to provide commercial UUCP and Usenet access. Originally an experiment by Rick Adams and Mike O'Dell.

1000th RFC: "Request For Comments reference guide"

Number of hosts breaks 10,000.

Number of BITNET hosts breaks 1000.

1988

1 November—Internet worm burrows through the Net, affecting about 6000 of the 60,000 hosts on the Internet (:ph1:).

CERT (Computer Emergency Response Team) formed by DARPA in response to the needs exhibited during the Morris worm incident.

> Number of advisories-reports/years: 1/88, 7/89, 12-130/90, 23/91, 21-800/92, 18-1,300/93, 15-2,300/94 .

DoD chooses to adopt OSI and sees use of TCP/IP as an interim. US Government OSI Profile (GOSIP) defines the set of protocols to be supported by Government-purchased products (:gck:).

Los Nettos network created with no federal funding, instead supported by regional members (founding: Caltech, TIS, UCLA, USC, ISI).

NSFNET backbone upgraded to T1 (1.544 Mbps).

CERFnet (California Education and Research Federation network) founded by Susan Estrada.

Internet Relay Chat (IRC) developed by Jarkko Oikarinen (:zby:).

First Canadian regionals join NSFNET:

> ONet via Cornell,
>
> RISQ via Princeton,
>
> BCnet via University of Washington (:ec1:)

FidoNet gets connected to the Net, enabling the exchange of e-mail and news. (:tp1:)

Countries connecting to NSFNET: Canada, Denmark, Finland, France, Iceland, Norway, Sweden.

1989

Number of hosts breaks 100,000.

RIPE (Reseaux IP Europeens) formed (by European service providers) to ensure the necessary administrative and technical coordination to allow the operation of the pan-European IP Network. (:glg:).

First relays between a commercial electronic mail carrier and the Internet: MCI Mail through the Corporation for the National Research Initiative (CNRI), and CompuServe through Ohio State University (:jg1,ph1:).

Corporation for Research and Education Networking (CREN) is formed by the merge of CSNET into BITNET.

Internet Engineering Task Force (IETF) and Internet Research Task Force (IRTF) comes into existence under the IAB.

AARNET— Australian Academic Research Network—set up by AVCC and CSIRO; introduced into service the following year (:gmc:)

The Cuckoo's Egg, written by Clifford Stoll, tells the real-life tale of a German cracker group who infiltrated numerous US facilities.

Countries connecting to NSFNET: Australia, Germany, Israel, Italy, Japan, Mexico, Netherlands, New Zealand, Puerto Rico, UK.

1990s

1990

ARPANET ceases to exist.

Electronic Frontier Foundation (EFF) is founded by Mitch Kapor.

Archie released by Peter Deutsch, Alan Emtage, and Bill Heelan at McGill University.

Hytelnet released by Peter Scott (University of Saskatchewan).

The World comes on-line (world.std.com), becoming the first commercial provider of Internet dial-up access.

ISO Development Environment (ISODE) developed to provide an approach for OSI migration for the DoD. ISODE software allows OSI applications to operate over TCP/IP (:gck:).

CA*net formed by 10 regional networks as national Canadian backbone with direct connection to NSFNET (:ec1:).

The first remotely operated machine to be hooked up to the Internet, the Internet Toaster, (controlled via SNMP) makes its debut at Interop.

Countries connecting to NSFNET: Argentina, Austria, Belgium, Brazil, Chile, Greece, India, Ireland, South Korea, Spain, Switzerland.

1991

Commercial Internet eXchange (CIX) Association, Inc. formed by General Atomics (CERFnet), Performance Systems International, Inc. (PSInet), and UUNET Technologies, Inc. (AlterNet), after NSF lifts restrictions on the commercial use of the Net (:glg:).

Wide Area Information Servers (WAIS), invented by Brewster Kahle, released by Thinking Machines Corporation.

Gopher released by Paul Lindner and Mark P. McCahill from the University of Minnesota.

World Wide Web (WWW) released by CERN; Tim Berners-Lee developer.

PGP (Pretty Good Privacy) released by Philip Zimmerman (:ad1:).

US High Performance Computing Act (Gore 1) establishes the National Research and Education Network (NREN).

NSFNET backbone upgraded to T3 (44.736 Mbps).

NSFNET traffic passes 1 trillion bytes/month and 10 billion packets/ month.

Countries connecting to NSFNET: Croatia, Czech Republic, Hong Kong, Hungary, Poland, Portugal, Singapore, South Africa, Taiwan, Tunisia.

1992

Internet Society (ISOC) is chartered.

Number of hosts breaks 1,000,000.

First MBONE audio multicast (March) and video multicast (November).

IAB reconstituted as the Internet Architecture Board and becomes part of the Internet Society.

Veronica, a gopherspace search tool, is released by University of Nevada.

World Bank comes on-line.

Internet Hunt started by Rick Gates.

Countries connecting to NSFNET: Cameroon, Cyprus, Ecuador, Estonia, Kuwait, Latvia, Luxembourg, Malaysia, Slovakia, Slovenia, Thailand, Venezuela.

1993

InterNIC created by NSF to provide specific Internet services: (:sc1:):

directory and database services (AT&T)

registration services (Network Solutions Inc.)

information services (General Atomics/CERFnet)

US White House comes on-line (http://www.whitehouse.gov/):

President Bill Clinton: president@whitehouse.gov

Vice-President Al Gore: vice-president@whitehouse.gov

First Lady Hillary Clinton: root@whitehouse.gov (-:rhz:-)

Worms of a new kind find their way around the Net - WWW Worms (W4), joined by Spiders, Wanderers, Crawlers, and Snakes.

Internet Talk Radio begins broadcasting (:sk2:).

United Nations (UN) come on-line (:vgc:).

US National Information Infrastructure Act.

Businesses and media really take notice of the Internet.

Mosaic takes the Internet by storm; WWW proliferates at a 341,634% annual growth rate of service traffic.

Gopher's growth is 997%.

Countries connecting to NSFNET: Bulgaria, Costa Rica, Egypt, Fiji, Ghana, Guam, Indonesia, Kazakhstan, Kenya, Liechtenstein, Peru, Romania, Russian Federation, Turkey, Ukraine, UAE, Virgin Islands.

1994

ARPANET/Internet celebrates 25th anniversary.

Communities begin to be wired up directly to the Internet (Lexington and Cambridge, Mass., USA).

US Senate and House provide information servers

Shopping malls arrive on the Internet.

First cyberstation, RT-FM, broadcasts from Interop in Las Vegas.

The National Institute for Standards and Technology (NIST) suggests that GOSIP should incorporate TCP/IP and drop the "OSI-only" requirement (:gck:).

Arizona law firm of Canter & Siegel "spams" the Internet with e-mail advertising green card lottery services; Net citizens flame back.

NSFNET traffic passes 10 trillion bytes/month.

Yes, it's true—you can now order pizza from the Hut online.

WWW edges out Telnet to become second most popular service on the Net (behind FTP-data) based on percentage of packets and bytes traffic distribution on NSFNET.

Japanese Prime Minister goes on-line (`http://www.kantei.go.hp/`).

UK's HM Treasury goes on-line (`http://www.hm-treasury.gov.uk/`).

New Zealand's Info Tech Prime Minister on-line (`http://www.govt.nz/`).

First Virtual, the first cyberbank, open up for business.

Radio stations start rockin' (rebroadcasting) round the clock on the Net:

> WXYC at University of North Carolina
>
> WJHK at University of Kansas—Lawrence
>
> KUGS at Western Washington University

Trans-European Research and Education Network Association (TERENA) is formed by the merge of RARE and EARN, with representatives from 38 countries as well as CERN and ECMWF. TERERNA's aim is to "promote and participate in the development of a high quality international information and telecommunications infrastructure for the benefit of research and education."

Countries connecting to NSFNET: Algeria, Armenia, Bermuda, Burkina Faso, China, Colombia, French Polynesia, Jamaica, Lebanon, Lithuania, Macau, Morocco, New Caledonia, Nicaragua, Niger, Panama, Philippines, Senegal, Sri Lanka, Swaziland, Uruguay, Uzbekistan.

1995

NSFNET reverts to being a research network. Main US backbone traffic now routed through interconnected network providers.

Hong Kong police disconnect all but one of the colony's Internet providers in search of a hacker. 10,000 people are left without Net access. (:api:)

Radio HK, the first 24 hr., Internet-only radio station, starts broadcasting.

WWW surpasses FTP-data in March as the service with greatest traffic on NSFNet based on packet count, and in April based on byte count.

Traditional online dial-up systems (CompuServe, American Online, Prodigy) begin to provide Internet access.

A number of Net related companies go public, with Netscape leading the pack with the third-largest-ever NASDAQ IPO share value.

Thousands in Minneapolis-St.Paul lose Net access after transients start a bonfire under a bridge at the University of Minnesota, causing fiber-optic cables to melt.

Registration of domain names is no longer free. Beginning 14 September, a $50 annual fee has been imposed, which up until now was subsidized by NSF. NSF continues to pay for .edu registration, and on an interim basis for .gov.

The Vatican comes online (`http://www.vatican.va/`).

The Canadian government comes online (`http://canada.gc.ca/`).

The first official Internet wiretap was successful in helping the Secret Service and Drug Enforcement Agency (DEA) apprehend three individuals who were illegally manufacturing and selling cellular phone cloning equipment and electronic devices.

Operation Home Front connects, for the first time, soldiers in the field with their families back home via the Internet.

Technologies of the Year: WWW, search engines.

Emerging Technologies: mobile code (JAVA, JAVAscript,) virtual environments (VRML), collaborative tools.

1996

The Internet 1996 World Exposition—the first World's Fair to take place on the Internet.

"A Day in the Life of the Internet" begs to be published (:rhz:)

Internet Growth Table

Date	Hosts	Date	Hosts	Networks	Domains
1969	4	07/89	130,000	650	3,900
04/71	23	10/89	159,000	837	
06/74	62	10/90	313,000	2,063	9,300
03/77	111	01/91	376,000	2,338	
08/81	213	07/91	535,000	3,086	16,000
05/82	235	10/91	617,000	3,556	18,000
08/83	562	01/92	727,000	4,526	
10/84	1,024	04/92	890,000	5,291	20,000
10/85	1,961	07/92	992,000	6,569	16,300
02/86	2,308	10/92	1,136,000	7,505	18,100
11/86	5,089	01/93	1,313,000	8,258	21,000
12/87	28,174	04/93	1,486,000	9,722	22,000
07/88	33,000	07/93	1,776,000	13,767	26,000

Date	Hosts	Date	Hosts	Networks	Domains
10/88	56,000	10/93	2,056,000	16,533	28,000
01/89	80,000	01/94	2,217,000	20,539	30,000
		07/94	3,212,000	25,210	46,000
		10/94	3,864,000	37,022	56,000
		01/95	4,852,000	39,410	71,000
		07/95	6,642,000	61,538	120,000

Appendix B

User Guidelines: Two Views

THIS appendix presents two documents that offer different but overlapping guidelines for "behaving yourself" on the Internet—using shared resources responsibly, avoiding harassment by others, and generally staying out of trouble.

The first, the "official" RFC on Netiquette, is addressed to users, administrators, and moderators.

The second, by Hilarie Gardner (calliope@well.sf.ca.us), is addressed to all new users learning their way around the Internet. Hilarie's guidelines help you protect your personal privacy and the privacy of others.

RFC 1855: Netiquette Guidelines

Status of This Memo

This memo provides information for the Internet community. This memo does not specify an Internet standard of any kind. Distribution of this memo is unlimited.

Abstract

This document provides a minimum set of guidelines for Network Etiquette (Netiquette), which organizations may take and adapt for their own use. This memo is the product of the Responsible Use of the Network (RUN) Working Group of the IETF.

1.0 Introduction

In the past, the population of people using the Internet had "grown up" with the Internet, were technically minded, and understood the nature of the transport and the protocols. Today, the community of Internet users includes people who are new to the environment. These "Newbies" are unfamiliar with the culture and don't need to know about transport and protocols. In order to bring these new users into the Internet culture quickly, this Guide offers a minimum set of behaviors that organizations and individuals may take and adapt for their own use. Individuals should be aware that no matter who supplies their Internet access, be it an Internet service provider through a private account, or a student account at a university, or an account through a corporation, those organizations have regulations about ownership of mail and files, about what is proper to post or send, and about how to present yourself. Be sure to check with the local authority for specific guidelines.

We've organized this material into three sections: One-to-one communication, which includes mail and talk; One-to-many communications, which includes mailing lists and NetNews; and Information Services, which includes FTP, WWW, Wais, Gopher, MUDs, and MOOs. Finally, we have a Selected Bibliography, which may be used for reference.

2.0 One-to-One Communication (electronic mail, talk)

We define one-to-one communications as those in which a person is communicating with another person as if face-to-face: a dialog. In general, rules of common courtesy for interaction with people should be in force for any situation and on the Internet it's doubly important where, for example, body language and tone of voice must be inferred. For more information on Netiquette for communicating via electronic mail and talk, check references [1,23,25,27] in the Selected Bibliography.

2.1 User Guidelines

2.1.1 For mail: Unless you have your own Internet access through an Internet provider, be sure to check with your employer about ownership of electronic mail. Laws about the ownership of electronic mail vary from place to place.

Unless you are using an encryption device (hardware or software), you should assume that mail on the Internet is not secure. Never put in a mail message anything you would not put on a postcard.

Respect the copyright on material that you reproduce. Almost every country has copyright laws.

If you are forwarding or re-posting a message you've received, do not change the wording. If the message was a personal message to you and you are re-posting to a group, you should ask permission first. You may shorten the message and quote only relevant parts, but be sure you give proper attribution.

Never send chain letters via electronic mail. Chain letters are forbidden on the Internet. Your network privileges will be revoked. Notify your local system administrator if your ever receive one.

A good rule of thumb: Be conservative in what you send and liberal in what you receive. You should not send heated messages (we call these "flames") even if you are provoked. On the other hand, you shouldn't be surprised if you get flamed; and it's prudent not to respond to flames.

In general, it's a good idea to at least check all your mail subjects before responding to a message. Sometimes a person who asks you for help (or clarification) will send another message which effectively says "Never Mind." Also make sure that any message you respond to was directed to you. You might be cc:ed rather than the primary recipient.

Make things easy for the recipient. Many mailers strip header information, which includes your return address. In order to ensure that people know who you are, be sure to include a line or two at the end of your message with contact information. You can create this file ahead of time and add it to the end of your messages. (Some mailers do this automatically.) In Internet parlance, this is known as a ".sig" or "signature" file. Your .sig file takes the place of your business card. (And you can have more than one to apply in different circumstances.)

Be careful when addressing mail. There are addresses that may go to a group, but the address looks like it is just one person. Know to whom you are sending.

Watch cc's when replying. Don't continue to include people if the messages have become a two-way conversation.

In general, most people who use the Internet don't have time to answer general questions about the Internet and its workings. Don't send unsolicited mail asking for information to people whose names you might have seen in RFCs or on mailing lists.

Remember that people with whom you communicate are located across the globe. If you send a message to which you want an immediate response, the person receiving it might be at home asleep when it arrives. Give them a chance to wake up, come to work, and log in before assuming the mail didn't arrive or that they don't care.

Verify all addresses before initiating long or personal discourse. It's also a good practice to include the word "Long" in the subject header so the recipient knows the message will take time to read and respond to. Over 100 lines is considered "long."

Know whom to contact for help. Usually you will have resources close at hand. Check locally for people who can help you with software and system problems. Also, know whom to go to if you receive anything questionable or illegal. Most sites also have "Postmaster" aliased to a knowledgeable user, so you can send mail to this address to get help with mail.

Remember that the recipient is a human being whose culture, language, and humor have different points of reference from your own. Remember that date formats, measurements, and idioms may not travel well. Be especially careful with sarcasm.

Use mixed case. UPPER CASE LOOKS AS IF YOU'RE SHOUTING.

Use symbols for emphasis: "That *is* what I meant." Use underscores for underlining: "_War and Peace_ is my favorite book." Use smileys to indicate tone of voice, but use them sparingly. :-) is an example of a smiley (look sideways). Don't assume that the inclusion of a smiley will make the recipient happy with what you say or wipe out an otherwise insulting comment.

Wait overnight to send emotional responses to messages. If you have really strong feelings about a subject, indicate it via FLAME ON/OFF enclosures. For example:

```
FLAME ON:
This type of argument is not worth the bandwidth it
takes to send it. It's illogical and poorly reasoned.
The rest of the world agrees with me. FLAME OFF
```

Do not include control characters or non-ASCII attachments in messages unless they are MIME attachments or unless your mailer encodes these. If you send encoded messages make sure the recipient can decode them.

Be brief without being overly terse. When replying to a message, include enough original material to be understood but no more. It is extremely bad form to simply reply to a message by including all the previous message: edit out all the irrelevant material.

Limit line length to fewer than 65 characters and end a line with a carriage return.

Mail should have a subject heading that reflects the content of the message.

If you include a signature keep it short. A rule of thumb is no longer than four lines. Remember that many people pay for connectivity by the minute, and the longer your message is, the more they pay.

Just as mail (today) may not be private, mail (and news) are (today) subject to forgery and spoofing of various degrees of detectability. Apply common sense "reality checks" before assuming a message is valid.

If you think the importance of a message justifies it, immediately reply briefly to an e-mail message to let the sender know you got it, even if you will send a longer reply later.

"Reasonable" expectations for conduct via e-mail depend on your relationship to a person and the context of the communication. Norms learned in a particular e-mail environment may not apply in general to your e-mail communication with people across the Internet. Be careful with slang or local acronyms.

The cost of delivering an e-mail message is, on the average, paid about equally by the sender and the recipient (or their organizations). This is unlike other media, such as physical mail, telephone, TV, or radio. Sending someone mail may also cost them in other specific ways like network bandwidth, disk space, or CPU usage. This is a fundamental economic reason why unsolicited e-mail advertising is unwelcome (and is forbidden in many contexts).

Know how large a message you are sending. Including large files such as Postscript files or programs may make your message so large that it cannot be delivered or at least consumes excessive resources. A good rule of thumb would be not to send a file larger than 50 Kilobytes. Consider file transfer as an alternative, or cutting the file into smaller chunks and sending each as a separate message.

Don't send large amounts of unsolicited information to people. If your mail system allows you to forward mail, beware the dreaded forwarding loop. Be sure you haven't set up forwarding on several hosts so that a message sent to you gets into an endless loop from one computer to the next to the next.

2.1.2 For talk: Talk is a set of protocols that allow two people to have an interactive dialog via computer. Use mixed case and proper punctuation, as though you were typing a letter or sending mail.

Don't run off the end of a line and simply let the terminal wrap; use a Carriage Return (CR) at the end of the line. Also, don't assume your screen size is the same as everyone else's. A good rule of thumb is to write out no more than 70 characters, and no more than 12 lines (since you're using a split screen).

Leave some margin; don't write to the edge of the screen.

Use two CRs to indicate that you are done and the other person may start typing. (blank line).

Always say goodbye, or some other farewell, and wait to see a farewell from the other person before killing the session. This is especially important when you are communicating with someone a long way away. Remember that your communication relies on both bandwidth (the size of the pipe) and latency (the speed of light).

Remember that talk is an interruption to the other person. Only use as appropriate. And never talk to strangers.

The reasons for not getting a reply are many. Don't assume that everything is working correctly. Not all versions of talk are compatible.

If left on its own, talk re-rings the recipient. Let it ring one or two times, then kill it.

If a person doesn't respond you might try another TTY. Use Finger to determine which are open. If the person still doesn't respond, do not continue to send.

Talk shows your typing ability. If you type slowly and make mistakes when typing it is often not worth the time of trying to correct, as the other person can usually see what you meant.

Be careful if you have more than one talk session going!

2.2 Administrator Issues

Be sure you have established written guidelines for dealing with situations, especially illegal, improper, or forged traffic.

Handle requests in a timely fashion—by the next business day.

Respond promptly to people who have concerns about receiving improper or illegal messages. Requests concerning chain letters should be handled immediately.

Explain any system rules, such as disk quotas, to your users. Make sure they understand implications of requesting files by mail such as:

▶ Filling up disks;

▶ Running up phone bills,

▶ Delaying mail, etc.

Make sure you have "Postmaster" aliased. Make sure you have "Root" aliased. Make sure someone reads that mail.

Investigate complaints about your users with an open mind. Remember that addresses may be forged and spoofed.

3.0 One-to-Many Communication (Mailing Lists, NetNews)

Any time you engage in One-to-Many communications, all the rules for mail should also apply. After all, communicating with many people via one mail message or post is quite analogous to communicating with one person with the exception of possibly offending a great many more people than in one-to-one communication. Therefore, it's quite important to know as much as you can about the audience of your message.

3.1 User Guidelines

3.1.1 General Guidelines for Mailing Lists and NetNews
Read both mailing lists and newsgroups for one to two months before you post anything. This helps you to get an understanding of the culture of the group.

Do not blame the system administrator for the behavior of the system users.

Consider that a large audience will see your posts. That may include your present or your next boss. Take care in what you write. Remember too, that mailing lists and Newsgroups are frequently archived, and that your words may be stored for a very long time in a place to which many people have access.

Assume that individuals speak for themselves, and what they say does not represent their organization (unless stated explicitly).

Remember that both mail and news take system resources. Pay attention to any specific rules covering their uses your organization may have.

Messages and articles should be brief and to the point. Don't wander off-topic, don't ramble and don't send mail or post messages solely to point out other people's errors in typing or spelling. These, more than any other behavior, mark you as an immature beginner.

Subject lines should follow the conventions of the group.

Forgeries and spoofing are not approved behavior.

Advertising is welcomed on some lists and Newsgroups, and abhorred on others! This is another example of knowing your audience before you post. Unsolicited advertising that is completely off-topic will most certainly guarantee that you get a lot of hate mail.

If you are sending a reply to a message or a posting be sure you summarize the original at the top of the message, or include just enough text of the original to give a context. This will make sure readers understand when they start to read your response. Since NetNews, especially, is proliferated by distributing the postings from one host to another, it is possible to see a response to a message before seeing the original. Giving context helps everyone. But do not include the entire original!

Again, be sure to have a signature that you attach to your message. This will guarantee that any peculiarities of mailers or newsreaders

Appendix B

which strip header information will not delete the only reference in the message of how people may reach you.

Be careful when you reply to messages or postings. Frequently replies are sent back to the address that originated the post—which in many cases is the address of a list or group! You may accidentally send a personal response to a great many people, embarrassing all involved. It's best to type in the address instead of relying on "reply."

Delivery receipts, nondelivery notices, and vacation programs are neither totally standardized nor totally reliable across the range of systems connected to Internet mail. They are invasive when sent to mailing lists, and some people consider delivery receipts an invasion of privacy. In short, do not use them.

If you find a personal message has gone to a list or group, send an apology to the person and to the group.

If you should find yourself in a disagreement with one person, make your responses to each other via mail rather than continue to send messages to the list or the group. If you are debating a point on which the group might have some interest, you may summarize for them later.

Don't get involved in flame wars. Neither post nor respond to incendiary material.

Avoid sending messages or posting articles which are no more than gratuitous replies to replies.

Be careful with monospacing fonts and diagrams. These will display differently on different systems, and with different mailers on the same system.

There are Newsgroups and Mailing Lists which discuss topics of wide varieties of interests. These represent a diversity of lifestyles, religions, and cultures. Posting articles or sending messages to a group whose point of view is offensive to you simply to tell them they are offensive is not acceptable. Sexually and racially harassing messages may also have legal implications. There is software available to filter items you might find objectionable.

3.1.2 Mailing List Guidelines   There are several ways to find information about what mailing lists exist on the Internet and how to join them. Make sure you understand your organization's policy about joining these lists and posting to them. In general it is always better to check local resources first before trying to find information via the Internet. Nevertheless, there are a set of files posted periodically to news.answers which list the Internet mailing lists and how to subscribe to them. This is an invaluable resource for finding lists on any topic. See also references [9,13,15] in the Selected Bibliography.

Send subscribe and unsubscribe messages to the appropriate address. Although some mailing list software is smart enough to catch these, not all can ferret them out. It is your responsibility to learn how the lists work, and to send the correct mail to the correct place. Although many mailing lists adhere to the convention of having a "-request" alias for sending subscribe and unsubscribe messages, not all do. Be sure you know the conventions used by the lists to which you subscribe.

Save the subscription messages for any lists you join. These usually tell you how to unsubscribe as well.

In general, it's not possible to retrieve messages once you have sent them. Even your system administrator will not be able to get a message back once you have sent it. This means you must make sure you really want the message to go as you have written it.

The auto-reply feature of many mailers is useful for in-house communication, but quite annoying when sent to entire mailing lists. Examine "Reply-To" addresses when replying to messages from lists. Most auto-replies will go to all members of the list.

Don't send large files to mailing lists when Uniform Resource Locators (URLs) or pointers to FTP-able versions will do. If you want to send it as multiple files, be sure to follow the culture of the group. If you don't know what that is, ask.

Consider unsubscribing or setting a "nomail" option (when it's available) when you cannot check your mail for an extended period.

When sending a message to more than one mailing list, especially if the lists are closely related, apologize for cross-posting.

If you ask a question, be sure to post a summary. When doing so, truly summarize rather than send an accumulation of the messages you receive.

Some mailing lists are private. Do not send mail to these lists uninvited. Do not report mail from these lists to a wider audience.

If you are caught in an argument, keep the discussion focused on issues rather than the personalities involved.

3.1.3 NetNews Guidelines

NetNews is a globally distributed system that allows people to communicate on topics of specific interest. It is divided into hierarchies, with the major divisions being:

sci	science-related discussions
comp	computer-related discussions
news	for discussions which center around NetNews itself
rec	recreational activities
soc	social issues
talk	long-winded never-ending discussions
biz	business-related postings
alt	the alternate hierarchy

Alt is so named because creating an alt group does not go through the same process as creating a group in the other parts of the hierarchy. There are also regional hierarchies and hierarchies that are widely distributed such as Bionet; and your place of business may have its own groups as well. Recently, a "humanities" hierarchy was added, and as time goes on it's likely that more will be added. For longer discussions on News see references [2,8,22,23] in the Selected Bibliography.

In NetNews parlance, "Posting" refers to posting a new article to a group, or responding to a post someone else has posted. "Cross-Posting" refers to posting a message to more than one group. If you introduce Cross-Posting to a group, or if you direct "Followup-To:" in the header of your posting, warn readers! Readers will usually assume that the message was posted to a specific group and that followups will go to that group. Headers change this behavior.

Read all of a discussion in progress (we call this a thread) before posting replies. Avoid posting "Me Too" messages, where content is limited to agreement with previous posts. Content of a follow-up post should exceed quoted content.

Send mail when an answer to a question is for one person only. Remember that News has global distribution and the whole world probably is NOT interested in a personal response. However, don't hesitate to post when something will be of general interest to the Newsgroup participants.

Check the "Distribution" section of the header, but don't depend on it. Because of the complex method by which News is delivered, Distribution headers are unreliable. But if you are posting something that will be of interest to a limited number of readers, use a distribution line that attempts to limit the distribution of your article to those people. For example, set the Distribution to "nj" if you are posting an article that will be of interest only to New Jersey readers.

If you feel an article will be of interest to more than one Newsgroup, be sure to CROSSPOST the article rather than individually post it to those groups. In general, probably only five-to-six groups will have similar enough interests to warrant this.

Consider using Reference sources (Computer Manuals, Newspapers, help files) before posting a question. Asking a Newsgroup where answers are readily available elsewhere generates grumpy "RTFM" (read the fine manual—although a more vulgar meaning of the word beginning with "f" is usually implied) messages.

Although there are Newsgroups that welcome advertising, in general it is considered nothing less than criminal to advertise off-topic products. Sending an advertisement to each and every group will pretty much guarantee your loss of connectivity.

If you discover an error in your post, cancel it as soon as possible. DO NOT attempt to cancel any articles but your own. Contact your administrator if you don't know how to cancel your post, or if some other post, such as a chain letter, needs canceling.

If you've posted something and don't see it immediately, don't assume it's failed and re-post it.

Some groups permit (and some welcome) posts that in other circumstances would be considered to be in questionable taste. Still, there is no guarantee that all people reading the group will appreciate the material as much as you do. Use the Rotate utility (which rotates all the characters in your post by 13 positions in the alphabet) to avoid giving offense. The Rot13 utility for Unix is an example.

In groups discussing movies or books it is considered essential to mark posts that disclose significant content as "Spoilers." Put this word in your Subject: line. You may add blank lines to the beginning of your post to keep content out of sight, or you may Rotate it.

Forging of news articles is generally censured. You can protect yourself from forgeries by using software that generates a manipulation detection "fingerprint," such as PGP (in the US).

Postings via anonymous servers are accepted in some Newsgroups and disliked in others. Material that is inappropriate when posted under one's own name is still inappropriate when posted anonymously.

Expect a slight delay in seeing your post when posting to a moderated group. The moderator may change your subject line to have your post conform to a particular thread.

Don't get involved in flame wars. Neither post nor respond to incendiary material.

3.2 Administrator Guidelines

3.2.1 General Issues   Clarify any policies your site has regarding its subscription to NetNews groups and about subscribing to mailing lists.

Clarify any policies your site has about posting to NetNews groups or to mailing lists, including use of disclaimers in .sigs.

Clarify and publicize archive policy. (How long are articles kept?)

Investigate accusations about your users promptly and with an open mind.

Be sure to monitor the health of your system.

Consider how long to archive system logs, and publicize your policy on logging.

3.2.2 Mailing Lists   Keep mailing lists up-to-date to avoid the "bouncing mail" problem.

Help list owners when problems arise.

Inform list owners of any maintenance windows or planned downtime.

Be sure to have "-request" aliases for list subscription and administration.

Make sure all mail gateways operate smoothly.

3.2.3. NetNews   Publicize the nature of the feed you receive. If you do not get a full feed, people may want to know why not.

Be aware that the multiplicity of newsreader clients may cause the News server to be blamed for problems in the clients.

Honor requests from users immediately if they request cancellation of their own posts or invalid posts, such as chain letters.

Have "Usenet," "Netnews," and "News" aliased and make sure someone reads the mail.

3.3 Moderator Guidelines

3.3.1 General Guidelines   Make sure your Frequently Asked Questions list (FAQ) is posted at regular intervals. Include your guidelines for articles/messages. If you are not the FAQ maintainer, make sure they do so.

Make sure you maintain a good welcome message, which contains subscribe and unsubscribe information.

Newsgroups should have their charter/guidelines posted regularly.

Keep mailing lists and Newsgroups up to date. Post messages in a timely fashion. Designate a substitute when you go on vacation or out of town.

4.0 Information Services (Gopher, Wais, WWW, FTP, Telnet)

In recent Internet history, the Net has exploded with new and varied Information services. Gopher, Wais, World Wide Web (WWW), Multi-User Dimensions (MUDs), and Multi-User Dimensions which are Object Oriented (MOOs) are a few of these new areas. Although the ability to find information is exploding, "Caveat Emptor" remains constant. For more information on these services, check references [14,28] in the Selected Bibliography.

4.1 User Guidelines

4.1.1. General Guidelines   Remember that all these services belong to someone else. The people who pay the bills get to make the rules governing usage. Information may be free—or it may not be! Be sure you check.

If you have problems with any form of information service, start problem-solving by checking locally: Check file configurations, software setup,

Appendix B

network connections, etc. Do this before assuming the problem is at the provider's end and/or is the provider's fault.

Although there are naming conventions for file-types used, don't depend on these file naming conventions to be enforced. For example, a ".doc" file is not always a Word file.

Information services also use conventions, such as www.xyz.com. While it is useful to know these conventions, again, don't necessarily rely on them.

Know how file names work on your own system.

Be aware of conventions used for providing information during sessions. FTP sites usually have files named README in a top-level directory, which have information about the files available. But don't assume that these files are necessarily up-to-date and/or accurate.

Do NOT assume that ANY information you find is up-to-date and/or accurate. Remember that new technologies allow just about anyone to be a publisher, but not all people have discovered the responsibilities that accompany publishing.

Remember that unless you are sure security-and-authentication technology is in use, any information you submit to a system is being transmitted over the Internet "in the clear," with no protection from "sniffers" or forgers.

Since the Internet spans the globe, remember that information services might reflect culture and life-style markedly different from your own community. Materials you find offensive may originate in a geography which finds them acceptable. Keep an open mind.

When wanting information from a popular server, be sure to use a mirror server that's close if a list is provided.

Do not use someone else's FTP site to deposit materials you wish other people to pick up. This is called "dumping" and is not generally acceptable behavior.

When you have trouble with a site and ask for help, be sure to provide as much information as possible in order to help debug the problem.

When bringing up your own information service, such as a home page, be sure to check with your local system administrator to find what the local guidelines are in affect.

Consider spreading out the system load on popular sites by avoiding "rush hour" and logging in during off-peak times.

4.1.2 Real Time Interactive Services Guidelines (MUDs, MOOs, IRC) As in other environments, it is wise to "listen" first to get to know the culture of the group.

It's not necessary to greet everyone on a channel or room personally. Usually one "Hello" or the equivalent is enough. Using the automation features of your client to greet people is not acceptable behavior.

Warn the participants if you intend to ship large quantities of information. If all consent to receiving it, you may send; but sending unwanted information without a warning is considered bad form, just as it is in mail.

Don't assume that people who you don't know will want to talk to you. If you feel compelled to send private messages to people you don't know, then be willing to accept gracefully the fact that they might be busy or simply not want to chat with you.

Respect the guidelines of the group. Look for introductory materials for the group. These may be on a related FTP site.

Don't badger other users for personal information such as sex, age, or location. After you have built an acquaintance with another user, these questions may be more appropriate, but many people hesitate to give this information to people with whom they are not familiar.

If a user is using a nickname alias or pseudonym, respect that user's desire for anonymity. Even if you and that person are close friends, it is more courteous to use his nickname. Do not use that person's real name online without permission.

4.2 Administrator Guidelines

4.2.1 General Guidelines Make clear what's available for copying and what is not. Describe what's available on your site, and your organization. Be sure any general policies are clear.

Keep information, especially READMEs, up-to-date. Provide READMEs in plain ASCII text.

Present a list of mirrors of your site if you know them. Make sure you include a statement of copyright applicable to your mirrors. List their update schedule if possible.

Make sure that popular (and massive) information has the bandwidth to support it.

Use conventions for file extensions:

> .txt for ASCII text
>
> .html or .htm for HTML
>
> .ps for Postscript
>
> .pdf for Portable Document Format
>
> .sgml or .sgm for SGML
>
> .exe for non-Unix executables, etc.

For files being transferred, try to make filenames unique in the first eight characters.

When providing information, make sure your site has something unique to offer. Avoid bringing up an information service which simply points to other services on the Internet.

Don't point to other sites without asking first.

Remember that setting up an information service is more than just design and implementation. It's also maintenance.

Make sure your posted materials are appropriate for the supporting organization.

Test applications with a variety of tools. Don't assume everything works if you've tested with only one client. Also, assume the low end of technology for clients and don't create applications that can only be used by Graphical User Interfaces.

Have a consistent view of your information. Make sure the look and feel stays the same throughout your applications.

Be sensitive to the longevity of your information. Be sure to date time-sensitive materials, and be vigilant about keeping this information well maintained.

Export restrictions vary from country to country. Be sure you understand the implications of export restrictions when you post.

Tell users what you plan to do with any information you collect, such as WWW feedback. You need to warn people if you plan to publish any of their statements, even passively by just making it available to other users.

Make sure your policy on user information services, such as home pages, is well known.

5.0 Selected Bibliography

This bibliography was used to gather most of the information in the sections above as well as for general reference. Items not specifically found in these works were gathered from the IETF-RUN Working Group's experience.

[1] Angell, D., and B. Heslop, *The Elements of E-mail Style*, New York: Addison-Wesley, 1994.

[2] "Answers to Frequently Asked Questions about Usenet" Original author: `jerry@eagle.UUCP` (Jerry Schwarz) Maintained by: `net-announce@deshaw.com` (Mark Moraes) Archive-name: usenet-faq/part1

[3] Cerf, V., "Guidelines for Conduct on and Use of Internet", at: `http://www.isoc.org/policy/conduct/conduct.html`

[4] Dern, D., *The Internet Guide for New Users*, New York: McGraw-Hill, 1994.

[5] "Emily Postnews Answers Your Questions on Netiquette" Original author: `brad@looking.on.ca` (Brad Templeton) Maintained by: `netannounce@deshaw.com` (Mark Moraes) Archive-name: emily-postnews/part1

[6] Gaffin, A., *Everybody's Guide to the Internet*, Cambridge, Mass., MIT Press, 1994.

[7] "Guidelines for Responsible Use of the Internet" from the US house of Representatives gopher, at: `gopher://gopher.house.gov:70/0F-1%3a208%3aInternet%20Etiquette`

[8] How to Find the Right Place to Post (FAQ) by `buglady@bronze.lcs.mit.edu` (Aliza R. Panitz) Archive-name: finding-groups/general

[9] Hambridge, S., and J. Sedayao, "Horses and Barn Doors: Evolution of Corporate Guidelines for Internet Usage", LISA VII, Usenix, November 1-5, 1993, pp. 9-16. `ftp://ftp.intel.com/pub/papers/horses.ps` or `horses.ascii>`

[10] Heslop, B., and D. Angell, *The Instant Internet Guide : Hands-on Global Networking*; Reading, Mass., Addison-Wesley, 1994.

[11] Horwitz, S., "Internet Etiquette Tips", `ftp://ftp.temple.edu/pub/info/help-net/netiquette.infohn`

[12] Internet Activities Board, "Ethics and the Internet", RFC 1087, IAB, January 1989. `ftp://ds.internic.net/rfc/rfc1087.txt`

[13] Kehoe, B., *Zen and the Art of the Internet: A Beginner's Guide*, Netiquette information is spread through the chapters of this work. 3rd ed. Englewood Cliffs, NJ., Prentice-Hall, 1994.

[14] Kochmer, J., *Internet Passport: NorthWestNet's Guide to our World Online*, 4th ed. Bellevue, Wash., NorthWestNet, Northwest Academic Computing Consortium, 1993

[15] Krol, Ed, *The Whole Internet: User's Guide and Catalog*, Sebastopol, CA, O'Reilly & Associates

[16] Lane, E. and C. Summerhill, *Internet Primer for Information Professionals: A Basic Guide to Internet Networking Technology*, Westport, CT, Meckler, 1993.

[17] LaQuey, T., and J. Ryer, *The Internet Companion*, Chapter 3 "Communicating with People", pp 41-74. Reading, MA, Addison-Wesley, 1993.

[18] Mandel, T., "Surfing the Wild Internet", SRI International Business Intelligence Program, Scan No. 2109. March, 1993. `gopher://gopher.well.sf.ca.us:70/00/Communications/surf-wild`

[19] Martin, J., "There's Gold in them thar Networks! or Searching for Treasure in all the Wrong Places", FYI 10, RFC 1402, January 1993. `ftp://ds.internic.net/rfc/rfc1402.txt`

[20] Pioch, N., "A Short IRC Primer", Text conversion by Owe Rasmussen. Edition 1.1b, February 28, 1993. `http://www.kei.com/irc/IRCprimer1.1.txt`

[21] Polly, J., "Surfing the Internet: an Introduction", Version 2.0.3. Revised May 15, 1993. `ftp://ftp.nysernet.org/pub/resources/guides/surfing.2.0.3.txt`

[22] "A Primer on How to Work With the Usenet Community" Original author: `chuq@apple.com` (Chuq Von Rospach) Maintained

by: netannounce@deshaw.com (Mark Moraes) Archive-name: usenet-primer/part1

[23] Rinaldi, A., "The Net: User Guidelines and Netiquette", September 3, 1992. http://www.fau.edu/rinaldi/net/index.htm

[24] "Rules for posting to Usenet" Original author: spaf@cs.purdue.edu (Gene Spafford) Maintained by: netannounce@deshaw.com (Mark Moraes) Archive-name: posting-rules/part1

[25] Shea, V., *Netiquette*, San Francisco: Albion Books, 1994(?)

[26] Strangelove, M., with A. Bosley, "How to Advertise on the Internet", ISSN 1201-0758.

[27] Tenant, R., "Internet Basics", ERIC Clearinghouse of Information Resources, EDO-IR-92-7. September, 1992. gopher://nic.merit.edu:7043/00/introducing.the.internet/internet.basics.eric-digest; gopher://vega.lib.ncsu.edu:70/00/library/reference/guides/tennet

[28] Wiggins, R., *The Internet for Everyone: a Guide for Users and Providers*, New York, McGraw-Hill, 1995.

6.0 Security Considerations

Security issues are not discussed in this memo.

7.0 Author's Address

Sally Hambridge

Intel Corporation

2880 Northwestern Parkway SC3-15

Santa Clara, CA 95052

Phone: 408-765-2931

Fax: 408-765-3679

E-Mail: sallyh@ludwig.sc.intel.com

General Hints for the New Online User

by Hilarie Gardner

The benefits of being online far outweigh the risks, but being aware of the risks, the tools, and the support available better prepares the newcomer for the adventure.

Understand the Impediments to Perceived Safety

1. That system footprints or tracks may be read to see:
   - ► when and where your logins occurred
   - ► when and what commands you've executed
   - ► even information deleted that may be retrieved from backups

2. That your account is only as secure as its password.

3. That sysops or root-holders (those with unlimited system permission):
   - ► may read mail, files or directories without leaving footprints
   - ► may undelete files you've erased
   - ► may release your files, etc., under warrant

4. That default file protection may not be secure for newly created files.

5. That mail:
   - ► may be compromised by each forwarding site
   - ► if it bounces may appear in entirety to the postmaster
   - ► is owned by *both* the sender and the receiver

6. That identifying biographies may be system-searched or remotely fingered.

7. That other users' identities:
   - ► may not be what they appear.
   - ► may be falsely registered.
   - ► may have had their own account compromised.

Be Aware of the Social Dangers Possible Online

▶ Harassment, or frequent or unsolicited messages from another user, occasionally sent randomly to women's IDs.

▶ Stalking, or being watched or followed online, occasionally coupled with physical confrontation.

▶ Flaming, or emotional verbal attacks.

▶ Addiction, or the need for support/feedback available online outweighing a reasonable budget of time or money.

Know How to Protect Yourself (Privacy Begins at Home)

1. Protect your password:

   ▶ Choose a strong password (a combination of upper- and lowercase characters, and not a name or a dictionary word).

   ▶ Do not leave your terminal logged in unattended.

   ▶ Do not let anyone watch you log in.

   ▶ Log out cleanly.

2. Protect your files:

   ▶ Know the default (permissions) for newly created files.

   ▶ Occasionally monitor your files.

3. Protect your information:

   ▶ Never send compromising information (your phone number, password, address, or vacation dates) by *chat, sends, mail,* or in your *bio.*

   ▶ See if encryption is available, if necessary.

See What Education/Communication Means are Available

▶ Join a support group like the Santa Monica PEN's PEN Femmes, or the online groups BAWiT or SYSTERS.

▶ Attend seminars, classes, or study groups.

▶ Make use of private, special interest forums online.

▶ Use peer pressure in public online to settle disputes.

▶ Answer harassment and inappropriate behavior directly and unambiguously, and then post for comment and discussion.

▶ Advocate for grievance procedures, tolerance guidelines and the discouragement of false or anonymous user registrations.

▶ Do not submit to unreasonable pressure.

▶ Speak up for what you want.

Please distribute this advice wherever appropriate, and please contact me with any questions, comments, or suggestions.

Appendix C
Internet Protocols for Business Users

by Daniel P. Dern

Copyright © 1994 Daniel P. Dern

From "The Internet Business Handbook," ed/auth. Daniel P. Dern, Prentice-Hall, 1996, by permission of the author.

THIS appendix summarizes major Internet protocol standards related to networking, applications, and use of Internet facilities, which any organization making use of the Internet should be aware of.

(Note: This material was reviewed by members of the Internet Engineering Steering Group—and many Internet developers helped suggest/cull what information belonged in a summary such as this—but there is no guarantee as to the accuracy or currency of the information in this document.)

How much of this do you need to know? Answer: The degree of in-depth familiarity you will need depends on the nature of your activities and the manner in which your organization provisions its Internet service.

In many cases, you will only need to know enough to be able to recognize key terms and numbers for purposes of discussion, such as referencing a standard as a selection criterion, e.g., "Does your e-mail gateway support RFC 822 format?"

Naming and IDs for Internet Standards

Most Internet efforts are defined in documents called RFCs (Requests for Comments). RFCs are created by members of the Internet community—developers, users, etc. The nature of RFCs ranges widely, from protocol definitions through informational documents, glossaries, history, and humor.

RFCs are identified by a number, e.g., RFC 1541, and a text name, e.g., Dynamic Host Configuration Protocol.

Standards-related RFCs also have an STD number, e.g. STD 01; introductory overview RFCs also have FYI numbers, e.g., FYI 01. STD numbers don't change, but the RFC associated with it may; this ensures that the STD always refers to the most recent RFC.

Bear in mind that not all RFCs are "standards track"—if the RFC a vendor claims to follow is Informational, for example, it doesn't mean any other vendors will also follow it.

The State or Status of a standards-track RFC is either Proposed, Draft, or Internet Standard (Full). Each standard also has a Primary Relevant Documents section. "Internet-drafts" reflect in-progress activity by Internet Engineering Task Force groups and individuals; as such, they are subject to change or deletion and therefore are not for longer-term citation.

To Get Current Status and More Info about RFCs

You can get a current "snapshot" of what's happening by retrieving and reading STD 1, "Internet Official Protocol standards." STD 1 is a quarterly updated RFC index containing citations for all RFCs, including Status; more information can be found in the similarly updated "Standards Track RFCs Eligible for Advancement," "IAB Standards Index," and "IESG Protocol Tracking Report" documents.

For more information on RFCs, see RFC 1310 "The Internet Standards Process"; also see draft-iab-standards-processv2-02.txt in the Internet Drafts directory of ds.internet.net and other Internet document repositories. For more information on the IETF, see FYI 17, "The Tao of the IETF: A Guide for New Attendees of the IETF" and FYI 18, "Internet Users' Glossary." (It's worth reading FYI 17 in any case.)

In any case, your best source of up-to-date information about these Internet standards, the standards themselves, and RFCs in general, is via the Internet itself (e-mail, anonymous-FTP, Gopher, World Wide Web), hard copy, and CD-ROM.

RFCs

Network, Transport, and Routing

NAME: TCP/IP

Brief Description: The Transmission Control Protocol/Internetworking Protocol (TCP/IP) suite is the general protocol suite of the Internet, encompassing protocols for network activities such as datagram delivery and acknowledgment, and protocols for user activity such as remote login (Telnet) and file transfer (FTP). A given implementation of TCP/IP typically contains a dozen or more protocols and facilities essential to the use of TCP/IP applications in a TCP/IP environment.

Status: Full.

Primary Relevant Documents: The Host Requirements Specifications Documents, RFC 1122 (Communications) and 1123 (Applications). These documents are intended to serve as the official specification for users and vendors of how TCP/IP protocol specs are to be applied in computers used on the Internet, to help ensure that they do the proper tasks and interoperate (work with each other).

The book *TCP/IP* by Douglas Comer is considered a definitive technical text on TCP/IP.

Name: IP (Internetworking Protocol)

Brief description: The network layer protocol of TCP/IP, IP provides the functions needed "to deliver a 'package of bits' (Internet datagram) from source to destination over an interconnected system of networks" (e.g., the Internet).

Status: Full.

Primary relevant document(s): RFC 791 "Internet Protocol"; also see RFCs 919, 922, 950, 1122

NAME: TCP (Transmission Control Protocol)

Brief Description: One of the Internet's two predominant transport layer protocols, TCP provides a reliable connection-oriented, byte stream service.

Status: Full.

Primary Relevant Document(s): RFC 793; also RFCs 1122, 1323

NAME: User Datagram Protocol (UDP)

Brief Description: A simple, datagram-oriented transport layer protocol—sends and receives datagrams for Internet applications; service is defined as "unreliable."

Status: Full.

Primary Relevant Documents: RFC 768, 1122

NAME: Internet Control Message Protocol (ICMP)

Brief Description: ICMP is used by the IP layer in hosts and routers (and by applications such as ping) to exchange error messages and other information.

Status: Full.

Primary Relevant Document(s): RFC 792, 1122

NAME: Internet Group Multicast Protocol (IGMP)

Brief Description: Host functions for multicasting applications such as audio, video and shared-document real-time teleconferencing over the Internet and other IP environments; also involves the Real Time Protocol (RTP).

Application and other related protocols under development include the Internet Whiteboard (W), Visual Audio Tool (VAT), Network Video (NV), Resource Reservation Setup Protocol (RSVP), Multimedia Multiparty Session Control (MMUSI), and INRIA Videoconferencing System (IVS).

Primary Relevant Document(s): RFC 1112.

NAMES: RIP, OSPF, IS-IS, BGP Network Routing Protocols

Brief Description: There are a variety of routing protocols and schemes in use within the Internet today, notably RIP (Routing Information Protocol), OSPF (the Open Shortest-Path First protocol for TCP/IP), IS-IS (Intermediate System to Intermediate System),

Appendix C

and BGP (Border Gateway Protocol) for use between separate Autonomous Systems.

Having some understanding of the Internet's decentralized routing environment is essential, especially if you're coming from a traditional point-to-point private-line network, or going to a frame-relay backbone.

Protocol	Status
RIP v1	FULL
RIP v2	PROPOSED
OSPF	Version 1 FULL, Version 2 Draft
BGP version 3	Draft
BGP version 4	Submitted for Proposal

Primary Relevant Document(s):

Protocol	Document
RIP	RFC 1058, 1388
OSPF	RFC 1248, 1249, 1349
Dual IS-IS	1195
BGP3	RFC 1267
BGP4	RFC 1467

NAME: PPP, SLIP Serial Line Protocols

Brief Description: Serial line protocols provide packetizing services, to enable network communication over phone lines (versus LANs, etc. The Point-to-Point Protocol (PPP) and its predecessor Serial Line Internetworking Protocol (SLIP) are used by routers to communicate over telephone lines; PPP (and SLIP) enable a user's personal computer to establish a network connection (multiple sessions, running TCP/IP applications) over a phone line, versus asynchronous terminal emulation. There are also serial protocols to support X Windows over serial lines.

Protocol	Status
PPP	FULL
SLIP	FULL

Primary Relevant Document(s):

Protocol	Document
PPP	RFC 1570, 1331, 1332
SLIP	RFC 1055

Network Management

NAME: Simple Network Management Protocol (SNMP)

Brief Description: The SNMP provides a framework for monitoring and control of network and computing devices over a TCP/IP network, including of non-TCP/IP devices.

Protocol	Status
SNMP version 1	FULL
SNMP version 2	Proposed/In process

Primary Relevant Document(s): RFC 1098, 1157

Network Services

NAME: Domain Name System (DNS)

Brief Description: DNS provides a way to map an Internet-wide structure of unique alphanumeric names (e.g., is.internic.net) for computer hosts against TCP/IP numeric host addresses and the methods by which these "names" can be managed and mapped to identifiers.

Status: Full.

Primary Relevant Document(s): RFC 1034, 1035, 1123

NAME: Network Time Protocol (NTP)

Brief Description: NTP provides a way to define time within the Internet's distributed environment, for time-stamping, synchronizing and sequencing events.

Status: Full

Primary Relevant Document(s): RFC 1119

Electronic Mail

NAME: RFC 822 MAIL

Brief Description: The format of Internet electronic mail message headers and content is defined by RFC 822; if your site's e-mail systems or gateways can't "speak RFC 822" you won't be able to swap Internet e-mail. RFC-compliant mail systems and/or gateways are available for most leading environments. Be sure they work reliably.

Status: Full.

Primary Document(s): RFC 822

NAME: Multipurpose Internet Mail Extensions (MIME)

Brief Description: The MIME standard specifies extensions to RFC 822 message body formats to include "multimedia" and other binary data—such as word processing documents, PostScript, graphic, binary files, video, fax, and voice messages—as attachments to Internet e-mail messages. MIME also specifies how to encode binary data into 7-bit form using ASCII characters, and convert it back at the other end. MIME avoids the problems traditionally associated with e-mail "protocol converter" gateways such as loss of data; MIME is being used for multimedia mail and EDI applications.

The HARPOON extension (Proposed Status) uses MIME to provide interworking between the 1984 and 1988 X.400 specifications, enabling 1988 X.400 body parts that can't be represented in 1984 X.400 to be encapsulated as MIME objects, which can then be received by 1984 X.400 systems.

Status: Draft.

Primary Relevant Document(s):

Protocol	Document
MIME	RFC 1563; also 1522, 1521
HARPOON	RFC 1494, 1495, 1496 (Status: Proposed)

NAME(S): Simple Mail Transfer Protocol (SMTP)

Brief Description: SMTP defines how systems will exchange RFC 822-formatted messages over IP.

Status: Full

Primary Relevant Document(s):

Protocol	Document
SMTP	RFC 821, 1425
Message formats	RFC 822
X.400/SMTP Gateway Tutorial	RFC 1506
Gatewaying between RFC822 and X.400(88)	RFC 1327 (Status: Proposed Standard), 1506 (Tutorial on RFC 1327)

NAME: Post Office Protocol(s) Versions 2 and 3

Brief Description: The Post Office Protocols (POP2, POP3) define how systems may act as "post offices" for users' messages, queuing them until the user retrieves them with a client program (e.g., Eudora, ZMail), and letting the POP2/POP3 mail client upload messages for delivery.

Status: POP3, Draft.

Primary Relevant Document(s): RFC1460.

NAME: Interactive Mail Access Protocol (IMAP)

Brief Description: IMAP will let PC users browse and read their e-mail on remote mail servers without, unlike POP2/POP3, having to transfer and be responsible for storage of read/stored messages.

Status: Experimental.

Primary Relevant Document(s): RFC 1176

Usenet News, a.k.a. "NetNews"

NAME: Network News Transport Protocol (NNTP)

Brief Description: NNTP defines how Usenet News articles are propagated across the Internet (i.e., over IP connections) and over dial-up UUCP connections. The Usenet currently comprises over 7000 newsgroups with daily traffic averaging 100 Mbytes (however, business sites may not need to receive more than a fraction of the "full feed").

Status: Full.

Primary Relevant Document(s): RFC 977

Appendix C

Tools

NAME: Telnet (Remote Login) Protocol

Brief Description: The Telnet protocol defines how remote-login terminal-emulation sessions may be established between IP hosts. Protocols supporting 3270 emulation are also available.

Status: Full.

Primary Relevant Document(s): RFCs 854, 855, 1123

NAME: File Transfer Protocol (FTP)

Brief Description: The File Transfer Protocol (implemented as the File Transfer Program, also known as FTP) defines how IP-connected hosts may transfer ASCII and BINARY files and perform related activities (e.g., obtaining directory listings). "Anonymous-FTP" is a mechanism to provide shareable-access to files, e.g., group projects, publicly-accessible archives.

Status: Full.

Primary Relevant Document(s): RFC 959

NAME: Finger, WHOIS

Brief Description: The Finger and WHOIS protocols support local and remote look-up of user-related information which may include data in user-created files (.signature, .plan, .project) and system information about the user.

Status: Draft

Primary Relevant Document: Finger: RFC 1288

NAME: Gopher, World Wide Web, WAIS, Archie, etc.

Brief Description: These (and other) Network Information Discovery Resource (NIDR) tools provide a variety of indexing, searching, browsing, access and retrieval facilities for Internet-based ASCII and multimedia information, and other resources and services. They have become de facto standard protocols and tools for Internet navigation and information-mounting, but are not, as yet, standards themselves.

Status: Widely deployed—millions and millions served!

Primary Relevant Document(s): FAQs and related documents.

NAME: MOSAIC, CELLO, LYNX, TurboGopher, etc.

Brief Description: These and other "Internet front ends" help provide single-program point-and-click access to Internet resources and services. ASCII and color bitmapped GUI clients are available for popular user computing platforms. (Dial-up users may find transfer rates useful only for ASCII text.)

Status: Widely deployed.

Primary Relevant Document(s): FAQs and other documents.

NAME: Universal Resource Names (URNs)

Brief Description: URNs arc location-independent "persistent" names for resources on the Internet; just as, say, domain names provide a stable ID for objects whose numeric IP address may change, URNs will provide stable pointers to files, archives and other Internet information resources.

Status: Under development.

Security

NAME: Privacy Enhanced Mail (PEM)

Brief Description: PEM offers author/message authentication and privacy for end-to-end transmission of electronic mail, by using a combination of RSA public-key and DES private key encryption technologies.

Status: Proposed standard

Primary Relevant Document(s): RFCs 1319, 1321, 1421-1424. For more on Internet security, see the Site Security Handbook (RFC 1244) and the various books on the subject.

For More Information

For additional information regarding RFCs and Internet standards, read the following documents:

Request for Comments on Request for Comments [RFC 1111]

On FYI: Introduction to the FYI notes [RFC 1150]

Introduction to the STD Notes [RFC 1311]

Guidelines to Authors of Internet Drafts [GAID]

The Internet Activities Board [RFC 1160]

The Internet Standards Process [RFC 1310]

IAB Official Protocol Standards [STD1]

To Obtain Copies

To obtain copies of RFCs, Internet-Drafts and other Internet standard information, you can use any of the following methods.

Online via the Internet

1. Via e-mail, send a message to any of the following

    ```
    info@internic.net
    mailserv@ds.internic.net
    rfc-info@isi.edu
    ```

    with these lines in the message body:

    ```
    help: help
    help: manual
    help: ways_to_get_rfcs
    ```

2. Via Gopher or anonymous FTP to:

    ```
    ds.internic.net
    isoc.org
    nic.near.net
    ```

    (or do a VERONICA/archie search for "RFCs").

CD-ROM

Collections of RFCs are available from several CD-ROM publishers, including:

Walnut Creek CD-ROM

SRI International

Appendix D

K-12 Internetworking Guidelines

THIS excellent guide to K-12 Internet connections is an informational memo (RFC 1709) from the Network Working Group of the Internet Engineering Task Force. We include it here as a more technical supplement to Chapter 18's discussion of K-12 educational uses of the Internet.

Network Working Group
Request for Comments: 1709
FYI: 26
Category: Informational
November 1994

J. Gargano
University of California, Davis

D. Wasley
University of California, Berkeley

Status of this Memo

I. Introduction

Many organizations concerned with K-12 educational issues and the planning for the use of technology recognize the value of data communications throughout the educational system. State-sponsored documents such as the California Department of Education's "Strategic Plan for Information Technology" recommend the planning of voice, video, and data networks to support learning and educational administration, but they do not provide specific technical direction. The institutions that built the Internet and connected early in its development are early adopters of technology, with technical staff dedicated to the planning for and implementation of leading edge technology. The K-12 community traditionally has not had this level of staffing available for telecommunications planning. This document is intended to bridge that gap and provides a recommended technical direction, an introduction to the role the Internet now plays in K-12 education and technical guidelines for building a campus data communications infrastructure that provides internetworking services and connections to the Internet.

For a more general introduction to the Internet and its applications and uses, the reader is referred to any of the references listed in the following RFCs:

1392 "Internet Users' Glossary" (also FYI 18)

1432 "Recent Internet Books"

1462 "What is the Internet" (also FYI 20)

1463 "Introducing the Internet - A Short Bibliography of Introductory Internetworking on Readings for the Network Novice" (also FYI 19)

II. Rationale for the Use of Internet Protocols

In 1993, the Bank Street College of Education conducted a survey of 550 educators who are actively involved in using telecommunications. (Honey, Margaret, Henriquez, Andres, "Telecommunications and K–12 Educators: Findings from a National Survey," Bank Street

College of Education, New York, NY, 1993.) The survey looked at a wide variety of ways telecommunications technology is used in K-12 education. Their findings on Internet usage are summarized below.

"Slightly less than half of these educators have access to the Internet, which is supplied most frequently by a university computer or educational service."

"Internet services are used almost twice as often for professional activities as for student learning activities."

"Sending e-mail is the most common use of the Internet, followed by accessing news and bulletin boards and gaining access to remote computers."

The following chart shows the percentage of respondents that use each network application to support professional and student activities.

Applications	Professional Activities	Student Activities
Electronic mail	91	79
News or bulletin board	63	50
Remote access to other computers	48	32
Database access	36	31
File transfer	34	19

The value of the Internet and its explosive growth are a direct result of the computer communications technology used on the network. The same network design principals and computer communications protocols (TCP/IP) used on the Internet can be used within a school district to build campus-wide networks. This is standard practice within higher education, and increasingly in K-12 schools as well. The benefits of the TCP/IP protocols are listed below.

Ubiquity

TCP/IP is available on most, if not all, of the computing platforms likely to be important for instructional or administrative purposes. TCP/IP is available for the IBM compatible personal computers (PCs) running DOS or Windows and all versions of the Apple Macintosh. TCP/IP is standard on all UNIX-based systems and workstations and most mainframe computers.

Applications

TCP/IP supports many applications including, but not limited to, electronic mail, file transfer, interactive remote host access, database access, file sharing and access to networked information resources. Programming and development expertise is available from a wide variety of sources.

Flexibility

TCP/IP is flexible, and new data transport requirements can be incorporated easily. It can accommodate educational and administrative applications equally well so that one set of network cabling and one communications system may be used in both the classroom and the office.

Simplicity

TCP/IP is simple enough to run on low-end computing platforms such as the Apple Macintosh and PCs while still providing efficient support for large minicomputer and mainframe computing platforms. TCP/IP benefits from over twenty years of refinement that has resulted in a large and technically sophisticated environment.

Capacity

TCP/IP supports local area network and wide area network services within the entire range of network data rates available today, from dial-up modem speeds to gigabit speed experimental networks. Communications can occur reliably among machines across this entire range of speeds.

Coexistence

TCP/IP can coexist successfully with other networking architectures. It is likely that offices and classrooms that already have networks may be using something other than TCP/IP. Networks of Apple Macintosh computers will probably be using AppleTalk; networks of PCs may be using any of the common network operating systems such as Novell NetWare or LANManager. Mainframe computers may be using IBM's System Network Architecture (SNA). None of these proprietary protocols provides broad connectivity on a global scale. Recognizing this, network technology vendors now provide many means for building networks in which all of these protocols can coexist.

Multimedia

TCP/IP networks can support voice, graphics, and video as part of teleconferencing and multimedia applications.

Compatibility

All of the major universities, as well as thousands of commercial and governmental organizations use TCP/IP for their primary communications services. Commercial networks such as CompuServe and America Online are also connected to the Internet. Many State Departments of Education have sponsored statewide initiatives to connect schools to the Internet and many K-12 school districts have connected based upon local needs.

NREN

The High Performance Computing Act of 1991 and the Information Infrastructure and Technology Act of 1992 provide the foundation for building the national telecommunications infrastructure in support of education and research. The National Research and Education Network (NREN) will be based upon Internet technology.

The benefits of internetworking technology have been demonstrated through twenty years of use by thousands of organizations. This same experience also provides tested technical models for network design that can be adapted to K-12 campus-wide networking in schools of all sizes and technical development.

III. A Technical Model for School Networks

The vision of a modern communications network serving all primary and secondary schools has been articulated and discussed in many forums. Many schools and a few school districts have implemented ad hoc network systems in response to their own perception of the importance of this resource. This section of the Internet School Networking (ISN) Working Group RFC presents a standard network implementation model to assist county offices of education and school districts in their planning so that all such implementations will be compatible with each other and with national networking plans intended to enrich K-12 education.

The future goal of "an integrated voice, data, and video network extending to every classroom" is exciting, but so far from what exists today that the investment in time and dollars required to realize such a goal will be greater than most districts can muster in the near term. We suggest that a great deal can be done immediately, with relatively few dollars, to provide modern communications systems in and between all schools around the nation. Our present goal is to define a highly functional, homogeneous, and well-supported network system that could interconnect all K-12 schools and district, county, and statewide offices and that will enable teachers and administrators to begin to use new communications tools and network-based information resources. It takes considerable time to adapt curricula and other programs to take full advantage of new technology. Through the use of standard models for implementation of current network technologies, schools can begin this process now. Many states have already developed communications services for their schools.

A notable example is Texas, which provides terminal access to central information resources from every classroom over a statewide network. Modem-accessible systems are available in many states that serve to encourage teachers to become familiar with network resources and capabilities. Although modem-access may be the only practical option today in some areas, it always will be limited in functionality and/or capacity. In anticipation of emerging and future bandwidth intensive information resource applications and the functionality that they will require, we believe it is essential to provide direct network access to the National Research and Education Network (NREN) Internet from computers in every classroom.

Appendix D

the planning of a school network implementation. The strategic decision to use Internet protocols in developing school networks provides the opportunity to avoid the major expense of building new statewide backbone infrastructures in the near term. Interconnection of schools, districts, county offices of education and the State Department of Education can be accomplished by acquiring Internet connection service from any of the existing Internet service providers in the state. (*Connecting to the Internet*, Susan Estrada, O'Reilly & Associates, Inc. (ISBN 1-56592-061-9) lists Internet service providers in California and the nation.) It is critical that Internet connection service meet criteria for reliability and capacity, but connection to any Internet service provider will provide communication capability to all other Internet subscribers within the state, the nation, and the world. Internet technology is designed to allow very flexible intersite topologies, but a hierarchical topology is the simplest to engineer. Generally this will mean hierarchical connection of school facilities to district offices, in many cases further aggregated at county offices, and finally a link to an Internet service provider.

Coordination of circuit services and a single point of connection to an Internet service provider serves both to minimize overall costs and increase opportunities to make use of newer technologies. The basic school network implementation model is quite simple: create a local area network (LAN) within each school building or cluster of buildings, provide at least one network server for that LAN, interconnect that LAN with the local school district offices where a similar LAN should be installed and where centrally managed information resources should exist, and connect the district offices to the nearest Internet service provider, possibly through the county office of education. Primary technical support for network monitoring and problem resolution, and for managing network resource servers should come from the district or county offices initially to avoid unnecessary duplication at the local level. As expertise is developed at the local level, more of the responsibility for daily operation and problem resolution can be assumed by individual schools. It is impossible to cover all conceivable scenarios for implementation of this model in specific schools. However, it is possible to state general principles that should be followed in designing school network implementations. The discussion below is organized into sections corresponding to the basic model summarized in the previous paragraph. It includes a description of the general principles that are important to each level of the implementation.

Step 1: School Local Area Network Implementation

A "school" is used here to mean a building or cluster of buildings that are managed as a unit and typically are on contiguous, district-owned property. Implementation of a LAN in this setting will involve installation of a cabling system to distribute the network throughout the structure(s), installation of premise wiring to support connections of computers and terminals to the network distribution system, installation of one or more network server machines in a central location (other protocols, such as AppleTalk or Novell's IPX, may be supported on a school's local area network (LAN) as needed for local function such as printer sharing or local resource servers), and provision of a network router and telecommunications circuit or radio link to connect that school to the district offices. The most common LAN technologies in use today are Ethernet and LocalTalk. (IEEE 802.5 Token Ring is not recommended for new installations. It is more expensive and it is not available for as wide a range of computers.) Both are quite inexpensive and easy to install and maintain. Ethernet is adaptable to most modern computers and is built-in to high performance workstations such as Sun, Hewlett-Packard, SGI, or Digital Equipment Corporation computers. LocalTalk is built-in to all Macintosh computers and is adaptable to DOS PC computers as well. Ethernet is roughly 20 to 40 times faster than LocalTalk. Therefore Ethernet is recommended for all computer connections, when possible, and for the school LAN "backbone" or network distribution system.

1.1 Network Adapters and Software

Individual computers will require network or communications adapters and appropriate software. Table D.1 gives basic recommendations for the computers most commonly found in schools. Basic communications software is available in the public domain for many personal computers at no cost. More sophisticated software is being developed by a number of vendors for applications such as electronic mail, distance learning, and multimedia database access. For example, the California Technology Project is developing very easy to use software for Macintosh and DOS or Windows PC computers that will enable access to a wide variety of information resources and services. Schools should look at all the available software and base choices on required functionality and support costs as well as acquisition costs. In locations where computers will be purchased, the choice of computer type should be driven by the availability of software for the particular application(s) to be supported. Almost all modern computers can be attached to the type of network described in this document.

Equipment Type	Network Adapter	Communication Software
Simple terminal	"Network Access Server" located centrally	Built-in to the network access server.
Apple II, Amiga, Tandy, Commodore, older IBM PCs, etc.	Serial asynchronous port that will allow connection to the above.	Serial communications software that emulates a simple terminal
Newer IBM PC	Ethernet adapter card with "10-base-T" port. "Thin-net" port may be used in lab clusters.	TCP/IP "TSR" software, for example "FTP Software" package. Additional software for special applications.
Older Apple Macintosh computers	PhoneNet adapter (external) and shared LocalTalk to Ethernet router, for example the Shiva FastPath.	MacTCP or equivalent plus Telnet and FTP. For example, NCSA Telnet. Additional software for special applications, e.g., "electronic mail client."
Newer Apple Macintosh computers	May use same as the above. For higher performance, use an Ethernet adapter card with "10-base-T" port. "Thin-net" port may be used in lab clusters.	Same as the above.
UNIX workstations	Ethernet adapter card, if not already built in.	Typically comes with the basic system. Additional software may be needed for special applications.

Table D.1. **Network Adapters and Software for Typical Computers**

1.2 Premise Wiring

A major component of the implementation will be installation of cabling to connect individual computers or clusters of computers to the LAN. The recommended topology is a "star" where each computer is wired directly to a "hub site" within the building as shown in Figures D.1 and D.2. A cluster of computers, typically found in a teaching lab or library, may be interconnected within the room where they are installed, and the cluster connected to the hub site with a single cable as shown in Figures D.3 and D.4.

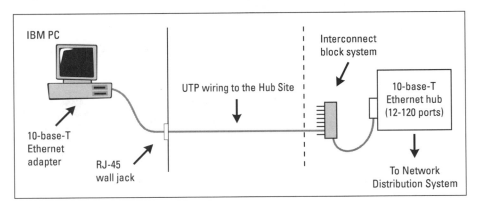

Figure D.1. **Individual Ethernet connection to the network.**

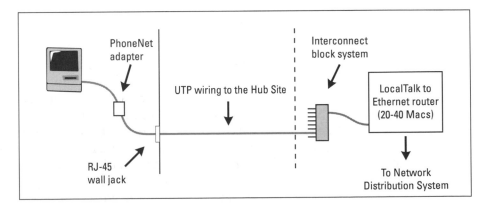

Figure D.2. **LocalTalk connection to the network.**

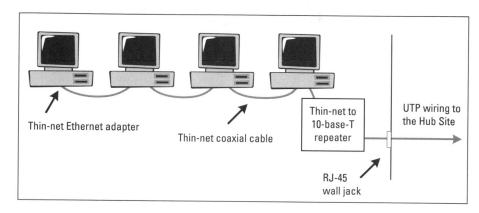

Figure D.3.   *A cluster of computers connected to the network.*

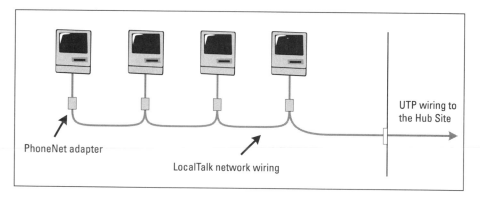

Figure D. 4.   *A Macintosh cluster connection to the network.*

The recommended premise wiring is "unshielded twisted pair" (UTP) wire that meets the Electronic Industries Association (EIA) category 5 standards for high-speed data communication service. (See EIA/TIA-568 "Commercial Building Telecommunications Wiring Standard.") While 2-pair cable may be adequate for most purposes, industry standards recommend installation of 4-pair cable. The difference in cost is minimal, so we recommend installation of the latter. One end of each cable terminates in a category 5 RJ-45 jack located near the computer. (A standard RJ-45 jack can be used for Ethernet or lower speeds if initial cost is a major factor. Such jacks can be replaced with category 5 versions later as needed.) The other end terminates on a standard "110 distribution block" at the hub site utility closet. (In older sites, M66 distribution blocks may already be installed. These can be used for the time being but will not support newer, higher-speed technologies.)

A labeling scheme must be chosen and strictly adhered to so that cables can be identified at both ends later, as needed.

In most cases, the hub site utility closet will be shared with telephone services. It is essential that a separate wall area be set aside within the closet for data service interconnections. Typically there will be a "field" of interconnect blocks for termination of all premise wires, another field for termination of trunk cables (used for low-speed data terminals), and a third field for hub equipment ports. Interconnections between premise wiring blocks and hub or trunk blocks are installed as needed in order to provide the appropriate service to each location where communication service is required.

Installation of wiring in a building typically is performed by a qualified data wiring contractor. This is a critical aspect of the program and must be planned and installed professionally with both current and future requirements in mind. (See "Virtual Schoolhouse—A Report to the Legislature on Distribution Infrastructures for Advanced Technologies in the Construction of New Schools, K through 12," Department of General Services, State of California, February, 1993, for example conduit and utility closet plans.)

To be prepared for future distribution of video signals, school network planners should consider installation of RG-59 coaxial cable to those locations where video may be required at the same time that the UTP premise wiring is being installed. The coaxial cable would terminate on a wall-plate mounted "F" connector in the classroom, and would be left unterminated in the utility closet. Future technologies may support video signals over other media so the installation of RG-59 cable should be limited to near-term potential requirements. It will be cost effective to install premise wiring to as many locations as might ever serve a computer. This will include administrative offices as well as classrooms, laboratories as well as libraries. In high-density locations such as offices, consideration should be given to installation of two UTP cables to each outlet location in order to provide the potential for several computers or workstations. Terminating both cables on the same wall plate will add little to the overall wiring project costs and will add greatly to the flexibility of the system. Premise wiring that is not to be used initially will not be connected to any electronics in the hub site. Hub sites should be utility closets or other protected, non-occupied areas. Hub sites can be created by construction of small closets or cabinets in low-use areas. A hub site must be located within 300 feet of any connection. Typically, multiple hub sites are required in large or multi-story buildings.

1.3 Network Distribution System

All hub sites within a school must be interconnected to complete the school LAN. The design of this network distribution system will depend greatly on the physical layout of the school buildings. We assume that Ethernet technology will be used since higher speed technology is still quite expensive.

If all hub sites are within 300 cable feet of a central location, then 10-base-T wiring can be used from a central hub to connect each hub site, as shown in Figure D.5. If longer distances are required, either thin-net or standard thick Ethernet can be used. Fiber optic cable can be used if distance requires it and funding permits. (If fiber optic cable is installed, consideration should be given to including both multimode fiber for current and future data requirements and single mode fiber for video and future very high speed data systems.) Specific design of the "backbone" network distribution system will depend on the layout of the buildings to be served. With proper design as many as 250 computers can be connected to a single Ethernet segment. Most often the practical maximum number will be much lower than this due to the amount of data sent onto the network by each computer. For planning purposes, one can assume 100–125 computers per segment. Beyond that size the network must be subdivided using "subnetworks." Design of a such a system is not difficult, but is beyond the scope of this document. The network distribution system cabling should include unshielded multi-pair trunk cabling as well as Ethernet trunk cabling. The multi-pair trunk cable will be needed to connect terminals or older computers emulating terminals to a central "network access server" (NAS). A typical NAS can serve from 8 to 128 such connections. It is most cost effective to provide one per LAN, if needed. The NAS connects directly to the Ethernet LAN.

1.4 Local Network Server

It is highly recommended that each school install a "network server" to support local storage of commonly used information, software, electronic mail, and other functions that may require high-speed communication to the users computer. Since the connection to the outside network will be much slower than the school LAN, it will be most efficient to access information locally. In particular, software that is to be shared among the schools computers must be stored locally since it would be very tedious to transfer it across the slower external link. The network server will be connected directly to the Ethernet network. The location of the server should be chosen carefully to ensure its protection from abuse and

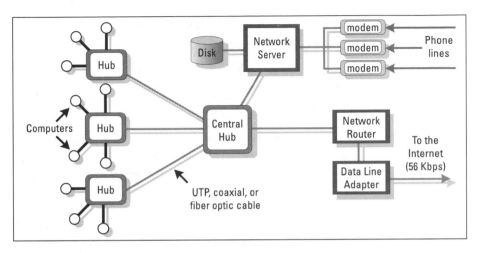

Figure D.5. *A complete small school LAN.*

environmental damage. Traditionally the school library is the focus of information gathering and storage activities, and many school libraries have clusters of computers or terminals already installed. The library would be a very logical place to locate the network server computer. The Network Router (see below) might also be located there if a suitable utility space is not available.

The network server will be a small but powerful computer with a large amount of disk storage capacity, typically 1-4 gigabytes. It will run software capable of supporting access by a large number of users simultaneously. It could also support dial-in access from teachers' or students' homes using standard inexpensive modems. (Access control with user authentication is essential if dial-in service is to be provided.) If more than a few modems are to be installed, an NAS might prove more cost effective. If dial-in access is to be provided to more than a few school sites within a district, a single central modem pool maintained at the district offices will be the most cost effective.

1.5 External Connection

A single communication circuit will connect the school LAN to the local school district offices. In the school, there will be a Network Router attached between the LAN and this circuit. On the LAN side, the connection will be a typical Ethernet cable. On the external side, the connection will depend on the type of communication circuit used, as discussed in step 2 below.

Step 2: Interconnection of Schools with District Offices

All schools within a district should be connected individually to the network router at the school district offices. This "star topology" will be much easier to manage, and the capacity of each school's connection can be increased appropriately as needs change. Several standard communication circuit services may be used to effect this connection. The least expensive for situations where only limited use is needed will be dial-up using high-speed modems. However, this type of connection is not recommended for serious usage because of its very limited capacity. Also, since most schools receive telephone service under business tariffs, usage will be measured and the cost will be dependent on how long the connection is maintained. This will be true in general for other "switched services" as well such as "switched-56" and ISDN. Dedicated (permanently installed) communications circuits are strongly recommended since they will allow unattended access to and from the school network at all hours. This will be particularly important if information files are to be downloaded during the night to local network servers or teachers and students are to access the schools information resources from home. Table D.2 shows the most common options for dedicated circuit services. Costs are indicated in relative terms since they vary greatly by location and as tariffs are modified. The exact costs must be determined by contacting local communications service providers. Total cost must take into account the equipment needed at each location as well.

Communications Options

Frame Relay communication services are becoming available in many areas. Frame Relay is a shared, packet-based data transport service. A school site would contract for Frame Relay service as part of a larger service group that includes the school district office and may include the Internet service provider. All members of that group would share the communications capacity. The advantage of this service is that only one end of the circuit needs to be ordered (each member orders a connection to the common service) and the capacity offered to each member can be upgraded independently. Also, in many areas the cost of Frame Relay service is not dependent on distance to the service provider, which will make service to rural schools much less expensive than equivalent services. Overall system costs will be minimized since

Type of Circuit	Data Rate	Relative cost
Voice grade leased telephone line	20 kilobits per sec (Kbps)	modest*
ADN-56	56 Kb/s	high
ISDN, where available	64 or 128 Kb/s	modest**
Low power radio	64 to 256 Kb/s	high startup cost
Frame Relay	56 Kb/s to 1.5 Mb/s	modest to high
DS1	1.5 megabits per sec	very high

* Measured service charges must be taken into account.

** At this time, most ISDN tariffs include message unit charges which can make the use of ISDN prohibitively expensive for full-time connectivity. [Author's note: ISDN tariffs vary widely across the U.S. Be sure to get cost quotes from at least two providers, if possible, for ISDN.]

Table D.2. **External connection Communication Options**

the central router at the district office will need fewer connections. If Frame Relay is chosen, the overall service group must be carefully engineered. For example, since all schools would share the connection to the district office (and possibly to the Internet service provider), that must be a high-capacity connection. For the initial design, the aggregate capacity of all school links should not exceed the capacity into the district office (or the Internet service provider) by more than a factor of 3 or there may be noticeable congestion and variability in response times across the system. There are many other factors that must be considered as well, such as the virtual connection topology and how best to connect to an Internet service provider. Therefore, it is recommended that an experienced network engineer be utilized to develop an operational plan for Frame Relay if it is chosen as the school interconnection service. Future options for interconnecting schools and district offices will include:

Community Access Television (CATV) cable systems offering either shared or dedicated bi-directional data communication services

Metropolitan area fiber optic communications service providers

Switched Multi-megabit Digital Service (SMDS) providing data transport service at speeds up to 34 megabits per second

Asynchronous Transfer Mode (ATM) connection services supporting voice, data, and video communications at speeds into the gigabit per second range

(Many more options will become available as new technologies come to market.) The costs for the last three options are unknown at this time, but may be generally higher than those indicated in Table D.2. The cost for the CATV option may be negotiable as part of the local CATV contract with the community. As demands for network speed develop due to heavy use of multimedia or other bandwidth-intensive applications, higher-speed communications circuits can replace the initial circuits with minimal change in the equipment or LAN. This gives great flexibility in tailoring service to funding levels and application needs.

Step 3: School District Office LAN and Support Systems

The School District offices should form the focal point for interconnection of all schools in the district. Within the District offices, network operations can be monitored and problem resolution managed. One or more network servers can provide essential network support as well as central archiving of common information and software. A critical role of the district office will be to manage Internet "Domain Name System" (DNS) (see STD 13, RFCs 1034, 1035 for the full explanation of DNS, and also, RFC 1480) service for the districts schools. DNS is required of all Internet networks. It defines the basic network-level identity of each computer, workstation, server, and active network component. This function is described more fully below under Network Management and Operational Monitoring. The district offices should be wired in a manner similar to a typical school, as shown above. This will allow teachers, superintendents, and principals to communicate and share information easily. In addition, an NAS connected to a central pool of modems could provide dial-in access to the district network.

Step 4: Interconnection of the School District with the Internet

Connection of the entire school district to the Internet will take place through the district office interconnect site, as shown in Figure D.6. This hierarchical model can be extended another level to interconnection of the school district offices through the county office of education facilities. Many administrative information resources could be located at the county level, and there might be cost savings if the entire county connects to an Internet service provider through a single point. The bandwidth required for this single connection, however, will be much greater than that required for each school district since traffic will be aggregated. This hierarchical topology also provides a logical model for network support and information resource management. The school district or county offices can provide continuous monitoring of the network and provide high level technical expertise for problem resolution, relieving the individual schools of this burden. Interactions with communications circuit providers and Internet service providers will be more effective if handled through a central "trouble desk."

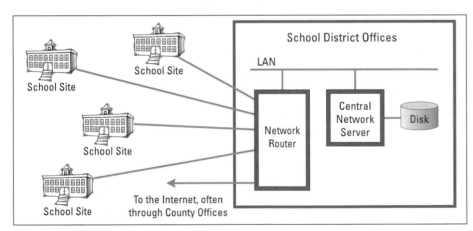

*Figure D.6. **Interconnection of schools to the Internet through local school district offices.***

Similarly, it is highly desirable that network users have a single, well known point of contact in case of problems or questions. Internet service should be acquired from the most cost-effective, reliable Internet service provider. Circuit services can be similar to those shown in Table D.2 above. The higher-speed services should be considered if traffic demands increase and funding permits. Circuit costs usually will be lowest when connecting to the provider with the nearest "point of presence" (POP), but newer technologies such as Frame Relay and SMDS make circuit costs less dependent on distance. (At this time, SMDS services are not widely available.) The Internet connection will require a high quality router that can be configured to interact correctly with the service providers routers. In most cases, this can be the same router used to support the local school connections.

Integration of Existing School Networks

Many schools have developed LAN systems in support of particular classroom activities or administrative functions. In some cases the technologies used are not those recommended for new installations. If these older LAN systems are capable of transporting Internet protocols they may be integrated into a new LAN system and replaced later as funding permits.

For example, IEEE 802.5 Token Ring is often used to interconnect DOS PC-type computers and IBM minicomputer servers. Token Ring networks can transport Internet protocols and software is available for DOS computers to support basic Internet functions. Many Internet routers support optional Token Ring adapters. This is the recommended way that existing Token Ring LANs can be integrated into a wider school LAN system in order to extend Internet information resources to those PC users.

Another example is a Novell Network system using Ethernet as a LAN. The Ethernet LAN, if implemented well, is perfectly capable of transporting Internet protocols as well as Novell protocols, simultaneously. Each PC or Macintosh can be given software that will allow both Novell and Internet services to be used as needed. This coexistence is important so that, for example, a person using a PC that depends on the Novell server for disk file space can transfer a large file from a remote Internet server to the PC's pseudo-disk. It also permits each user to run client software such as Eudora (electronic mail), Gopher (information services), and Mosaic (World Wide Web information services), which require direct Internet access. To integrate the Novell Ethernet LAN into the wider school LAN system, a simple Ethernet repeater can be used in a manner similar to Figure D.3 above.

An alternative to supporting both protocols that is sometimes suggested in cases such as the one cited above, in which a network server already exists, is to use the server as a "network application gateway." This approach is strongly discouraged. It is essential that each computer and workstation support Internet protocol data communication directly so that modern client/server applications can be supported where the server or servers may be located anywhere on the Internet. The "gateway" approach severely restricts the workstations' potential ability to access multimedia and other important information resources. Some technologies, such as "arcnet," may not be capable of supporting Internet protocols but may offer "terminal emulation" shared access to something like a "modem pool." The modem adapter might be rewired to connect to ports on a network access server instead. This would provide simple access to information resources for the arcnet users. In any case, older LAN technologies should not be expanded and should be phased out as funding permits. It is critical that there be a relatively homogeneous installed base of technology in order that new applications of information resources can be provided to the entire school community.

Network Management and Operational Monitoring

All networks require some level of network management in order to ensure reliable service. Monitoring of the health of the network can help identify problems before they become detrimental to network users. It also can help predict trends in traffic patterns and volume. Internet technology network management consists primarily of determining the proper routing parameters for optimal and reliable network operation, assignment of network Internet Protocol (IP) addresses and maintenance of a network-accessible database of node names corresponding to each address (see RFC 1480 for a discussion of Internet naming conventions for school networks), and monitoring the daily operation of the network. These functions typically are performed by the staff of a Network Operations Center (NOC).

Domain Name System

The Internet Domain Name System (DNS) is the mechanism for documenting and distributing information about the name and address of each computer attached to the network (the network nodes). The DNS service is provided by software that runs on the main network server. It uses a database that is created and maintained by the NOC staff. An Internet address is the numerical identifier for a node, and it must be unique among all nodes associated with the network. Furthermore, if the network is to be part of the global Internet, all addresses must be legitimate within the worldwide Internet system. Associated with each numerical address can be one or more "node names." Although computers have no difficulty using numerical addresses, it is often easier for computer users to remember and use the node names rather than the numerical addresses. In particular, electronic mail addresses use node names. DNS node names are hierarchical, and by appropriately using this hierarchy, "subdomains" can be assigned to each school site or district office. In this way, naming can be structured to be flexible as well as meaningful in the context of the whole organization.

A plan for the assignment of IP network addresses and node names should be developed early in the planning for the network installation. Initially, the database serving the DNS should reside on the "district server" so that there is one site at which all assignments are officially registered. As the network grows and expertise is developed, secondary DNS service can be run on the servers at larger school sites. The main DNS server for the district should be located as close to the Internet connection (topologically) as possible. This proximity is to help ensure that network problems within the district network will have minimal impact on access to the server. This design is illustrated in Figure D.1, where the district server is on an Ethernet connected directly to the main distribution router. Associated with the assignment of node names and addresses should be a database of specific information about the computers connected to the network. When trying to resolve problems or answer user questions, it is very important to know where the computers and other nodes are located, what type of computer and software are in use, and what type of network connection is installed. With proper software this database can be used to extract the DNS database discussed above.

Network Monitoring

Internet network monitoring serves three primary purposes:

1. **Constant observation of the "health" of the network, network components, and external network connectivity.** Standard Simple Network Management Protocol (SNMP) support is built-in to most active components today. Even network servers and workstations can be monitored in this way. Operations staff can be provided with

network monitoring stations that will display alerts immediately upon detecting a wide variety of problems or anomalies.

2. **Collection of statistics on the performance of the network and patterns of traffic in order to identify needed enhancements or re-engineering.** Using the same SNMP capabilities mentioned above, data on packet forwarding and total traffic volume can be collected and used to generate periodic reports on network utilization.

3. **More rapid problem resolution. When problems do occur, SNMP tools can help to pinpoint the source of the problem(s).** Such problems include transient routing anomalies, DNS query failures, or even attempts at breaking into network-accessible host computers.

Since network management and monitoring is a technically demanding task and requires special equipment and software, it should be a centralized function in the initial design of school network systems, as discussed above.

Summary

The model for school network implementation described above is based on broad experience with this technology in higher education and administrative environments. Many schools have already installed networks very similar to this model. We believe that it is a practical first step towards bringing a powerful resource to bear for enriching all of the nation's school programs.

None of the suggestions above preclude or postpone in any way future development of an integrated voice, data, and video network for the nation's schools. Use of existing Internet carriers does not in any way preclude future development of a separate "backbone" for the K-12 community if such a "backbone" is determined to be cost effective or required for enhanced functionality. Rather, the infrastructure recommended above can be the foundation at the local level in preparation for future high-capacity networks.

Appendix D

IV. Network Support

The installation of a campus-wide network or Internet connectivity will also require a commitment to ongoing network support and its related resource requirements. There are two major areas of network support: network operations and user services. These support functions are usually performed through the establishment of a Network Operations Center (NOC) and Network Information Center (NIC); however, both functions can be performed by the same individual or groups of individuals.

Network Operations Center (NOC)

The Network Operations Center (NOC) oversees the performance of the physical network and some of its software support systems. The staff may install networks, configure network devices and provide configurations for computers attached to an organization-wide network. Real-time monitoring of the network can be performed using the Simple Network Management Protocol and many vendors produce monitoring systems that graphically display network performance, log events and usage, and produce trouble tickets. The use of this type of network monitoring allows NOC staff to quickly detect problems and greatly reduces the personnel required to perform this function. Routine monitoring of the network can help to anticipate problems before they develop and lead to reconfigurations and upgrades as indicated.

If problems do arise, NOC personnel may go on-site to troubleshoot a problem and repair it. If the problem is not local, NOC personnel will work with school district, county, or regional network technical staff to resolve the problem.

NOC personnel also assign addresses to network computers and devices and maintain the Domain Name service (DNS) for their organization. Domain Name service is a machine registry service that runs on a network server and enables access to machines by easy to remember names, rather than a network number. DNS is required for any organization connected to the Internet and critical to the establishment of an electronic mail system.

It is most cost effective to have the Network Operation Center serve an entire organization or region. In order to ensure timely service all the way out to the most remote LAN, it is recommended that an organization assign local area network administration duties to on-site personnel to interact with NOC staff and assist with the maintenance of the network. In the case of a school district, administrative support staff, teachers, librarians or school based technical staff can each take responsibility for a LAN or group of LANs. If a problem arises, it can be reported to the LAN administrator. The LAN administrator can determine if the problem is local or remote and if NOC staff need to be notified. If so, the LAN administrator acts as the single point of contact for the NOC to provide a good communications channel for information and ensure efficient coordination of problem resolution. This method of delegating responsibility provides for a high level of service for each LAN and optimally uses the time of NOC staff to provide economies of scale.

Network Information Center (NIC)

The Network Information Center (NIC) provides information and support services to facilitate the use of the network. The NIC often provides a help-desk service to answer questions about use of the network, references to useful resources, and training in new tools or applications. The NIC may also provide services such as an online directory of network users and their electronic mail addresses, bulletin board services of information, and notices about the network and online training materials. These NIC services could be provided on a school district or county level. Most of the information would not be site-specific and can be delivered electronically using electronic mail, electronic conferencing, online bulletin boards or other document delivery mechanisms. These types of services may be well suited for a school or school district librarian. Other types of support services may be performed by NIC personnel such as maintenance of the electronic mail system or Postmaster duties, coordination of an online bulletin board or campus-wide information system (CWIS), and management of an online conferencing system. These duties are more technical in nature and will require technical staff to maintain them.

Postmaster

Every organization that uses electronic mail should have an Electronic Mail Postmaster and a mailbox, named postmaster, for the receipt of messages regarding use of the electronic mail system, mail problems, and general inquiries about reaching people within the organization.

The Postmaster is responsible for reading postmaster mail and responding to inquiries. These duties can be performed by nontechnical staff with forwarding of messages to the appropriate technical support person as required.

CWIS Administrator

Campus-wide information systems or bulletin boards are one of the most useful applications on the network. These systems allow people to share timely notices, documents, and other resources with large groups of people. These systems typically provide a hierarchical or tree-like structure of menus that lead to online documents or other services. Common types of information include deadline notices, grant announcements, training schedules, and lists of available resources such as videos in a library or reference materials.

Information need not be stored all in one location. Figure D.7 shows a set of distributed servers. These servers can receive new information automatically from a central server and can also contain information generated locally that may pertain only to the local school. Users of the information need not know where the information is stored: the information access software will present choices on an integrated menu. A CWIS or bulletin board must have an administrator or sponsor to oversee the design and maintenance of the system so that it is easy to navigate and find information, provides a professional presentation of information and ensures that information remains timely and relevant. This function can be performed by NIC staff, or trained librarians or administrative staff as appropriate.

Management of Online Conferences

Online conferences provide a way for groups of people to share information, discuss ideas, and pose questions. Conferences usually are set up to serve the needs of a group of people sharing a common interest. For example, an online conference might be established for teachers to discuss a new science teaching framework or a teacher may establish a conference for the discussion of the Civil War as part of an American History class. Some conferences are on-going and may exist for years. Others are short-term and may exist for only one semester. Conferences may be created using the electronic mail system or a facility called Usenet News. Online conferencing systems require a server computer on the network that collects messages posted to a conference and

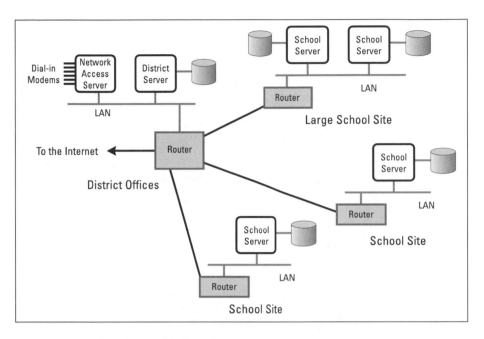

*Figure D.7. **Distributed network information servers.***

distributes them when requested. Usually these systems are managed by a systems administrator and someone must configure the system to establish and delete groups upon request. Other management duties include scheduling the deletion of old messages and archiving especially valuable conversations. Typically these duties are performed by a systems administrator or technical staff.

Staffing Considerations

The duties described above do not necessarily require hiring new staff, and they may be shared by people already within an organization. Small schools or districts may rely on County Office of Education Information Systems staff to perform all functions. Larger schools or districts may have staff to take on any combination of duties and rely on the County Office of Education for others. Access to the network and the use of electronic communications allows people throughout the organization to perform these functions remotely. The assignment of responsibility for any of these duties is flexible and should be approached with the goal of providing the highest quality of service in the most cost effective and workable manner.

V. References

Honey, Margaret, Henriquez, Andres, "Telecommunications and K-12 Educators: Findings from a National Survey", Bank Street College of Education, New York, NY, 1993.

Susan Estrada, *Connecting to the Internet*, OReilly & Associates, Inc. (ISBN 1-56592-061-9)

Carole Teach, Editor, "Building the Future: K-12 Network Technology Planning Guide", California Department of Education, Research, Evaluation & Technology Division, 1994.

VI. Special Thanks

Special thanks to Brian Lloyd of Lloyd Internetworking, Inc. for his contributions to this document. Brian was one of the contributors to the California Department of Education "K-12 Network Technology Planning Guide" which served as the motivation for writing most of this document. Brian contributed significantly to Section II, "Rationale for the Use of Internet Protocols" and thoroughly reviewed Section III, "A Technical Model for School Networks," providing valuable feedback.

VII. Security Considerations

Security issues are not discussed in this memo.

VIII. Authors' Addresses

Joan C. Gargano

Information Technology

Distributed Computing Analysis and Support

University of California at Davis

Davis, CA 95616

E-Mail: jcgargano@ucdavis.edu

David L. Wasley

Data Communication & Network Services

Information Systems and Technology

University of California at Berkeley

Berkeley, CA 94720

E-Mail: dlw@berkeley.edu

Appendix E

Electronic Access to Potentially Offensive Material and Pornography

Virginia E. Rezmierski, Ph.D.

1132 Argus Building

535 West William Street

University of Michigan

Ann Arbor, MI 48106

E-Mail Address: Virginia_Rezmierski@umich.edu

[Note: Dr. Rezmierski has stated that this is not a position paper for K–12 administrators. The issues facing college campuses are clearly different because of the age of the students and the history of academic freedom and responsibility on college and university campuses. McG.&C.]

Introduction

As rapidly as the technology is changing, college and university administrators are being faced with ethical and values issues regarding the use of information technology on their campuses. In many cases when a behavioral incident happens involving the technology, the administrator is pressed to respond—to react—even before they have had sufficient opportunity to understand the competing values and issues at hand. In some cases the issues are so fraught with emotion that not only does the urgency for a response cause stress, but the smoke of anger and the haze of disbelief over the incident cause stress as well. Electronic access to pornography on the networks and from other sources on campuses is one such issue for some administrators. It is important in this, as in other ethical and values-laden issues, to carefully remove the smoke and haze and to think the issues through before responding.

This paper addresses the issues pertaining to electronic access to potentially offensive material and pornography on campuses. It provides one proactive course of action thought to empower both those individuals on campuses who wish to access the materials and those who do not.

Access to Information

The electronic availability of information has increased exponentially in the last ten years. Of course this includes information containing all types of content. It includes information in a variety of written, graphic, audio, and animated forms as well. University and college faculty, staff, and students are increasingly able to access materials, from a variety of sources, that would be considered offensive to some others on the campus. Most prominent among the electronic sources of potentially offensive materials are the newsgroups and electronic bulletin boards that are available through the Internet.

The information that might fall into this category covers, as you would expect, the full spectrum. It is possible to access a range of information, from written material with minor sexual innuendo and pictures or drawings of partially or fully nude figures to explicitly written descriptions of sexual acts, descriptions of violent sexual torture, and color graphics of acts of bestiality, bondage, and child pornography. Not only is it possible to access this material but it is also possible to send the material with great speed to one or hundreds of others, to send the material to a common printer where others are retrieving their work, to place the material in accounts that others are required to access for class work, and so on.

Difficult Issues and Balances

University and college administrators are faced with difficult decisions in regards to this issue and the related behaviors of some of the members of their community. Balances must be reached; balances between community values, existing laws and protections, and the sensitivities of members of the community need to be found. Policies and guidelines can be useful in clarifying community values and guiding responses. In regard to policy making in this area however, as one Stanford administrator expressed it, "There is no clear winning position on this set of issues."

Appendix E

Values Continuum

Some portion of each campus community will feel strongly that no access to this material should be allowed on the campus. They feel that, in its existence, it is an act of violence against a group of individuals—women. They advocate that no university resources should be expended to facilitate in any way access, transport, or storage of this material. And they maintain that not to restrict this material is to minimize or ignore the rights of an entire segment of the community. Conversely, some portion of each campus community will feel strongly that access to information of all types is critical to academic freedom. For this group, the material is a form of expression and not an act in and of itself. They argue that it is the university's appropriate role to facilitate access to information and not to predetermine by content the usefulness of any information for the purposes of its community. For this segment of the community, any act of screening, restriction, or selection is a critically dangerous step towards loss of liberty. Admittedly, these are the more purely extreme positions. However, these positions and the many variations in between are found on most university and college campuses. The topic stimulates high emotions and heated discussions.

One might ask, "If there is no political win in this arena, is there a reason to engage this set of issues or should administrators wait until the courts have produced more clarity in this area or until there is an explicit complaint or suit?" There are important reasons to address these issues—reasons that are integrally related to the missions of institutions of higher education. On an issue such as this, where the values of different segments of the community seem to be at such extreme odds, there is a need to foster social cognitive development, social thinking, and to encourage the sharing of points of view. There is a need to increase the valuing of diversity in the college community, a community that will become increasingly diverse over time and that will live within an increasingly diverse nation. And there is a need to promote the development of conflict management skills around issues such as this, issues that stimulate conflict and reduce reasoned discourse.

Ernest Boyer is eloquent in his writing about university and college life. Three of the principles he identifies for campus educational purposefulness are directly related to why this issue needs to be engaged. He writes:

"A college or university is an open community, a place where freedom of expression is uncompromisingly protected and where civility is powerfully affirmed.";

"A college or university is a just community, a place where the sacredness of each person is honored and where diversity is aggressively pursued"; and,

"A college or university is a disciplined community, a place where individuals accept their obligations to the group and where well-defined governance procedures guide behavior for the common good."

A look now at the balances and decisions that must be made will illustrate the complexity of the issues.

Art vs. Pornography

Many individuals, as they begin to discuss the issue of electronic access to potentially offensive material, try immediately to discern whether the material is art or pornography. It is probably impossible to make this determination and therefore this is probably not the place to begin discussions. The judgment will vary with each piece of material, with each viewer, and perhaps for a given viewer, will vary at different times. Other than where specific legal interpretations exist, e.g., child pornography which is determined to be illegal, the judgments vary by community and cannot be generalized. While for some of the material there would readily be an agreement on a campus that the material is pornographic and offensive, the community would quickly split on the question of whether it threatens and intimidates as an act or whether it constitutes artistic expression. Rather than expending community energy trying to make these determinations, questions about access appear to be more critical.

Institutional Provision of Service

To analyze these questions it is important to separate the issue of a university or college providing access to a service from the issue of an individual accessing certain material. The first question to be asked is, "Should the university or college provide access to the newsgroups in general and to the Internet?" As a service provider, if access is provided to the news service, most likely it is provided to all of the groups within the news service. Likewise, if access is provided to the networks, it is to the service in its entirety. The value of the overall service is the determinant for whether the service is provided. A decision about access to a part, e.g., the bulletin boards that exist on the networks, is subordinate to the decision to provide access to the service in general.

It is possible to apply selection criteria in order to allow only certain portions of the news service to be received. By doing so, however, an institution moves away from the question of whether to provide the service to the question of whether to allow individuals to access certain material. This very important distinction gets blurred in discussion of this issue. It gets blurred because issues of service provision become mixed with issues of institutional vs. individual power.

Some administrators have tried to address the second question indirectly. They argue that while in the case of Usenet News, for example, they provide access to the service, but they do not provide access to those pieces of the service that are storage-space-intensive, e.g., the graphics. The argument falls apart when it becomes clear that some graphics are provided as part of the service but not those that are pornographic in content. In reality, a content judgment has determined service, mixing again the issues of service provision and institutional vs. individual power.

Many institutions, like the University of Michigan, provide extensive access to the Internet and to News services, generally to anything on those services for which there is a request. The decision to do this is based on the recognition that a diverse community of scholars requires a diverse set of information sources and contents and that for a service provider to make the determination based on anything other than expressed demand would be inappropriate.

Institutional vs. Individual Power: Access to Information

Having determined that providing access to the service is valuable to a university or college community, the issue of power between institutions and individuals can be addressed with more clarity. Does a university or college have a role in determining whether individuals should access certain material? In addressing this question it is helpful to restrict our focus, for the moment, to one individual accessing material for his/her own personal use. (The ramifications of a broader, multiperson focus will be considered in later sections of this paper.)

It needs to be recognized that a university or college essentially has no control in this regard. Once the decision has been made to provide individuals access to the networks and to information services, and once the decision has been made to allow members of a community to use information technology to interact with, store, and potentially transport information of all types, the options and possibilities are nearly endless. Individuals no longer need to go to specifically designated locations—adult book stores—to obtain pornographic materials. Such materials are available on the networks, on bulletin boards, from other users, and from servers where other students, faculty and/or staff may be storing the information. It can be scanned from hard copy and photographs or integrated with material from movies and videos.

One might ask, "Should individuals be allowed to use university property to access, store and transport this material? Can we establish the fact that such property is to be used only for the business of the university, the teaching, learning, research, administrative, and service behaviors of the members?" While the answers to these questions may help to shape a community response, they do not provide reason for assertion of institutional power over the individual in the form of censorship.

Universities, if doing so is consistent with their values, need to make a strong and frequently heard statement about appropriate and intended use of information technology resources on the campuses. Perhaps these resources are clearly provided only for, or primarily for, the purposes of teaching, learning, research, administration, and service. At the author's institution, the University of Michigan, the word "primarily" needs to be emphasized. Resources have been provided to enable the community to communicate, socialize, and exchange points of view electronically, as well as to specifically participate in class-related learning and teaching. However, even with emphasis on the primary missions of the institution, one must ask, What is learning and how might this material fit into that process? What is research and how might this material fit into that process? What is teaching and how might this material fit into that process? Who can determine this for another? And, how would the institution go about identifying the moments when the question should be asked? Without access to this material, those who most oppose it cannot know what exists and cannot speak out against it. John Stuart Mill wrote:

"If all mankind minus one, were of one opinion and only one person were of the contrary opinion, mankind would be no more justified in silencing that one person, than he, if he had the power, would be justified in silencing mankind… The peculiar evil of silencing the expression of an opinion is, that it is robbing the human race; posterity as well as the existing generation; those who dissent from the opinion, still more than those who hold it; If the opinion is right, they are deprived of the opportunity of exchanging error for truth; if wrong, they lose, what is almost as great a benefit, the clearer perception and livelier expression of truth, produced by its collision with error."

Without access, the researchers cannot study the effects of its existence. Dan W. Lacy wrote: *"The goal of freedom in information and communication is a double one, with its two aspects inseparably complementary: for all who wish to speak or write to be free to do so, and for all who wish to hear or read them to have that opportunity."*

Without discussions about these differing positions, members of the community cannot begin to understand the effects of this material on each other. In a previous paper, I wrote:

"I have discovered that there is a war going on within me around this topic. My body and feelings scream out for censorship and even violence against the creators of some of the material—reactions that are quite foreign to my usual manner of doing business. My mind reasons and rallies energy to maintain reasoned discourse about liberty, about freedoms, about fairness and about balance of power."

Many administrators would argue that most of the access to this material is not for assignments, research, or explicit teaching duties. To claim to be able to determine which is which, however, or to say that teaching and learning are not happening, would be foolish. The important Liberty and First Amendment Rights must take precedence in this question. They demand that the power to decide whether to access this material remain in the hands of the individuals, where decisions about the value of the information and the purposes for which it is to be used can best be made. They demand a position against censorship.

Ensuring Empowerment to All: Institutional Responsibility

Having made this critical decision to protect against censorship for the individual, to empower individuals to make their own choices about accessing information, and to restrain institutional power, it is now important to widen our focus from one individual accessing the material for their own personal use in order to examine the interaction between individuals. What are the effects of one person's access to potentially offensive material on another who wishes not to access or to be exposed to the material?

Changing focus in this way, from the question of whether an individual at a university or college should be able to access potentially offensive material to a focus on rights within a two- or multiperson interaction, moves decisions from the arena of First Amendment constitutional rights to the arena of community sensitivities, standards, civilities and the specific protections that are provided under derivative constitutional law. Many universities have taken a position to protect freedom of speech and press. However, the grayer areas ahead, in this more extended focus, require that a balance be achieved between freedom of speech and freedom from harassment and intimidation.

Individual Access: Unconscious Intrusion

It has been argued that individuals within a university community must be empowered to select what they need to access for their learning, teaching, research, and personal purposes. Further, it has been argued that the choice about what to access and how to use the information should best be left to the individual without institutional censorship (albeit with strong standards for using resources primarily for the purposes for which they were provided where those have been specified). Are there interpersonal conditions that must be considered if universities and colleges are to achieve the educational purposefulness about which Boyer writes? What are the limits to this individual empowerment? Are there boundaries between individuals that must be observed? Does one empowered individual who chooses to access information that may be considered offensive and even threatening by another have the right to access it in a way that crosses beyond his/her own personal space and boundaries?

The questions of interpersonal boundaries and information access are central to decisions regarding all types of potentially offensive material, not just that which is considered pornographic. These questions are complicated by the different forms in which information may be delivered. Some information will exist in graphic form, some in text only. Some information will contain, or primarily consist of, sound. If material that is accessed by one individual contains audible sound, for example, are there reasons to restrict access in a shared worksite where others, who may not wish to access or be exposed to the material, also work? e.g., a public computing site? A recent incident at one university will illustrate the issue.

A student, bored with his current assignments, developed a method for loading a sound segment onto machines in a public computing site. He placed the faked orgasm sound segment from the movie "When Harry Met Sally" onto all of the machines. When any other user turned on a machine, the entire sound segment played without the user having a method for disengaging the sequence until the segment was completed.

For information contained in the form of sound, the potential disturbance can be readily recognized. Administrators may decide that sound is intrusive to the personal work space of others and therefore should be restricted regardless of content.

Visual images or printed content may be harder to understand in terms of interpersonal space, however. Is a visual image, accessed by one individual, intrusive to the personal work space of others and therefore to be restricted, particularly if the content is offensive? University and college communities will need to contemplate the scope and importance of an individual's work space. Within a public computing site for instance, does such individual space comprise the workstation, desk, and chair, or does it include all of the workstations, desks, and chairs within the viewing range of the individual? What can we say to individuals who access offensive messages or visual images of any type about intrusion into the space of the others who are working within those shared resources? Does a university or college have any responsibility in this regard?

The Opportunity

Universities and colleges have an opportunity to lead through an educational effort, not to censor, but to proactively encourage individuals to think about the needs, rights and values of others. Other options such as to restrict a person's access to potentially offensive material to only certain machines within a public site, or to require only nonpublic access for material that might be considered offensive, move the community unnecessarily and dangerously toward censorship. Instead, encouraging and empowering individuals to interact, to ask each other to be considerate of their reactions to offensive material, to ask them to CONSIDER a more private and less intrusive site for accessing it, is to encourage community sensitivity and social thinking.

For an institution to proactively anticipate such situations because they will happen and are already happening is to make a topic that can be divisive a topic that can lead to community growth. To provide discussions and education about empowerment and about the rights of all individuals, those who wish or need to access such material and

those who do not, does not cross the line to censorship, but instead purposefully crosses a line towards community consciousness raising and responsiveness. Experience with this approach at two universities has found that the majority of those who engage in unconscious intrusion into another's space respond positively to such suggestions and learn from the encounter.

At one university, students working in a multiple-window environment on powerful public site workstations were accustomed to displaying a variety of material beside their text documents, while they worked. On several machines, students had one of their available windows displaying, at one-minute intervals, pictures of nude women in various provocative poses. While the student typed a paper, he was "entertained" by the changing photos. Women at that university, a significant minority of the campus population, found that working in the public sites was often uncomfortable and felt intrusive. They found it difficult to work next to public stations where such multiple window displays were active. They questioned their rights to a work and learning environment free from such stress and embarrassment. When the male students were asked to consider accessing that material from a more private space, the vast majority of them agreed to do so, expressing regret for their unconscious insensitivity.

Individual Access and Purposeful Intrusion

Within each community, however, there are those who access material that may be offensive to others and then purposefully send or otherwise deliver the material to another person. Should we consider all such purposeful acts as harassment? The answer has to be "no," because what is offensive to one may not be offensive to another. Some will appreciate, enjoy, or find useful, the delivery of the material.

There are increasing numbers of incidents on university and college campuses involving individuals who, after exercising their right to access material that they themselves do not find offensive, purposefully use it to intrude on the work or private space of another individual. They send it to the machine of an unsuspecting user, place it into the files of an unsuspecting group, or send it to a public printer that is used by an unsuspecting group. These acts are generally designed for "comic or shock value." Sometimes, they are designed to target, threaten, intimidate, and/or harass another person. In these cases the

empowered individual anticipates that the recipient will find the material offensive, yet purposefully intrudes.

At one university, a student sent a racist message in broad print to a public printer and waited for the reactions which she received. At another, a student sent a file of pornographic images to a class account that a group of students were required to access for their daily assignment. At another college, a young student, though asked to stop sending electronic mail to an unwilling recipient, continued to send daily solicitations for homosexual sex, including in them increasingly intimidating descriptions of the acts to be committed and the violence that would be included.

Should a university or college administrator intervene in these interpersonal conflicts? Should a university take a position regarding the kind of work and study environment it provides on its campus? Is there a critical educational and disciplinary process that should be followed if we are to achieve the sensitive educationally purposeful community of reasoned discourse about which Boyer writes?

It would be difficult to view even a sampling of the pornography that exists on the networks, in the selected newsgroups, or in some of the files collected by individuals on the campuses, as benign artistic expressions. Few women could view the bestial reduction of females in pornographic pictures involving animals and not feel hurt or frightened—hurt for the women who participated in the making of the pictures, frightened that the possibility even exists that someone could place them in such a situation against their will or for monetary gain. Few women could see the repeated emphasis placed on dominance and power in pornography and not rage at the possibilities of such dominance. Few could recognize the themes of violence or, minimally, the symbolized hurtful sexual entry into all orifices, and not quiver with fear that such acts might be possible or cry for those for whom such acts have occurred in real life. To suggest that being forced to view these pictures unwittingly or unwillingly is anything but an act of intimidation and violence is to be so involved in the power struggle for rights as to be blinded by the obvious.

This is not about an individual's right to access material. It is about an individual's rights to choose NOT to access or be exposed to the material. This is about a small number of individuals intentionally intruding into the private, personal, work and psychological space of other people—to assert their power at the expense of another's, in the name of rights.

Conclusions

The university's proactive role begins through education and awareness when an individual's access to potentially offensive materials results in unintentional intrusion for another. Its role in discipline and intervention increases significantly when acts of purposeful intrusion and harassment occur. To ignore or take lightly such acts is to enable the disintegration of a community, to allow hostilities and misunderstandings to increase, and to allow the disempowering of some individuals within the community AS an expense for the empowering of others.

This is a topic that may not have a political win within it, but which has a tremendous learning-teaching win for institutions of higher education. This is a learning moment. If we are to achieve Boyer's notions of an open, just, and disciplined community where freedom of expression and civility are affirmed, where persons are honored and valued, and where individuals will self discipline for the sake of others, "electronic access to potentially offensive material" is a topic to be engaged. This is a topic around which learning and teaching can be built. This is an opportunity to empower all individuals.

Endnotes

1. Boyer, Ernest L. 1990. *Campus Life: In Search of Community*, The Carnegie Foundation for the Advancement of Teaching, Princeton, New Jersey, p.17

2. Ibid, p. 25.

3. Ibid, p. 37.

4. Mill, John S., 1859. in *Civil Liberties*, "On Liberty" Of the Liberty of Thought and Discussion" Syracuse University Press, Syracuse, New York. p. 24, 25.

5. Lacy, Dan M.,1986. *Freedom and Equality of Access to Information: A Report to the American Library Association,* Commission on Freedom and Equality of Access to Information, American Library Association, Chicago. p. 3.

6. Rezmierski, V. "No Ostriches, Only Eagles: It's Time to Speak", Paper presented to Women's Studies, The University of Michigan, Ann Arbor, MI, 1994.

Appendix F

Windows 95 and the Internet

N August 1995, Microsoft officially released the latest version of its flagship operating environment, Windows 95. This version of Windows completely redesigned the desktop. It also added networking support.

Network Drivers Integrated into the Operating System

From the beginning of DOS, networks have been treated like any other peripheral: the vendor of the peripheral had to write the DOS drivers to make it run. For example, Panasonic has had to provide the software that would allow all of the various word processing programs to print with Panasonic's printers. (Occasionally, the software vendor would provide the drivers; for many years, the advantage of WordPerfect over other word processors was the huge number of printers for which it had drivers.) The development of Winsock (WINdows SOCKets) was an attempt to provide a standard interface for Windows applications to use when talking to the network. In effect, it allows any vendor's application to work with any other vendor's network drivers. Now, with Windows 95, the network drivers are bundled with the operating system. (At this point, Macintosh users are probably saying, "We've had that from the beginning!" They're right.)

Using Win95 with Installed Software

If you install Windows 95 on a machine that already has networking software installed, you may find that your old software doesn't work any more. Many programs copy vital files into the Windows directory.

Installing a new version of the operating system will overwrite those files with newer versions. If the files aren't in the Windows directory, they probably will not be used, since the Windows versions would be found first. However, if you prefer your current networking software, you can reinstall it after installing or upgrading to Windows 95. (It is possible that older versions of networking software will not work properly with Windows 95. Many programs, not just networks, have had to be upgraded to work with the new version of Windows.)

Configuring Win95 for Your Network

After you have installed Windows 95, you will need to configure it to connect to a network.

To find the Network Control Panel, you can either double-click on MyComputer, then double-click Control Panel and then double-click the Network icon, or you can click the Start icon on the task bar, point to Settings, click Control Panel and then double-click the Network icon.

There are three pieces that need to be installed: a client, an adapter, and a protocol.

First, check the list of things under *The following network components are installed.* If the Microsoft Client, Dial-Up Adapter, and either TCP/IP or TCP/IP ➤ Dial-Up Adapter are installed, you can move on to configuring a connection to your network service provider. If not, follow the steps below:

1. To install the client choose Microsoft from the list of manufacturers, click Client for Microsoft Network under Network Clients, and then click OK. The client will then be installed.

2. At this point, a Select Network Adapters window may be open. If it isn't, click Adapter and then Add in the Select Network Component Type window. As you did for the client, choose Microsoft from the list of manufacturers and then select Dial-Up Adapter from the list of Network Adapters. Click OK to confirm your choice.

3. Finally, to install the protocol, click Protocol and then Add in the Select Network Component Type window. As before, choose Microsoft from the list of manufacturers and then click TCP/IP from the list of Network Protocols.

In the process of installing the client, protocol and adapter, Windows 95 may have automatically installed others as well. Any that you don't want can be uninstalled by highlighting them and then clicking the Remove button.

Customizing for an Internet Service Provider

If you are not planning on using the Microsoft Network (MSN), you will need to configure Win95 to work with the software you use to connect to your provider. There are two ways to do this: Use the Control Panel settings, as we describe below, or use SetupWizard which comes with Internet Explorer. We'll talk about Wizard more at the end of the chapter.

 MASTER WORDS We talked about most of these properties and terms in Chapter 6, "Once You're Connected: Working with Direct and Dialup Links." We describe them briefly here, but if you need more information, please go back and review that chapter.

Using the Control Panel

For every service provider that you use, you will need to create a connection icon with the settings for that provider. There are three parts to this connection and its configuration: the Client (we use the one built in to Win95), the Dial-Up Adapter, which understands how to talk to your modem, and the TCP/IP Dial-Up Adapter, which knows which protocol you want to use to talk to the network. Let's get started!

Click the Configuration tab in the Network window, shown in Figure F.1. The Client for Microsoft Networks, Dial-Up Adapter, and TCP/IP ➤ Dial-Up Adapter will all be listed (you may have to scroll through the list to see them all). You will have to select each one in turn and click the Properties button.

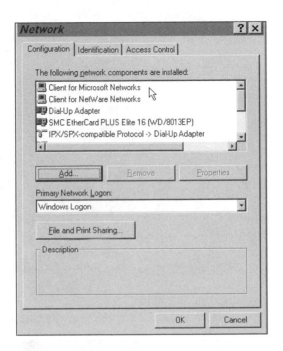

Figure F.1. Checking the Configuration tab of the Network window.

The Client for Microsoft Networks

First, select the Client for Microsoft Networks and click on the "Properties" button. Figure F.2 shows the client settings. If you want to use a provider that is *not* MSN, or if your provider is not using WinNT servers, make sure Log on to Windows NT Domain is *not* selected. This property is used only if you are using Win95 to connect to a WinNT server. Choose Quick Logon and then click OK.

The Dial-Up Adapter

Next, go back to the Network window and select Dial-Up Adapter, as shown in Figure F.3, to connect via a modem to network servers running PPP, RAS (Microsoft's Remote Access Server), and Novell NetWare.

In the Dial-Up Adapter Properties window, there are several tabs. Under the Driver Type tab, select the Enhanced mode (32-bit and 16-bit) NDIS driver, as shown in Figure F.4. This will install a custom Win95 TCP/IP driver.

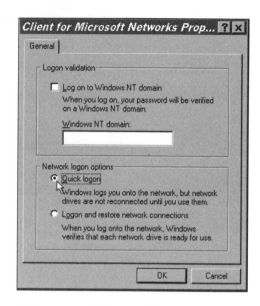

Figure F.2. Do not select "Log on to Windows NT domain."

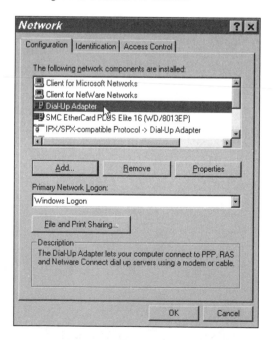

Figure F.3. Selecting Dial-Up Adapter from the Configuration tab.

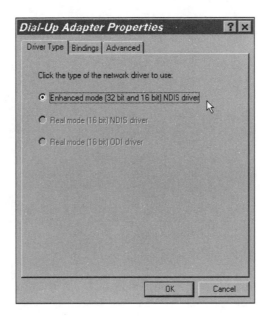

Figure F.4. **Choosing the driver.**

Under the Bindings tab, shown in Figure F.5, choose **only** the "TCP/IP" option. (If you want to use a Novell Network, or to connect to the Microsoft Network, you will need to go through this process again to create a new connections icon. Follow the MSN directions or your NetWare administrator's directions to create the connection type you need.)

You should not need to make any changes under the Advanced tab; the default settings should work just fine.

The TCP/IP Dial-Up Adapter

Go back to the Network window and under TCP/IP ➤ Dial-Up Adapter, choose Properties, as shown in Figure F.6.

The TCP/IP properties depend upon your service provider. Start with the IP Address tab, as shown in Figure F.7. If your provider has given you a permanent IP address, choose Specify an IP address and record your IP address. If you are assigned a different IP address every time you dial in, choose "Obtain an IP address automatically."

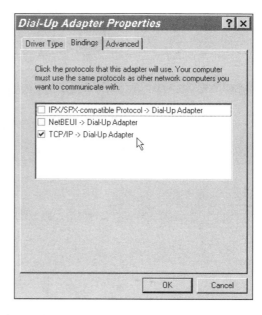

Figure F.5. **Choose the TCP/IP option.**

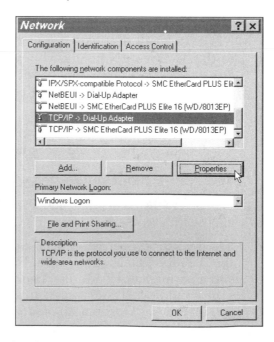

Figure F.6. **Configuring the TCP/IP properties.**

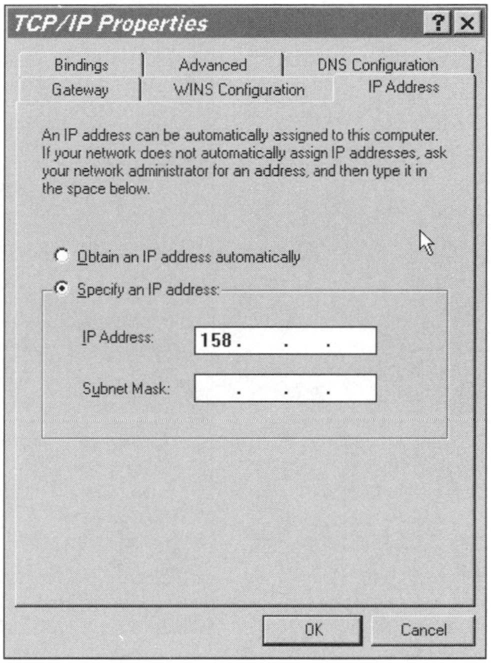

Figure F.7.   Recording your IP address.

Now you may need to configure a default gateway to the Internet, depending on your Internet service provider. If you need a default gateway address, your provider should have given you one. Record that address in the Gateway tab, as shown in Figure F.8; otherwise, you should leave that tab blank.

If you change gateways depending on network conditions (congestion, etc.) your provider may have you install several gateways in this section. Check with your provider for more information.

Next, click the WINS tab. Unless you are an NT user connecting to a Windows NT server, you should choose Disable WINS Resolution, as shown in Figure F.9, under the WINS Configuration tab. WINS is Microsoft's proprietary solution for Domain Name Service, and unless your provider is running Microsoft networking, you should use regular DNS. If you are connecting to a Windows NT server, you will need to ask your system administrator for the information needed in this tab.

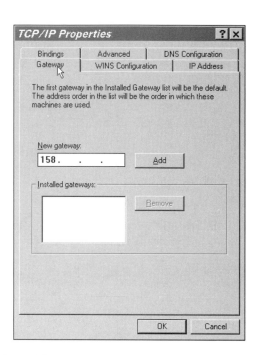

Figure F.8.   Configuring a default gateway to the Internet.

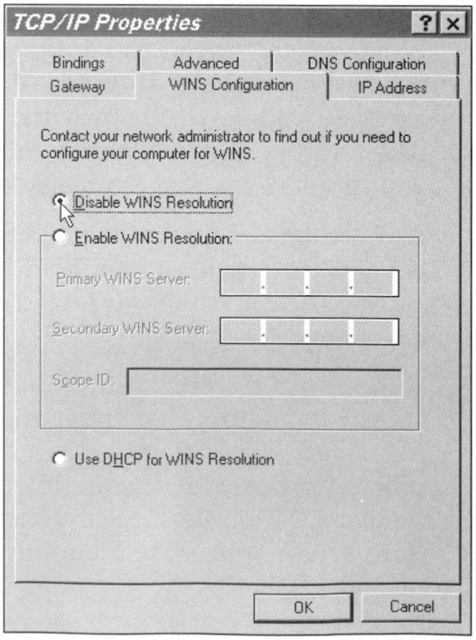

Figure F.9.   Disabling WINS.

Next, click the DNS Configuration tab, where you will want to choose the Enable DNS option. Figure F.10 shows the DNS configuration tab. Enabling DNS lets your computer talk to the Domain Name Service servers used by your provider.

Your service provider will tell you what address to put in the Host box. They will also be able to tell you the domain name to put in the Domain box, the IP addresses of your Domain Name Servers (DNS) for the DNS Server Search Order list, and the host or domain names to enter in the Domain Suffix Search Order list box.

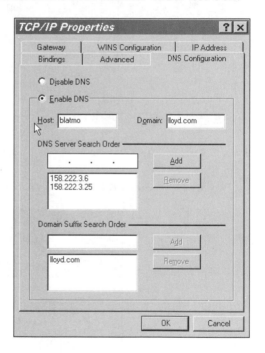

Figure F.10. **Configuring for DNS.**

 WARNING Do *not* copy the settings shown in Figure F.10. They are illustrated only for example. If you do, your connection will not work. Use the settings given to you by your service provider. This is *very* important.

The Advanced tab, shown in Figure F.11, allows you to choose the default protocol; until and unless you add other protocols (such as Microsoft RAS or NetWare), you will want to "Set this protocol to be the default protocol."

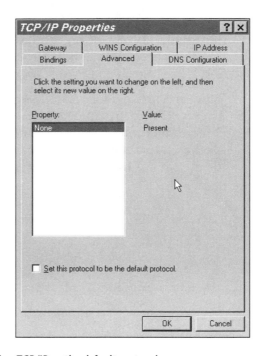

Figure F.11. **Selecting TCP/IP as the default protocol.**

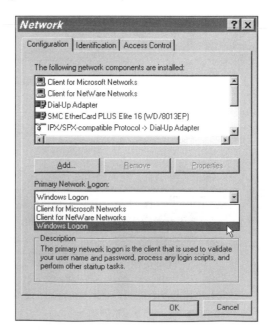

Figure F.12. **Selecting Windows Logon as the Primary Network Logon.**

Finally, click the Bindings tab and click the Client for Microsoft Networks option. Now click OK to confirm your selections. This tells Win95 that your Win95 Client will use these TCP/IP settings to access your service provider.

After all of these are configured, choose the Primary Network Logon box, which is just below the Add, Remove, and Properties buttons in the Network box. Select Windows Logon, as shown in Figure F.12, and click on the Identification tab. Most likely, everything is already set up here.

Unless you don't have a workgroup, in which case you should enter None, you shouldn't change the Workgroup setting.

Your service provider may want you to use a particular name for the Computer Name. The Computer Description can be anything you like. You will not want to make any changes in the Access Control tab. Unless you are on a LAN, the settings there aren't likely to be of use.

Finally, click OK to close the Network window, and then reboot your computer. In the System Settings Change window, click Yes to restart.

Creating a Connection Icon

When the machine has finished rebooting, double-click again on MyComputer and then on the Dial-Up Networking icon, as shown in Figure F.13.

If you get a Welcome to Dial-Up Networking window, as shown in Figure F.14, click Next. If you have installed other connection icons before, you may see the "Make New Connection" dialogue. If so, double-click the Make New Connection icon.

Give the new connection a name that makes sense to you. (If you use several different providers, or different phone numbers for one provider, you may want to name it for the provider or with the phone number.) In Figure F.15, we called it "Innercite."

Choose your modem from the list of modems, as shown in Figure F.15, and click Configure. Everything in the window should be correct, but check to make sure.

Under the General tab, as shown in Figure F.16, the maximum speed should be set to at least 19200; however, do NOT select Only Connect at This Speed. If you do, your modem will not be able to use compression, nor will it be able to detect what speed your provider's modems are running at and adapt accordingly.

Make sure that the Port is set to your modem's COM port; you may also want to make sure that the Speaker Volume is set to at least the first mark, so you can know that the modem is getting a dial-tone.

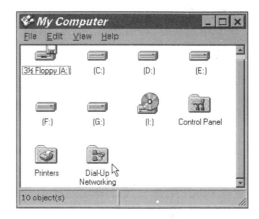

Figure F.13.   **Choose Dial-Up Networking again.**

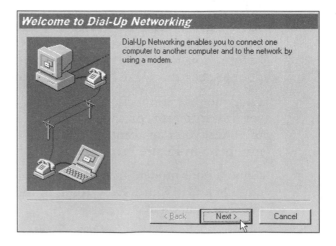

Figure F.14.   **The Welcome to Dial-Up Networking window.**

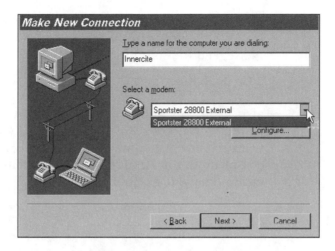

Figure F.15. Name your connection icon, and then choose your modem model and type.

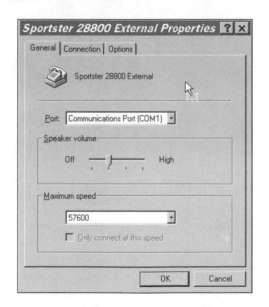

Figure F.16. The General tab of the Dialup Networking window.

Under the Connection tab, shown in Figure F.17, you can set the data bits, which should probably be 8, the parity, which should probably be None, and the stop bits, usually 1.

The default settings in the Call Preferences frame should be satisfactory. Wait for Dial Tone Before Dialing is selected. You will probably also want to Cancel the Call if Not Connected within 60. You will probably NOT want to Disconnect a Call if Idle. (You will, though, want to close the connection and hang up when you are finished with a dial-up connection, though, since most providers charge for the entire time you are connected.)

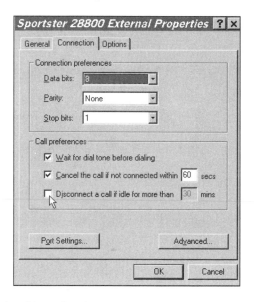

Figure F.17.   Setting data bits and parity.

Click Advanced to see the Advanced Connection Settings, shown in Figure F.18. The Use Flow Control option should be set to Hardware. This is critical, as we explained in Chapter 6. If you are not using hardware flow control, you will not be able to view large graphics, receive large mail messages, or download large graphics. The other default settings should be fine: Use Error Control is selected, Compress Data is selected, the Modulation type is Standard, Extra Settings are blank, and Record a Log File is not selected. Click OK to leave Advanced Connection Settings.

In the Options tab, shown in Figure F.19, you should choose Display Modem Status. If your network service provider does not support PAP with PPP, you will also need to choose Bring Up a Terminal Window AFTER Dialing. Finally, click OK to close the Modem Properties window.

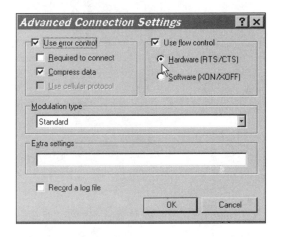

Figure F.18. **Configuring the Advanced Connection Settings.**

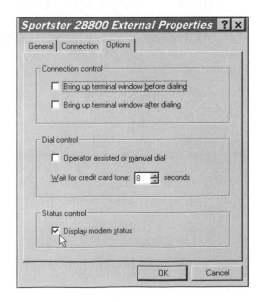

Figure F.19. **The Options tab.**

Back in the Make New Connection window, click Next, type in the telephone number and area code for your provider, and, under Country Code, select the appropriate country, as in Figure F.20. You do not need to include dashes or hyphens.

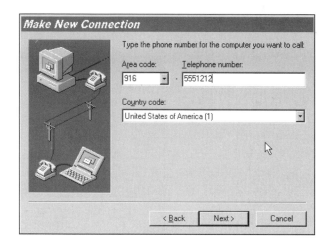

Figure F.20. **Putting in the telephone number of your provider.**

Click the Next button again, check the name of your connection icon as shown in Figure F.21, and then click Finish.

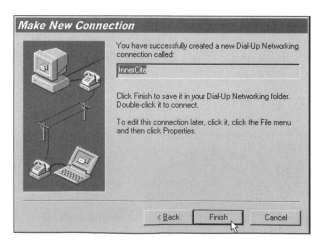

Figure F.21. **Naming the icon for your modem connection.**

Now, from the Dial-Up Networking window, select Settings from the Connections menu. Here you can select the Redial option, set Before Giving Up Retry to 20 times (more or less, depending upon how busy your provider's numbers tend to be),set Between Retries Wait to 30 seconds, and leave the Prompt to use Dial-Up Networking option selected, as in Figure F.22. Click OK to confirm your choices.

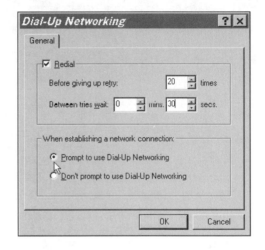

Figure F.22. **Choosing settings for modem retries.**

Now that you have created a connection, you have to tell it how to connect to your service provider.

In the Dial-Up Networking window, click the connection that you just created once to highlight it and then select Properties from the File menu. (Alternatively, you can click on it with the right mouse button and then select Properties.)

Click Server Type and, in the window that opens up, as shown in Figure F.23, choose the appropriate connection from the Type of Dial-Up Server list. For example, for a PPP connection, select "PPP: Windows 95, Windows NT 3.5, Internet." Make sure that the Allowed Network Protocols include TCP/IP.

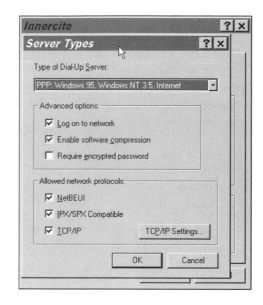

*Figure F.23.   **Choosing the Server Type.***

Unless your provider supports other protocols, and you know that you will be using them, you will probably want to make sure that TCP/IP is the only option selected. Click OK, and you are done. You should reboot your computer yet again, to make sure that all of the changes take effect.

Dialing In

To use this connection you have created, double-click MyComputer, then Dial-Up Networking, and then the icon for your connection. A Connect To window will open up and prompt for your user name and password. If your provider uses PAP, you can enter the information now. If you chose Bring Up a Terminal Window After Dialing when setting up the connection, you can wait and enter the information while logging in manually.

> **WARNING** Unless you are completely confident that your computer will never be stolen from your home or office, do *not* enter your user name and password in the PAP script. Increasingly, thieves who take computers rely on the owners to have the user name and password in an automated process. This allows them to steal even more from you, by connecting to your service provider. They can then send e-mail under your name and rack up charges on your account. Be especially careful if you have a laptop and travel with it. Physical security for your machine is very important.

Once the connection is established, a dialog box with a counter will be displayed. There is no other indication that the network connection is up and operating. You can now run any of your Winsock applications, such as Netscape or Eudora.

Win95 Setup Wizard

If you download a copy of Microsoft Explorer from the Microsoft Web site (http://www.microsoft.com), the compressed file you receive has an excellent utility called Setup Wizard. This utility uses dialog and questions to set up Win95 to work with Explorer and other Internet tools.

Setup Wizard is not available on the Win95 distribution CD-ROM, even if that CD contains Explorer. It is only available from the Microsoft Internet archive.

Setup Wizard is very good at setting up Win95 to use Internet protocols. However, some users have experienced problems getting it to save settings for using other mailers than Microsoft Exchange, and other browsers than Explorer. You should still understand the material in the first part of this appendix to give you the greatest flexibility in using Win95, with its built-in TCP/IP support, to access the Internet.

Appendix G

Internet Content Regulation in the Telecommunications Act of 1996

Ronald L. Plesser and James J. Halpert,
Piper & Marbury, L.L.P.

CONGRESS passed the Communications Decency Act of 1995 and related provisions as part of the Telecommunications Act of 1996. These provisions principally regulate the content provided on the Internet and through online services, and establish criminal penalties for violators. They pose serious difficulties for both users and the Internet/online industry.

Of greatest concern is the "indecency" standard used in Section 502 of the bill to limit material available to children through the Net and online services. Because the standard is both overbroad and quite vague, it risks chilling a significant amount of valuable expression on the Net. However, the standard has already been challenged in court, and may be enjoined as unconstitutional. With a major Supreme Court ruling on the indecency provision possible as early as the winter of 1996–97, we may know quite soon whether the restriction on indecent communications in Section 502 is an unconstitutional limitation on free expression over the Net.

Public attention has naturally focused upon the Act's troubling indecency prohibition. However, Congress included other provisions of equal importance. The Act contains several compromises designed to minimize its impact on the Net and online services. Most importantly, Congress rejected efforts by some hard-liners to force Internet and online providers to police indecency on the Net by exposing them to criminal liability unless they prevented indecency content from being accessed through their networks. This appendix examines the Internet/online content regulation provisions of the Telecommunications Act of 1996 in detail, with emphasis upon what the provisions do to the role of Internet and online service providers. Individual users, however, should be mindful that these compromises often do not protect them when they act as content providers on the Net and online services.

I. PRINCIPAL FEATURES

With the notable exception of the Act's adoption of the FCC's broadcast indecency standard, the results of the conference report are very favorable to Internet access providers and Internet software providers. The compromise legislation includes:

provisions targeting liability at creators and distributors of indecent or obscene content, rather than providers of the means of online communication,

a broad defense for entities that simply provide general access to the Internet and other interactive computer services, even if these services include browser software, uploading and downloading capacity, and similar added features,

a broad defense for providers of access software, including proxy server software, and for access providers who offer users access software to facilitate navigation of the Internet,

a defense from the indecency prohibition for content providers who use debit (checking) or credit accounts or personal access codes to establish that subscribers are not minors,

broad preemption of inconsistent state or local criminal standards, as well as of imposition of civil liability upon "Good Samaritans," and

eliminating indecency prohibitions in Title 18 and obscenity prohibitions in Title 47 to avoid inconsistent standards of liability.

II. STRUCTURE OF THE COMPROMISE

The Internet content provisions, Sections 502, 507 and 509 of the Act, generally follow the structure of the "three-way" compromise proposal put forward by industry in mid-November.

Section 507 amends the federal criminal code's provisions prohibiting trafficking in obscenity and certain abortion related materials to clarify that they apply to trafficking using interactive computer services. It is based closely upon the Hyde amendment to the House bill. It differs from the Hyde amendment by:

punishing trafficking only in obscenity, rather than both obscenity and indecency;

clarifying that there is no vicarious liability for online/Internet Service Providers whose systems are used by others to traffic in obscenity;

Section 502 broadens the "Dial-a-porn" statute to create a new subsection 223(d) applying to communications by interactive computer service. However, Section 502 establishes a separate regulatory regime for interactive computer services that differs from the rest of "Dial-a-porn" regulation. The sections of the statute relating to harassing, obscene or indecent telephone communications do not apply to online/ Internet Service Providers.[1] The Section is based upon the Exon amendment approved by the Senate. It differs from the Senate-passed version with:

a narrower and separate offense that avoids creating vicarious liability for access providers;

broader defenses (including a defense for access software providers and for content providers who require use of a debit account);

broader preemption;

vastly reduced and specifically limited FCC authority;

and no prohibition against Internet/online obscenity in Title 47 (the only prohibition is in Title 18, framed in narrow language)

Section 509 is based closely upon the Cox-Wyden-White "Good Samaritan" amendment to the House bill. It alters that amendment principally by:

making access software providers and providers of non-subscriber systems eligible for the amendment's Good Samaritan defense to civil liability;

making preemption of state and local liability for Good Samaritans much clearer;

eliminating the amendment's prohibition against FCC regulation of the Internet and other interactive computer services.

In addition, the Act contains a separate provision, inserted as Section 508, that criminalizes use of **"any facility or means of interstate or foreign commerce"**[2] to entice or coerce a minor to engage in prostitution or any sexual act.

III. SECTION 507:
TITLE 18 OBSCENITY PROVISIONS (HYDE AMENDMENT)

A. SHELTERING THE ONLINE AND SOFTWARE INDUSTRIES FROM LIABILITY

Section 507's amendments to federal obscenity law are crafted very narrowly to target traffickers in obscenity. Their narrow formulation avoids targeting providers of the means of communication without the need for any defenses.

They amend Sections 1462 and 1465 of the federal criminal code to punish knowingly using **"an interactive computer service"** to import, transport or receive in interstate or foreign commerce any obscene material. In addition to obscenity, Section 1462 also criminalizes importing, transporting or receiving material concerning where or how to obtain or to make products to induce abortion. These amendments treat interactive computer services like express companies and other common carriers and means of distribution. They punish the "knowing" use of interactive computer services to traffic in obscenity, rather than punishing the operation of such services that are used by others to traffic in obscenity.

Section 507 reflects modifications of the House-passed Hyde amendment clarifying that an interactive computer service used by another for importation of obscenity, like a common carrier, is not criminally liable. The Hyde amendment passed by the House had prohibited

"bring[ing] into the United States, or any place subject to the jurisdiction thereof (including by computer) … any obscene material … ."

H.R. 1555, Section 403. By replacing this formulation with **"knowingly uses … an interactive computer service,"** Section 509 avoids imposing vicarious liability on online service providers for obscenity. To our knowledge, no common carrier or express company has ever been convicted under Sections 1462 or 1465. Consequently, the entire Internet industry should be protected from fear of prosecution for obscenity. This formulation offers a significant and very helpful model for other areas of potential online liability. It also constitutes an improvement upon existing law, under which a provider could be indicted for knowingly importing or transporting obscene material.

Although its liability structure is favorable to the online/Internet industry, Section 507's restriction against using an interactive computer service to transport abortion-related material is a content-based restriction on expression that has been challenged in litigation and will in all likelihood be invalidated by the courts.

Section 508 criminalizes use of any facility in interstate or foreign commerce—presumably including use of most interactive computer services—to knowingly persuade, entice or coerce a minor to engage in prostitution or any sexual act for which any person may be criminally prosecuted. Criminal penalties include up to ten years in prison and/or a fine under the federal criminal code. Because, like Section 507, this provision penalizes use of a facility, it poses no threat of vicarious liability for online/Internet Service Providers.

IV. SECTION 502:
TITLE 47 INDECENCY PROVISIONS (EXON AMENDMENT)

A. THE INDECENCY STANDARD

The conference committee compromise has placed the indecency standard only in Section 502, the conference committee's proposed amendment to the "Dial-a-porn" statute. It applies to any content that:

" in context, depicts or describes, in terms patently offensive as measured by contemporary community standards, sexual or excretory activities or organs … ."

Sec. 223(d)(1). This standard appears to pose significant vagueness problems. It is not limited to pornography, and might be construed to criminalize a variety of other depictions of or descriptions of **"sexual activities or organs,"** from sex education materials to highly vulgar, Howard Stern-type discourse.

However, the Joint Explanatory Statement of the Committee of Conference (the conference report language) explaining the standard attempts to narrow the standard to safeguard its constitutionality. It asserts that by focusing upon the **"context"** of the communication, the standard requires *"two distinct elements: the intention to be patently offensive, and a patently offensive result."* Joint Explanatory Statement, at 70. Accordingly, the conference report concludes that *"[m]aterial with serious redeeming value"* will not be criminalized under the standard. *Id.*

Courts are likely either to invalidate the indecency standard in the Act or to construe it fairly narrowly along the lines suggested by the report language. Thus this legislative history may prove helpful in narrowing the range of content affected by the standard so that it more closely resembles the narrower *"harmful to minors"* standard that the conferers rejected.

Industry should receive further guidance fairly quickly on the meaning and constitutionality of the indecency standard and its restriction on online expression. Section 561 establishes a procedure for expedited review of Section 502's constitutionality. The Section specifies that civil lawsuits challenging the facial constitutionality of the Act's content regulation sections shall be heard by a special court of three judges, with an appeal as of right directly to the Supreme Court. This is likely to produce a major Supreme Court ruling on the meaning and constitutionality of the indecency provision in the next few years. The Section should help to reduce confusion over the indecency provision, and to give the online industry authoritative guidance about how and whether it must comply with the indecency standard and other restrictions in the Act.[3]

Section 561 also improves the chances for a successful challenge somewhat by leaving the plaintiffs free to file suit in what they consider to be the most advantageous federal district court. A draft of the Act during a late stage of negotiations had specified that the challenge must be brought in the District of Columbia District Court, a jurisdiction with bad precedent on the indecency standard. Section 561 permits the challenge to be heard in a more sympathetic initial forum before being appealed to the Supreme Court.

B. PENALIZING THE PROVIDERS OF PROHIBITED CONTENT, NOT THE UNINTENTIONAL PROVIDERS OF THE MEANS OF COMMUNICATION

The portion of Section 502 setting forth offenses committed by means of online communications provides:

" **Whoever—**

(1) in interstate or foreign communications knowingly—

(A) uses an interactive computer service to send to a person or persons under 18 years of age, or

(B) uses any interactive computer service to display in a manner available to a person under 18 years of age, any comment, request, suggestion, proposal, image, or other communication that, in context, depicts or describes, in terms patently offensive as measured by contemporary community standards, sexual or excretory activities or organs, regardless of whether the user of such service placed the call or initiated the communication; or

(2) knowingly permits any telecommunications facility under such person's control to be used for an activity prohibited by paragraph (1) with the intent that it be used for such activity, shall be fined under title 18, United States Code, or imprisoned not more than two years, or both."

The conference report language elaborates that:

"New subsection 223(d)(1) applies to content providers who send prohibited material to a specific person or persons under 18 years of age. Its "display" prohibition applies to content providers who post indecent material for online display without taking precautions that shield that material from minors.

★ ★ ★ ★

Each intentional act of posting indecent content for display shall be considered a separate violation of this subsection, rather than each occasion upon which indecent material is accessed or downloaded from an interactive computer service or posted without the content provider's knowledge on such a service. New subsection 223(d)(2) sets forth the standard of liability for facilities providers who intentionally permit their facilities to be used for an activity prohibited by subsection 223(d)(1)."

Joint Explanatory Statement, at 69, 71.

Subsection (d)(1) has been modified from the version passed by the Senate so that it applies only to content providers who **"use"** interactive computer services, and not to facilities providers. As passed by the Senate, the Exon amendment's Section (d)(1) had penalized knowingly "making available" to a minor any indecent material. This formulation would have likely targeted criminal penalties at facilities providers who received notice that indecent content on the Internet could be accessed by minors through their systems and who then failed to deny access to all such content. Under current Section 502, these facilities providers are instead covered only by subsection (d)(2).

This change is significant because subsection (d)(2) includes a much higher standard of proof—not only **"knowingly permit[ting]"** one's facility to be used for a violation, but also having **"the intent that it be used for such activity"** (emphases added). It therefore minimizes potential liability for Internet Service Providers based upon a letter or tip that indecent content could be accessed through their systems. It penalizes only providers who have a "specific intent" to distribute indecency or to permit others to distribute indecent material through their systems.

The legislative history for this provision reinforces this point, specifying that *"subsection 223(d)(1) applies to content providers"* and later explaining that *"subsection 223(d)(2) sets forth the standard of liability for facilities providers."* Joint Explanatory Statement at 69, 71.

C. BROAD DEFENSES FOR ENTITIES THAT PROVIDE GENERAL ACCESS TO THE INTERNET AND OTHER INTERACTIVE COMPUTER SERVICES

Subsection 223(e) sets forth a list of defenses to prosecution under the prohibitions in Section 502 (the indecency provision). The first of these defenses is the "access provider" defense of subsections 223(e)(1), (2) and (3), which provides:

"(e) In addition to any other defenses available by law:

(1) No person shall be held to have violated subsection (a) or (d) solely for providing access or connection to or from a facility, system, or network not under that person's control, including transmission, downloading, intermediate storage,

Report language explaining these provisions elaborates that:

> "*The conferees also recognize the critical importance of access software in making the Internet and other interactive computer services accessible to Americans who are not computer experts. Accordingly, provision of "access software" is included within the access provider defense. As defined in new subsection 223(h)(3), the term includes software that enables a user to do any of an enumerated list of functions that are set forth in technical language. It includes client and server software, such as proxy server software that downloads and caches popular Web pages to reduce the load of traffic on the Internet and to permit faster retrieval. The definition distinguishes between software that actually creates or includes prohibited content and software that allows the user to access content provided by others.*"

Joint Explanatory Statement, at 72.

The term **"access software"** in Section 502 and the term **"access software provider"** in Section 509 are given expansive definitions. The "access software" definition of subsection 223(h)(3) is somewhat narrower:

> **"(3) The term 'access software' means software (including client or server software) or enabling tools that do not create or provide the content of the communication but that allow a user to do any one or more of the following:**
>
> **(A) filter, screen, allow, or disallow content;**
>
> **(B) pick, choose, analyze, or digest content; or**
>
> **(C) transmit, receive, display, forward, cache, search, subset, organize, reorganize, or translate content."**

(emphasis added). The definition of subsection 230(f)(4), relating to the Cox-Wyden-White "Good Samaritan" protection, is identical, except that it does not contain the underlined phrase, and therefore applies to software that actually supplies content, in addition to permitting the user to navigate the Internet and other networks.

The conference report language explaining these definitions makes clear that proxy server software is encompassed by the terms **"client or server software."** See Joint Explanatory Statement, at 72 ("*As defined in new subsection 223(h)(3), the term includes ... client and server software, such as proxy server software that downloads and caches popular Web pages*") & 75 (Good Samaritan protections "*apply to all access* *software providers, as defined in Section 230(f)(5), including providers of proxy server software.")*

The access software provisions and their legislative history should act to protect not only access software companies, but also Internet Service Providers who license and use access software as part of their service.

E. EMPLOYER DEFENSES ENCOURAGING USE OF ONLINE COMMUNICATIONS SERVICES

Section 223(e)(4) sets forth a defense for employers whose employees violate the prohibitions of Section 502. It provides:

"(4) No employer shall be held liable under this section for the actions of an employee or agent unless the employee's or agent's conduct is within the scope of his employment or agency and the employer (A) having knowledge of such conduct, authorizes or ratifies such conduct, or (B) recklessly disregards such conduct."

The conferees' explanatory statement elaborates that:

"New subsection 223(e)(4) provides a defense to employers whose employees or agents make unauthorized use of office communications systems. This defense is intended to limit vicarious or imputed liability of employers for actions of their employees or agents. To be outside the defense, the prohibited action must be within the scope of the employee's or agent's employment. In addition, the employer must either have knowledge of the prohibited action and affirmatively act to authorize or ratify it, or recklessly disregard the action. Both conditions must be met in order for employers to be held liable for actions of an employee or agent."

Joint Explanatory Statement, at 71.

As passed by the Senate, this defense had made the employer's knowledge of the employee/agent's conduct, coupled with the employee/agent acting within the scope of employment, an independent basis for liability. The conference compromise now requires both knowledge and authorization or ratification, as well as action within the scope of employment to trigger liability. However, the defense has also been narrowed somewhat in conference by making reckless disregard for an employee/agent's violation, coupled with action within the scope of employment, a possible basis for liability.

F. GOOD FAITH DEFENSES FOR PROVIDERS OF INDECENT CONTENT

Subsections 223(e)(5) and (6) of Section 502 set forth "good faith" screening defenses available both to content and access providers. They provide:

> "(5) It is a defense to a prosecution under subsection (a) or (d) that a person—
>
>> (A) has taken, in good faith, reasonable, effective, and appropriate actions under the circumstances to restrict or prevent access by minors to a communication specified in such subsections, which may involve any appropriate measures to restrict minors from such communications, including any method which is feasible under available technology; or
>>
>> (B) has restricted access to such communication by requiring use of a verified credit card, debit account, adult access code, or adult personal identification number.
>
> (6) The Commission may describe measures which are reasonable, effective, and appropriate to restrict access to prohibited communications under subsection (d). Nothing in this section authorizes the Commission to enforce, or is intended to provide the Commission with the authority to approve, sanction, or permit, the use of such measures. The Commission has no enforcement authority over the failure to utilize such measures. The Commission shall not endorse specific products relating to such measures. The use of such measures shall be admitted as evidence of good faith efforts for purposes of this paragraph in any action arising under subsection (d). Nothing in this section shall be construed to treat interactive computer services as common carriers or telecommunications carriers."

The report language elaborates that:

> *The good faith defenses set forth in new subsection 223(e)(5) are provided for "reasonable, effective, and appropriate" measures to restrict access to prohibited communications. The word "effective" is given its common meaning and does not require an absolute 100% restriction of*

access to be judged effective. The managers acknowledge that content selection standards, and other technologies that enable restriction of minors from prohibited communication, which are currently under development, might qualify as reasonable, effective, and appropriate access restriction devices if they are effective at protecting minors from exposure to indecent material via the Internet.

Subsection 223(e)(6) permits the Commission to describe its view of what constitute "reasonable, effective and appropriate" measures and provides that use of such measures shall be admissible as evidence that the defendant qualifies for the good faith defense. This subsection grants no further authority to the Commission over interactive computer services and should be narrowly construed."

Joint Explanatory Statement, at 71-72.

These defenses differ from the good faith defenses in the Exon amendment in several important respects:

Requiring Convenient Payment Method Qualifies for the Defense: Adding debit accounts to a list of methods for establishing that recipients of indecent content are at least 18 years of age creates a very practical way for service providers to take legally sufficient steps to ensure that recipients are not of minor age. The list of methods had been limited to credit cards, adult access codes and personal identification numbers—all methods that the FCC had approved in the "Dial-a-porn" context. Debit (checking) accounts are used as methods of payment by a number of online providers, who would have been ineligible for the good faith defense unless they changed their method of payment;

Parental Empowerment and Other Potential Defenses: The compromise contains broad statutory language making clear that any effective technological method of restricting access by minors to indecent communications could qualify for the good faith defense. This open-ended language is coupled with report language stating that "content selection standards" might qualify, if effective. Together, they permit rating systems, such as those built around the M.I.T. "PICS" platform, to provide a broad-based defense to liability, if effective. Accordingly, when rating systems become effective at screening indecent content from minors, content providers will be covered by the good faith defense simply by rating their content. Use of more elaborate screening techniques, such as credit or debit accounts, adult access codes, or personal identification numbers, would then no longer be necessary.

Very Narrow and Clear Limits on the FCC's Role: Subsection 223(e)(6) specifically forecloses FCC authority to enforce the prohibitions of subsection 223(d), which had been authorized in the Senate-approved Exon amendment. This restriction limits enforcement to the Department of Justice and United States Attorneys offices, which will be far less focused on online indecency than would the FCC. It also facilitates a constitutional challenge to the indecency provision by preventing the FCC from issuing regulations to cure constitutional defects in the indecency prohibition. In addition, subsection 223(e)(6) eliminates FCC authority to approve or require other methods of restriction that qualify for the good faith defense. Instead, the subsection limits the FCC solely to describing its view of what methods of restriction should qualify for the good faith defense, and makes evidence of use of such measures admissible in court;

Flexible "Effectiveness" Definition: The report language clarifies that the requirement that restriction techniques be **"effective"** does not require 100% effectiveness. See Joint Explanatory Statement, at 71 (*"The word 'effective' is given its common meaning and does not require an absolute 100% restriction of access to be judged effective."*)

Together, these changes enlarge the scope of the good faith defenses, explicitly permit them to expand with technological changes, and significantly restrict FCC regulatory authority.

At this juncture, the good faith defenses may continue to pose difficulty for less sophisticated and lower-budget content providers. However, they offer content providers several specific, technologically feasible ways to offer indecent, non-obscene content to adults without fear of criminal liability.

G. BROADENING PREEMPTION

Like Section 509 of the conference compromise discussed below, Section 502 contains a broad preemption provision that has been significantly expanded as part of the conference compromise.

Section 230(f)(2) provides:

> **"(2) No State or local government may impose any liability for commercial activities or actions by commercial entities, nonprofit libraries, or institutions of higher education in connection with an activity or action described in subsection (a)(2) or (d) that is inconsistent with the treatment of those activities or actions under this section:** Provided, however, **That nothing herein shall preclude any State or local government from enacting and enforcing complementary oversight, liability, and regulatory systems, procedures, and requirements, so long as such systems, procedures, and requirements govern only intrastate services and do not result in the imposition of inconsistent rights, duties or obligations on the provision of interstate services. Nothing in this subsection shall preclude any State or local government from governing conduct not covered by this section."**

Conference report language explains:

> *"Subsection 223(f)(2) preempts inconsistent State and local regulation of activities and actions described in subsections 223(a)(2) and (d). This provision is intended to establish a uniform national standard of content regulation for a national, and indeed a global medium, in which content is transmitted instantaneously in point-to-point and point-to-multipoint communications. As originally passed by the Senate, this subsection excluded non-commercial content providers. The conferees have expanded this section to provide for consistent national and State and local content regulation of both commercial and non-commercial providers. The Committee recognizes and wishes to protect the important work of nonprofit libraries and higher educational institutions in providing the public with both access to electronic communications networks like the Internet, and valuable content which they are uniquely well-positioned to provide. Accordingly, nonprofit libraries and educational institutions, like commercial entities, are assured by this provision that they will not be subjected to liability at the State or local level in a manner inconsistent with the treatment of their activities or actions under this legislation."*

Joint Explanatory Statement, at 72. This change helps to encourage continued participation by libraries and higher education institutions in the development of online communications.

Subsection 223(f)(2) is also broader than the Exon amendment's preemption provision in another important respect. The Exon amendment had offered preemption only for violators of the facilities provider offense (subsection 223(d)(2)). By extending preemption to the content provider offense (subsection 223(d)(1)), this amended provision ensures that the structure of defenses set forth in subsection 223(e) cannot be undermined in state legislation.

H. AVOIDING INCONSISTENT STANDARDS OF LIABILITY AND NARROWING THE SCOPE OF THE INDECENCY STANDARD

The compromise eliminates an indecency prohibition in the Hyde amendment and an obscenity prohibition in the Exon amendment. This approach eliminates inconsistent standards for obscenity and indecency in the Hyde and Exon approaches that would have created considerable uncertainty.

It also eliminates a second indecency crime that had been part of the Hyde amendment. This provision amended 18 U.S.C. § 1465 to provide that:

> "Whoever intentionally communicates by computer, in or affecting interstate or foreign commerce, to any person the communicator believes has not attained the age of 18 years, any material that, in context, depicts or describes, in terms patently offensive as measured by contemporary community standards, sexual or excretory activities or organs, or attempts to do so, shall be fined under this title or imprisoned not more than five years or both."

H.R. 1555, Section 403. This indecency crime was somewhat broader than the indecency crime included in Section 502 of the conference compromise, including an attempt crime and covering communications that are not directed to **"a specific person or persons under 18 years of age."** Although including an relatively high intent standard, it used the "by computer" formulation present elsewhere in the Hyde amendment that would have established a harmful precedent if followed in other legislation without including its intent standard.

V. SECTION 509: CIVIL LIABILITY PROTECTIONS (COX-WYDEN AMENDMENT)

A. BROAD ELIGIBILITY FOR THE CIVIL LIABILITY DEFENSE

Section 509 is crafted broadly—both in terms of the type of content that may be blocked or destroyed without fear of civil liability and in terms of the entities eligible for the "Good Samaritan" defense.

Its subsection 230(c)(2)(A) provides that the "Good Samaritan" defense applies to restricting:

> **"material that the provider or user considers to be obscene, lewd, lascivious, filthy, excessively violent, harassing, or otherwise objectionable, whether or not such material is constitutionally protected ... ."**

Thus there is no requirement that the **"objectionable"** material be either obscene or indecent in order for providers or users to receive the defense.

Furthermore, the "Good Samaritan" protections are available to a very broad range of entities and individual users. As discussed in Section IV D above, the definition of the term **"interactive computer service"** in subsection 230(f)(2) of the Cox-Wyden-White amendment has been expanded in conference to include access software providers, thereby including them among **"provider[s] ... of an interactive computer service"** eligible for the "Good Samaritan" defense of subsection 230(c)(2).

Section 509 contains a similar expansion of the definition of **"interactive computer service"** that makes non-subscriber systems—such as those operated by many businesses for company use—eligible for the Good Samaritan defense. This change, coupled with the employer defense in subsection 230(e)(4) of Section 502, gives further encouragement to businesses to use interactive computer services.

Subsection 230(f)(2) of Section 509 expands the Cox-Wyden-White amendment's definition of **"interactive computer service"** to include **"systems,"** in addition to **"information services,"** as entities eligible for the Good Samaritan defense. The conference report specifies that the Cox-Wyden-White protections now *"apply to all interactive computer services … including non-subscriber systems."* Joint Explanatory Statement, at 75.

With the changes incorporated into the conference compromise, Section 509 now protects a very broad range of entities and individuals who restrict or enable restriction of objectionable content on interactive computer services.

B. BROAD PREEMPTION

The compromise expands and clarifies the Cox-Wyden-White amendment's preemption provision in subsection 230(e)(3). It provides:

> **"(3) State Law.—Nothing in this section shall be construed to prevent any State from enforcing any State law that is consistent with this section. No cause of action may be brought and no liability may be imposed under any State or local law that is inconsistent with this section."**

Report language elaborates that:

> *"One of the specific purposes of this section is to overrule Stratton-Oakmont v. Prodigy and any other similar decisions which have treated such providers and users as publishers or speakers of content that is not their own because they have restricted access to objectionable material. The conferees believe that such decisions create serious obstacles to the important federal policy of empowering parents to determine the content of communications their children receive through interactive computer services."*

Joint Explanatory Statement, at 75.

The second sentence of subsection 230(e)(3) was added in conference in response to the conferees' decision to add a "no implied preemption" provision, Section 601(c), in conference. By clearly expressing Congress' intent to preempt decisions such as Stratton-Oakmont v. Prodigy, the new sentence ensures that preemption is not defeated by Section 601(c).

Although it is unclear how state courts will apply the Good Samaritan provision in state tort law actions, the Cox-Wyden-White amendment's protections are useful principally to limit these state tort actions. Accordingly, this broad preemption language is essential if the amendment is to have broad effect.

C. BROADENING ONLINE SERVICES' PROTECTION FOR ERASING MESSAGES WITHOUT EXTENDING "GOOD SAMARITAN" PROTECTIONS TO "CANCELBOTTING"

Section 509 contains another change in the Cox-Wyden-White amendment that should aid the stability of online communications. The change broadens the amendment's "Good Samaritan" protections to permit online providers to erase inappropriate messages. It is accompanied by report language safeguarding against extending these protections to "cancelbotting" users.

Subsection 230(c)(2)(A) has been amended to extend the Good Samaritan civil liability protection to **"any action voluntarily taken in good faith to restrict access to or availability of [objectionable] material ... "** (modification underlined). This change clearly permits individuals and entities that have the contractual right to eliminate material from their systems or other systems to which a message may have been sent, to eliminate the material without fear of civil liability.

However, there is some risk that "cancelbotting"—the unauthorized destruction by a user of messages on the communications systems of others—might be sheltered from liability under this broadened formulation. The conference report guards against this risk by specifically providing:

> "The conferees do not intend, however, that these protections from civil liability apply to so-called "cancelbotting," in which recipients of a message respond by deleting the message from the computer systems of others without consent of the originator or without having the right to do so."

Joint Explanatory Statement, at 75. This language should be helpful in avoiding creating immunity for this destructive practice without in any way limiting the ability of Internet users and online service providers to screen out objectionable content.

Appendix G

Footnotes

1. Section 502 also amends the current "Dial-a-porn" statute to address harassing, obscene and indecent telephonic communications by devices other than interactive computer services. Because these provisions, found in subsection 223(a) of the bill, do not affect the online/ Internet industry, they are not discussed in this memo.

2. Boldface type is used in this memo to denote statutory language. Italics are used to denote citations to the "Joint Explanatory Statement of the Committee of Conference" (the report language explaining the conference committee's legislative language). Citations to previous conference committee drafts and to language in the Exon, Hyde, or Cox-Wyden-White amendments are in plain text.

3. "Facial challenges" are across-the-board attacks against the constitutionality of a statute, and are more difficult to win than challenges to the application of a statute to a particular defendant. In the event that a facial challenge failed, defendants could still mount constitutional challenges to the application of the statute to them.

Appendix H
Using the Compact Disk

THE accompanying CD-ROM contains tools, files, and other information that we think will aid you in navigating the Internet. You will find:

Eudora LIGHT, a shareware version of the Eudora e-mail client.

Microsoft's Internet Explorer, a Web browser.

The FTP-List, Perry Rover's famous comprehensive list of nearly all the public FTP archives on the Internet.

HotDogPro, an exceptional HTML editor to let you create your own WWW pages quickly and easily. It also includes an FTP client, so that you can not only get files from the Internet, but load your created HTML files onto an Internet server.

Microsoft's Internet Assistants for Word, Excel, and Power-Point, to help you convert documents, spreadsheets, and presentations into HTML format.

Doran's Mudlist, so those of you interested in exploring the world of MUDs can find all the games you might be interested in.

The Webspinners list, where you can find a professional HTML creation and hosting service if you would like someone else to create your Web page.

WinZip for both Windows and Win95, a compression tool to help you receive and send files across the Internet most economically.

Netcom's NetCruiser, an integrated graphical interface to the Internet for Windows. NetCruiser includes a Web browser, as well as client software to read and send e-mail, to read and post Usenet news, and to use Gopher, Telnet, FTP, Internet Relay Chat, and Finger. It also includes the connection software to connect your computer to the Netcom network. To use it you will need an account with Netcom.

Some of these tools are evaluation copies, and if you like them, licensing information is available on the disk to help you register your copy. (The Microsoft license agreement appears at the back of the book.) Be sure to read and abide by the copyright and licensing information for each item on the disk.

If you need help with these tools beyond the installation, please contact your service provider or the software company directly.

Eudora LIGHT

Eudora is an excellent e-mail client. With it you can connect to your local provider and receive your e-mail using a POP (Post Office Protocol) server. You can send attachments, such as spreadsheets and word-processing files, with your e-mail. (In fact, Pat used Eudora LIGHT to attach files from her hard disk to e-mail she was sending to our editor at Sybex. In the course of writing and editing this book, hundreds of files were exchanged, mostly as attachments to e-mail.)

Two self-extracting archives come with your CD-ROM: the documentation, in the file eud15man.exe, and the program itself, in the file eudor152.exe.

The manual included with Eudora LIGHT is quite good, and we described how to use Eudora LIGHT in Chapter 8. Therefore, we just give you a brief overview here of how to install Eudora LIGHT.

Installing Eudora LIGHT

1. Create a new directory on your hard drive, called\eudora\.

2. Using the File Manager in Windows 3.1 or the Explorer in Win95, open the directory \eudora\ on the CD.

3. Copy the files eudor152.exe and eud15man.exe into the new \eudora\ directory you have created.

4. Click on the eudor152.exe file. This will launch a self-extraction program that will unpack Eudora LIGHT on your hard drive.

5. Click on the eud15man.exe file.

These two operations will install Eudora LIGHT on your hard drive, as shown in Figure H.1.

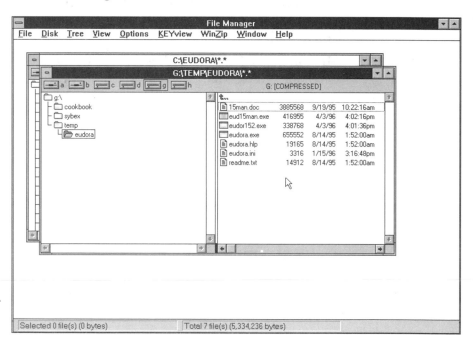

*Figure H.1.   **Unpacked Eudora LIGHT files after extraction.***

Now you need to configure Eudora for use with your service provider.

1. Click on the eudora.exe file. This will launch Eudora LIGHT.

2. The Settings menu will come up, as shown in Figure H.2. Your POP account is your e-mail account name at your provider, which they should have given you. Your real name is, of course, your given name.

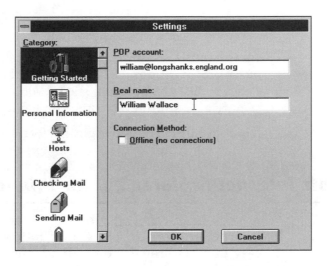

Figure H.2. Enter your account name and your real name in the Settings menu.

3. Do *not* click OK. Instead, click on the Personal Information button. This will let you add your return address, if it is different from your popmail account. Check with your provider to be sure.

4. Now, click on the Hosts icon, as shown in Figure H.3. Here you enter your SMTP host, as provided by your ISP, the phone number which you use to connect, and (optionally) a host where your information is accessible via Finger.

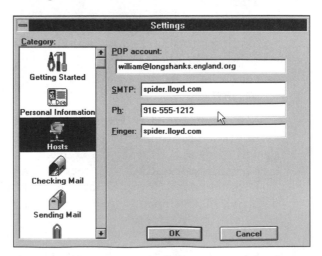

Figure H.3. The Hosts information lets Eudora LIGHT make your mail connection.

Next you will need to configure the Checking Mail and Sending Mail panels, as described in the documentation and/or information given you by your ISP. We recommend *strongly* that you do NOT store your password in Eudora LIGHT, even though this box is checked by default when the program starts. For security, set up your software to require a password every time you launch it.

(Eudora LIGHT is copyright © 1991-1996 by QUALCOMM, Inc.)

Microsoft Internet Explorer 2.0 for Windows 95

Microsoft Internet Explorer 2.0 for Windows 95 is Microsoft's Internet browser designed for Windows 95. Internet Explorer is an easy Internet browser to set up and use with the Windows 95 operating system, and it supports all major World Wide Web standards.

Microsoft Internet Explorer 2.0 embraces existing HTML standards, such as tables, while using new improvements such as inline video, background sounds, and marquee effects. Internet Explorer 2.0 delivers support for secure Internet shopping applications.

What's in Version 2.0?

Tables

Internet Explorer now supports tables. You can check these out by loading the table demonstration from the Microsoft Web site at

```
http://www.microsoft.com
```

Security

Microsoft Internet Explorer now supports SSL security, with an upgraded random-number generator. In addition, Internet Explorer will support STT (Secure Transaction Technology—jointly developed by Microsoft and VISA International) for financial transactions, and PCT (Private Communication Technology)—a new secure channel protocol developed by Microsoft and industry partners.

NNTP News

Read Usenet newsgroups with Microsoft Internet Explorer. No need for a separate newsreader.

Sound and Video

Microsoft Internet Explorer incorporates HTML extensions that let background sounds and inline video be used on Web pages. Now you can hear and see what the Web page programmer intended, without configuring special viewers or players.

Scrolling Text Marquees

Now you can see those eye-catching callouts on Web pages for special offers and other time-critical information.

Client Pull

Microsoft Internet Explorer can pull a sequence of graphics from a Web server to run simple animations, such as the front page of the Levi-Strauss Web server (http://www.levi.com) or the Batman Forever server (http://www.batmanforever.com).

Search Button

You can jump quickly to your favorite search page on the Internet.

Send Shortcut Command

The File menu now contains a command that enables you to mail a Win95 shortcut to a favorite Web site directly to your colleagues and friends from Microsoft Internet Explorer.

Installing Internet Explorer

Internet Explorer comes in a self-extracting archive file. On the CD, look for the directory \ms\explore\. If you want to use Explorer with Win95, choose the directory \win95\. If you want to use it with Windows 3.1, choose \win31\.

Using the File Manager or File Explorer, click on the file msie20.exe. This will launch the self-extractor and begin the installation process. In general, it's best to accept the defaults for disk location and names that Microsoft provides.

Easy to Set Up and Use

The Internet Setup Wizard configures Windows 95 to use TCP/IP Networking, Dial-up Networking, and Microsoft Exchange e-mail. If you don't already have an account with an Internet service provider, the Internet Setup Wizard can sign you up for MSN (the Microsoft Network), reducing the whole signup and setup procedure to nothing more than typing in your name and address, selecting a payment method, and swapping disks.

If you already have a provider, the procedure is not much harder. You will need to have ready:

> The name of your service provider, your account name, password, and dial-up telephone number

> Your IP address and subnet mask (these may not be required if your service provider automatically assigns these)

> The address of your DNS server

To Try the Internet Setup Wizard

1. Click the Start button, point to Programs, point to Accessories, and click Internet Tools.

2. Click Internet Setup Wizard.

Explorer Is Easy to Use

Using Microsoft Internet Explorer is a "natural" for Windows 95 users. Internet Explorer has many of the user interface improvements and system services that Windows 95 introduced, such as context menus, shortcuts, and drag-and-drop.

To start Microsoft Internet Explorer, just double-click the Internet icon on the Windows 95 desktop. The user interface is simple and easy to use, in a deliberate attempt to simplify working with the Web. At the top of the window is a short toolbar of buttons for common activities. As you would expect, if you pause the mouse over each button in turn, a short description of each is displayed. At the bottom of the window is the status bar, showing descriptive status text on the left and a download status meter on the right.

The FTP-List

Perry Rover's FTP List is one of the most comprehensive resources on the Internet about FTP archives. For the FTP FAQ and other FTP resources, check out Perry's WWW page at

`http://www.iaehv.nl/users/perry/ftp-list.html`

On the disk, in the directory \ftp-list\, we have the most recent version of the list in ASCII format. There are two ways to use this file: open it in a word processor, or open it with your WWW browser.

Either way, you can then search for an archive that has what you need. For example, if you are looking for archives with information on Dr. Who, you could search for "Dr. Who" or, perhaps, "drwho."

(The FTP-List is copyright © 1993-1996, Perry Rovers. Used with permission. Rovers additionally places this restriction on the electronic media version, in case you wish to use the electronic version for some other purpose than reference: "Text may be quoted in on-line documents and written publications, but please notify me so I can add a reference and make sure that you add pointers to the places where people can get the latest version. You may make this file available on public servers, like FTP, Gopher or WWW servers as well, but please let me know. Do not modify the info itself (i.e. converting it to some other format) before consulting me. All rights reserved. This may seem stricter than the last versions, but I only want to make sure I'm notified of how this file is used and for what purpose. If you contact me, I'm sure we can work something out." Rover's e-mail address is available in both files in the ftp-list.zip archive.)

The Webspinners List

Mary E. S. Morris, author of *HTML for Fun and Profit,* and her company, Finesse, sponsor a comprehensive list of Web designers. You can hire these folks to create a Web presence for you, be it a single page or a comprehensive site with hundreds of documents, query forms, interactive software, or what have you.

We have included this list in ASCII text format on the CD-ROM, in the directory \webspin\.

As with the FTP-list, you should open the file with a word processor, and browse. Because of the global nature of the Internet, you can

Appendix H

choose designers who are close to you geographically or remotely located. Cut and paste the URLs for these designers' Web pages right into your browser and take a look at what they can do.

(Copyright © 1993-1996 Mary E. S. Morris. Used with permission.)

Doran's MUDlist

Not so long ago, MUDs were mostly underground and kept secret from "the establishment." A player named Doran compiled a list of every MUD he could find, much as Perry Rovers compiled a list of FTP archives. Soon Doran's MUDlist became *the* roadmap into the MUD community. Taken over on Doran's retirement by a player named Indium, this list is still the most comprehensive resource to finding MUDs around the globe.

On the CD, in the directory \mudlist\, look for the file mudlist.txt.

Use the MUDlist to search for games that look interesting: Star Trek, Sword and Sorcery, Pern, what-have-you. Open the MUDlist in a word processor like Microsoft Word (it's too big for Notepad), and use the Search function, or just browse.

You can cut and paste the URLs for the MUDs right into your browser, Telnet client, or MUD client.

Additions to the list can be found at:

    http://www.csc.calpoly.edu/~kamundse/mudlist.html

The MUDlist is published every once in a while and posted to the USENET newsgroups rec.games.mud.diku, rec.games.mud.lp, rec .games.mud.misc, rec.games.mud.tiny, and rec.games.mud.admin.

(Doran's Mudlist is copyright © 1989-1996, Doran. Used with Permission. Send any additions/corrections/gripes/complaints/praise/cash to mudlist@merlyn.punk. Indium says, "Complete, explicit instructions for sending mail to this address appear at the end of the mudlist. Please read them carefully. If you do not follow the instructions, your mail will be sucked into /dev/null and never be seen by human eyes again.")

HotDog Pro

Although you can use any text editor or word processor that will let you save your file as straight ASCII text to create HTML code for WWW pages, the new breed of HTML editors lets you create the files more easily. HotDog Pro is one of the best available, and we include an evaluation copy on the CD-ROM in the directory \html-edi\.

You can find out more about the Sausage company, which created Hot-Dog Pro, at their Web site:

```
http://www.sausage.com/
```

With HotDog Pro, you can:

Create HTML code.

See what you've created without having to go out to a separate browser.

Create tables and frames.

Debug your HTML code simply.

To install HotDog Pro, click on the hd251pro.exe file on the CD-ROM. This will launch the installation program, as shown in Figure H.4. You will be warned about a library (called a DLL file) which you may not already have in your Windows System folder. We have included it on the CD-ROM for convenience, or you can get it from the Web site above. You will then be asked to complete the license agreement.

Click OK to accept the evaluation license agreement and continue the setup.

Next you will be asked where to install your software. The default is c:\htdogpro, as shown in Figure H.5. If this is OK, click OK. If you want the software in some other directory, enter the disk and directory, and then click OK.

Next you will be asked if you want Hot Dog to create backups of any files it has to replace during installation. This is a safe choice: Click OK. Hot Dog will then confirm the directory where it will place these backup files.

*Figure H.4.   **The HotDog Pro setup program includes the evaluation license agreement.***

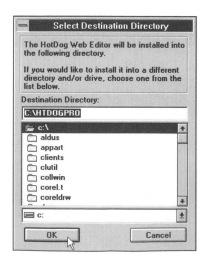

*Figure H.5.   **Creating a HotDog Pro directory.***

Next, as shown in Figure H.6, you will see a status bar while HotDog Pro unpacks and installs the various files that make up the program.

Figure H.6. **HotDog keeps you informed of the status.**

Next, the installation program will ask if you want to add icons for HotDog Pro to the Program Manager. Click OK. You can put HotDog in an existing Program group, or, by default, in one of its own. Click OK. The installation will complete, and you will be left at the Program Manager with the new HotDog icon, as shown in Figure H.7. Click on the cute dog to launch the Web editor.

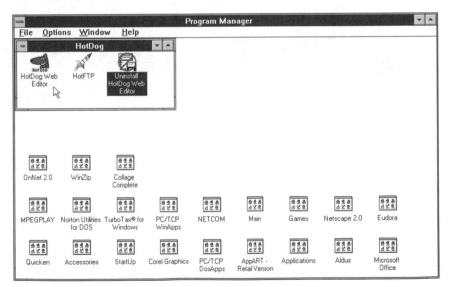

Figure H.7. **Hot Dog is installed: Click on the Dog icon to start creating a Web page!**

Once you launch HotDog, the program starts a new HTML file and also brings up a really good tutorial about HTML and HotDog, shown in Figure H.8. Rather than repeat that information here, we recommend you take the tutorials and learn how to use this tool. Be sure to check out the HotFTP, an FTP client which comes as part of HotDogPro.

(Hot Dog is copyright © 1996 Sausage Software Limited.)

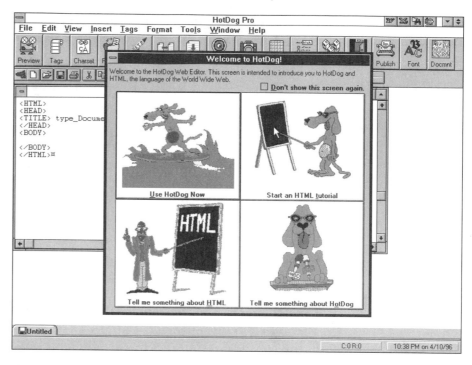

Figure H.8.   HotDog offers 4 tutorials—Use them!

Microsoft's Internet Assistants for Word, Excel, and PowerPoint

One of the major frustrations of creating Web sites has been converting existing documents into HTML. Microsoft offers a shareware solution to this problem, in the form of "Internet Assistants" for Word 6.0 and Word for Windows 95, for Excel, and for PowerPoint.

These three programs let you take your existing documents, spreadsheets, or presentations and convert them. They work in different ways, but each produces good basic HTML code that can be viewed on your WWW site.

In the \ms\ directory on the CD you'll find the software for each of these programs, the system requirements, installation instructions, a FAQ from Microsoft, and other documentation. Please read it carefully to install your Internet Assistants.

(The Internet Assistants are copyright © 1995–1996 Microsoft Corporation. All rights reserved.)

WinZip

One of the fastest ways to spend excess money on the Internet is to stay connected for a long time. Transferring large files will keep you hooked up for a long time, longer than you probably want to pay for. Therefore, most FTP archives, WWW sites with downloadable files, and other places to obtain files from the Internet will have those files in *compressed* format.

In addition, if you want to attach files to your e-mail, it's polite to compress the file first.

WinZip is a Windows tool to help you compress, uncompress, and extract just the file you want from a compressed group of files. We have both the 16-bit version for Windows 3.1 and the 32-bit version for Win95 on the CD-ROM.

To install WinZip from the CD, click on the file you want to install. For Windows 3.1, this is wz60wn16.exe. For Win95, this would be winzip95.exe.

Clicking on the file will open a self-extracting archive, as shown in Figure H.9. Click on Start to begin the process.

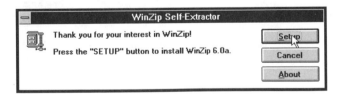

Figure H.9.   *WinZip installs with a self-extracting archive.*

Next, WinZip's installation program will ask you into which directory you want to install the program. If the default, c:\winzip, is acceptable, click OK, as in Figure H.10. If not, type in the name of the preferred directory now.

Now you can decide what kind of installation to use. Unless you are short on disk space, click OK to choose the default express setup, as shown in Figure H.11.

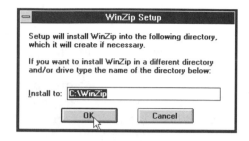

Figure H.10.   **Confirm the installation directory.**

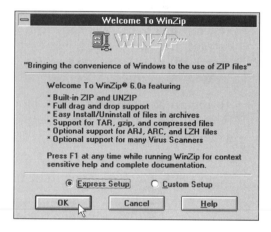

Figure H.11.   **Use the Express Setup.**

Like most of the other software on this disk, WinZip is an evaluation copy. If you want to continue using it beyond the evaluation period, you must register and pay for it. You will next be asked, as in Figure H.12, to explicitly agree to this: be sure to read the license agreement first.

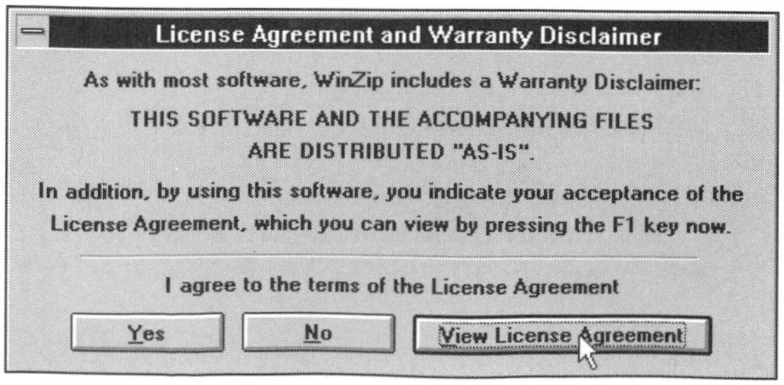

Figure H.12.   **The License agreement.**

After you click to show your acceptance, WinZip will finish the installation, and the program will launch. As shown in Figure H.13, you can create a new archive or open a previously "zipped" file.

Figure H.13.   *Use WinZip to create New archives or open existing ones.*

If you choose Open, you can unzip files you have received from other folk or downloaded. In Figure H.14, you see that we used WinZip to extract files for this book. When the Open Archive dialog box appears, highlight the name of the file you want to uncompress and then click OK.

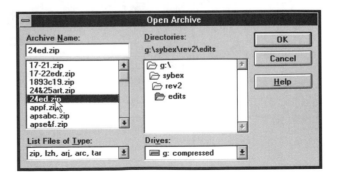

Figure H.14.   *You can select an existing archive by highlighting the file name.*

Once you have selected the archive you want to work with, WinZip tells you about the files inside. You can find out how big the file will be uncompressed, the compressed size, and the compression ratio. You can also find out when the files were created.

To work with an archive, you need to either click on the Add button to add more files into the archive, or click on Extract to uncompress what's currently there, as in Figure H.15. If you only want one of many files, you can highlight that file name only and then click on Extract.

Figure H.15.   Select the files you want to extract.

Next, you need to select the directory where you want the extracted files to go, as shown in Figure H.16.

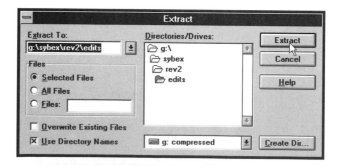

Figure H.16.   Choose the destination directory for the extracted files.

WinZip has many more features you can use. There is excellent online help available within the program itself.

(WinZip® Copyright © 1991–1994 Nico Mak Computing, Inc. All rights reserved.)

NetCruiser

If you've got a modem and a PC running Windows 3.1 or later, Netcom's NetCruiser is the only other thing you'll need to get up and running on the Internet. (OK, you'll also need to set up an account with Netcom, but you can do that through NetCruiser.) This program provides access to e-mail, Gopher, the Web, Telnet, and more; in short, it provides you with complete Internet access. *Access the Internet*, by David Peal (Sybex, third edition 1996) is the "official guide" to NetCruiser and an excellent starting point for exploring this "one-stop" Internet tool.

Installing and Registering NetCruiser

Before you can use NetCruiser, you need to install the NetCruiser program on your computer and then register an account with Netcom. This section describes how to do these things. You will find instructions on how to:

Install the NetCruiser program.

Run the NetCruiser registration program to register a new account.

Run the NetCruiser program to connect to the Netcom network.

Check to see if there is a later version of NetCruiser and download the new version.

Configure your startup options.

Checking Your Equipment

Before you get started, you should review your computer equipment to make sure you can successfully run the program. To run NetCruiser, you will need the following:

An IBM-compatible personal computer that uses an 80386 (also called a "386") or greater processing chip. This means that computers that use an 80486 or Pentium processing chip will work, too. Computers using the 80286 chip will not work.

MS-DOS 5.0 or greater and Microsoft Windows 3.1 or greater. This means you can be running MS-DOS 6.2 and Microsoft Windows 3.11, for example. NetCruiser also runs on Windows 95

CHANGING THE AUTOEXEC.BAT FILE

If you think you will ever use other Internet applications that use the NetCruiser *WinSock,* you need to include the directory that contains NetCruiser in the path of the directories that DOS and Windows will search when they begin executing programs. This means that the PATH statement in your AUTOEXEC.BAT file will need to have in it the directory that contains NetCruiser. This statement is read by the operating system and used to construct a list of places to look for programs that may be requested by other programs. If something is not listed in the PATH statement, it is effectively hidden, unless the program is *invoked* (started) with a complete directory path (for instance, C:\Netcom\NETCRUZ.EXE for the NetCruiser program itself).

WinSock is the name of the Windows-based program that connects Internet communications programs to the network. "Open WinSock" programs are designed to meet standards that allow programs written by other people and published and distributed by other companies to work together. NetCruiser versions 1.6 and later meet the Open WinSock standards for compatibility to allow other programs that are not originally part of NetCruiser to be used with NetCruiser. You will probably want to try other programs as you become more proficient with NetCruiser, so make sure that the NetCruiser directory is listed in your PATH statement.

Joining Netcom via NetCruiser

The first display screen you will see is your welcome to Netcom and NetCruiser (Figure H.17). *Registration* is the name that Netcom gives to the process where you supply Netcom with your name and address, where you choose your username, and where the credit card account that you have chosen to use with Netcom will be validated. There are special computers at Netcom, called registration servers, where your account information is stored. These computers are not on the global Internet, so your account information remains private. Because the computers are separate from the Internet, the registration program will use your modem and telephone line to connect to the registration servers using a different telephone number than you will use to connect to the Netcom network.

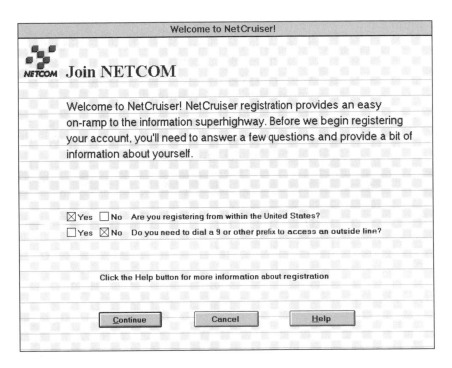

Figure H.17. **The NetCruiser registration screen.**

If you live within the United States, the registration number is a toll-free number that the registration program will dial automatically. If you live within the United States, click Yes so that the program will use the toll-free connection.

If you live outside the United States, the registration number may not be toll-free. Check with the Netcom people where you live. You may want to get a copy of NetCruiser specifically for the country in which you reside. The registration program on this disk will dial a number in San Jose, California, and you will be charged for the telephone call. You may need to add additional access codes before the number before the connection is made. If you click No, the registration program will not use the toll-free number for registration.

If you need to dial a line outside your organization's telephone system, click the Yes box. The registration program will present a dialog box for you to enter a dialing code. Here's where you should enter any numbers you may require to turn off your call-waiting function, for instance. If you don't turn off call-waiting, you may suddenly lose your connection if someone tries to call when you are logged on. Consult your local telephone service provider to find the correct sequence of codes to turn call-waiting off.

If you need to enter a calling card number, enter it here, too. Or you can choose to enter the code for your long-distance provider here, as we've done in Figure H.18.

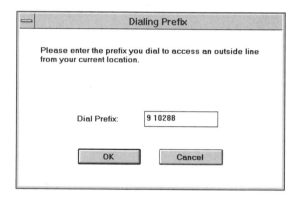

Figure H.18.   Entering a "dial-out" prefix and a code for a long-distance provider.

Click Continue when you are ready to go on to the next registration action.

If you click Help, you will start the NetCruiser Help program. This program gives you additional information prepared by Netcom to help you in registering for your NetCruiser account.

If you click Cancel, you will exit the registration program. If you already have a registered NetCruiser account, you can start a NetCruiser session by clicking on the NetCruiser icon in the appropriate program group.

Entering Your User Information

In the Enter User Information screen (Figure H.19), you enter your name, address, and telephone numbers. Use upper- and lowercase letters in the name and address portion of the form. Press the Tab key to move from one part of the form to the next.

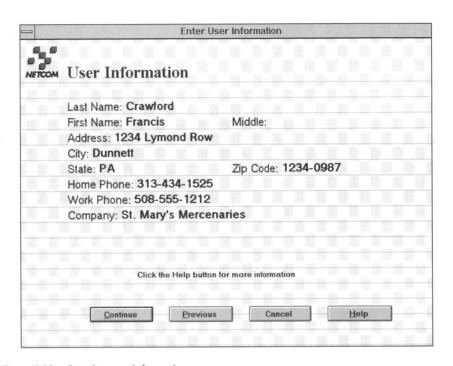

Figure H.19. **Entering user information.**

 MASTER WORDS   The name that you enter here is used in the field called "full name" in e-mail and Usenet headers. This means that other people will see this name. If you don't want this name to be seen by others, use the Edit/User Account Information command under the Settings menu after you are connected to the Netcom network.

Click Continue when you are ready to go on to the next registration step.

Choosing Your Username

Next you are asked to choose your username (Figure H.20). Your username will be combined with the NetCruiser domain name (ix.netcom .com) to form your new Internet e-mail address. If you don't like the way it looks or sounds, or you simply would rather use something else, now is the best time to change it. A good username (the name that identifies you to the authorization system and that will be part of your Internet address) is between six and eight characters long. It should not begin with a number, but it may contain numbers. The Netcom system will make sure that it is unique so that your username is the only one among NetCruiser users.

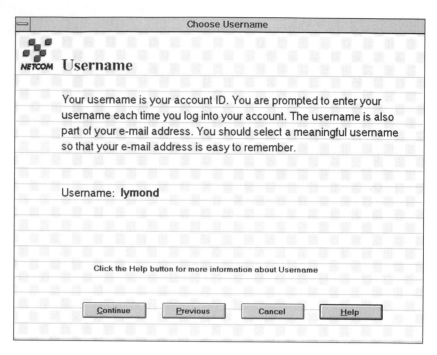

*Figure H.20. **Entering a username.***

Click Continue when you are ready to go on to the next registration action.

Choosing a Password

The Choose Account Password screen (Figure H.21) asks you to enter a password for your account. You are asked to repeat your password so that the system is certain of it (and so are you). You will need to enter your password each time you connect to the Internet using NetCruiser, so be sure to choose something that is relatively easy for you to remember, yet safe and secure.

 MASTER WORDS A safe password is one that is six or more characters long and contains both upper- and lowercase characters and numbers. Avoid using special characters like ") (* & ^ . Password-cracking programs look for complete words (in forward or reverse order) in a number of different languages. Therefore, it is safest to avoid using words. It is an especially good idea to avoid the password "aardvark."

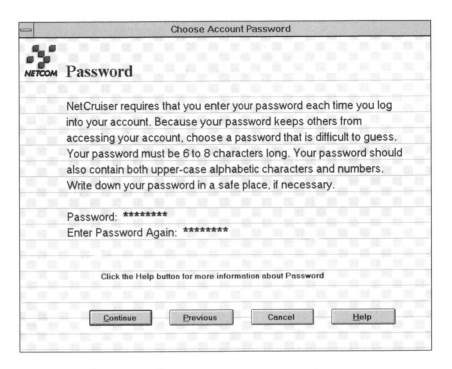

Figure H.21.   **Entering a password.**

Another good idea, of course, is to record your password, as you do PIN(s) for your bank card(s), in a safe place *away* from the computer on which the NetCruiser software resides.

Click Continue when you are ready to go on to the next registration action.

Verification Information

NetCruiser registration next asks that you supply your mother's maiden name or a secret word (Figure H.22). This word will be stored with your user account information. When you call Netcom technical support (at 408-983-5970) or Netcom accounting (at 408-983-5950) and ask that changes be made to your account, you will be asked for this word so that Netcom can be certain that the person requesting the changes is, in fact, authorized to request the changes. This protects you and your account.

Appendix H

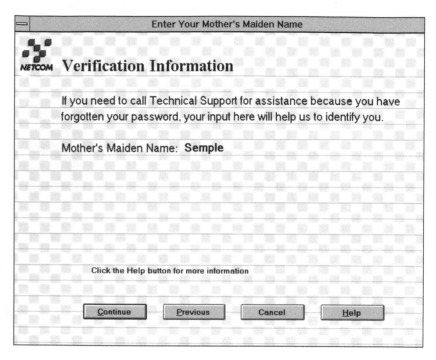

*Figure H.22.   **As verification information, NetCruiser requests your mother's maiden name.***

Click Continue when you are ready to go on to the next registration action.

Registration Code

In the next screen, you enter any registration code assigned to the program by Netcom. A brief message that varies with the registration code may appear above the registration code. Do not worry if you don't have a special code. All you need to do is press Enter or click on Continue to accept the supplied code and continue the registration process. Some codes may only be used once. If you are not able to use the supplied code, perhaps because you have installed NetCruiser before, you will need to call Netcom technical support for another registration code. The registration code will be validated during the program's connection to the registration server. If you enter a code that is not valid, a message to that effect will be displayed at that time. Then you can change or erase the code that you entered.

Click Continue when you are ready to go on to the next registration step.

Registration Status

NetCruiser will now connect you to the special registration server. At this time, the information you have supplied is added to Netcom's records. If your username is already being used, you will be asked to supply another one. Your credit card number will be verified. While NetCruiser is making the connection and sending data to the server, it will report its progress on this screen (Figure H.23). When you need to supply additional information, NetCruiser will interrupt the progress report and display a dialog box. You should enter the requested information into the displayed dialog box and then click Continue.

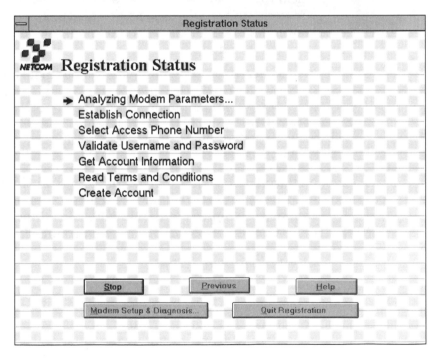

Figure H.23. **The registration server displays its progress.**

Setting Up Your Modem

In order for NetCruiser registration to pass your collected information to the Netcom servers, your modem must be configured (set up) correctly to communicate with the Netcom network. Different types of services require different modem settings. Each time you connect to the Netcom network, NetCruiser will set your modem so that it can communicate with the network. This is like making sure that we all agree what language to use in conducting a conversation. Here are some things to check before you start that will help the process along.

First make sure that no other application is using the modem. Some fax programs run as TSRs (*terminate and stay resident* programs)—they run whenever you start up DOS or Windows and are resident in memory in order to receive a fax that is transmitted to you. If you are running a program like this, you will need to restore it and then exit the program before NetCruiser can use your modem.

Then, you'll need to make sure that your modem is turned on. If you have an internal modem, your modem will have power as soon as you turn on your computer. An external modem, however, usually has its power supplied separately.

NetCruiser has a lot of information about modems already stored within it. NetCruiser will use Automatic Modem Setup to find your modem and supply a configuration string that will connect your modem to the network properly. If you know a lot about what type of modem you have, or if NetCruiser is unable to set up your modem accurately, click on Manual Setup.

NetCruiser starts testing your modem and COM port (communications port) setup. It will try combinations of modems and communications ports until it finds a match. Click Modem Setup & Diagnosis if NetCruiser is unable to detect and configure your modem.

Manual Modem Settings

If NetCruiser is unable to detect what type of modem is installed or connected to your computer a dialog box is presented with the COM port, speed, and modem name filled in with the information which was obtained from the automatic modem detection process. You will need to change the information to reflect what you can determine about your modem from your modem manual or with the help of the NetCruiser Technical Support team.

WARNING   If your modem is not configured correctly, you will be unable to connect to the Netcom network reliably. Symptoms of incorrect configuration include not hanging up on exit (could result in larger telephone bills), large transfers (many bytes) not completing, and connections dropped unexpectedly.

If you are unsure what to do to configure your modem correctly, call Netcom technical support, at (408) 983-5970.

Choose a Phone Number

After your modem is configured and you are connected to the registration server and your account data has been transferred and stored, you will be asked to choose an access number (Figure H.24). Netcom has many access numbers. You can choose to connect to *any* of them. Naturally, not all of them will be a local call for you. Local calls are the least expensive way to use the NetCruiser service. Netcom will display several numbers that may be local to either the office or home telephone number that you supplied with your account data. To select a number, you can scroll through the list of numbers in the Directory chosen by clicking on Directory in the Access Phone Number box.

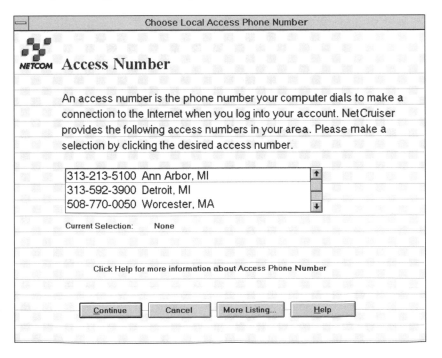

Figure H.24. Scrolling through a list of Netcom access numbers within your area code(s).

The numbers are in order first by area code and then by the first three digits of the telephone number, called the exchange. The name of the metropolitan area that the number serves is listed next. The first thing to look for is a number in the area code from which you will be calling. Compare the numbers listed with the local calling area given in the front of your telephone book. Just because a number is in your area code does not make it a local call. Conversely, just because a number is not in your area code does not make it a long-distance call. Some large metropolitan areas, Washington DC, for example, have several area codes within a local calling area.

If none of the numbers proposed are suitable, click More Listing for a display of all the telephone numbers available (Figure H.25). Again, the telephone numbers are organized by area code and then by number within area code. Click to select a number.

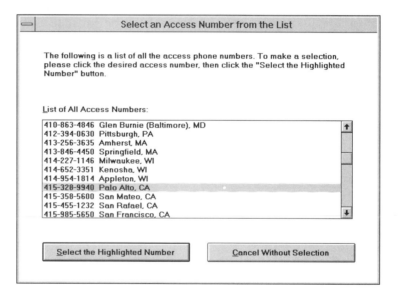

Figure H.25.   Netcom's complete list of access numbers.

Click Select the Highlighted Number to choose a particular number.

Click Cancel without Selection to return to the previous display.

You can change the number you use to connect to Netcom before each session. Choosing a number here as part of registration selects the number to be stored and dialed for your first connection.

If there is no local number for you to dial, you should investigate your options to call a number in a state that is near you as well as your in-state calling options. Sometimes out-of-state toll calls are considerably less expensive than in-state toll calls. You should ask both your local and long-distance telephone providers to tell you how much the calls would be to several possible access numbers. Some people may be able to use the Dial Netcom service. There is a surcharge to use this service; you will be charged with your NetCruiser service bill.

Billing Information

Your credit card information is now collected after a thank-you message. The billing information and subscription charges are explained. You are given the opportunity to save the billing information for your own later reference. At the bottom of the display are text boxes to record the number, type, and expiration date for your credit card. If you enter an invalid number, a message will be displayed. Be sure to enter two digits for the month (e.g. 02 for February if your credit card expires in February).

Read the Terms and Conditions

After you click on Continue, the terms and conditions of your NetCruiser account are displayed. To save them so that you can refer to them later, click on Save. If you wish to cancel the registration process, click on Cancel.

After you click on Continue, your credit card information is sent over a secure line from the NetCruiser registration server to a credit card authorization server. This transaction takes place over a system other than the Internet in order to better protect the information. Since this process can take some time, a status report is given. Occasionally, the connection to the credit card authorization is not completed. If that happens, you will have to try again later. Remember that your information will be saved on your computer to be used next time.

User Name Confirmation

If you choose a username that is being used by another user, you will receive a message like the one shown in Figure H.26.

You'll need to select another name. NetCruiser will suggest that you add a number to the end of the name to make it unique. If you'd like to do that, click Continue. Or select and enter another name in the dialog box and click Continue.

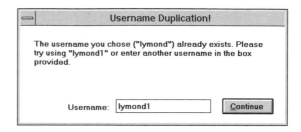

Figure H.26.   The dialog box for changing a duplicate username.

Congratulations!

You are now the proud possessor of a NetCruiser account and a new e-mail address. Click on OK to bring up the final message, shown in Figure H.27. You can now use your new account to connect to the Internet. Just click on the Login Now button to begin.

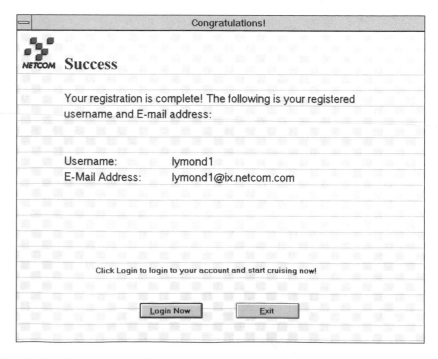

Figure H.27.   Netcom congratulates you for a successful registration.

Connecting to Netcom

Now that you've successfully registered with Netcom, you can launch NetCruiser and go online. In the "Congratulations!" window, click on Login Now to start the program.

You'll see the opening NetCruiser screen. Before you log in, take this opportunity to check the settings you've just entered. You cannot change modem settings while you are logged into NetCruiser. And if your modem settings are incorrect, you cannot log in at all. You may also need to change your password, address or billing information, or modem settings at some point in the future. If you need to be security-conscious, it's a good idea to change your password frequently. Again, the time to make such changes is before you log in for a NetCruiser session.

Checking Your Settings

Whenever you need to check or change your program configuration, click on the Settings menu on the main NetCruiser menu bar. Then, for instance, click on the Phone Number menu item. You can also use your keyboard to move among the menus. Press the Alt key to enable the menus, press S to reach the Settings menu, and then press N to display the Phone Number dialog box. This is the same dialog box as the one you saw in the Select an Access Number portion of the registration process.

If you take advantage of the many Netcom access numbers as you travel, you will need to check your Phone Number settings each time you connect. NetCruiser retains the *last number dialed* in the Phone Number settings. Generally, people use the same number, so this is convenient. However, you may inadvertently find yourself dialing a number that isn't a NetCruiser access number or isn't even a modem number. For example, the number 323-4304 in Elyria, Ohio (area code 216), would be a valid number in Palo Alto, California, if you dialed it from there (area code 415). However, the access number for Palo Alto is 328-9940. You can see that dialing the Elyria number from Palo Alto will have unexpected results.

If you have changed your modem since you last connected, you will want to choose Modem Settings and reconfigure your NetCruiser program settings.

When you have finished checking and/or changing your settings, click OK to return to the Login sequence.

Enter Your Password

In the NetCruiser Login screen, enter your password in the text box below your username. (If you have just registered, NetCruiser will display your password in the text box. After that, you'll need to enter it each time.) You'll see that NetCruiser automatically displays the username. NetCruiser remembers what username to use from session to session. If you have more than one NetCruiser account or you are letting a friend use your computer to connect to the NetCruiser service, you can replace the displayed username with the one you want to use.

Click on Start Login

NetCruiser will dial the access number you have selected. You can also press Enter or first press Alt+L and then Enter.

Observe the Connection Progress

NetCruiser reports the progress of the connection process in the top line of the center message box. Typical messages include, "Dialing Netcom, Palo Alto" and "NetCruiser Starting Session."

Your modem was configured to turn on the modem speaker so that you can hear the connection process, too. This helps to diagnose connection problems if you have them. The annoying noises are a small price to pay for the ability to determine if your modem has connected properly to the network. NetCruiser will turn off the modem speaker when the connection is established.

You will also see a message, "Logging In." This message appears just before the "NetCruiser Starting Session" message.

If you see the message "Call Failed," you know that NetCruiser could not establish a connection. There are several reasons why this can happen. One is that the access number is busy. You will be able to hear the busy signal on your modem speaker. NetCruiser records the busy signal each time it is encountered, and when the connection is finally established, NetCruiser reports the number of busy signals encountered to Netcom so that the network access engineers can review network status and expand the number of access ports as appropriate.

Another reason you may receive a Call Failed message is that the access number is not working at the given time. Occasionally access points are "down" for maintenance, or some network disaster prevents your connection. Sometimes a modem on the Netcom end fails. In that case, you may hear the telephone on the Netcom end of the connection ring and ring. This is called a "ring, no answer" condition or "RNA." When this happens, you can either click on Stop Login or simply wait until NetCruiser stops the login process and tries again. When you do establish a connection, it is considered good network citizenship to send an e-mail message to support@ix.netcom.com and report the problem. Sometimes if you call back right away (or let NetCruiser try again for you), you will connect to the same line again and the call will continue to fail. If you have access to a second telephone line, a quick trick is to use your voice telephone line to dial the access number. Then when you have the "bad" modem on that line, start the NetCruiser login process on your computer. You will then get bumped to the "next" modem in the pool of modems, and a connection will be established.

Another connection failure can happen when a modem on the Netcom end has lost the correct configuration. When this happens, the modem on the Netcom end picks up and yet nothing happens—you get the equivalent of someone answering the telephone and not talking to you. This is called a "Connect, No Login" condition. You can use the same trick involving a second line to call the access number. Be sure to report the situation to support@ix.netcom.com when you do establish a connection.

The connection could, of course, fail on your end. If you have made changes to your computer's configuration (installing a new modem, switching the devices around on your COM ports, or whatever) and not reconfigured the NetCruiser settings, NetCruiser will not be able to find and use the modem. If your modem is not turned on, NetCruiser will not be able to use it. And so on. NetCruiser tries to give diagnostic messages to help you see what the problem might be.

If you cannot connect to the access number you selected and you are sure that the problem is not your configuration, the next thing to try is to connect to another access number. Choose a different access number from the Phone Settings menu to test your configuration. If you are successful in establishing a connection, you will know that the error is on the Netcom end. To report the problem, you should telephone Netcom Technical Support, at (408) 983-5970.

If you still cannot establish a connection, you may want to try an access number that is quite geographically distant. Sometimes network problems may be located in a hub connection that is geographically between you and the rest of the network. When that happens, network access points near you may also not be working. To confirm a significant network outage like this, you should call Netcom Technical Support.

Go Online with Netcom NetCruiser

Welcome to the Internet! You're ready to cruise. NetCruiser has excellent help about all the different tools you can use to access the Internet. With this book and the NetCruiser help, you'll become a NetCruiserUser easily and quickly.

Downloading the Latest Version of NetCruiser

Running the latest version of the NetCruiser software provides you with better service and more features, so check periodically to see whether there is a later version of NetCruiser for you to download.

To check if you have the latest version, click on the File menu in the upper-left corner of the menu bar. You can also display this menu by pressing Alt+F. Select Download New Version.

The Download New Version dialog box estimates how long it will take to transfer the new parts of the NetCruiser program to your computer. Click on Download to begin the transfer. The bottom part of the Download dialog box shows messages from the Netcom server, reporting on the progress of the connection and the transfer. A gauge and byte count are also displayed to let you know how much longer you need to wait. When the "Download complete!" message appears, the transfer is done. Click on OK to continue.

Upgrading Your Software

To take advantage of whatever is new about the latest version of NetCruiser, you will need to upgrade the software on your computer. You cannot be connected to the network while the program is being upgraded, so you need to think about whether you want to complete the upgrade process now or defer it to some time when you are not connected. If you choose not to upgrade now, click on Exit and you will be returned to NetCruiser. If you choose to upgrade, click on Upgrade. A warning message will be displayed.

If you don't want to close your connection now, click on No and then click on Exit, and you will be returned to NetCruiser. If you want to continue the upgrade, click on Yes.

After NetCruiser has closed, you will see the Upgrade dialog box. Click on Upgrade to continue the upgrade process.

You may be shown a dialog box reporting that some parts of the NetCruiser program will be cleared from memory.

The Upgrade program replaces and/or adds the new parts of the NetCruiser program to your computer. When this process is complete, click on OK to finish the process.

Scroll through the Release Notes that are sent with the program updates. They tell you what changes have been made. The information in this file is saved on your computer as RELEASE.TXT in the program directory where you store NetCruiser. You can view it at any time by using a word-processing program to read the file, or you can use the View Text File command found on the NetCruiser File menu.

If you decide that the newer version does not work as well as the older version, you can return to the previous version by clicking on the Restore button in the NetCruiser Upgrade dialog box.

Click on Exit to return to the Program Manager.

If you already have the latest version, NetCruiser will report that with a message box. Click on OK and then click on Exit in the previous dialog box to return to NetCruiser.

Exploring the Startup Options

Your version of NetCruiser may have been configured to start up a particular function automatically, such as the World Wide Web. You can control which functions are started when you connect via the Startup Options dialog box, which you can reach through the last item of the Settings menu.

If you are using the Web browser or if you are using Telnet, you will not see the Startup Options choice. You will need to close the Web session and/or the Telnet session before you can see this choice. When you click on Startup Options or press Alt+T and then S, you will see the Startup Options dialog box. The most common choices for startup options are None (meaning don't load anything automatically), Read Mail (to check if there is new mail), or World Wide Web (to start a Web session automatically). You can select only one function to start automatically.

Click on the button next to your choice and then click on OK. If you wish to return to the previous settings, on the other hand, click on Cancel to return to NetCruiser without making any changes.

Cruising with NetCruiser

Look at all you've accomplished. You've installed your NetCruiser software, configured your modem, and selected your preferred access number. You've connected to the Netcom network, checked to see if there is a later version to download, downloaded it, and upgraded your NetCruiser software to the latest version. You've learned how to configure the startup options to meet your own needs. You know how to change the configuration and the access number. You're ready to cruise the Internet.

NetCruiser is copyright © 1993–1996 NETCOM On-Line Communication Services, Inc. All rights reserved.

Index

Note to the Reader: First-level entries are in **bold**. Page numbers in **bold** indicate the principal discussion of a topic or the definition of a term. Page numbers in *italic* indicate illustrations.

S

V

W

END-USER LICENSE AGREEMENT FOR MICROSOFT SOFTWARE

IMPORTANT—READ CAREFULLY: This Microsoft End-User License Agreement ("EULA") is a legal agreement between you (either an individual or a single entity) and Microsoft Corporation for the Microsoft software accompanying this EULA, which includes computer software and associated media and printed materials, and may include "online" or electronic documentation ("SOFTWARE PRODUCT" or "SOFTWARE"). By opening the sealed packet(s) OR exercising your rights to make and use copies of the SOFTWARE PRODUCT, you agree to be bound by the terms of this EULA. If you do not agree to the terms of this EULA, promptly return this package to the place from which you obtained it.

SOFTWARE PRODUCT LICENSE

The SOFTWARE PRODUCT is protected by copyright laws and international copyright treaties, as well as other intellectual property laws and treaties. The SOFTWARE PRODUCT is licensed, not sold.

1. **GRANT OF LICENSE.** This EULA grants you the following rights:

   - **Installation and Use.** You may install and use an unlimited number of copies of the SOFTWARE PRODUCT.

   - **Reproduction and Distribution.** You may reproduce and distribute an unlimited number of copies of the SOFTWARE PRODUCT; provided that each copy shall be a true and complete copy, including all copyright and trademark notices, and shall be accompanied by a copy of this EULA. The copies may be distributed as a standalone product or included with your own product.

2. **DESCRIPTION OF OTHER RIGHTS AND LIMITATIONS.**

   - **Limitations on Reverse Engineering, Decompilation, and Disassembly.** You may not reverse engineer, decompile, or disassemble the SOFTWARE PRODUCT, except and only to the extent that such activity is expressly permitted by applicable law notwithstanding this limitation.

   - **Separation of Components.** The SOFTWARE PRODUCT is licensed as a single product. Its component parts may not be separated for use on more than one computer.

   - **Software Transfer.** You may permanently transfer all of your rights under this EULA, provided the recipient agrees to the terms of this EULA.

   - **Termination.** Without prejudice to any other rights, Microsoft may terminate this EULA if you fail to comply with the terms and conditions of this EULA. In such event, you must destroy all copies of the SOFTWARE PRODUCT and all of its component parts.

3. **COPYRIGHT.** All title and copyrights in and to the SOFTWARE PRODUCT (including but not limited to any images, photographs, animations, video, audio, music, text, and "applets" incorporated into the SOFTWARE PRODUCT), the accompanying printed materials, and any copies of the SOFTWARE PRODUCT are owned by Microsoft or its suppliers. The SOFTWARE PRODUCT is protected by copyright laws and international treaty provisions. Therefore, you must treat the SOFTWARE PRODUCT like any other copyrighted material.

4. **U.S. GOVERNMENT RESTRICTED RIGHTS.** The SOFTWARE PRODUCT and documentation are provided with RESTRICTED RIGHTS. Use, duplication, or disclosure by the Government is subject to restrictions as set forth in subparagraph (c)(1)(ii) of the Rights in Technical Data and Computer Software clause at DFARS 252.227-7013 or subparagraphs (c)(1) and (2) of the Commercial Computer Software—Restricted Rights at 48 CFR 52.227-19, as applicable. Manufacturer is Microsoft Corporation/One Microsoft Way/Redmond, WA 98052-6399.

LIMITED WARRANTY

NO WARRANTIES. Microsoft expressly disclaims any warranty for the SOFT-WARE PRODUCT. The SOFTWARE PRODUCT and any related documentation is provided "as is" without warranty of any kind, either express or implied, including, without limitation, the implied warranties or merchantability, fitness for a particular purpose, or noninfringement. The entire risk arising out of use or performance of the SOFTWARE PRODUCT remains with you.

NO LIABILITY FOR CONSEQUENTIAL DAMAGES. In no event shall Microsoft or its suppliers be liable for any damages whatsoever (including, without limitation, damages for loss of business profits, business interruption, loss of business information, or any other pecuniary loss) arising out of the use of or inability to use this Microsoft product, even if Microsoft has been advised of the possibility of such damages. Because some states/jurisdictions do not allow the exclusion or limitation of liability for consequential or incidental damages, the above limitation may not apply to you.

Miscellaneous

If you acquired this product in the United States, this EULA is governed by the laws of the State of Washington.

If this product was acquired outside the United States, then local laws may apply.

Should you have any questions concerning this EULA, or if you desire to contact Microsoft for any reason, please contact the Microsoft subsidiary serving your country, or write: Microsoft Sales Information Center/One Microsoft Way/Redmond, WA 98052-6399.

About This CD

This CD contains a wealth of shareware, freeware, and licensed software that will help you make a connection—or a better connection—to the Net. The directories of the CD are organized as follows:

Directory	Contains
\eudora\	The Eudora e-mail program and its documentation.
\ftp-list\	The FTP-List, an ASCII document listing virtually every publicly accessible FTP archive.
\html-edi\	The HotDog HTML editor and its accompanying files.
\ms\	Shareware or freeware from Microsoft Corporation
\excel\	Internet Assistant for Microsoft Excel
\explore\	Internet Explorer for Microsoft Windows 95 and Windows 3.*x*.
\powerpt\	Internet Assistant for Microsoft Powerpoint
\word60\	Internet Assistant for Microsoft Word 6
\word95\	Internet Assistant for Microsoft Word 95
\mudlist\	A list of publicly accessible sites for MUD client software
\webspin\	The Webspinners list of Web information publishers
\netcruis\	The NetCruiser package from Netcom, described below.
\winzip\	The WinZip file compression/decompression software for Windows 95 and Windows 3.*x*.

NetCruiser

NetCruiser is a product of Netcom Online Communications, Inc., a leading Internet service provider. It provides a friendly Windows interface and the following Internet tools: e-mail, a Web browser, Internet Relay Chat (IRC), a Usenet newsreader, a Gopher program, File Transfer Protocol (FTP), and Telnet. The monthly rate for a Netcom account is $5.00 for the first month and $19.95 thereafter. (Rates are current as of the publication date and are subject to change.) This is charged to the credit card number you provide. **Customer support:** For billing questions, call (408) 983-5950. For installation and technical support questions, call (408) 983-5970.

For More Information

See Appendix H for a more complete description of all the files on this CD. Also, be sure to read the README files that accompany various programs on the CD. Where specified in files on the CD, the owners retain copyright to their respective contents. Where not otherwise noted, all contents copyright © 1996 SYBEX Inc.

Mastering the Internet contains hundreds of addresses for useful, informative, or just plain fun Web sites. The *Mastering the Internet Companion Page*, the Web page we created to accompany this book, contains links to the most important of these resources. You'll find it at http://www.lloyd.com/~patmcg/mastering.html.